MW00577425

Rogue Diplomats

Many of America's most significant political, economic, territorial, and geostrategic accomplishments from 1776 to the present day came about because a U.S. diplomat disobeyed orders. The magnificent terms granted to the infant republic by Britain at the close of the American Revolution, the bloodless acquisition of France's massive Louisiana territory in 1803, the procurement of an even vaster expanse of land from Mexico forty years later, the preservation of the Anglo-American "special relationship" during World War I—these and other milestones in the history of U.S. geopolitics derived in large part from the refusal of ambassadors, ministers, and envoys to heed the instructions given to them by their superiors back home. Historians have neglected this pattern of insubordination—until now. *Rogue Diplomats* makes a seminal contribution to scholarship on U.S. geopolitics and provides a provocative response to the question that has vexed so many diplomatic historians: is there a distinctively "American" foreign policy?

SETH JACOBS is Professor of History at Boston College and the author of *The Universe Unraveling: American Foreign Policy in Cold War Laos* (2012), *Cold War Mandarin: Ngo Dinh Diem and the Origins of America's War in Vietnam, 1950–1963* (2006), and *America's Miracle Man in Vietnam: Ngo Dinh Diem, Religion, Race, and U.S. Intervention in Southeast Asia, 1950–1957* (2004).

Cambridge Studies in US Foreign Relations

Edited by

Paul Thomas Chamberlin, *Columbia University*
Lien-Hang T. Nguyen, *Columbia University*

This series showcases cutting-edge scholarship in US foreign relations that employs dynamic new methodological approaches and archives from the colonial era to the present. The series will be guided by the ethos of transnationalism, focusing on the history of American foreign relations in a global context rather than privileging the US as the dominant actor on the world stage.

Also in the Series

Sarah Steinbock-Pratt, *Educating the Empire: American Teachers and Contested Colonization in the Philippines*

Walter L. Hixson, *Israel's Armor: The Israel Lobby and the First Generation of the Palestine Conflict*

Aurélie Basha i Novosejt, *"I Made Mistakes": Robert McNamara's Vietnam War Policy, 1960–1964*

Greg Whitesides, *Science and American Foreign Relations since World War II*

Jasper M. Trautsch, *The Genesis of America: US Foreign Policy and the Formation of National Identity, 1793–1815*

Hideaki Kami, *Diplomacy Meets Migration: US Relations with Cuba during the Cold War*

Shaul Mitelpunkt, *Israel in the American Mind: The Cultural Politics of US-Israeli Relations, 1958–1988*

Pierre Asselin, *Vietnam's American War: A History*

Lloyd E. Ambrosius, *Woodrow Wilson and American Internationalism*

Geoffrey C. Stewart, *Vietnam's Lost Revolution: Ngô Đình Diệm's Failure to Build an Independent Nation, 1955–1963*

Michael E. Neagle, *America's Forgotten Colony: Cuba's Isle of Pines*

Elisabeth Leake, *The Defiant Border: The Afghan-Pakistan Borderlands in the Era of Decolonization, 1936–1965*

Tuong Vu, *Vietnam's Communist Revolution: The Power and Limits of Ideology*

Renata Keller, *Mexico's Cold War: Cuba, the United States, and the Legacy of the Mexican Revolution*

Rogue Diplomats

The Proud Tradition of Disobedience in American Foreign Policy

SETH JACOBS

Boston College

CAMBRIDGE
UNIVERSITY PRESS

CAMBRIDGE
UNIVERSITY PRESS

University Printing House, Cambridge CB2 8BS, United Kingdom

One Liberty Plaza, 20th Floor, New York, NY 10006, USA

477 Williamstown Road, Port Melbourne, VIC 3207, Australia

314–321, 3rd Floor, Plot 3, Splendor Forum, Jasola District Centre, New Delhi – 110025, India

79 Anson Road, #06–04/06, Singapore 079906

Cambridge University Press is part of the University of Cambridge.

It furthers the University's mission by disseminating knowledge in the pursuit of education, learning, and research at the highest international levels of excellence.

www.cambridge.org
Information on this title: www.cambridge.org/9781107079472
DOI: 10.1017/9781139941884

First published 2020

Printed in the United Kingdom by TJ International Ltd, Padstow Cornwall

A catalogue record for this publication is available from the British Library.

Library of Congress Cataloging-in-Publication Data
NAMES: Jacobs, Seth, 1964– author.
TITLE: Rogue diplomats : the proud tradition of disobedience in American foreign policy / Seth Jacobs, Boston College.
OTHER TITLES: Proud tradition of disobedience in American foreign policy
DESCRIPTION: Cambridge, United Kingdom ; New York : Cambridge University Press, 2020. |
SERIES: Cambridge studies in US foreign relations | Includes bibliographical references and index.
IDENTIFIERS: LCCN 2020004503 | ISBN 9781107079472 (hardback) | ISBN 9781107438743 (paperback)
SUBJECTS: LCSH: United States–Foreign relations–Case studies. | Diplomatic and consular service–United States. | United States. Foreign Service–Biography.
CLASSIFICATION: LCC E183.7 .J33 2020 | DDC 327.73–dc23
LC record available at https://lccn.loc.gov/2020004503

ISBN 978-1-107-07947-2 Hardback

For Panda and Phie

Contents

Acknowledgments

I often tell people that I teach for free. Boston College, I say, pays me to grade papers and attend faculty meetings. The lectures, seminars, and colloquia are on the house. It's no joke. Teaching is my passion, and I never feel more alive than when I'm in the classroom. That's why I don't take sabbaticals, and why I won't retire while there's breath in me.

Yet, ironically, this is the first of my books to grow out of a course. I've been offering a survey of United States foreign relations for two decades, and around six years ago I began to notice that students sat up a little straighter, listened a bit more attentively, when the discussion turned to episodes in which American diplomats disobeyed orders. This was especially the case when we talked about how the peace commission charged with ending America's Revolutionary War defied the Continental Congress by circumventing the court of Louis XVI, and how Nicholas Trist hammered out the Treaty of Guadalupe Hidalgo with Mexico despite being fired – not once but twice – by President James K. Polk. Students laughed in amazement when I quoted from John Adams's shockingly blunt letters to Congress explaining why he and his fellow commissioners had betrayed the government that had sustained the Revolution since Lexington. Citations from Trist's tornadic correspondence from the field drew gasps and, on one occasion, applause. (Trist, drama queen that he was, would've appreciated that.) Since student enthusiasm is infectious, I yielded to my performer's instinct and started devoting more class time to those two geopolitical milestones. It didn't take long for a student to point out to me that the Louisiana Purchase had to rank alongside them as an example of U.S. envoys disregarding instructions and steering American foreign policy down a path contrary to that sanctioned by the

White House and State Department. Maybe Robert Livingston and James Monroe weren't as deliciously quotable as Adams and Trist, the student observed, but what they brought off in the spring of 1803 was pretty damn audacious. So, of course, the Purchase began receiving greater attention in class as well.

Eventually, as BC's bright students are wont to do, a young woman posed a challenging question: "Did other nations have this problem with their diplomats?"

I couldn't answer. I also found it noteworthy that she used the word *problem* when, by just about everyone's assessment, the United States obtained favorable results in the Revolution, the Purchase, and the Mexican War. In any event, I posted her question on H-Diplo, H-Net's network for diplomatic historians, and the responses came flooding in from scholars who specialized in the foreign policies of other countries. With a few minor deviations, it was a chorus of no's: not only do non-American diplomats *not* have a similar record of rebelliousness, but the mere notion of, say, a mid-nineteenth-century Russian envoy doing what Trist did was preposterous. He would've been likelier to flap his arms and fly to Pluto.

More detailed and far-reaching conversations followed, as I picked my colleagues' brains via telephone and email and at the yearly conference of the Society for Historians of American Foreign Relations. It gradually dawned on me that American diplomatic indiscipline was a much more recurrent phenomenon than I'd imagined, that it persisted well past the 1840s, and that historians had, for the most part, ignored it. Sure, they sometimes spiced up their texts with accounts of John Jay dashing his pipe into the fireplace as he announced his refusal to follow Congress's commands in 1782, but no one had attempted a systematic analysis of why American diplomats were so insubordinate and what the effects of that defiance had been on the United States's ascendancy to global power. There was, in other words, a lacuna in the literature. I determined to fill it. Friends and co-workers kicked around potential titles – an early favorite, believe it or not, was *Diplomats Behaving Badly* – and we settled on *Rogue Diplomats* as most sweeping and succinct.

Fortunately, Cambridge University Press found the project promising. My first heartfelt thanks must therefore go to senior editor Deborah Gershenowitz and the two anonymous reviewers she enlisted to review my book proposal. I'm also grateful to Lien-Hang Nguyen and Paul Thomas Chamberlin for including *Rogue Diplomats* in their U.S. Foreign Relations series. In a foretaste of the good luck that graced the book from the beginning, I received word that Cambridge was going to offer me a contract just minutes before delivering my "promotion talk" to the BC History Department. The glad tidings sent me into that typically nightmarish ordeal with the wind at my back and doubtless contributed to my becoming a full professor. A propitious start!

Research took longer than anticipated, largely because I failed to consider the fact that, for the first time in my career, I'd be working with handwritten archival sources. Trist, thank goodness, had exquisite penmanship, but the same cannot be said for the majority of policymakers whose chicken scratches I had to decipher. (Yes, Mr. Livingston, I'm talking about *you*.) That skull-splitting chore was leavened by the good cheer and professionalism of the staffs at the Library of Congress and National Archives I and II, to whom I extend my gratitude.

I'm also indebted to the archivists at the Eisenhower and Kennedy Presidential Libraries, chief among them Steve Plotkin, who has worked with me on no fewer than three books and served as a mentor to many of my undergraduate and graduate students. If you've got to spend hours sounding the depths of Joseph P. Kennedy's fetid psyche, it helps to have an encyclopedically knowledgeable hail-fellow-well-met like Steve as your guide.

Harvard's Widener Library proved a gold mine, not only of published materials – books, magazines, newspapers, and government transcripts – but of unpublished diaries, correspondence, and other documents that, in many cases, I wasn't even aware existed until I ran across them by serendipity. I passed so many days at Widener roaming the stacks that Harvard would've been justified in charging me rent. The same was true, to a lesser extent, of Yale's Sterling Library, which has the priceless Edward M. House Papers and a crew of knowledgeable, enthusiastic administrators eager to hunt down whatever a researcher requests.

Indeed, throughout my multiyear journey exploring the history of U.S. rogue diplomacy, the librarians and archivists with whom I dealt were, without exception, superb. Thanks to them all.

When the manuscript was finally complete, it passed into the hands of some of the ablest people it's been my privilege to work with. I refer in particular to Cynthia Col, my ever-patient and unfailingly meticulous indexer; Rosemary Morlin, my copy-editor, whose lynx-eyed inspection of the text ensured stylistic consistency throughout (and who caught me in several whopping errors of fact that would've caused great embarrassment had they been allowed to stand uncorrected); Rachel Blaifeder, senior editorial assistant, who, alongside Deborah, invested immense

talent, time, and energy in determining how to market a hefty, methodologically old-fashioned monograph like *Rogue Diplomats* to audiences
both lay and academic; and Stephanie Taylor, the content manager, who
oversaw the book's progress through production with a laudable mix of
rigor and bonhomie. Cambridge's reputation for giving its authors – and
their work – first-class treatment is well deserved. Hopefully, *Rogue
Diplomats* won't be the only book I publish with this press.

I moreover acknowledge with appreciation the guidance and assistance
of Rabia Akhtar, Alessandro Antonello, Stephen Azzi, Joseph Blady,
Mark Bradley, James Cameron, Ted Cogan, Frank Costigliola, Charles
Giovanni Vanzan Coutinho, Andy DeRoach, Rogério de Souza Farias,
George Egerton, Robin Fleming, Sinan Kuneralp, Sung-Yoon Lee, Kevin
Levin, Diane Labrosse, Peter Layton, Fred Logevall, Lynn Lyerly, Patrick
Maney, Asa McKercher, Edwin Moise, Nina Monafo, James O'Toole,
Andrew Preston, Marinko Raos, Gideon Remez, Heather Cox Richard-
son, Simon Rofe, Andrew Rotter, Joseph Siracusa, Mark Stout, Ken
Weisbrode, and Joe Wippl.

To those kind individuals whom I've inadvertently neglected to mention by name: apologies for the oversight and thank you for your comments, criticisms, corrections, and suggestions. *Rogue Diplomats* is a
better work because you contributed to its growth. All errors and omis-
sions herein are entirely my own.

This book is dedicated to my children, Miranda and Phie, the two most
important people in my life. Work on the manuscript overlapped with
their graduation from high school and abandonment of "the nest"
(indeed, Panda began grad study before the book hit the shelves), and
it's been a wondrous, humbling experience to see them grow into such
brilliant, gracious, and strong adults committed to bringing a measure of
compassion and justice to a world badly in need of both. My many, and
grievous, parental missteps notwithstanding, my kids have always been
the source of my greatest joy.

Introduction

Many of the most important political, economic, territorial, and geo-strategic triumphs enjoyed by the United States during its first two hundred years of national existence came about because an American diplomat disobeyed orders. The spectacularly generous terms granted the fledgling republic by Great Britain after the Revolutionary War, the acquisition of half a continent via the Louisiana Purchase, the seizure of a larger expanse of land from Mexico in 1848, the preservation of Anglo-American ties in the years leading up to U.S. cobelligerency in World War I – these and other watersheds in the history of American foreign relations derived in great part from the refusal of ambassadors, envoys, and other diplomatic agents to follow the instructions given them by their superiors back home.

And when I say "disobeyed," I mean *disobeyed*. American diplomats did not misunderstand their orders or fail to receive them. They struck out on courses that they knew were contrary to Washington's wishes but that they felt were in the best interest of their country. In nearly every instance, with one infamous exception, they were right. America profited from their insubordination.

This pattern of defiance has, as a rule, been neglected by scholars, who either address it anecdotally or ignore it altogether. Such inattention is surprising given the contrast between America's record and that of other nations. British, French, German, Japanese, and Russian diplomats almost never displayed comparable refractoriness. The idea of doing so would have struck them as absurd, if not suicidal. Yet Washington's foreign representatives habitually stepped out of line. A generalized inquiry into the causes and consequences of this behavior is essential, for it goes to the heart of one of the weightiest issues a diplomatic historian can tackle: Is there a distinctive "American" foreign policy?

Some scholars say no, that the United States behaves like any great power in the international arena. Others argue to the contrary that there are certain episodes – notably the Wilsonian crusade to make the world safe for democracy in World War I and the later, ill-contrived interventions in Vietnam and Iraq – that do not conform to the dictates of realpolitik and that grew out of idiosyncratic strains in American culture like evangelism, racism, or hubris. This debate has raged for decades and shows no sign of waning, but disputants have thus far failed to address the vital dimension of *protocol*, of permissible, even conceivable, self-direction on the part of the diplomat. When Soviet Foreign Minister Vyacheslav Molotov attended the 1947 Paris conference to coordinate plans for a European recovery program, he refused to answer the most innocuous questions without first telephoning Moscow for guidance, and although his plight constituted an extreme case of bureaucratic subjugation, it was more representative of the strictures under which most diplomats operated than the extraordinary latitude granted to – or, rather, assumed by – U.S. statesmen like Benjamin Franklin, James Monroe, and their successors. No non-American diplomat ever responded to a notice of dismissal the way envoy Nicholas Trist did when President James K. Polk fired him in October 1847. Trist, then negotiating with a moderate Mexican faction to end America's first major military intervention abroad, flung down the president's dispatch and announced his intention to finish what he had started. The result was the Treaty of Guadalupe Hidalgo, whereby Mexico relinquished all claims to Texas north of the Rio Grande and ceded an imperial domain that ultimately formed the states of California, Arizona, New Mexico, Nevada, Utah, and parts of Colorado and Wyoming. American diplomats have always been a disobedient lot, to the immense good fortune of the United States.[1]

What accounts for this perennial contrariness? The answer lies in the attitude toward professional diplomacy expressed by the Founding Fathers and translated by them and their descendants into the apparatus

---

[1] For Molotov in Paris, see D. F. Fleming, *The Cold War and Its Origins, 1917–1960* (Garden City, NY: Doubleday & Company, 1961), 1:480. In fairness to the foreign minister, he sometimes managed to rise above the obsequiousness so evident at this conference. He was never insubordinate, though. Self-preservation dictated that all civil and military officials in Joseph Stalin's Soviet Union bend over backwards to avoid crossing the boss. See Geoffrey Roberts, *Molotov: Stalin's Cold Warrior* (Washington, D.C.: Potomac Books, 2012), 15–18, 96–98, 129–130.

through which foreign policy is conducted. Novelist John Dos Passos famously observed that "rejection of Europe is what America is all about," and one European institution Americans rejected during much of their nation's history was Old-World geopolitics. They felt that republican institutions were incompatible with diplomacy and that foreign intercourse made people effete, aristocratic, and unproductive – in a word, un-American. The Continental Congress went so far as to pass a resolution limiting U.S. diplomats' tenure abroad to no more than three years. A longer enlistment, they believed, would endanger the diplomats' integrity. Secretary of State John Quincy Adams endorsed this policy in the early 1800s, writing the U.S. minister to Sweden, "Americans. . .should for their own sake, as well as for that of their country, make no long residences in a public capacity at the courts of Europe." The "air of those regions," Adams declared, was "so unfriendly to American constitutions that they always require after a few years to be renovated by the wholesome republican atmosphere of their own country."[2]

Adams's sentiments were not unique to the early national period. The first five or six generations of Americans viewed diplomacy with suspicion and distaste. Complaints about its corrupting effects abound in the congressional record. In 1834, during Martin Van Buren's presidency, a southern legislator insisted that diplomacy "spoil[ed] the good republicans we send abroad," that U.S. diplomats came home "with their heads as full of kings, queens, and knaves as a pack of cards," and that the "brilliant, gaudy, laced, jeweled, and plumed finery" of foreign courts was "unsuited to an agricultural, distant, peaceful people." A quarter-century later, Representative Jabez Curry of Alabama said of the U.S. diplomatic corps, "Here is the evil, the fungus, the excrescence, a pinchbeck imitation of the pomp and pageantry of royalty, and we should put the knife to it and cut it out." Thirty years after that, New York Senator William Robinson called diplomacy "an ulcer on the body of republicanism" and demanded that the "fops," "profligates," "snobs," and "dandies of our diplomacy" be "quarantined as we quarantine foreign rags through fear of cholera" upon reentry to America. Their "offensive and polluting influences," Robinson proclaimed, left "a stench in the nostrils

---

[2] Dos Passos cited in Lou Cannon and Carl M. Cannon, *Reagan's Disciple: George W. Bush's Troubled Quest for a Presidential Legacy* (New York: Public Affairs, 2007), 109; Adams to Hughes, 22 June 1818, *Writings of John Quincy Adams*, Worthington Chauncey Ford, ed. (New York: Macmillan, 1916), 6:357. Ironically, Adams himself served for longer periods of time as minister to Britain, Russia, and Prussia without need of such cultural delousing.

of the American people." This association of diplomacy with contamin-
ation persisted in the halls of Congress until the early twentieth century,
and to a considerable extent beyond then.[3]

Not only did Americans find diplomacy repugnant; they also believed
it was unnecessary, a luxury. In their view, European nations employed
diplomats to calm mutual jealousies, work out complicated defensive
pacts, calibrate and re-calibrate the balance of power, agree on whose
grand-nephew got to control the Duchy of Pomerania, and so on. But
Americans did not concern themselves with such nonsense. Why, then,
did they need representatives overseas? To facilitate commerce? No
befrilled plenipotentiary was necessary for that. "If we want to do any
business abroad," Connecticut Senator Chauncey Goodrich wrote Treasury Secretary Oliver Wolcott in 1794, "give some good fellow a letter of
attorney and let him do it." That neatly summed up the American view.
Most nineteenth- and early twentieth-century U.S. politicians believed
that their country's interaction with the rest of the world would always
be predominantly commercial in nature. When they wrote and spoke
about foreign policy, they wrote and spoke in economic terms. None of
the activities that people in other nations identified with geopolitics –
forging or maintaining alliances, avoiding or limiting wars, annexing or
surrendering territory – struck Americans as important. These were Old-
World issues, the kind of decadent, tradition-bound entanglements the
Founding Fathers had fought a revolution to escape. The United States
needed Europe as a market for its goods and as a provider of other goods,
but few Americans saw any reason to create a European-style professional
diplomatic service on their side of the Atlantic.[4]

---

[3] Speech by Representative Warren R. Davis of South Carolina, 30 April 1834, *Register of Debates in Congress* (Washington, D.C.: Gales and Seaton, 1835), 10:3879–3880; speech by Representative Jabez Curry of Alabama, 27 January 1859, *Congressional Globe* (Washington, D.C.: John C. Rives, 1860), 35:593; speech by Senator William E. Robinson of New York, 10 January 1885, *Congressional Record* (Washington, D.C.: U.S. Government Printing Office, 1885), 16:613–615.

[4] Goodrich to Wolcott, 10 March 1784, *Memoirs of the Administrations of Washington and Adams Collected from the Papers of Oliver Wolcott*, George Gibbs, ed. (New York: Printed for the Subscribers, 1846), 1:131. Representative Champ Clark of Missouri made the same case over a century later, with the United States standing on the threshold of world power. "It would be better really to withdraw the entire diplomatic corps," Clark mused, "and then, when we need a representative at a foreign court, whenever we have need for anyone to attend to these delicate duties,... pick out a man of the highest capacity in this country" and "send him there." Speech by Representative James Beauchamp Clark of Missouri, 18 April 1908, *Congressional Record* (Washington, D.C.: U.S. Government Printing Office, 1908), 42:4926. At least Clark's expression *"these delicate duties"* could

American diplomacy was therefore an amateur affair from the Declaration of Independence to the Jazz Era. Whereas candidates for diplomatic work in Europe and elsewhere had to pass competitive examinations, entered their countries' services at the lowest grade, were promoted on a merit basis, and continued practicing statecraft in some capacity until reaching retirement age, American diplomats were, on balance, novices. There were no formal qualifications for diplomatic jobs in the United States, no criteria by which to judge an applicant's competence. A man could receive senatorial confirmation as a diplomat without knowing the language of the nation to which he was assigned or understanding anything of its history and customs. He usually took up his post late in life after having distinguished himself in another field. In many cases, he was appointed for a single task, like negotiating a treaty, and he expected to return home after completing it. Certainly, he did not view diplomacy as a career. The spoils system, a constant feature of American politics after 1828, ensured that few diplomatic positions carried tenures longer than that of the administration in power, and even after the campaign for civil service reform exempted a range of government jobs from partisan considerations, U.S. diplomacy remained spoils-ridden. Tellingly, this did not disturb most Americans. Although they could work up enthusiasm about other efforts to make the American economic or political system more efficient – antitrust laws, income taxes, women's suffrage, the initiative, referendum, and recall – diplomacy left them unmoved. Well into the twentieth century, it was purely fortuitous if a U.S. diplomat possessed the experience and talent to discharge his duties.[5]

One thing he did have to possess, however, was an independent income. Americans' antipathy toward professional statecraft, and concomitant doubts about its utility, led Congress to starve America's diplomatic institutions of funding, with the result that only wealthy men, men whose principal means of support lay in the private sector, or men intending to serve for a short time could accept foreign appointments. For eighty years after the Declaration of Independence, American ministers scarcely drew salaries. They also received little in the way of expense accounts, being expected to pay out of pocket for housing, food,

be construed to encompass matters of war and peace, not just economic affairs. That went above the mental ceiling of most Americans of his day.

[5] William Barnes and John Heath Morgan, *The Foreign Service of the United States: Origins, Development, and Functions* (Washington, D.C.: Department of State, Historical Office, Bureau of Public Affairs, 1961), 68, 80, 89–90, 105–106, 125, 132–133.

transportation, clerical help, and entertainment. Thomas Jefferson went bankrupt as a result of his diplomatic outlays while U.S. representative to France. John C. Calhoun declined offers to assume the top diplomatic post in Paris – not because he did not want the assignment, he explained, but because he could not afford it. The same conditions obtained during Woodrow Wilson's administration, when Charles Eliot, former president of Harvard, and Richard Olney, former secretary of state, refused diplomatic appointments on financial grounds. Congressional parsimony ironically led to the United States developing a first line of defense more high-caste than that fielded by Britain, France, or Spain.[6]

This had momentous consequences. America's diplomats did not feel as beholden to the government they served as did representatives of other countries. The rich and prominent American lawyers, soldiers, politicians, journalists, educators, or businessmen who lent prestige to an administration by performing important diplomatic duties often concluded that their principal obligation was to their country rather than to the president. They therefore ignored directives that, in their view, ran counter to the national interest. For example, the U.S. commission that hammered out an end to America's Quasi-War with France in 1800 disregarded John Adams's insistence that they demand compensation for seized American ships because they decided that the United States would have to drop its financial claims against Paris if there was to be peace. Similarly, when Henry Clay, John Quincy Adams, and Albert Gallatin confronted an inflexible British delegation at Ghent toward the close of the War of 1812, they declined to insist that London stop impressing sailors from American vessels on the high seas, even though James Madison had made abandonment of this policy the sine qua non of any agreement.[7]

U.S. diplomats became even more brazen after Andrew Jackson introduced the practice of rotation in office, for obvious reasons. A campaign contributor or ward heeler who received his ministership as a patronage

---

[6] For Jefferson's financial straits, see Merrill D. Peterson, *Thomas Jefferson and the New Nation: A Biography* (New York: Oxford University Press, 1970), 302. For Calhoun's, see Charles M. Wiltse, *John C. Calhoun: Nationalist, 1782–1828* (Indianapolis: Bobbs-Merrill, 1944), 200. For Eliot's and Olney's, see Warren Frederick Ilchman, *Professional Diplomacy in the United States* (Chicago: University of Chicago Press, 1961), 121.

[7] For the U.S. commission's indiscipline while crafting the Convention of 1800, see Alexander DeConde, *The Quasi-War: The Politics and Diplomacy of the Undeclared War with France, 1797–1801* (New York: Charles Scribner's Sons, 1966), 247–256. For Clay, Adams, and Gallatin at Ghent, see Bradford Perkins, *Castlereagh and Adams: England and the United States, 1812–1823* (Berkeley: University of California Press, 1964), 50–53.

plum when his party took power was likely to assume that the president owed *him*, not the other way around, and to interpret presidential instructions as friendly suggestions from a peer rather than orders from the commander in chief. Thus when Jackson fired Minister to Mexico Anthony Butler in 1834, Butler took no notice of the recall order and remained at his post for two more years, repeatedly attempting to purchase Texas despite having no authority to do so. Elijah Hise, sent to Central America by James K. Polk in the late 1840s to negotiate commercial treaties with Guatemala and El Salvador, instead signed a treaty with Nicaragua giving the United States the right to construct a canal or railway through that republic's territory, an act that grossly exceeded his instructions. William Brent, Polk's representative in Buenos Aires, offered to mediate a dispute between Argentina and Paraguay even though Secretary of State James Buchanan told him numerous times that this was not administration policy. Neither Butler, Hise, or Brent had any thought of making diplomacy a life's work, and this liberated them from executive control to an extent undreamt of in the foreign services of other nations, where, according to a nineteenth-century British commissioner, "We consider ourselves as little more than pens in the hands of the government at home." America's amateur diplomats had a more expansive understanding of their function.[8]

Victory in the Spanish-American War established the United States as a world power and led progressive legislators and muckraking journalists to call for the professionalization of American statecraft. In a representative piece in the *North American Review*, Edward Bourne demanded that the United States do "what England, Holland, France, and Germany are doing for their colonial and diplomatic services" by instituting a "regular system of preparation" free of the "blight of spoils" in which candidates mastered "such subjects as colonial problems, administrative law, civil law, comparative religions, [and] ethnology." Bourne further prescribed "permanency of tenure" and a salary sufficient for the diplomat's

---

[8] For Butler's ministership, see Quinton Curtis Lamar, "A Diplomatic Disaster: The Mexican Mission of Anthony Butler, 1829–1834," *The Americas* 45 (July 1988): 1–17. For Hise's, see David Shavit, *The United States in Latin America: A Historical Dictionary* (New York: Greenwood Press, 1992), 165; T. Ray Shurbutt, *United States-Latin American Relations, 1800–1850: The Formative Generations* (Tuscaloosa: University of Alabama Press, 1991), 35, 41–43. For Brent's, see Graham H. Stuart, *The Department of State: A History of Its Organization, Procedure, and Personnel* (New York: Macmillan, 1949), 107. British diplomat cited in Thomas A. Bailey, *A Diplomatic History of the American People*, Seventh Edition (New York: Appleton-Century-Crofts, 1964), 43.

"comfortable support." But Bourne recognized that congressional and public opinion was not favorable for such reforms. "We lack not only trained men," he lamented, "but the belief that training is necessary." At a moment when Americans were exulting in the triumph of their state-of-the-art navy, the product of a modern building program that enjoyed overwhelming popular support, U.S. diplomacy had changed little since Jackson's day. It was still ad hoc, part-time, and dependent on partisan considerations. And Americans, by and large, did not care. They might grumble when they read articles in *Harper's Weekly* or the *Forum* inveighing against "the white-spat brigade" who represented the United States overseas, but the subject never engaged their attention for long. As far as most Americans were concerned, if a few bored bluebloods and party hacks wanted to debauch themselves at foreign courts, there was no harm in giving them the opportunity, provided they more or less paid their own way. After all, it was not as though they were doing anything important.[9]

Congress finally took some steps toward placing diplomacy on a career footing after the outbreak of the Great War. That conflict imposed overwhelming demands on the staffs of every U.S. legation or embassy in Europe: among other things, officials had to ensure the relief, protection, and transportation of American citizens caught in the path of hostilities, respond to a deluge of inquiries from home regarding the welfare and whereabouts of loved ones, and carry out widespread reporting and intelligence work. America's foreign affairs establishment proved altogether inadequate to these challenges. Legislators, shaken for the moment out of their indifference, passed the 1915 Stone-Flood Act, which extended the merit principle of the Civil Service (Pendleton) Act of 1883 to the diplomatic service, mandated qualifying examinations for appointment, and set up a board of examiners to evaluate candidates. It also provided for promotion within the service on the basis of demonstrated skill. Postwar distresses, mostly of an economic nature, prompted Congress to pass a supplementary bill in 1924. The Rogers Act consolidated the diplomatic and consular branches into a single foreign service, established a school in the Department of State for the instruction of candidates who passed the qualifying exam, authorized

---

[9] Edward Gaylord Bourne, "A Trained Colonial Civil Service," *North American Review* 169 (October 1899): 528–535. Warren Frederick Ilchman notes that the greatest obstacles to reform in America's diplomatic service at the dawn of the twentieth century were "the silence of Congress" and "public apathy." Ilchman, *Professional Diplomacy*, 64.

higher salary scales, and made provisions for retirement and disability. American diplomacy had, at long last, seemingly become professionalized and specialized.[10]

This was an illusion. Salaries for diplomats on the various levels of seniority were inferior to the amounts paid to officers of an equivalent rank in other countries. As before, anyone who wanted the privilege of serving the United States abroad had to be a wealthy man willing to dip into his private fortune. The exam system hardly guaranteed a level playing field either, as candidates had to go to Washington, D.C. to take their exams and remain in the city for at least two weeks, the usual gap between the written and oral sections. (It was sometimes longer.) Many aspiring diplomats found the travel costs beyond their means. Those who managed to scrape together enough money to cover train fare and lodging had, of course, to pass the exam, a much easier task for the scion of a rich, politically connected family than for a lower- or middle-class man. For one thing, the written part emphasized knowledge of international law, economics, and political science, subjects that only men who had been educated in exclusive private schools and colleges were likely to have studied. It was also organized into a short-answer format that tested recall more than intelligence; moneyed candidates could afford to attend one of several "cram-schools" specializing in the rote memorization of responses to likely questions. As for the oral half, examiners evaluated candidates on the basis of such vague but clearly classist categories as "disposition," "discretion," "judgment," "polish," and "address." Given these factors, it was not difficult for the diplomatic branch of the newly minted U.S. Foreign Service to preserve its patrician cliquishness.[11]

More importantly, promotion by merit stopped below the level of minister or ambassador. Diplomatic officers of the highest rank could still be appointed for reasons other than demonstrated competence over a long tenure of service. They could, that is, still be amateurs, and many of them were. For example, three years after the Rogers Act passed, during a

[10] Barnes and Morgan, *Foreign Service*, 188–210; J. Robert Moskin, *American Statecraft: The Story of the U.S. Foreign Service* (New York: St. Martin's Press, 2013), 245–281, 345–352; Robert D. Schulzinger, *The Making of the Diplomatic Mind: The Training, Outlook, and Style of United States Foreign Service Officers, 1908–1931* (Middletown, CT: Wesleyan University Press, 1975), 68–78.
[11] Barnes and Morgan, *Foreign Service*, 233–234; Lawrence E. Gelfand, "Towards a Merit System for the American Diplomatic Service, 1900–1930," *Irish Studies in International Affairs* 2 (1988): 54–57; Ilchman, *Professional Diplomacy*, 91, 97, 117, 167–170.

period of tension between the United States and Mexico, President Calvin Coolidge nominated his former Amherst College classmate Dwight Morrow to be ambassador to Mexico City. Morrow had donated handsomely to Coolidge's 1924 presidential campaign, but he had no diplomatic experience, spoke no Spanish, and was a partner in the House of Morgan – scarcely a profession likely to endear him to the ultra-liberal Mexican president, Plutarco Calles. Yet Morrow's nomination did not stir a ripple of protest and he received speedy Senate confirmation. Americans remained blasé about diplomacy, in contrast to other professions, like, say, the military. It is hard to imagine the American people or their representatives in Congress tolerating the practice of four-star generals or admirals being chosen from the ranks of campaign contributors. Diplomacy, however, still occupied a marginal, out-of-the-way place in the American popular imagination.[12]

Another bill intended to professionalize U.S. statecraft, the 1931 Moses-Linthicum Act, removed some of the barriers keeping non-wealthy Americans out and overhauled the examination process to a degree, but its effects were minimal. The Great Depression restricted government expenditures so severely that those salaries that the act increased on paper were in fact cut or abolished. Washington's "cram-schools" adjusted to fit the new exam, and the men who passed continued to be disproportionately affluent. (Over half graduated from Harvard, Yale, or Princeton.) Also, the act retained the principle of stopping the promotional ladder below the highest level. Career men might be appointed ambassadors if the country in question was not deemed significant, or if it was such a

---

[12] Donald R. McCoy, *Calvin Coolidge: The Quiet President* (Lawrence: University Press of Kansas, 1988), 102–105, 109, 111, 114. Morrow's amateurism did not prevent him from being an effective ambassador. Indeed – in keeping with the theme of this book – it may have been an asset, as he brought a freshness in perspective to the job that allowed him to make such small but symbolically significant gestures as changing the sign outside his workplace to read "United States Embassy" instead of "American Embassy." He also got his future son-in-law, Charles Lindbergh, who had just completed a solo flight across the Atlantic, to fly from Washington to Mexico City as a sign of U.S. goodwill. More substantively, Morrow persuaded President Calles to conciliate American oilmen whose subsoil properties the Mexican government had expropriated. Calles ultimately accepted the terms of the so-called Bucarelli agreement, whereby foreign companies that had begun working their properties before 1917 could retain ownership. Contemporaries viewed Morrow's ambassadorship as a success, and that verdict has been sustained by most historians. See for example Richard Melzer, "The Ambassador Simpatico: Dwight Morrow in Mexico, 1927–1930" in *Ambassadors in Foreign Policy: The Influence of Individuals on U.S.-Latin American Policy*, C. Neale Ronning and Albert P. Vannucci, eds. (New York: Praeger, 1987), 1–27.

notorious hardship post that few officers wanted to serve there. But when
it came to the critical nations – nations whose conduct with respect to the
United States could seriously jeopardize American physical and economic
security – the ambassador was normally a non-career man who did not
owe his appointment to merit recruitment and promotion. Thus in the
fateful period leading up to U.S. cobelligerency in World War II, nearly
all of Franklin Roosevelt's ambassadors in vital countries were dilettan-
tes: Joseph Kennedy in London, Jesse Straus in Paris, Claude Bowers in
Madrid, William Dodd in Berlin, and Josephus Daniels in Mexico City.
Only the U.S. ambassador in Tokyo, Joseph Grew, was a career
diplomat.[13]

It appeared a recipe for disaster. And, as I argue later, it *was* in
Kennedy's case. Daniels, though, proved one of America's more successful foreign representatives, and his success rested on those characteristics
that had distinguished U.S. diplomacy from the start: amateurism and the
attendant willingness to disobey orders. When he assumed his ambassadorship in 1933, Daniels was seventy years old; he did not expect to serve
for long. He was also rich, one of the wealthiest newspaper editors
in America; he could not have cared less about salary. Furthermore,
Roosevelt was indebted to him. Daniels's paper, the Raleigh *News and
Observer*, had been one of the first to promote Roosevelt's candidacy
for president, and Daniels had been instrumental in getting the North
Carolina delegates to the 1932 Democratic National Convention to vote
for FDR. The Mexican assignment was Daniels's reward for his support.
He accepted it without undue gratitude; in fact, he was miffed that
Roosevelt had not offered him a cabinet post. Like many of his predeces-
sors, Daniels did not go abroad to be anyone's errand boy, least of all
Secretary of State Cordell Hull's.[14]

Consequently, when in 1938 Mexican President Lazaro Cardenas
nationalized Mexico's petroleum industry and Hull cabled Daniels the
text of a protest note, instructing the ambassador to deliver it to Cardenas
at once, Daniels refused. He argued that an American reprimand would
destroy Roosevelt's Good Neighbor Policy and drive Mexico into Adolf
Hitler's arms. The U.S. oil cartel moguls whom Cardenas had offended

---

[13] Ilchman, *Professional Diplomacy*, 204–207, 227; Graham H. Stuart, *American Diplomatic and Consular Practice* (New York: Appleton-Century-Crofts, 1952), 103–106.
[14] E. David Cronon, *Josephus Daniels in Mexico* (Madison: University of Wisconsin Press,
1960), 1–9; Carroll Kilpatrick, *Roosevelt and Daniels: A Friendship in Politics* (Chapel
Hill: University of North Carolina Press, 1952), vii–xvi, 131–138.

would just have to bite the bullet, he said. Furious, Hull ordered Daniels to present the State Department's complaint without delay. He also instructed the ambassador to return to the United States immediately. Daniels flouted both orders, stalled for time, and waited for what he called the secretary's "Tennessee temper" to cool. At length, Hull agreed to soften the tone of the note and to withhold it from publication. That was not good enough for Daniels. When he read Hull's dispatch to Cardenas, he told the Mexican president that it ought not to be regarded as a formal diplomatic communication from Washington. It was, he declared, just an unofficial expression of American attitudes.[15]

E. David Cronon, the most astute analyst of Daniels's service in Mexico, concludes that the ambassador's "actions were clearly insubordinate" and that he "had no authority" to take the steps he did. But Cronon considers Daniels's performance praiseworthy. Interviews with former members of the Cardenas government convince Cronon that "Mexico would have broken diplomatic relations if Ambassador Daniels had presented the note officially." The ramifications of such a rupture can be imagined. Mexican defection from the hemispheric alliance would have been a godsend to the fascists, especially if Hitler had succeeded in gaining access to Mexican oil, a resource vital to U.S. defense interests. In Cronon's view, "Daniels almost single-handedly prevented a break between the United States and Mexico." This verdict is borne out by the fact that the Cardenas government *did* break relations with Great Britain when British Minister Owen St. Clair O'Malley, as per his instructions from the Foreign Office, demanded a return of confiscated oil properties. Alas for London, it had an obedient diplomat in Mexico City.[16]

Daniels is not one of the diplomats given chapter-length treatment in this book, because he could be reasonably confident that Roosevelt would take his side against Hull. With fascism ascendant in Europe and Hitler and Benito Mussolini casting covetous eyes on the Western Hemisphere, FDR considered preservation of his Good Neighbor Policy essential to

[15] Josephus Daniels, *Shirt-Sleeve Diplomat* (Chapel Hill: University of North Carolina Press, 1947), 231–245; Hull to Daniels, 26 March 1938, *Foreign Relations of the United States* (hereafter *FRUS*), 1938 (Washington, D.C.: U.S. Government Printing Office, 1956), The American Republics, 5:734–735; Daniels to Hull, 27 March 1938, ibid., 5:735; Hull to Daniels, 27 March 1938, ibid., 5:735–736; Daniels to Hull, 31 March 1938, ibid., 5:739–741; Welles, Memorandum of Conversation, 31 March 1938, ibid., 5:737–738, 756.

[16] Cronon, *Josephus Daniels in Mexico*, 197–198; Daniels, *Shirt-Sleeve Diplomat*, 244–245.

national security. The president's anti-Big Business stance moreover left him unsympathetic to the oilmen condemning Cardenas as a Bolshevik. Finally, as Daniels knew, FDR ran the State Department. Hull may have been America's longest-serving secretary of state, but he was also one of its least influential. The president rarely asked his advice and often overruled him. So Daniels's defiance of Hull did not rise to the same level of insubordination as that displayed by other U.S. diplomats who broke ranks and made history. But Daniels was representative of a tradition in U.S. statecraft that I call rogue diplomacy, a bold, even cocky rebelliousness that is uniquely American. No other nation's foreign service can claim such a remarkable track record of diplomats telling their bosses to go to hell.[17]

This book examines that record through a case-study approach. Each of its chapters addresses a milepost in U.S. foreign relations: the American Revolution, the Louisiana Purchase, the Mexican War, World War I, World War II, and the 1963 coup in South Vietnam. My organization is chronological, and the thread holding these foreign-policy turning points together is the rogue diplomat, the policymaker who becomes a law unto himself and whose vision is not only influential but decisive. I argue that, apart from Kennedy's calamitous ambassadorship in London, these diplomats' insurgentism redounded to America's benefit. The United States would have been worse off – weaker, smaller, poorer, and less secure – had men like U.S. Minister to France Robert Livingston not departed from their marching orders.

Such a claim entails counterfactual reasoning, normally taboo among historians, but less of a problem here because, more often than not, the superior officer whose instructions went unheeded himself acknowledged that the undutiful diplomat had obtained the best possible result. In no instance did presidents or secretaries of state attempt to undo the handiwork of their mutinous underlings. Even Polk, who bent every effort to destroy Trist's reputation after the latter returned from Mexico City, privately admitted that the Treaty of Guadalupe Hidalgo met or exceeded all of Washington's war aims. It also, I contend, prevented national disaster. Had Trist accepted his ouster and come home without completing negotiations, the Mexican government, whose foothold was shaky,

---

[17] For FDR's relationship with Hull, see Robert Dallek, *Franklin D. Roosevelt and American Foreign Policy, 1932–1945* (New York: Oxford University Press, 1995), 149, 421, 532–533; David Mayers, *FDR's Ambassadors and the Diplomacy of Crisis* (Cambridge: Cambridge University Press, 2013), 2.

would have fallen, and Mexico would have descended into anarchy. The United States would then have been confronted with the prospect of prolonged guerrilla resistance, and the House of Representatives, recently captured by the antiwar Whigs, might have blocked further appropriations for America's armies in the field. By disobeying his commander in chief's instructions, Trist saved his nation from a Vietnam-like quagmire and played an indispensable role in securing the greatest territorial acquisition in U.S. history.

Trist, in many ways the hero of this book, was shabbily repaid for his efforts, but he might have taken solace in the words of John Adams, one of the original rogue diplomats, who, after joining John Jay and Benjamin Franklin at Paris for the final round of negotiations concluding the Revolutionary War, was disgusted to learn that the Continental Congress had ordered its peace commissioners to make no overtures to Great Britain unless America's ally, France, approved. Aware that the French foreign minister sought to confine the infant United States east of the Appalachians, and certain he could persuade war-weary British agents to agree to the Mississippi River as a western boundary, Adams ignored Congress's directive and proclaimed, "It is glory to have broken such infamous orders."[18]

I should note by way of disclaimer that rogue diplomacy is not unheard of in other countries. It does happen, but with nothing like the regularity with which it occurs in the United States. Also, non-American governments tend to be much less indulgent of the maverick diplomat's actions than is Washington. Illustrative examples include David Erskine and Craig Murray, British dignitaries whose ambassadorships were separated by nearly two centuries but who suffered the same fall from grace when they flouted the Foreign Office's instructions: both were recalled – Erskine from America, Murray from Uzbekistan – and both found it impossible to secure another diplomatic post. Furthermore, London disavowed their iconoclastic stratagems; neither Erskine's promise to withdraw British Orders in Council on the eve of the War of 1812 nor Murray's attempt to isolate his country from the American-led war on terror became British policy. The contrast between this harsh response and the kid gloves treatment accorded most American rogue diplomats is striking. Indeed, of the insubordinates assessed in the following pages, only two, Trist and Kennedy, sustained any punishment as a result of disobeying their

[18] Diary Entry, 18 February 1783, *The Works of John Adams*, Charles Francis Adams, ed. (Boston: Little, Brown, and Company, 1851) (hereafter *WJA*), 3:359.

superiors' orders. The rest either completed their missions undamaged or with reputations enhanced.[19]

Another caveat: I am not the first historian to note the atypical refractoriness of U.S. representatives abroad. That distinction would appear to belong to Bradford Perkins, who declared in a 1986 essay that "[p]robably no other Western diplomatic corps has ever been so disobedient" as America's pre-Civil War ministers. Perkins ascribed this noncompliance to "the breadth of the Atlantic." Messages took as long as two months to cross the ocean in the days of sail, he observed, and American diplomats often did not have time to petition their government for new instructions if breaking events called for a change. They were therefore obliged to exercise greater freedom of action than would have been the case had communication been swifter. Perkins was onto something – three thousand miles of blue sea did indeed pose a formidable obstacle to coordinated action – but there are two problems with his argument. First, as we will see, U.S. diplomats continued their wayward ways after the advent of the telegraph, when dozens of cables flew back and forth between Washington and Saigon in an afternoon. (Email's arrival in the 1980s and 1990s likewise failed to make American diplomats more tractable.) Second, European ambassadors, ministers, and consuls stationed in the United States during the late eighteenth and early nineteenth centuries were nowhere near as insubordinate as their Yankee contemporaries, despite facing the same hurdles in corresponding with their superiors on the Continent. U.S. diplomatic indiscipline, contrary to Perkins's claim, arose from factors other than technological primitivism. It was a consequence of American diplomats' deep-rooted beliefs about the role they played in managing U.S. relations with the wider world.[20]

---

[19] For Erskine's dereliction, see Paul A. Gilje, *Free Trade and Sailors' Rights in the War of 1812* (Cambridge: Cambridge University Press, 2013), 164, 167, 193. For Murray's, see Nick Paton Walsh, "The Envoy Who Said Too Much," *Guardian*, 15 July 2004. Another non-American whose diplomatic misconduct short-circuited his career – and his life – was Francis Garnier, the "inspector of indigenous affairs" for French Indochina. Garnier proclaimed Paris's ownership over Hanoi in 1873 only to have Prime Minister Jacques-Victor Albert repudiate the gesture and hand the city back to the Vietnamese. Native bandits calling themselves the Black Flag Army assassinated Garnier before the Quai d'Orsay could sack him. See Milton Osborne, "Francis Garnier (1839–1873): Explorer of the Mekong River" in *Explorers of Southeast Asia: Six Lives*, Victor T. King, ed. (New York: Oxford University Press, 1995), 51–106.

[20] Bradford Perkins, "The Peace of Paris: Patterns and Legacies" in *Peace and the Peacemakers: The Treaty of 1783*, Ronald Hoffman and Peter J. Albert, eds. (Charlottesville: University Press of Virginia, 1986), 222–223.

Two more preliminary points are in order. All of my actors are white
men. This is not by design but because of institutional racism and sexism.
U.S. diplomacy was a profession closed to women and minorities until the
1930s, at least at the ambassadorial level, and while there have been many
female and nonwhite diplomats of that grade since Franklin Roosevelt's
administration, they make up a small percentage of the historical whole.
They include, to be sure, some powerful and outsized personalities –
Ralph Bunche, Clare Boothe Luce, Susan Rice, Pearl Mesta, Pamela
Harriman, Jean Kirkpatrick, Bill Richardson, Gary Locke, Samantha
Power – and at least one of them was a genuine rogue diplomat: Andrew
Young, Jimmy Carter's ambassador to the United Nations, who in
1979 met with representatives of the Palestine Liberation Organization
despite White House assurances to Israeli Prime Minister Menachem
Begin that it would not initiate contact with the PLO until that group
recognized Israel's right to exist. I have not included Young among my
subjects because his action had little effect on U.S. policy. Begin protested
the ambassador's behavior, but U.S.-Israeli relations, already strained in
the post-Camp David period, did not become appreciably worse, and
America's posture toward the PLO remained hostile. What pundits called
the "Andy Young affair" was soon overshadowed by such world-shaking
events as the Iranian hostage crisis and the Soviet invasion of Afghanistan.
Young did prove himself a spiritual kinsman to Adams and Trist, though,
when he told reporters after stepping down as UN ambassador, "I really
don't feel a bit sorry for anything that I've done," adding, "I could not say
to anybody that, given the same situation, I wouldn't do it again almost
exactly the same way." Had Young's conduct led to substantive change,
either positive or negative, in Washington's handling of the Israeli-
Palestinian conflict, he would have merited a chapter in this book. In
any event, his stormy tenure at the UN proves that rogue diplomacy is not
exclusively a white man's affair.[21]

My other point relates to methodology. This is a traditional book in a
field undergoing a renaissance. Ever since G. M. Young derided diplomatic history in 1936 as nothing more than "the record of what one clerk
said to another clerk," those of us who study U.S. foreign policy have
suffered from inferiority complexes. Critics blasted us for our America-
centrism, state-centrism, elitism, adherence to conventional forms of

---

[21] Andrew DeRoche, *Andrew Young: Civil Rights Ambassador* (Wilmington, DE: Scholarly
Resources, 2003), 111–113; Young cited in Don Oberdorfer, "Young Resigns as UN
Ambassador; Envoy Faulted for Talks with PLO," *Washington Post*, 16 August 1979.

explanation, lack of theoretical sophistication, resistance to interdisciplinarity, unfamiliarity with foreign languages, and a slew of other defects that kept us, as Charles Maier put it in 1980, far from "the cutting edge of scholarship." Roughly a generation ago, however, diplomatic history began to shed its reputation as an intellectual backwater. Younger scholars borrowed approaches from related disciplines like political science, anthropology, sociology, psychology, and economics. They acquired language skills that allowed them to mine archives in nations as far-flung as China, Chile, Egypt, Niger, and Indonesia. They acknowledged the importance of non-state, nongovernmental actors like multinational corporations, interest groups, and religious communities. They included the marginalized and powerless in their accounts of events that had heretofore been written about from the top down. Many of them took the so-called "cultural turn" of the 1990s by adopting such categories of analysis as race, gender, and religion. A few even abandoned the empiricism long at the core of their specialty and embraced postmodernism. "The field of U.S. diplomatic history," Andrew Rotter marveled at the dawn of the new millennium, "has been overrun by culture vultures, gender heads, theory heads, even users of the 'D' word – discourse." And the trend toward ever-greater diversity continues.[22]

Amid such pluralism and innovation, this book will strike some twenty-first-century diplomatic historians as a museum piece. No grand theory, postmodern or otherwise, informs it. The reader will encounter no abstractions: "metanarrative," "discursive regime," "imaginary" as a noun. My sources are all in English, and they come from time-honored founts in the United States: government archives, presidential libraries,

---

[22] G. M. Young, *Portrait of an Age: Victorian England* (New York: Oxford University Press, 1936), 110; Charles S. Maier, "Marking Time: The Historiography of International Relations" in *The Past Before Us: Contemporary Historical Writing in the United States*, Michael Kammen, ed. (Ithaca: Cornell University Press, 1980), 355; Andrew J. Rotter, "Christians, Muslims, and Hindus: Religion and U.S.-South Asian Relations, 1947–1954," *Diplomatic History* 24 (Fall 2000): 593. Space does not allow me to list all the monographs and articles that have galvanized the field since Maier's critique, but one can get a feel for diplomatic historians' growing confidence that their work matters within the larger discipline by comparing the first and third editions of the historiographical survey *Explaining the History of American Foreign Relations*, Frank Costigliola, Michael J. Hogan, and Thomas Paterson, eds. (Cambridge: Cambridge University Press, 1991 and 2016). The first strikes a cranky, defensive tone; the third is a love-fest celebrating diplomatic history's robust ferment. One sees the same shift in attitude in the two editions of *America in the World: The Historiography of American Foreign Relations since 1941*, Frank Costigliola and Michael J. Hogan, eds. (Cambridge: Cambridge University Press, 1995 and 2014).

and diplomats' private papers. I have not interrogated these sources to get at their authors' underlying assumptions about women, people of color, or God, taking it as given that my subjects were men of their respective eras who, enlightened as some of them were, shared the values, attitudes, and prejudices of the time. Methodologically, this book breaks no ground unplowed at the time Young fired his broadside at diplomatic history during the New Deal years. It is fitting that my most important actor, Trist, was, in fact, a clerk, and that much of the record of his historic mission to Mexico consists of what he said – and wrote – to other clerks.

Traditional approaches to the study of U.S. foreign policy remain valuable even as scholars push the boundaries of the field. In the case of rogue diplomacy, where the crucial relationship is between the diplomat at his post and his government back home, a detailed examination of official American correspondence and related sources, the same methodology practiced by diplomatic historians during the genre's putative dark age, is not only appropriate but obligatory. This correspondence, after all, was the channel through which diplomat and government wrestled over policy. When analyzed in conjunction with personal letters, diaries, and other materials generated by the rogue diplomat and his superiors over the course of a foreign-policy crisis, such written communication offers the best means of explaining why the United States followed the course that it did.

And that is, at bottom, what this book seeks to do. Had I intended to explore these various geopolitical defining moments from a multinational perspective, weighing the roles played by other powers, then it would have been incumbent upon me to employ foreign sources, but mine is an American story, and, as Robert McMahon reminds us, "American decisions are invariably predicated upon perceptions of reality rather than upon reality itself (if the latter can ever be accurately gauged)." In each of the events I address, America's rogue diplomats acted upon perceptions at variance with those of stateside policymakers. I do not claim that either party fully grasped the "truth" of the situation – indeed, I join McMahon in questioning whether such comprehension is possible – but I propose to demonstrate how, time and again, the diplomat's vision prevailed despite his inferior rank. Making that clear requires me to pursue such old-fashioned goals as establishing a relationship between cause and effect. It also perforce restricts my cast of characters to officials in a policy-making capacity. This is, in brief, a classic study of high politics, bound to displease those who believe every new book should redefine the field, but no less important for that because many of the features of U.S. diplomacy that encouraged insubordination in the past are with us today.[23]

America is still the only great power on earth where a large percentage of key diplomatic posts are held by non-career men and women. The two major legislative renovations of the Foreign Service since World War II, the Foreign Service Acts of 1946 and 1980, brought about significant reforms, but they, like previous bills, failed to change matters at the highest level of diplomatic representation: the ambassadorships. Presidents continue to appoint individuals to this rank who owe their jobs to factors other than their previous documented fitness to discharge diplomatic duties.[24]

Usually, these factors are economic. Campaign contributors often receive prestigious overseas assignments. Richard Nixon was caught on one of his White House tapes telling Chief of Staff H. R. Haldeman, "Anybody who wants to be an ambassador must give at least $250,000." (When she learned of Nixon's bare minimum, would-be ambassador to Costa Rica Ruth Farkas allegedly exclaimed, "Isn't $250,000 an awful lot of money for Costa Rica?") As the cost of presidential campaigns has passed the $1 billion mark, ambassadorships have increasingly gone to so-called "bundlers," those well-connected men and women who not only donate millions of dollars of their own money but get their rich friends to kick in. George Tsunis, a wealthy lawyer and CEO, bundled or contributed around $1.3 million to Barack Obama's reelection campaign as well as to the campaigns of other Democratic candidates, and Obama nominated him for the ambassadorship to Norway. During his confirmation hearing, Tsunis revealed that he had never been to that country and that, moreover, he did not know that a prime minister and not a president headed its government. Clearly, his appointment was based on money rather than merit, a pay-to-play arrangement that is, two-time ambassador Dennis Jett observes, "as American as apple pie, because no other serious country has such a practice."[25]

---

[23] Robert McMahon, "The Study of American Foreign Relations: National History or International History?" in *Explaining the History Of American Foreign Relations*, First Edition, 16.

[24] Moskin, *American Statecraft*, 454–455, 483, 723–726, 765.

[25] Nixon cited in Meryl Gordon, *Mrs. Astor Regrets: The Hidden Betrayals of a Family beyond Reproach* (Boston: Houghton Mifflin, 2008), 87; Farkas cited in Dennis C. Jett, *American Ambassadors: The Past, Present, and Future of America's Diplomats* (New York: Palgrave, 2014), 81; Al Kamen, "Obama Ambassador Nominees – Baucus, Bell, and Tsunis – Hit Bumps in Hearings," *Washington Post*, 30 January 2014; Dennis

Apart from their pecuniary support for the right candidates, super-donors receive ambassadorial appointments for another reason, one that would have been familiar to Thomas Jefferson and John C. Calhoun. Because Congress is still notoriously tight-fisted when it comes to providing funds for representational entertaining – the parties, banquets, and other events an ambassador is expected to host – a rich ambassador-wannabe willing to dig into his or her own fortune to cover the costs of such festivities has an advantage over applicants of more modest means. In 2013, when ambassadors earned a maximum base salary of $179,700, they had to spend hundreds of thousands of dollars a year at certain posts wining and dining foreign elites. Thus, when Obama signaled his intention to nominate ex-congressman Timothy Roemer as ambassador to India, Roemer asked the president not to put his name forward. Roemer later informed the *New York Times*, "I told the White House and the State Department [that] I can't afford a job like that." The financial requirement for high diplomatic service remains a distinctive feature of U.S. foreign policy.[26]

Not all non-career ambassadors buy their appointments. Some receive them because of a personal relationship with the president. William Wilson, who became friends with Ronald Reagan when the latter was a movie actor and pitchman, was named first U.S. ambassador to the Holy See by President Reagan in 1984. George W. Bush nominated his former college roommate, Robert Johann Dieter, to head the U.S. Embassy in Belize in 2005. Dieter was succeeded in 2009 by Vinai Thummalapally, who had shared a dorm room with Barack Obama at Occidental College. Crystal Nix-Hines, named U.S. ambassador to the United Nations Educational, Scientific, and Cultural Organization in 2014, earned her undergraduate degree at Princeton, where she befriended the future Michelle Obama, and then attended Harvard Law School with the future President Obama. All of these individuals lacked any significant background in international affairs at the time they were sworn in as ambassadors. They got their positions because of the belief, more widespread in American policymaking circles than in the foreign services of other countries, that the president benefits from having friends in charge of U.S. embassies,

C. Jett, "Those Ignorant Ambassadors," *Huffington Post*, 26 February 2014. Embarrassed by his performance before the Senate Foreign Relations Committee, Tsunis withdrew his nomination.

[26] Roemer cited in Nicholas Confessore and Sheryl Gay Stolberg, "Well-Trod Path: Political Donor to Ambassador," *New York Times*, 18 January 2013.

that such an arrangement ensures loyalty and candor, and that these qualities are often more important than ability.[27]

Then there are the political appointees, those party stalwarts who receive ambassadorships as consolation prizes or thank-you gifts. Embassy Tokyo has served both functions. Former Vice-President Walter Mondale, cast into the political wilderness for eight years after his defeat by Reagan, became U.S. ambassador to Japan when the Democrat Bill Clinton took office in 1993. Mondale's successor, also appointed by Clinton, was the just-defeated former speaker of the House, Tom Foley. Caroline Kennedy, who enhanced Obama's prospects for victory in the 2008 election by writing an op-ed piece in which she compared the then-senator from Illinois to her father, obtained the Tokyo ambassadorship under President Obama. While one might argue that Mondale and Foley at least had valuable administrative and governmental experience, Kennedy lacked even that, aside from her work on the boards of various nonprofit organizations. None of the three ambassadors spoke Japanese. In any first-world country except the United States, they would never have been trusted with such responsibility, but Washington has its own criteria for selecting what Lewis Bollard calls "the bearers of the American eagle abroad." Friends, fundraisers, lobbyists, bundlers, and wheelhorses repeatedly beat out career men and women to represent their nation overseas, and, once installed in their posts, they often act with greater license than their foreign counterparts.[28]

William Wilson's stint in Rome is a case in point. Along with being one of Reagan's oldest friends, Wilson was a longtime trustee of the president's finances, and Reagan had absolute faith in his judgment. Thus, when in 1981 Reagan appointed Wilson special envoy to the Vatican, he persuaded the State Department and Office of Government Ethics to grant Wilson a dispensation permitting him to keep his seat on the Pennzoil Petroleum Company's board of directors, a privilege Wilson retained after being promoted to ambassador. Wilson saw no conflict of interest in this arrangement. In late 1985, after terrorists funded by Libyan dictator Muammar el-Qaddafi conducted deadly attacks at the Rome and Vienna airports and Reagan tried to get the governments of

[27] James Bruno, *The Foreign Circus: Why Foreign Policy Should Not Be Left in the Hands of Diplomats, Spies, and Political Hacks* (Canastota, NY: Bittersweet House Press, 2014), 20; Jett, *American Ambassadors*, 85–86.
[28] Jett, *American Ambassadors*, 88; Caroline Kennedy, "A President Like My Father," *New York Times*, 27 January 2008; Lewis E. Bollard, "America's Shaky Ambassadors," *Harvard Crimson*, 26 April 2006.

Western Europe to join America in imposing economic and political sanctions on Libya, Wilson defied a White House travel ban and secretly met with Qaddafi in Tripoli. The story broke, sparking rumors that the two men had discussed business dealings between Libya and Pennzoil. Wilson denied the allegation, but otherwise refused to answer reporters' questions about what he had been doing in a nation branded by Reagan as a center of global terrorism. Secretary of State George Schultz insisted that no one in the State Department had authorized Wilson's trip and claimed to have chewed the ambassador out after learning of his back-channel activity. "I knew that only the president could make the decision," he recalled in his memoir, but the unanimous sentiment at State was that "Wilson had to go, for the president's sake as well as to protect the integrity of our policy."[29]

Wilson did not go. Reagan expressed confidence in his old friend through the White House press secretary and declined to reprimand Wilson, even privately. The affair prompted columnist William Safire to write several blistering pieces lashing Wilson as a "loose-cannon envoy" who engaged in "diplomatic Lone Rangerism" and "arrogated to himself the right to make American policy." The ambassador's "mutiny," Safire wrote, required that he "be fired forthwith." But Safire acknowledged that this was unlikely to happen. Echoing a refrain sounded by reformers since the turn of the century, he noted the "absence of outrage at apparent dereliction of duty" and predicted that Wilson would leave his post "in honor and dignity, probably with a glowing letter from the president." That is how events played out. Wilson stepped down several months after his meeting with Qaddafi, telling journalists that "We are leaving because we feel that what had to be done has been done." With that, Wilson returned to his previous life as a California real estate and investments magnate.[30]

A non-American diplomat whose behavior triggered such a scandal would have been dismissed, disgraced, and possibly jailed. Even if we take

[29] Leslie Gelb, "U.S. Diplomat Reportedly Held Talks in Libya," *New York Times*, 22 March 1986; "Envoy Admits Visiting Libya in 1985," *New York Times*, 19 June 1986; Schultz cited in "Qaddafi Describes Meeting with U.S. Envoy to Vatican," *Washington Post*, 15 June 1986; George P. Schultz, *Turmoil and Triumph: Diplomacy, Power, and the Victory of the American Ideal* (New York: Charles Scribner's Sons, 1993), 678–679.

[30] Gerald M. Boyd, "Reagan Backs Envoy Despite Trip to Libya," *New York Times*, 24 March 1986; William Safire, "Cronyism at Its Worst," *New York Times*, 24 March 1986; Safire, "Loose-Cannon Crony," *New York Times*, 16 June 1986; Wilson cited in E. J. Dionne, "Envoy to Vatican Denies an Ouster," *New York Times*, 22 May 1986.

Wilson at his word that he did not talk about private commercial matters with Qaddafi, the fact that he talked to him at all, at a time when Reagan was calling on civilized nations to quarantine the "mad dog of the Middle East," was enough to warrant punishment. It constituted a violation of the administration's antiterrorist policy and was, in its way, as audacious as what Adams, Franklin, and Jay did in 1782. Like Young's dalliance with the PLO, however, Wilson's diplomatic freelancing had little impact on U.S.-Middle Eastern relations. There was no rapprochement between Washington and Tripoli. On the contrary, Qaddafi proclaimed a "line of death" north of the Gulf of Sidra and Reagan ordered a series of air strikes against Qaddafi's headquarters. Wilson thus joins Young as a rogue diplomat whose rebelliousness stamped him as quintessentially American but who did not influence the course of events to the degree that the protagonists of my six case studies did.[31]

Those studies, and the subject of American rogue diplomacy in general, have especial bearing on our time, as the United States faces myriad challenges to its hegemony and as the institutions developed over the last seventy-plus years to ensure stability and predictability in international affairs – the UN, North Atlantic Treaty Organization, Organization of American States, European Union, World Trade Organization, and others – become increasingly irrelevant due to resurgent nationalism, isolationism, protectionism, and militarism. With more geopolitical flash-points than any period since the end of the cold war and fewer accepted norms and rules governing actions among states, U.S. foreign policy will come to depend, to an even greater extent than heretofore, on the judgment of diplomats who, like their predecessors, not only implement but formulate strategies that shape the world we inhabit in the twenty-first century. Whether they enjoy the same improbable success as in the past is an issue to which no one can be indifferent.

[31] Reagan cited in Richard Downie, "Five Myths about Muammar Qaddafi," *Washington Post*, 11 March 2011; Qaddafi cited in James Gerstenzang, "U.S. Navy Ends Maneuvers in Gulf of Sidra," *Los Angeles Times*, 28 March 1986; Schultz, *Turmoil and Triumph*, 683–688.

I

"It Is Glory to Have Broken Such Infamous Orders"

Adams, Jay, and Franklin Midwife the Republic

Historian Samuel Flagg Bemis called it "the greatest victory in the annals of American diplomacy," and he was not exaggerating. The treaty that ended America's Revolutionary War in 1783 was all the rebels could have hoped for. Great Britain, the former mother country, not only recognized American independence but agreed to generous boundaries: the newborn United States was to stretch from the Atlantic seaboard to the Mississippi River and from Canada to the frontier of Spanish Florida, meaning that, in addition to the area comprising the original thirteen colonies, Americans gained title to a trans-Appalachian domain they had neither conquered nor occupied. The British moreover acknowledged American rights to fish in the waters off Newfoundland and granted extensive onshore curing and drying privileges. In addition, London pledged to withdraw its military forces from U.S. territory "with all convenient speed" and affirmed that navigation of the Mississippi from its source to the ocean would be open to British and American subjects. The government of George III and Prime Minister William Petty Fitzmaurice, Earl of Shelburne, even gave ground on an issue that had stymied peace negotiations: rather than insisting that British Loyalists in the United States be compensated for property lost during the revolution, they accepted American assurances that Congress would "earnestly recommend" indemnification, an arrangement that diplomats on both sides of the Atlantic knew amounted to royal abandonment of the Tories. America's overseas representatives won every point they considered requisite, while Britain effectively surrendered. In Paris, Foreign Minister Charles Gravier, comte de Vergennes, marveled at the outcome, writing to his undersecretary that British "concessions ... exceed all that I should have thought possible."[1]

Yet the men who brought off this diplomatic miracle – John Adams, Benjamin Franklin, and John Jay – received scorching criticism in the American Continental Congress. Legislators could find no fault with the pact itself, but many were chagrined by what Secretary for Foreign Affairs Robert Livingston termed "the management of it." The 1778 treaty of alliance between the United States and France, a bond essential for American victory in the revolution, had stipulated that neither country could conclude a settlement with the British without prior consent by the other power. Furthermore, Congress had ordered its envoys in Paris to place themselves under French control during the peacemaking process. The American diplomats, however, had not consulted Vergennes or any other French official before drawing up and signing preliminary articles of peace; indeed, they had not even informed their ally that negotiations toward that end were underway. Adams, Franklin, and Jay had shut the French out, and Livingston was aghast. "I am persuaded that the old maxim 'honesty is the best policy' applies with as much force to states as to individuals," he spluttered to President of Congress Elias Boudinot after the good ship *Washington* docked in Philadelphia bearing the provisional treaty. Could Congress ratify a document drafted in defiance of its own instructions and solemn commitments?[2]

Several congressmen demanded that the diplomats be censured. Charles Carroll of Maryland thought that "unless something expressive of our disapprobation" was done, the peace commission's handiwork would "be an indelible stain on our character." New York's Alexander Hamilton urged the "necessity of vindicating our public honor by renouncing ... the conduct of our ministers." Two delegates from Virginia were especially adamant. "The separate and secret manner in which

---

[1] Samuel Flagg Bemis, *The Diplomacy of the American Revolution*, Second Edition (Bloomington: Indiana University Press, 1965), 256; Preliminary Terms of Peace between Britain and the United States, 30 November 1782, *Treaties and Conventions Concluded between the United States of America and Other Powers since July 4, 1776* (Washington, D.C.: U.S. Government Printing Office, 1889), 370–373; Vergennes to Gérard, 4 December 1782, *The Revolutionary Diplomatic Correspondence of the United States*, Francis Wharton, ed. (Washington, D.C.: U.S. Government Printing Office, 1889) (hereafter *RDC*), 6:107.

[2] Livingston to Peace Commissioners, 25 March 1783, *RDC*, 6:339; Livingston to Boudinot, 18 March 1783, ibid., 6:315.

our ministers proceeded with respect to France," James Madison said, was "inconsistent with the spirit of our alliance and a dishonorable departure from the candor, rectitude, and plain dealing professed by Congress." If, after having "repeatedly assured" Vergennes that they would "take no step in negotiations but in concert and in confidence with him," Madison's colleagues did not "disclaim the policy followed by our ministers," America would "be considered by all nations as devoid of constancy." John Mercer went further. Just arrived in Philadelphia after service in the Continental Army and intent on proving himself rhetorical heir to Patrick Henry, Mercer delivered a scenery-chewing harangue against the "chicane and low cunning" exhibited by the commission, so contrary to "the honesty and good faith which became all nations, particularly an infant republic." The diplomats' behavior was "a mixture of follies which had no example," he said, a "tragedy to America, and a comedy to all the world beside." It proved that the United States had "at once all the follies of youth and the vices of old age." Mercer warned that unless Congress made plain their "inexpressible indignation" at the commission's "treachery," they would "realize the case of those who kicked down the ladder by which they had been elevated." When Hugh Williamson of North Carolina questioned whether such brickbats should be applied to men who had, after all, "shown great ability," Mercer shot back that his "language with respect to the ministers" was "justified by their refusal to obey instructions."

This obloquy filled many pages in Madison's record of congressional debate, and an observer could be forgiven for concluding that Adams, Franklin, and Jay did in fact face censure or worse. But, Madison noted, it gradually became apparent that, for all the remonstrances showered on the diplomats, "a large proportion" of legislators were "against any measure which seemed in any manner to blame" them for acting as they did. Connecticut's Oliver Wolcott spoke for the majority when he expressed confidence that Congress would "never censure ministers who had obtained such terms for this country." Richard Henry Lee also felt it "highly improper to censure ministers who had negotiated well." Although he detested Franklin and had no desire to help America's most celebrated figure win further acclaim, Lee reminded his fellow Virginians that "in particular emergencies" a diplomat might consider it expedient to "swerve from strict instructions" in order to obtain the best outcome. That appeared to be the case here, with the policy of hard and fast fidelity to France running counter to "our interests." Most outspoken in his defense of the peace commissioners was South Carolina's John Rutledge.

Adams, Franklin, and Jay had "done right," he affirmed. They had "maintained the honor of the United States after Congress had given it up" by making any peace treaty subject to French approval. In Rutledge's opinion, "instructions ought to be disregarded" whenever they conflicted with the public good. He himself "would never be bound by them" if he found them "improper."

Mercer, thunderstruck, excoriated "the dangerous tendency of the doctrine maintained by Mr. Rutledge with regard to instructions." Did the legislators intend to embrace this doctrine and let the commission's misconduct go unpunished? How could the United States conduct a coherent foreign policy if its diplomats felt free to flout orders? More important, how could Americans, who prided themselves on being above Old-World Machiavellianism, countenance an act of bad faith worthy of the slipperiest intriguer in the most corrupt European country? Mercer was certain that "His Most Christian Majesty," Louis XVI of France, would never so "betray or injure us." The least Congress could do was censure Adams, Franklin, and Jay and repudiate the preliminaries they had concluded behind French backs.

Debate continued off and on for nearly two weeks, and the halls of Congress echoed with some of the feistiest commentary yet voiced in that chamber. At one point, a delegate asked François Barbé-Marbois, head of the French legation in America, if the court of France planned to file a complaint about the diplomats' double-dealing, to which the Frenchman responded that "great powers never *complained*, but they *felt* and *remembered*," a barely disguised threat that lent force to the arguments advanced by Mercer and Madison. Hugh Williamson, torn between joy at British concessions and dismay at American perfidy, proposed a compromise that avoided "harsh treatment of the ministers" but still communicated to them Congress's unhappiness, thereby leaving them to "get over the embarrassment as they should find best." Some congressmen dismissed this as a slap on the wrist; others thought it insulting treatment for patriots who had ably served their country. Neither side could win out, and Congress never went on record as commending or condemning its negotiators.

It did, however, ratify the preliminaries, which stood as tacit endorsement of the commission's maneuvering – and which might have been prompted by the appearance in numerous newspapers of reports of what Adams, Franklin, and Jay had wrought. (Congressional proceedings were supposed to be secret, but members leaked information when it served their ends.) To no one's surprise, the provisional treaty was popular with the American people. Congress would have diminished its prestige had it rejected so felicitous an agreement. Britain's "terms," Madison admitted, were "extremely liberal."[3]

An ocean away, the envoys could only guess at congressional response to their disobedience. Adams, the most anxious and pessimistic of America's first generation of diplomats, was uncharacteristically sanguine. When Henry Laurens, who had joined the commission at the last moment, ventured that "John Adams & Co. may be hanged" as traitors, Adams replied, "I cannot think our country will hang her ministers merely for their simplicity in being cheated into independence, the fisheries, and half of the Great Lakes." But if Congress were foolish enough to "get J. A. hanged," Adams said, he was "pretty well prepared for this, or to be recalled, or censured, ... or slandered, just as they please." Adams knew he had acted properly. Had he and his cohorts not forsaken the French, he insisted, "our country would have lost advantages beyond computation."[4]

Jay, possibly the best lawyer in America, justified the commission's actions with some ingenious reasoning. He admitted that "Congress positively instructed us to do nothing without the advice and consent of the French minister, and we have departed from that line of conduct." They had done so, however, assuming "the object of that instruction" to be "the supposed interest of America, and not of France." From Jay's perspective, "we were directed to ask the advice of the French minister because it was thought advantageous to our country that we should receive and be governed by it." Yet everything Jay had observed since arriving in Paris in mid-1782 convinced him that Vergennes's "plan for a treaty for America was far from being such as America would have preferred." The French wanted America independent, but they had no desire to see another great power rise in the West. They sought to keep the United States weak, confined between the Allegheny Mountains and the sea, a French satellite. Since this agenda was contrary to American interests, Congress's instructions were not binding, and the commission was under no obligation to obey them. Jay's conscience was clear.[5]

---

[3] Reports of Debates during the Congress of Confederation, 12–24 March 1783, *Papers of James Madison*, Gaillard Hunt, ed. (New York: J. & H. G. Langley, 1841), 1:380–412 (emphasis in the original).

[4] Adams to Laurens, 12 March 1783, *RDC*, 6:284–285; Adams to Livingston, 9 July 1783, ibid., 6:531.

[5] Jay to Livingston, 19 July 1783, *The Life of John Jay: With Selections from His Correspondence and Miscellaneous Papers*, William Jay, ed. (New York: J. & J. Harper, 1833) (hereafter *LJJ*), 1:174–178.

Franklin's was not. Alone among the commissioners, he felt pangs of regret. In his five-and-a-half years in France, he had developed considerable affection for his host country; unlike Adams and Jay, he was fond of the French and adapted to the ceremony, complex etiquette, and subtle diplomatic traditions of Paris and Versailles. Furthermore, he was aware of how invaluable French aid had been to American victory. Whereas Adams and Jay tended to downplay France's contribution, their elder colleague knew the United States owed its metamorphosis from colony to republic to Louis XVI. Rather than questioning French motives, Franklin was more likely to express vehement – often toadying – gratitude and preface even the mildest criticism of America's ally with a surfeit of compliments and affirmations of eternal allegiance. Nonetheless, he had joined Adams and Jay in end-running the government that kept America afloat from Lexington to Yorktown. The commissioners had concluded an Anglo-American treaty without the blessings or even the knowledge of the French because London offered such tempting, and apparently time-sensitive, terms. Had they erred? Had the territorial and other gains been worth the sacrifice of American rectitude? Franklin could not be certain. "We did what appeared to all of us best at the time," he wrote Livingston, "and if we have done wrong, Congress will do right ... to censure us."[6]

The New World's paramount philosopher finally took refuge in a kind of bemused fatalism. As he had warned his fellow envoys over a year earlier, any treaty they managed to put together, no matter how favorable for the United States, would have its detractors. "I have never known of a peace that did not occasion a great deal of popular discontent, clamor, and censure," Franklin pronounced, citing the Treaties of Utrecht and Aix-la-Chapelle. Even the Pact of Paris ending the Seven Years' War, "the most advantageous and glorious for England that ever she made" was "violently decried" and its authors "as violently abused." So the American commissioners should not expect universal applause. "[T]he blessing promised to peacemakers," said Franklin, "relates to the next world, for in this they seem to have a greater chance of being cursed."[7]

That forecast proved wrong. Although a few legislators kept up their attacks on the diplomats after ratification of the provisional treaty, most of Franklin's countrymen recognized it for the magnificent accomplishment it was. (Tellingly, Hamilton, one of the commission's critics on the

---

[6] Franklin to Livingston, 22 July 1783, *RDC*, 6:581.
[7] Franklin to Laurens, 25 May 1782, *RDC*, 5:560.

floor of Congress, sent a private letter to Jay conveying his "warmest approbation of your conduct.") When the definitive treaty, identical to the preliminary version, was borne back to the United States in November 1783, Congress ratified it unanimously. Jay and Franklin returned home to rapturous receptions, and only Adams's assumption of his duties as the first U.S. minister to Great Britain prevented him from receiving a similar hero's welcome. None of the diplomats suffered any political damage as a consequence of their having disobeyed orders. Franklin lived to participate in the Constitutional Convention and hold the prestigious office of president of Pennsylvania, a position equivalent to today's governorship. Jay went on to serve as secretary of foreign affairs and chief justice of the Supreme Court. And Adams, of course, became president.[8]

Contemporary reaction to the commissioners' exploits presaged most scholarship on Revolutionary War diplomacy. Generations of historians have hewed to the Bemis line, lauding Adams, Franklin, and Jay for their "astounding diplomatic victory," a settlement "as advantageous to their country as any in their history." Authors differ as to which Founding Father deserves credit for this masterstroke – in some versions Franklin restrains his two headstrong comrades and preserves the Franco-American partnership until independence is won; in others Jay, or Adams, or both, strong-arm a timid Franklin into closing a deal with the British before America's ally can undercut U.S. war aims – but the story line remains constant: the Americans, despite holding a weak negotiating hand, overcome their naïveté, capitalize on European rivalries, exploit time and distance factors, and, most significantly, violate Congress's orders when circumstances call for it. As a result of their cunning, the United States enters the family of nations as a world power with boundaries outstripping those of any republic since ancient Rome. Richard Morris is only slightly more effusive than most scholars when he writes of Adams, Franklin, and Jay, "a free people is eternally in their debt."[9]

---

[8] Hamilton to Jay, 25 July 1783, *The Papers of Alexander Hamilton*, Harold C. Syrett, ed. (New York: Columbia University Press, 1962), 3:416.

[9] Stacy Schiff, *A Great Improvisation: Franklin, France, and the Birth of America* (New York: Henry Holt and Company, 2005), 327; David McCullough, *John Adams* (New York: Simon & Schuster, 2001), 285; Richard B. Morris, *The Peacemakers: The Great Powers and American Independence* (New York: Harper & Row, 1965), 459. For other accounts in this vein, see Elmer Bendiner, *The Virgin Diplomats* (New York: Alfred A. Knopf, 1976); Thomas Fleming, *The Perils of Peace: America's Struggle for Survival after Yorktown* (New York: Smithsonian Books, 2007); Lawrence F. Kaplan, *Colonies*

Overlooked in the literature is the fact that the commissioners set a precedent that shaped America's foreign policy for the next two centuries and ensured that U.S. diplomacy would differ from that practiced by representatives of any other government. In defying the orders of stateside superiors, and in profiting so immensely thereby, both in terms of their personal fortunes and the welfare of their country, Adams, Franklin, and Jay made it likelier that future U.S. diplomats would step out of line. Censure – or hanging – might have nipped this rebelliousness in the bud, but it would also have kept the United States from receiving everything its leaders demanded with regard to the West, the fisheries, the Loyalists, the Mississippi, and other matters deemed essential to national survival. Congress therefore followed the remunerative path of least resistance, and the architects of peace escaped punishment. American independence was, to a great extent, founded on diplomatic insubordination.

"DIMINISH THE POWER OF ENGLAND AND PROPORTIONATELY RAISE THAT OF FRANCE"

The United States could never have won its revolution singlehanded. Outmatched by the mother country in wealth, population, and military power, America would have been crushed had Vergennes not persuaded Louis XVI to covertly supply George Washington's army in the summer of 1776. Thereafter Paris moved war goods westward in such quantity that French powder comprised 90 percent of the American stock for the first two years of the revolution. France also provided uniforms, medicine, muskets, and even cannons with the king's monogram graven upon them. In the pivotal Battle of Saratoga, nearly all of the rebels' arms and ammunition came from French merchants. And France did more than furnish military articles: it emptied its treasury making loans to the American government; it safeguarded American commerce on the high seas by protecting rebel vessels from seizure by British warships; and Vergennes permitted American privateers to operate out of French ports and dispose of prizes on French soil, a breach of France's duties as a neutral. When France shed that fictive status, declaring war on Britain in

into Nation: American Diplomacy, 1763–1801 (New York: Macmillan, 1972); David Schoenbrun, *Triumph in Paris: The Exploits of Benjamin Franklin* (New York: Harper & Row, 1976). For rare exceptions to the orthodox treatment, see Jonathan R. Dull, *A Diplomatic History of the American Revolution* (New Haven: Yale University Press, 1985), 144–151; Perkins, "Peace of Paris," 190–229.

1778, its contribution to the American cause swelled. The French fitted out thousands of troops for combat. A joint Franco-Spanish armada threatened to invade southern England, obliging the British to keep many of their ships close to home instead of employing them in America. French attacks on the British East and West Indies diverted more men-of-war. At Yorktown, the final engagement, it was not only French ground forces but the appearance of a French fleet in adjacent waters that made impossible General Charles Cornwallis's reinforcement or escape. Indeed, more Frenchmen participated in the battle of Yorktown than Americans. By almost every historian's reckoning, French assistance tilted the scales of war in favor of the fledgling republic.[10]

This succor, however, was not prompted by love for Americans or zeal for democracy, despite myths to that effect. Although a few French intellectuals did enthuse over the noble savages fighting for liberty in the New World, and while the young firebrand Gilbert du Motier, Marquis de Lafayette, drew notice in Paris with his pleas on behalf of Washington's ragtag army, King Louis and his court viewed the rebels with mistrust, a natural response given French values, interests, and history. France was a Catholic country ruled by an absolute monarch; if the mostly Protestant Americans succeeded in their insurrection, they planned to establish a republic, which could serve as a dangerous example to France's colonial subjects in the Caribbean and elsewhere. Moreover, Americans had fought against the French in four previous wars, the last of which – known as the Seven Years' War in Europe and the French and Indian War in America – ended with a crushing French defeat. France lost nearly all of its North American possessions, including Canada and Louisiana, and suffered reverses in Europe and India as well. No French statesman could forget that the rustics extolled by Lafayette had helped Britain to its greatest victory to date and enabled their then-mother country to achieve a position of unprecedented political supremacy at France's expense.

Yet it was precisely the humiliation of this thrashing, and the belief that Americans played an essential role in bringing it about, that underlay

---

[10] For representative works, see R. W. Van Alstyne, *Empire and Independence: An International History of the American Revolution* (Hoboken, NJ: John Wiley and Sons, 1965); Edward S. Corwin, *French Policy and the American Alliance* (Princeton: Princeton University Press, 1916); J. H. Plumb, "The French Connection: The Alliance That Won the Revolution," *American Heritage* 26 (1974): 4; James Brown Scott, *The United States and France: Some Opinions on International Gratitude* (New York: Oxford University Press, 1926); William C. Stinchcombe, *The American Revolution and the French Alliance* (Syracuse, NY: Syracuse University Press, 1969).

French policy after 1763. From the moment Britain took the French sword in surrender, Étienne François, duc de Choiseul, Vergennes's predecessor in the foreign office, made *revanche* his prime objective. He rebuilt France's navy, improved its army, carried out financial reforms, and, above all, tried to sow dissension between America and Britain. His logic was compelling. Britain had replaced France as the strongest nation on earth. The chief source of Britain's strength was its colonial empire, in particular its holdings in North America. Therefore, if France deprived Britain of these possessions, it would redress the balance of power in its favor.

American complaints about Parliamentary overbearance in the 1760s struck Choiseul as a heaven-sent opportunity to effect a schism. He dispatched several missions across the Atlantic for that purpose, instructing his agents to gauge the popular temper in the middle colonies, the south, and especially New England. How intense was American wrath over the Sugar Act, the Stamp Act, the Townshend Acts? Were American vows to defy these measures sincere? If so, would the colonists welcome trained officers and engineers from a foreign power? Choiseul accumulated scores of reports on America's military resources, its strong points and entrenched forts, and its potential leaders. For a time, he thought the bonds of imperial loyalty so frayed that a few expressions of encouragement from Paris would suffice to ignite revolt. Parliament's repeal of its most offensive duties, however, and the consequent easing of tensions between crown and colonies made Choiseul revise his opinion. He left office convinced that the Americans remained allegiant to Britain and would not seek independence until the distant future.[11]

Needless to say, he was wrong. Vergennes confronted a different situation, becoming foreign minister during the fraught period between the Boston Tea Party and the assembly of the first Continental Congress, when a series of ill-considered decrees reinvigorated anti-British feeling in America. The ministry of Frederick, Lord North, dubbed these the Coercive Acts, colonists called them "intolerable acts," but regardless of their label they had an effect opposite from what was intended: instead of bringing America to heel, they sparked protests from Georgia to New Hampshire. Vergennes did not initially appreciate how close Britain was to an imperial civil war – during his first few months in office, he

---

[11] Most scholarship on Choiseul's policy is in French, but a useful English-language examination is C. H. Van Tyne, "French Aid before the Alliance of 1778," *American Historical Review* 31 (October 1925): 21–31.

concentrated on Eastern European affairs – but the shots heard round the world in mid-1775 caught his attention. Lexington made reconciliation unlikely; Bunker Hill made it impossible. Here was a chance to humble the British and reverse the verdict of 1763.

Vergennes connived with the playwright, journalist, and sometime arms contractor Pierre-Augustine Caron de Beaumarchais to set up a sham trading company through which military supplies could be funneled to the colonists, and he overcame Louis XVI's opposition to this project by assuring him the risks were slight. Paris would maintain a posture of neutrality, he insisted. Absent some direct provocation it was doubtful that the cash-strapped British would renew hostilities with their arch-enemy. If the American rebellion succeeded, as Vergennes thought it might, France would glean the fruits of victory without the hazards of combat. And what fruits! In a *mémoire* remarkable for its frankness, Vergennes explained why American independence would redound to Louis's benefit: "First, it will diminish the power of England and proportionally raise that of France. Second, it will cause irreparable loss to English trade, while it will considerably extend ours. Third, it presents to us as very probable the recovery of a part of the possessions which the English have taken from us." While conceding the unattractiveness of American political principles, Vergennes saw nothing to fear from them. Republics were by nature weak and fractious, he noted. Americans, once independent, would be unable to menace European dominions in the New World.[12]

So persuasive were Vergennes's arguments that he not only got Louis to transfer 1 million livres worth of munitions from the royal arsenals to the bogus firm of Roderigo Hortalez and Company; he convinced Louis's uncle and fellow Bourbon monarch, Charles III of Spain, to match the contribution. (Spain had fought alongside France in the Seven Years' War and paid a similar price for losing.) Ships laden with money, arms, ammunition, and clothing began sailing to the colonies before any American diplomat set foot in France – indeed, even before the Continental Congress issued its Declaration of Independence.[13]

---

[12] Vergennes cited in Samuel Flagg Bemis, *A Diplomatic History of the United States* (New York: Henry Holt, 1946), 20.

[13] For France's military subsidies under the guise of private trade, see Maurice Lever, *Beaumarchais*, trans. Susan Emanuel (New York: Farrar, Straus, and Giroux, 2009); Brian N. Morton and Donald C. Spinelli, *Beaumarchais and the American Revolution* (Lanham, MD: Lexington Books, 2003); Joel Richard Paul, *Unlikely Allies: How a Merchant, a Playwright, and a Spy Saved the American Revolution* (New York:

By the time of Franklin's arrival in Paris in December 1776, then, French assistance was an established fact. Franklin's task – and that of his two colleagues, Silas Deane and Arthur Lee – was to transform covert support into recognition of American independence and a Franco-American alliance. This was no easy assignment. Franklin, Deane, and Lee, the first accredited diplomats in U.S. history, had their introductory encounters with Vergennes in the wake of a British campaign that saw King George's redcoats seize New York City and almost apprehend General Washington. Given that setback, and other recent rebel defeats, Vergennes was hardly eager to raise France's profile in America. The near destruction of the Continental Army on Brooklyn Heights served as a vivid reminder of British military power, and the program of rearmament inaugurated by Choiseul was not yet complete. Premature recognition of the United States, much less official French commitment to the rebel cause, was likely to bring on war. Vergennes consequently preferred to keep his country's aid *sub rosa*. Not even the tumultuous reception accorded Franklin in Paris, where the Sage of Philadelphia attracted crowds so massive that the curious bought tickets to view him from afar, could budge the French court. Franklin may have been the most famous man in the world after Voltaire, but his philosophical writings and electrical experiments meant nothing to Vergennes, who judged all events by the criterion of what was good for France. Until the Americans gave some sign that they could hold their own against British forces, the foreign minister saw no reason to chance a replay of the conflict that had shorn France of its great-power status less than twenty years before.[14]

Historians disagree about what caused Vergennes to change his mind. For a long time they identified the Battle of Saratoga as the deciding factor. Major General Horatio Gates's victory in the Hudson Valley, they argued, won Americans new respect at Versailles and made an alliance with the United States look more propitious. Recent treatments deemphasize Saratoga's importance and contend that Vergennes had decided by late 1777 that war with Britain was inevitable. If France was going to

---

Riverhead Books, 2009). The best treatment of Vergennes's foreign policy is Orville T. Murphy, *Charles Gravier, Comte de Vergennes: French Diplomacy in the Age of Revolution* (Albany: State University of New York Press, 1982).

[14] Franklin's taking of Paris by storm is one of the most written-about episodes in American diplomatic history. The better accounts include Claude-Anne Lopez, *Mon Cher Papa: Franklin and the Ladies of Paris* (New Haven: Yale University Press, 1966); Schiff, *Great Improvisation*; Schoenbrun, *Triumph in Paris*; Gordon S. Wood, *The Americanization of Benjamin Franklin* (New York: Penguin Books, 2004).

have to fight its ancient foe again anyway, he felt, it was better to do so at once, when the British were hemorrhaging men and money in America, rather than later, when London would have both hands free. Vergennes moreover seems to have concluded that France's fleet was ready to engage Britain on the high seas. Whatever his motivation, he persuaded his sovereign to move from surreptitious aid to open conflict, and on 6 February 1778, Franklin, Deane, and Lee joined Conrad Alexandre Gérard, Vergennes's chief assistant, at the Hotel de Lautrec in Paris to initial the historic treaty. After the four men affixed their signatures, Gérard traveled by carriage to Versailles to hand the document to Vergennes, who presented it to the king. Louis gave it his blessing. While the Continental Congress had yet to ratify the alliance, their assent was certain. France and America had become cobelligerents. Echoing Bemis almost word-for-word, historian Edmund Morgan dubs this "the greatest diplomatic victory the United States has ever achieved."[15]

Perhaps, but it was not an unmixed blessing. There were, in fact, two treaties signed that day. The first, a treaty of amity and commerce, followed almost exactly the principles laid down by John Adams two years earlier, when he drafted his Plan of 1776, a definition of maritime rights that formed the basis of what later became America's policy of "freedom of the seas." Franklin had brought a copy of Adams's plan to Paris to guide him in negotiations, and the French acquiesced to every provision: the treaty included rules protecting neutral commerce in wartime and permitted American ships free entry into French ports; it also granted the United States most-favored-nation status. More consequential than these agreements was France's recognition of America as an independent country. Franklin, Deane, and Lee had at last achieved this cherished objective.[16]

[15] Edmund S. Morgan, *The Birth of the Republic, 1763–1789*, Second Edition (Chicago: University of Chicago Press, 1977), 83. For the orthodox view of Saratoga's significance, see Helen Augur, *The Secret War of Independence* (New York: Greenwood Press, 1955), 251; Bemis, *Diplomacy of the American Revolution*, 58–61; Piers Mackesy, *The War for America, 1775–1783* (Cambridge: Harvard University Press, 1964), 147; Van Tyne, "French Aid before the Alliance of 1778," 40; Van Tyne, "Influences Which Determined the French Government to Make the Treaty with America, 1778," *American Historical Review* 21 (April 1916): 531–534. For studies giving less weight to American heroics in the woods of northern New York, see Dull, *Diplomatic History of the American Revolution*, 89–96; Jonathan R. Dull, *The French Navy and American Independence: A Study of Arms and Diplomacy, 1774–1787* (Princeton: Princeton University Press, 1975), 89–94; Van Alstyne, *Empire and Independence*, 132–133.

[16] Treaty of Amity and Commerce, 6 February 1778, *Treaties and Other International Acts of the United States of America,* Hunter Miller, ed. (Washington, D.C.: U.S. Government Printing Office, 1931) (hereafter *TOIA*), 2:3–29. See also Plan of a Treaty with France,

The second accord, a treaty of conditional and defensive alliance, was to take effect only in the event that French recognition triggered war between France and Britain. (Since it was inconceivable that George III and North would respond to such provocation with anything less than a call to arms, all signatories considered this pact in force before the ink was dry.) Article 2, the clause most important to Americans, stipulated, "The essential and direct end of the present defensive alliance is to maintain effectually the liberty, sovereignty, and independence absolute and unlimited of the said United States." America's diplomats paid a steep price for that article. Although Vergennes disclaimed any intention of reconquering Canada, the United States had to recognize French acquisitions in the Caribbean and guarantee "from the present time and forever" all territories on the North American continent France might obtain at the peace table. Vergennes moreover insisted on a clause stating that "Neither of the two Parties shall conclude either Truce or Peace with Great Britain without the formal consent of the other first obtain'd." If, in other words, London decided to cut its colonies loose, the Americans could not declare victory and disband their army; they had to keep fighting until Paris's aims were satisfied.[17]

"OUR GENEROUS ALLY"

Fear of overseas involvement, especially in European affairs, is a persistent theme in United States history. It predates the 1778 treaties. Those agreements, however, and the events that flowed from them brought Americans' fear to the level of pathology, made "entangling alliances" the most hot-button term in their foreign-policy lexicon, and underlay such bedrock American texts as Washington's Farewell Address and the Monroe Doctrine. So keenly did Americans resent the obligations imposed upon them by the Faustian bargain of 1778 that they did not become party to another formal alliance for a century and a half.[18]

To Franklin, Deane, and Lee, though, this limitation on the United States' freedom of action was essential for military victory, and they

---

24 September 1776, *Journals of the Continental Congress, 1774–1789*, Galliard Hunt, ed. (Washington, D.C.: U.S. Government Printing Office, 1912) (hereafter *JCC*), 5:765–789.

[17] Treaty of Conditional and Defensive Alliance, 6 February 1778, *TOIA*, 2:35–41.

[18] The classic study of American political isolationism in the early national period remains Felix Gilbert, *The Beginnings of American Foreign Policy: To the Farewell Address* (Princeton: Princeton University Press, 1961).

concluded, with good reason, that Vergennes had been something of a soft touch in not demanding more by way of quid pro quo. Congress felt the same; after ratifying the pacts in early May, it instructed its ministers to convey "grateful acknowledgements ... to his Most Christian Majesty for his truly magnanimous conduct respecting these states in the said generous and disinterested treaties." Pro-French feeling was high among Americans on both sides of the Atlantic – for a time.[19]

Several developments combined to dampen this enthusiasm. Charles III, initially reluctant to join his cousin Louis in hostilities against Britain, realized by early 1779 that the war presented an excellent chance to recover Gibraltar, the famous fortress on the southern tip of the Iberian Peninsula that the British had taken from Spain seventy-five years earlier. While Charles would neither ally his kingdom with the United States nor commit himself to American independence, he did sign the Convention of Aranjuez, a Franco-Spanish accord that, among other things, bound the French to do battle until Gibraltar was once again attached to Spanish soil. In some ways this partnership proved advantageous to the Americans: by pooling their fleets, France and Spain gained naval superiority over Britain, and their maneuvers in the English Channel compelled George III to divert resources from the American theater. On the other hand, the two Bourbon kings saddled the United States with a potentially fatal burden. Franklin, Deane, and Lee had guaranteed that their nation would not make a separate peace without French approval, and France was now obliged to wage war until the Spanish flag flew over Gibraltar. Hence, Americans found themselves tied, indirectly, to a problem in which they had no strategic or economic interest. Little did Adams, who hailed the Franco-American alliance in 1778 as "a rock upon which we may safely build," anticipate that events on an actual rock in the Mediterranean could derail his country's revolution![20]

---

[19] Congressional Resolution, 4 May 1778, RDC, 2:569. Vergennes's magnanimity was calculating. He wanted to stay on good terms with the neutral maritime powers of Europe, and he feared that a too-selfish French policy in the New World would jeopardize those relations, possibly driving countries like Portugal and the Netherlands into the British camp. See Corwin, *French Policy and the American Alliance*, 21–22, 170–172; Bemis, *Diplomacy of the American Revolution*, 65; Murphy, *Charles Gravier*, 256–257.

[20] Adams to Wharton, 4 August 1778, RDC, 2:676. For a Spain's role in turning a localized North American insurgence into a global conflict, see Thomas E. Chavez, *Spain and the Independence of the United States: An Intrinsic Gift* (Albuquerque: University of New Mexico Press, 2002); Anthony McFarlane, "The American Revolution and the Spanish Monarchy" in *Europe's American Revolution*, Simon P. Newman, ed. (New York:

Just as distressing was the fact that French cobelligerency did not lead to an upturn in U.S. military fortunes. The war continued to go badly for the rebels despite the dispatch of French soldiers and ships of the line to America. Indeed, the first joint Franco-American campaign was a fiasco, as French Admiral Charles Hector d'Estaing and rebel General John Sullivan failed to coordinate their forces at Newport, Rhode Island, thereby missing the opportunity to overrun the British garrison there. French attempts to blockade New York Harbor likewise came a cropper. Vergennes began receiving despondent reports from Gérard, who arrived in Philadelphia five months after the treaties' signing as the first French minister to the United States and who was appalled by the indiscipline of Washington's army. The revolution was near collapse, he wrote. No matter what Versailles did, these frontier outposts would never make good their escape from the British Empire. Gérard's verdict seemed borne out when the British shifted their focus south and took Savannah with a loss of only seven men. A combined French and American siege to recapture the city flopped; miscommunication kept the allies from acting in concert, and insufficient secrecy ensured that the defenders knew their enemy's every move beforehand. Allied casualties were nearly six times those suffered by the British, who maintained their hold on Georgia's capital.[21]

Congress, frustrated by these reverses and put off by the hauteur of the French officers sent to America, nonetheless saw no alternative other than to beseech Vergennes for more money, men, and *matériel*. American entreaties grew especially shrill after the British seized Charleston in the spring of 1780, taking almost 5,000 continental troops prisoner, the largest surrender of a U.S. armed force until the Civil War. Another British victory followed at Camden, where Gates, hero of Saratoga, allowed his army to be outflanked by a numerically inferior enemy. The British also made territorial gains in Virginia. For Americans, this was the bleakest time in the war, and their desperation affected their compact with France. William Stinchcombe, author of the most thorough study of Franco-American policy during the revolution, notes, "The 1778 alliance

Palgrave, 2006), 26–50; Buchanan Parker Thomson, *Spain: Forgotten Ally of the American Revolution* (North Quincy, MA: Christopher Publishing House, 1976).
[21] Dull, *French Navy and American Independence*, 120–124, 161; Orville T. Murphy, "The View from Versailles: Charles Gravier Comte de Vergennes's Perceptions of the American Revolution" in *Diplomacy and Revolution: The Franco-American Alliance of 1778*, Ronald Hoffman and Peter J. Albert, eds. (Charlottesville: University Press of Virginia, 1981), 131–140.

changed from a relation of partnership, although assuredly not on an equal basis, to one of dependence by 1780."[22]

Vergennes was quick to capitalize on this change, using his increased leverage to direct the war effort toward French rather than American ends. When Congress called for a joint expedition into Canada, Vergennes vetoed the proposal because he preferred to see the rebels' northern neighbor remain under British control. Having ceded French claims to the region, and seeking to maximize French influence over an independent United States, Vergennes concluded that it was in his country's interest for the new republic to be as insecure as possible. British retention of Canada, he advised Gérard, would keep the Americans "uneasy" and "make them feel to an even greater extent the need which they have for friendship and alliance with the king."[23]

This consideration also led Vergennes to discourage plans to extend the United States's western boundary to the Mississippi River, a congressional aim that became doubly odious in French eyes when the Spanish government objected to it. Charles III had no desire to share navigation of that vital waterway with the Americans, much less give up what he considered Spanish possessions on its east bank. Vergennes therefore informed Congress through Gérard that Versailles would not interpret Article 11 of the 1778 treaty of alliance, a mutual guarantee of territory acquired as a result of the war, to include land west of the Alleghenies. Vergennes moreover refused to assist the Americans in any campaign to capture East or West Florida. The Spanish foreign minister, José Monino y Redondo, conde de Floridablanca, wanted to keep the United States away from the Gulf of Mexico, and, as Gérard flatly told American legislators, Versailles valued Spain more highly than America in the contest with Britain. If Congress compelled the French to choose between Spain and the United States with regard to territorial claims, Louis XVI's Bourbon ally would receive preference. In other words, Vergennes envisaged the sovereign American republic as a narrow coastal strip hemmed in by the dominions of two empires.

Such constraints were bad enough, but they paled beside the instructions Vergennes obliged Congress to send to Franklin and his colleagues in August 1781. Vergennes was dissatisfied with the commission's existing

---

[22] Stinchcombe, *American Revolution and the French Alliance*, 134. See also Robert Middlekauff, *The Glorious Cause: The American Revolution, 1763–1789*, Second Edition (New York: Oxford University Press, 2005), 442–463.

[23] Vergennes cited in Stinchcombe, *American Revolution and the French Alliance*, 27.

orders, issued in 1779, a time when America's military prospects had seemed more promising. The earlier charge gave the diplomats considerable license, directing them to govern themselves "by the alliance between His Most Christian Majesty and these states, by the advice of our allies, by your knowledge of our interests, and by your own discretion, in which we repose the fullest confidence." That was too much slack for Vergennes, who wanted the envoys under his thumb, particularly after Congress named John Adams to replace Deane. Adams's impatience with the *politesse* of Versailles, his oft-voiced conviction that France was not doing enough to aid America, and his seeming ingratitude toward the monarchy that had opened its coffers and veins to keep the revolution afloat infuriated Vergennes, who predicted that the prickly New Englander "will only incite difficulties and vexations, because he has an inflexibility, a pedantry, an arrogance, and a conceit that renders him incapable of dealing with political subjects." Efforts to get Adams recalled came to nothing, but Vergennes had enough clout with Congress to ghostwrite what amounted to a diplomatic straitjacket.[24]

A rough draft of the new instructions included the command:

You are to make the most candid and confidential communications upon all subjects to the ministers of our generous ally, the King of France; to undertake nothing in the negotiations for peace or truce without their knowledge and concurrence; and to make them sensible how much we rely upon His Majesty's influence for effectual support in every thing that may be necessary to the present security or future prosperity of the United States of America.

Even the most imaginative diplomat would have had trouble finding elbowroom in that passage, but it was insufficiently stringent for Anne-César, Chevalier de la Luzerne, Gérard's successor as French minister to America. Luzerne persuaded the committee tasked with revising the orders to insert a safeguarding codicil, so that the final version read: "You are ... to undertake nothing in the negotiations for peace or truce without their knowledge and concurrence; *and ultimately to govern yourselves by their advice and opinion, endeavoring in your whole*

---

[24] Congressional Instructions, 14 August 1779, *RDC*, 3:302; Vergennes to Luzerne, 7 August 1780, *Documents of the Emerging Nation: U.S. Foreign Relations, 1775–1789*, Mary Giunta, ed. (Wilmington, DE: Scholarly Resources, 1998) (hereafter *DEN*), 74. Accounts of Adams's bull-in-a-china-shop conduct during his early months in Europe include James H. Hutson, *John Adams and the Diplomacy of the American Revolution* (Lexington: University Press of Kentucky, 1980), 33–74; McCullough, *John Adams*, 187–215, 225–242.

conduct to make them sensible how much we rely upon His Majesty's influence for effectual support . . ."[25]

"Never in history," Bemis thundered in 1935, "has one people voted to put its entire destiny more absolutely, more trustfully, under the control of a foreign government." A recent appraisal by Bradford Perkins comes to the same conclusion, to wit, that "the instructions of 1781 were a disgrace." Why would Congress forfeit American honor by handcuffing its ministers like this? Certainly, the state of the war was a factor; many legislators felt that French support was so essential that ensuring its continuance outweighed all other considerations. Madison took this position when he conceded that the instructions were "a sacrifice of national dignity" but went on to affirm that it was "a sacrifice of dignity to policy." The "situation of affairs," he said, rendered the "sacrifice necessary." A number of congressmen, however, were actuated by baser motives. As historians have shown, Luzerne, in addition to being a more industrious diplomat than the oft-bedridden Gérard, was also more unscrupulous; from the moment his frigate docked in Boston Harbor, he began a study of the corruptibility of Congress and identified men whose loyalty was for sale. By a judicious use of bribes, he induced those legislators to vote according to France's wishes. He even took credit for the election of Robert Livingston over the Francophobe Arthur Lee as secretary of foreign affairs, and while that boast cannot be substantiated, many congressmen were in fact on Luzerne's payroll. There seems little doubt that congressional approval of the new instructions derived in great part from French funds sprinkled in the right places. The fact that the instructions sailed through in less than a week, whereas the 1779 mandate took the assembly eight months to hammer out, lends credence to Walter LaFeber's contention that Congress had become "a slave to Vergennes" by the summer of 1781.[26]

---

[25] Report of Committee, Instructions to the Ministers Plenipotentiary to Negotiate a Peace, 8 June 1781, *JCC*, 20:617; Deliberations, 11 June 1781, ibid., 20:626 (emphasis added). Some congressmen tried to strike that clause as "too abject and humiliating," but their motion failed.

[26] Bemis, *Diplomacy of the American Revolution*, 190; Perkins, "Peace of Paris," 196; Congressional Actions on Engagements with France, 8 August 1782, *RDC*, 5:647; Walter LaFeber, *The American Age: U.S. Foreign Policy at Home and Abroad, 1750 to the Present*, Second Edition (New York: W. W. Norton & Company, 1994), 24. For Luzerne's backstairs influence with Congress, see George Dangerfield, *Chancellor Robert R. Livingston of New York, 1746–1813* (New York: Harcourt, Brace, and Company, 1960), 114, 135–148, 153; Morris, *Peacemakers*, 197–198, 209–217; Stinchcombe, *American Revolution and the French Alliance*, 85–88, 153–169.

Vergennes's victory was not yet complete. Since he had been unable to eliminate Adams from the peacemaking process, he strove to dilute the New Englander's influence by expanding the U.S. commission and giving it a stronger pro-French tinge. Congress bridled at this suggestion, but a few days of lobbying by Luzerne sufficed to overcome most resistance, and on 11 June 1781 the legislators added Thomas Jefferson, Henry Laurens, and John Jay to the American team in Paris. Lee having returned home to take a congressional seat, this meant that the number of commissioners had risen to five, three of whom – Franklin, Jefferson, and Jay – enjoyed reputations as Francophiles. (Laurens, a hardliner in the Adams mode, was acceptable to Luzerne if Versailles could count on his proposals being overruled by the majority.) As it happened, Jefferson never left his estate at Monticello until the war was over, Laurens was a prisoner in the Tower of London for almost all of the negotiations, and Jay, despite his French ancestry, turned out to be more anti-Gallican than Adams – but Vergennes had no way of knowing this when he received the tidings from Luzerne. He could be forgiven for thinking the American commission was in his pocket.[27]

Ironically, Congress handed the checkreins to Vergennes just five months before Yorktown changed the complexion of the war, forcing North's resignation and ushering in the ministry of Charles Watson-Wentworth, Second Marquess of Rockingham, who was sworn to a restoration of peace. For the rebels, the outlook suddenly appeared brighter, and some congressmen began having second thoughts about the emasculating instructions they had issued. All motions for revision or repeal were defeated, though, for obvious reasons. Apart from Luzerne's generosity, which continued to weigh in the calculations of powerful legislators like John Witherspoon of New Jersey, there was the uncomfortable truth that Yorktown did not lessen America's dependence on France. Quite the contrary: if, as Robert Ferrell observes, Saratoga had been "almost a French victory," that was even truer of the war's final battle. Indeed, Admiral de Grasse originally intended to accept Cornwallis's surrender himself, and was only persuaded by Lafayette at the last moment to let Washington share in the glory. No American could

---

[27] Deliberations, 11 June 1781, *JCC*, 20:628; Deliberations, 14 June 1781, ibid., 20:648. Many leading figures in the American press were also recipients of French gold, among them Tom Paine, and they generated a steady stream of articles favorable to France from mid-1779 until the war's conclusion. See Schoenbrun, *Triumph in Paris*, 346–347; Stinchcombe, *American Revolution and the French Alliance*, 118–132.

pretend that the continentals had achieved this result unaided. Still less could anyone imagine that the United States was capable of fending for itself if London elected to prolong hostilities, which was a possibility in late October 1781. Contemporaries did not invest Yorktown with the finality we assign it today: Rockingham's government was shaky; many members of Parliament continued to advocate a policy of bringing the colonies to submission; and the British, despite their defeat in the Chesapeake, still fielded 30,000 troops in North America, held New York and most of the major southern ports, and remained masters of the greatest navy on earth. The flush of victory after Yorktown could not obscure these facts.[28]

Moreover, Rockingham had only pledged to end the war; he had said nothing about granting American independence. It was rumored that he sought to conclude a treaty of union like the one England had with Scotland, whereby both countries recognized the same king. In addition, even if Britain acknowledged the nationhood of its former colonies, that would not cancel out America's obligation to fight on until Versailles – and, by extension, Madrid – came to terms with London. Charles III's determination to capture Gibraltar had not diminished; the American Revolution might conceivably drag along until Spanish forces overran that naval choke point, a dubious prospect even if French forces fought at their side. And a Bourbon reconquest of the rock would still result in the United States taking its place among the nations of the world as a littoral with almost indefensible borders.

In all, America's diplomats faced a fearful challenge – or, rather, the challenge was fearful if they chose to face it. They could have simply followed instructions. That was Luzerne's expectation when he wrote to Vergennes in triumph after Congress dispatched its new charge to the peace commission. "[T]hese changes appear suitable to fulfill the desired objective," Luzerne exulted. "In fact, I view the negotiations as presently being in the hands of His Majesty." Had Franklin, Adams, and Jay been typical eighteenth-century envoys, they would have sought and obeyed French advice at every turn of the peacemaking, deferring to Vergennes's wisdom even when the foreign minister proposed policies contrary to American interests. To do otherwise would fly in the face of accepted diplomatic practice, as Franklin himself acknowledged in a letter to Livingston. "There is, I imagine, no minister who would not think it safer

---

[28] Robert H. Ferrell, *American Diplomacy: A History* (New York: W. W. Norton & Company, 1959), 11; Bendiner, *Virgin Diplomats*, 206.

to act by orders than from his own discretion," the Philadelphian wrote his stateside boss.[29]

Yet this was not a time for playing it safe, and the American commissioners had no intention of serving as Versailles's stooges after six years of war. French efforts to lead them by the nose would prove as unavailing as had British attempts to crush their rebellion.

"DOCTOR DOUBLEFACE"

Jay, Adams, and Franklin reacted differently to the 1781 instructions. Gouverneur Morris, a former congressman and Jay's friend, predicted that the stiff-necked New Yorker would be so appalled by Congress's willingness to "prostitute the very little dignity our poor country is possessed of" that he would refuse to serve, and this nearly proved true. From his post in Madrid, where he had spent two-and-a-half years endeavoring unsuccessfully to obtain Spanish recognition of American independence, Jay composed a courteous but still searing letter to Livingston in which he confessed that his new assignment "embarrasses me." "I know it to be my duty, as a public servant, . . . faithfully to execute my instructions without questioning the policy of them," he wrote. Nonetheless, the stipulation requiring America's diplomats to take their leads from Versailles "occasions sensations I have never before experienced, and induces me to wish that my name had been omitted." He swore that "personal pride" had nothing to do with it, noting, "My ambition will always be more gratified in being useful than conspicuous." *National* pride was the issue: "As an American I feel an interest in the dignity of my country, which renders it difficult for me to reconcile myself to the idea of the sovereign, independent States of America submitting, in the persons of their ministers, to be absolutely governed by the advice and opinions of the servants of another sovereign."

On the other hand, Jay was far from the scene of action and, by his own admission, imperfectly informed. Events in North America or elsewhere may have so altered the strategic calculus as to necessitate Congress's new approach. For the present, then, Jay felt "it would not be proper to decline this appointment." He did, however, ask Livingston "to take an early opportunity of relieving me from a station where . . . I must necessarily receive and obey the directions of those on whom

---

[29] Luzerne cited in Stinchcombe, *American Revolution and the French Alliance*, 161; Franklin to Livingston, 5 December 1782, *RDC*, 6:111.

I really think no American minister ought to be dependent." Although he would not leave Congress in the lurch, he deplored the spectacle of America "casting herself into the arms of the King of France," a policy he doubted would "advance either her interest or reputation" with Versailles. "What the sentiments of my colleagues on this occasion may be," he concluded, "I do not as yet know."[30]

That last line must have been written tongue in cheek. No one acquainted with Adams could have failed to anticipate his sulfuric response. He did not receive the news until later – indeed, as we shall see, until after Jay and Franklin had worked out the essentials of a peace settlement between Britain and the United States – but his diary left no confusion as to where he stood. "I am disgusted, affronted, and disappointed," he wrote. "I have been insulted, and my country has joined in the injury; it has basely prostituted its own honor by sacrificing mine." Adams found the new orders "servile and intolerable," roared that Congress had "surrendered their own sovereignty to a French minister," and concluded, "Blush! Blush! ye guilty records. Blush and perish! ... How can such a stain be washed out? Can we cast a veil over it and forget it?" Not for the Duke of Braintree Jay's polite disapproval; some offenses were too grievous to be borne.[31]

By contrast, Franklin accepted the instructions without complaint. In fact, he seemed pleased, telling the president of Congress, "I have had so much experience of his majesty's goodness to us, ... that I cannot but think the confidence well and judiciously placed, and that it will have happy effects." As directed, Franklin showed a copy of the orders to Vergennes, who already knew about them but pretended to learn their contents for the first time. The comte expressed "satisfaction," said Congress "never would have cause to regret" entrusting its fate to Versailles, and assured Franklin that Louis XVI had "the honor of the United States at heart, as well as their welfare and independence." Franklin's reply was a cascade of honeyed words. He praised the "sincerity" of the "upright and able" Vergennes and noted that the French court "never promised me anything" that it did "not punctually perform." America's diplomats would, he said, "submit dutifully" to the commands of their government.[32]

---

[30] Morris to Jay, 17 June 1781, *LJJ*, 130; Jay to Livingston, 20 September 1781, *RDC*, 4:716–717.
[31] Diary Entry, 18 February 1783, *WJA*, 3:359
[32] Franklin to McKean, 13 September 1781, *RDC*, 4:709.

Franklin appeared to do just that when the Earl of Shelburne, secretary of state for colonial affairs under Rockingham, sent the Scottish slave merchant Richard Oswald to Paris to unofficially sound out the U.S. commissioners about the possibility of a separate Anglo-American peace. Shelburne had been a critic of George III's policy toward America since the beginning of the Revolution, and while he had yet to reconcile himself to independence, he adopted a more accommodating approach than had his predecessor under North. He felt that by lavishing the rebels with concessions, he might persuade them to accept an arrangement that kept America in the empire, but with its own parliament (the so-called "Irish solution"). Above all, he was determined to prevent Versailles from reestablishing a foothold in the New World, and he recognized that the surest way to accomplish that objective was to drive a wedge between America and France. He was therefore willing to be generous with respect to boundaries, debts, and other issues certain to arise at the negotiating table, and he chose Oswald as his envoy because he believed the Scot – elderly, philosophical, and pro-American – was a man after Franklin's heart.[33]

Franklin, however, brought Oswald up short by informing him upon arrival that the United States would not negotiate with Britain "but in concert with France." He then took Oswald to Versailles, where Vergennes told him the same thing through an interpreter: any attempt to divide the allies was doomed; if the British wanted peace with America, they had to satisfy French demands. Vergennes looked over to Franklin, who nodded his assent. To all appearances, the American was a puppet, and that did not bode well for British negotiators since there was no other high-ranking U.S. diplomat in Paris at the time with whom to deal. With Jay en route from Madrid and Adams in the Netherlands soliciting a loan, Franklin was the entire American commission. Oswald must have left Versailles feeling defeated.[34]

The next day, though, as Oswald prepared to return to London, Franklin dropped his flunky's mask. He paid Oswald a call, ostensibly to say goodbye but really because he wanted to talk to him out of French earshot. It was his impression, he said, that the British aimed at "much

---

[33] For Shelburne's policymaking as secretary of state and prime minister, see C. R. Ritcheson, "The Earl of Shelburne and Peace with America, 1782–1783: Vision and Reality," *International History Review,* 5 (August 1983): 322–345.

[34] Diary Entry, 1 July 1782, *RDC,* 5:537–539. Franklin kept a diary of this period, including copies of his correspondence, and it is one of the principal sources for historians studying American diplomacy during the final act of the Revolutionary War.

more than a mere peace" between their nation and its former colonies. They desired *"reconciliation* with the Americans," and, since he sought the same outcome, he would speak frankly. Britain had inflicted "cruel injuries" on the United States, burning American towns and massacring women and children. This had created "impressions of resentment" that would "long remain" unless London did something to indemnify its victims. Franklin knew the perfect reparation. "Britain possesses Canada," he observed, and if Britain gave this snow-clad landmass to the Americans, they might forgive and forget. If Britain continued to hold onto it, though, "that would necessarily oblige us to cultivate and strengthen our union with France." In other words, transfer of Canada could relax or dissolve that union – the 1778 treaty of alliance and Congress's 1781 instructions notwithstanding.

Franklin neither cleared this proposal with Vergennes before making it nor informed him of it afterward. As noted above, Vergennes aimed to keep Canada British, both for the purpose of limiting U.S. expansion and ensuring that the new republic remained dependent upon France. He would have vetoed Franklin's suggestion had the doctor run it by him, but Franklin did not, thereby violating the letter and spirit of Congress's orders. When Oswald seemed receptive to the idea of surrendering Canada in the interest of Anglo-American relations, Franklin gave him a letter to pass along to Shelburne. "I desire no other channel of communication between us than that of Mr. Oswald," Franklin told the colonial secretary. The Scot was "a wise and honest man," and Franklin hoped he would be formally commissioned to negotiate a peace that would "expedite the blessed work which our hearts are engaged in."[35]

Shelburne rejected Franklin's Canada scheme, but he retained Oswald as his go-between and in a short time came to the conclusion – "*decidedly* tho' *reluctantly*," as he put it – that Britain would have to set the colonies free. There was one condition. "[I]f America is to be independent," he declared, "she must be so of the whole world. No secret, tacit, or ostensible connections with France." Towards that end, he sent Oswald back across the Channel with a quid pro quo offer: "the allowing of American independence" in exchange for "England being put into the same situation that she was left by the peace of 1763." London would relinquish sovereignty over the United States, but it expected to retain everything else

[35] Diary Entry, 1 July 1782, *RDC*, 5:539–542 (emphasis in the original); Franklin to Shelburne, 18 April 1782, ibid., 5:538–539. See also Grenville to Fox, 4 June 1782, ibid., 5:474–477.

it had possessed at the end of the Seven Years' War. The French would receive no territory in North America.[36]

This was a blatant attempt to sever the Franco-American alliance, and if Franklin had felt bound by his instructions he would have broken off the discussion and reported Shelburne's ploy to Vergennes. He did neither. Perhaps he rationalized that his talks with Oswald did not constitute formal negotiations, since the Scot as yet lacked full plenipotentiary powers, but the deal Shelburne proposed was so clearly adverse to French interests and so obviously designed to pry America from Versailles's grasp that not even a tortured interpretation of the 1781 orders could excuse the U.S. commissioner's keeping Vergennes in the dark.

Within a short time, then, Franklin and Oswald had established the relationship that would endure until the signing of a preliminary treaty in late November. They bargained seriously one-on-one; their speeches and silences at Versailles were a façade. Complicating matters was the fact that Shelburne was at that moment engaged in a turf war with Charles James Fox, secretary of state for foreign affairs, over control of Britain's geopolitics, and Fox soon dispatched his own envoy to Paris. His choice of representative – Thomas Grenville, son of former prime minister George Grenville, whose Stamp Act precipitated the American Revolution – was either a slap in the face to the U.S. commissioners or indicative of gross naïveté. Franklin, though, handled the matter with aplomb. He greeted Grenville cordially, pronounced him an "intelligent, good-tempered, and well-instructed young man," and listened with apparent attentiveness to his proposals. He also treated him to a shameless display of hypocrisy. After a two-hour meeting at the palace at which Franklin nodded while Vergennes repeatedly told the British minister that London could expect no separate peace from either France or the United States, Franklin lectured Grenville during the carriage ride back to Paris on what he termed "the general subject of benefits, obligation, and gratitude." People often had "imperfect notions of their duty on those points," the doctor said, and could become "ingenious in finding out reasons and arguments to prove that they had been under no obligation at all." He was happy to note that Americans did not engage in such casuistry.[37]

---

[36] Shelburne to Oswald, 27 July 1872, *DEN*, 91 (emphasis in the original); Shelburne cited in George C. Herring, *From Colony to Superpower: U.S. Foreign Relations since 1776* (New York: Oxford University Press, 2008), 30; Shelburne to Franklin, 27 April 1782, *The Private Correspondence of Benjamin Franklin*, William Temple Franklin, ed. (London: Henry Colburn, 1817), 2:161–162.

[37] Diary Entry, 1 July 1782, *RDC*, 5:550–556.

The inconvenience of dealing with Grenville ended on 1 July, when Rockingham died and George III directed Shelburne to assume the post of prime minister. Fox resigned, Grenville lost his commission, and Oswald became the sole British agent in Paris. With the field thus cleared, Franklin felt it time to present Oswald with specific terms for peace, which he read to him from a memorandum that has been lost to history; the only account we have of it is in Oswald's report to Shelburne. According to the Scot, Franklin divided his terms into *necessary* and *advisable* provisions. The necessary articles were "full and complete" American independence, withdrawal of British troops from American soil, acknowledgment that the United States extended from the Great Lakes to the Mississippi, and "freedom of fishing on the banks of Newfoundland." Advisable articles included an official British apology for "distressing" the Americans and the "giving up [of] every part of Canada." When Oswald asked Franklin to turn over his memorandum, the doctor declined; he did not want to leave proof that he had broken faith with his ally. He moreover recommended that Oswald introduce both the necessary and advisable terms to Shelburne as his own suggestion rather than Franklin's. Vergennes was again left out of the loop.[38]

As the events just described make clear, Franklin, not Jay or Adams, first violated the instructions of 1781. Franklin was a subtler statesman than his fellow commissioners, but he was no less devoted to American interests, and although he never went on record as opposing Congress's directive to be guided by French advice, he never heeded it either, except rhetorically. To be sure, his circumvention of Vergennes did not approach the blatancy of Jay's subsequent efforts – the comte knew *of* Franklin's meetings with Oswald, even if he did not know what the two men discussed – and Franklin liked the French, whereas Jay and Adams held them in contempt. Nonetheless, when presented with an opportunity to secure British recognition of American independence and liberal boundaries for the United States, Franklin did not allow fondness for his hosts or respect for congressional prerogatives to divert him. In the spring and summer of 1782, he lived up to the "Doctor Doubleface" sobriquet coined by his detractors in Britain. His correspondence during these months, whether with superiors back home, adversaries in London, or abettors on the Continent, teemed with expressions of gratitude to Louis XVI and affirmations of American loyalty to the 1778 alliance, while his

---

[38] Oswald to Shelburne, 10 July 1782, DEN, 88–90. See also Bemis, *Diplomacy of the American Revolution*, 207.

actions demonstrated a readiness to defy Congress and Versailles if such behavior benefited his country.[39]

A vivid example of this dissonance between word and deed was Franklin's reply to David Hartley, a member of Parliament and longtime acquaintance who wrote to ask whether there was any truth to rumors that "America was disposed to enter into a separate treaty with Great Britain." Since Hartley played no role in the negotiations, Franklin did not address him with the candor he showed Oswald and Shelburne. Instead, he affected indignation, declaring, "I never had such an idea, and I believe there is not a man in America . . . that would not spurn at the thought of deserting a noble and generous friend for the sake of a truce with an unjust and cruel enemy." How could anyone imagine that Franklin and his associates were capable of "treachery to our first friend," France? "Congress will never instruct their commissioners to obtain a peace on such ignominious terms," the doctor pronounced, "and although there can be few things in which I would venture to disobey their orders, yet if it were possible for them to give me such an order as this, I certainly should refuse to act, I should instantly renounce their commission, and banish myself forever from so infamous a country." As Franklin wrote these lines, of course, he was disobeying Congress's instructions in order to facilitate the treachery he inveighed against.[40]

"LET US THINK FOR OURSELVES"

It was therefore not so much the strategy as the tone of American diplomacy that changed when Jay joined the talks in late July. He had arrived in Paris a month earlier, but an attack of influenza confined him to his bed and left Franklin in command of relations with Great Britain, an assignment the doctor managed so dexterously that Shelburne swallowed the bitter pill and told Oswald he was prepared to make peace on the basis of Franklin's necessary conditions. Oswald expected the American diplomats to be ecstatic when he brought this news, but Jay was more interested in the language of Oswald's just-drafted commission. He noted that the document, written by Shelburne and signed by George III, empowered Oswald "to treat with commissioners named by the said

---

[39] Sarah Knott, *Sensibility and the American Revolution* (Chapel Hill: University of North Carolina Press, 2008), 248.

[40] Franklin to Hartley, 15 January 1782, *RDC*, 5:112. See also Franklin to Hartley, 16 February 1782, ibid., 5:169–170.

colonies or plantations ... in North America." That was unacceptable, Jay declared. He, Franklin, and the absent Adams represented a sovereign nation made up of free states. There were no colonies on the eastern seaboard. What kind of trickery was this?[41]

Oswald argued that Jay was being unnecessarily legalistic. As long as Britain conferred independence in the final treaty, as Shelburne intended to do, what difference did it make what titles were used during negotiations? Franklin agreed. While admitting that he was no lawyer, he thought this a technicality that should not hold up the peace process. Jay stood fast. Formal titles mattered, he said. If Shelburne was sincere in his claims, he ought to have no hesitation acknowledging America's independence from Britain *prior* to a treaty. Independence was not a gift for London to give the United States as the price of peace. Americans had already won their independence. Now the diplomats had come together to hash out the terms of that independence. Jay wanted Oswald's commission revised to mention a country calling itself the United States of America. He moreover wanted independence "expressly granted by act of Parliament." When Oswald protested that this was impracticable because Parliament had recessed for the summer, Jay said that George III could recognize American independence "by proclamation." Jay did not care how this issue was resolved, but resolved it must be before he would negotiate. He was too fervent a patriot to move forward on anything other than an equal footing.

Accustomed to dealing with Franklin, Oswald found Jay's combativeness deplorable, and Jay made matters worse by remarking how much better the situation would be for all parties if the king had liberated his North American colonies years ago, "before such deep wounds had been given to the bias and attachment which then subsisted all over the country in favor of Great Britain." According to Oswald's notes of the meeting, Jay then "ran into a detail of particulars too unnecessary and unpleasant here to be repeated." He spoke "with such a freedom of expression and

---

[41] My treatment of Jay's role in the negotiations draws for the most part upon his report to Livingston on 17 November 1782, which one historian describes as the most important document in the archives "detailing the steps leading up to the preliminary treaty with England and emphasizing the success of the American commissioners." Henry P. Johnston, *The Correspondence and Public Papers of John Jay* (New York: G. P. Putnam's Sons, 1890), 2:366. Also crucial is *The Diary of John Jay during the Peace Negotiations of 1782, Being a Complete and Faithful Rendering of the Original Manuscript, Now Published for the First Time*, Frank Monaghan, ed. (New Haven: Bibliographical Press, Yale University, 1934).

disapprobation of our conduct," the Scot wrote, "as shows we have little to expect from him in the way of indulgence." Franklin stopped by Oswald's lodgings after this encounter to assure his friend that Jay meant no harm, that he was impetuous and suffering from the aftereffects of flu, and that in the long run the British would appreciate his keen legal mind. There was, however, no mistaking the chill that had descended on the heretofore pleasant Anglo-American dialogue.[42]

If Oswald aggravated Jay's suspicions, the Spanish ambassador to France – Pedro Pablo Abarca de Bolea, conde de Aranda – made him downright panic-stricken. Ironically, Aranda was one of the few Spaniards Jay liked; after meeting the conde for the first time in late June 1782, Jay described him as "frank," "candid," and "sagacious." Yet their first discussion of peace terms revealed how far apart the two were. Aranda got down to business, spreading a map of North America on a table and proposing that he and Jay establish a demarcation line between Spanish territory and the lands the United States expected to control in the postwar period. With his finger, Jay traced along the Mississippi River from its source almost to its mouth and then drew a boundary east along the 31st parallel to the border between Florida and Georgia. Aranda's smile faded. When Jay asked what Spain offered by way of alternative, Aranda said he needed time to think it over. A few days later, a courier delivered Aranda's map to Jay's quarters. The conde had drawn a longitudinal line nearly 500 miles to the east of the Mississippi, so that what are today the states of Indiana, Illinois, Tennessee, Kentucky, and Mississippi fell within the Spanish zone. An appalled Jay wrote Livingston that this line "would leave near as much country between it and the Mississippi as there is between it and the Atlantic Ocean." Jay saw little prospect of reconciling the two visions of America's western border.[43]

Unsurprisingly, Oswald's commission and Aranda's boundary line were the two subjects under review when Jay and Franklin met with Vergennes at the palace on 10 August. Also in attendance was Joseph

---

[42] Draft commission, 25 July 1782, *RDC*, 5:613; Richard Oswald: Minutes of His Conversations with Benjamin Franklin and John Jay, 7 August 1782, 11 August 1782, 13 August 1782, *DEN*, 91–94; Oswald to Townshend, 7 August 1782, *The Works of Benjamin Franklin*, Jared Sparks, ed. (Philadelphia: Childs and Peterson, 1840), 9:378; Oswald cited in George Pellew, *John Jay* (Boston: Houghton Mifflin, 1890), 9:159.

[43] Jay to Montmorin, 26 June 1782, *RDC*, 5:524; Jay to Livingston, 17 November 1782, ibid., 6:22–24; Jay cited in Norman A. Graebner, Richard Dean Burns, and Joseph M. Siracusa, *Foreign Affairs and the Founding Fathers: From Confederation to Constitution, 1776–1787* (Santa Barbara: ABC-CLIO, 2011), 16.

Mathias Gérard de Rayneval, undersecretary of state for foreign affairs, a man for whom Jay contrived an immediate dislike. On both issues, the Frenchmen gave advice that seemed to go against American interests. Vergennes told Jay and Franklin to accept the British commission as it stood. The term *colonies* "signified little," he said. What, after all, was in a name? Whenever British plenipotentiaries communicated with Versailles, they used an ancient form of address designating George III king of France as well as king of Britain, and that was no obstacle to French diplomats negotiating with them. Besides, if Oswald received the American commissions, in which Jay and Franklin were identified as representatives of the United States, that would constitute recognition of the United States as an independent nation. Franklin, impressed, said that the arrangement the comte proposed "would do." Jay disagreed. He had no use for "all this singular reasoning," he complained, and Vergennes's formula did not satisfy him. It was "descending from the ground of independence to treat under the description of colonies."

Jay and Franklin concurred when it came to the western boundary, both denouncing what they called the "extravagance" of Aranda's line. They not only refused to give up any territory east of the Mississippi to Spain; they demanded the right of free navigation on that mighty river. (Franklin had earlier proclaimed that "a neighbor might as well ask me to sell my street door" as to "sell a drop of its waters.") Vergennes made no reply to these statements, but Rayneval did. According to Jay's memorandum, the undersecretary "thought we claimed more than we had a right to," a view Jay was certain Rayneval's boss shared. The meeting adjourned with ill feeling all around.[44]

What took place in the next few hours is the stuff of legend, a thrice-told tale worth retelling here because it underscores the novelty of the path America's diplomats chose. Franklin and Jay began arguing on the ride to Passy, a village just outside Paris where Franklin had lived since early 1777. Jay insisted that Vergennes was colluding with the Spanish to keep the United States small and weak, and that the comte's enjoinder to accept Oswald's commission was an attempt to postpone British acknowledgment of U.S. independence until France and Spain had "made all their uses of us." If the American commissioners did what Vergennes recommended, Jay said, Spanish reconquest of Gibraltar (an unlikely prospect)

---

[44] Jay to Livingston, 17 November 1782, *RDC*, 6:14–15, 22–23; Franklin to Jay, 2 October 1780, *Selected Letters of John Jay and Sarah Livingston Jay*, Landa M. Freeman, Louise V. North, and Janet M. Wedge, eds. (Jefferson, NC: McFarland & Co., 2005), 94.

and French recovery of all North American territory lost in the Seven Years' War (an impossible one) would have to precede the birth of a sovereign United States – meaning, in effect, that America might never become independent. Jay asked why, if this was not Vergennes's objective, he was "advising us to act in a manner inconsistent with our dignity"? The comte had "too much understanding not to see the fallacy of" his ratiocination.

Franklin felt his colleague was being unfair to the French. While admitting that Spain sought "to coop us up within the Allegheny mountains," he saw no reason to ascribe such malice to Versailles, whose representatives had "hitherto treated us very fairly." He observed that Vergennes's counsel was susceptible to a more benign interpretation: maybe the comte was just trying to please two allies. Furthermore, Franklin said, French advice that the Americans receive Oswald's commission could be taken as evidence of a desire to hasten British confirmation of U.S. independence, not defer it.

The debate continued at Franklin's house, where the two men moved into the study, Jay puffing furiously on his churchwarden pipe. When Franklin again contrasted Spanish covetousness with French altruism, Jay fired back that there was no difference between Madrid and Versailles. "I have no faith in any court in Europe," he declared. "Let us forget the pretty sentiments that they profess to entertain. We know they are motivated by self-interest." And, he pointed out, it was not in the self-interest of either Spain or France that "we should become a great and formidable people." Therefore, "they will not help us to become so." Jay said that he and Franklin should insist upon the Mississippi as the United States's western boundary despite Aranda's claims, and that they should refuse to treat without prior British acknowledgment of American independence, no matter what Vergennes prescribed.

Franklin assured Jay that he was of like mind with respect to the Mississippi. "It is true that we owe Spain nothing," he said. But challenging Vergennes over Oswald's commission seemed dastardly recompense for an ally who had underwritten America's revolution for six years and whose troops had contributed to the victory at Yorktown. "Have we any reason to doubt the good faith of the king of France?" Franklin asked. Jay shot back, "We can depend upon the French only to see that we are separated from England." Beyond that, American and French interests diverged. "Let us be grateful to the French for what they have done for us," Jay contended, "but let us think for ourselves. And, if need be, let us act for ourselves."

The doctor then turned to the elephant in the room. Congress had ordered its diplomats to comply with French wishes, he observed, and Vergennes's counsel was unequivocal. Did Franklin need to remind Jay of the text of the 1781 instructions? Jay grimaced. "With the wording of those letters I am too familiar," he said. "I am likewise familiar with the means by which they were forced upon a subservient Congress," meaning French bribery. Raising the obvious question, Franklin asked, "Would you deliberately break Congress's instructions?" Jay replied, "Unless we violate these instructions, the dignity of Congress will be in the dust." Franklin bore down. "Then you are prepared to break our instructions," he said, "and intend to take an independent course now." Jay, in high dudgeon, thundered, "*If* the instructions conflict with America's honor and dignity, I would break them – *like this!*" He then flung his pipe into the fireplace.[45]

It is a classic story. Did it really happen that way? Probably not. As Richard Morris notes, both Franklin and Jay kept diaries, and neither contains an entry relating to this exchange. Jay did mention it in a letter to Livingston, but only in passing, and his account ended with Franklin's remark that the 1781 instructions required "our acquiescence in the advice and opinion of the [French] minister"; he said nothing about what came next. While Jay's son William wrote about the pipe shattering years later, there are no contemporary reports of the commissioner's famous gesture. The dialogue, too, has the feel of having been embellished for posterity; it does not read like spontaneous discourse between human beings. Most implausible is Franklin's purported astonishment that Jay would dare betray America's French ally when, as we have seen, the doctor had been double-crossing Vergennes for months before Jay came to the negotiating table.[46]

---

[45] Jay to Livingston, 17 November 1782, *RDC*, 6:15–16, 49; Jay to Livingston, 18 September 1782, *RDC*, 5:740; Franklin and Jay cited in Fleming, *Perils of Peace*, 221–222; Frank Monaghan, *John Jay* (New York: Bobbs-Merrill, 1935), 195–196; Morris, *Peacemakers*, 309–310 (emphasis in the original).

[46] Morris, *Peacemakers*, 310; Jay to Livingston, 17 November 1781, *RDC*, 6:15, 49; Monaghan, *John Jay*, 449; Jay to Morris, 13 October 1782, *RDC*, 5:819. This encounter is such a durable component of the Revolutionary-War narrative that Monaghan titles a chapter "Mr. Jay Smashes His Pipe" and Morris designates one "The Long Clay Pipe of Mr. Jay." See also Bendiner, *Virgin Diplomats*, 226; Jerald A. Combs and Arthur G. Combs, *The History of American Foreign Policy*, Second Edition (New York: McGraw-Hill, 1997), 10; William M. Fowler, Jr., *American Crisis: George Washington and the Dangerous Two Years after Yorktown, 1781–1783* (New York: Walker & Company, 2011), 121–122; James H. Hutson, "The American Negotiators: The Diplomacy of Jealousy" in *Peace and*

Then again, Franklin may have feigned shock to test Jay's resolve. Was the New Yorker bold enough to overturn centuries of diplomatic tradition and thereby risk dismissal, public disgrace, and perhaps a date with the gibbet? Jay certainly left Passy convinced Franklin was in Vergennes's thrall. At the end of a dispatch to Livingston lashing the French for duplicity, he wrote, "Dr. Franklin does not see the conduct of this court in the light I do, and he believes they mean nothing in their proceedings but what is friendly, fair, and honorable," adding, "Facts and future events must determine which of us is mistaken." Some of the most pungent phrases attributed to Jay at that 10 August meeting – "let us think for ourselves," "the dignity of Congress will be in the dust" – did issue from his pen on later occasions, and he could have been recycling them.[47]

Furthermore, the standard account of the Franklin-Jay faceoff accurately reflects Jay's hostility toward continental Europeans in general and the Bourbons in particular. Nearly three years as an unrecognized minister to Spain had left Jay disgusted with His Most Catholic Majesty, Charles III, who dangled the Americans at the end of a line of promises but gave them precious little aid. Jay considered Charles and his grandees lazy, backward, and unscrupulous, and he took an even dimmer view of Versailles. In one of the crowning ironies of the Revolutionary War, Vergennes and Luzerne had intrigued to get Jay appointed peace commissioner because they thought his French lineage would make him sympathetic to their position, but they were unaware that Jay's paternal ancestors had been Huguenots (Calvinists) who fled France after Louis XIV revoked the Nantes Edict of Tolerance. Two of the most profound cultural inheritances in the Jay family were Francophobia and anti-Catholicism. These were matched by Anglophilia – Great Britain had, after all, offered refuge to the Huguenots – and devotion to the Church of England. Few Americans were less likely to turn into a jelly of obeisance before Louis XVI than John Jay, and none was more eager to forsake Versailles for London. While Jay probably did not dash his long clay pipe into the fireplace on 10 August 1782, he might as well have. That flourish, apocryphal or not, summed up his attitude.[48]

---

the Peacemakers, 65; Thomas G. Paterson, J. Garry Clifford, Shane J. Maddock, Deborah Kisatsky, and Kenneth J. Hagan, *American Foreign Relations: A History*, Seventh Edition (Boston: Wadsworth, 2010), 1:2; Schiff, *Great Improvisation*, 310.

[47] Jay to Livingston, 18 September 1782, *RDC*, 5:740; Adams to Livingston, 31 October 1782, ibid., 5:839.

[48] For a vivid account of Jay's Gethsemane in Madrid, see Bendiner, *Virgin Diplomats*, 143–167. For his Huguenot ancestry, see Monaghan, *John Jay*, 13–22.

"RATHER JEALOUS THAN PARTIAL TO AMERICA"

At almost the same time that Jay and Franklin had their colloquy, the Continental Congress took up the question of whether or not "to revise the instructions to the ministers plenipotentiary of the U.S. for negotiating and concluding a treaty of peace." Legislators weighed in on both sides, and the most passionate advocates for and against revision were two Virginians: Richard Henry Lee and James Madison. Lee appealed to his colleagues' patriotism, declaring that the instructions, by entrusting Versailles with "the whole, the absolute disposal of our affairs," were so supine as to "expose us to the contempt and scorn of all the nations of Europe." What self-respecting people obliged their envoys to submit to such trammels? "Our dignity is stained," he pronounced. "We must revoke the instructions in order to wipe off that stain and restore its luster." He also insisted that France's "long and close connection with Spain" would induce Versailles to give Spanish claims on the North American continent "preference to those of these States." Since everyone knew Madrid coveted lands west of the Appalachians – and, in fact, sought to make the Mississippi a Spanish river – it was obvious that, unless the instructions were revised, "we shall be so circumscribed in our boundaries that our independence will be a nugatory independence."

Madison carried the burden of the argument against revision. Yes, he conceded, the instructions looked excessive post-Yorktown and were, perhaps, unworthy of an independent nation. Nonetheless, for Congress to change them would be disastrous to the Franco-American alliance. It would appear an "act of ingratitude" toward France, "awaken her suspicions and jealousies," and "abate her zeal in our favor." America could ill afford to estrange Versailles "at this critical moment" with the treasury empty and Britain still seemingly full of fight. Besides, Madison contended, the instructions were not as restrictive as Lee and others made out: "Our ministers may still, notwithstanding the instructions given, state and assert our claims and contend with the utmost earnestness for our rights, and it is only in the last extremity, when all their pleas, all their reasoning, and all their most earnest endeavors prove ineffectual, that they are ultimately to govern themselves by the advice and opinion of the court of France." Madison could not imagine a case in which, America's representatives having exhausted every means of persuasion, Versailles still said no.[49]

---

[49] Congressional Action on Engagements with France, 8 August 1782, *RDC*, 5:645–651.

Across the Atlantic, Jay *could* conceive of such a situation, and although the non-revisionists triumphed in Congress – the 1781 orders remained unchanged until peace rendered them moot – Congress was not setting policy. Its commissioners were, principally Jay, who seized control of the negotiations in the last week of August when Franklin was incapacitated by a kidney stone. With the doctor laid up, Jay was free to follow through on his threat to suspend talks with the British pending an alteration of Oswald's powers. He told Oswald that he would not treat with any agent whose commission described the Americans as British subjects, and that until the Scot could show him a document, under the Great Seal of George III, recognizing U.S. independence, there was nothing more to discuss.[50]

Jay's inflexibility on this issue, while justifiable from a legal standpoint, proved counterproductive. It delayed negotiations for seven weeks, during which Britain's military fortunes improved, with a commensurate hardening of British peace terms. As it happened, Jay would have been well advised not to stand on ceremony. Had he begun bargaining in earnest in late August, according to several historians, Shelburne's government would have been more amenable to American pressure and might have agreed to greater concessions. When Jay broke off talks with Oswald, the Bourbon powers were intensifying their two-year siege of Gibraltar with a frontal assault that employed battery-mounted fire boats specially designed for this operation, and for a few days it looked as though the Franco-Spanish forces might succeed. The British garrison on Gibraltar, however, held out until a fleet commanded by one of Britain's best admirals arrived to lift the siege and inflict defeat on the attackers. By the time Oswald received a new commission from Shelburne removing the colonial designation and mentioning the United States by name, Gibraltar, gateway to the Mediterranean, was firmly in British hands, French and Spanish morale was depressed, and Shelburne had sent Henry Strachey, a veteran foreign-office diplomat with no love for the Americans, to Paris to stiffen Oswald's negotiating stance. Jay won his point, but at considerable cost.[51]

---

[50] Walter Stahr, *John Jay: Founding Father* (New York: Bloomsbury Academic, 2005), 156.

[51] Richard Oswald's Second Commission for Negotiating Peace, 21 September 1782, *RDC*, 5:748. A number of scholars point out that Oswald's revised commission was not the explicit royal or parliamentary statement of recognition that Jay had demanded. Shelburne's cabinet merely empowered Oswald "to treat with the commissioners ... under the title of Thirteen United States," and then listed the states one by one. This language

In any event, concerns about the wording of Oswald's commission soon faded in importance compared to three developments that spurred Jay to his boldest violation of Congress's orders. First, British agents showed Jay a translated copy of a dispatch the British had intercepted on the high seas from François Barbé-Marbois, chargé d'affaires of the French embassy in Philadelphia, for Vergennes. In it, Barbé-Marbois argued against supporting the American claim to a postwar right to fish in waters off the Grand Banks. If the United States secured that right, Barbé-Marbois noted, New Englanders would cut into France's share of the North American fisheries and Versailles would lose revenue. The Americans should therefore be encouraged to abandon their "pretension" before they, the French, and the British sat down to the anticipated trilateral talks. Barbé-Marbois compounded his affront in Jay's eyes by gloating that the Continental Congress's 1781 instructions left Louis XVI "master of the terms of the treaty of peace." This letter convinced Jay even more forcibly than before that Versailles was not a faithful guardian of the American national interest.[52]

The second incident that unsettled Jay was a 5 September meeting he had with Rayneval to discuss U.S.-Spanish differences. Rayneval expanded on the point he had made earlier: that the Americans should cut back on their territorial demands, that Spain had legitimate claims to land west of the Appalachians, and that Native Americans who occupied parts of the area deserved a measure of sovereignty too. After delivering what Jay called a "long disquisition," Rayneval suggested a compromise that looked like Aranda's proposal of several months past. He produced a map and drew a line along various rivers, stopping at the intersection of the Cumberland and the Ohio. "The savages to the westward of the

---

left Parliament and George III free to forswear any acknowledgment of U.S. independence. One historian deems the new commission "an easily discardable, unilateral, purely executive-level document" that should not have been allowed to interrupt talks. Frank W. Brecher, *Securing American Independence: John Jay and the French Alliance* (Westport, CT: Praeger, 2003), 193. See also Dull, *Diplomatic History of the American Revolution*, 148; Perkins, "Peace of Paris," 202–204. For an account of the final Bourbon campaign to wrest Gibraltar from Britain, see Dull, *French Navy and American Independence*, 304–324.

[52] Translation of an Intercepted and Decyphered Letter from M. Barbé-Marbois to M. Vergennes, 13 March 1782, *Life and Writings of Benjamin Franklin*, William Dean, ed. (New York: Derby and Jackson, 1859), 1:473. Although Barbé-Marbois, Vergennes, and other French diplomats protested that this dispatch was a British forgery, historians have deemed it authentic. See Morris, *Peacemakers*, 325; Carl Van Doren, *Benjamin Franklin* (New York: Viking Press, 1939), 686.

line ... should be free under the protection of Spain," he said, while "those to the eastward should be free under the protection of the United States." Since, by this formula, the Americans would not receive a boundary on the Mississippi, it would be foolish for them to assert the prerogatives of a riparian power. Rayneval therefore recommended that they drop all demands for navigation rights. Jay, stone-faced, asked Rayneval to commit these suggestions to paper, and the deputy complied, furnishing Jay the next afternoon with a memorandum whose arrogance of tone made the American see red.[53]

Far more explosive than these occurrences was the report Jay received on 9 September from Matthew Ridley, a member of the British secret service stationed in Paris. Ridley informed Jay that Rayneval had left on a covert mission to Shelburne two days earlier – that is, hard on the heels of his meeting with Jay. Worse, Ridley revealed that on the morning of his departure for the enemy capital, Rayneval had met with Vergennes and Aranda for "two or three hours" at Versailles. For Jay, the conclusion was inescapable. What purpose could this trip have other than a betrayal of the United States? Why would Vergennes have neglected to inform the American commissioners of his right-hand man's visit to London unless he and Aranda were plotting to make a separate peace with the British that deprived America of the Mississippi boundary, access to the fisheries, and who could tell what else?[54]

We know now, because the relevant documents have been declassified, that Jay overreacted. Rayneval's mission did not have the sinister character Jay gave it. It was prompted by an interview Vergennes had with Admiral de Grasse, hero of Yorktown and until recently a British prisoner of war. (De Grasse had been captured after his fleet went down to defeat.) The just-released de Grasse assured Vergennes that the British were willing to negotiate peace with their European rivals on honorable terms, and were in fact prepared to cede Gibraltar to the Spanish if that would expedite matters. To Vergennes, this sounded too good to be true – it was – but he sent Rayneval to London to ask Shelburne whether de Grasse's message accurately reflected the prime minister's position.

---

[53] Jay to Livingston, 17 November 1782, *RDC*, 6:24; Rayneval to Jay, 6 September 1782, ibid., 6:25; M. de Rayneval's Memoir Respecting the Right of the United States to the Navigation of the Mississippi, 6 September 1782, ibid., 6:25–27.

[54] Jay to Livingston, 17 November 1782, *RDC*, 6:28–29; Diary Entry, 9 September 1782, "Matthew Ridley's Diary during the Peace Negotiations of 1782," Herbert E. Klingelhoffer, ed., *William and Mary Quarterly* 20 (January 1963): 104.

American issues were not on the agenda when Rayneval met Shelburne at the latter's country home in Wiltshire.[55]

Still, one can hardly fault Jay for thinking a plot was afoot. Rayneval's conduct looked shady, as did Vergennes's secretiveness. And it must be noted that while Rayneval's formal instructions did not address the American situation, he did make a number of remarks during his exchanges with Shelburne that smacked of an anti-United States deal. On the first day of their talks, Rayneval told Shelburne, "*We do not want the Americans to share in the fisheries.*" He moreover belittled American claims that their nation should stretch to the Mississippi and insisted that France's commitment to the United States bore only on independence; it did not require Versailles to fight for every territorial, legal, and commercial demand the Americans put forth. Shelburne reported to George III after this discussion, "The point of independence once settled, [Rayneval] appears rather jealous than partial to America upon other points." Rayneval manifested this jealousy repeatedly as he strolled with Shelburne through the earl's wooded park, at one time noting that he had no doubt of Louis XVI's intention to "contain the Americans." He also said that such containment would be easier if the U.S. delegation were kept ignorant of negotiations between Britain, Spain, and France. These were not innocuous statements. While the records of the Rayneval-Shelburne talks include no smoking-gun evidence that Versailles intended to violate the terms of its alliance with America, a reasonable person could infer from what went on that Jay's misgivings had substantial basis in fact.[56]

Furthermore, quite apart from Rayneval's trip to London, Jay was correct in the three larger conclusions he drew and communicated to Livingston in early September: first, "that this court would, at a peace, oppose our extension to the Mississippi"; second, "that they would oppose our claim to free navigation of that river"; and third, that they would seek to "divide" the fisheries with Britain "to the exclusion of all

---

[55] Jared Sparks, one of the first historians to examine the paper trail left by diplomats in France, Spain, Britain, and America during the Revolutionary War, exonerated Rayneval of any wrongdoing and lamented that "some grave particulars have crept into our history which have slender foundation in fact and which bestow but scanty justice on the motives, conduct, and policy of the first ally of the United States." Observations on the Above Letter by Mr. Sparks, *RDC*, 6:49–51.

[56] Rayneval cited in Morris, *Peacemakers*, 329–330 (emphasis in the original); Shelburne cited in Bradford Perkins, *The Creation of an American Empire, 1775–1865* (Cambridge: Cambridge University Press, 1993), 40; Conferences of M. de Rayneval (Extracts), October 1782, *RDC*, 5:821–822.

others." Those had been Versailles's policy goals since the American Revolution began. From the moment the first French ambassador, Gérard, arrived in Philadelphia, Vergennes directed him to support Spanish claims to sovereignty over lands east of the Mississippi. To Gérard's successor, Luzerne, the comte wrote in October 1782 that American demands for navigation rights were "foolishness not meriting serious refutation." As for the fisheries, the words of Alleyn Fitzherbert, Shelburne's assistant, make plain French designs for postwar North America. Fitzherbert recalled years later, "M. de Vergennes never failed to insist on the expediency of a concert of measures between France and England for the purpose of excluding the American states from these fisheries, lest they should become a nursery for seamen." Jay was right to assume that the French wanted to keep the United States a miniature East Coast nation with no access to the river that was the key to future aggrandizement, and that they sought to deprive Americans of a resource so essential to the U.S. economy that, by the time of the peace treaty's signing, the value of the fishing business in Massachusetts alone was nearly $2 million.[57]

Animated, then, by a mix of well-founded surmise and anti-Bourbon bias, Jay resolved to steal a march on Vergennes. His instrument was one Benjamin Vaughan, who seemed at first blush a curious choice, being not only an Englishman but a protégé of Shelburne whom the prime minster had sent to Paris to spy on the American delegation. Vaughan, however, possessed qualifications that lent themselves to Jay's purpose. His mother was from Boston and he was dedicated to preserving Anglo-American amity despite the sundering of the colonial tie. He was related to Henry Laurens, the then-absent American peace commissioner, by marriage. He was an impulsive young man with a taste for adventure. Most important, he was among Franklin's most ardent admirers. In 1779 he had published an edition of the doctor's writings in London, and he fell under the spell of his idol after arriving on the Continent, regularly signing letters to him "Your ever devoted, affectionate, and obliged [friend]." Jay perceived that Vaughan's allegiance to Franklin, and by extension to the United States, eclipsed his commitment to Shelburne, and that he would agree to

---

[57] Jay to Livingston, 17 November 1782, *RDC*, 6:27, 29; Vergennes cited in Richard Kluger, *Seizing Destiny: The Relentless Expansion of American Territory* (New York: Alfred A. Knopf, 2005), 155; Fitzherbert cited in *Narrative and Critical History of America*, Justin Winsor, ed. (Boston: Houghton Mifflin, 1888), 7:120; Richard B. Morris, "The Durable Significance of the Treaty of 1783" in *Peace and the Peacemakers*, 243–244.

undertake a risky mission if it might help subtract America from Britain's list of enemies.[58]

Accordingly, Jay dispatched Vaughan to London bearing a message for Shelburne that put in plain language what Franklin had been insinuating through his correspondence with the prime minister and his parleys with Oswald: the American commissioners were willing to establish a bilateral negotiating track from which the French were excluded, and they would sign a separate peace with Britain provided they got good terms. Jay told Shelburne that "a little reflection must convince" him that it was in the interest of France, but not of Britain or the United States, to delay an Anglo-American settlement. Vergennes wanted the Americans to keep fighting their former mother country because that would oblige George III to maintain a force in North America that he could otherwise unleash on his continental adversaries. But neither the British nor the Americans benefited from this policy. Parliament had already granted U.S. independence, so what was the purpose in prolonging a conflict between peoples united by blood? And why should Americans battle redcoats for European ends like the retrocession of Gibraltar? These considerations, Jay wrote, highlighted "the obvious interest of Britain immediately to cut the cords which tied us to France." Shelburne could cut those cords if he satisfied the Americans on a few points.

First, the fisheries: "we could not make peace," Jay said, at the "expense" of Britain dividing the fisheries with France and shutting out the United States. Such an arrangement "would irritate America, would perpetuate her resentments, and induce her to use every possible means of retaliation by ... imposing the most rigid restraints on a commerce with Britain." This was a shrewd hortatory tactic by Jay, who knew his man. Shelburne was a free-trade zealot, a convert to the principles of Adam Smith. Although he regretted Britain's loss of sovereignty over its American colonies, he considered territorial empire less essential to British greatness than the maintenance of an environment in which trade could thrive. Jay stressed commercial advantages in his other two demands as well. It would be "impolitic," he declared, "to oppose us on the point of boundary and the navigation of the Mississippi," because a United States extending to that river and free to ply its waters would furnish Britain with a market that could not fail to enhance its already dominant position

---

[58] Vaughan cited in Fleming, *Perils of Peace*, 216. For Vaughan's role in crafting the 1783 peace, see Charles R. Ritcheson, "Britain's Peacemakers, 1782–1783: 'To an Astonishing Degree Unfit for the Task'?" in *Peace and the Peacemakers*, 72–77.

in Europe. No Anglo-French entente promised such benefits. Vergennes aimed to reduce British power, not magnify it; that was the reason he had allied France with the United States to begin with. Why would the British conciliate the French behind American backs when it was so much more profitable to conciliate the Americans behind French backs?

There was, of course, a problem. Vergennes, along with Franklin, had for months been drumming into the ears of Shelburne's envoys the message that France and the United States were bound by a treaty that forbade either party to enter into a peace with the enemy without the other's concurrence. Did not that treaty prohibit the settlement Jay was proposing? Here Jay's legal skills failed him, as he resorted to sophistry. Although the American commissioners were "determined faithfully to fulfill our treaty and engagements with this court," he wrote, it was *"a different thing to be guided by their or our construction of it."* He left unexplained what possible construction of the 1778 alliance, a pact barring bilateral settlements, could allow for a bilateral settlement. Shelburne took the hint. The Americans were offering to violate their treaty in exchange for generous concessions, but then again, it appeared, so were the French. Jay bet that Shelburne would see greater value in an Anglo-American double-cross than an Anglo-French one. He was right.

As might have been expected, Jay did not inform Vergennes or Congress of Vaughan's mission. Less predictably, he did not tell Franklin about it, and he revealed why in a report to Livingston written over a month later. "It would have relieved me of much anxiety and uneasiness to have concerted all these steps with Dr. Franklin," he said, "but on conversing with him about M. Rayneval's journey, he did not concur with me in sentiment respecting the objects of it, but appeared to have a great deal of confidence in this court." In other words, Franklin did not believe Rayneval had gone to London to stab the Americans in the back, and he did not find Vergennes's silence on the matter as troubling as Jay did. Moreover, Jay observed, the doctor was "much embarrassed and constrained by our instructions." Jay, feeling no such inhibition, had therefore decided to forge ahead alone. At the denouement of the American Revolution, U.S. foreign policy had become a one-man show, and that man was disobeying orders.[59]

---

[59] Jay to Livingston, 17 November 1782, *RDC*, 6:29–32 (emphasis in the original). For Shelburne the free trader, see Bernard Semmel, *The Rise of Free Trade Imperialism: Classical Political Economy, the Empire of Free Trade, and Imperialism, 1750–1850* (Cambridge: Cambridge University Press, 1970), 30–32.

"I AM OF YOUR OPINION"

Jay's solo act did not last long. Franklin emerged from his sickbed in early October to rejoin the talks, and Adams arrived in Paris from Amsterdam on the twenty-sixth of that month. By the time the U.S. commission became a trio, though, the outlines of a separate Anglo-American treaty had already been established.

Vaughan got back from London in late September with word of Shelburne's enthusiastic reaction to Jay's proposal, and the pace of negotiations accelerated. On 8 October, Jay and Oswald completed the first draft of America's first peace treaty. It contained all of the "necessary" conditions Franklin had listed in July plus a demand for navigation rights on the Mississippi, and Jay fended off Oswald's efforts to include provisions for compensating Loyalists or paying debts owed to British creditors. When Jay presented this document to a still-bedridden Franklin, the doctor approved it but urged that it be shown to Vergennes before submitting it to Shelburne. Jay refused. Vergennes deserved "no such confidence," he said. Franklin objected. Still, he went along.[60]

Oswald crossed the Channel confident of the draft's acceptance, but political motives compelled Shelburne to reject it. He did not believe his government could survive unless he made some gesture on behalf of the creditors and Tories. His counterproposal laid down a number of conditions, among them the demand that Americans discharge their debts in specie, not continental currency. He also insisted on compensation for Loyalists whose property had been destroyed, and he denied U.S. fishermen the right to dry their catches on Newfoundland shores "on account of the danger of disputes." Although he sought to adjust Jay's suggested boundary between Nova Scotia and Maine so as to give Britain more land, he was flexible on this point, advising Oswald that if Jay and Franklin proved obdurate the matter could be referred to a postwar commission. Other than that, Shelburne did not challenge the Americans' territorial claims. The region lying to the eastward of the Mississippi would, he acknowledged, become part of the United States. He moreover agreed that Britain and America would share freedom of navigation on that river (a concession that, absent Spanish concurrence, was of limited value). Indeed, while Shelburne's cabinet complained about the

---

[60] Articles Agreed on between the American and British Commissioners, 8 October 1782, *RDC*, 5:805–808; Franklin to Livingston, 5 December 1782, ibid., 6:112; Jay cited in Diary Entry, 2 October 1782, "Matthew Ridley's Diary," 117.

preliminary terms Oswald showed them – and while Shelburne lashed the Scot for "the principle which you seem to have adopted of going before the American commissioners in every point of favor" – much of Jay's first draft made it into the final treaty.[61]

A chastened Oswald, Strachey in tow, returned to France to find Adams among his American opposite numbers. The Bostonian had reached Paris just days before, and had learned of Congress's new instructions during his introductory meeting with Jay. His reaction was immediate and savage. The orders, he wrote to Livingston, had the effect of "subjecting us to the French ministry, . . . taking away from us all right of judging for ourselves, and obliging us to do whatever the French ministers should advise us to do, and to do nothing without their consent." He had not imagined, when Congress asked him to represent the United States abroad, that he would become Vergennes's clerk. "If I had, I never would have accepted the commission." He took the "utmost satisfaction" in Jay's noncompliance, noting that Jay had "been all along acting here upon the same principles" that animated Adams's own diplomacy. "There is no man more impressed with the obligation of obedience to instructions [than I]," Adams declared, but what Congress required was absurd. "If the French minister advises us to cede to the Spaniards the whole river of the Mississippi and five hundred miles to the eastward of it, are we bound by our instructions to put our signature to the cession when the English themselves are willing we should extend to the river and enjoy our natural rights to its extension?" Did the same strictures obtain if Vergennes told the American commissioners "to relinquish our right to the fishery on the Grand Bank of Newfoundland" despite British readiness to grant that right? If so, Adams snarled, "I really think it would be better to constitute the Comte de Vergennes our sole minister and give him full powers to make peace." Certainly Adams had no intention of surrendering his nation's diplomatic autonomy. To his diary he confided, "It is glory to have broken such infamous orders."[62]

That remark raises a provocative issue: the degree to which some writers have cast Adams in a starring role in these deliberations because, to continue the theatrical metaphor, he had most of the good lines. No Founding Father wrote or spoke with greater ferocity. Beside his

---

[61] Ritcheson, "Britain's Peacemakers," 95–96; Shelburne cited in *Narrative and Critical History*, Winsor, ed., 7:132.

[62] Adams to Livingston, 31 October 1782, *RDC*, 5:839; Adams to Livingston, 18 November 1782, ibid., 6:52–54; Diary Entry, 18 February 1783, *WJA*, 3:359.

broiling correspondence Jay's matter-of-fact reports blend into the background. Yet Adams himself admitted that Jay was instrumental in fashioning treaty terms. In another, less frequently cited diary entry, Adams mused that if the French had appreciated Jay's labors, they would have accorded him "the title with which they inconsiderately decorated me, that of '*Le Washington de la négotiation*': a very flattering compliment indeed, to which I have not a right, but sincerely think it belongs to Mr. Jay." Given Adams's notorious reluctance to share credit, that was high praise, and he was not alone in considering Jay principally responsible for the Anglo-American settlement. Hamilton, who crossed swords with Adams on other questions, agreed with him that Jay deserved the lion's share of glory. Several historians also make that case. In a popular turn-of-the-century survey of United States foreign policy, Willis Fletcher Johnston sounded a note that continues to echo in scholarship on the Revolutionary War. Jay, he asserted, was "the giant and hero of all these negotiations."[63]

We may ask, however, what Jay's initiatives in the late summer of 1782 gained for the United States. Shelburne had been prepared to negotiate on the basis of Franklin's "necessary" conditions as early as July, before Jay took center stage in the talks. Jay did make navigation of the Mississippi a more categorical U.S. demand than Franklin had during his meetings with Oswald, and Jay and Adams clarified the sloppy language of the doctor's original memorandum with regard to the fisheries, but the Americans could probably have achieved these objectives without the two-month delay caused by Jay's insistence on a reworded commission, a hiatus during which, as noted above, the Franco-Spanish assault on Gibraltar failed and Britain's position improved. The bluster over Oswald's powers was much ado about nothing. Altering them did not foil any British designs to reconsolidate the empire, since Shelburne had abandoned his dream of reunion between mother country and colonies

---

[63] Diary Entry, 30 November 1782, *WJA*, 3:339; Hamilton cited in Stahr, *John Jay*, 245; Willis Fletcher Johnston, *America's Foreign Relations* (New York: Appleton-Century-Crofts, 1916), 1:122. David McCullough's Pulitzer-Prize-winning biography celebrates – and occasionally exaggerates – Adams's contribution, a tendency even more pronounced in the Home Box Office miniseries based on the book. See McCullough, *John Adams*, 273–286; *John Adams* (dir. Tom Hooper, 2008), Episode 3: "Don't Tread on Me" and Episode 4: "Reunion." For texts in which Jay appears the indispensable man, see L. Nathan Ellis, *A Short History of American Diplomacy* (New York: Harper & Brothers, 1951), 35–37; Reginald Horsman, *The Diplomacy of the New Republic, 1776–1815* (Chicago: Harlan Davidson, 1985), 25–27; Kaplan, *Colonies into Nation*, 134, 140, 141–142.

before George III asked him to form a government. Furthermore, as Bradford Perkins notes, "There is no evidence that the ministry intended to use recognition as a bargaining chip." Neither Shelburne nor any of his colleagues ever suggested withholding acknowledgment of U.S. independence until the Americans gave way on other points. To Shelburne, independence was an accomplished fact, however disagreeable. Had Jay let the issue slide and begun substantive discussions in August, when Britain faced an uncertain military fate in the Mediterranean, the Americans might have been able to secure some of Franklin's "advisable" provisions, such as the surrender of all or part of Canada, or they might have obtained more expansive fishing rights than the British agreed to in the final treaty. As it turned out, Jay's finickiness helped take the heat off Shelburne at a time when the prime minister was vulnerable. Jay the lawyer won out over Jay the diplomat, and the result was a sacrifice of American leverage.[64]

Moreover, the Vaughan mission, while dramatic, would have been unnecessary had Jay not suspended talks with the British over a matter of semantics. Franklin had already inaugurated the bilateral dialogue Jay sought to create. Negotiations between the doctor and Oswald had led to Shelburne's tacit acceptance of most key U.S. demands, and Franklin had kept this information from Vergennes. The Americans were thus on course to signing a separate agreement with their enemy before the skulking exploits of Vaughan – or, for that matter, Rayneval, who may not have had the welfare of the United States uppermost in his mind but who was not the agent of Gallic perfidy Jay imagined. Vaughan's trip did help solve the problem of interrupted talks, but Jay himself had caused this problem by making a fuss over the commission and breaking off contact with Oswald when Franklin was too ill to stop him. A dispassionate analysis of the events following Franklin's incapacitation must conclude that Jay, rather than being *"Le Washington de la negotiation,"* unnecessarily slowed the momentum toward an Anglo-American treaty. His stretch as sole negotiator of the peace was not his finest hour.

If Jay's tactics left something to be desired, though, his strategy was sound. National self-interest demanded that he disobey Congress's orders. Jay lacked Adams's penchant for hyperbole, but he would have applauded the mid-November tirade the Bostonian wrote to Livingston, in particular its concluding yowl that "there is nothing that humbles and

---

[64] Perkins, "Peace of Paris," 201.

depresses, nothing that shackles and confines – in short, nothing that renders totally useless all your ministers in Europe so much as these positive instructions to consult and communicate with French ministers upon all occasions and follow their advice."[65]

Adams's arrival came as a godsend to Jay. From that point on, Jay believed, Franklin would have no choice but to go along with his younger colleagues, who, together, comprised a majority of the peace commission. As for Adams, he found Jay a second self. "Nothing that has happened," he later wrote, "has ever struck me more forcibly, or affected me more intimately than the entire coincidence of principles and opinions between him and me." The two lawyers were so alike in personality that it is difficult to determine which man hated the French more or had scanter patience with Franklin's approach to statecraft. It did not take them long to conclude that they were the only American patriots in Paris and that the future greatness of the United States depended on their defying Congress, Versailles, and the doctor. After his initial meeting with Jay, and after introducing himself to Oswald and Strachey, Adams headed off to Passy to tell Franklin that the days of adherence to French advice and opinion were finished.

The resulting encounter was bizarre. Adams clearly expected Franklin to argue with him, and he delivered a lecture that must have set the old man's teeth on edge. According to Adams's diary, "I told him without reserve my opinion of the policy of this [French] court, and of the principles, wisdom, and firmness with which Mr. Jay had conducted the negotiation in his [Franklin's] sickness and my absence, and that I was determined to support Mr. Jay to the utmost of my power." A diplomat's first duty was to his country, not to Congress, Adams declaimed. Had Americans shed their blood at Monmouth, Camden, and Brandywine only to make the United States a tail to the French kite?

Instead of responding in kind, Franklin said nothing, a reaction Adams chalked up to his still being weak from his battle with the stone. The next day, however, when the three American diplomats met to thrash out strategy before sitting down with the British negotiators, Franklin told Adams and Jay, "I am of your opinion and will go on with these gentlemen [Oswald and Strachey] without consulting this [French] court." An astonished Adams had to report on 30 November that Franklin "has gone with us in entire harmony and unanimity

---

[65] Adams to Livingston, 18 November 1782, *RDC*, 6:52–54.

throughout, and has been able and useful, both by his sagacity and his reputation, in the whole negotiation."[66]

Franklin handled – one is tempted to say played – his fellow commissioners as nimbly as he managed Vergennes, Oswald, and their respective sovereigns. He would have been within his rights to protest that Jay and Adams had achieved no breakthroughs, that he had adopted their policy of negotiating without French knowledge before either man arrived in Paris, and that the only difference between the approach they were pursuing and the one he had followed was that he had been more attentive to French sensibilities. But a quarrel with Adams and Jay would have been detrimental to the commission's efforts at a time when it was imperative for the Americans to present a united front. Franklin therefore let his colleagues believe he was acting out of deference to their wishes, and his self-effacement went a long way toward mollifying them. Assured of Franklin's support, both lawyers felt free to concentrate their argumentative skills on the adversary.

There followed two months of discussions, the specifics of which need not concern us. The essential point is that the Americans failed to keep Vergennes informed of these talks, and in fact orchestrated a campaign of disinformation that so misled the comte that as late as 23 November he was writing to Luzerne about how far apart the United States and Great Britain were from reaching an agreement. (By that date, nearly all of the issues in dispute between the two sides had been resolved in America's favor.) Congress was likewise left unapprised. Livingston wrote the commissioners to express his perplexity "that we have not yet been favored with such minute information on many points as we have reason to expect." That was the arrangement Franklin, Adams, and Jay wanted, and it facilitated a nearly comprehensive diplomatic triumph. Adams did make a concession on the fisheries, permitting the British to substitute the word "liberty" for "right" in the treaty passage referring to curing and drying claims, a distinction that generated over a century of controversy, but otherwise the Americans got everything they wanted: boundaries to their liking, freedom of navigation and commerce on the Mississippi, acknowledgment of U.S. independence, and a British pledge to withdraw their troops.[67]

---

[66] Diary Entry, 30 November 1782, *WJA*, 3:336.
[67] Vergennes cited in Brecher, *Securing American Independence*, 307; Livingston to Jay, 23 November 1782, *RDC*, 6:71; Livingston to Franklin, 5 September 1782, ibid., 5:66. For Adams's yielding on the fisheries, see John Adams's Journal of Peace Negotiations,

Ironically, given his younger colleagues' reputation for stubbornness, it was Franklin who proved most obdurate on a key article. The doctor was opposed to Loyalist indemnification. His son William was a Loyalist, and he felt the personal and political betrayal keenly. Shelburne would have been happy to pass over this matter in silence, but the Tories had a powerful lobby in Parliament and he believed his survival in office depended on appeasing them. Negotiations were deadlocked for several days on the question until Oswald proposed a "compromise" that became Article 5 of the treaty, which stipulated that Congress would recommend to the legislatures of the individual American states the restitution of property and estates. Both parties were aware that this provision meant nothing. It was designed to save Shelburne's face rather than protect Tory rights, and, predictably, the states ignored congressional recommendations in the coming years. Shelburne in effect sold the Loyalists out. Franklin had his victory.[68]

On the last day of talks, Henry Laurens finally arrived to take his place on the commission. His imprisonment in the Tower of London had left him feeble, and he could do little more than join Franklin, Jay, and Adams in signing the treaty at Oswald's lodgings at the Grand Hotel Muscovite. Before putting his name to the document, he expressed surprise that the Americans had not consulted Vergennes during their deliberations, but he did not press the point, and the business concluded without incident. Franklin then invited the signers and their staffs to a celebratory dinner at the Hotel Valentinois in Passy, where they drank toasts to an independent United States. "Thus drops the curtain upon this mighty tragedy," Adams wrote his wife a few days later, a premature claim but one that indicates his – and the other negotiators' – confidence that the preliminary articles were definitive. Although they would have to be ratified by Congress and Parliament, and while they would not become effective until France, Spain, and Holland made peace, these were technicalities. Having entered the family of nations and won a territorial bonanza by coming to terms with Great Britain, the United States could hardly be expected to plunge back into war against its former sovereign over

---

28 November 1782, *RDC*, 6:85–88. For the terms agreed upon by the British and American commissioners, see Provisional Articles of Peace, 30 November 1782, *RDC*, 6:96–99.

[68] "Franklin is very staunch against" the Loyalists, Adams recorded toward the close of talks, "more decided a great deal on this point than Mr. Jay or myself." Diary Entry, 26 November 1782, *WJA*, 3:332.

Gibraltar or any other European issue. For all practical purposes, the American Revolution ended on 30 November 1782.[69]

"THIS LITTLE MISUNDERSTANDING"

Someone had to break the news to Vergennes. Adams would have relished that assignment. He believed the comte had been conniving with the British commissioners, especially Strachey, whose proposals, he noted, "appeared to me to come piping hot from Versailles," and he exulted in having beaten Europe's most accomplished chess player at his own game. "There is a Vulcan at Versailles whose constant employment has been to forge chains for American ministers," he wrote fellow diplomat Francis Dana. "But his metal has not been fine and strong enough, nor his art of fabricating it sufficiently perfect, to be able to hold a giant or two who have broken them to pieces like morsels of glass."[70]

Fortunately for the future of Franco-American relations, Franklin volunteered to explain matters. He had taken the precaution of sending a note to Vergennes the night before the signing ceremony, although he did not provide any details about what the commissioners had agreed to. The next day he forwarded a copy of the treaty to the palace along with the information that it had been signed that morning. There was no reply for several days. When Franklin broke the silence by paying a call on Vergennes, he was received with icy formality. The "abrupt signature of the articles," Vergennes observed, had "little in it which could be agreeable to our king." Franklin offered lavish apologies and the best excuses he could devise, and at length Vergennes softened, reasoning that, although the Americans "had not been particularly civil," at least the damage was minor, since the agreement just signed would not become valid till a general European settlement. To avoid any misconceptions in America or elsewhere, the comte urged Franklin not to send a copy of the provisional treaty to Congress for the time being. Such an "intelligence with England," he said, "might make the people in America think a peace was consummated." Franklin made polite murmurings that Vergennes interpreted as assent.[71]

[69] Diary Entry, 30 November 1782, *WJA*, 3:335–339; John Adams to Abigail Adams, 22 January 1783, *The Adams Papers: Adams Family Correspondence*, Richard Alan Ryerson, Joanna M. Revelas, Celeste Walker, Gregg L. Lint, Humphrey J. Costello, eds. (Boston: Massachusetts Historical Society, 1993), 5:74.
[70] Diary Entry, 25 November 1782, *WJA*, 3:328; Adams cited in Henrietta Dana Skinner, "New Light on Revolutionary Diplomacy," *Harper's* 104 (December 1901): 784.
[71] Vergennes to Luzerne, 19 December 1782, *RDC*, 6:107.

Vergennes was therefore blindsided when Franklin sent him a note ten days later informing him that an American ship, the *Washington*, was preparing to depart for the United States with a copy of the treaty. Even more shocking was Franklin's comment that, in view of the fact that the British had given the ship a safe-conduct pass, it would be helpful if he could also send home 6 million livres in aid. "I fear the Congress will be reduced to despair when they find that nothing is yet obtained," he wrote. The *Washington* set sail at ten o'clock the following morning, and if Vergennes could come up with the cash by then, Franklin said, he would be happy to dispatch a courier to collect it.[72]

Vergennes's reply to this letter was revealing. He had ample grounds for protest. The Americans had disregarded their instructions to take no steps without French permission and had violated the terms of the 1778 alliance. Having rushed to close a deal with the British, they were now, it seemed, dropping out of the war. And they had the effrontery to ask for more money! Franklin might have expected a wrathful message. Instead, Vergennes sounded almost plaintive. "I am at a loss, sir, to explain your conduct and that of your colleagues on this occasion," he wrote. "You have concluded your preliminary articles without any communication between us, although the instructions from Congress prescribe that nothing shall be done without the participation of the [French] king." This was curious behavior for a "wise and discreet" man like Franklin. How was Versailles to construe it as anything other than an act of bad faith?[73]

Franklin spent a day and a half working on his response, one of the most famous pieces of correspondence in the annals of U.S. diplomacy. He began by pointing out that it was the American commissioners' responsibility to "give Congress as early an account as possible of our proceedings," lest they hear of them from the British first, which would be confusing. Then he assured Vergennes that he and his colleagues had not made a separate peace; they had simply agreed on preliminary articles that would not be valid until France and Britain concluded their negotiations. He admitted, however, that by failing to consult Vergennes before signing, "we have been guilty of neglecting a point of *bienséance* [propriety]," but not "from want of respect for the King, whom we all love and honor." It would be a shame if this "single indiscretion" were to undermine "the great work which has hitherto been so happily conducted"

[72] Franklin to Vergennes, 15 December 1782, *RDC*, 6:137–138.
[73] Vergennes to Franklin, 15 December 1782, *RDC*, 6:140.

between France and the United States, because if that happened all of their years of shared sacrifice would be for naught. Expressions of gratitude for King Louis's "many and great benefits" followed, capped by a statement that could be read either as an entreaty or a threat: *"The English, I just now learn, flatter themselves that they have already divided us.* I hope this little misunderstanding will therefore be kept a secret, and that they will find themselves totally mistaken." That was blarney; Franklin had not "just now" learned anything of the sort, but it was a signal to Vergennes that he should moderate his criticism if he wanted to preserve Franco-American friendship.[74]

Again, Vergennes did not react with the fury that might have been anticipated. Rather than responding to Franklin right away, he wrote Luzerne in Philadelphia, suggesting that "the most influential members of Congress should be informed of the very irregular conduct of their commissioners in regard to us." According to Congress's instructions, "they ought to have done nothing without our participation," and yet they had clandestinely met with British agents for weeks, signed a preliminary treaty, and sprung it on Versailles with no advance notice. While Vergennes was hurt by the Americans' treachery, though, he told Luzerne not to speak of it "in the tone of complaint." Shortly thereafter he sent the ambassador another letter countermanding even that mild remonstrance. What was done was done, he said. There was no point in forcing a confrontation that could drive the Americans into an alliance with the British. Remarkably, when the *Washington* weighed anchor a few days behind schedule, it carried 600,000 livres from the French treasury, a down payment on Vergennes's commitment to pay the full 6 million in quarterly installments throughout 1783.[75]

Why was Vergennes so serene in the face of the commissioners' double-dealing? Three considerations seem to have shaped his response. First, as he indicated to Luzerne, he did not want to risk a breach with the United States at a time when France was still at war. Second, he recognized that, had he been in Franklin's position, he would have done the same thing. The terms Britain offered were too good to decline. "You will notice that the English buy the peace more than they make it," the comte remarked to Rayneval. "What can be the motive that they could have brought terms so easy that they could have been interpreted

---

[74] Franklin to Vergennes, 17 December 1782, *RDC*, 6:143–144 (emphasis in the original).
[75] Vergennes to Luzerne, 19 December 1782, *RDC*, 6:150–152; Vergennes to Luzerne, 21 December 1782, ibid., 6:153.

as a kind of surrender?" Finally, and most important, he understood that the Anglo-American settlement benefited France, relieving Versailles of its obligation to fight until Spain achieved its war aims. Vergennes could now tell the Spanish that American actions made recovery of Gibraltar impracticable. The Bourbons had been unable to overrun the rock with the Americans in their camp; without them, Spanish reconquest was a pipe dream. Britain, freed from fighting in North America, was certain to fight even more tenaciously for Gibraltar, meaning that Spain would have to accept something less than fulfillment of the Treaty of Aranjuez. The Americans' duplicity actually helped break a diplomatic logjam.[76]

Thus it was that Vergennes received news of the separate peace with greater equanimity than some U.S. Congressmen, notably Livingston, who lambasted Jay, Adams, and Franklin for "forfeit[ing] the confidence of an ally to whom we are much indebted." As noted above, Livingston's fellow legislators swallowed whatever moral qualms they had and ratified the commissioners' handiwork. The preliminary peace agreement initialed by Britain and the Bourbon powers on 20 January 1783 ensured that the United States escaped any reprisals for what its diplomats had done. Definitive treaties were signed all around several months later, and the European war was over.[77]

Vergennes had accomplished his principal objective, depriving Britain of its North American colonies, but France had recovered none of the territory taken from it in 1763 and its army and navy were exhausted. Worse, it was bankrupt. The war had cost the government an estimated 1 billion livres. Vergennes could not look with satisfaction on the results of French diplomacy. "If we may judge the future from what has passed here under our eyes," he wrote to Luzerne, "we shall be but poorly paid for all we have done for the United States, and for securing them a national existence."[78]

In the short term, he was right. The financial crisis brought about by the war compelled Louis XVI to call the Estates General, which had not assembled in 175 years, and France was soon convulsed by a revolution of its own. By the time that world-shaking event ran its course, the map of

[76] Vergennes to Rayneval, 4 December 1782, *RDC*, 6:107.
[77] Livingston to Boudinot, 18 March 1783, *RDC*, 6:316; Dull, *Diplomatic History of the American Revolution*, 152–158.
[78] Vergennes to Luzerne, 19 December 1782, *RDC*, 6:152; Murphy, *Charles Gravier*, 397–404.

Europe had changed dramatically, and not in France's favor. Yet in the second decade of the twentieth century, millions of Americans would cross the Atlantic to fight to preserve French independence, repaying many times over "the debt to Lafayette," in part because another American diplomat disobeyed orders.[79]

---

[79] Jonathan R. Dull, "France and the American Revolution Seen as Tragedy" in *Diplomacy and Revolution*, 73–106.

2

"Service without Authority"

Livingston and Monroe Buy Louisiana

The two diplomats assumed an almost apologetic tone when they broke the news. "An acquisition of so great an extent was, we well know, not contemplated by our appointment," Robert Livingston and James Monroe wrote Secretary of State James Madison in mid-May 1803. They had been sent to Paris to acquire New Orleans and as much territory east of that city as the government of Napoleon Bonaparte could be persuaded to cede. Instead, they had pledged $15 million for the vast area from the Mississippi River to the Rocky Mountains, a region of over 800,000 square miles. This arrangement, they admitted, went beyond "the principles laid down in our instructions," but they argued that "the circumstances and conditions which induced us to make it will justify us, in the measure, to our government and country."[1]

They were correct. Reaction in the United States was overwhelmingly positive. Madison conveyed his "entire approbation" of the envoys' "zealous exertions." Horatio Gates, the seventy-five-year-old hero of the Battle of Saratoga, wrote President Thomas Jefferson that the pact was "the greatest and most beneficial event that has taken place since the Declaration of Independence." Ohio Senator John Smith called it the foremost contribution toward "peace and harmony among us since the establishment of the federal constitution." Even Alexander Hamilton, Jefferson's bitter enemy, admitted that Livingston and Monroe had made

---

[1] Livingston (hereafter RL) and Monroe to Madison, 13 May 1803, *The Papers of James Madison: Secretary of State Series*, Mary A. Hackett, J. C. A. Stagg, Jeanne Kerr Cross, Susan Holbrook Perdue, and Ellen J. Barber, eds. (Charlottesville: University Press of Virginia, 1998) (hereafter *JMP:SS*), 4:601–602.

"an important acquisition ... essential to the peace and prosperity of our western country."[2]

This applause echoes through scholarship on the Louisiana Purchase, starting with the earliest attempts by historians to grapple with the subject. On the first anniversary of Jefferson's triumph, David Ramsay declared, "The acquisition of Louisiana is the greatest political blessing ever conferred on these states." A century later, Henry Adams wrote that Jefferson "achieved the greatest diplomatic success recorded in American history." Bernard DeVoto, commissioned by *Collier's* magazine to assess the Purchase on its sesquicentennial, did not equivocate. "No event in all American history," he said, "not the Civil War, nor the Declaration of Independence, nor even the signing of the Constitution, was more important." The flood of books and articles published in 2003, as the Purchase turned two hundred, rang variations on the same theme, with authors extolling it as "the greatest real estate transaction in history," "the greatest diplomatic triumph in the history of the United States," and even "the greatest event since the nation was founded." Scholars have crossed swords over many features of the Purchase, but none dispute its significance.[3]

Equally undisputable is the fact that it grew out of two American diplomats' refusal to follow orders. Livingston and Monroe had no authority to act as they did, a point historians note but decline to pursue. Few studies devote much attention to the envoys' day-to-day actions in Paris. The principal scholarly debate is over whether or not Jefferson deserves credit for the Purchase. Some historians portray the president as lucky, the beneficiary of a combination of events – slave rebellion in Santo Domingo, yellow fever on that island, Napoleon's icebound fleet

---

[2] Madison to RL and Monroe, 29 July 1803, *JMP:SS*, 5:238–239; Gates and Smith cited in Jon Kukla, *A Wilderness So Immense: The Louisiana Purchase and the Destiny of America* (New York: Alfred A. Knopf, 2003), 287; Hamilton cited in Douglass Adair, "Hamilton on the Louisiana Purchase: A Newly Identified Editorial from the New York Evening Post," *William and Mary Quarterly*, 12 (April 1955): 273.

[3] Ramsay cited in Robert W. Tucker and David C. Hendrickson, *Empire of Liberty: The Statecraft of Thomas Jefferson* (New York: Oxford University Press, 1999), 89; Henry Adams, *History of the United States of America during the First Administration of Thomas Jefferson* (New York: Charles Scribner's Sons, 1909), 2:48; DeVoto cited in Dennis W. Johnson, *The Laws That Shaped America: Fifteen Acts of Congress and Their Lasting Impact* (New York: Routledge, 2009), 1; Stephen E. Ambrose and Douglas G. Brinkley, *The Mississippi and the Making of a Nation: From the Louisiana Purchase to Today* (Washington: National Geographic, 2003), 5; Thomas Fleming, *The Louisiana Purchase* (New York: John Wiley and Sons, 2003), 1; Charles A. Cerami, *Jefferson's Great Gamble* (Naperville, IL: Sourcebooks Incorporated, 2003), x.

in Holland, the prospect of renewed war in Europe – that he did not control or even influence, while others argue that he played a more active role, combining pressure with forbearance to extract maximum benefit out of a perilous situation. Neither side in this debate gives Livingston or Monroe much claim to glory. Both Jefferson's detractors and defenders argue that it took no special courage or foresight to disobey orders, as the diplomats could be certain that Jefferson would uphold, indeed applaud, their actions.[4]

These accounts do a disservice to Monroe and especially Livingston. Their disobedience was daring and even reckless, and they knew it. They were not at all confident that the president would go along with what they had done. Had they believed he would, they would not have prefaced their report with a virtual *mea culpa*. They understood that the transaction required Jefferson to abandon two of his most cherished and oft-proclaimed principles: economy in government and strict construction of the Constitution. Jefferson had vowed to reduce the national debt, and the Purchase increased it. He had also consistently upbraided the Federalists for strengthening the central government at the expense of the states by loose constitutional construction, and the Purchase required him to arrogate more power to himself than George Washington or John Adams ever had. To present Jefferson with the Purchase was to confront him with a political Pandora's box that Monroe and Livingston rightly feared he might reject.

More important, as we will see, the Purchase did not represent Livingston and Monroe's only act of defiance while in Paris. In negotiations with his host government, Livingston raised the possibility of the United

---

[4] For works that depict Jefferson as passive observer rather than master strategist, see James K. Hosmer, *History of the Louisiana Purchase* (New York: D. Appleton and Company, 1902); Frederick Austin Ogg, *The Opening of the Mississippi: A Struggle for Supremacy in the American Interior* (London: Greenwood Press, 1904); Perkins, *Creation of a Republican Empire*. For works claiming that Jefferson's diplomacy was instrumental in bringing about the Purchase, see Francis D. Cogliano, *Emperor of Liberty: Thomas Jefferson's Foreign Policy* (New Haven: Yale University Press, 2014); Alexander DeConde, *This Affair of Louisiana* (Baton Rouge: Louisiana State University Press, 1976); Lawrence S. Kaplan, *Entangling Alliances with None: American Foreign Policy in the Age of Jefferson* (Kent, OH: Kent State University Press, 1987); Walter LaFeber, "Jefferson and American Foreign Policy" in Peter S. Onuf, ed., *Jeffersonian Legacies* (Charlottesville: University Press of Virginia, 1993), 370–391. "[W]hen considering the Louisiana Purchase," Francis Cogliano notes, "it seems that a positive view of Jefferson's handling of the Mississippi crisis and the negotiations over Louisiana between 1801 and 1803 has prevailed." Francis D. Cogliano, *Thomas Jefferson: Reputation and Legacy* (Charlottesville: University of Virginia Press, 2006), 244.

States extending west of the Mississippi long before anyone in Bona-parte's inner circle made a formal offer to that effect. He also, without prompting from the White House or State Department, prepared and disseminated a brilliant memorandum that laid out, point by point, why France ought not take possession of Louisiana. As for Monroe, he orchestrated an advance payment of $2 million to Napoleon when he had no power to do so. This action saved the Purchase at a time when the French dictator seemed about to back out of the deal.

Why did Livingston and Monroe violate their instructions so fla-grantly? As in many cases of American rogue diplomacy, the key factor was how the two men conceived of their mission in Paris. They did not view themselves as subordinates executing plans developed stateside but, rather, as policy*makers* on a more or less equal footing with the president. Livingston, the leading plutocrat of Duchess County and head of one of the oldest dynasties of New York, was accustomed to having things his own way and giving rather than receiving orders. Monroe, for his part, took the Paris job after Jefferson sent him two remarkable letters all but begging him to serve and insisting that he, and only he, could save the United States at a moment of existential crisis. Ego stroked, Monroe left for France expecting that Jefferson and Madison would trust his judg-ment and that he would steer events.

If historians have overlooked Livingston and Monroe's contribution to the Purchase, Jefferson did not. Shortly after learning that his envoys had agreed to buy Louisiana, the president wrote a friend that "both men have a just portion of merit, and, were it necessary or proper, it could be shown that each has rendered peculiar service, and of important value." Their service was all the more peculiar and important for having been rendered in the absence of authorization from back home.[5]

"CIRCUMSTANCES OF DESPAIR"

By the time the soon-to-be-inaugurated Jefferson nominated Livingston as minister to Paris, Spain's transfer of Louisiana to France was the worst-kept secret on either side of the Atlantic. French and Spanish representatives had formalized the agreement in the Treaty of San Ilde-fonso in early October 1800, but the governments in Paris and Madrid continued to deny that a transaction had taken place out of fear that

---

[5] Jefferson to Gates, 11 July 1803, *Works of Thomas Jefferson*, Paul Leicester Ford, ed. (New York: G. P. Putnam's Sons, 1899) (hereafter *WTJ*), 10:13.

either the British or the Americans would react by capturing Louisiana before Bonaparte could take possession. Nonetheless, rumors were rife in Washington and London, and in late March 1801 Rufus King, U.S. minister to Britain, could report with near-certainty to Madison that "Spain has ... ceded Louisiana and the Floridas to France. ... I am apprehensive that this cession is intended to have, and may actually produce, effects injurious to the union and consequent happiness of the people of the United States."[6]

King's concern was warranted. As long as weak, distracted Spain occupied America's borderlands, Jefferson had nothing to fear. Spain could offer little resistance to U.S. expansionism, and the 1795 Treaty of San Lorenzo between Washington and Madrid granted the United States unrestricted navigation of the Mississippi River. But if Bonaparte took control of Louisiana, the future would be grim. France's army, the mightiest in the world, could use the territory as a springboard for an attack on the United States, or Napoleon might revoke American access to the Mississippi, thereby closing off the only cheap and speedy route for sending trans-Allegheny produce to market. Denied use of the river, farmers would have to transport their agricultural produce across the mountains, a prohibitively expensive endeavor. "The Mississippi is to our Western farmers everything," Madison observed. "It is the Hudson, the Delaware, the Potomac, and all the navigable rivers of the Atlantic states formed into one stream." Americans could not surrender control of that all-important waterway to the mercurial Bonaparte.[7]

On paper, few people were better equipped to represent the United States in Paris at this tense time than Livingston. He was one of the most prominent men in America, and his appointment as minister would make plain to Napoleon how seriously the U.S. government took the Louisiana matter. As chancellor (secretary) of New York, Livingston had administered the oath of office to George Washington. He had been the first U.S. secretary of foreign affairs, precursor to the position of secretary of state, and thus had diplomatic experience. He was more-over, like the president, a Francophile who, despite qualms about the excesses of the Terror, had sided repeatedly with France in its conflict with America's former mother country. While he did not speak French,

---

[6] King to Madison, 29 March 1801, *American State Papers: Foreign Relations* (Washington, D.C.: Gales and Seaton, 1832) (hereafter *ASP*), 2:509.

[7] Madison cited in Joseph J. Ellis, *American Sphinx: The Character of Thomas Jefferson* (New York: Vintage Books, 1998), 205.

he read the language with ease. Perhaps most important, he was wealthy enough to support himself in a position whose expenses could be killing. Louis André Pichon, the French chargé in Washington, was delighted when he learned of Livingston's nomination. "No one," he assured Jefferson, "could receive this mission with qualities more apt to maintain and increase the good understanding ... between the two states."[8]

Yet Livingston had a few handicaps that ought to have given Jefferson and Madison pause. He was hard of hearing, which made verbal negotiations, even in English, a chore for him. He was also, one historian notes, impulsive and unreflective, his mind "a fertile seedbed for the reception of unlikely schemes." Finally, he was intensely ambitious, anxious to play a leading role in global developments. He knew that the laurels he had won prior to the Paris assignment came for the most part from family connections, and he longed to leave his own mark on the world. At fifty-five, he felt that time was running out. His ambition, harnessed to his fortune, made him, like future rogue diplomat Joseph Kennedy, a difficult man to control.[9]

The Senate confirmed Livingston by a party-line vote of fifteen to twelve, and the minister, in accordance with Jefferson's wishes, delayed his departure until ratification of the treaty ending the naval Quasi-War between the United States and France. That war had kept America from having a representative in Paris for years. The Directory, which governed France during the Adams administration, had refused to receive Adams's minister-designate and had actually expelled him from the country. Now that the Directory had given way to the Consulate, commanded by First Consul Bonaparte, many Americans feared that relations between Washington and Paris would grow even more hostile. Livingston, it appeared, had a formidable task before him.[10]

Madison did not make matters easier. Over the course of several months, while the administration waited for news that the undeclared Franco-American conflict was in fact finished, the secretary of state met often with Livingston and worked out a complicated strategy designed to meet a number of contingencies. First, Livingston was told to convey America's opposition to any change in the status of Louisiana. If a transfer had not taken place, Livingston was to persuade Napoleon to

---

[8] Pichon cited in Dangerfield, *Livingston*, 305.

[9] Ibid., 339. George Dangerfield's biography of Livingston is admirably even-handed in its presentation of the diplomat's faults and virtues.

[10] The best study of the Quasi-War is DeConde, *Quasi-War*.

forgo one. If, as everyone in Washington assumed, Napoleon had accepted Louisiana from Spain, Livingston was to find out whether the cession included the Floridas, and if it did, he was to convince the French dictator to give those territories, "or at least West Florida," to America. Livingston was also to pressure Bonaparte to "make over to the United States" the port city of New Orleans, which controlled the mouth of the Mississippi.

This approach would have stood a greater chance of success if Livingston had been given something to bargain with, but Jefferson was convinced that the threat of an Anglo-American alliance would be sufficient to bring the French to terms. France had been at war with Great Britain for over a decade, and the president did not think Bonaparte would dare risk driving the United States, whose independence France had helped win, into the arms of the British by denying the Americans what they demanded. Livingston was therefore not authorized to offer Napoleon money for New Orleans or the Floridas. The most he could do was promise that the U.S. government would assume the claims of its citizens against France arising out of the Quasi-War, a sum amounting to around $3,500,000. Given the financial requirements of a war-bent tyrant, this paltry reward was no enticement at all.[11]

Livingston left for Paris in the royal style to which he was accustomed. Sailing with him were his wife, his two daughters and their husbands, numerous ministry and household servants, and several friends. "I don't know where the devil they'll store themselves," the ship's captain complained, "for every apartment that is decent is filled with stores." So it seemed, as Livingston not only brought a huge quantity of trunks and suitcases but also a barnload of livestock – "poultry, hogs, sheep, and a cow and a calf, and they say that's not half!" Finally, the New Yorker brought his carriage, which he ordered lashed to the quarterdeck to serve as a parlor for the ladies. A man who traveled in such fashion was unlikely to be intimidated by anyone, including Bonaparte, and he was even less likely to play the role of hireling.[12]

Unbeknownst to Livingston, conditions worsened for the United States during his month-long ocean voyage. Napoleon's agent in London signed preliminary articles of peace with the British government, which freed the first consul from the menace of the Royal Navy as he prepared to take over Louisiana. Charles-Victor Leclerc, Napoleon's brother-in-law, set sail

[11] Madison to RL, 28 September 1801, *ASP*, 2:510–511.
[12] Captain cited in Dangerfield, *Livingston*, 309.

from Brest with a fleet of sixty-seven ships carrying 20,000 soldiers to suppress a slave rebellion in the Caribbean island of Santo Domingo, France's most valuable sugar colony. After completing this task, Leclerc was under orders to proceed to Louisiana and make a show of force. Napoleon intended to establish an empire in the Western Hemisphere before the Americans could organize any opposition.[13]

It was thus a seemingly doomed ministership that began when Livingston arrived in Paris in early December 1801. Waiting for him was a letter from King urging him to "perform the duties of hope" despite "circumstances of despair," hardly an exhortation calculated to improve his mood. Livingston's biographer notes that the minister "was tempted almost from the beginning – a temptation which he fortunately resisted – to ask for his recall." Only the most masochistic of diplomats would have enjoyed confronting the Napoleonic juggernaut armed with nothing more substantive than a pledge to assume a few private claims.[14]

In due course, Livingston was presented to Bonaparte in the state apartments in the royal palace of the Tuileries. After exchanging pleasantries communicated through an interpreter, Napoleon asked whether Livingston had been to Europe before, to which the American replied that he had not. "You have come," the first consul remarked, "to a very corrupt world." Napoleon turned to Foreign Minister Charles Maurice de Talleyrand Périgord, who was standing beside him, and said, "Explain to him that the Old World is very corrupt. You know something about that, don't you?" The first consul then moved on to another guest.[15]

Livingston was aware of Talleyrand's reputation. The foreign minister was more Machiavellian than Machiavelli. Over his long career in the diplomatic corps he had served several masters – the *ancien régime*, the Directory, the Consulate – and he would serve others after Napoleon's fall, filling posts abroad until the late 1830s. He had no principles or convictions apart from self-interest, and his keen political sense, what contemporaries termed his *prescience barométrique*, led him to gravitate toward whichever group or individual was in the ascendancy at a given

[13] R. S. Alexander, *Napoleon* (New York: Oxford University Press, 2001), 74–75; Robert D. Bush, *The Louisiana Purchase: A Global Context* (New York: Routledge, 2014), 48; Alan Schom, *Napoleon Bonaparte* (New York: Harper-Collins, 1997), 342–343.

[14] King to RL, 3 December 1801, *The Original Letters of Robert R. Livingston, 1801–1803*, Edward Alexander Parsons, ed. (New Orleans: Louisiana Historical Society, 1953) (hereafter *OLRL*), 24; Dangerfield, *Livingston*, 315.

[15] Napoleon cited in Buckner F. Melton, Jr., *Aaron Burr: Conspiracy to Treason* (New York: John Wiley and Sons, 2002), 42.

time. Scholars invariably praise his diplomatic finesse while condemning him for moral delinquency so pronounced that his name has become synonymous with corruption. Negotiating a treaty with this man would take patience, a virtue not normally associated with Americans and one Livingston conspicuously lacked.[16]

The first round of talks between Livingston and Talleyrand prefigured much of what followed. Talleyrand refused to acknowledge that France possessed Louisiana, conceding only, as Livingston reported, that "it had been a subject of conversation, but nothing had been concluded or even resolved on that affair." Livingston decided to play along. Regardless of who held the territory, he said, "perhaps both France and Spain might find a mutual interest in ceding the Floridas to the United States." He observed that such a cession would go a long way toward settling France's obligations to American merchants. Talleyrand replied, "None but spendthrifts satisfy their debts by selling their lands." Then, recognizing what he had just tacitly admitted, he added, "But it is not ours to give."[17]

Talleyrand continued to insist that no transaction had taken place even when that claim became too preposterous to sustain. He also declined to give direct answers to questions about Louisiana's boundaries or the likelihood that France and Britain might soon be at peace. Since it was in Paris's interest to keep the Jefferson administration guessing on these subjects, Talleyrand put Livingston off with one evasion after another, always taking care to maintain what historian George Dangerfield calls "an exquisite amenity of address" that veiled "almost imperceptible snubs and frail but deadly sarcasms." Livingston, with his partial deafness and imperfect French, probably did not pick up on these *sous-entendus*, but he was aware that he was being stonewalled, and he did not appreciate it.[18]

So matters stood for the first months of Livingston's ministership. Try as he might, he could not penetrate Talleyrand's façade of sophistry and

---

[16] The French foreign minister has attracted the attention of numerous biographers. See for example Crane Brinton, *The Lives of Talleyrand* (New York: Norton, 1963); Robin Harris, *Talleyrand: Betrayer and Savior of France* (London: John Murray, 2007); David Lawday, *Napoleon's Master: A Life of Prince Talleyrand* (New York: Thomas Dunne, 2007); Lewis Madelin, *Talleyrand: A Vivid Biography of the Amoral, Unscrupulous, and Fascinating French Statesman* (New York: J. Rolls Book Company, 1948).

[17] RL to Madison, 10 December 1801, *State Papers and Correspondence Bearing upon the Purchase of the Territory of Louisiana* (Washington, D.C.: U.S. Government Printing Office, 1903) (hereafter *SPC*), 9; RL to Madison, 12 December 1802, ibid., 9–10.

[18] Dangerfield, *Livingston*, 319.

denial. His letters home bristled with indignation: "On the business of Louisiana, they have, as yet, not thought it proper to give me any explanations, although I have omitted no opportunity to press the subject"; "The minister will give no answer to any inquiries I make"; "The same silence is observed by the minister. I can get him to tell me nothing"; "Today's talk ... terminated, as all my conversations on the subject have done, in nothing." The more Livingston importuned, the slipperier Talleyrand became, often avoiding contact altogether. In mid-October, Livingston wrote him a note protesting "the indignity offered [the United States] in my person yesterday – when, in violation of the established rules of your office, four different gentlemen who arrived after me were admitted to audience while I remained in waiting." It was hard to avoid the conclusion that Talleyrand enjoyed tormenting his American opposite number.[19]

Talleyrand's low opinion of Livingston was reinforced by a message the latter penned after learning that the Treaty of San Ildefonso transferring Louisiana from Spain to France had been secretly concluded a whopping sixteen months earlier. "The undersigned minister plenipotentiary of the United States," Livingston wrote, "has seen with some concern the reserve of the French government with respect to the cession they have received from Spain of Louisiana." *Reserve* was a gracious substitute for *deceit*, as *concern* was for *outrage*, and Talleyrand must have smiled at these euphemisms – and at what followed, as Livingston expressed regret that the foreign minister had not made "frank and open communications" to him that would have enabled him to "satisfy the government of the United States that neither their boundary nor the navigation of the Mississippi ... would be affected by the measure." Livingston's tone was that of an ally betrayed. Why were the French, who surely had the tenderest feelings for their American cousins, being so cloak-and-dagger? Why had they not informed the Jefferson administration about a treaty vital to American interests? Had Napoleon abandoned "the policy of the former government of France," which "led it to avoid all ground of controversy with the United States"? Did the first consul not appreciate how dishonorable this was?[20]

[19] RL to Madison, 24 March 1802, *SPC*, 20; RL to Madison, 24 April 1802, ibid., 23; RL to Madison, 16 August 1802, ibid., 50; RL to Madison, 20 May 1802, ibid., 28–29; RL to Talleyrand, 19 October 1802, Reel 8, Robert Livingston Papers, New York Historical Society, New York City, New York (hereafter RLP).
[20] RL to Talleyrand, 20 February 1802, *SPC*, 14.

It was an appeal to friendship and fair dealing, directed at perhaps the most amoral diplomat in history. Talleyrand did not reply. In more ways than one, the American and the Frenchman spoke different languages.[21]

"CAUTIONARY CONNECTIONS WITH BRITAIN"

As Livingston fumed at Talleyrand's evasions, developments in the Old and New Worlds complicated the international picture. Joseph Bonaparte, Napoleon's older brother, signed the Treaty of Amiens, confirming the preliminaries of the peace with Great Britain and ensuring that the British fleet would not stand in the way of French maneuvers in North America and the Caribbean. Leclerc, however, ran into greater difficulty than anticipated in quelling the rebellion on Santo Domingo, where the slaves, under the leadership of Toussaint L'Ouverture, waged a guerrilla campaign that bled the French army dry. Napoleon, realizing that Leclerc would need all his forces to subdue the island, appointed Claude Victor, duc de Bellune, commander of an occupying expedition scheduled to leave from Hellevoetsluis in the western Netherlands to seize Louisiana. Livingston and other American officials in Paris believed, with good cause, that if Victor succeeded, French military might could not be dislodged by any army that the U.S. government was capable of mustering.[22]

Jefferson did not know about all of these moves, but he was sufficiently attuned to the trend of events to send a letter to Livingston on 18 April 1802 that has become one of his most famous public papers. "There is on the globe one single spot, the possessor of which is our natural and habitual enemy," the president wrote. "It is New Orleans, through which the produce of three-eighths of our territory must pass to market. ... France, placing herself in that door, assumes to us the attitude of

[21] I am indebted to Charles Cerami for bringing this letter to my attention and to Dangerfield for noting Talleyrand's lack of response. Cerami, *Jefferson's Great Gamble*, 67–68; Dangerfield, *Livingston*, 328.
[22] For the Treaty of Amiens, see Robert B. Asprey, *The Rise of Napoleon Bonaparte* (New York: Basic Books, 2000), 410–432; Robert Harvey, *The War of Wars: The Great European Conflict, 1793–1815* (New York: Carroll and Graf, 2006), 312–324; R. B. Mowat, *The Diplomacy of Napoleon* (New York: Russell and Russell, 1971), 87–101. For the Santo Domingo revolution, see C. L. R. James, *Toussaint L'Ouverture: The Story of the Only Successful Slave Revolt in History* (Durham, NC: Duke University Press, 2013); Ronald Angelo Johnson, *Diplomacy in Black and White: John Adams, Toussaint L'Ouverture, and Their Atlantic World Alliance* (Athens: University of Georgia Press, 2013).

defiance." Jefferson affirmed his administration's goodwill toward France – "we have ever looked to her as our *natural friend*, as one with which we never could have an occasion of difference" – but he insisted that that friendship could not survive Napoleon's present policy: "The day that France takes possession of New Orleans fixes the sentence which is to restrain her forever within her low-water mark. .... From that moment, we must marry ourselves to the British fleet and nation." Jefferson, the Francophile, Anglophobe, and pacifist, was proposing a military alliance with Britain against France unless Napoleon gave the United States New Orleans and territories east of that city. "Every eye in the United States is now fixed on the affairs of Louisiana," Jefferson pronounced. "Perhaps nothing since the Revolutionary War has produced more uneasy sensations through the body of the nation."[23]

The president made sure his threat reached Napoleon by entrusting delivery of the message to Pierre Samuel du Pont de Nemours, an aristocratic friend of long standing who had fled France during the Terror and to whom Jefferson often turned for advice on European matters. Du Pont was returning to Paris to seek a position in the government, and Jefferson instructed him to "deliver the letter to Chancellor Livingston with your own hands," noting, "You will perceive the unlimited confidence I repose in your good faith ... when you observe that I leave the letter for Chancellor Livingston open for your perusal." Jefferson was confident du Pont would convey to his fellow French grandees the concern with which Washington viewed Napoleon's intentions to establish hegemony in the New World.[24]

Upon receipt of the president's letter, and a more agitated one from Madison declaring that French control of the Mississippi would bring about "the worst events," Livingston began work on a memorandum titled "Whether It Will Be Advantageous to France to Take Possession of Louisiana." This document, the highlight of Livingston's service in Paris, was written on his own initiative. No one in Washington asked him to

[23] Jefferson to RL, 18 April 1802, SPC, 15–18 (emphasis in the original). See also Mary P. Adams, "Jefferson's Reaction to the Treaty of San Ildefonso," *Journal of Southern History* 21 (May 1955): 173–188.

[24] Jefferson to du Pont, 25 April 1802, *Correspondence between Thomas Jefferson and Pierre Samuel du Pont de Nemours, 1798–1817*, Dumas Malone, ed. (Boston: Houghton Mifflin Company, 1930), 46–49. In his letter to Livingston, Jefferson wrote, "I pray you to cherish du Pont. He has the best disposition for the continuance of friendship between the two nations, and you may be able to make good use of him." Jefferson to RL, 18 April 1802, SPC, 18.

do it. While Jefferson and Madison expected their minister to petition Talleyrand, and by extension Bonaparte, to give America New Orleans and the Floridas, they never instructed Livingston to undertake anything like the analysis he produced in late spring 1802. In arguments totaling over 12,000 words, Livingston made an almost invincible case that Napoleon's government would be better off, financially and politically, if it spurned the territory Spain had handed over.[25]

Nations cannot make profitable use of colonies, Livingston wrote, unless they have two things: a "superfluous population" unable to find employment at home and "superfluous capital that cannot otherwise be rendered productive." France had neither. The country was "not over-stocked with inhabitants" and capital was so short "that no manufacturer has any quantity of goods on hand to answer an immediate demand." Why, then, would Napoleon want to acquire an "immense wilderness" in the Western Hemisphere when domestic problems were so pressing? Transoceanic colonies, Livingston pointed out, "are guarded at great expense of men and money, more particularly when they are placed in warm and unhealthy climates," as was the case with New Orleans. Lacking soldiers and cash, Napoleon would be foolish to assume this burden.

Livingston was not, he hastened to add, arguing that his host country should have no colonies at all. "France possesses colonies," he noted. "She has urged her citizens to remove themselves, and invest their prop-erty therein, and she is bound in good faith to retain and protect them. But she is not bound to create new colonies, to multiply her points of defense, and to waste a capital which she needs both at home and abroad." While the minister acknowledged that France's sugar colonies were lucrative, or at least had been until the uprising on Santo Domingo, he observed that they had been lucrative in a particular context. They provided commodities that were "equal to every demand in France, and, indeed, of Europe." If France generated those same commodities in Louisiana, it "would only reduce the price, without adding to the value," and Napo-leon's regime would find itself obliged, in order to rescue the Frenchmen who had invested their capital in the colonies, "to imitate the Dutch, who destroy their spices and teas when they find that the quantity debases the value." All the work involved in putting Louisiana into a thriving condi-tion – years of clearing the land and making it suitable for coffee and sugar cultivation – would result in a glut that benefited no one.

---

[25] Madison to RL, 1 May 1802, *SPC*, 24.

What about the oft-invoked argument that Louisiana could serve as breadbasket or granary for the sugar islands, supplying them with wood, rice, and wheat? Here Livingston concentrated on his most compelling point: the lumber-for-molasses exchange between the northern American states and the French West Indies, an arrangement that had worked well for both parties for years. "The islands may ... be truly said to have their lumber from the United States for nothing," Livingston observed, since molasses (which the Americans turned into rum) was valueless to them. Yet Louisiana would not consume molasses and French island planters would have to pay for their lumber with cash, something Livingston had already indicated was in short supply. Rather than profit from the new setup, France would sustain a punishing loss.

As for the other items a French-controlled Louisiana might furnish the West Indies, Livingston reminded his readers that "in the case of a war, supposing Britain to maintain her naval superiority, those supplies would be rendered extremely precarious." The Mississippi would be "blocked up" and the planters of the French colonies "reduced to the utmost distress." But if Louisiana were under the sway of a neutral nation – like Spain or, conceivably, the United States – London would have to respect the right of neutral ships to carry, in wartime, all belligerent property except contraband. Ironically, Louisiana's products would be safer without formal French ownership of the territory.

Livingston then turned his attention to those French entrepreneurs who foresaw making a fortune by selling their commodities in the western United States by means of the Mississippi. At this point the minister's prose turned almost derisive. Only "the most perfect ignorance of the navigation of that river and of the wants of the inhabitants" could give rise to such schemes, he said. Passage upriver, against the current, was "slow and expensive," which was why dry goods, hardware, glass, tableware, and other items reached the west for the most part through Baltimore or Philadelphia. America's canals and roads were improving rapidly, making it ever easier to transport commodities overland to the Ohio and other rivers. Even the British, who shared free navigation of the Mississippi with the United States, rarely used that route when transporting goods to the west.

Besides, Livingston argued, the American west did not want French products. This was a disagreeable but undeniable truth. The "wines of France are ill calculated for so warm a climate as they must pass through to arrive in the Western states," the minister declared, "and worse suited to the palates or purses of the inhabitants, both of which are better adapted to their own liquors, cider, beer, [and] whisky." Frenchmen seeking to line their pockets by exploiting a chimerical western market were courting bankruptcy or worse.

"In a commercial view, then," Livingston proclaimed, "the settlement of Louisiana shall not be advantageous to France, but, on the contrary, really injurious. . . . In a political one, it will be found still more inconsistent with her interests." On this score, the minister felt the need to tread carefully. "I am aware," he said, "of the delicacy of touching upon the political evils that may result to France and the United States from the former possessing itself of" Louisiana, and he wanted neither to "leave unsaid what truth requires to be spoken" nor to "give umbrage by freedom which haughty spirits may construe into menace." He navigated Scylla and Charybdis by paying "homage to the wisdom of those [French] statesmen who, at the end of a successful war, conceived it more advantageous to France to ensure the lasting friendship of the United States than to acquire a territory which might excite their jealousy." The consequence of this wisdom was that "France and the United States are so happily placed with respect to each other as to have no point of collision."

But Franco-American harmony, so precious to both nations, was menaced by France's impending capture of Louisiana. "[H]ow strong, how powerful should the inducement be," Livingston proclaimed, "that compels France to lose these advantages and convert a natural and warm ally into a jealous and suspicious neighbor, and, perhaps, in the progress of events, into an open enemy!" To Livingston, history proved that "no two nations can border upon each other without having the spirit of rivalry excited; and if this is true with respect to neighboring nations, it will be found to apply more forcibly to the colony of a great and powerful nation placed at a distance from home, and a sovereign adjoining such nation." Why? Because the colonial governor might commit acts of hostility against the native population that could not be readily settled by the home government, and bitterness could fester for months or even years until justice prevailed. "The commander and his troops," Livingston predicted, "will look down upon surrounding people," and insult and abuse them in a variety of ways. "No vigilance on the part of the parent country can control the oppressions that will be practiced by men at such a distance," and inevitably the Americans, "rather than wait for the tardy justice that they may hope for from diplomatic representations," would "avenge themselves" on their tormentors, making an already explosive situation more dangerous. Before long, the worst possible outcome would eventuate: "the government of the United States . . . will find itself unavoidably placed in such a situation as to change its connection and to guard against the supposed hostility of its old ally, by forming cautionary connections with Britain." Then the balance of power would revert to what it had been during the close of the Seven Years' War, when France lost its North American possessions.

How, then, was a Franco-American clash, followed by an Anglo-American alliance, to be avoided? The simplest solution, Livingston said, was for France to allow Spain to retain Louisiana. Americans did not fear the Spanish as neighbors. If that settlement was unacceptable – if all the arguments Livingston had mustered for the disadvantageousness of Louisiana to France had landed on stony ground – then the Jefferson administration would be content with Napoleon's "cession of New Orleans to the United States," along with one or both of the Floridas. Livingston noted that U.S. control of that territory would make it impossible for another country to deny American rights to navigate the Mississippi and would remove "a source of endless jealousy" between Washington and Paris. The presence of a French army west of the Mississippi would still "excite the fear" of many Americans, especially Anglophile Federalists, but the most pressing issue dividing France and the United States would have been resolved.

Livingston's memorandum ended with the minister promising, on behalf of his government, that if Napoleon gave up New Orleans, the Jefferson administration would preserve France's "right of entry, at all times, free of any other duties than such as are exacted from the vessels of the United States." Livingston went so far as to predict that France would soon replace Britain as America's chief trading partner, an odd forecast given his earlier assertion that westerners did not want French commodities. But if the conclusion was unworthy of the rest, the memorandum superbly complemented Jefferson's famous letter of 18 April. In addition to demolishing French mercantilist rationales for colonization, it raised a specter Bonaparte feared: that Britain and the United States might join forces against him.[26]

It is, of course, impossible to measure the impact of Livingston's memorandum on Napoleon's policy. The minister had it translated into French, and, he reported to Madison, "struck off twenty copies. . . . I have placed some of them in such hands as I think will best serve our purposes." Among the recipients were Talleyrand, Finance Minister François

---

[26] Memorandum: "Whether It Will Be Advantageous to France to Take Possession of Louisiana," undated, *SPC*, 36–50.

Barbé-Marbois, and the first consul himself. Joseph Bonaparte told Livingston that he and Napoleon had read the document "with attention," which may or may not have been true. What *is* irrefutable is that when leading French statesmen later explained the sale of Louisiana, they often seemed to be paraphrasing Livingston. Indeed, as Jon Kukla, one of the few historians to examine Livingston's ministership in depth, observes, by April 1803 Napoleon and Talleyrand had "adopt[ed] Robert Livingston's arguments as their own."[27]

"A DESERT AND AN INSIGNIFICANT TOWN"

That denouement, however, lay months down the road. For the present, all was frustration for the American minister. "There never was a government in which less could be done by negotiation than here," Livingston complained to Madison. Talleyrand was inaccessible and Bonaparte, who became consul for life in a rigged plebiscite in August 1802, was determined to prosecute France's "wild expedition" in the New World regardless of American sensibilities. Stymied, Livingston left his post for a two-week vacation in Belgium and Holland.[28]

Upon returning to Paris, he struck out on a bold course. If he could not get through to Napoleon via Talleyrand, he would circumvent the foreign minister and make Joseph Bonaparte his go-between. Then Talleyrand might be jolted into behaving more responsibly. On 26 October, Livingston had what he described as a "very interesting conversation" with Joseph, who seemed eager to play a role in affairs of state. "[Y]ou must not ... suppose my power to serve you greater than it actually is," Joseph reportedly said. "My brother is his own counselor, but we are good brothers, he hears me with pleasure, and ... I have an opportunity of turning his attention to a particular subject that might otherwise be passed over." Livingston then set forth his by-now familiar proposition that Napoleon return Louisiana to Spain while retaining New Orleans and the Floridas, which he would then give to America in exchange for an assumption of U.S. claims against France. Joseph, seemingly out of the blue, asked whether Washington "should prefer the Floridas or Louisiana?"

---

[27] RL to Madison, 10 August 1802, *SPC*, 35; Joseph Bonaparte cited in RL to Jefferson, 28 October 1802, ibid., 59; Kukla, *Wilderness So Immense*, 282.

[28] RL to Madison, 1 September 1802, *ASP*, 2:525. See also Michael Broers, *Europe under Napoleon, 1799–1815* (London: Arnold, 1996), 55–56; Steven Englund, *Napoleon: A Political Life* (New York: Charles Scribner's Sons, 2004), 217–223.

A stunned Livingston replied that there was "no comparison" between the two. "I told him ... that we had no wish to extend our boundary across the Mississippi, ... that all we sought was security, and not extension of territory." But the idea was out there. Joseph had raised it almost casually, and he and Livingston soon moved on to other subjects. Nonetheless, Napoleon's brother was the first to suggest that France might cede Louisiana to the United States. While Livingston did not capitalize on the suggestion at the time, he recovered his bearings and began advancing schemes that exceeded anything Jefferson or Madison had authorized him to propose.[29]

Thus sometime in early December (the record is unclear), Livingston made the first of several offers to Joseph, arguing that, in return for Washington assuming claims, France should cede to the United States New Orleans, West Florida, and the two-thirds of Louisiana that lay west of the Mississippi and above the mouth of the Arkansas River. That would calm any American fears of French encroachment in the New World and prevent an Anglo-American alliance. It would also establish a belt of U.S. territory between French and British possessions that would lessen the chance of friction between those two inveterate rivals. If Napoleon was worried about jeopardizing French navigation of the Mississippi, Livingston ventured, he could build a port at Leon, opposite New Orleans, and share access to the river with the United States. Joseph agreed to lay this proposal before his brother, and he presumably did so, with little immediate effect.[30]

Livingston, however, would not be put off, and shortly thereafter he submitted another note to Joseph making the same case in stronger terms and revisiting the themes of his memorandum. He was, he said, "honored by the first consul's attention" but anxious lest Napoleon let an opportunity escape. "Not a moment, sir, should be lost," Livingston wrote. The "peace between France and Britain has been too disadvantageous to the latter to be of long duration." When hostilities broke out again, Britain would seize the Floridas and Louisiana, "unite them to her other American possessions" – Canada, Newfoundland, and Nova Scotia – and "annihilate the external trade of every other nation in Europe." The only way to prevent this was for France to "ced[e] to the United States the portion I have proposed above the Arkansas" and "New Orleans and West Florida." If Napoleon did so, he would "cheaply purchase the

---

[29] RL to Jefferson, 28 October 1802, *SPC*, 58–60.
[30] RL cited Dangerfield, *Livingston*, 341–342.

esteem of men and the favor of Heaven by the surrender of a distant wilderness." On the other hand, if he stubbornly chose to hang on to Louisiana and territory east of the Mississippi, he would lose everything by driving the United States into "alliances, both offensive and defensive, which it has heretofore been her policy to avoid."[31]

A third note, dated 24 December, was almost threatening in tone, as Livingston pointed out to Joseph that the U.S. Congress was in session and that it would be difficult for Jefferson to resist pressure to take drastic action. France's plans for Louisiana were shrouded in "obscurity," the minister complained; its American creditors were "ruined"; its statesmen (meaning Talleyrand) spoke a language "painful to the feelings of the American government." This left "a fair field for the enemies of France," especially since the British, contrary to their usual behavior, now paid "the most scrupulous attention" to American demands. Circumstances rendered "every day important in what relates to the United States and France," and Livingston felt the "utmost anxiety to know whether my project, which you had the goodness to submit for the inspection of the first consul, is likely to meet with his concurrence." Americans did not want to ally with their former mother country against France, Livingston insisted, but French policy was making such a union unavoidable.[32]

Livingston's last extant note to Joseph was drafted on 7 January 1803, and it was more emotional than the others, for the minister had just learned of rumors (as yet unconfirmed but correct) that the Spanish intendant at New Orleans, Juan Ventura Morales, had forbidden American merchants to deposit their goods there. Many Americans, including Jefferson, believed that Morales had acted at Napoleon's direction and that this was the French tyrant's first step toward closing the Mississippi to U.S. commerce. "Now, sir, I will frankly confess to you," Livingston wrote Joseph, "that the United States will rather hazard their very existence than suffer the Mississippi to be shut against them." This latest outrage could not fail to "wind up the American people and government to so high a pitch of resentment as shall lead them to a close and intimate connection with Britain." Was that what Napoleon wanted? If not, then it was "peculiarly the interest of France and the United States to come to an immediate arrangement" whereby Napoleon gave America New Orleans, West Florida, and Louisiana above the Arkansas in return for a discharge of the U.S. debt. "I speak, sir, perhaps with too much freedom on the

[31] RL to Joseph Bonaparte, undated, *SPC*, 103–108.
[32] RL to Joseph Bonaparte, 24 December 1802, *ASP*, 2:530.

views of your country and my own," said Livingston. "But I speak with freedom from a conviction of the integrity of my own intentions and the absolute certainty that the measures I suggest are not less the interest of the one than of the other."[33]

Joseph waited four days before replying, and his response was brief. He told Livingston to conduct all future negotiations through the foreign minister, "who alone could inform you of the intentions of the government." Talleyrand had evidently gotten wind of Livingston's correspondence with Joseph and resented being outflanked. No matter: the elder Bonaparte had served his purpose; he had brought Livingston's propositions under Napoleon's eye and lured Talleyrand down from Mount Olympus and back into the game.[34]

Now Livingston went on the offensive, demanding in a note to Talleyrand that France cede to the United States "West Florida, New Orleans, and ... so much of Louisiana as lays [sic] above the mouth of the river Arkansas." Under any other arrangement, he declared, "the whole of this establishment must pass into the hands of Great Britain, who has, at the same time, the command of the sea and a martial colony [Canada] containing every means of attack." While the British fleet "block[ed] up the seaports," hordes of British troops would "attack New Orleans from Canada" and overrun it with ease. Livingston also invoked, again, the prospect of an Anglo-American alliance. France, "by grasping at a desert and an insignificant town" was in danger of "throw[ing] the weight of the United States into the scale of Britain," an outcome that could not fail to "render her mistress of the New World." While Livingston felt it would be best for France to give New Orleans, West Florida, and Louisiana above the Arkansas "gratuitously" to the United States, he said that Washington would "purchase them at a price suited to their value."[35]

By volunteering to buy these territories, Livingston was, of course, exceeding his instructions. Indeed, since his arrival in Paris a year earlier, he had sent numerous messages to Madison complaining that he was not

---

[33] RL to Joseph Bonaparte, 7 January 1803, *ASP*, 2:536–537. Morales claimed that he had revoked the right of deposit on his own authority, and historians took him at his word for over a century. It was not until the 1920s that Edward Channing uncovered and published an order from Spanish King Charles IV telling Morales to close the port to Americans. Edward Channing, *History of the United States* (New York: Macmillan, 1926), 4:326–327.

[34] Joseph Bonaparte to RL, 11 January 1803, Reel 8, RLP.

[35] RL to Talleyrand, 10 January 1803, *SPC*, 89–92.

empowered to offer any inducement to the French beyond assumption of the claims of U.S. merchants. That was not enough, Livingston insisted in a representative dispatch. He needed "gold to operate here. But it must be plentifully and liberally bestowed, not barely in the assumption of debts, but in active capital." Napoleon's projected military endeavors would require funding, and his government was so corrupt that no business could be done without resort to bribery. Livingston repeatedly asked Madison to "communicate to me what are precisely the utmost limits of the sum I may venture to offer in cash," since, "if left to myself, I may go beyond the mark." Madison never obliged, and Livingston, rather than being inhibited by the lack of explicit orders, became more audacious.[36]

In an especially daring move, he wrote directly to Napoleon in late February. He opened with a veiled swipe at Talleyrand – "Though I am satisfied that my notes to the minister of exterior relations have been truly represented to you" – and went on to describe the situation in the American west in dark terms, noting that if the French did not restore the right of deposit at New Orleans, Jefferson's administration "will be compelled to follow the impulse of the people." Americans would descend upon that entrepôt by the thousands and "a fatal blow will be struck at the future peace and harmony" of France and America. The time for diplomatic tergiversation had passed, Livingston declared. He renewed his proposal for territory. "France will never derive any advantage from the colonization of New Orleans and the Floridas," he wrote. "These have always remained weak and languid and an expensive burden to the possessor. . . . They are, however, important to the United States," which would gladly pay a "warrantable" sum for them. Washington would also fund the American debt, computed by Livingston at 20 million livres. Livingston closed by assuring Napoleon that such a comprehensive settlement would in be "the interest both of France and the United States, and of humanity."[37]

Napoleon did not reply, but Talleyrand did, with a strange note that failed to acknowledge Livingston's demand for New Orleans and the Floridas. Instead, the foreign minister focused on the 20 million livres

---

[36] RL to Madison, 24 April 1802, *SPC*, 23; RL to Madison, 30 July 1802, ibid., 35; RL to Madison, 20 December 1802, ibid., 65. See also RL to Madison, 20 May 1802, ibid., 28–29; RL to Madison, 2 November 1802, ibid., 61.

[37] RL to Napoleon, 27 February 1803, *SPC*, 115–122. Curiously, Livingston did not ask for Louisiana above the Arkansas in this communication, perhaps because he assumed that Joseph Bonaparte had already raised that issue numerous times with his younger brother and that it did not bear repeating.

figure, arguing that it was excessive but that Paris would honor its obligations. "No embarrassment exists in the finances of France," Talleyrand asserted. "The French government has the means as well as the inclination to be just." If Livingston furnished an exact statement of the U.S. debt, "every claim will be promptly and fully discharged." Livingston must have been puzzled by this message, but he could not help but have noticed that Talleyrand's tone was less supercilious than usual, or that the promise to satisfy American creditors was the first genuine concession by the Bonaparte regime to the United States. After almost fifteen months of misery, Livingston could report progress to Washington, albeit not the boundary-stretching triumph he sought.[38]

"ALL EYES, ALL HOPES, ARE NOW FIXED ON YOU"

Although Livingston was not aware of it, his negotiations were being conducted against the backdrop of the dissolution of Napoleon's projected New World empire. Leclerc could not crush the slave rebellion on Santo Domingo. "These men may be killed," he reported to Napoleon, "but they will never surrender. They laugh at death, and it is the same with the women." Not even the capture of Toussaint in April 1802 brought the insurrection to a close. Over 20,000 French soldiers died in combat before yellow fever swept the island, carrying off thousands more. In November, Leclerc himself succumbed to the disease. Meanwhile, the fleet that Napoleon had ordered to Louisiana could not set sail; it was icebound and then delayed by storms. Worst of all, from the first consul's perspective, was the fact that the Peace of Amiens gave every indication of collapsing. None of the sources of friction between France and Britain had been eliminated, and it was a matter of time before hostilities resumed. When that happened, the British Navy would again pose a barrier to French adventurism in the Western Hemisphere.[39]

Napoleon also had to weigh the factor Livingston had been at pains to emphasize: the growing belligerence of the Americans, especially those who lived west of the Blue Ridge. After Morales revoked the right of deposit at New Orleans, many western legislatures passed resolutions demanding seizure of the city and an alliance with England against

---

[38] Talleyrand to RL, 10 March 1803, *ASP*, 2:546.
[39] Leclerc cited in Bailey, *Diplomatic History of the American People*, 107. See also Vincent Cronin, *Napoleon Bonaparte: An Intimate Biography* (New York: William Morrow and Company, 1972), 224–236; Harvey, *War of Wars*, 335–346.

France. In mid-February 1803, Senator James Ross of Pennsylvania asserted America's "indisputable right to the free navigation of the river Mississippi" and moved to give Jefferson authority to raise 50,000 troops "to take immediate possession of ... a convenient deposit for [American] produce ... in the island of New Orleans." Jefferson managed to get a milder form of words adopted, but the west was clearly spoiling for a fight.[40]

It was partially out of a desire to placate the west and slow the stampede toward war that Jefferson decided to appoint his friend, fellow Virginian, and onetime law student James Monroe as envoy extraordinary to Paris. Monroe had earned a reputation as a champion of western interests during negotiations between Spain and the United States over navigation of the Mississippi in 1785–1786. He had spoken out vehemently in defense of western rights during the debates over ratification of the Constitution. He owned land in the west and knew many prominent people there. Frontiersmen disinclined to trust Livingston, the New York aristocrat, had no such misgivings about Monroe. In addition, Monroe had served as George Washington's minister to France in the chaotic period following the Terror. He was acquainted with some of the leading French republicans, although not many members of Napoleon's government, and he spoke fluent French.[41]

Jefferson knew Monroe would not welcome the assignment. The latter was just retiring as governor of Virginia and planned to open a law practice in Richmond. His years of public service had left him deeply in debt, and he was looking forward to making some money. The president, however, appealed to Monroe in terms he knew would touch a chord. First came a brief note dated 10 January 1803 lamenting "the fever into which the western mind is thrown by the affair at N. Orleans." Jefferson informed his friend, "I shall tomorrow nominate you to the Senate for an

[40] Ross Resolution, 16 February 1803, *The Debates and Proceedings of the Congress of the United States* (Washington, D.C.: Gales and Seaton, 1851), 12:143–144. The substitute resolution was introduced by Kentucky Senator John Breckenridge and empowered Jefferson "to organize, arm, and equip" as many as 80,000 militia and "hold [them] in readiness to march at a moment's warning." While this arrangement gave Jefferson more time to work the diplomatic levers, Congress's overall tone was still militant. Breckenridge cited in Kukla, *Wilderness So Immense*, 267.
[41] The most comprehensive biography of Monroe is Harry Ammon, *James Monroe: The Quest for National Identity* (Charlottesville: University Press of Virginia, 1990). For Jefferson's personal and professional relationship with Monroe, see Noble E. Cunningham, Jr., *Jefferson and Monroe: Constant Friendship and Respect* (Chapel Hill: University of North Carolina Press, 2003).

extraordinary mission to France, and the circumstances are such as to render it impossible to decline, because the whole public hope will be rested on you." Having presented Monroe with a fait accompli, Jefferson followed up with a letter three days later that pulled out all the stops:

All eyes, all hopes are now fixed on you; and were you to decline the chagrin would be universal, and would shake under your feet the high ground on which you now stand. Indeed, I know nothing which would produce such a shock, for on the event of this mission depends the future of this republic. . . . I am sensible of the measures you have taken for getting into a different line of business, and that it will be a great sacrifice on your part, and presents from the season and other circumstances serious difficulties. But some men are born for the public. Nature by fitting them for the service of the human race on a broad scale has stamped them with the evidence of her destination and their duty.[42]

How could Monroe say no? Jefferson had invoked the call to greatness, and Monroe, a faithful public servant, acquiesced. The Senate approved Jefferson's nomination, and the House appropriated $2 million for "any expenses which may be incurred in relation to the intercourse between the United States and foreign nations" – in other words, for the purchase of New Orleans and the Floridas.[43]

Monroe took a devastating financial hit from this assignment. He stood to make only $9,000 a year, and he had to pay for his own staff and transportation. To cover the costs of his mission, he sold all his plate and much of his china and furniture. From his standpoint, he was doing the president a favor by accepting the job, and, in this frame of mind, he, like Livingston, went to Paris intent on making, not following, U.S. foreign policy.[44]

The orders issued by Madison to Monroe offered the French considerably greater temptation than Livingston had been authorized to dangle before them in 1801. Washington, the secretary declared, would give Paris as much as 50 million livres ($9,375,000), along with the $2 million authorized by Congress, in exchange for "a cession to the United States of New Orleans and of West and East Florida, or as much thereof as the actual proprietor can be prevailed to part with." Madison made a point of assuring Napoleon's government that France would retain "all the territory on the west side of the Mississippi." The Jefferson administration, unaware of Livingston's efforts to obtain Louisiana above the Arkansas,

[42] Jefferson to Monroe, 10 and 13 January 1803, *WTJ*, 9:416–420.
[43] Representatives cited in Kukla, *Wilderness So Immense*, 262.
[44] Ammon, *Monroe*, 205; Fleming, *Louisiana Purchase*, 82.

had not modified its territorial demands, which remained confined to the eastern bank.[45]

Livingston, understandably, was not thrilled by news of Monroe's appointment, even though Madison told him that Jefferson had "undiminished confidence" in his regular minister. Sure that he was on the verge of some breakthrough in negotiations, Livingston did not want to share the laurels he expected to win. Still, he replied civilly to the secretary, writing, "I shall do everything in my power to pave the way for him and sincerely hope it may be attended with the desired effect. It will, however, cut off one resource on which I greatly relied; because I had established a confidence which it will take Mr. Monroe some time to inspire." To Rufus King, Livingston complained that the Monroe mission "has greatly embarrassed my operations." Napoleon and Talleyrand, he said, had been anxious about western threats to New Orleans and susceptible to American coercion, but "the appointment of Mr. Monroe has tranquilized everything." Now the French "might safely defer their negotiations" for weeks, if not months.[46]

These statements did not augur well for a smooth partnership between Livingston and Monroe, and indeed the two men, heretofore friends, would clash bitterly in Paris and afterwards over which one deserved the lion's share of glory for the Louisiana Purchase. It was a regrettable sidelight to the greatest achievement of their lives.

"TAKE THE WHOLE COUNTRY"

Historians have been unable to determine when Napoleon decided to sell Louisiana to the United States, but he had almost certainly made up his mind by 12 March 1803, when he confronted Lord Whitworth, the British ambassador, at a salon hosted by Madame (Josephine) Bonaparte. Livingston was present, along with the rest of the diplomatic corps, and he reported the events to Jefferson and King. After "going the usual round," he wrote, the first consul spoke briefly with the Danish ambassador and then "went up to Lord Whitworth" at "the other end of the room." Napoleon remarked that France and Britain "would probably have a storm." Whitworth responded that he "hoped not," to which

[45] Madison to RL and Monroe, 2 March 1803, *ASP*, 2:540–544. Despite the March date, the instructions were written on 31 January. Dangerfield, *Livingston*, 355.
[46] Madison to RL, 18 January 1803, *ASP*, 2:529; RL to Madison, 3 March 1803, ibid., 2:537–538; RL to King, 23 March 1803, *OLRL*, 108–109.

Napoleon snapped, "I find, my lord, your nation wants war again." "No, sir," Whitworth said, "we are very desirous of peace." Napoleon shot back, "You have just finished a war of fifteen years." Whitworth agreed, noting, "That was fifteen years too long." "But you want another war of fifteen years," Napoleon insisted. According to Livingston, the first consul then expressed "a few more very strong terms evoking the vengeance of heaven upon those who broke the treaty [of Amiens]" and concluded by thundering, "I must have Malta or war." Whitworth, gobsmacked, sputtered that he was "not prepared, sir, to speak on that subject," at which point a servant told Napoleon that the ladies in the next room awaited him. Napoleon stalked out.

Whitworth, Livingston wrote, "came up to me and repeated the conversation as I now give it to you." The first consul's intent could not have been clearer. Malta, that strategically placed island in the middle of the Mediterranean, was essential to the protection of Britain's imperial interests in the Near East. London had agreed to give it to Napoleon in the Peace of Amiens, but British forces had made no move to evacuate, and now that the treaty was visibly unraveling there was no way George III would surrender such a valuable possession. Napoleon had apparently determined that France would be better off if war came now rather than later. He knew, moreover, that once hostilities broke out he would not be able to hold onto Louisiana, which in any event was an unprofitable encumbrance without Santo Domingo. Ever the willful man of action, he chose to cut his losses and seek glory elsewhere.[47]

Hence the two famous meetings between Napoleon and his minister of the treasury, Marquis François de Barbé-Marbois, on 10 and 11 April. As recalled by Barbé-Marbois, the first consul summoned him to the palace at St. Cloud and told him that he feared the British would capture Louisiana in the opening salvo of the coming war. "The conquest of Louisiana would be easy, if they only took the trouble to make a descent there," he said. "I have not a moment to lose in putting it out of their reach. ... I think of ceding it to the United States." Barbé-Marbois, who had lived in Philadelphia during the American Revolution and had married an American, voiced his support for the cession. Agreement or dissent meant nothing to Napoleon, who continued, in words that echoed Livingston's memorandum, "They only ask of me one town in Louisiana, but I already consider the colony as entirely lost, and it appears to me that

---

[47] RL to Jefferson, 12 March 1803, *SPC*, 144–146; RL to King, 15 March 1803, *OLRL*, 106–108.

in the hands of this growing power, it will be more useful to the policy and even to the commerce of France, than if I should attempt to keep it."[48]

The following morning found Napoleon ready to take the plunge. He again sent for Barbé-Marbois and delivered his verdict. "Irresolution and deliberation are no longer in season," he said. "I renounce Louisiana. It is not only New Orleans that I will cede; it is the whole colony without any reservation. . . . I direct you to negotiate this affair with the envoys of the United States. Do not even await the arrival of Mr. Monroe. Have an interview this very day with Mr. Livingston."[49]

Livingston, who did not know of these conversations, was meanwhile unhappily preparing for Monroe's appearance. He learned on 10 April that the envoy extraordinary had landed at Le Havre, and, to his subsequent regret, dashed off a quick note of welcome. "I congratulate you on your safe arrival and have long and anxiously wished for you," he wrote. "God grant that your mission may answer yours and the public expectations. War may do something for us – nothing else would. I have paved the way for you, and if you could add to my means an assurance that we were now in possession of New Orleans, we should do well." That he had prepared the ground for Monroe was true enough, but he was anything but pleased by his coming, and the self-deprecatory tone he adopted would later furnish Monroe with grounds for claiming that Livingston had made no headway while in Paris. This was unfortunate because, just one day after penning the note, Livingston received a payoff for his months of hard work that exceeded his most soaring expectations.[50]

For reasons that remain unclear, it was not Barbé-Marbois but Talleyrand who unleashed the thunderbolt on the afternoon of 11 April. As Monroe's carriage rolled toward the capital, the foreign minister

---

[48] Napoleon cited in François de Barbé-Marbois, *The History of Louisiana: Particularly of the Cession of that Colony to the United States*, William Beach Lawrence, trans. (New York: Carey and Lea, 1830), 264. I am obliged to Marshall Sprague for noting Napoleon's near-paraphrase of Livingston's argument. See Marshall Sprague, *So Vast, So Beautiful a Land: Louisiana and the Purchase* (Boston: Little, Brown, and Company, 1974), 300.

[49] Napoleon cited in Barbé-Marbois, *History of Louisiana*, 274–275. See also E. Wilson Lyon, *The Man Who Sold Louisiana* (Norman: University of Oklahoma Press, 1974), 118–119.

[50] RL to Monroe, 10 April 1803, Reel 8, RLP. In his autobiography, Monroe recalled that "Mr. Livingston gave a very discouraging prospect of the success of the mission." James Monroe, *The Autobiography of James Monroe*, Stuart Gerry Brown, ed. (Syracuse, NY: Syracuse University Press, 2017), 184.

asked Livingston to call at his headquarters in the Rue de Bac and casually inquired whether the United States "wished to have the whole of Louisiana."

Livingston's astonishment may be imagined. He had been laboring for over a year to extract territorial concessions from the French government, and now Talleyrand was offering him half a continent. It is hardly surprising that his first response was halting. "I told him no," Livingston reported to Madison, "that our wishes extended only to New Orleans and the Floridas." Talleyrand responded that if France gave up New Orleans, "the rest would be of little value." What, he asked Livingston, would Washington "give for the whole?"

Steadying himself, Livingston opened with a modest bid: "I supposed we should not object to twenty millions provided our citizens were paid." (20,000,000 livres was roughly $3.75 million.) That was "too low an offer," Talleyrand said, and asked Livingston to "reflect upon it and tell him tomorrow." Livingston remarked that since Monroe would soon be in town, he would "delay my further offer until I had the pleasure of introducing him." Talleyrand shrugged, as if he had been discussing a subject of no importance, and commented that "he did not speak from authority but that the idea had struck him." Such humbuggery did not fool Livingston – he knew Talleyrand would not have made the proposal except at Napoleon's behest – and he ultimately decided *not* to wait until Monroe joined the negotiations. "I shall see the minister again tomorrow," Livingston wrote Madison, "in order to sound him out more fully."[51]

Alas, Talleyrand had retreated to his customary elusiveness the next day, and Livingston's talk with him was excruciating. "He ... thought [it] proper," Livingston reported, "to again declare that his proposition was only personal." The American ignored the lie and "told him I had been long endeavoring to bring him to some point, but unfortunately without effect – that I wished merely to have the negotiation opened by any proposition on his part." Livingston then presented Talleyrand with a note requesting a specific price tag for Louisiana. What did the first consul want in return for this munificent grant of territory? Talleyrand replied that "he would answer my note, but that he must do it evasively because Louisiana was not yet theirs."

"I smiled at this assertion," Livingston informed Madison, "and told him that I had seen the treaty recognizing it, that I knew the [first] consul

[51] RL to Madison, 11 April 1803, *JMP:SS*, 4:500–503.

had appointed officers to govern the country, and that [Bonaparte] had himself told me that General Victor was to take possession." Talleyrand stuck to his story: "He still persisted that they had it in contemplation to obtain it but had it not." Livingston, his temper rising, said that if they did not have it, there was no profit in continuing this exchange, and that when Monroe arrived the two envoys "would advise our government to take possession" of New Orleans, the Floridas, and perhaps all of Louisiana from Spain.

"He seemed alarmed at the boldness of the measure," Livingston wrote, "and again told me he would answer my note, but that it would be evasively." At this, Livingston declared that he was "not disposed to trifle," that "the times were critical," and that "tho' I did not know what instructions Mr. Monroe might bring, I was perfectly satisfied that they would require a precise and prompt notice." Livingston also lamented that he was "fearful from the little progress I had made that my government would consider me a very indolent negotiator." Talleyrand "laughed and told me that he would give me a certificate that I was the most importunate he had yet met with." The foreign minister then excused himself, citing another engagement. Any hopes Livingston had of pulling off a diplomatic coup before Monroe's arrival were dashed.

A post chaise dropped Monroe and his family off at a Paris hotel that afternoon, and the envoy extraordinary called upon Livingston at his house the following day. Livingston welcomed him cordially. The two men spent several hours in discussion, with Monroe showing Livingston the instructions Madison had given him and Livingston telling his colleague about Talleyrand's stupendous offer. Toward evening, they sat down to dinner with two other Americans: U.S. Consul General Fulwar Skipwith and Colonel James Mercer, who had come to Paris to serve as Monroe's secretary. In the middle of the meal, Skipwith noticed someone lurking in the garden. "Doesn't that look like Barbé-Marbois out there?" he asked. Livingston squinted and determined that it was indeed the finance minister. As he reported to Madison, he sent an aide out to greet Barbé-Marbois, who said that he would "return when we had dined."[52]

A few hours later, while the men were having coffee, Barbé-Marbois reappeared, and he and Livingston "strolled into the next room." Barbé-Marbois ventured that Livingston "might have something particular to

[52] Skipwith cited in Cerami, *Jefferson's Great Gamble*, 175; RL to Madison, 13 [*sic*] April 1803, *JMP:SS*, 4:511–512. Livingston actually completed this letter in the predawn hours of 14 April. Sleep deprived and overwrought, he misdated it.

say to him." Unsure of what that meant, Livingston revealed that he had had two meetings with Talleyrand in the previous forty-eight hours. He also noted "the extraordinary conduct of the [foreign] minister" in their second conversation. This probably confirmed Barbé-Marbois's suspicions that Talleyrand had attempted to commandeer the negotiations Napoleon had entrusted to him, and he whispered to Livingston that "something important" had been "mentioned to him at St. Cloud." Since Livingston's "house was full of company," Barbé-Marbois invited the American minister to "call upon him any time before eleven that night." Livingston agreed, and the men parted for the moment.[53]

For what happened next, it is best to cite Monroe, who described the events to Madison in a letter sent shortly thereafter. Livingston returned to the table "much agitated" and announced that he would "go to Mr. Marbois's as soon as the company left." Monroe "hesitated on the idea of his going alone" and volunteered to tag along, but Livingston said that this was "altogether impossible" because Monroe had yet to be formally presented to Napoleon and Talleyrand; the "rigorous etiquette observed by the government" required that the minister undertake this errand by himself. Monroe then counseled his colleague that "too much zeal might do harm" and that "a little reserve might have a better effect." Livingston, though, "could not see the weight of these objections" and insisted on the "necessity of dispatch." Monroe finally "ceased to oppose his going" but "most earnestly pressed on him the propriety of his being reserved in the conference, . . . in short, to hear and not to speak." The advice fell on (partially) deaf ears, as Livingston was itching to conclude a deal.[54]

After his guests went home, Livingston hastened to Barbé-Marbois's office, where, he reported, the finance minister "told me that he wished me to repeat what I had said relative to Mr. Talleyrand requesting a proposition from me as to the purchase of Louisiana." Livingston obliged, "conclud[ing] with the extreme absurdity of [Talleyrand's] evasions." Barbé-Marbois confirmed that Talleyrand was lying. The decision to sell Louisiana, he said, came directly from Napoleon; it was not some fleeting notion of the foreign minister's. Barbé-Marbois also revealed that, in his discussion with Napoleon at St. Cloud two days earlier, the first consul had said to him, "Let [the Americans] give you one hundred millions and pay their own claims and take the whole country." Since

[53] RL to Madison, 13 [sic] April 1803, *JMP:SS*, 4:512.
[54] Monroe to Madison, 17 September 1803, *JMP:SS*, 5:440.

American creditors maintained that French citizens owed them at least 25 million livres, Napoleon was asking for approximately $22,500,000.

Noting Livingston's shock "at so extravagant a demand," Barbé-Marbois said that "he considered the demand as exorbitant" and that he had told Napoleon that the Americans "had not the means of raising it." Napoleon's reply was that they "might borrow it." Livingston countered by minimizing American interest in Louisiana. In view of the fact that the Jefferson administration "would be perfectly satisfied with New Orleans and the Floridas and had no disposition to extend across the river," he declared, "of course we would not give any great sum for the purchase" – definitely not $22 million. Nonetheless, Livingston continued, "we would be ready to purchase provided the sum was reduced to a reasonable limit."

Barbé-Marbois then asked Livingston to "name the sum." Livingston demurred, protesting that he would "make the offer only after mature reflection." Barbé-Marbois said that if Livingston could mention "any sum that came near the mark that could be accepted," he would "communicate it to the first consul." Still reluctant to put forward a figure, Livingston tried to get Barbé-Marbois to make the first move. "I told him," Livingston reported to Madison, "that we had no sort of authority to go to a sum that bore any proportion to what he mentioned, but that as he himself considered the demand as too high, he would oblige me by telling me what he thought to be reasonable." To this, Barbé-Marbois suggested that "if we would name sixty millions, and take upon us the American claims to the amount of twenty more, he would try how far this would be accepted." Sixty million livres was about $11,250,000 and 20 million $3,750,000, for a total of $15 million.

In two weeks, Livingston and Monroe would sign a treaty pledging that amount, but for now Livingston protested that "it was vain to ask anything that was so greatly beyond our means." He argued that if the Jefferson administration paid it, they would lose the next election, and the Federalists – "men who were most hostile to a connection with France" – would come to power. Livingston also reminded Barbé-Marbois of the "ardor of the Americans to take [New Orleans] by force and the difficulty with which they were restrained by the prudence of the president." Barbé-Marbois, Livingston recorded, "admitted the weight of all this" but "feared the [first] consul would not relax."

"Try, then, if you cannot come up to my mark," Barbé-Marbois entreated. "Consider the extent of the country, the exclusive navigation of the river, and the importance of having no neighbors to dispute you, no war to dread." Livingston, sensing that the conversation was nearing a climax, came on strong. "I asked him," he wrote Madison, "in case of a purchase, whether they would stipulate that France would never possess the Floridas ... and would relinquish all right that she might have to them." Barbé-Marbois assented to that proposition.

Then the American made what must have been his most satisfying demand, phrased diplomatically but freighted with over a year's frustration: "[I]f any negotiation should go on, I would wish that the first consul would depute somebody to treat with us who had more leisure than the minister for foreign affairs." In other words, he did not want to spend one more second in Talleyrand's presence. Barbé-Marbois obligingly replied that "there would be no difficulty, when this negotiation was somewhat advanced, to have the management of it put into his [Barbé-Marbois's] hands."[55]

It was midnight, and the two men had just concluded the most portentous exchange in the chronicle of American diplomacy. As Jon Kukla notes, "They were no longer discussing *whether* France might sell Louisiana or *whether* the United States might buy it. Livingston and Barbé-Marbois had begun to negotiate a price." Heart hammering, giddy with triumph, Livingston raced back to his house to write a report of the meeting to Madison.[56]

"Thus, sir," he declared after scribbling furiously for three hours, "you see a negotiation is fairly opened and upon grounds that I confess I prefer to all others. ... We shall do all we can to cheapen the price, but my present sentiment is that we shall buy." Although he acknowledged that "the field opened to us is infinitely larger than our instructions contemplated," he argued that the enormity of the acquisition justified bending the rules. Still hoping to garner sole credit for doubling the size of the republic, he added, "[I]t is so very important that you should be apprised that a negotiation is actually opened even before Mr. Monroe has been presented."[57]

"THE UNITED STATES TAKE THEIR PLACE AMONG THE POWERS OF THE FIRST RANK"

Monroe's reaction to news of the midnight meeting between Livingston and Barbé-Marbois was telling. He took no relish in the progress the two

[55] RL to Madison, 13 [sic] April 1803, *JMP:SS*, 4:512–514.
[56] Kukla, *Wilderness So Immense*, 275.
[57] RL to Madison, 13 [sic] April 1803, *JMP:SS*, 4:514–515.

men had made. Instead, he wrote an angry letter to Madison complaining about how he had been treated. Skipwith, he said, had told him that "Livingston, mortified at my appointment, had done everything in his power to turn the occurrences in America, and even my mission, to his account"; that he had "press[ed] the [French] government on every point with a view to show that he had accomplished what was wished without my aid"; and that he had even intimated "that my mission had put in hazard what might otherwise have been easily obtained." Monroe had by this time had the opportunity to review Livingston's official correspondence, and this, he wrote, "sufficiently proves that he did not abstain, even on hearing that I was on my way, from the topics entrusted to us jointly." Surely the secretary did not approve of such behavior. "You will perceive the dilemma into which ... I am placed," Monroe wrote, "since I have not only to negotiate with the French government, especially its ministers, but my colleague also."[58]

While we can fault Monroe for pettiness, his attitude was understandable. He had come to Paris at great difficulty and expense, and he intended to wring from his mission all the acclaim he could. Moreover, he viewed the virtual simultaneity of his arrival in France and Bonaparte's decision to sell Louisiana as proof that the former caused the latter. It was not Livingston's persistent efforts over a year-and-a-half, he thought, but the appearance of a U.S. minister extraordinary that had convinced the first consul that the Americans meant business and that the wisest course was to appease them. The accuracy of this interpretation is impossible to establish, but Monroe never wavered in his belief that he, not Livingston, tipped the scales.

Fortunately for the United States, the two men had too strong a sense of public responsibility to allow mutual jealousies to impede their service in Paris. When the great work was done, and the central region of North America became part of the United States, they would engage in a nasty public tug-of-war over credit, but for the present they worked together effectively. It did not take long for the grandeur of the first consul's offer to dawn on Monroe, who concurred with Livingston that they must disobey their orders. They were far from home, it would take months to petition Washington for new instructions, and Napoleon was an impatient man. He might decide to sell to a more appreciative purchaser. The wisest course was to strike while the iron was hot and hope that Jefferson,

---

[58] Monroe to Madison, 15 April 1803, *SPC*, 164–165.

despite his parsimony and deference to Constitutional niceties, would endorse their actions.[59]

Two weeks of negotiations ensued while an imperial domain hung in the balance. On 14 April, Monroe was presented to Talleyrand. On the fifteenth, Livingston reported, the two envoys agreed to offer as much as 50 million livres, "including our debts," but "only to mention forty in the first instance." Barbé-Marbois "expressed great sorrow" at this opening bid "because he was sure that it would not be accepted and that perhaps the whole business would be defeated." Still, he said that he would communicate the offer to Bonaparte at St. Cloud. The next day, he informed the Americans that the first consul had received the news "very coldly" and that he believed the negotiations were "no longer in his hands." Livingston and Monroe then offered 50 million, to which Barbé-Marbois said that "he had very little hopes that anything short of [Napoleon's] proposition would succeed." He also warned the envoys that if nothing came of the overture when he relayed it to Bonaparte, they would have to conclude that the first consul had taken the offer of Louisiana off the table. Livingston and Monroe held their ground: 50 million was Washington's upper limit. "Thus we stand at present," Livingston wrote Madison, "resolving to rest a few days upon our oars."[60]

The delay was due in part to a back injury suffered by Monroe that confined him to his bed. Livingston met alone with Barbé-Marbois on a few occasions, but he took care to keep his colleague informed of what had been discussed. The looming threat of renewed Franco-British hostilities lent the whole process a sense of white-knuckle urgency. Livingston and Monroe knew that the transaction would become immeasurably more complex if talks were still ongoing when war broke out.[61]

On 27 April Monroe was able to receive Livingston and Barbé-Marbois at his apartment to continue the negotiations as he reclined on a sofa. Barbé-Marbois brought two draft treaties with him, one drawn up by Napoleon and the other by himself. The first, he confessed, was "hard and unreasonable"; Bonaparte's asking price was the same 100 million livres Barbé-Marbois had suggested in his midnight talk with Livingston at the Treasury. The second, "to which [Barbé-Marbois] presumed the first consul would assent," reduced the demand to 80 million "including the debt." Barbé-Marbois's draft also granted France limited commercial

[59] Ammon, *Monroe*, 211–212.   [60] RL to Madison, 17 April 1803, *JMP:SS*, 4:524–527.
[61] Roger Knight, *Britain against Napoleon: The Organization of Victory, 1793–1815* (New York: Penguin, 2013), 251–284.

privileges in New Orleans. Monroe and Livingston spent the rest of the afternoon and the following day going over this document, and then called on Barbé-Marbois at his office on 29 April with a revised draft that, Monroe recorded, "proposed to offer 50 millions to France and 20 on account of her debts to the U[nited] States." Barbé-Marbois replied that "it would be useless" for him to bring a treaty to Napoleon offering less than 80 million livres, "as the [first] consul had been sufficiently explicit on that point."

By now, the two Americans had had time to reflect on how colossal a prize was within their reach. "We agreed to accede to his idea and give 80 millions," Monroe noted: 60 million for Louisiana and 20 million for the claims. They had pledged more money than they had been authorized to spend for a province they had not been instructed to purchase.[62]

An elated Barbé-Marbois carried the offer to Napoleon at St. Cloud the following morning. No announcement issued from the palace, and the envoys remained in suspense until 1 May, when Monroe was presented at the Louvre to Napoleon. The first consul kept the conversation brief: "You speak French?" "A little." "You had a good voyage?" "Yes." "You came in a frigate?" "No, in a merchant vessel." Then, Monroe noted in his diary, Napoleon "turned to Mr. Livingston and observed that our affairs stood as settled." That night, Monroe and Livingston met with Barbé-Marbois, who confirmed that the first consul had accepted the terms.[63]

The Louisiana Purchase treaty was signed on 2 May 1803. Apart from the French territorial cession and the American commitment to pay $15 million, the agreement contained the vital stipulation that the inhabitants of Louisiana were to be incorporated into the United States and given the rights of citizenship as soon as possible under the Constitution. After the three men set their names to the treaty, toasts were drunk, and Livingston declared, "We have lived long, but this is the noblest work of our whole lives. ... From this day the United States take their place among the powers of the first rank. ... The instruments which we have just signed will cause no tears to be shed. They prepare ages of happiness for innumerable generations of human creatures." Under almost any other circumstances, such rhetoric would have been excessive. Here, it was apt.[64]

---

[62] Diary Entries, 27 and 29 April 1803, *The Writings of James Monroe*, Stanislaus Murray Hamilton, ed. (New York: G. P. Putnam's Sons, 1900) (hereafter *WJM*), 4:12–15.

[63] Diary Entry, 1 May 1803, *WJM*, 4:15–17.

[64] Livingston cited in Barbé-Marbois, *History of Louisiana*, 310–311. For the complete text of the treaty, see Kukla, *Wilderness So Immense*, 350–358.

"AN ACT BEYOND THE CONSTITUTION"

News of the Louisiana settlement took eight weeks to cross the Atlantic. Two newspapers, the *Boston Independent Chronicle* and the *New York Evening Post*, broke the story on 30 June 1803, the same day Rufus King, recently relieved of his post as U.S. minister to London, arrived in a New York port bearing notes from Livingston and Monroe detailing what they had accomplished. Jefferson and Madison learned of the deal just before the nation celebrated the twenty-seventh anniversary of the Declaration of Independence. Neither the newspapers nor King said anything about how much the envoys had bound their government to pay. Jefferson informed his son, "[W]e are in hourly expectation of the treaty by a special messenger."[65]

After an anxious wait of over a week, the Purchase treaty arrived in Washington on 14 July. An attached letter from Livingston and Monroe explained their departure from instructions. "Before the negotiation commenced," they wrote, "we were apprised that the first consul had decided to offer to the United States, by sale, the whole of Louisiana and not a part of it." This had forced them to decide "whether we would treat for the whole, or jeopardize, if not abandon, the hope of acquiring any part." The choice seemed obvious: "We did not long hesitate, but proceeded to treat for the whole." If Napoleon had opted to sell only New Orleans, they conceded, the acquisition of that city would have fulfilled their orders, but they felt they had obtained a vastly better deal. "A divided jurisdiction over the river," they wrote, "might beget jealousies, discontents, and dissensions, which the wisest policy on our part could not prevent or control." Now that America controlled both banks of the Mississippi, "the apprehensions of these disasters is banished for ages from the United States." And there were other benefits. The Purchase made it less likely that America would be drawn into the vortex of Old-World "wars and intrigues." It would profit the United States economically. And, as Livingston had pronounced on the occasion of the treaty's signing, it rendered America a great power, with "a more imposing attitude in respect to all." On balance, then, the envoys felt that they had acted appropriately. "The terms on which we have made this acquisition," they affirmed, "when compared with the objects

[65] Kukla, *Wilderness So Immense*, 284–285; RL and Monroe to King, 9 May 1803, *OLRL*, 122–123; Jefferson to Randolph, 5 July 1803, *Papers of Thomas Jefferson*, Barbara B. Oberg, ed. (Princeton: Princeton University Press, 2014), 40:660.

attained by it, will, we flatter ourselves, be deemed advantageous to our country."[66]

Jefferson summoned his cabinet to consider what to do. Since Bonaparte had laid down a 30 October deadline for ratification, the cabinet members decided to convene both houses of Congress on 17 October, three weeks earlier than usual. Madison said he would send copies of the treaty to the congressmen with accompanying letters explaining why the early assembly was necessary. Every cabinet member voiced approval of Livingston and Monroe "having treated for Louisiana and the price given," and they agreed not to make an issue of the fact that the envoys had not acquired the Floridas.[67]

The president's response to the Purchase was noteworthy for its ambivalence. He perceived the advantages America would derive from such a massive transfer of territory, but the price appalled him. In 1803, $15 million was a huge amount of money. As one critic pointed out, Jefferson, who had pledged his administration to rigid economy, was being asked to cough up a sum that equaled 433 tons of pure silver and that, if piled in silver dollars, would make a stack three miles high.[68]

More important than issues of cost, though, was Jefferson's strict constructionism. Nowhere in the Constitution was there any clause granting the president the power to buy land or bring the inhabitants of that land into the United States as citizens. Jefferson admitted as much, calling the Purchase "an act beyond the Constitution." As he wrote to Pennsylvania statesman John Dickinson, "The general government has no powers but such as the Constitution has given it, and it has not given it a power of holding foreign territory and still less of incorporating it into the Union. An amendment to the Constitution seems necessary for this." And, indeed, for almost a month, Jefferson worked on crafting an amendment that would permit him to carry through the deal Livingston and Monroe had made.[69]

This was a quixotic enterprise. Getting the amendment ratified by a sufficient number of states would take a long time, maybe years, and Napoleon was in a hurry. Slightly more than two weeks after the first consul ratified the Louisiana treaty on his own authority, the British violated the Peace of Amiens by declaring war on France. Napoleon

---

[66] RL and Monroe to Madison, 13 May 1803, *SPC*, 191–196.
[67] Kukla, *Wilderness So Immense*, 288–289.
[68] Federalist cited in DeConde, *This Affair of Louisiana*, 179.
[69] Jefferson to Breckenridge, 12 August 1803, *WTJ*, 10:7; Jefferson to Dickinson, 9 August 1803, ibid., 10:29.

needed ready cash. He did not appreciate the Americans dragging their feet, and he let Livingston and Monroe know this, telling them that the Louisiana treaty would become void unless the White House made its first payment within the three-month period stipulated for U.S. ratification. Talleyrand turned up the heat by informing the envoys that Napoleon considered the treaty under his control until ratifications were exchanged, and that he might alter the document drastically.[70]

Panicked, Monroe sent Madison an urgent letter that arrived on 18 August. He warned that Napoleon was having second thoughts. If the president wanted Louisiana, he said, "It is highly important that Congress be immediately called and the treaty ... be carried into immediate effect. No delay should occur in performing what we are to perform, since a failure in any one point in the time specified may defeat and I think will defeat the whole." Three weeks after Monroe wrote that letter, Livingston composed an even more frantic one, telling the secretary, "I hope [to] God that nothing will prevent your immediate ratification and without altering a syllable of the terms. . . . Be persuaded that France is sick of the bargain . . . and the slightest pretense will lose you the treaty."[71]

With Napoleon seemingly on the verge of scuttling the Purchase, Monroe saved it through an inspired bit of rogue diplomacy. As noted above, Monroe had arrived in France with a $2 million appropriation from Congress to purchase New Orleans and West Florida. He now decided to exceed his orders by using the special appropriation as a down payment on Louisiana. Livingston balked, pointing out that this would expose the two envoys to serious difficulties if the U.S. Senate rejected the treaty. Monroe agreed but argued that the risk was worth running. Livingston saw the logic in this argument and did not want to be blamed for losing Louisiana at the eleventh hour. He therefore co-signed an order to the British banking firm of Hope and Co. for $2 million. This arrangement, Monroe informed Madison, amounted to "a guarantee of the stipulations of the treaty." He urged speedy action: "I consider the present moment an all-important one in our history. . . . [T]he most prompt and decisive measures appear to me to be necessary."[72]

[70] Ammon, *Monroe*, 220. See also Ines Murat, *Napoleon and the American Dream*, trans. Frances Frenaye (Baton Rouge: Louisiana State University Press, 1976), 5–16.

[71] Monroe to Madison, 8 June 1803, *WJM*, 4:34; RL to Madison, 25 June 1804, *ASP*, 2:566.

[72] Monroe to Madison, 15 August 1803, *JMP:SS*, 5:310–312. See also Monroe to Madison, 31 August 1803, ibid., 5:363–367; Ammon, *Monroe*, 221; Monroe, *Autobiography*, 197–200.

In the end, Jefferson, with what historian Thomas Bailey terms "much anguish of spirit," abandoned one of his core political beliefs. "The less we say about constitutional difficulties respecting Louisiana, the better," he wrote Madison. "What is necessary for surmounting them must be done sub-silentio." He sent the treaty to the Senate, as he put it, "to secure a good which would probably never again be in reach," and hoped that a later constitutional amendment would legalize the transaction.[73]

The Republicans in the Senate were more than willing to join Jefferson in casting aside constitutional scruples. They voted twenty-four to seven to ratify the treaty, more than the necessary two-thirds majority required for passage. Debate in the House of Representatives was more spirited, but legislators ultimately gave their approval by a narrow margin. The exchange of ratifications took place in Washington on 20 October, and Jefferson declared the Louisiana treaty the law of the land.[74]

"THE ZEAL OF OUR FRIENDS OFTEN CARRIES THEM TOO FAR"

Jefferson's Federalist opponents were put in an awkward position by the Purchase. Only a few months before, they had been urging a military descent on New Orleans, a policy that might have led to war with France, or Spain, or both. Now that Jefferson had obtained that vital outlet, and the huge hinterland of Louisiana besides, without firing a shot, the Federalists struggled to find a way to discredit his accomplishment. "For the moment," the French chargé in Washington wrote Talleyrand, "the enemies of the president seem to be truly stupefied."[75]

They did not remain so for long. A Boston Federalist newspaper sneered that Louisiana was "a great waste, a wilderness unpeopled with any beings except wolves and wandering Indians. . . . We are asked to give money, of which we have too little, for land, of which we already have too much." Another Federalist organ lashed the president for "tearing the Constitution to tatters." Many Federalists warned, as did the editor of the *Noristown Herald*, that Louisiana, "if ever admitted into the Union, will give such a preponderance to Virginia and the south that the northern states can never afterwards maintain any considerable consequence in the

---

[73] Bailey, *Diplomatic History of the American People*, 111; Jefferson to Madison, 18 August 1803, *WTJ*, 10:245; Jefferson to Breckinridge, 12 August 1803, *Public Documents Printed by Order of the Senate of the United States* (Washington, D.C.: Gales and Seaton, 1845), 3:79.

[74] DeConde, *This Affair of Louisiana*, 187–192.

[75] Chargé cited in Kukla, *Wilderness So Immense*, 287.

general government." These men feared that a group of agricultural states would be carved out of the new territory, and that the industrial East would henceforth be outvoted in Congress.[76]

Alexander Hamilton broke with his party by giving the Purchase his blessing. Louisiana, he argued in an unsigned *New York Evening Post* editorial, would furnish "a free and valuable market to our commercial states." He did not consider the price "too dear" and admitted that the "exultation which the friends of the administration display" was justified. "The purchase has been made during the period of Mr. Jefferson's presidency," he wrote, "and will, doubtless, give éclat to his administration." But, he continued, Jefferson deserved little glory: "Every man ... possessed of the least candor and reflection will readily acknowledge that the acquisition has been solely owing to a fortuitous concurrence of unforeseen and unexpected circumstances." Hamilton ran through those circumstances – Franco-British tensions, slave revolt, icebound ports, ferocious storms – and concluded that they had allowed the administration to achieve "what the feebleness and pusillanimity of its miserable system of measures could never have acquired." As for the negotiation of the treaty, Hamilton declared, "the merit of it ... is due to our ambassador, Chancellor Livingston, and not to the Envoy Extraordinary," Monroe. After all, he pointed out, "[t]he cession was voted in [Napoleon's] Council of State on the 8th of April, and Mr. Monroe did not even arrive until the 12th."[77]

Hamilton's chronology was off, but this was not his fault. Sadly, and to his great discredit, Livingston began misrepresenting what had happened in Paris almost as soon as he and Monroe wrapped up their talks with Barbé-Marbois. Convinced that Monroe was about to reap the honor for gaining Louisiana despite having done little more than show up, Livingston wrote numerous letters to prominent people in Europe and America in which he altered the timeline of events to make himself the sole author of the Purchase.

While he had told Madison in his 3:00 a.m. communication of 14 April that Napoleon made the decision to sell Louisiana on 10 April, it occurred to him, as it had to Monroe, that people might draw a causal connection between the envoy extraordinary's arrival at Le Havre on the eighth and

---

[76] Federalist newspapers cited in William E. Foley, *The Genesis of Missouri: From Wilderness Outpost to Statehood* (Columbia: University of Missouri Press, 1989), 134; Bailey, *Diplomatic History of the American People*, 112; Carol Sue Humphrey, *The Press of the Young Republic, 1783–1833* (Westport, CT: Greenwood Press, 1996), 77.

[77] Hamilton cited in Adair, "Hamilton on the Louisiana Purchase," 273–278.

the first consul's change in policy two days afterwards. Thus Livingston attempted to propagate the notion that Napoleon made up his mind earlier, and that his decision was owing to the regular minister's skillful and dogged diplomacy, not to the appearance of Monroe. Livingston was not consistent in his accounts of when Napoleon chose to divest himself of Louisiana. In a letter to Rufus King, he asserted, "About ten days before Mr. Monroe arrived, the resolution was taken." To other friends, he dated the first consul's decision from 8 or 6 April. He even tried to counteract his previous letter to Madison by sending another in which he told the secretary that Napoleon's "determination to sell" had been "communicated ... on the 8th April." The most shameful instance of Livingston's attempting to rewrite the record was discovered by his biographer, George Dangerfield, who found that the envoy changed the date of an important note to Talleyrand in his letter book from 12 April to 10 April by superimposing a zero over the two.[78]

Livingston's supporters in the United States sought to bolster his version of events. In July 1803, newspapers in Boston, Washington, Philadelphia, and New York printed the envoy's 1802 memorandum, "Whether It Will Be Advantageous to France to Take Possession of Louisiana," in which he argued that the colony would be an economic and political liability to Napoleon's government. Publication of the memorandum was accompanied by a covering note from "an American in Paris," who said that the document proved that Livingston had been the key player in acquiring Louisiana. Madison, appalled, wrote Monroe, "You will find in the gazettes a letter from Paris ... enclosing a copy of [Livingston's] memorial [and] representing it as the primary cause of the cession, praising the patriotism which undertook so great a service without authority, and throwing your agency out of any real merit." The "publication of the memorial is so improper," the secretary declared, as to "invite ... strictures." Yet his reprimand to Livingston was mild, consisting of a request to "trace the indiscretion to its author."[79]

The envoy responded with the most unseemly dispatch of his mission: petulant, self-pitying, and arrogant. He began by protesting that "it could

---

[78] RL to King, 7 May 1803, *OLRL*, 60; RL to Armstrong, 1 September 1803, Reel 8, RLP; RL to Gates, 8 June 1803, ibid.; RL to Graham, 10 July 1803, ibid.; RL to Mitchell, 23 July 1803, ibid.; RL to Watson, 25 June 1803, ibid.; RL to Madison, *JMP:SS*, 12 May 1803, 4:594; Dangerfield, *Livingston*, 378.

[79] Dangerfield, *Livingston*, 378–379; Madison to Monroe, 30 July 1803, *JMP:SS*, 5:248–249; Madison to RL, 29 July 1803, *SPC*, 222. When he read the memorandum, Monroe dismissed it as "long winded and empty." Cited in Ammon, *Monroe*, 218.

hardly be expected that [the memorandum] could be kept secret, since, as I informed you at the time, I had delivered printed copies of it not only to the first and other consuls and to the French ministers but to most of those persons who I believed would be consulted upon the occasion." Although he was "sorry that a bad translation of it has found its way into the papers," he felt that "it may serve, in some measure, to justify the president's appointment of me by showing that I had not been inattentive to the great interests of my country." As for the identity of the "American in Paris," Livingston could only remark, "The zeal of our friends often carries them too far." He ventured that "some of them ... finding some endeavor here to impress a belief that [Monroe] was the principal agent in treating with France ... [sought] to do me the justice they felt I was entitled to."

Besides, the envoy pointed out, "Mr. Monroe's particular friends" were promoting *his* cause in the United States as well. Livingston had it on good authority that certain politically influential Americans were passing around a copy of that private letter to Monroe of 10 April in which Livingston apparently despaired of the chance for a treaty – "as proof that he had been the principal agent in the negotiation." Would Madison reprove Monroe for this indiscretion, and would the latter apologize? Livingston hoped that Monroe had "too much candor not to be displeased that his friends should publicly endeavor to depreciate me."

In any event, Livingston declared, such efforts would fail, "because facts and dates are too well known to be contradicted. ... [I]t is known to everybody here that the [first] consul had taken his resolution to sell previous to Mr. Monroe's arrival." Livingston conceded that "[t]here is no doubt that Mr. Monroe's talents...would have enabled him, had he been placed in my circumstances, to have effected what I have done. But he unfortunately came too late to do more than assent to the propositions that were made to us." In other words, for all practical purposes, Livingston had bought Louisiana without any help from Monroe.[80]

Madison must have deplored this letter. Nonetheless, despite Livingston's backdating, his charge against Monroe was accurate. Monroe had in fact written a note in late May 1803 "to Virginia senators" explaining his part in the Purchase. In it, he employed a lighter touch than had Livingston, adopting the bureaucrat's technique of disclaiming credit

---

[80] RL to Madison, 15 November 1803, *SPC*, 266–269. The "American in Paris" was probably James Swan, a speculator who promised to promote Livingston's candidacy for the vice-presidency. Dangerfield, *Livingston*, 379.

and lavishing it on his superiors. "Personally, I pretend to nothing but zeal and industry after I got here," he wrote. "If my mission produced any effect, it was altogether owing to the motive which induced the president to nominate me." Still, the idea that "the decision to offer us the territory by sale" was taken "before I reached Paris" flew in the face of the evidence: "I enclose a copy of a letter from Mr. Livingston bearing [the] date of the 10th of April, in answer to one from me on the 8th announcing my arrival, which establishes the facts." Monroe asked that the letter be circulated among members of Congress. It certainly seemed to indicate that negotiations had reached a stalemate prior to Monroe's appearance – legislators must have been especially struck by Livingston's assertion that only a war could rescue the situation – and Monroe's self-effacing insistence that the success of his mission was due to the firmness of the administration's policy and not to any initiatives of his own contrasted favorably with Livingston's shrill self-promotion. Livingston came off as a narcissistic glory hound, while Monroe appeared to be setting the record straight.[81]

Of course, Monroe's posture was strategic. Ascribing the Purchase to Jefferson's wise and forceful policy had the fortunate corollary of ensuring that the president's personal representative in Paris, his fellow Virginian, and his friend and protégé would share in the limelight – definitely more so than the regular minister. It was this fact that galled Livingston and fueled his efforts to establish himself in the public mind as the man who secured Louisiana for the United States. The campaign was bound to fail. Among other things, Livingston's letters in the files of the State Department and the French archives established the true sequence of events in April 1803 and exposed his clumsy attempts to rewrite history. Also, the aggressiveness with which he waged his crusade for recognition alienated many Americans, chief among them Madison, who spread the word throughout Washington that the Jefferson administration was displeased with its envoy.[82]

Ultimately, Monroe was able to extract the most benefit out of the Purchase. While Livingston hoped that his role in acquiring Louisiana would put him in line for the governorship of New York, or even the vice presidency when Jefferson ran for reelection in 1804, the highest office he held after his time in Paris was grand master of a Freemason Lodge. Monroe, by contrast, went on to serve as U.S. minister to Britain,

---

[81] Monroe to Virginia Senators, 25 May 1803, *WJM*, 4:31–34.
[82] Dangerfield, *Livingston*, 380–387.

secretary of state and war in the Madison administration, and president for two terms. Livingston had been in his grave for over a decade when Monroe entered the White House, but his feud with his former colleague endured, as John Armstrong, Livingston's brother-in-law, published several editorials in the press claiming that the president had stolen the laurels belonging to the real purchaser of the westside vastness of the Mississippi valley.[83]

The saddest aspect of this quarrel was that even if Livingston's fictional timeline had been accurate, it would have made no difference in terms of cementing his status as one of America's most important diplomats. He had indeed been a vital contributor to the acquisition of Louisiana, the first American to suggest that Washington might be willing to extend the United States's borders west of the Mississippi. His memorandum on Louisiana's usefulness to France probably did find its place in the complex of motives that induced Napoleon to sell. The choice to bypass Talleyrand and communicate with Joseph Bonaparte – and the first consul himself – was a courageous, unorthodox maneuver that advanced negotiations considerably, as did Livingston's repeated offer to buy New Orleans, the Floridas, and Louisiana above the Arkansas at a time when he had no authority to do so. And the minister's midnight parley with Barbé-Marbois was arguably the most important single event in gaining the United States the heart of the North American continent. As for Monroe, he ably complemented Livingston's efforts during his stay in Paris, and he made the crucial decision to use his special appropriation of $2 million as a down payment on Louisiana, reasoning that such an installment would make it difficult for Napoleon to withdraw prior to the ratification of the treaty. Both men had served their country well, and, in the tradition of the diplomats who negotiated an end to America's revolution against Great Britain, they had done so by disobeying their stateside bosses.

---

[83] Ammon, *Monroe*, 215.

3

"Instructions or No Instructions"

Trist Makes Peace with Mexico

As he approached his seventieth birthday, Nicholas Philip Trist wrote a message "to be opened after my death." In it, he described how he had played a crucial part in ending the Mexican War, an act that saved thousands of lives and spared Americans the ignominy of a protracted occupation of Mexico. He also wrote that he had received virtually no compensation for this feat. Too proud to go to the White House hat in hand, he had spent the last quarter-century working poorly paid jobs to scrape by. Now, old and sick, he was terrified of leaving his family penniless. Although he did not like to dredge up ancient history when America had moved on, he insisted that the issue went beyond him. "Why and wherefore is this service recalled to your minds, my countrymen?" he wrote. "It is done on behalf of my wife and children. It is brought forward as the title by which I call upon you from the grave, saying *Do not let them suffer from want.*"[1]

Few could match Trist when it came to self-dramatizing, but on this occasion he spoke the truth. He had in fact been the catalytic figure in America's war with Mexico. "There are few examples in history of how a single person can so greatly affect the destinies of so many people, or of two countries," notes historian Miguel Soto of Trist's all but single-handed forging of the Treaty of Guadalupe Hidalgo in 1848. If not for Trist, Soto observes, "the war would have continued, and the consequences would

---

[1] Nicholas Trist (hereafter NT), undated message, Folder 253, Nicholas Philip Trist Papers, Southern Historical Collection, Louis Round Wilson Special Collections Library, University of North Carolina, Chapel Hill (hereafter NPTP-UNC). All emphases throughout this chapter are in the originals.

have been very different." Moreover, Trist performed this function, in diplomatic terms, "without portfolio," meaning that he lacked authority to make a treaty. President James K. Polk fired him four months before the enemy agreed to terms. Trist disregarded the order for his recall and continued negotiations with the Mexican government, ultimately securing vast stretches of territory that enlarged the United States by almost one-third.[2]

This achievement should have earned Trist a bonus and promotion. Instead, it destroyed him professionally. Polk saw to it that Trist left Mexico City under armed escort, like a criminal. The discredited emissary died forgotten, having brushed the pages of history for a few months and faded into oblivion. Yet no one did more to make Manifest Destiny a reality.

Trist's epochal piece of statecraft was incongruous because, on paper, he did not fit the profile of an American rogue diplomat. Born into straitened circumstances that he never rose above, he lacked the financial safety net enjoyed by Robert Livingston, Joseph Kennedy, and other men whose insubordination determined the course of U.S. foreign relations. He was also an obscure figure; unlike Benjamin Franklin or Henry Cabot Lodge II, he could not leverage his personal prestige to obtain the outcome he wanted. In addition, he alone among the men examined here was a career civil servant. Dependent on the federal government for his livelihood, he could not threaten to resign or run the risk of dismissal secure in the knowledge that a job awaited him outside the State Department. Removal from office meant ruin.

Nonetheless, Trist's tenure as Polk's special representative in Mexico marked the zenith of U.S. rogue diplomacy. Trist was the most brazen of all envoys in defying orders, and the yield of his obstreperousness eclipsed in importance that brought about by any other act of diplomatic indiscipline. Thanks to his refusal to do as he was told, the United States grew by half a million square miles, acquired a Pacific coastline and a storehouse of natural resources, and all but finished building the geographic base for its future as a superpower. Not even Monroe and Livingston's negotiation of the Louisiana Purchase could match what Trist pulled off in the winter of 1847–1848.

The Treaty of Guadalupe Hidalgo grew out of one thing Trist *did* have in common with other rogue diplomats: a distinctively American capacity

---

[2] Soto cited in Carol and Thomas Christensen, *The U.S.-Mexican War* (San Francisco: Bay Books, 1998), 216.

to justify disobedience on the grounds that Washington had issued its commands in ignorance of actual conditions. Like Adams, Franklin, Jay, Monroe, and Livingston before him, Trist reasoned that if the president and the secretary of state had the facts at their disposal, they would approve his action. As the man on the spot at the moment of truth, he did what he felt was appropriate and counted on his superiors' good sense, when informed, to back him up. He was half right. Polk embraced the treaty – it fulfilled his war aims, after all – but refused to pay Trist for the time spent in Mexico after receipt of the discharge notice.

Equally important to the success of Trist's mission was his personality, for which the term *difficult* could have been invented. Trist had a genius for alienating people and burning bridges. In particular, his tendency to relieve his anger by writing puerile, interminable letters to men in a position to do him damage made him his own worst enemy. Although some of his contemporaries, including such illustrious figures as Thomas Jefferson and Andrew Jackson, found his brash spirit attractive and developed affection for him, the muster roll of his adversaries was longer. When he crashed and burned after defying Polk, many Americans enjoyed the spectacle.

Historians, for the most part, find Trist as disagreeable as his peers did. Arthur Smith calls him a "cadaverous man, bereft of charm, ... sickly, testy, and very limited in intellectual equipment." Polk biographer Eugene Irving McCormac has nothing good to say about the envoy. "Vain," "arrogant," "tiresome," and "devoid of judgment" are among his descriptors, and he takes every opportunity to lash Trist for "bad taste," "desire for notoriety," "want of sincerity," "audacity," "unwarranted insolence," "excessive vanity," and "small mental caliber." Other scholars sound the same note: Trist was "long-winded and tactless," "thin-skinned and touchy," "a man of modest attainments" with "delusions of grandeur" who "behav[ed] far below the threshold of dignity, let alone ordinary civility" and made U.S. diplomacy a "laughing stock."[3]

[3] Arthur D. Howden Smith, *Old Fuss and Feathers: The Life and Exploits of Lt.-General Winfield Scott* (New York: Greystone Press, 1937), 294; Eugene Irving McCormac, *James K. Polk: A Political Biography* (New York: Russell & Russell, 1922), 496, 499, 524–527, 538; David M. Pletcher, *The Diplomacy of Annexation: Texas, Oregon, and the Mexican War* (Columbia: University of Missouri Press, 1973), 501; Christensen and Christensen, *The U.S.-Mexican War*, 193; Bailey, *Diplomatic History of the American People*, 274; John S. D. Eisenhower, *So Far from God: The U.S. War with Mexico, 1846–1848* (Norman: University of Oklahoma Press, 1989), 298; David and Jeanne Heidler, *The Mexican War* (Westport, CT: Greenwood Press, 2006), 124; Nathaniel W. Stephenson, *Texas and the Mexican War* (New Haven: Yale University Press, 1971), 230. For rare positive appraisals, see Dean B. Mahin, *Olive Branch and Sword: The United States and*

This abuse notwithstanding, one would be hard pressed to find an author who disputes Robert Morgan's assertion that the Treaty of Guadalupe Hidalgo was an "achievement rarely surpassed in American diplomatic history." Furthermore, it was in great measure a one-man creation. Trist deserved more credit for this treaty than any other U.S. diplomat could claim for a comparable pact; indeed, even minor international bargains usually involve more participants than did the agreement that rounded out the southern and western boundaries of the United States. During negotiations with representatives of the Mexican government, Trist was the entire American delegation: he had no assistants, translators, or rapporteurs; he served as his own stenographer and secretary; and he kept minutes of the deliberations while taking part in them. No American envoy ever juggled more responsibilities, and none was more poorly rewarded.[4]

Norman Graebner captures the dissonance in scholarship on Trist. On the one hand, he marvels that "Trist's diplomacy secured a treaty of peace with Mexico at a time when American generals, politicians, the press, members of the cabinet, and the president himself believed it impossible," adding, "Perhaps few other Americans could have succeeded at the task." Even so, he considers Trist's day-to-day conduct throughout his service in Mexico scandalous. Trist, Graebner notes, "lacked two important qualities, good judgment and humility." This led him to respond to every slight, real or imagined, with an "epistolary flood" in which he "pour[ed] forth invectives with remarkable facility." As a result, Trist's correspondence from the field was so "lengthy" and "verbose" as "to wear out even the Spanish patience, thought durable enough to last a thousand years." The standard account of the Trist mission makes little attempt to reconcile substance with style, or product with process. Historians extol the treaty that gained California and the Southwest while holding its architect in contempt.[5]

Mexico, 1845–1848 (Jefferson, NC: McFarland & Co., 1997), 187–200; Louis Martin Sears, "Nicholas P. Trist: A Diplomat with Ideals," *Mississippi Valley Historical Review* 11 (June 1924): 85–96.

[4] Robert Morgan, *Lions of the West: Heroes and Villains of the Western Expansion* (Chapel Hill: Algonquin Books, 2011), 365.

[5] Norman Graebner, *Empire on the Pacific: A Study in American Continental Expansion* (New York: Ronald Press Company, 1955), 206, 193–194, 197. See also Graebner, "Party Politics and the Trist Mission," *Journal of Southern History* 19 (May 1953): 141. For other works in this vein, see Alfred H. Bill, *Rehearsal for Conflict: The War with Mexico, 1846–1848* (New York: Alfred A. Knopf, 1947), 304; Ray A. Billington, *Westward Expansion* (Albuquerque: University of New Mexico Press, 2001), 583–585; R. M.

Neither Graebner nor anyone else who has studied this subject appears to recognize that Trist's mission succeeded because of his personality, not in spite of it. A stabler man would never have scored such a triumph. Had Trist *not* been perhaps the most undiplomatic diplomat his country ever produced, he would have returned from Mexico empty handed.

"GREAT SERVICE TO YOUR COUNTRY"

Mexico was a defeated nation by March 1847, when U.S. General Winfield Scott launched the first large-scale amphibious operation in American history against the seaport of Veracruz. What contemporaries called "Mr. Polk's War" had been a disaster for the Mexicans. They lost every battle and were often routed from the field. Yet the government of Antonio López Santa Anna remained defiant; even after U.S. troops drove deep into northern Mexico, shellacking larger armies at Monterey and Buena Vista, the Mexican leader refused to sue for peace. This irritated President Polk, who did not relish the prospect of a long war, especially since, from his perspective, the United States had already won its objectives: American forces controlled California, with its three harbors, and had seized disputed territory between the Nueces and Rio Grande rivers. All that remained was for Santa Anna to surrender, a move Polk sought to make unavoidable by directing Scott's army to march north from Veracruz and capture Mexico City.

Polk was still eager to explore diplomatic channels, however, and he hit upon the novel scheme of sending an envoy along with Scott to conclude a settlement with the Mexicans as soon as they recognized that their cause was hopeless. When the president raised this possibility at a cabinet meeting on 10 April, the response was enthusiastic, but he and his advisers could not agree on a suitable candidate. Although Polk preferred to have Secretary of State James Buchanan take on the job, that was impracticable; the Mexicans had not even named commissioners of their own to negotiate, and Polk could not spare his chief cabinet member for the months it might take for serious talks to get underway. This uncertain time frame also ruled out distinguished figures like Senate Foreign

McElroy, *The Winning of the Far West* (New York: Carpenter Press, 1914), 299; Robert W. Merry, *A Country of Vast Designs: James K. Polk, the Mexican War, and the Conquest of the American Continent* (New York: Simon & Schuster, 2009), 359–360, 366–374, 383–386, 393, 397–401, 407–410, 424–426; Jesse S. Reeves, *American Diplomacy under Tyler and Polk* (Baltimore: Johns Hopkins University Press, 1906), 311.

Relations Committee Chair Ambrose Sevier, who would not appreciate being kept waiting at Scott's headquarters while the Mexicans made up their minds. Indeed, Polk noted in his diary, it was "impossible to appoint any prominent man."

After a few minutes' discussion, Buchanan suggested Nicholas Trist, chief clerk of the State Department. This seemed an inspired choice. Trist was fluent in Spanish and, according to Buchanan, "familiar with the Spanish character," having served as U.S. consul in Havana. He was also sufficiently unrenowned that, if negotiations went badly, Polk could recall him, a move that would be awkward in the case of an eminent emissary. Most important, from Polk's perspective, was the fact that Trist's Democratic credentials were beyond reproach: he had married Thomas Jefferson's granddaughter, studied law under Jefferson, been private secretary to Andrew Jackson, and proved himself a gifted publicist for party causes. This clinched the matter for Polk; as his biographers have shown, the eleventh president valued loyalty above all else. A scarred veteran of political wars, he had difficulty trusting anyone or delegating authority, which led him to do much of the administration's work himself. If he was going to take the unprecedented step of assigning a diplomat to accompany the United States army in battle, he wanted someone he could control.[6]

Polk's cabinet agreed that Trist possessed the necessary credentials. They moreover approved the president's decision to make Trist an executive agent to avoid the necessity of Senate confirmation. Judging from the sketchy accounts left by those who attended this meeting, all participants, including Polk, conceived of Trist's mission in modest terms; it involved traveling with Scott, draft treaty in hand, and waiting for Santa Anna to accept American conditions for peace. If the Mexican leader would not yield everything Polk demanded but indicated a willingness to negotiate, Trist was to report this fact to Washington so that Buchanan could be rushed to the scene. Neither Polk nor any of his cabinet intended Trist to play a dominant role in the treaty-making process.[7]

[6] Diary Entry, 10 April 1847, *The Diary of James K. Polk*, Milo Milton Quaife, ed. (Chicago: A.C. McClurg & Co., 1910) (hereafter *DJKP*), 2:465–469. Useful Polk biographies include Sam W. Haynes, *James K. Polk and the Expansionist Impulse* (New York: Longman, 1997); Thomas M. Leonard, *James K. Polk: A Clear and Unquestionable Destiny* (Lanham, MD: Scholarly Resources, 2001); McCormac, *James K. Polk*. See also Mark E. Byrnes, *James K. Polk: A Biographical Companion* (Santa Barbara: ABC-CLIO, 2001).

[7] Later, after Trist had repeatedly exceeded instructions, Buchanan admonished him, "Your mission was a mere precautionary measure." Buchanan to NT, 13 July 1847, Reel 11,

That afternoon, Polk summoned Trist to the White House and told him of his new assignment. Trist, surprisingly, was less than overjoyed. As he recalled over a decade later, his first thought was for his family, and of what effect his absence would have on them. He was also concerned about his health; physically delicate and something of a hypochondriac, he had always sought to avoid unwholesome climates, and Mexico was on the cusp of the yellow-fever season. While he accepted the president's commission, his failure to take delight in it puzzled Polk, who pointed out, "If you succeed in making a treaty, you will render a great service to your country, and earn great distinction for yourself."

"I care nothing for the distinction," Trist replied. "But I will do all I can to render the service."

Polk snorted. All men desired glory, he said. There was no need for false modesty. Trist insisted that he was telling the truth; his only ambition, he declared, was to become a military storekeeper somewhere because that job would allow him a decent income while leaving time for intellectual pursuits. Polk regarded Trist with a combination of amusement and disbelief that the clerk still remembered years after leaving government service. "Had [Polk] been at all capable of attaining insight into character, he would thereby have obtained at least a glimpse into mine," Trist wrote a friend in 1861. "But it remained a sealed book for him."

Changing the subject, Polk gave Trist a suggestion that has troubled students of the Mexican War for generations. In view of the responsibilities weighing on General Scott, the president ventured, it might be wise to avoid pestering him with the specifics of Trist's mission. Instead, the envoy should make Gideon Pillow, Scott's second-in-command, his principal contact with the army. Trist, who knew that Polk and Scott disliked one another, accepted this advice nonchalantly, unaware that it guaranteed quarrelsome civil-military relations. Polk then dismissed Trist with a wave.[8]

Nicholas Philip Trist Papers, Library of Congress, Washington, D.C. (hereafter NPTP-LOC). The archival record of Polk's cabinet meetings is frustratingly meager. Rarely did the president have minutes kept, and few of his advisers committed their recollections to paper. Polk's diary is a better source of information. See Henry Barrett Learned, "Cabinet Meetings under President Polk," *Annual Report of the American Historical Association* (Washington, D.C., 1916), 229–242.

[8] Nicholas Philip Trist Memorial to Congress, 7 August 1848, Record Group 58, National Archives, Washington, D.C. (hereafter Trist Memorial); NT to Scott, 12 January 1861, Folder 209, NPTP-UNC. Trist's memorial is not paginated.

Several conferences with Buchanan followed, during which the secretary explained to Trist what he was empowered to do. Polk's main demands were nonnegotiable, Buchanan said; Mexico must acknowledge the Rio Grande as the southern boundary of Texas and yield upper California and the New Mexican territory to the United States. The price tag for this acquisition, however, had yet to be determined. While Polk wanted to get it for $20 million, he recognized that this might be unrealistic. Trist was therefore authorized to offer as much as $30 million, especially if Mexico could be persuaded to give up lower California and a passageway across the Isthmus of Tehuantepec (which Polk envisioned as the site for a future inter-oceanic canal). Buchanan noted that Washington might further sweeten the deal by canceling claims by American citizens against the Mexican government. But any attempt by Santa Anna to recover at the bargaining table those lands he had lost on the battlefield was to be met with refusal. Moreover, if it looked as though extended negotiations would be required to finalize peace, Trist was to stand aside and wait until Buchanan could arrive and take over.

In their final meeting, Buchanan gave Trist a sealed copy of the *projet*, or treaty proposal, along with other documents he would need in Mexico. Among these was a letter from Secretary of War William Marcy for Scott asserting that Trist had been "directed" to show the general Washington's peace terms. In another gaffe whose repercussions have received considerable scholarly attention, Buchanan told Trist that he was "authorized" to do this. It seemed a semantic matter, but it would let loose the furies.[9]

Trist's account of his sendoff is illuminating. Buchanan, he recalled, accompanied him partway downstairs and then grasped his hand, declaring, "If you succeed, we shall have to take you up as the Democratic candidate for the presidency." That statement drew a reaction even more idiosyncratic than Trist's earlier comeback to Polk. "To these words," Trist remembered, "I answered only by the thought, 'How little you understand me.'"[10]

[9] Buchanan's Instructions for NT, 15 April 1847, Reel 112, Diplomatic Instructions of the Department of State, 1801–1906, Mexico, Record Group 59, National Archives II, College Park, Maryland (hereafter DIDS); *Projet*, undated, ibid.; Polk's Letter of Appointment, undated, Reel 8, NPTP-LOC; Buchanan to Mexican Minister of Foreign Relations, undated, ibid.; Walker to NT, 15 April 1847, ibid.; Marcy to Scott, 14 April 1847, Outgoing Correspondence, Volume 13, William L. Marcy Papers, Library of Congress, Washington, D.C. (hereafter WLMP).
[10] Trist Memorial.

"NOT ALTOGETHER OBSERVANT OF THE APPROVED STYLE"

What did Buchanan fail to understand? Who was Nicholas Trist?

A survey of Trist's life before 1847 reveals one constant feature. He could not recognize and respect a chain of command. Again and again, he broke ranks regardless of consequence and irrespective of who was giving the orders. A historian reviewing Trist's numerous abortive careers often feels that this was a man who stepped out of line simply because he could; each act of resistance was its own justification, and no reward, professional or otherwise, was worth surrendering the freedom to say no. This intractability was often the despair of those powerful men, chiefly Jefferson and Jackson, who liked Trist and sought to save him from himself. Trist's story is one of talents wasted and opportunities squandered, and of a social and political order remarkably forgiving of its wayward son. Despite repeated, flagrant misbehavior, Trist was always able to find patrons to take care of him – until, ironically, he did something great, whereupon all sources of support vanished and he suffered the ostracism he had courted for years.[11]

The circumstances of Trist's upbringing were paradoxical but hardly unusual in his native state of Virginia. He was an aristocrat in constant combat with pauperism. Acquainted from an early age with some of the most prominent figures of his time, he never enjoyed the financial security that normally accompanies such status. Jefferson and James Madison lodged at his great-grandmother's boardinghouse in Philadelphia while attending the Continental Congress, and his grandmother, Elizabeth, became a virtual second parent to Jefferson's daughter after the great man's wife died. Indeed, the Trists moved to Charlottesville at Jefferson's request; according to Trist family lore, Jefferson wanted them near his home. This relocation proved a godsend socially but a dry well financially, as few Trist men were able to find work in the shadow of Monticello. When Nicholas reached the age of eighteen, his parents told him there was no money for college.

---

[11] For monographic treatments of Trist's life, see Robert A. Brent, "Nicholas P. Trist: Biography of a Disobedient Diplomat" (Ph.D. Dissertation: University of Virginia, 1950); Robert W. Drexler, *Guilty of Making Peace: A Biography of Nicholas P. Trist* (Lanham, MD: University Press of America, 1991); Wallace Ohrt, *Defiant Peacemaker: Nicholas Trist in the Mexican War* (College Station: Texas A & M University Press, 1997). See also Robert A. Brent, "Nicholas Philip Trist's Search for a Career" (M.A. Thesis: University of Virginia, 1946).

Jefferson intervened. The former president, who had taken a paternal interest in Nicholas, used his influence with the James Monroe administration to get him admitted to West Point as a cadet in 1818. Nicholas earned excellent grades at the academy but proved incapable of following orders. If he did not respect a superior officer – and there were few he deemed worthy of respect – he could not bring himself to pay due deference. Furthermore, he had a tendency to interpret instructions as invective and respond in kind. After receiving a number of complaints about Nicholas's behavior, the superintendent wrote his parents to warn them that the young man faced dismissal. This prompted a letter from home whose admonition would become an oft-repeated refrain. "[Y]ou must be subordinate," Elizabeth Trist lectured her grandson. "I hope there will be no more trials or heartburnings against those who are appointed to command you." There were, in fact, many more, and although Nicholas managed to avoid expulsion, he grew disgusted with the institution on the Hudson and announced after his third year that he had no intention of returning for the fourth. A military life was not for him.[12]

He tried his hand at the law. Since he could not afford to attend law school, he petitioned Edward Livingston, father of one of his boyhood playmates and a distinguished attorney, to tutor him. Livingston agreed, and even put Trist up in his own home in New Orleans for three years. Far from being grateful, Trist chafed under the discipline of legal studies. His letters to friends and family bristled with lamentations about having to memorize hundreds of cases by rote, and these grievances reached Jefferson, who, in a remarkable gesture, invited Trist to come to Monticello to train for the bar under his supervision. Jefferson had been dismayed to learn of Trist's washout at West Point. He wanted to spare this promising young man the blow of another career dead end.[13]

Trist accepted the offer and moved into Jefferson's hilltop mansion. There followed the happiest time of his life. Jefferson assigned fourteen hours of reading a day, but this included volumes of poetry, philosophy, physical science, and religion in addition to law books, and Trist found the work intellectually stimulating. Also, because he admired Jefferson, he followed this regimen without protest. Jefferson, impressed by Trist's

[12] Elizabeth Trist to NT, 2 January 1819, Folder 17, NPTP-UNC.

[13] NT to Virginia Randolph, 12 April 1823, Folder 31, NPTP-UNC; NT to Virginia Randolph, 4 November 1823, Folder 33, NPTP-UNC; Elizabeth Randolph to NT, 30 March 1824, Reel 2, NPTP-LOC.

dedication, engaged him as a private secretary, and it did not take long for Trist to make himself indispensable in this role. He catalogued Jefferson's personal library, organized his daily schedule, and managed his correspondence. While at Monticello, Trist also successfully courted the ex-president's granddaughter, Virginia, thereby cementing a connection that gained him entrée to Washington's top governmental and social circles. Shortly before his death, Jefferson named Trist executor of his estate.[14]

This was heady stuff, but it ought not to obscure the fact that Trist did not get around to passing the Virginia bar exam until age twenty-six, or that he brought only one case to court before deciding that the world had enough lawyers. While he kept busy for a few years auctioning off Monticello's art and books to satisfy the bankrupt Jefferson's creditors, he made little money from this activity. Equally unlucrative was his work at the University of Virginia, where Madison had succeeded Jefferson as rector. Stricken in years, the Father of the Constitution could not handle his administrative responsibilities, and Trist wound up discharging many of them in his stead, a kindness that earned him another well-placed friend but only $200 in income.[15]

In 1828, Trist decided to give journalism a whirl. He purchased a half share in a newspaper, the Charlottesville *Advocate*, which had been promoting Andrew Jackson's candidacy for the presidency, and composed a number of Jacksonian editorials. Circulation was slack, though, and the paper folded without turning a profit. By this time Trist had three children, one of them a deaf-mute. He was in desperate need of funds.[16]

The tie to Jefferson opened an unlikely door: Henry Clay, secretary of state in the John Quincy Adams administration, offered Trist a State Department clerkship despite his anti-Adams pieces in the *Advocate*. Clay

---

[14] Always more comfortable with written rather than face-to-face communication, Trist proposed to Virginia in a series of notes, despite the fact that they were both living under the same roof. Elizabeth Trist to Mary Trist Tournillon, 14 August 1824, Folder 35, NPTP-UNC.

[15] Madison would write several letters of introduction for Trist when the latter applied for employment in Washington. To then-Secretary of State Henry Clay, Madison enthused, "This young gentleman is, I believe, regarded by all best acquainted with him as possessing a fine understanding, as respectable for his scientific and literary accomplishment as for his strict honor and good habits of every sort." Madison to Clay, 18 October 1828, Reel 3, NPTP-LOC.

[16] Contract and Bill of Sale, 22 March 1828, Reel 4, NPTP-LOC; Hore Brown Trist to NT, 3 August 1828, ibid.

extended this offer out of concern for Martha Jefferson, Virginia's mother and the Sage of Monticello's only surviving child, whom he knew to be in financial distress and dependent on her son-in-law for support. Trist moved his family to Washington to begin work, for the first time in his life, as a salaried employee.[17]

Predictably, he hated it. He had no authority, as Clay would not delegate important tasks to subordinates. Trist's daily grind consisted of copying, filing, and mailing letters. He was a functionary, and it galled him. Even the assurance of a regular paycheck did not last, as Jackson won the presidential election of 1828 less than a year after Trist took up his new duties. Trist felt that the spoils system would cost him his job.[18]

He was pleasantly surprised. Jackson's secretary of state, Martin Van Buren, kept his department patronage-free, and officials close to the new president were aware of Trist's previous career as a Democratic newspaper editor. These factors helped Trist survive the changing of the guard. Equally important was his association with Jefferson, whose name was invoked often by the Democrats during the 1828 campaign. Jackson fancied himself an ideological heir to Jefferson, and he sought Trist out for information. What, he asked, had the great thinker said privately about those political and social issues plaguing the country: slavery, sectionalism, tariffs, the national bank? Trist, flattered by this attention, found Jackson an appreciative listener. Their conversations became more frequent. In 1830, Jackson, following Jefferson's example, named Trist his private secretary.[19]

Trist quickly became one of the most valued members of Jackson's inner circle. During the nullification crisis of 1832–1833, the president encouraged Trist to write articles for publications ridiculing states' rights advocates, and Trist, who had come to venerate Jackson, complied; he published a number of pieces whose go-for-the-jugular tone attracted a

---

[17] Clay to NT, 10 October 1828, Reel 3, NPTP-LOC; NT to Van Buren, 24 March 1829, ibid.; NT to Jackson, 12 April 1830, ibid.

[18] Virginia Trist (hereafter VT) to NT, 26 November 1828, Folder 44, NPTP-UNC; NT to VT, 3 April 1829, Folder 48, NPTP-UNC.

[19] Livingston to Van Buren, 17 March 1829, Reel 3, NPTP-LOC; Rives to NT, 19 March 1829, ibid.; Jackson to NT, 15 December 1831, ibid. James Parton, one of Jackson's first biographers, wrote in 1860, "Among the many young men who surrounded General Jackson during the early years of his presidency, there was none who enjoyed more of his affection and none more worthy of it than Mr. Nicholas P. Trist of Virginia." James Parton, *The Presidency of Andrew Jackson* (New York: Mason Brothers, 1861), 3:601.

wide readership. Jackson rewarded Trist with his most prestigious assignment to date. When, in the spring of 1833, the American consul at
Havana retired, Old Hickory named Trist to replace him, passing over
more qualified applicants.[20]

Professionally, Trist appeared to have arrived. The post was a plum,
with light duties and an annual salary of $2,000. It seemed the sinecure he
had sought, and felt he deserved, all his life. Now he was free to read,
write, and contemplate, and his title commanded respect. Trist rented
a house outside of Havana and sent two of his children to Paris for
schooling; the third attended an expensive institute for the deaf in Philadelphia. Jackson even allowed Trist, who was concerned about the possible effects of the Cuban climate on his health, to spend the summer
months of each year in the United States. In all, the consulship represented
the high point of Trist's fortunes.[21]

It also, unfortunately, gave him free rein to indulge his gift for self-
sabotage. While he made a favorable first impression on the international
community at Havana, charming civilian and military officials at social
functions and mastering the Spanish language, he grew revolted by the
corruption and incompetence of the people around him. His letters home
became jeremiads. He condemned the shady practices of resident American businessmen, dismissed U.S. sailors at the port as drunken brutes, and
found the Spanish colonial authorities "utterly unfit, ... *morally* and
intellectually, for the offices which they fill."[22]

Had these views been confined to his personal correspondence, they
would not have set off any avalanches, but he also expressed them in his
reports on the activities of the consulate, documents that frequently ran to
over fifty pages. Trist was incapable of brevity. He also lacked any sense
of proportion, harping on all subjects, however trifling, at ludicrous
length. (One dispatch strove for fifty-two pages to find the English
equivalent for *hacienda*.) Furthermore, as had been the case at West
Point, he was so hypersensitive to slights that every difference of opinion
became an affront to be answered with storms of obloquy that must have
bewildered his superiors at State. Some of the Americans who bumped

[20] Brent, "Nicholas Philip Trist," 80–90; Livingston to NT, 24 April 1833, Reel 3, NPTP-
LOC; Jackson to NT, 1 May 1833, Reel 4, NPTP-LOC.
[21] For Trist's years as consul, see Matthew Rafferty, "Our (Unhappy) Man in Havana:
Nicholas P. Trist, American Networks of Capital, and U.S. Consular Authority in Cuba,
1833–1845," *Society for Historians of American Foreign Relations 2015 Annual Meeting*
(Washington, D.C.: 25 June 2015).
[22] NT to VT, 5 May 1834, Folder 72, NPTP-UNC.

heads with Trist in Havana called for his dismissal. Yet he remained Jackson's fair-haired boy and escaped reproof for years.[23]

That changed in the summer of 1839, when a number of Washington journals reported widespread dissatisfaction with the consul. Trist, readers learned, had alienated American skippers, shipowners, and sailors with his arrogance, remoteness, and failure to uphold their interests, and had even imprisoned them without cause. Scoffing at such assertions, Trist claimed to be the victim of a conspiracy; if given the chance to defend himself before Congress, he would do so, but he would not descend to a "newspaper war" with his enemies.[24]

Another charge could not be so easily shrugged off. Soon after the worrisome articles appeared, two British abolitionists, members of a commission sent to Havana to enforce an Anglo-Spanish treaty outlawing the slave trade, accused Trist of violating that treaty. They complained that the consul had refused to allow the boarding and inspection of ships flying the American flag and suspected of slave-running; in so doing, they said, he had encouraged maritime transportation of human chattel. The British Foreign Office was at the time under the direction of one of the giants of European diplomacy, Henry John Temple, Viscount Palmerston, who took these accusations seriously. An avowed abolitionist, he lodged protests in Washington demanding that Trist be fired and publicized these admonitions in the British press and Parliament.[25]

What made the ensuing spectacle so silly is that Trist could have averted any penalties by holding his tongue – or, rather, his pen. The offense with which he was charged was, despite Palmerston's pique, minor. After all, no American had signed the treaty that Trist had allegedly been lax in fulfilling. It was an agreement between London and Madrid, and everyone in Cuba knew the Spanish government was unenthusiastic about it, suspecting that the British really wanted to subvert the slave-based Cuban sugar industry and eliminate all competition with sugar growers in the British West Indies. Spanish authorities in

---

[23] See for example NT to McLane, 9 August 1833, Dispatches from U.S. Consuls in Havana, 1783–1906, Reel 6, Record Group 59, National Archives II, College Park, Maryland (hereafter DUSCH); NT to Forsyth, 29 September 1835, ibid.; NT to Forsyth, 23 November 1836, Reel 7, DUSCH; NT to Van Buren, 9 January 1838, Reel 2, NPTP-LOC.

[24] NT cited in Dodman to Hore Browse Trist, 27 January 1840, Reel 7, NPTP-LOC. A selection of these critical press accounts may be found in Reel 11, DUSCH. See also Ferdinand Clark, *The American Captives in Havana, Being Ferdinand Clark's Reply to Nicholas P. Trist, Consul at That Place* (Boston: Jonathan Howe, 1841).

[25] See R. R. Madden, *A Letter to W. E. Channing, D.D., on the Subject of the Abuse of the Flag of the United States in the Island of Cuba* (Boston: William D. Ticknor, 1839).

Havana made little effort to discharge their obligations under the treaty. Many of them flagrantly circumvented it. Had Trist just told his British detractors that he had done his best to uphold enforcement but that the crookedness of the host government made perfect observance impossible, the whole affair would have died out.

Instead, he answered the commissioners' charges in a letter than runs to almost 100 pages in its printed, published version and that must have been much longer in original handwritten form. Reading this document is a surreal experience. It is so senselessly protracted, so freakish in its inability to distinguish the essential from the trivial, that it crosses the line from unprofessionalism into performance art. The reader feels like a witness to self-immolation. By the time he set down his pen, Trist had not only destroyed his credibility with the commissioners and their supervisors in London; he had left them questioning his sanity.

He began well enough, denying that had ever knowingly issued ship's papers to U.S. flag vessels taking part in the slave trade. He also said that the commissioners had overstepped their authority by contacting him because Washington was not a signatory to the Anglo-Spanish treaty outlawing slave trafficking. But if his logic was unassailable, his tone was not. "You are agents," he wrote, "created for a definite special purpose, existing solely in consequence of precise treaty stipulations, and as instruments for their effectuation between particular members of the family of nations, and consequently it would be absurd (and, in one aware of the absurdity, wrong and criminal) in any officer of any nation not one of the parties of those stipulations to allow himself to be made an instrument for practically placing his country into the predicament of such a party." As the commissioners learned, Trist could not let a declarative sentence alone; he had to pin to its tail a tin can of word clusters that left the reader gasping for air by the time a period hove into view. Thus Trist's indignation at British attempts to involve him in European affairs found vent in the following blast of ink:

Before I would submit to your pretension, or meet it when persisted in, in any other tone than that defiance which I now hurl, my daughter should make a bonfire of her books and her music, and bidding adieu to those pursuits which are to qualify her for the womanly employment which she has been taught to look forward to for support – that of training the minds and hearts of her young fellow citizens of our magnificent republic in the same way that her mother, and her paternal grandmother's countrywoman (Maria Edgeworth) have trained her own – she should dedicate herself to the *rifle*, until to her eye and finger its cunning should be as obedient as it proved to the Tennessee man who drew the closest sight and touched the surest hair spring trigger in New Orleans!

Most of these passages were shot through with abuse, as Trist called the commissioners "indecent," "unprincipled," "impertinent," "stupid," and "calumnious." Their mission, he said, was a "wretched farce," a "despicable mockery," a "wasteful superfluity," an "empty show of counterfeit zeal and efficiency" that "meets no sympathy in my bosom." He berated them for demanding "miracles" of enforcement from him when he was running the consulate "single-handed" and charged them with hypocrisy, noting that the slave shackles available for sale in Havana were "products of British Vulcan industry" that arrived at Cuban ports "direct from the mouth of the Thames." Whose nation was the true abettor of the slave trade?

Warming to his task, Trist professed indignation that the commissioners would dare to instruct him on points of egalitarianism and justice when they represented a decadent monarchy from which his countrymen had blessedly escaped. In another marathon sentence that reads as though written under the influence of amphetamines, he roared that no one "look[ed] forward with more heartfelt pleasure" than he did "to the time when the people of England shall be free," when "the House of Lords shall exist only upon the page of history," and "a real representation shall take the place of that detestable simulacrum" by which British subjects "have been plundered," their wealth "shamelessly squandered in every imaginable mode in which it could subserve the selfishness of a sordid few." Anglophobia was common among Americans during the Jacksonian era – Alexis de Tocqueville remarked on it in *Democracy in America* – but for an agent of the U.S. government to express such sentiments in his official correspondence was improper to say the least. The commissioners must have wondered whether Trist was aware that the War of 1812 had ended a quarter-century earlier.

Worse, Trist yoked his Britain-bashing to a passionate defense of slavery. "The condition of the American Negro slave," he preached, "is, under every aspect – the religious and the moral, no less than the physical – better than that of the poorer classes in Great Britain." He had "not a shade of doubt" that there were "hundreds of thousands" of Britons "whose condition would, in every possible particular, be immensely benefited" if they were "set down" in the American South as slaves. For evidence, Trist cited articles in the *Edinburgh Review*, speeches by Irish political leader Daniel O'Connell to the House of Commons, and a lurid exposé called "The Factory Child" by the British reformer Douglas Jerrold, all of which, Trist wrote, proved that England's industrial laborers inhabited "a hell upon earth." Their working conditions were "diabolical," their hours "brutal," their pay barely sufficient to stave off "famine" – and they had to surrender much of these meager earnings to "that hateful system of robbery called parliamentary taxation." If a worker objected to such fleecing, he risked being shot by a "secret committee of assassination" or having "sulphuric acid dashed into his eyes and flesh." By contrast, slaves in America enjoyed "a chance of plenty and long life." Jerrold's factory child – a "little blue-eyed, flaxen-haired maiden" – would be better off "metamorphosed" into a "little wooly-headed Ethiop on the coast of Guinea, ready to be embarked upon a slaver" for the American South, where at least she would be secure from the "pangs of hunger" and enjoy "the glories of God's creation" in the open air. "To judge from this comparison," Trist wrote, "slavery is a blessed thing."

The more copiously the ink flowed, the drunker Trist became on his rhetoric. In his final ranting pages, he insisted that the abolitionist "dream" of "raising the black race to political equality with the white" was "chimerical in the extreme." Blacks were "decidedly, inherently, and irremediably inferior" to whites; they were, moreover, "incurably incapable of improvement, except when in contact with, and in subjection to, some higher variety of the species." Trist backed up this "settled point in natural history" with quotations from Jefferson's works, and advised the commissioners that if emancipation were to occur, it would have to be accompanied by the return of all freed slaves to Africa, where they would "yield to the propensities which draw them downward." Furthermore, Trist declared, the blacks knew this; he was personally acquainted with many slaves who "preferred to be sold from hand to hand" in Virginia rather than "live as freemen" in Liberia. If the commissioners failed to appreciate these sentiments, that was because they did not possess "*any*, the slightest, personal knowledge of the black race," who, in Britain, were "creatures of the imagination purely." In any event, their errand in Havana was "the very height of absurdity," and this, Trist declared in a line that must have elicited peals of laughter, explained why "I should seem to have been not altogether observant of the approved style for diplomatic composition."[26]

Even allowing that Trist's views on slavery mirrored those of millions of his fellow Southerners, this letter was an outrage. Scarcely foremost among its sins was its irrelevance. While the commissioners were

---

[26] NT to Commissioners, 2 July 1839, *Public Documents Printed by Order of the Senate of the United States during the Second Session of the Twenty-Sixth Congress* (Washington, D.C.: Blair & Rives, 1841), 3:49–144.

abolitionists, their quarrel with Trist had nothing to do with manumission; they were in Havana to ensure enforcement of a bilateral treaty banning the slave *trade*, and they sought to foil traffickers who hoisted the American flag to escape inspection. Trist's disquisition on the happiness of bondsmen in Virginia and the misery of Lancashire proletarians was beside the point, as was his cannonade against the British system of government. Rarely, if ever, has a diplomat wandered so far afield from the matter at hand. That Trist broadcast his off-topic convictions in language more appropriate to a sanitarium than a consulate only added to the document's grotesqueness.

As might have been expected, the commissioners forwarded this diatribe to Palmerston, whose choleric response left the Van Buren administration no alternative: to avoid a rupture in Anglo-American relations, Van Buren asked Congress to conduct an investigation into Trist's conduct. Secretary of State John Forsyth included the consul's letter in the collection of official correspondence transmitted to the House Committee of Commerce. Trist, typically defiant, returned to America to meet the charges against him. "You may have heard the rumor of my having been *ordered* to Wash[ington]," he wrote his wife. "No such thing. And if I had been, I should not have gone." In light of Trist's subsequent career, that statement takes on special significance.[27]

The committee concluded its investigation by declining to take any action, but, as historian David Pletcher notes, "the weight of complaints against Trist suggests that he was lucky not to be censured." One of Trist's biographers speculates that Jackson, out of office but widely viewed as the power behind Van Buren's throne, influenced the representatives' verdict. At any rate, Trist's consulship was almost over. The Whigs regained the White House in the 1840 presidential election, and soon after William Henry Harrison's inauguration Trist received notice that he had been replaced.[28]

Ever quixotic and tired of working for others, Trist resolved to stay in Cuba. He would be a gentleman farmer and writer. His family settled on a

[27] NT to VT, 30 November 1839, Folder 104, NPTP-UNC.
[28] Pletcher, *Diplomacy of Annexation*, 502; Brent, "Nicholas Philip Trist," 113–114; Webster to NT, 15 July 1841, Reel 7, NPTP-LOC; NT to Tyler, 14 September 1841, ibid.; NT to Webster, 7 December 1841, ibid. See also *Report from the Committee on Commerce, to Whom Was Referred the Petition of Certain Shipmasters, Shipowners, and Other Citizens, in Relation to the Conduct of N. P. Trist, Consul of the United States in Havana*, 26th Cong., 1st Session, 1839–1840 (Washington, D.C.: U.S. Government Printing Office, 1840).

farm southwest of Havana. The farm, however, proved a nonstarter and Trist had to sell many of his belongings; within a year, he and his wife were advertising rooms with board. The only literary work he produced was a translation of a French essay on dairy cows. Several business ventures in Havana failed. By 1845 he was on the verge of putting his farm up for sale at a loss when an elderly Jackson rescued him again. Jackson prevailed upon the just-installed president, fellow Democrat James K. Polk, to find something for Trist.[29]

Polk's many biographers note his admiration of Jackson – he wore the nickname "Young Hickory" with pride – but there is no question that if he had known what kind of man his idol was asking him to hire, he never would have consented. The president liked to surround himself with sycophants who would not question his judgment, and Trist was the farthest thing from a "yes man." In the summer of 1845, though, Polk confronted a number of foreign-policy crises, the direst of which was a looming war with Mexico, and he appointed Trist without giving the matter much thought. After over a decade, Trist was back at State, this time as chief clerk to Secretary of State James Buchanan.[30]

Trist's independent streak was not in evidence for the first two years of the Polk administration. Perhaps because he found Buchanan an agreeable boss, he performed his duties faithfully, working long hours every day and often returning to the department after dinner to toil away until eleven o'clock. This assiduousness impressed Buchanan, who began entrusting Trist with responsibilities more important than screening and logging correspondence. Trist's fluency in Spanish made him valuable as the White House sought to resolve Mexican-American tensions through means short of war, and Buchanan frequently summoned his chief clerk to serve as translator in cabinet meetings. On those occasions when Buchanan found it necessary to be out of town, he left Trist in charge as acting secretary. By all accounts, Trist kept a low profile and did not use these opportunities to aggrandize himself at Buchanan's expense. He seemed the ideal number two.[31]

[29] NT to Jackson, 1 December 1842, Reel 2, NPTP-LOC; NT to Donelson, 3 December 1842, ibid.; NT to Burton, 18 February 1843, ibid.; Jackson to NT, 9 September 1844, Reel 5, NPTP-LOC; Donelson to NT, 5 February 1845, ibid.; NT to Polk, 2 April 1845, ibid.; NT to Polk, 2 May 1845, ibid.
[30] Buchanan to NT, 28 August 1845, Reel 5, NPTP-LOC.
[31] For Buchanan's increasing dependence on his chief clerk, see Buchanan to NT, 31 March 1846, Reel 5, NPTP-LOC; Buchanan to NT, 9 April 1846, ibid.

It was not surprising, then, that Polk felt comfortable sending Trist to join Winfield Scott's army in Mexico. As far as the president was concerned, this middle-aged Virginian was a bureaucrat without ambition who would do as he was told. No chief executive ever misjudged a subordinate more completely.

"A FARRAGO OF INSOLENCE, CONCEIT, AND ARROGANCE"

Trist approached his Mexican assignment with characteristic melodrama. He had not sought the post, but he convinced himself of its importance and took extreme measures to ensure its success. Informed by Polk that the mission must remain secret, he covered his departure from Washington with the story that he was visiting a sick relative. Then he traveled incognito by mail coach and steamer to New Orleans, where he registered at a hotel as "Docteur Tarreau" and traveled about the city in a closed carriage looking for Denis Prieur, the customs collector. When he found Prieur, he handed him a letter from the secretary of the treasury authorizing travel expenses, whereupon Prier arranged for a revenue steamer to take Trist to Veracruz. Before boarding, Trist bought a brace of pistols and engaged a young Catalan as his bodyguard – "an expensive luxury," he explained in a letter to Buchanan, but desirable since "I shall be surrounded on all sides by the enemy." None of this hugger-mugger activity served its purpose. Several newspapers revealed details of Trist's "secret" mission days after he left the capital.[32]

The envoy arrived in Veracruz to discover that Scott had already departed. There had been an engagement at Cerro Gordo that saw the Mexicans put to flight, and the main force of Scott's army was now on its way to Jalapa, seventy-five miles distant, where they would await reinforcements before launching the final assault on Mexico City. Weakened by the stormy voyage from New Orleans, Trist did not feel well enough to join Scott immediately, but, believing that haste was imperative, he wrote the general a note and sent it, along with Secretary of War Marcy's letter and a sealed copy of Buchanan's draft treaty, by courier. He then prepared to travel to Jalapa with the next supply train, which was due to leave in two days.[33]

[32] NT to Buchanan, 25 April 1847, Reel 11, NPTP-LOC; NT to VT, 18 April 1847, Reel 2, NPTP-LOC; NT to VT, 25 April 1847, ibid.; Merry, *Country of Vast Designs*, 361–362.
[33] NT to Buchanan, 6 May 1847, Reel 8, NPTP-LOC; NT to Buchanan, 7 May 1847, ibid.; NT to VT, 26 April 1847, Reel 2, NPTP-LOC; NT to VT, 8 May 1847, ibid.

Trist's note has not survived, but its contents may be guessed at. He apparently ordered Scott to deliver the treaty to the Mexican government and asserted that he, Trist, as the president's special representative, had the power to suspend military operations if he felt that might expedite the peace process. Equally important was what the message did not say. It made no mention of the Polk administration's peace terms, an omission Scott found galling when he read Marcy's assurance that Trist had been "directed" to divulge this information. Trist – assuming, on the basis of his final briefing with Buchanan, that he was merely "authorized" to tell Scott what the treaty contained – chose to keep the general in the dark.

Scott, who was almost as thin-skinned as Trist, and who resorted just as readily to his pen when angry, wrote an irate reply to the envoy's directive. Perhaps Trist was unaware of this, he said, but the arrangement he proposed "degrades me by requiring that I, the commander of the army, shall defer to you, the chief clerk of the Department of State, on the question of continuing or discontinuing hostilities." That was unthinkable. Scott had no intention of permitting a civilian to take charge of his war. He was also furious that Trist had given him a sealed document to transmit to the enemy. Did Trist think he could not be trusted with the treaty's terms? And was Trist not cognizant of the fact that there *was* no government in Mexico City to receive a treaty? Santa Anna had taken command of his nation's armies in the field, leaving a nonentity to act in his place, and the Mexican Congress had passed a decree making it a crime for any Mexican official to negotiate with the Americans. Under the circumstances, Scott did not think the chances of getting the president *ad interim* to consider Buchanan's proposal were good. If, however, Trist wished to deliver the treaty himself despite these conditions, Scott would be happy to "lend an escort to your flag of truce."[34]

Such sarcasm was uncalled for but understandable. Scott – along with being a national hero, the highest-ranking officer in the army, and twenty years Trist's senior – had just orchestrated the capture of Veracruz, one of the enduring masterpieces in the annals of warfare. Yet Trist addressed him as though he were a servant. Small wonder he took offense. Furthermore, Scott was under tremendous stress, which did nothing to improve his mood. He had landed at Veracruz with over 10,000 men, but sickness, battle casualties, and desertion had reduced his force to just 5,300, and he had received less than half the supplies he had ordered. With justification,

[34] Scott to NT, 7 May 1847, Reel 8, NPTP-LOC.

he suspected Polk of withholding equipment for partisan reasons. Scott was a Whig, and the president mistrusted him, fearful lest he gain enough military glory to seize the White House. It was common knowledge in Washington that Polk had only given Scott command of this campaign because no one else was qualified for the job. Now Trist's appearance in Mexico seemed a ploy to deny Scott the honor of concluding a peace, which was vexing because the general took pride in his diplomatic talent. He had been a member of the U.S. commission that fashioned the Treaty of Ghent ending the War of 1812; he had helped negotiate settlement of the 1832 Black Hawk War; and President Van Buren had twice called upon him to resolve disputes with the British along the Canadian border. Scott's success in those ventures had earned him the title of the Great Pacificator. Why, then, had Polk appointed a State Department paper pusher to treat with the Mexicans? Scott had good cause to feel that he was facing two adversaries that spring: Santa Anna's army and his own government.[35]

Trist, on the other hand, had no excuse for the missive he composed after receiving Scott's note on the road from Veracruz to Jalapa. Like much of Trist's correspondence, it was labor-intensive: he began writing by candlelight on the night of 13 May, added paragraphs whenever he had a free moment during the weeklong march inland, and did not finish until after he arrived at his destination – where, rather than calling on Scott and clearing the air, he had an intermediary deliver the letter. Then he secluded himself in his tent.

Stripped of hyperbole, Trist's dispatch made a simple point. His mission, he said, did not degrade Scott, and no one was asking the general to defer to the wishes of a clerk. Scott should understand that Trist spoke for Polk, not for himself; his relation to the president was comparable to that of an aide-de-camp to Scott, "when entrusted with a verbal order to a subordinate officer." Trist explained that the treaty was sealed not to hide its contents from Scott but because Buchanan wanted it to look impressive when presented to the Mexicans. Scott's concerns about civilian usurpation of his authority, in short, were groundless.

Had Trist just conveyed the above message respectfully, he could have avoided two months of feuding that threatened to wreck Polk's military-diplomatic plans. But, as usual, he refused to let a statement of fact speak for itself, lecturing Scott, "The course determined upon by our

---

[35] For the Polk-Scott rivalry, see Otis A. Singletary, *The Mexican War* (Chicago: University of Chicago Press, 1960), 102–127.

government ... is what any man of plain unsophisticated common sense would take for granted that it must be; and it is not what your exuberant fancy and over-cultivated imagination would make." He chided the general for having written a "tirade against our government," said that his refusal to forward Buchanan's letter to the Mexicans constituted "contempt" of presidential orders, and warned him "not to step one single hair's breadth beyond the limits which circumscribe the strictly military duties and powers of a general." Noting that "I was most assuredly not sent to Mexico for any such purpose as that of engaging in a correspondence with you," Trist declared that he would do so "in the hope that it may – ere you allow your passions to precipitate you into acts most mischievous to your country, as well as most disloyal to her – have the effect of bringing you to your senses." In a letter to his wife written during the same period that he composed this thirty-page harangue, Trist judged Scott "utterly incompetent," "a man of bitter selfishness and egregious vanity," and "decidedly the greatest imbecile ... I have ever had anything to do with." He noted that he had sent copies of his exchange with the general to Buchanan. "If I have not *demolished* him," Trist gloated, "then I give up."[36]

Scott, who had a war to fight, did not get around to reading Trist's epistle until 29 May, by which time, having been reinforced by 1,000 members of the Tennessee dragoons, he had moved his troops 116 miles to Puebla. That city, Mexico's second largest, had fallen to an advance division of the American army two weeks earlier and afforded a healthier environment than did the coastal lowlands, but the change in climate failed to sweeten Scott's disposition. His heatedly scribbled reply denounced Trist as "the personification of Danton, Marat, and St. Just – all in one," called his message "a farrago of insolence, conceit, and arrogance," and threatened, "If you dare to use this style ... again, or indulge yourself in a single discourteous phrase, I shall throw back the communication with the contempt and scorn you merit at my hands." Like Trist, Scott forwarded copies of these letters to Washington, along with a note to Secretary of War Marcy complaining about "a flank battery planted against me amidst critical military operations." Not only was Trist trying to sabotage the campaign, Scott protested; he "has not done me the honor to call upon me. Possibly he thought the compliment of a first visit was due to him!" If so, the ink-stained upstart was in for a long wait. Indeed, although Trist

[36] NT to Scott, 20 May 1847, Reel 8, NPTP-LOC; NT to Buchanan, 21 May 1847, ibid.; NT to VT, 15 May 1847, Reel 2, NPTP-LOC.

arrived in Puebla just a few days after Scott, he and the general continued to shun each other. Brigadier General Persifor Smith, who hosted Trist during this pause on the drive to Mexico City, tried to bring the two men together, but neither would relent. Scott was about to undertake the first American assault on an enemy capital, and he and the president's personal representative were not on speaking terms.[37]

In due course, Polk received word of the feud, and, predictably, he blamed Scott for it. Certain that the general was preparing to run for president as the Whig candidate in 1848, Polk reasoned that Scott sought exclusive control of the peacemaking process because that would make him unbeatable at the polls. Why else, the president asked, would Scott decline to "cooperate with Mr. Trist in accomplishing the object of his mission"? Polk found Scott's conduct "not only insubordinate but insulting to Mr. Trist and the government." He told his cabinet he wanted the general court-martialed. Marcy managed to talk Polk out of this idea, but the president directed his secretary of war to send a harsh reprimand to Scott. Buchanan, he said, should issue a less severe admonition to his clerk.[38]

Ironically, by the time these rebukes reached their respective targets, the donnybrook between Trist and Scott was over and the administration was reacting to a situation that no longer existed. Throughout Trist's mission, the transit time between Mexico and Washington proved a critical factor, sometimes operating to the envoy's detriment but often furnishing him with breathing space in which to pursue initiatives his superiors would have vetoed in an era of more rapid transmittal. It took at least a month for reports from the army to arrive at the White House and vice versa, and that was under optimal conditions. As Scott pushed deeper into the interior, lines of communication grew increasingly frayed. Guerrillas and bandits menaced the road back to Veracruz, and no one dared make the trip without an escort, which Scott, short of cavalry, was loath to provide. Heavy rains also frequently rendered the route impassable. Buchanan therefore did not learn from Trist until early August that he and Scott had patched things up.[39]

---

[37] Scott to NT, 29 May 1847, Reel 8, NPTP-LOC; Scott to Marcy, 20 May 1847, Reel 11, NPTP-LOC.

[38] Diary Entry, 12 June 1847, *DJKP*, 3:57–59; Buchanan to NT, 14 June 1847, Reel 112, DIDS; Marcy to Scott, 31 June 1847, Outgoing Correspondence, Volume 13, WJMP. Buchanan took the sting out of his official rebuke by sending a chatty, collegial follow-up letter that philosophized, "What can't be cured must be endured." Buchanan to NT, 13 July 1847, Reel 8, NPTP-LOC.

[39] NT to Buchanan, 24 June 1847, Reel 2, NPTP-LOC.

Trist's reconciliation with Scott is one of the legends of the Mexican War, although the facts veer from the standard narrative. According to most accounts, Trist fell ill after arriving in Puebla and was confined to his bed for days, unable to keep food down. Scott, who had thus far declined to meet with the envoy, softened and sent Trist a jar of guava marmalade to speed his convalescence. Touched by this gesture, Trist returned fond thanks to the sender, who soon dropped by Smith's tent to visit his erstwhile antagonist, whereupon the two men recognized each other as kindred spirits and the clouds of acrimony dissolved.[40]

In truth, relations between Trist and Scott began to improve two weeks before the famous gift of marmalade, and the trigger for this *entente cordiale* was Trist's first act of insubordination in Mexico. After reviewing newspapers from the capital left in a stable by travelers, Trist concluded that Scott's description of the Mexican government was exaggerated; it was not in such disarray as to preclude delivery of the sealed treaty – and, moreover, the Mexican Congress had begun considering British offers of mediation. Trist therefore wrote to Charles Bankhead, British minister to Mexico, and asked him to forward the treaty Scott had refused to deliver. Bankhead agreed, and sent chargé Edward Thornton to Puebla to meet Trist. Soon thereafter, Thornton presented Washington's terms to Santa Anna, who seemed receptive. While the generalissimo could not officially treat with Trist due to congressional constraints, he promised to do his utmost to get the legislature to lift the ban on negotiations. Perhaps because he took sick around the time he received this response, Trist passed it along to Scott in a letter notable for its brevity. More important, Trist included with the letter a list of the American peace terms, information he ought to have shared with Scott sooner. Its arrival did much to placate the general.[41]

What really impressed Scott, though, was Trist's chutzpah. The envoy had no authorization to involve the British as intermediaries. Quite the

---

[40] For examples of this orthodox version, see Alexander DeConde, *A History of American Foreign Policy*, Second Edition (New York: Charles Scribner's Sons, 1971), 202; Howard Jones, *Crucible of Power: A History of American Foreign Relations to 1913*, Second Edition (Lanham, MD: Rowman & Littlefield, 2009), 171; Paterson et al., *American Foreign Relations*, 1:114–115; Julius W. Pratt, *A History of United States Foreign Policy* (Englewood Cliffs, NJ: Prentice-Hall, 1955), 255.

[41] NT to Bankhead, 6 June 1847, Reel 8, NPTP-LOC; NT to Bankhead, 7 June 1847, ibid.; NT to Bankhead, 11 June 1847, ibid.; NT to Scott, 26 June 1847, ibid. To Trist's credit, he did not allow any ill feelings from his spat with the British in Havana to prevent him from exploring this diplomatic avenue.

contrary: as both Trist and Scott knew, Polk was highly suspicious of British motives. The British had tried to prevent American annexation of Texas, and Polk thought they coveted California. At the time the Mexican War broke out, the president had nearly precipitated another armed clash with Britain over the Oregon Territory. He would have been appalled to learn that his representative had asked Bankhead for assistance without obtaining permission from the White House. Scott, who yielded to few in his loathing of Polk, had to admit that Trist was no presidential puppet.

Trist, for his part, reciprocated Scott's olive branch with gratitude as manically over-the-top as his earlier petulance had been. A day after Smith brought the marmalade to Trist's sickbed, the envoy wrote to Buchanan that he and Scott had patched things up "in a way which should at once preclude all restraint and embarrassment between us." Trist concluded that the administration, through whose eyes he had heretofore viewed Scott, had allowed the general's status as a prominent Whig to mask his many "sterling qualities of heart and head." Scott was "the soul of honor and probity," Trist effervesced. "All who have been near him, and have enjoyed opportunities of knowing him which I have possessed, acknowledge his title to the highest esteem." Sheepish at having so "misconceived" Scott's character, Trist asked that his earlier, insulting dispatches be "withdrawn from the files of the Department." This attempt at damage control failed. Trist's letters not only remained in the files; within a short time they became public.[42]

Scott and Trist went on to forge an effective partnership that succeeded, despite Polk's often maladroit management of the war effort, in giving the president his greatest glory: a republic that straddled the Continent. No one but Trist could have established this bond with Old Fuss and Feathers, and this is the feature of the Trist-Scott collaboration that has eluded most historians. It is impossible to envision Buchanan or any other accomplished diplomat so completely winning Scott's trust, much less convincing him to risk his political neck the way Trist did over the second half of this campaign. The similarities between Trist and Scott were striking. Both were Virginians. Both were well educated and widely read. Both had trained as lawyers and abandoned the profession. Both

[42] NT to Buchanan, 7 July 1847, Reel 11, NPTP-LOC; NT to VT, 18 November 1847, Reel 2, NPTP-LOC. See also Scott to Marcy, 25 July 1847, Reel 8, NPTP-LOC. For an especially florid tribute by Trist to Scott, see NT to VT, 18 October 1847, Reel 2, NPTP-LOC.

were, frankly, prima donnas whose stiff-necked pride, theatricality, and bent for expressing themselves in longiloquent prose inspired ridicule among contemporaries.[43]

Most important, both were prepared to ignore orders that conflicted with their judgment. Over the next eight months, their increasingly insubordinate course, while not free of blunders and false starts, resulted in Mexico giving up half of its territory to the United States for half of what Polk was willing to pay. Polk never appreciated how essential Trist and Scott were to this outcome, and the diplomat and the general left Mexico in disgrace, sacked and slandered by the president whose every objective they had won.

"DUTY TO DISREGARD"

Paradoxically, the Trist-Scott comradeship upset Polk more than their feud. When Polk learned that Scott and Trist were meeting regularly for long conversations, he drew the conclusion that they had joined in league against him. "Mr. Trist has become General Scott's tool," Polk confided to his diary, "and his mental instrument."[44]

Encouraging Polk in this delusion was Gideon Pillow, Scott's second-in-command and the man whom Polk had identified for Trist as the likeliest contact for smooth civil-military relations. Pillow was carrying on his own squabble with Scott. Angry not to have received supreme field command, he took every opportunity to discredit the general in Polk's sight, an easy task given the president's readiness to believe the worst of political rivals. Now Pillow began undercutting Trist as well – and this was a problem for Trist because no military figure enjoyed greater access to the president than Pillow. Polk and Pillow had been law partners before the former embarked on a political career; Pillow successfully defended Polk's brother against a murder charge in 1838; and Pillow was one of the managers of Polk's candidacy in the 1844 Baltimore convention that nominated him for the presidency. A just-inaugurated Polk rewarded Pillow with a high position in the American army. For Polk, whose obsession with loyalty was notorious, Pillow's uncertain military abilities mattered less than his allegiance. When Pillow forwarded

---

[43] I am obliged to Robert Morgan for pointing out the resemblance between Trist and Scott, both in terms of temperament and background. Morgan, *Lions of the West*, 377.

[44] Diary Entry, 2 September 1847, *DJKP*, 3:57–59.

dispatches from Mexico warning of a Trist-Scott cabal, the president took them seriously.[45]

Trist soon gave Pillow grist for his slander mill. In early June, Santa Anna told Trist, via Thornton, that he might be able to persuade the Mexican Congress to open negotiations if the Americans paid him a bribe. The amount was unclear, but Santa Anna suggested $10,000 to get the ball rolling and another $1,000,000 when the treaty was ratified in both Washington and Mexico City. Trist leaped at this opportunity. He told Scott that it would save lives and preserve Mexican honor, which would make diplomacy proceed more amicably than would be the case if the United States ground Mexico into the dust. There was no shame in accepting Santa Anna's offer, Trist said; any moral blight attached solely to the party soliciting a bribe. Yet Trist foresaw a snag: "Nothing of this sort has, I positively know, been in the contemplation of our government." Polk had not authorized him to pay bribes. That did not trouble him, though. As he explained to Scott, he had a "duty to disregard" his instructions in the interest of securing Washington's objective. Polk, he felt sure, would understand.[46]

Polk did not, but the tortoiselike pace of communications ensured that news of the bribery venture took five months to reach Washington, by which time it was, like the Trist-Scott quarrel, old news. Remarkably, Trist declined to mention his plan to purchase a peace in his reports to Buchanan, reasoning, perhaps, that the White House would trust him to handle the matter. On his own prerogative, Trist persuaded Scott to give him the army's entire contingency fund for emergencies ($10,000) and arranged for it to be brought to Santa Anna.[47]

As anyone familiar with the generalissimo's record of opportunism could have predicted, this secret payment did not lead to the promised results. Santa Anna knew he lacked sufficient congressional support to overturn the prohibition, and he made his appeal to the legislators without hope of prevailing. Then, having pocketed the cash, he informed Thornton that only an American descent upon Mexico City would cause the *Puros*,

---

[45] See for example Pillow to Polk, 15 November 1847, Reel 51, James Knox Polk Papers, Library of Congress, Washington, D.C. (hereafter JKPP); Pillow to Polk, 22 November 1847, ibid.; Pillow to Polk, 23 November 1847, ibid.; Pillow to Polk, 24 November 1847, ibid.; Pillow to Polk 26 November 1847, ibid. The best study of Pillow's controversial career is Nathaniel Cheairs Hughes and Roy P. Stonesifer, Jr., *The Life and Wars of Gideon Pillow* (Chapel Hill: University of North Carolina Press, 1993).

[46] NT to Scott, 16 June 1847, Reel 9, NPTP-LOC.

[47] NT to Scott, 16 July 1847, Reel 8, NPTP-LOC; Scott to NT, 17 July 1847, ibid.

or hawks, to amend their position. He also said that his generals had entreated him to try one last time to reverse the tide of the war on the battlefield. There would be no negotiations. Trist's gambit had fizzled. Pillow gleefully reported the details to Polk in letters that wended their slow, uncertain way by wagon train or courier to the coast for dispatch to New Orleans and thence overland to the capital. It would be mid-December before the president learned of his agent's misconduct.[48]

Scott, meanwhile, had no alternative other than to continue his advance. The Americans overwhelmed the Mexicans at a key defensive position along the Churubusco River that Santa Anna had ordered held at all costs. Although U.S. casualties were high, Santa Anna lost fully one-third of his army, and the victory brought the Americans within sight of Mexico City. Panicky, Santa Anna contacted Scott through the British legation, stating that his government was willing to receive Trist as a plenipotentiary. Scott, whose policy was to wage war in a way that minimized loss of life, agreed to a brief armistice. Four months after arriving at Veracruz, Trist at last had the opportunity to perform the task Polk had appointed him to do.[49]

He began by once again violating instructions. When he met with the Mexican peace commission on 27 August, its members informed him that they had authority merely to accept his proposals and pass them along to Santa Anna. They would see to it that the president read any document Trist presented to them; if he preferred to convey America's terms verbally, they were to listen, nothing more.

This news ought to have caused Trist to break off the exchange, as he was under orders to confer only with persons empowered to conclude a treaty. Yet he dismissed that stipulation as "mere etiquette" and pressed ahead. With an ingenuousness that must have nonplused the ex-presidents and prominent lawyers sitting across the table from him, he did not open with extravagant demands in the expectation that they

---

[48] NT to Thornton, "Wednesday," Reel 8, NPTP-LOC; NT to Thornton, 30 July 1847, ibid. For a biography of the general – and five-time president – see Will Fowler, *Santa Anna of Mexico* (Lincoln: University of Nebraska Press, 2007).

[49] Pacheco to Buchanan, 20 August 1847, *Diplomatic Correspondence of the United States: Inter-American Affairs, 1831–1860*, William R. Manning, ed. (Washington, D.C.: Carnegie Endowment for International Peace, 1937) (hereafter *DCUS*), 8:922 (this note, given to the British minister, who was to place it in Trist's hands, was left open so that Trist could read it, even though it was addressed to Buchanan); Scott to Santa Anna, 21 August 1847, Reel 11, NPTP-LOC; NT to Pacheco, 25 August 1847, ibid.; NT to Pacheco, 26 August 1847, ibid.; Robert Selph Henry, *The Story of the Mexican War* (New York: Da Capo Press, 1950), 338–345.

would be scaled back; instead, he laid out Polk's minimum conditions for peace and tried to persuade his opponents that these were reasonable. The commissioners made some noncommittal remarks before retiring to discuss the matter with Santa Anna.[50]

In subsequent meetings, they countered with their own terms. Mexico, they said, would give up nothing more than the traditional Texas boundary at the Nueces River and a small portion of California – which meant, in effect, that the Americans would have to evacuate nearly all of the territory they had conquered. Santa Anna had directed his representatives to behave as though Mexico held the battlefield advantage. These propositions were unacceptable, but Trist did not despair. "It is to be expected that they will attempt to reduce as low as possible the extent of territory which Mexico will part with," he wrote Buchanan. He believed their position would weaken.[51]

While the talks were complex, the pivotal moment occurred when Trist suggested that the United States might be willing to retreat from its initial demand that the Rio Grande form the boundary of Texas. Perhaps, Trist ventured, the swath of land between the Rio Grande and Nueces might be made a neutral zone, possibly under European auspices. This was not a radical proposal – the territory in question was so arid as to be worthless even for cotton cultivation until the 1920s – and Trist floated the notion confidentially while continuing to insist, in formal negotiations, on the Rio Grande boundary. Nonetheless, he ought to have known that, for Polk, any ambivalence on this issue was unthinkable. The president needed Texas to extend to the Rio Grande in order to maintain the fiction that Mexico, not the United States, started the war by shedding American blood on American soil. Trist compounded the error when he agreed to refer the boundary question to the White House. He did tell the Mexicans that he considered it "in the very highest degree improbable" that Polk would agree to a boundary at the Nueces, but said he would sound out the president to avoid a breakdown in the negotiations that would "scatter to the winds all hope of bringing the war to close." Since it would take at least forty-five days to obtain a reply, Trist informed the commissioners that he was prepared to ask Scott to extend the armistice that long.[52]

Trist's buck-passing was reckless, and he should not have been surprised by the volcanic reaction it drew, but it proved, in the long run, an

[50] NT to Buchanan, 29 August 1847, DCUS, 8:932.
[51] NT to Buchanan, 4 September 1847, DCUS, 8:934, 936.
[52] NT to Buchanan, 4 September 1847, DCUS, 8:935.

effective tactic. As the envoy explained afterwards, with perhaps a degree of self-justification, "I expected ... that the answer from Washington would be a peremptory refusal to accede to this modification of the boundary... [with] the effect of conclusively satisfying them that the determination of our government, on this point, was *unchangeable*." And indeed, when the Mexicans learned months later of Polk's insistence that the Rio Grande boundary remain inviolate, they recognized that there was no alternative to accepting this arrangement. By the time Trist began his second round of negotiations in January 1848, his opposite numbers had relinquished all claims above the Rio Grande.[53]

Those developments, however, lay in the future, when a different man would be president of Mexico. In the fall of 1847, Santa Anna held that office, and he called the American demands "extravagantly extortionate." He also interpreted Trist's offer to extend the armistice as a trick to gain time while Scott waited for the arrival of reinforcements. Under fire from *Puros* in Congress, Santa Anna declared that he had never contemplated making a treaty with the invaders and that he remained committed to a military resolution of the conflict. Further parleys were pointless. Trist and the commissioners met for the last time on 6 September to acknowledge the failure of their efforts, and Scott notified Santa Anna that the armistice was over. The last major military operation of the war began.[54]

It lasted little more than a week. Scott's capture of Mexico City was a tactical tour de force that moved no less an authority than the Duke of Wellington to exclaim, "He is the greatest living soldier!" Against the advice of his senior officers, Old Fuss and Feathers ordered an attack on the city from the west while launching a feint to fool Santa Anna into thinking it would come from the south. This approach required the Americans to overrun the fortress of Chapultepec, which Santa Anna thought impregnable but which Scott's men took in two hours before storming across the western causeways and bursting through the city gates. Once inside, the Americans faced several days of street-to-street, building-to-building conflict, made worse by Santa Anna's decision to open the prisons and unleash thousands of criminals. The generalissimo did not linger to see the results of this measure; he renounced the presidency and fled north with his army, but his departure did not mean an end to the fighting, as irregular forces sniped at the Americans from rooftops and windows and rioting convulsed much of the capital. By 14 September,

---

[53] NT to Buchanan, 6 December 1847, *DCUS*, 8:1012.
[54] Santa Anna cited in NT to Buchanan, 4 September 1847, *DCUS*, 8:936.

however, Scott had the situation in hand. He imposed martial law, ordered his troops to execute anyone who offered opposition to American patrols, and appointed a U.S. major general as Mexico City's military governor. Mob violence grew sporadic, then died out. The Stars and Stripes flew over the National Palace.[55]

Yet the war was not over. Santa Anna's army, beaten and demoralized, remained intact. The Mexican government, led now by elderly Supreme Court justice Manuel de la Peña y Peña, withdrew to Querétaro, a town about 100 miles northwest of the capital, where they tried to heal the divisions between conservative and liberal wings and made no effort to reopen talks with Trist. It was a frustrating period for the American soldiers. Despite their string of victories, prospects for a peace settlement seemed dim.

"YOU HAVE PLACED US IN AN AWKWARD POSITION"

Exasperation and anxiety were even more acute in Washington. News of the fall of Mexico City had not yet arrived by early October, and Polk, who had envisioned a brief conflict, faced the final year of his administration without having fulfilled his main campaign promise. The Whigs were making political capital out of the war; they seized control of the House of Representatives in the off-year elections, and Polk knew that when the new Congress convened, it would challenge his leadership more energetically than had the previous, Democratically dominated legislature. Pro-peace and anti-Polk editorials appeared daily in the nation's papers. And some members of Polk's cabinet began advising the president that the Trist mission had been a mistake. Trist's presence with the army, they argued, had sent the wrong message to the Mexicans, who interpreted it as a sign that the United States was eager to stop fighting, hardly the impression Polk wanted to convey. As early as 7 September, Attorney General Nathan Clifford urged that Trist be recalled. "Mexico and the world should be informed that we have no further propositions of peace to make," Clifford said, "and that we will ... overrun and subdue the whole country until Mexico herself has sued for peace." Secretary of the Treasury Robert Walker concurred.[56]

---

[55] Wellington cited in Christensen, *U.S.-Mexican War*, 211. For accounts of the battle for Mexico City, see K. Jack Bauer, *The Mexican War, 1846–1848* (New York: Macmillan, 1974), 306–325. Eisenhower, *So Far from God*, 329–342; Henry, *Story of the Mexican War*, 357–369; Smith, *Old Fuss and Feathers*, 317–335.

[56] Diary Entry, 7 September 1847, *DJKP*, 3:161–166.

Polk declined for the moment to take this measure, reasoning, "We should keep our minister with the headquarters of the army ready to receive any propositions or overtures of peace which the Mexicans might have to make." Over the next few weeks, however, information drifted into the White House from various sources that Scott had agreed to an armistice on the outskirts of Mexico City and that the Mexicans had proposed preposterous peace terms, among them the fixing of Texas's border at the Nueces. Polk was furious with Scott for halting his advance, certain that the Mexicans were not negotiating in good faith, and convinced that Clifford and Walker were right: any peace would have to be a conquered one. On 4 October, the president decided to fire Trist. He explained his decision in his diary the following day: "Mr. Trist is recalled because his remaining longer with the army could not, probably, accomplish the objects of his mission and because his remaining longer ... would impress the Mexican government with the belief that the U.S. were so anxious for peace that they would ultimately conclude one on Mexican terms."[57]

It bears note that, contrary to most accounts of the Trist mission, Polk's choice to cashier Trist did not stem from dissatisfaction with the envoy's performance. At the time, the president did not know about Trist's offer to submit the Nueces-Rio Grande dispute to Washington or the other occasions on which he had twisted or disobeyed orders. In fact, Buchanan made a point of telling Trist not to interpret his dismissal as a rebuke. No one in Washington thought he had mismanaged the negotiations, the secretary wrote. The villains in this matter were the Mexicans, whose propositions were "a mere mockery" that exposed the hollowness of their professed desire for peace. From Polk's perspective, the Americans had shown "moderation and forbearance," only to be repaid with "treachery," and it was now time to double down on the war effort. Buchanan therefore instructed Trist "to return to the United States by the first safe opportunity." If he had concluded a treaty by the time the recall notice arrived, he might bring it with him. If, on the other hand, he was in the middle of negotiations, he must break them off and not delay his departure on that account. He should, moreover, tell the Mexicans to present any future peace proposals to Scott, who would forward them to Polk.[58]

---

[57] Polk cited in Mahin, *Olive Branch and Sword*, 127; Diary Entry, 5 October 1847, *DJKP*, 3:186.

[58] Buchanan to NT, 6 October 1847, Reel 112, DIDS.

As if to assure Trist that he remained in good standing with the administration, Buchanan attached a personal note to the official letter of recall. This message was warm and gossipy, full of news about the Department and events in Washington. Among other things, Buchanan revealed that Trist's replacement, James Derrick, had been sick, leaving the secretary swamped with work at a time when he could not afford to take on additional responsibilities. For that reason, and because Derrick was a member of the Whig Party, Buchanan looked forward to having Trist back as his chief clerk. Buchanan also urged Trist not to run any unnecessary risks in returning to Veracruz. The envoy, he said, should wait until there was safe transportation down the outlaw- and guerrilla-beset National Highway.[59]

That was the last cordial piece of correspondence Trist would receive from a member of the Polk administration. Shortly after Buchanan sent off the notice of dismissal, four of Trist's dispatches arrived at State reporting on the August-September negotiations. These letters were over six weeks old, and they made clear that Trist had volunteered to ask his superiors if they could be flexible on the boundary question – and, worse, that he had told the Mexicans of his willingness to extend the armistice until Washington had a chance to reply. Polk was beside himself when he learned the news. "Mr. Trist has managed the negotiation very bunglingly," he confided to his diary. "He has done more. He has departed from his instructions." How could Trist misinterpret "the simple duty with which he was charged, which was to submit and enforce the ultimatum of his government"? "I am much embarrassed by Mr. Trist's course," Polk fumed. "I thought he had more sagacity and more common sense than to make the propositions he has made." Polk instructed Buchanan to write to Trist again, "expressing in strong terms my disapprobation" and demanding the envoy's "immediate recall."[60]

Buchanan handled this task with delicacy, but there was no mistaking the chill in his tone. "The president," he declared, "could not for a single moment entertain the question of surrendering that portion of Texas" called for by the Mexicans, and Trist ought to have known as much. For Polk to accept this arrangement, he would have to dismember a state of the union, "expel by force" those American citizens who lived between the Nueces and the Rio Grande, and "convert this territory into a desert." The mere suggestion was offensive. Equally so was Trist's plan to halt

[59] Buchanan to NT, 7 October 1847, Reel 8, NPTP-LOC.
[60] Diary Entries, 21 and 23 October 1847, *DJKP*, 3:199, 200–201.

"our victorious army at the gates of the capital," thereby giving the Mexicans "an opportunity to recover from their panic ... and to prepare for further resistance." Buchanan conveyed Polk's "profound regret that you should have gone so far beyond the carefully considered ultimatum to which you were limited by your instructions." He told Trist a second time that his mission was at an end. To soften the blow, he again included a personal message, noting, "My dear sir, I am extremely sorry to be obliged to write you this dispatch. It was unavoidable. You have placed us in an awkward position, and the president feels it deeply." Buchanan ended by expressing hope that the "portion of your conduct which the president disapproves may not subject you to any public criticism" – an absurd statement given Polk's vindictiveness. Anyone who enraged the president as Trist had was certain to reap the whirlwind.[61]

Even Buchanan's insincere solicitude had evaporated by the time he sent his next letter, a blistering epistle prompted by the arrival in Washington of news of Trist's failed June attempt to bribe Santa Anna. Polk, apoplectic, condemned this act "in the strongest terms," told his cabinet that Trist did not have "the slightest authority to make such a proposition," and thundered, "It must be investigated, and the censure fall where it is due, whatever may be the consequences." At Polk's direction, Buchanan berated Trist for considering "a transaction which would cover with merited disgrace all those who participated in it, and fix indelible stain upon the character of our country." He demanded that the envoy furnish him with "a precise and minute history of all of the particulars," presumably in preparation for a congressional inquiry, and maybe even a criminal indictment. There was no personal note enclosed with this dispatch.[62]

"MAKE THE TREATY, SIR!"

So slow were communications between Washington and Mexico City that Trist did not learn his fate until over a month after Polk sealed it. During those five weeks, the envoy kept busy monitoring the Mexican political situation, which was, he reported, "chaotic." According to the Mexican Constitution of 1824, if the office of president of the republic

---

[61] Buchanan to NT, 25 October 1847, Reel 112, DIDS; Buchanan to NT, 27 October 1847, Reel 8, NPTP-LOC.

[62] Diary Entries, 11 and 20 December 1847, *DJKP*, 3: 245–246, 252–253; Buchanan to NT, 21 December 1847, Reel 112, DIDS.

became vacant, the president of the Supreme Court should step in, but that office was also vacant, the man who held it having died. Peña, as senior justice, was acting in the capacity of president of the tribunal when Santa Anna resigned, and thus he became chief executive by virtual default. "The validity of his title," Trist noted, was "questionable." A diffident, infirm man, Peña had not coveted the presidency and could not be expected to take up his duties with zeal. Moreover, Congress had difficulty forming a quorum in Querétaro, which meant that it could not officially receive Santa Anna's resignation and clear the way for Peña's installment.

Even if Peña managed to organize a new ministry and win legislative backing for it, his hold on power would be shaky. Several factions challenged his *Moderado* party. On one hand were the monarchists and *Santanistas*, who believed that only one-man rule could bring law and order to the country and who wanted to abolish the republic in favor of a dictatorship. On the other were the *Puros*, who fought for a liberal democracy and opposed any peace agreement with the American army. The group that most worried Trist, though, consisted of those powerful elements, notably the clergy, who favored U.S. annexation of Mexico. Trist wrote Buchanan that many high church officials, although aware that "freedom of worship would be the immediate consequence" of such a union, were prepared to endure this "evil" in exchange for "the security of their property."

Not only men of the cloth desired this outcome. Sentiment for American rule had been spreading since the seizure of Mexico City. Some felt that Washington was responsible for the anarchy in Mexico and that the Americans had an obligation to stay and clean up the mess they had made. Others despaired of Mexican abilities to create a stable government. The nation's twenty-plus years of turbid political life, they argued, proved that Mexico could not survive independently; its salvation lay in becoming part of the United States. Trist marveled at "how rapidly the wish that we may retain the country is extending itself." People who a short time before would have bridled at the suggestion that Mexico surrender Texas were now extolling the benefits of annexation.[63]

Those benefits were not apparent to Trist. He advised Buchanan that U.S. absorption of Mexico would pose "incalculable danger to every

[63] NT to Buchanan, 25 October 1847, *DCUS*, 8:958–964.

good principle ... which is cherished among us." A man of his times when
it came to racial matters, Trist viewed Mexicans as inferiors who lacked
the intelligence, industry, and virtue to assimilate into Anglo-Saxon democracy. He also felt that annexation was militarily impracticable, since it
would require the long-term occupation and pacification of a heavily
populated, hostile region. Most important, he was certain that any
attempt to incorporate Mexico into the United States would upset the
balance between slave and free states in Congress and inflame sectional
conflict. When Trist heard reports that the so-called "all-Mexico" movement was gaining ground in Washington during the period after Mexico
City fell, he grew anxious. Delay clearly whetted the appetite of the
annexationists. The sooner he concluded a treaty, the better.[64]

Toward that end, Trist wrote Luis de la Rosa, Peña's foreign minister,
with an account of his mission, emphasizing the fact that he had taken
extraordinary steps to achieve peace. Although those measures had not
borne fruit, he said, his powers to treat stood "unrevoked," and, "so long
as that shall be the case," he would continue "to cherish the wish that they
may not have been conferred in vain." De la Rosa responded with
assurances that Peña would soon announce the appointment of commissioners to resume talks.[65]

Unfortunately, several weeks passed before those commissioners were
named, as Peña did not feel strong enough to take such decisive moves.
He was, after all, only a caretaker head of state pending the selection of
the interim president, whose investiture required a congressional quorum.
Not until 5 November did enough members arrive in Querétaro, the
temporary Mexican capital, to meet that prerequisite; some were delayed
by the inability of local governments to cover traveling expenses, others
by their own reluctance to come to terms with the *yanquis*. Once a
sufficient number assembled, however, the results were dramatic. Congress not only repealed the ban on negotiations; it defeated, by a majority
of forty-six to twenty-nine, a measure that would have forbidden the
cession of territory held by Mexico before the war. Even better, the
legislators chose Pedro Anaya, a leading *Moderado*, to serve as president
ad interim until a newly elected Congress met in January. Anaya
appointed Peña his foreign minister and Brigadier General Ignacio Mora
y Villamil his minister of war. Trist, who considered the latter an

[64] NT to Buchanan, 6 December 1847, *DCUS*, 8:998.
[65] NT to de la Rosa, 20 October 1847, Reel 11, NPTP-LOC; De la Rosa to NT, 31 October
      1847, *DCUS*, 8:971.

"avowed apostle of peace," informed Buchanan, "In the present instance, the prospect of a treaty is, I know, very good."[66]

Then the roof caved in. At 3:30 in the afternoon on 16 November, Trist received a courier pouch containing Buchanan's first two dispatches recalling him to Washington. (The third letter, prompted by news of the envoy's bribery attempt, arrived shortly thereafter.) Trist was shocked. He found his new instructions baffling, based upon a total misconception of political and military realities in Mexico, and he resented the distant manner in which Buchanan conveyed the ill tidings. Nowhere in either of the secretary's messages was there a word of appreciation for the five months of effort Trist had invested in his mission, the hardships undergone, the challenges met, the risks run. Trist had shouldered an assignment unprecedented in American diplomatic history, and he remains the only envoy to accompany a U.S. army into combat with power to negotiate a peace treaty on the battlefield, but the administration did not acknowledge how demanding his situation was or make allowances for the fact that he sometimes had to improvise. Instead, Buchanan accosted him in the manner of a shopkeeper scolding a delinquent delivery boy. For the proud, high-strung Trist, this was the unkindest cut of all.

Nevertheless, his initial reply indicated that he would obey the president. He was, of course, upset, observing that, should he ever find time, he might examine the "grounds for the censure" Polk had cast on his conduct. That, though, was a theme so insignificant that he would take it up only when he had nothing else to occupy him. For now, as he saw it, the one way in which he could be said to have exceeded his "carefully considered instructions" was in his willingness to explore whether Polk could be accommodating on the Rio Grande boundary issue, and he had only agreed to refer that question to Washington because he believed such a gesture was necessary to "preserve a chance for a peace." Had he stood firm, he argued, Santa Anna would have ordered his representatives to break off talks and the war would have resumed. Surely Polk understood that negotiations involved more than one party telling another what to do, no matter how great the imbalance of power between them! The key passage in Trist's letter came toward the end, however, when he described for Buchanan how, upon learning of the recall order, Anaya and his lieutenants begged the envoy to stay on, as did other Mexican peace

[66] NT to Buchanan, 6 December 1847, *DCUS*, 8:993; NT to Buchanan, 7 November 1847, ibid., 8:972.

advocates. "To these entreaties," Trist wrote, "I have turned a deaf ear." He would depart for Veracruz, and thence to the United States, as soon as practicable.[67]

On the surface, that was an accurate account of developments in Mexico after the arrival of Buchanan's bombshell. Trist called on British chargé Edward Thornton to tell him the news, and Thornton rode to Querétaro to convey it to Peña, who wept, lamenting, "All is lost." Apparently at Thornton's suggestion, Peña decided to act as though he had not received this message. He sent an already-drafted letter to Trist announcing that the new government had at last appointed a peace commission; the negotiations begun in August, he said, "may be continued" and "bring to an end the calamities of the war." In forwarding the letter, Thornton enclosed a note of his own. "I leave it to your charity for this unhappy nation to lend a hand toward the preservation of her nationality," he declared. "I look upon this as the last chance for either party of making peace." Despite this appeal, Trist dutifully informed Peña that his mission was over and that he had to return "without delay to the U.S." He expressed his hope that a treaty would be concluded soon, even if "another hand than mine" must sign it.[68]

Trist's response to Thornton, though, struck a more equivocal note. It was here that he first hinted that he might break ranks on the weightiest of all foreign-policy matters, war or peace – although he seemed to dismiss the notion after bringing it up. A typical Trist treatise, the letter was wordy and histrionic, with sentences that devoured entire pages and the author alternating between excesses of self-pity and self-importance. He was, he wrote, "divested entirely of the official character which I lately held, and with it all shadow of authority to do anything whatever." Yet he remained committed to serving his country. Career meant nothing to him: "My position is the very reverse of that of a person entertaining aspirations which would make him dread the displeasure of those entrusted with the power of dispensing office." He told Thornton that, "in a case of such magnitude as this, no personal consequence to myself ... could deter me from assuming responsibilities to any extent, if by so doing I could substantially promote the object of my government in sending me here." Indeed, he proclaimed, "I would stop short of

---

[67] NT to Buchanan, 18 November 1947, *DCUS*, 8:981–984.

[68] Peña cited in Ohrt, *Defiant Peacemaker*, 134; Peña to NT, 22 November 1847, *DCUS*, 8:973–974; Thornton to NT, 22 November 1847, Reel 9, NPTP-LOC; NT to Peña, 24 November 1847, Reel 11, NPTP-LOC.

nothing, ... not even the point of disobeying positive and peremptory instructions, such as those which have come to me."

Then he backed away from the brink, concluding that this was "an impossibility," that "the cause of peace could not fail to be seriously prejudiced were I to pursue any other course than that of the most absolute and unqualified acquiescence in the executive will." As a private citizen without portfolio, fallen from the president's good grace, he could not make a treaty acceptable to his government. Perhaps he could accomplish more at home than he had been able to in Mexico. Meanwhile, he took solace in the knowledge that, after he left, Scott would spare no effort to assist the Anaya government. Bidding his hosts to "be of good cheer," Trist set about packing his bags.[69]

Yet he could not travel from Mexico City to the coast right away. Three considerations made that unfeasible. First, he felt obliged to await the arrival of his replacement, whom he planned to bring up to speed on events in Mexico. Second, the journey was too dangerous to undertake without a strong escort, and Scott had few men to spare. Rather than deplete the general's forces, Trist informed Buchanan that he would accompany the next wagon train to Veracruz, which was scheduled to depart on 5 December. Finally, Scott had brought court martial proceedings against Gideon Pillow for dereliction of duty, and Trist had agreed to appear as a witness. He could not leave before testifying.[70]

It was an assignment Trist relished. Aware by now that Pillow had been badmouthing him, Trist concluded, not unreasonably, that the general's poison letters to Polk had played a role in his dismissal. "A baser villain and dirtier scoundrel does not exist out of the penitentiary nor *in* it than General Pillow," Trist wrote his wife. "This is not an *opinion* but a matter of fact." Pillow had done "infinite mischief" over the past months, and only incarceration could prevent him from "deepening the already unfathomable disgrace which he has brought on Mr. Polk." Since Trist was aware of Polk's fondness for Pillow and dislike of Scott, he must have known that his contribution to this military court of inquiry would further incense the president, but he yielded to his passions, more interested in vengeance than survival. "I have bid adieu *forever* to official life," he declared. "The decision is irrevocable." He went so far as to instruct Virginia Trist to personally tell Buchanan that he would not be returning to State, as though it were still an option: "He will soon see the impossibility of this or of my having *anything* to do with Mr. Polk." A subsequent letter contained the pronouncement, "I will live on bread and water before I will again hold office of any kind." That proved an accurate forecast.[71]

As Trist lingered at army headquarters, he encountered daily reminders of how precarious the political situation was. *Moderados* called on him to find out if rumors of his dismissal were true, and upon discovering that they were, expressed dismay. It was, he said, "the coup de grace for them." They told Trist that if peace did not come soon, the Anaya government would collapse, and it might be years before such an opportunity arose again. Trist, alarmed, wrote to Buchanan demanding "the immediate appointment of a commissioner" to take charge of the peace talks. The next Mexican Congress was set to convene on 8 January, he observed, and the *Moderados* had a majority, but their control of the legislature would be short-lived. Mexican and American diplomats needed to forge a treaty *now* if they wanted to be sure of Congress ratifying it. Days passed, however, and no one showed up to relieve Trist, whose concern turned to panic when he received copies of prominent U.S. newspapers announcing, among other things, that Polk had chosen not to send a new peace commissioner, that he had "fully decided" on "the military occupation of the country," and that his cabinet was weighing the question of whether "the nationality of Mexico should be annihilated."[72]

Polk had not, in fact, joined the all-Mexico movement, but reports of his refusal to appoint a replacement for Trist were accurate, and he was increasingly tempted by suggestions that the United States punish Mexico for prolonging the war by insisting on greater territorial concessions than those outlined in the April 1847 draft treaty. In any event, Trist had no way to distinguish between truth and falsehood at so great a remove from Washington. These stories contributed to his impression that U.S. foreign policy had gone off the rails. He read and reread his letters of dismissal, finding in them nothing to indicate that Polk had any aim other than that of obtaining peace. Quite the contrary: Buchanan explicitly stated that the reason the president had fired Trist was because he felt this gesture would expedite the peace process. How to reconcile that modest motive with the grandiose claims of the journalists and editors? And what to make of those senior U.S. army officials like General William Worth who voiced

---

[71] NT to VT, 28 November 1847, Reel 2, NPTP-LOC; NT to VT, 1 February 1848, ibid.
[72] NT to Buchanan, 27 November 1847, *DCUS*, 8:982–983; newspapers cited in Mahin, *Olive Branch and Sword*, 142–143.

their desire to absorb America's neighboring republic? "That our race is finally destined to overrun the whole continent is too obvious to need proof," Worth boasted around the time Trist's recall order arrived. "It is our decided policy to hold the whole of Mexico." While Trist hoped the jingoistic general spoke only for himself, he was tormented by fear that such views had won favor in the White House.[73]

The "Memorial to Congress" Trist wrote in early 1848, when events were still fresh in his memory, provided a graphic account of how he wrestled with his emotions during this crucial time. "Benumbing despair had taken possession of me," he remembered, "and all power of thought was occupied exclusively in tracing and brooding over the fatal consequences which stood out in bold relief before me, as things which had become inevitable through the loss of this last chance for restoring peace." Those consequences were indeed fatal. Anaya's administration would not survive a complete shutdown in negotiations. His adversaries, once in command, were likely to draw the U.S. army of occupation into a long, inconclusive guerrilla war. Unable to sleep, Trist wrote Thornton with the question that consumed him: "What is my line of duty to my government and my country in this extraordinary position in which I find myself?"[74]

Several accounts of Trist's mission credit Thornton with helping the envoy frame an answer to that question. According to these texts, Thornton pressed Trist to stay and complete a treaty, assuring him that if he extracted favorable terms from Mexico, the White House and Congress would have to accept the result. Certainly, Trist was aware that Thornton disapproved of Polk's directive, but there is no evidence that the chargé tipped the scales in favor of mutiny. He was in Querétaro when Trist chose that path, and while his letters did depict a Mexican government keen on peace, they also took as given that Trist was closing up shop and that someone else would have to renew negotiations for the Americans. As for Scott, whom historians have also identified as a source of encouragement, he never counseled his young colleague to defy Polk.[75]

---

[73] Worth cited in John D. P. Fuller, *The Movement for the Acquisition of All Mexico, 1846–1848* (Baltimore: Johns Hopkins University Press, 1936), 94.

[74] Trist Memorial; NT to Thornton 4 December 1847, *DCUS*, 8:985.

[75] For works which stress Scott's or Thornton's contribution to this act, see Bauer, *Mexican War*, 382; Eisenhower, *So Far from God*, 361; Morgan, *Lions of the West*, 383; Merry, *Country of Vast Designs*, 399; Ohrt, *Defiant Peacemaker*, 139; Pletcher, *Diplomacy of Annexation*, 538–539. In his memorial to Congress, Trist insisted, "The truth is that the emperor of China had as much to do with this determination of mine as General Scott or any other man . . . had." Trist Memorial.

Only one person played a direct role in Trist's decision, and even he appears to have served as a launching pad for measures already determined upon. James Freaner, a reporter for the New Orleans *Delta* whom Trist had befriended and whose assignment was to travel with the army, dropped by Trist's quarters for a chat on 4 December, the day before the envoy planned to leave for Veracruz. Freaner was shocked to learn that Polk had stripped Trist of authority. When Trist told Freaner something he had not revealed to anyone, that he was thinking of disobeying the president and staying to conclude peace, Freaner's response was enthusiastic. Trist recalled him urging, "Mr. Trist, make the treaty. Make the treaty, sir! It is now in your power to do your country a greater service than any living man can render her. … Make the treaty, sir! You are bound to do it. Instructions or no instructions, you are bound to do it. Your country, sir, is entitled to this service from you. Do it, sir! She will support you in it, instructions or no instructions!" To which Trist, afire, bolted from his chair and declared, "I *will* make the treaty!" In spite of professional and economic ruin, in spite of possible executive charges of treason, he would perform the great work providence had assigned him – instructions or no instructions.[76]

Whether that conversation took place as Trist remembered is debatable. His narrative is so histrionic as to strain credibility, and he amped up the blood and thunder when he described his inner monologue at the moment of decision. "I stood there as the only man living by whom the work could be done," he wrote. "It must be done by *me* or remain undone long enough for any chances of its being done to be lost. … The only doubtful point was the *possibility* of its being done. That possibility was universally believed to have received its deathblow by my recall. Its resuscitation was, at best, a slender chance – a forlorn hope." Trist, however, made up his mind to grasp that last straw "as an act of solemn duty to my country." Conscious of the enormity of his decision, he called it "an event that stands alone in history, and is not likely ever to have a parallel."[77]

Trist's correspondence for that evening throbbed with vainglory. A letter to his wife contained the following postscript, in cipher: "Knowing it to be the very last chance, and impressed with the dreadful consequences

---

[76] Trist Memorial.
[77] NT to Felton, 5 April 1870, Reel 7, NPTP-LOC; Trist Memorial. See also Thomas J. Farnham, "Nicholas Trist and James Freaner and the Mission to Mexico," *Journal of the Southwest* 11 (Autumn 1969): 247.

to our country which cannot fail to attend the loss of that chance, I will make a treaty, if it can be done." He insisted that the decision was "*altogether* my *own*" – which was doubtless true.[78]

To Thornton, he wrote a characteristically overlong dispatch almost comic in its "*You're not going to believe this*" breathlessness. "This letter will occasion you great surprise," he gushed, "but no greater than I should myself have experienced a few hours ago, had a seer, in whose prophetic powers I put faith, foretold to me that I was to write it." Although he knew he was cutting his professional throat, he had decided to be the instrument of Mexico's – and America's – salvation. As Thornton knew, "if the present opportunity be not seized *at once*, all chance for making a treaty *at all* will be lost." Therefore, "I am now resolved and committed to carry home with me a treaty of peace." Trist told Thornton, who he knew would relay the information to Peña and Anaya, that the only treaty terms he would accept were those contained in his earlier proposal, meaning the Rio Grande boundary for Texas and the cession of New Mexico and California. The Mexicans must decide either to relinquish this territory for around $20 million or "surrender at once to the *Puros* and dismiss all thoughts of a treaty." Trist's terms were the best Mexico could hope to get. Any new conditions issued from Washington would not be as lenient as those he was presenting now. Polk, impatient at the lack of progress, was certain to demand more land and offer less money for it. And time was not on the side of peace. Trist signed off with a gratuitous warning: "'Now or never' is the word."[79]

"INFALLIBILITY OF JUDGMENT . . . IS NOT AMONG THE ATTRIBUTES OF THE PRESIDENT"

While Thornton bore news of Trist's decision to the Mexican commissioners, the envoy set about justifying that decision to his government. For two days, he banged away at a letter that, when completed, filled sixty-one pages. Polk called it "the most extraordinary document I have ever heard from a diplomatic representative," which indicates that he had not run across Trist's dispatches from Havana. Compared to those philippics, this effort was restrained. It also stuck more or less to the topic at hand, as Trist organized it around the four assumptions that underlay his insurgentism: first, that "peace is still the desire of my government";

[78] NT to VT, 4 December 1847, Reel 2, NPTP-LOC.
[79] NT to Thornton, 4 December 1847, *DCUS*, 8:984–985.

second, that the "boundary proposed by me … is the utmost point to which the Mexican government can by any possibility venture"; third, if an American representative did not exploit the chance for peace immediately all hope of ending the conflict would disappear, "probably forever"; and fourth, that Polk had based his decision to relieve Trist on the "incorrect preconception" that conditions in Mexico were not favorable to peace, or were less favorable than when Trist began his exchanges with Santa Anna's delegates.

None of these premises was unwarranted, and had Trist communicated them temperately he might have brought Polk around to his view that the wisest course was indeed for him to continue talks under his original instructions. But, as always, such reserve was beyond him. He belabored each postulate for pages, with eye-glazing, mind-numbing sentences like the following defense of Scott's armistice after the victory at Churubusco:

His nature is too lofty, his perceptions of high principles too clear, his obedience to them too steady and habitual, to admit of his swerving, under the influence of ill feelings, from his line of duty as a servant of his country, and, governed as he was by this sense of duty, no servile tool of party could have been more earnestly or more anxiously solicitous to fulfill the wish, the all engrossing wish, of the administration, than he proved himself to be on this occasion, and on every occasion when the fulfillment of that wish could be in any degree affected by aught which he could do, or which he could omit doing.

Buried under that rock pile was a valid point about the armistice being unmotivated by political considerations, but one doubts that either Polk or Buchanan had the inclination to blast for it.

Since Trist knew that Pillow was the source of much of the misinformation that drove Polk's policy, he attacked the general, soaring to new heights of opprobrium. Pillow, he declared, "pollutes this glorious army by his presence." He was a "most worthy compeer of Santa Anna, so far as he can be made so by the same low craving for distinction and the same happy felicity for deviating from the ways of truth." He had been feeding the president "nonsense," "chicanery," and "*balderdash* – unworthy, disgraceful balderdash" that "insulted the intelligence of our country" and ought not to be credited by anyone, "however low in understanding." Yet this "intriguer" somehow enjoyed Polk's "blind confidence" despite "the unimaginable and incomprehensible baseness of his character." That Polk "allowed himself to be governed" by such a man, wrote Trist, was a "deep disgrace to our country – as she will ere long deeply feel."

Trist had by this point lost all chance of a sympathetic hearing, and he drove the final nail in his casket with the observation: "Infallibility of judgment ... is not among the attributes of the president of the United States, even when his sentences rest upon full and accurate knowledge of all the facts and circumstances on which their justice depends." Polk lacked such knowledge. Trist therefore felt justified in disregarding his order.[80]

While it is Trist's style that strikes the eye of a twenty-first-century audience – the hyperbole, the acrimony, the sentences that read like carelessly unwound rolls of toilet paper – those eccentricities should not detract from the fact that his assessment of the military and political state of affairs in Mexico in December 1847 was, for the most part, accurate. Trist was not an infallible observer, as his misjudgment of Santa Anna's calculations reveals, and he shared the paternalistic view of Mexicans common to Americans of his generation; nonetheless, analysts generally agree that he sized up matters well. Timothy Henderson, author of the most comprehensive treatment of the losing side in the Mexican-American War, argues that an immediate peace was essential to keep Mexico from "spinning wildly out of control." Had the *Moderados* fallen, he insists, other factions would have fought in vain among themselves to gain a majority in the legislature, and there would have been no government with whom to treat. Revolution might well have occurred, or the nation might have splintered into warring states. Meanwhile, the army, Mexico's chief instrument of law enforcement, was so demoralized that it would have been unable to prevent complete "social disintegration." Trist was right to worry that Washington, by its failure to capitalize on the break in the war clouds, risked plunging Mexico into chaos and the United States into a quagmire.[81]

Furthermore, although Trist exaggerated in his memorial to Congress when he claimed that Polk had a secret plot to annex America's southern neighbor, he was not far wrong in his estimation of the general trajectory of U.S. foreign policy. The all-Mexico movement, once a fringe campaign embraced only by diehard Manifest-Destiny zealots, had rapidly shifted from the margins to the mainstream of American political opinion after the capture of Mexico City. Protracted stalemate could have made it the

---

[80] Diary Entry, 15 January 1848, *DJKP*, 3:300; NT to Buchanan, 6 December 1847, *DCUS*, 8:984–1020.

[81] Timothy J. Henderson, *A Glorious Defeat: Mexico and Its War with the United States* (New York: Hill and Wang, 2007), 172–178. See also Pedro Santoni, *Mexicans at Arms: Puro Federalists and the Politics of War, 1845–1848* (Fort Worth: Texas Christian University Press, 1996), 232–233.

dominant view. In the only book-length examination of this phenomenon, John Fuller does not equivocate. "The movement for absorption had gained sufficient momentum" by "the fall and early winter of 1847," he writes, that if "the war had continued several months longer, ... Mexico would now be part of the United States." Among "the people, in the administration, and in Congress," there was "a widespread belief that peace could be established only by the extinction of Mexican independence," because Americans were becoming increasingly convinced of "the impossibility of forcing Mexico to agree to an honorable peace." By defying Polk and concluding the Treaty of Guadalupe Hidalgo, Trist proved that this was not an impossibility, thereby robbing the annexationists of their strongest argument. He also deprived them of another factor essential to their crusade: time. Fuller contends that the "most important" reason for "the failure of this country to annex Mexico in 1848" was the "lack of time for expansionist settlement to develop," and that the "unprecedented action of Nicholas P. Trist is largely responsible for this fact." All-Mexico devotees had not yet won over the majority of Americans as the new year dawned, but they were gathering steam, poised to make annexation the paramount issue of the 1848 presidential contest, when Trist removed it from the realm of politics by presenting Polk with a fait accompli that the president believed he had no choice but to accept. Those "who feel that the absorption of Mexico in 1848 would have meant permanent injury to the best interests of the United States," Fuller concludes, "should be extremely grateful" to Polk's ex-envoy, to whom "not a little credit is due for the fact that Mexico is today an independent nation."[82]

And absorption *would* have meant permanent injury. Americans had never before attempted to militarily occupy an enemy nation. They had

[82] Fuller, *Movement for the Acquisition*, 93, 100, 104–105, 125, 157, 163. Glyndon Van Deusen concurs, observing that the "formidable demand that the United States take over all of Mexico" was "coming to its peak in the winter of 1847–48. ... It is possible, even probable, that Trist's refusal to obey his final instructions prevented the absorption of Mexico by the United States." Glyndon Van Deusen, *The Jacksonian Era* (New York: Harper & Brothers, 1959), 239. Thomas Bailey, mentor to a generation of diplomatic historians, puts the case just as strongly. Trist's disobedience was critical "in stopping the all-Mexico boom," he affirms. "The discredited Trist, by courageously violating his instructions, probably saved the United States from prolonged guerrilla warfare and the staggering problems that would have arisen from trying to absorb the more densely settled portions of Mexico." Bailey, *Diplomatic History of the American People*, 265. For a recent statement of this thesis, see Timothy Evans Buttram, "'Swallowing Mexico without Any Grease': The Absence of Controversy over the Feasibility of Annexing All Mexico" (Ph.D. Dissertation: University of New Hampshire, 2008).

no idea how large a force would be required, but it would have had to be many times the size of the 24,000-man U.S. Army in Mexico in late 1847. Polk would have found it impossible to put that many men under arms, since the United States did not have a draft at the time. Those Americans who fought in Mexico did so as volunteers or as members of the regular army, and even during the war's early stages, when enthusiasm for the effort was high, most volunteers enlisted for a year or less. Few reenlisted after their terms expired. Given how unpopular the conflict had become after twenty months without victory, it is certain that the number of enlistments would have decreased had Polk decided to expand the war's aims to include acquisition of Mexico. In addition, the Whig-dominated House of Representatives, which in January 1848 resolved that the war had been "unnecessarily and unconstitutionally begun by the president of the United States," would have been reluctant to approve expenditures for such an expansion. Polk would have had neither the men nor the money to engage in a long-term, open-ended campaign to make Mexico part of the Union.[83]

Even if, as some historians claim, Polk was deaf to the all-Mexico siren song and only intended to seize territory between the Rio Grande and the 26th parallel – or a somewhat more northern boundary dubbed the "Sierra Madre line" – he would still have faced the same military, political, and financial difficulties involved in taking over the entire country. The northern provinces of Mexico would have resisted annexation. Despite claims by American politicians and newsmen at the war's outset that Coahuila, Chihuahua, Sonora, and Nueva León were eager to place themselves beneath the folds of the Stars and Stripes, the grim experience of Zachary Taylor's forces at Monterrey, Buena Vista, and elsewhere proved otherwise. Polk could only have held that zone by force, and he would have been unable to raise an army anywhere near the necessary strength for such an assignment. Guerrilla warfare and disease would have carried off U.S. soldiers by the thousands, deepening political divisions at home and exacerbating discontent with "Mr. Polk's War."[84]

---

[83] Resolution, 4 January 1848, *Congressional Globe*, 30th Congress, 1st Session (Washington, D.C.: Blair & Rives, 1848), 19:95.

[84] For studies contending that Polk's ambition stopped short of the forcible incorporation of Mexico into the Union, see Bauer, *Mexican War*, 370; E. G. Bourne, "The United States and Mexico, 1847–1848," *American Historical Review* 5 (April 1900): 491–502; Christensen, *U.S.-Mexican War*, 218; Graebner, *Empire on the Pacific*, 203; Pletcher, *Diplomacy of Annexation*, 552–555; Reeves, *American Diplomacy under Tyler and Polk*, 325.

In addition, no Mexican government would have agreed to territorial concessions below the Rio Grande. Trist was right when he admonished Buchanan in his 6 December dispatch, "However helpless a nation may feel, there is necessarily a point beyond which she cannot be expected to go, under any circumstances, in surrendering her territory as the price of peace." The government in Querétaro had reached that point: "Earnest as is their desire for peace and for the preservation of their nationality, the Peace Party will not go a hair-breadth further. . . . They *can*not go further. It would be utterly impossible to obtain the ratification of any such treaty." Anaya and his cabinet were already being condemned as traitors for surrendering Mexico's far north; had they yielded more land in the Rio Grande valley, they would either have been ejected from office by the Mexican Congress or overthrown in a military coup. Only a puppet regime installed and supported by Washington could have countenanced further sacrifice of national honor, and the imposition of such a government on the Mexican people would have done irreparable damage not only to U.S.-Mexican relations but also to relations between the United States and Latin America.[85]

Trist was also right to challenge Polk's presumption that the presence of an American negotiator in Mexico made the achievement of peace more difficult. Under pressure from war hawks and expansionists in his cabinet, Polk had recalled Trist because he did not want to embolden the Mexicans by giving them the impression that he was desperate to end the war. He hoped to signal Washington's resolve by withdrawing U.S. diplomatic representation and obliging the enemy to sue for peace. If carried out, this policy would have been disastrous. The Mexicans had proven unwilling to negotiate despite persistent entreaties by the president's envoy on the spot. It is doubtful that any Mexican government would have seized the initiative and proposed terms that satisfied Polk; at least they would not have done so until it was too late to prevent the demise of the Mexican republic. A few more months of war would have sufficed to make annexation a foregone conclusion for most Americans, and even if Polk's initial response to the lack of a Mexican peace offer was to demand something less than the whole country, the practical consequences of that demand would have been a military occupation, the establishment of a figurehead government propped up by American bayonets, and the arousal of anti-Yankee sentiment throughout South America that might never have died down.

[85] NT to Buchanan, 6 December 1847, *DCUS*, 8:997.

Finally, there was the all-consuming matter of slavery. Dean Mahin persuasively argues that if Trist had obeyed orders and left Mexico, the war would have continued throughout the presidential election of 1848, and this would have made it much more difficult for Whigs and Democrats to "paper over their internal divisions on the slavery issue." With the extent of annexed Mexican territory still in doubt, the question of whether slavery ought to be admitted into that territory would have dominated debate during the campaign and further envenomed America's already toxic political climate – a development which, Mahin contends, "could have prevented the great compromise masterminded in 1850 by Henry Clay" and led to civil war in the early 1850s, *before* "the increases in population, industry, agriculture, and railroads" above the Mason-Dixon Line gave the Union its decisive advantage over the Confederacy. Secession might have become an accomplished fact.[86]

We do not have to accept every dire counterfactual scenario to recognize that December 1847 was a watershed moment, a juncture at which the United States stood poised between two paths with drastically different implications for the country's future, and that one man made the decision that shaped the fates of millions. Mexicans and Americans alike can count themselves fortunate he chose as he did. Trist may have been a long-winded writer, but on this occasion the wind was blowing in the right direction.

"ENSLAVEMENT AND EXTINCTION"

The day after Trist finished writing his letter to Buchanan, and weeks before the secretary of state received it, Polk delivered his annual message to Congress. As in all such documents, the president addressed a range of matters, foreign and domestic. He reported on the effects of his tariff program, the record number of immigrants flooding into the country, friction with Indian tribes along the frontier, and other subjects. Appropriately, however, he devoted the bulk of the address to the Mexican War, and what he said seemed to confirm Trist's darkest suspicions. After giving a slanted account of how the conflict began, he praised the "unequaled bravery" and "glorious victories" of America's soldiers and acknowledged what had become an open secret: "Believing that, after these successes so honorable to our arms and so disastrous to Mexico, the

---

[86] Mahin, *Olive Branch and Sword*, 199–200.

period was propitious to afford her an opportunity ... to enter into negotiations for peace, a commissioner was appointed to proceed to the headquarters of our army with full powers ... to conclude a just and honorable treaty."

Alas, the Mexicans had "shown themselves to be wholly incapable of appreciating our forbearance." When Scott had halted the American army at the gates of Mexico City, Santa Anna's peace delegation had presented "inadmissible" terms that "they must have known ... could never be accepted." Polk had therefore taken off the white gloves. "Believing that his continued presence with the army could have been productive of no good, I determined to recall our commissioner," the president revealed, adding, "I shall not deem it proper to make any further overtures of peace."

Possibly as a sop to the antiwar Whigs, Polk insisted, "It has never been contemplated by me, as an object of the war, to make a permanent conquest of the Republic of Mexico." On the other hand, Washington had spent a great deal of blood and treasure and was entitled to indemnity for its sacrifices. "Mexico has no money to pay," Polk pointed out. "The only means by which she can reimburse the United States for the expenses of the war is a cession to the United States of a portion of her territory." And given the Mexican government's intransigence, Washington had every right to demand a large portion. California and New Mexico would surely become part of the Union – "I am satisfied that they should never be surrendered to Mexico" – but U.S. troops had conquered other provinces as well, and Polk hinted that he might seize them as compensation for war expenses incurred since he issued his initial peace terms. The fate of those territories, he said, "must depend on the future progress of the war, and the course which Mexico make think proper hereafter to pursue." If the Mexicans continued to frustrate American attempts to bring the conflict to a conclusion, they had only themselves to blame for the shrinkage of their national domain.

The above comments were alarming enough to Anaya and his cabinet, but Polk went a giant step further, declaring that it might be necessary "for our commanding generals in the field to give encouragement and assurances of protection to the friends of peace in Mexico in the establishment and maintenance of a free republican government, ... able and willing to conclude a peace." Polk predicted that such an outcome would be "an enduring blessing" to Mexico: "After finding her torn and distracted by factions and ruled by military usurpers, we should then leave her with a republican government in the enjoyment of real independence." To this naïve claim, which rested on the assumption that America in the mid-nineteenth century was capable of carrying out long-term democratization policies similar to those implemented in Japan and West Germany after World War II, Polk added another threat. "If, after affording this encouragement and protection, ... we shall ultimately fail" to establish a tractable Mexican government, he said, "then we shall have exhausted all honorable means in pursuit of peace, and must continue to occupy her country with our troops." A reasonable person could interpret this to mean that if the war did not end soon, and with Mexico's surrender, Mexico would lose its sovereignty.[87]

That was Trist's conclusion when he read the text of the president's message in late December 1847. He warned Buchanan that Polk was playing into the hands of those Mexicans who sought "the subjugation of their country and the enslavement and extinction of their race." To Trist, the measures Polk proposed, if not calculated to bring about annexation, could scarcely have a different result. The majority of Mexicans would never stand for a client regime imposed on them by Washington; they would resist it "at whatever risk, at whatever cost, and by whatever means," drawing the United States into a contest fatal "to the peace and welfare of both nations." Rather than establishing a new government, Trist argued, Washington should "*maintain* what is already established" and "*protect* it against military violence and usurpation." Anaya and his ministers had been working to conclude the war on terms that would both satisfy American demands and preserve Mexican independence, and they had been making headway until Polk's message appeared in every newspaper south of the Rio Grande. "The arrival of the message at this critical instant," wrote Trist, "may be attended with consequences similar to those produced by the appearance of Bulow and Blucher on the field of Waterloo!"[88]

Here Trist stretched the truth. December had been a frustrating month for the friends of peace even before Polk's address became public knowledge in Mexico. By taking the suicidal step of disobeying the president, Trist expected to jump-start negotiations and wrap up a treaty in days, but he failed to reckon with the peculiarities of the Mexican system of

---

[87] Third Annual Message, 7 December 1847, *A Compilation of the Messages and Papers of the Presidents, 1789–1897*, James D. Richardson, ed. (Washington, D.C.: U.S. Government Printing Office, 1898), 5:532–564.

[88] NT to Buchanan, 26 December 1847, *DCUS*, 8:1025; NT to Buchanan, 29 December 1947, ibid., 8:1028–1032.

government. An embarrassed Peña informed Trist that, anxious as he was to begin deliberation, proceedings could not commence before the Senate had confirmed all peace commissioners, and Congress was not due to convene again until 1 January. Trist's demands that the Mexicans find some way around this constitutional requirement proved fruitless. The wheels of diplomacy did not begin to turn until 2 January 1848, when Trist met with his opposite numbers in the town of Guadalupe Hidalgo, a few miles north of the capital.[89]

This seemed a propitious venue. It was the site of the most hallowed shrine in the Western Hemisphere, marking where the Virgin Mary allegedly appeared in 1531, and Trist felt that a treaty concluded in such a spot might gain acceptance among the devout Mexican people. Sadly, Anaya's commissioners were not awed by the sacrosanctity of the setting. While the terms they proposed were more moderate than anything Santa Anna had considered, they were still unacceptable, and some of them were absurd, especially the requirement that U.S. forces withdraw from Mexico during negotiations. The commissioners also insisted that the treaty be guaranteed by neutral powers and that it contain a provision stipulating that future disputes between Mexico and the United States be subject to arbitration.[90]

Trist recognized that these demands were designed in part to save face. Anaya needed to be able to counter charges that he had sold out the country with a record of his attempts to uphold Mexican honor. Nonetheless, the negotiators were racing against the clock, and Trist's patience, never his strong suit, wore thin. When the Mexicans tried to avoid complete capitulation on the Texas boundary issue by suggesting that the dividing line run parallel to, but a league north of, the Rio Grande, Trist exploded. "As to any other boundary than the middle of the river," he said, "it would be a waste of words to talk about it." Did Anaya's men not recall how harshly Polk had reprimanded Trist for giving ground on this point? Were they not aware that any day now another envoy, less sympathetic to Mexico's plight and bearing instructions to demand tougher treaty terms, might arrive to take Trist's place? Or that Scott might receive orders to undertake further operations involving, perhaps, the seizure of Querétaro? Trist protested that he was risking everything, even his freedom, to fashion an agreement that would ensure that Mexico

[89] Sierra to NT, 15 December 1847, *DCUS*, 8:1025.
[90] NT Notes, 2 January 1848, Reel 9, NPTP-LOC.

remained among the world's independent nations. The least the Mexicans could do was to stop dragging their feet.[91]

Adding to Trist's anxiety was the fact that these negotiations unfolded amid political bedlam. Less than a week after talks began, Anaya's term as president *ad interim* ran out. Delays in the election of several legislators meant that Congress could not muster a quorum to choose a successor, so Peña, who was still senior justice of the Supreme Court, assumed the office of president again, with greater reluctance than before. The *Santanistas* and *Puros* renewed their attacks on him and his party and he confronted an uprising in San Luis Potosí that looked as though it might spread to other states. Such developments left Trist even more convinced of the indispensability of a speedy peace. Yet he could report no progress to State. It appeared his gamble had failed.[92]

"I HAVE NEVER IN MY LIFE FELT SO INDIGNANT"

In Washington, Polk learned of Trist's insubordination by stages. On 30 December 1847, the envoy's initial response to the recall order arrived. While Polk was irritated by the bad grace with which Trist accepted a presidential directive, he had no reason to think it might be disobeyed. Then, four days into the new year, Polk received word from a British courier that Trist had resumed negotiations with Anaya's commissioners. The president was furious – although, tellingly, most of his anger was directed against Scott, whom he suspected of having encouraged Trist to flout orders. Trist "is acting, no doubt, upon General Scott's advice," Polk wrote in his diary. "He has become the perfect tool of Scott. ... He seems to have entered into all of Scott's hatred of the administration, and to be lending himself to all Scott's evil purposes." The next day, Buchanan read Polk the coded postscript of Trist's 4 December letter to his wife, which Virginia Trist had given to Buchanan and in which the envoy stated that the decision to ignore a Polk's decree was "altogether my own." Polk was aghast. "His conduct astonishes both the secretary of state and myself," he recorded, noting that Trist "has acknowledged the receipt of his letter of recall and has no power to treat." Unable to blame Trist's revolt on Scott, Polk nonetheless decided to take an action he had been contemplating for a long time: he removed Old Fuss and Feathers from

---

NT Notes 3 January 1848, Reel 9, NPTP-LOC.
Ohrt, *Defiant Peacemaker*, 142; Pletcher, *Diplomacy of Annexation*, 543; Santoni, *Mexicans at Arms*, 222–227.

command of the American army in Mexico and replaced him with General William Butler, a loyal Democrat.[93]

The president was thus already in a vengeful mood when, on 15 January, he received Trist's sixty-one-page dispatch explaining why he had chosen to remain in Mexico and complete a treaty. Now Polk's rage knew no bounds. He found the message "arrogant, impudent, and very insulting to the government, and even personally insulting to the president." That last quality, in Polk's view, was most objectionable. "I have never in my life felt so indignant," he fumed. Trist had "acted worse than any man in the public employ whom I have ever known. . . . If there is any legal provision for his punishment, he ought to be severely handled." Polk cut off Trist's compensation, both expenses and salary, beyond 16 November, the date the notice of removal was received, and ordered Buchanan to fire Trist *again.* Trist was "destitute of honor or principle," the president proclaimed. "He has proved himself to be a very base man." Polk moreover told Secretary of War Marcy to send a dispatch to the just-promoted Butler directing him to expel Trist from army headquarters and inform the government at Querétaro that Washington had canceled Trist's powers.[94]

Marcy demurred. He and other cabinet members raised a ticklish question. What if Trist had already signed a treaty? Trist's letters from early December indicated that he expected negotiations to begin at once. That was over a month ago. What if in the interim the Mexicans had agreed to Polk's peace terms, and the treaty was at that moment on its way back to Washington? Buchanan advised Polk that disavowing the envoy would be "proper" only if Polk had made up his mind to "reject any treaty which Mr. Trist might make." But if Polk found the treaty acceptable, how could he submit it to the Senate after having gone on record as repudiating its author? Perhaps he should wait until he had a chance to inspect the document. Secretary of the Treasury Walker agreed with Buchanan. Both wished to spare the president "embarrassments." Democratic Senators Lewis Cass and Ambrose Sevier likewise cautioned Polk against precipitate action. While they shared his outrage at Trist's "reprehensible conduct," calling it "not only insubordinate but infamous," they foresaw considerable awkwardness if Polk publicly spurned

---

[93] Diary Entries, 30 December 1847, 4, 5, and 8 January 1848, *DJKP*, 3:266–267, 283, 286, 293–294; Pillow to Polk, 12 December 1847, Reel 51, JKPP; Pillow to Polk, 21 December 1847, ibid.

[94] Diary Entry, 15 January 1848, *DJKP*, 3:300–302.

the renegade diplomat only to endorse his handiwork. Polk was not impervious to logic, especially if it was couched in terms of political advantage, but his anger toward Trist got the better of him and he had Marcy send the letter to Butler.[95]

Once again, the lag time in communication between Washington and Mexico worked to Trist's advantage. Butler would not learn of his promotion for weeks, and Scott, who supported Trist's effort to forge a peace, remained in charge of the U.S. army. As the president's order directing Scott to turn over his command was borne south, Scott and Trist tried to galvanize the negotiations to life by playing a good cop-bad cop routine in which Trist argued that acceptance of his treaty terms was the only way to prevent the general from making a descent upon Querétaro. The arrival in late January of thousands of fresh American troops lent force to this threat, as did a much-publicized banquet at which annexationist politicians offered Scott $1 million to take over the country. Scott had no intention of accepting this invitation, but he allowed Peña and his inner circle to think he might. Under the circumstances, it was not difficult for Trist to present himself as the voice of moderation.[96]

Yet he drove a hard bargain. Fears in Washington that he would accept peace at any price proved unfounded. However bitter he may have felt toward Polk, he strained every nerve and sinew to conclude a treaty consistent with the president's April instructions, and as the peace talks moved into their third week his efforts began to bear fruit. Peña's commissioners, who had earlier raised endless procedural objections and felt obliged to refer every sticking point to their government, came around to Trist's view that this approach was counterproductive. The American envoy was living on borrowed time. If the negotiators did not conclude their business soon, they might look up from their papers to find military policemen sent to place Trist under arrest. So the pace of deliberations accelerated. And Trist, normally fragile, seemed to grow haler by the moment. "At no other period of my life, so strong has my health become, could I have undertaken the same amount of labor," he wrote Buchanan. He kept an account of the daily sessions while participating in them and sent voluminous reports to Washington describing how the two sides sparred over a range of issues, chiefly the fixing of boundaries and the amount of money America would pay Mexico for its losses. It was, he said, an "exceedingly laborious" business, but he never

[95] Diary Entries, 23, 24, 25, and 26 January 1848, *DJKP*, 3:310–317.
[96] Smith, *Old Fuss and Feathers*, 339–340.

flagged. "My health is the admiration of everybody," he marveled in a letter to Virginia, noting that more than one person had told him, "You look younger every time I see you." Insubordination acted as a tonic.[97]

In determining the new border between the United States and Mexico, Trist and his counterparts confronted three territorial disputes involving the southern limits of Texas, New Mexico (which comprised the present states of New Mexico and Arizona), and California. The first dispute was most easily resolved. After making their bid for a cutoff point one league north of the Rio Grande, the Mexicans accepted Trist's argument that Washington had established the Rio Grande border by force of arms. Both parties agreed that the frontier line would follow that river until it reached 32 degrees north. New Mexico presented greater difficulty because the land being divided up had not been extensively surveyed and the map the negotiators used contained inaccuracies. Wrangling over the boundary would not cease until 1853, when the Gadsden Purchase completed the continental expansion of the contiguous United States, but Trist carried the day on this issue as far as his unreliable geographical information would allow. The language of the Treaty of Guadalupe Hidalgo with respect to New Mexico's southern border was virtually identical to that in the draft treaty Buchanan had given Trist in April.

As for California, Trist strove to ensure that the port of San Diego fell within the U.S. zone. He did not press for Baja California because Peña's commissioners showed him an intercepted dispatch from the State Department revealing that acquisition of the peninsula was not a sine qua non for the Polk administration. Mexican soldiers had seized this message, which State had neglected to encode, the previous summer, and thus the government in Querétaro knew that Trist would not jeopardize negotiations to obtain both Californias. Confronted with such evidence, Trist saw no point in challenging the commissioners' demand that Baja California remain Mexican.[98]

Where, however, did one California end and the other begin? "It appears," Trist wrote to Buchanan, "that no line of division was ever established between the two Californias." Trist therefore drew his own

---

[97] NT to Buchanan, 25 January 1848, *DCUS*, 8:1042–1043; NT to VT, 26 December 1847, Reel 2, NPTP-LOC. Trist's most detailed memoranda are from the first three days' discussion. After that, his notes become sketchier, probably due to time pressure. For a meticulous report of this bargaining written by Trist twenty years after it concluded, see NT to Felton, 8 June 1868, Reel 10, NPTP-LOC.

[98] See Eugene Keith Chamberlain, "Nicholas Trist and Baja California," *Pacific Historical Review* 32 (February 1963): 49–63.

line. Assisted by Scott's engineer and scout, Captain Robert E. Lee, he marked a boundary running from the mouth of the Gila River to a point seven miles south of San Diego. This diverged slightly from Buchanan's draft treaty, which stipulated that the 32nd parallel form the border, but it spared Mexico the humiliation of losing part of the states of Sonora and Chihuahua while still securing U.S. possession of a harbor that Polk considered as valuable as San Francisco's. After several days of debate, the Mexicans yielded and gave up their maritime prize. The unemployed diplomat had won another round.[99]

It was when discussion turned to the purchase price, though, that Trist truly shone. Perhaps because he had been dogged by financial difficulties most of his life, he proved an exceptionally frugal negotiator, intent on paying as little as possible for the domain the United States had wrenched from its southern neighbor. Peña instructed his commissioners to demand $30 million, a price Trist's original instructions permitted him to meet, but the envoy would not go beyond half of that. Mexico had unnecessarily prolonged the war after defeat was certain, Trist argued, and this had resulted in "increased expenditure of blood and treasure" by Washington. Any final figure must acknowledge that fact. Although he might have been willing to offer $20 million back in September when he first sat down with Santa Anna's representatives, the expense incurred since then was many times the $5 million he had taken off. All things considered, he felt he was being generous. The commissioners protested that $30 million was the minimum necessary to sustain the government in the face of attacks by the *Puros* and the rebellion in San Luis Potosí, but Trist stood his ground. He was "inflexible upon this point," he declared, "even at the risk of the treaty being lost." Indignant but stymied, the commissioners provisionally consented to the smaller sum, pending review by Peña and his cabinet.[100]

Trist was nearly as tight fisted with regard to the question of claims by American citizens against Mexico. Buchanan had authorized him to propose U.S. payment of all such claims up to $3 million, and Trist offered that amount, provided the claims had been filed before 13 May 1847. The commissioners complained that this was not enough. They sought an unqualified discharge from liability and demanded that no fixed amount appear in the treaty. Trist replied that the U.S. Senate would never approve an agreement "without their being informed what was the

[99] NT to Buchanan, 7 January 1848, *DCUS*, 8:1047.
[100] NT to Buchanan, 25 January 1848, *DCUS*, 8:1051.

extent of the obligation so incurred." He would raise the ceiling to three
and a quarter million, but not a penny more. It was "a waste of time" to
debate the matter further. Again, the commissioners gave way.[101]

A number of issues arose that Buchanan had not anticipated while
writing the draft treaty, and Trist had to play it by ear. With regard to the
status of Mexicans living in the ceded territories, he and the commissioners devised a flexible arrangement whereby such persons could depart if
they wished without being taxed for the removal of their property. If they
chose to stay, they could become American citizens after a year. Trist also
agreed to stipulations that the U.S. government would not seize churches
or church property and that Washington would assume responsibility for
cross-border raids by Native Americans.

The thorniest unforeseen issue involved a passage in Buchanan's draft
treaty that Trist initially thought immaterial but that the commissioners
recognized as vital. Buchanan had specified that "a suspension of hostilities" would take place after the *ratification* of the treaty by the Mexican
Congress. The commissioners insisted that hostilities end after the *signing*
of the treaty. Ratification could take weeks or months. How could Peña's
representatives allow what they called "the precious blood of our fellow
citizens" to flow during that interval? Trist saw the validity of this point,
but noted that "General Scott is totally without discretion on the subject,"
having clear orders from Marcy to keep fighting until the pact was
ratified. Still, Trist's heart was with the Mexicans. He sought to reassure
them. Scott's "instructions are to push the war with all possible vigor," he
said, but when the treaty was "ready for signature, ... I will lay it before
him, stating that its being signed depends upon his engaging to suspend
further movements until he can receive instructions from Washington."
Trist was certain that Old Fuss and Feathers would do the right thing. His
confidence, and his somewhat convoluted proposal, satisfied the
commissioners.[102]

By 25 January, both sides were in accord. Trist, who had taken care to
establish a greater degree of correspondence between the English and
Spanish versions of the treaty than was common in international agreements of that period, drafted copies in quintuplicate. All that was necessary to bring matters to a close was for Peña's government to give its
sanction, and Trist considered this a formality. Exhausted but triumphant, he reported to State, "The treaty agreed upon by myself and the

[101] NT to Buchanan, 22 January 1848, *DCUS*, 8:1052.
[102] NT to Buchanan, 12 January 1848, *DCUS*, 8:1032–1034.

Mexican plenipotentiaries will, according to every probability, be signed immediately upon the return of an express which has just been dispatched to Querétaro."[103]

It was not going to be that easy. At the last minute, Peña got cold feet. Fearful for his political life, desperate to avoid accusations that he had given away the store, he added new conditions for peace that he had Foreign Minister Luis de la Rosa pass along to his representatives. First, he demanded a more explicit guarantee that hostilities would cease upon signature of the treaty. He also insisted that the Americans withdraw from Mexico City, and that they turn over to Mexico all custom revenues. Finally, he asked for a payment to tide his government over during the transition period until it received some of the funds to be paid by Washington under the treaty. That final proviso was most urgent. As de la Rosa informed the commissioners on 26 January, "The government will never agree to close the negotiations without having here, at Querétaro, under its control, the sum of 300,000 to 400,000 dollars." Unless Peña had that cash, he said, "the government will inevitably succumb to anarchy."[104]

Trist's heart sank when the courier from Querétaro delivered de la Rosa's message. These conditions were impossible to fulfill. Trist could not come up with anything approaching as much money as Peña was demanding on short notice, and he knew Scott would never agree to evacuate the enemy capital before the war was over. Peace, so tantalizingly close a day earlier, seemed out of reach. To make matters worse, nearly two months had elapsed since Trist sent his defiant message to Washington. Polk's response was fast approaching, and Trist had every reason to believe it would come in the form of officers instructed to clap him in irons and bear him back to the United States in disgrace. Most diplomats would have given up.

Then again, most diplomats would never have disobeyed the president in the first place. Trist's actions over the next few days were characteristically unprofessional, impulsive, self-dramatizing – and effective. He determined that Peña's first demand, for a ceasefire upon the treaty's signature, was least far-fetched, and he dashed off a letter to Scott requesting "a pledge of your word that no more expeditions shall take place for the further occupation of the country until, the treaty having been received in Washington, new instructions from thence shall have reached you."

[103] NT to Buchanan, 25 January 1848, *DCUS*, 8:1034.
[104] De la Rosa cited in G. L. Rives, *The United States and Mexico* (New York: Charles Scribner's Sons, 1914), 2:608.

Unwilling to wait for a message-bearer, he took the dispatch to the general himself on the evening of the twenty-eighth. No record survives of their meeting, but Scott, while reluctant to do anything that might imperil the chance for peace, apparently declined to offer the pledge Trist sought, whereupon the two men devised a plan to compel Peña's government to accept the treaty.[105]

Their instrument would be British Chargé Percy Doyle. Trist had enjoyed good relations with Doyle's predecessor, Thornton, and felt that the Mexicans saw the British as honest brokers in this conflict. Hence, after conferring with Scott, Trist paid a midnight visit to the British legation, roused Doyle from bed, and told him that he had decided to break off negotiations unless the treaty was signed at once. The commissioners could shift for themselves. If they would rather deal with an envoy less committed to preserving Mexico's integrity, that was their business; he was heading home. As Doyle reported to the Foreign Office, Trist felt that "it was useless going on from day to day as they were doing" and that the government "did not give sufficient credit to what he had so frequently urged, namely, the danger of delay." Trist asked Doyle to convey his sentiments to the commissioners. The chargé promised to do so the following morning.[106]

Anxious lest Doyle fail to raise the proper hue and cry, Trist spent the next few hours composing a quintessentially Tristean ultimatum for Doyle to hand-deliver to Peña's delegates. "This whole time has passed, every day bringing with it a new death to the hope which, on the preceding, had taken the place of the one that then expired," he wrote. "And now the limit of these delays has been reached." True to his wont, he personalized the issue, complaining that the Mexicans did not appreciate the sacrifices he had made and that they had placed him in an "impossible position" vis-à-vis his government. Polk had fired him in the belief that the politicians in Querétaro were stalling for time, waiting for American public opinion to tire of the war and for the U.S. army to lose its combat effectiveness, and events seemed to prove the president correct. By contrast, Trist looked like a fool – or, worse, a traitor. He had staked everything on the good faith and competence of the Mexican government, but Peña and his associates, through their "idle, fruitless, and imbecile delays," had let him down. Although it caused him "infinite pain," he was

[105] NT to Scott, 28 January 1848, Reel 9, NPTP-LOC.
[106] Doyle cited in Mahin, *Olive Branch and Sword*, 161; Rives, *United States and Mexico*, 2:608.

abandoning his post, "after maintaining it as long as its nature rendered possible." He hoped the Mexicans were happy.[107]

This note had the intended impact. When a sleep-deprived Doyle gave it to the commissioners on the twenty-ninth, they pleaded for more time, insisting that they could not assume responsibility for signing the treaty without authorization from Querétaro, but, the chargé reported, "promising to write in such terms to their government as would ensure a decided answer with the least possible delay." Doyle relayed this information to Trist, who made a great show of impatience. He had waited too long already, he said. Why should he endure further humiliation at Mexican hands? At length, however, he relented. He told Doyle to advise the commissioners that he would sign the treaty if they could get Peña's approval by the following Tuesday, 1 February. But, he stressed, this was *it*, the last chance for a non-Carthaginian peace. And the Mexicans had better pray that no negotiation-ending dispatch arrived from the White House before the courier made his gallop from Guadalupe Hidalgo to Querétaro and back![108]

Doyle did as requested, with impressive results. The commissioners' message vibrated with the tones of Cassandra. "We regret beyond anything the supreme government can imagine that matters should have come to this point," they wrote, but there was no denying "the gravity of this business." None of Peña's requirements for peace would be met. Mexico had to swallow its medicine. The commissioners noted "Mr. Trist's exigencies, which he has never expressed with so much heat." Supplementing this message was a letter from Doyle borne to Querétaro by the same courier on the evening of the twenty-ninth. In it, Doyle informed de la Rosa of a recent conversation he had had with Scott, who was, to all appearances, on the verge of ordering a major offensive. Scott, Doyle reported, did not want to "take such a step," but "his orders were most peremptory to march upon Querétaro and not to allow the general government an opportunity of establishing itself in any other point of the republic."[109]

That was untrue. Marcy had issued only vague instructions to Scott, with his most recent dispatch urging the general to "deprive the enemy of the means of organizing further resistance." Nowhere in this or any other War Department communication was there an order to advance on

[107] NT to Couto, Atristain, and Cuevas, 29 January 1848, Reel 9, NPTP-LOC.
[108] Doyle cited in Rives, *United States and Mexico*, 609–610.
[109] Commissioners and Doyle cited in Rives, *United States and Mexico*, 610–611.

Querétaro or break up the government. While it is possible that Doyle misheard Scott, or that he deliberately deceived de la Rosa, both of those scenarios stretch credulity. The two men could not have misunderstood one another on a matter of such importance, and Doyle was not known to be an imaginative or daring diplomat. Scott biographer Charles W. Elliot is almost certainly right to conclude that Old Fuss and Feathers invented these "peremptory" orders as a means of leveraging the Mexican government into capitulation. In other words, the general took a page from his accomplice's playbook; although not bold enough to disobey instructions, as Trist had done, he claimed to be under instructions more Draconian than those he had received.[110]

Trist and Scott's one-two succeeded. On the last day of January, Peña told de la Rosa to transmit his endorsement to the commissioners. Given "the probability that the United States may prove every day more exacting and more exaggerated in their demands," he declared, his government had no choice but to accept the treaty, for it represented the only chance of "checking the projects of annexation to Northern America." The courier delivered the surrender to Trist and his fellow plenipotentiaries the following afternoon, and they signed the Treaty of Peace, Friendship, Limits, and Settlement at the Shrine of Our Lady of Guadalupe Hidalgo on 2 February. Signing for Mexico were former minister of justice José Bernardo Couto, former foreign minister Luis Gonzaga Cuevas, and prominent attorney Miguel Atristain. The only American to attach his signature to the treaty was Nicholas Trist – who, all parties were aware, had no authority to represent the United States.[111]

"UNINFLUENCED BY THE EXCEPTIONABLE CONDUCT OF MR. TRIST"

Polk had resolved to destroy Trist before the Treaty of Guadalupe Hidalgo arrived in Washington. His fury stoked by Pillow's letters, the president repeatedly inveighed against the envoy in cabinet meetings, making plain to all present that Trist's career in government was over and that criminal proceedings might be in order. Anyone listening to these

[110] Marcy to Scott, 14 December 1847, Outgoing Correspondence, Volume 13, WLMP; Charles W. Elliott, *Winfield Scott: The Soldier and the Man* (New York: Macmillan, 1937), 561.

[111] Peña cited in Rives, *United States and Mexico*, 612; NT to Buchanan, 2 February 1848, DCUS, 8:1059–1060.

bitter words must have concluded that Polk would tear up any document issuing from Trist's hand.[112]

The treaty, however, took Polk by surprise. On late Saturday afternoon, 19 February, a spent and unshaven James Freaner, having covered the distance between Mexico City and Washington in an astonishing seventeen days, knocked on the door of Buchanan's house and delivered the pact. Buchanan showed it to Polk that evening. According to the president's diary, he gave it a quick once-over and saw that it was almost identical to the draft treaty Trist had brought with him to Mexico in April. While noting that "there are many provisions in it which will require more careful examination than a single reading will afford," Polk had to admit that Trist had obtained terms "within his instructions." Polk then took the extraordinary step of summoning his cabinet to discuss the treaty the next morning, even though that meant violating his policy of never working on Sunday. "Mr. Trist has acted very badly," he wrote, "but notwithstanding this, if, on further examination, the treaty is one that can be accepted, it should not be rejected on account of his bad conduct."[113]

Polk received conflicting advice when the cabinet convened on 20 February. Buchanan and Treasury Secretary Walker told the president to reject the treaty because it gave the United States too little territory. (Walker, a diehard all-Mexico enthusiast, threatened to resign if Polk approved Trist's handiwork.) The other four cabinet members said Polk should submit the treaty to the Senate since it included everything Trist had been instructed to obtain. On one subject, though, they were agreed. Polk noted, "All condemned Mr. Trist's disregard of the order of his government to return to the United States when he was recalled." The president said he would defer his decision and asked the cabinet to meet again the following noon.[114]

Polk's diary records how he grappled with this predicament. On the one hand, he despised Trist and found his messages "arrogant, highly exceptionable, and even of an insulting character." On the other, he was in a bind. The Whigs controlled the House of Representatives and would take any opportunity to sabotage the war effort. If the president turned

[112] See for example Diary Entries, 4, 7, 12, and 16 February 1848, *DJKP*, 3:325–343.
[113] Diary Entry, 19 February 1848, *DJKP*, 3:345. See also VT to NT, 23 February, Reel 2, NPTP-LOC.
[114] Memorandum of Special Cabinet Meeting, 20 February 1848, Reel 77, JKPP; Diary Entry, 20 February 1848, *DJKP*, 3:347.

down "a treaty made on my own terms, as authorized in April last," Congress would probably refuse to appropriate funds for continuing hostilities. It might even vote to withdraw the American army from Mexico, meaning that New Mexico and California would be lost. Most important, from Polk's perspective, was the fact that failure to submit the treaty would all but guarantee a Whig victory in the next presidential election. The war had become very unpopular by the winter of 1847–1848. Polk needed peace to ensure that his party stayed in power. A politician to his marrow, he could not allow his personal feud with Trist to hand Henry Clay – or, worse, Winfield Scott – the White House. Accordingly, he informed the cabinet on 21 February that while he preferred stiffer terms than those Trist had agreed to, "under all the circumstances of the case," there was little he could do but submit the treaty for ratification.[115]

This did not mean that he forgave Trist. He told Marcy to instruct Butler to remove the emissary from Mexico, by force if necessary. Marcy, who had opposed expelling Trist before the result of the negotiations was known, had no such qualms now, and his dispatch to Butler dripped with scorn. Trist's behavior constituted "flagrant violation of duty and of decency," wrote the secretary of war. His dispatches were "grossly insulting," abounded in "extraneous and impertinent matter," and presented "such a commentary upon the course of his government as could only result from great ignorance." Polk would not "countenance Mr. Trist longer occupying a position in which he appears to the world as a representative of his government, and of which he avails himself to defy and insult the authority of that government." Butler was therefore directed to ensure Trist's return to the United States.[116]

Polk meanwhile sent the treaty to the Senate with a recommendation that it be ratified with a few minor modifications. "It was not expected that Mr. Trist would remain in Mexico or continue in the exercise of the functions of the office of commissioner after he received his letter of recall," the president explained. "He has, however, done so," and the result was a treaty "conforming ... substantially on the main questions of boundary and indemnity to the terms which our commissioner ... was authorized to offer." Maintaining civility by his fingernails, Polk noted that while the "extraneous circumstances attending" the treaty's

---

[115] Diary Entries, 21 and 24 February 1848, *DJKP*, 3:347–348, 357.
[116] Marcy to Butler, 25 February 1848, Outgoing Correspondence, Volume 14, WLMP.

"conclusion and signature ... might be objected to," he had put such matters aside with a view to the national interest. He asked the Senate to do the same.[117]

At first, that seemed unlikely. Most senators reacted negatively to the treaty, albeit for different reasons. All-Mexico men, bent on bringing the entire southern republic into the Union, refused to accept any pact that preserved an independent Mexican state. Other legislators did not seek the whole of Mexico but thought the United States was entitled to a larger part of it; they pointed out that Trist's treaty gave America no more land than had been demanded a year earlier, before Scott launched his campaign. Many Whigs wanted *less* territory. Some, like Daniel Webster, argued that the United States should take none. The debate grew ugly, but then came news that the eighty-year-old John Quincy Adams had been felled by a stroke on the House floor. As Adams lingered, semiconscious, in the speaker's private chambers, a new mood of sobriety descended on Congress, and by the time the former president died on the evening of the twenty-third the senators were ready to consider the treaty on its merits.[118]

They had to take several factors into account. After two years of fighting, Americans yearned for peace, and this agreement offered an end to the war. It also transferred to the United States what Polk aptly called "an empire, the value of which ... it would be difficult to calculate." Yes, that empire might be bigger, but there was no guarantee that the Mexican government would agree to part with more territory, or that the Mexican Congress would ratify a treaty dismembering their nation further. There was also no guarantee that additional combat would make the Mexican people reconciled to such humiliation. There was, indeed, no guarantee that additional combat was possible; Polk's fears of a Whig-dominated House cutting off funds for the war were well grounded. Furthermore, even if the White House could coax Congress into authorizing appropriations, it could only raise the money through borrowing. Over the course of Polk's administration, the national debt had increased from $18 to $66 million. America's credit was stretched to the limit by early 1848. The economic consequences of throwing Trist's treaty aside were likely to be dire, perhaps disastrous. And they paled beside the

---

[117] Message of the President, 23 February 1848, *The Treaty between the United States and Mexico: Proceedings of the Senate Thereon* (Washington, D.C.: U.S. Government Printing Office, 1848), 3–4.
[118] Merry, *Country of Vast Designs*, 428–430.

human costs. How many American soldiers would have to die before
Mexico met all of Washington's terms?[119]

Against those uncertainties, the senators weighed the treaty. Their
deliberations took place behind closed doors, but enough information
leaked to the press for reporters and editors to be informed as to the main
provisions of the instrument under review, and the result was, historian
George Rives notes, "a universal chorus of advice to the Senate from
newspapers all over the country" to accept what Trist had done. "Let
there be PEACE between the UNITED STATES and MEXICO," trum-
peted the Washington *National Intelligencer*, an anti-administration
paper. "We have attained all that honor and interest requires," said the
Washington *Daily Union*, a Democratic organ. Newsmen took issue with
various aspects of the treaty, but almost without exception they agreed
that it was preferable to continued hostilities. "Admit all its faults,"
argued Horace Greeley of the Whig New York *Tribune*, "and say if an
aimless and endless foreign war is not far worse than any honorable treaty
of peace could be." Every member of the House of Representatives and a
third of the senators had to face the voters in November 1848. Their
reelection prospects would be dim if their opponents could charge them
with having obstructed peace.[120]

Nonetheless, when the Senate Foreign Relations Committee took a
preliminary vote on the treaty, most members decided to reject it. Committee Chairman Ambrose Sevier informed Polk that his colleagues "did
not object to the terms of the treaty, ... but to Mr. Trist's authority to
make it after his recall as commissioner." How could the committee
legitimize such insubordination by approving its byproduct? Sevier told
the president that he, personally, was in favor of acceptance, but that he
was in the minority. He advised the president to discard the treaty and
send a "grand commission" to Mexico to negotiate a new one.

We may imagine Polk's disconcertment at hearing this. His dilemma
was profound. To save the treaty, and with it his party, he was obliged to
minimize Trist's misdeeds. Through gritted teeth, he told Sevier that while
he condemned "the insubordinate and insolent conduct of Mr. Trist,"

[119] Diary Entry, 28 February 1848, *DJKP*, 3:366.
[120] Rives, *United States and Mexico*, 631; *Intelligencer* and *Union* cited in Alice Katherine
Schuster, "Nicholas Philip Trist: Peace Mission to Mexico" (Ph.D. Dissertation: University of Pittsburgh, 1947), 184, 190; *Tribune* cited in Merry, *Country of Vast Designs*,
430. See also Robert A. Brent, "Reaction in the United States to Nicholas Trist's Mission
to Mexico, 1847–1848," *Revista de Historia de América* 35 (January–December 1953):
105–118.

that conduct had no bearing on the matter at hand, which was "the treaty itself," not the circumstances under which it had been negotiated. The Senate, Polk insisted, was assuming executive privileges. All the senators were empowered to do was to consider the treaty. The means of making it were up to the president, and Polk did not intend to surrender that prerogative. Since Sevier admitted that his fellow committee members had found no fatal flaws in Trist's arrangement, Polk did not see why they could not vote for ratification. Renegotiating the "same treaty" with the Mexicans would be an "idle ceremony." As for Trist, the president would deal with him.[121]

The committee ultimately sent the treaty to the Senate floor without recommendation. There ensued an extraordinary scene in which the venerable Sam Houston renewed the committee's main argument in language calculated to arouse. Trist, he thundered, had acted "contumaciously, ... in violation of his instructions, the laws of the land, and the Constitution of the Union, and to the great scandal of our national character." According to Houston, Trist's transgressions rendered the treaty "utterly void and ineffectual." Moreover, he declared, "it would be ... dangerous, if not ruinous, for the Senate, by their decision, to sanction such a flagrant disregard of the institutions of the country, as it would be holding out inducements to similar acts by vicious men, who may be actuated by the corrupt, treasonable intentions against the liberties of the country." Although Trist's motives had been anything but corrupt or treasonable, that did not excuse his disobedience or justify the precedent Congress would set if it endorsed his treaty. (Houston was apparently unaware that the Continental Congress had countenanced similar indiscipline in 1783.) Robert Baldwin of Connecticut tended to agree with Houston but said he would reserve judgment until he knew the full details of Trist's mission. He introduced a resolution requesting Polk to "communicate to the Senate, in confidence, the entire correspondence" between Trist and the Mexican negotiators, between Trist and Buchanan, and between Trist and Scott.[122]

Polk was happy to comply. At his direction, the State and War Departments delivered copies of every letter, along with a note from the president drily observing that "these documents are very voluminous." "It will be perceived," Polk noted, that Trist's writings "contain much matter that is impertinent, irrelevant, and highly exceptionable." Polk could not

---

[121] Diary Entry, 28 February 1948, *DJKP*, 3:362–237.
[122] Proceedings, 28 February 1848, *Treaty between the United States and Mexico*, 5–6.

"approve the conduct of Mr. Trist in disobeying the positive orders of this government contained in the letter recalling him, or do otherwise than condemn much of the matter with which he has chosen to encumber his voluminous correspondence." Still, the president contended, he felt it was his "solemn duty to the country, uninfluenced by the exceptionable conduct of Mr. Trist, to submit the treaty to the Senate with a recommendation that it be ratified." His reasons for doing so were, he believed, self-evident: first, the terms "conform substantially ... to those authorized by me in April last"; second, "if the present treaty be rejected, the war will probably be continued, at great expense of life and treasure, for an indefinite period." Always careful to protect his political flanks, Polk wanted the Senate, not the White House, to bear the blame for prolonging hostilities.[123]

For the next ten days, a free-for-all raged in the Senate, with supporters of the treaty battling expansionist Democrats and non-expansionist Whigs. Eventually, both groups of dissidents accepted the argument that an even worse treaty – "worse" from their very different perspectives – might follow repudiation of this pact, and the Treaty of Guadalupe Hidalgo passed by a vote of thirty-eight to fourteen, inspiring Whig politician Philip Hone's famous observation that "the peace, negotiated by an unauthorized agent, with an unacknowledged government, submitted by an accidental president, to a dissatisfied Senate, has, notwithstanding all of these objections in form, been confirmed." The Mexican Senate proved similarly willing to overlook irregularities and ratified the treaty in late May. America's first foreign war was over.[124]

"AN INTERMINABLE SERIES OF DISASTERS"

When Anaya's commissioners submitted the treaty they and Trist had fashioned to the Mexican legislature, they included an official statement praising their American counterpart. "The favorable conception which, in the first negotiation, we formed of the noble character and high endowments of Mr. Trist has been completely confirmed by the second," they declared. "Happy has it been for both countries that the choice of the American government should have been fixed upon a person of such

---

[123] Message of the President, 29 February 1848, *Treaty between the United States and Mexico*, 7–8.

[124] Hone cited in Robert A. Divine, *Perpetual War for Perpetual Peace* (College Station: Texas A & M University Press, 2000), 64.

worth, upon a friend to peace so loyal and sincere. Of him, there remain in Mexico none but grateful and honoring recollections." One commissioner privately expressed the hope that Trist would become U.S. minister to Mexico, noting that this would be just recompense for "the important services rendered by him to his government, to his country, and to humanity."[125]

Trist might have fulfilled that hope. Even though he had alienated Polk, he was still on good terms with powerful people in Washington. The obvious thing for him to do, after concluding negotiations, was to go home at once, explain his actions to Congress, and respond to reporters' questions. Most editors were willing to wink at his insubordination, since it had ended the war; some even celebrated it. Tellingly, of seventeen mainstream newspapers examined by historian Robert Brent, all but four praised Trist for doing what was necessary to secure peace. Had he returned with Freaner and the treaty, and had he exercised a modicum of tact in defending his mission to Mexico, a prestigious job in the next administration could have been his for the asking.[126]

Instead, he stayed in Mexico, waiting to testify at Pillow's trial. For ten weeks after signing the treaty, he idled at army headquarters. To pass the time, he turned to his favorite activity, writing, and the hundreds of pages he filled brooded on two subjects: his own gallantry and the wickedness of his rivals. "I have, all of a sudden, become a great man," he informed his wife. "I have earned *true* distinction – distinction sound, solid, unswerving, and never more visibly earned." Yet the wave of applause sure to greet him back in America would not go to his head: "Away with it, let it be blown about with the leaves of autumn. It shall not change me. It shall not obtrude itself upon me to mar the life upon which I have always been intent." Certainly, it would not induce him to descend to the level of "the pitiable being in the presidential chair." He forbade Virginia to petition Polk for payment beyond her husband's recall date: "I will accept of *nothing* – not even my due – which it depends on *his* decision, even his *official* decision, to give me. His official mind is too corrupt or too imbecile.... I say the same of every man capable of retaining a seat in

---

[125] Couto and Cuevas cited in Thornton to NT, 26 May 1848, Reel 9, NPTP-LOC; Couto cited in de Drusina to NT, 11 April 1848, ibid.

[126] Brent, "Nicholas Philip Trist," 220. Speaking for the majority, the Pittsburgh *Daily Dispatch* declared, "No one who carefully examines the history of Mr. Trist's mission can avoid concluding that he is superior to those who have placed him in his present position. ... [W]e would wish his continuance in the diplomatic service." Cited in Schuster, "Nicholas Philip Trist," 197, 199.

his cabinet during the last 3, 4, or 5 months." That included Buchanan. "My confidence in Mr. B. is gone," Trist proclaimed. "Accept no services at his hands." The secretary had some "good qualities," but ultimately he was just another in a long line of "schemers and plotters and cheats" driven by "the falseness and baseness of their own ignoble hearts." Worst of all was Pillow, "that *reptile*," whose every statement was "a string of barefaced falsehoods from beginning to end." Trist did not fear the forces of darkness arrayed against him. "Their crests are fated to fall, never more to rise," he raved. "With the spear of truth, I am an overmatch for the whole host."[127]

Principally, Trist worked on his memorial to Congress, the most outlandish document he ever produced, a screed that made his wildest dispatch from Havana seem tame by comparison. He began by likening himself to Martin Luther and citing the theologian's famous declaration, "If I am to have a fault, I would rather speak too harshly, and thrust forth the truth unwisely, than to have played the hypocrite to any, and held truth in." What truth did Trist thrust forth? That Polk sought "the conquest of Mexico and its absorption into the Union," and had set in motion "*a plot to deceive and betray our country*" for that purpose. "Should the American people fail to obtain this knowledge now," Trist declared, "the evil consequences to that people, now and in all future time, and through them to mankind, cannot fail to be such as no human mind can calculate." He called for Polk's impeachment. The French had just deposed Louis Philippe in the February Revolution, he said, because of "the corrupt use of executive influence." Yet the same outrage "has occurred among *ourselves* within the last six months, and it *cannot* have *been surpassed* by anything that formed part of the misrule of the 'Citizen King.'"

Every one of Trist's worst traits was on display in his memorial: paranoia, vanity, sanctimony, self-pity, and, above all, spleen. It was not enough to call Pillow an "egotistical fop" and "calculating intriguer"; Trist also deemed him "the *veriest lie incarnate* it has ever been my misfortune to know," "a person incapable, absolutely incapable, of a single thought that does not center upon *self*." For Polk to have given this "popinjay" a position in the American army was of a piece with the Roman emperor Caligula making his horse a consul, except that Polk's was the greater offense: "The steed could do no mischief as consul – he doubtless was a noble specimen of his kind – but what is the harm that

---

[127] NT to VT, 2 February 1848, Reel 2, NPTP-LOC; NT to VT 17 May 1848, ibid.; NT, "To My Country," undated, Reel 10, NPTP-LOC.

might *not* have resulted to us, the American people, to our republic, to our country, from James K. Polk's minion being dressed up in rank entitling him – *him*, Gideon J. Pillow! – to assume command over this army?" And Pillow was only one target. Trist fulminated against all of the "political mountebanks" and "barefaced criminals" in the Polk administration, "to every one of whom I would have been an object of obsequious praise instead of bitter hate and reckless calumny, had my character permitted me to court the one, or, through dread of the others, to shrink from anything which I believed it right for me to do ..." So it went, for 111 pages plus 116 pages of appendices and 67 pages of supporting material.[128]

Congress was preparing to adjourn when Trist's memorial arrived in Washington. It is doubtful that many legislators read the document in full. Eighty-three members of the House voted to publish it, but 96 voted not to, and it was tucked away in the National Archives to gather dust, a kindness to its author. Apart from the memorial's berserk tone, its entire premise had been invalidated by the time of its submission: Polk had sent the Treaty of Guadalupe Hidalgo to the Senate, which had agreed to ratify. How, then, could congressmen take seriously Trist's charge that the president wanted to annex all of Mexico? Many of them, even those previously sympathetic to Trist, must have concluded that Polk had been right to fire his envoy. The man was obviously mad.[129]

Trist's behavior fit that description during his final days in Mexico. After testifying against Pillow at the court of inquiry, he received a note from General Butler informing him that Polk wanted him back in Washington. "I have received instructions to require you to leave the headquarters of the army," Butler wrote, "and to furnish you the necessary escort." A decent fellow, Butler did not savor his task. He hoped Trist would leave of his own volition, but the ex-diplomat refused to oblige. Polk had no right to order him home, he said. The president had fired him, remember? That meant he was an ordinary American citizen, "and as such exempt from all right on the part of any earthly powers to assert control over my person, or over my freedom in any respect." He could go wherever he wanted and stay as long as he liked. In a letter all-too-typical for its self-righteous self-destructiveness, Trist told Butler that he had planned to leave Mexico "in the course of the ensuing week" but that now he could not because it might appear as "acquiescence in usurped authority."

[128] Trist Memorial.   [129] Mahin, *Olive Branch and Sword*, 189.

Butler replied that he had no intention of "entering into your discussion of
the rights of an American citizen." He was under orders. "Should it
become necessary," he wrote, "which I feel certain it will not, it will be
my unpleasant duty to enforce" Polk's command. Trist made sure it was
necessary. From the saddle of his very high horse, he pronounced, "My
liberty is at end." Butler had Trist placed under military arrest and
conducted by a troop of soldiers to Vera Cruz, where he had arrived a
year earlier, peace treaty in hand.[130]

The final third of Nicholas Trist's life was, as he put it in an 1857 letter
to his son, "an interminable series of disasters." While Polk chose not to
press criminal charges, he otherwise took his full measure of revenge on
the man who, he felt, had embarrassed him. The president declined to
meet with Trist upon the latter's return to Washington – indeed, he did
not include Trist among the invitees to witness his signature of the
proclamation that hostilities with Mexico had concluded, even though
Trist was at that time living a few blocks from the White House – and he
never reconsidered his decision to stop payment on Trist's salary and
expenses as of 16 November 1847, the day Trist received his recall notice.
It was customary for diplomats to be paid until they could arrange safe
transportation out of their countries of assignment, and Trist's defenders
pointed out that the earliest date when the envoy might have done that
was 9 December, but Polk was not subject to such guidelines; since Trist
had been an executive agent, unconfirmed by the Senate, he was paid out
of the president's secret fund, and Polk alone determined when his term of
service ended. To deepen the humiliation, Polk computed Trist's salary at
a rate lower than that normally allowed a "minister plenipotentiary,"
which had been Trist's formal title. In other words, Trist was underpaid
for his mission and received no compensation for the period in which he
negotiated the Treaty of Guadalupe Hidalgo.[131]

He would not appeal Polk's decision. Friends tried to get him to
petition Congress for his back pay, but he refused. He was no beggar.
Should an ungrateful government deny him his just due, he would bear
the wrong with dignity, if not in silence. Never at a loss for words, he
grew more prolix as he aged, writing long, digressive letters on a range of

[130] Butler to NT, 17 March 1848, Reel 9, NPTP-LOC; NT to Butler, 17 March 1848, ibid.;
Butler to NT, 18 March 1848, ibid.; NT to Butler, 18 March 1848, ibid. See also
Defense of Major General Pillow before the Court of Inquiry, 1848, Reel 11, NPTP-
LOC.
[131] NT to Jefferson Trist, 6 November 1857, Reel 2, NPTP-LOC; NT to Buchanan, 27 June
1848, ibid.

subjects. When an aspiring biographer of Jefferson or Jackson asked him a question, the response often ran to 100 pages, and inquiries about the Mexican War drew irruptions of ink whose wordiness was surpassed only by their rancor. Toward the end of his life, Trist declared that the war had been "an abuse of power on our part" and that he had taken no pride in signing the treaty that ended it. "Could those Mexicans have seen into my heart at that moment," he recalled, "they would have known that *my* feeling of shame as an American was far stronger than theirs could be as Mexicans. For though it would not have done for me to say so *there*, that was a thing for every right-minded American to be ashamed of, and I *was* ashamed of it."[132]

That was a peculiar assertion. Nothing in Trist's wartime correspondence supports it, and one suspects that it grew out of a desire to distance himself from the Polk administration. If the Mexican Cession had secured Polk's place in history, then Trist did not wish to be associated with that triumph. If he could not escape being identified with it, he wanted people to know it was a source of self-reproach for him. He preferred to belittle his own accomplishment rather than contribute to the legacy of someone he loathed.

This attitude derived, at least in part, from the financial problems that plagued Trist throughout the 1850s and 1860s. After being rebuffed by Polk and frozen out of Washington society, he moved his family to Westchester, Pennsylvania, where he and his wife opened, of all things, a charm school for girls. Unsurprisingly, it lost money, as did Trist's investment in a gold-mining operation in California and a British washing-machine business. He managed to earn some funds by working on Wall Street for a firm that handled cases for Spanish-speaking clients, but the job was temporary, and he could not find affordable housing in New York for his family. After moving back to Pennsylvania, he took a position as a railway clerk for the Wilmington and Baltimore Railroad Company. There, for the first time since his Havana consulship, he enjoyed a measure of job security, remaining in the company's employ until ill health forced him to retire in 1870. Even when he rose to the level of paymaster, however, his salary was a meager $1,200 per year,

[132] Trist cited in VT to Tuckerman, 8 July 1864, Folder 225, NPTP-UNC. I am indebted to Robert W. Drexler for drawing my attention to this document. Drexler, *Guilty of Making Peace*, 129–130. See also NT to Scott, 26 July 1851, Reel 6, NPTP-LOC; NT to the Editors of the *Daily Times*, 4 November 1857; ibid.; NT to the Editors of the *New York Evening Post*, 1850, Reel 10, NPTP-LOC; NT to Felton, undated, Reel 11, NPTP-LOC.

and he faced a grim old age, with debts exceeding assets and no income to speak of.[133]

Fortunately for Trist, Ulysses S. Grant assumed the presidency in 1869 and lent his support to a drive to pay the rogue diplomat for the second half of his Mexican mission. A veteran of the Mexican War, Grant was aware of how important Trist had been in ending that conflict. With the president's approval, Senator Charles Sumner made an appeal on Trist's behalf to his colleagues, and the Senate awarded Trist $14,599.90 – his salary plus twenty-two years' interest. This vindication was bittersweet, though, as Trist had to wait until 1872 to get the money; specious charges that a lobbyist had been hired to get the bill through Congress delayed payment. Grant also appointed Trist postmaster of Alexandria, Virginia, a job with the impressive annual salary of $2,900, but Trist was by this point too old and infirm to profit much by it. A stroke incapacitated him in 1873, and he died a year later.[134]

It was a dingy end for a man so instrumental in shaping the boundaries of his country, and doubtless just what Polk would have wanted had he not preceded Trist in death by almost a quarter-century. If Polk intended this comeuppance to serve as a warning to future would-be loose cannons, however, he failed. Trist was hardly the last American diplomat to take peace – or war – into his own hands.

---

[133] For a poignant description of Trist when his finances were at low ebb, see Gordon to Scott, 13 October 1858, Reel 6, NPTP-LOC.

[134] See Remarks upon the Case of Mr. N. P. Trist, Now before Congress, 5 April 1870, Reel 10, NPTP-LOC; Sumner Report and Related Documents, 14 July 1870, *Compilation of Reports of Committee on Foreign Relations, United States Senate* (Washington, D.C.: U.S. Government Printing Office, 1901), 3:752–763.

4

"I Have Now Read the Dispatch, But I Do Not Agree with It"

Page Preserves America's "Special Relationship"

Walter Hines Page was a terrible golfer. During the five and one-half years that he headed the U.S. Embassy in London, stories about his ineptitude on the links became legendary. Page often joked about the subject. "My golf this afternoon was too bad to confess," he wrote his son Arthur in mid-1916, remarking that his game might improve if he were allowed to "play with howitzers instead of clubs." By contrast, Joseph Patrick Kennedy began his ambassadorship to Great Britain in 1938 by shooting a hole in one at the Stokes Poges course in Buckinghamshire. It was, he noted in his diary, "the triumph of my diplomatic career." It was also the only respect in which Kennedy's stint at the Court of St. James compared favorably with Page's.[1]

Embassy London has traditionally been the most coveted post in the American foreign service, both as a status symbol – one historian observes that "its occupant was automatically placed at the very top of the nation's social ladder" – and as a springboard for higher office. Page's predecessors at the embassy included five future presidents, four future vice presidents, and nine future secretaries of state. These men had on occasion played critical roles in global politics, for good and ill, but never was America's chief representative to Great Britain more perfectly placed to direct the course of history than in the lead-up to World Wars I and II.

---

[1] Walter Hines Page (hereafter WHP) to Arthur Page, 22 May 1916, *The Life and Letters of Walter H. Page*, Burton J. Hendrick, ed. (Garden City, NY: Doubleday, 1922) (hereafter *LLWHP*), 2:132; Joseph Patrick Kennedy (hereafter JPK) Diary Entry, 5 March 1938, Diary, Box 100, Joseph Patrick Kennedy Papers (hereafter JPKP), John F. Kennedy Library, Boston, Massachusetts (hereafter JFKL).

During those anxious years, when the United States was officially neutral, two of the most incorrigible rogue diplomats in the annals of American foreign relations ran Embassy London. Page and Kennedy held passionate views about how America should cope with the conflicts convulsing Europe, and they defied their superiors again and again as they sought to bend U.S. policy to their will.[2]

In Page's case, such obstreperousness was heroic. Long before the Woodrow Wilson administration committed the United States to fight alongside the Allies in World War I, Page recognized the menace that German domination of the Continent posed to America. He kept up a fusillade of letters and cables to Wilson and the State Department arguing that American isolationism in the face of this threat was unrealistic. "This war," he wrote the president less than two months after the outbreak of hostilities, "is showing how we are part of the great world whether we wish to be or not." Worse than efforts to remain aloof from the struggle, in Page's view, were administration claims that the two sides were equally responsible for starting it and comparably guilty of violating American rights in their pursuit of victory. Britain and the other Allied Powers were *not* on the same moral plane as Germany and its collaborators, Page insisted. The war was a case of "English free institutions" versus "German military autocracy," and if Berlin won, "it would dash our Monroe Doctrine to the ground" and "even invade the U.S. in time."[3]

For nearly three years, Page waged a lonely battle to persuade Washington to join the Allied cause. Ranged against him were the four most powerful policymakers in America: Wilson; his two secretaries of state, William Jennings Bryan and Robert Lansing; and his chief political adviser, Colonel Edward House. In making the case for U.S. cobelligerency to these men, Page frequently expressed himself in language far from diplomatic. "Is that the way you write to the *president*?" gasped a British official after reading one of Page's missives, adding, "There is no other person in the world who dares talk to him like that!" British Foreign Secretary Arthur Balfour observed that he had "never seen any such communication [from] an ambassador to his master." Like Nicholas Trist – and, later, Henry Cabot Lodge II – Page refused to allow decorum

---

[2] David E. Koskoff, *Joseph P. Kennedy: A Life and Times* (Englewood Cliffs, NJ: Prentice-Hall, 1974), 115.

[3] WHP to Wilson, 22 September 1914, Reel 63, Woodrow Wilson Papers, Library of Congress, Washington D.C. (hereafter WWP); WHP to Wilson, 15 October 1914, ibid.; WHP to Wilson, 6 September 1914, Reel 62, WWP.

to muffle the message he drummed into Washington's ears, and his abrasive approach bore fruit. Anglo-American relations, strained almost to the snapping point between August 1914 and April 1917, never ruptured entirely. What policymakers on both sides of the Atlantic would come to call the "special relationship" between the United States and its former mother country endured until America, with dangerous belatedness, took up arms against Germany and Austria-Hungary and tipped the scales of war in favor of the Allies.[4]

Page has received harsh treatment from historians. During the interwar era, when scholars excoriated Wilson's generation of policymakers for sending Americans to die in a conflict allegedly unrelated to American interests, Page proved an irresistible whipping boy, the out-of-his-depth Anglomaniac whose slanted messages to Washington caused the United States to abandon its traditional, and wise, policy of isolationism. Charles Tansill denounced the ambassador as "far more British than American," judged his conduct "reprehensible," and found him "wholly unfit to represent the United States at London." C. Harley Grattan snarled that Page "swallowed the whole of the British propaganda, hook, bait, and sinker." Nastiest was Harry Elmer Barnes. "If we had possessed at London a competent, fair-minded, and judicious ambassador," he pronounced, "the story of American foreign policy from 1914–1919 would have been far different than what it was." Alas, Wilson appointed a man "more English than the English ... whose maladministration of his duties was a chief obstacle to American impartiality in dealing with the belligerent nations after 1914." To Barnes, "The offense of Benedict Arnold seems highly comparable." More recent studies by John Milton Cooper, Jr., and Ross Gregory take a milder tone and acknowledge the shared Anglo-American stake in preventing German victory, but still fault Page for "diplomatic naiveté" and for behavior "not warranted or correct for a diplomat." Page "sometimes acted with dubious propriety," writes Gregory. "An honorable man, his zeal for the British led him to positions that were not honorable." They were certainly positions at variance with those

---

[4] British official cited in *LLWHP*, 2:21–22 (emphasis in original); Balfour cited in Ross Gregory, *Walter Hines Page: Ambassador to the Court of St. James* (Lexington: University of Kentucky Press, 1970), 153. For recent works addressing the uniqueness of the Anglo-American tie, see John Dumbrell, *A Special Relationship: Anglo-American Relations from the Cold War to Iraq*, Second Edition (London: Palgrave, 2006); B. J. C. McKercher, *Britain, America, and the Special Relationship since 1941* (London: Routledge, 2016); Niklas Rossbach, *Heath, Nixon, and the Rebirth of the Special Relationship: Britain, the U.S., and the EC* (London: Palgrave, 2009).

of his government, but to the extent that they helped achieve a result favorable to the United States – that is, security against German militarism and aggression – they deserve a more positive reckoning.[5]

Embassy London took a toll on Page. His attempts to bring America into the war on the side of the Allies broke his health; he resigned in August 1918 and lived just long enough to learn of the armistice later that year. Like most rogue diplomats, he never expressed regret for his insubordination. He went to his grave believing he had honorably served his nation as the world marched toward war.

"BARBAROUS BEHAVIOR"

Unlike Kennedy, Page did not seek an ambassadorial appointment. One of America's foremost journalists and publishers, he had no diplomatic experience as of 1913 and had concerned himself almost exclusively with domestic issues, chief among them public education. His efforts on that front had brought him to the attention of a young lawyer named Woodrow Wilson in the 1880s. The two Southern progressives formed a friendship that endured throughout Wilson's rise through the political ranks, and, when Wilson won the White House, Page expected to become a cabinet member, perhaps secretary of the interior. He was taken aback by the offer of Embassy London. "I knew ludicrously little about the duties and opportunities of an ambassador," he admitted later. But he chose to regard the president's request as "the call of duty" and accepted. As he

---

[5] Charles Callen Tansill, *America Goes to War* (Boston: Little, Brown, and Company, 1938), 146, 148, 600; C. Harley Grattan, "The Walter Hines Page Legend," *American Mercury* 6 (September 1925): 41; Harry Elmer Barnes, *The Genesis of the World War* (New York: Alfred A. Knopf, 1929), 603, 606, 646; John Milton Cooper, Jr., *Walter Hines Page: The Southerner as American, 1855–1918* (Chapel Hill: University of North Carolina Press, 1977), 295; Gregory, *Walter Hines Page*, 215, 217. See also David M. Esposito, *The Legacy of Woodrow Wilson: American War Aims in World War I* (Westport, CT: Praeger, 1996), 72, 91, 93; M. Ryan Flood, *Abandoning American Neutrality: Woodrow Wilson and the Beginning of the Great War, August 1914–December 1915* (London: Palgrave Macmillan, 2013), 27, 39, 84, 87–88, 111, 114–115; Ernest R. May, *The World War and American Isolation, 1914–1917* (Cambridge, MA: Harvard University Press, 1959), 15, 21, 31, 143–144, 153, 320, 359, 427; Walter Millis, *Road to War: America, 1914–1917* (Boston: Houghton Mifflin, 1935), 20–21, 49–50, 52, 86, 88, 337; Robert W. Tucker, *Woodrow Wilson and the Great War: Reconsidering America's Neutrality, 1914–1917* (Charlottesville: University of Virginia Press, 2007), 21, 26, 33, 47, 104–105, 116, 165–166. *LLWHP*, while a financial success, was not a work of scholarship. Its editor, Burton Hendrick, was Page's friend and successor as managing editor of the journal *World's Work*. He made no claim to detachment; his commentary was unapologetically hagiographic.

wrote Colonel House in a line that rings ironic in light of his subsequent conduct, "A good soldier is subject to orders without question."[6]

At first, it seemed as though the assignment would be one continuous revel. Page arrived in London at the height of the social season and was caught up in a merry-go-round of dinners, dances, and receptions. "I'm having more fun than anybody else anywhere," he wrote a friend. He was soon on familiar terms with dukes, earls, and even the king himself – a heady experience for a man born in a small North Carolina town. Although he committed several faux pas, as when he broke off a conversation with Prince Louis of Battenberg before being formally dismissed, he adapted to the brave old world of British etiquette and in a short time moved with confidence among nobility and royalty. "In the last four weeks I've made twenty-six speeches on everything from the Monroe Doctrine to 'The Spirit of Christmas,'" he bragged to House. "I've had parties and I've gone to parties. I've had dinners and I've gone to dinners. ... I've worn two dress coats to a frazzle." There was little actual work for the top U.S. diplomat to do, but Page kept busy.[7]

His duties were not entirely ornamental. Two controversies complicated relations between the United States and Great Britain. The first arose out of the Wilson administration's refusal to recognize General Victoriano Huerta as president of Mexico. Wilson insisted that Huerta had come to power through force rather than constitutional procedures and was therefore not a legitimate national leader. Unfortunately, Britain had already recognized Huerta's regime, which was committed to protecting British oil interests in Mexico. Page managed to persuade his host government to withdraw recognition, a task made easier by the close working relationship he established with British Foreign Secretary Sir Edward Grey. He handled the second semi-crisis with equal success. The U.S. Congress in 1912 had passed a law exempting American vessels engaged in domestic coastal trade from paying tolls to use the soon-to-be-open Panama Canal. London accused Washington of bad faith, arguing

---

[6] Unpublished Essay: *The Ambassadorship*, undated, Walter Hines Page Papers, Houghton Library, Harvard University, Cambridge, Massachusetts (hereafter WHPP); WHP to House, 30 January 1914, Series I: Select Correspondence (hereafter SI:SC), Box 86, Edward M. House Papers, Sterling Library, Yale University, New Haven, Connecticut (hereafter EMHP). Most of Page's papers are unprocessed, which makes tracking down documents difficult.

[7] WHP to Houston, undated, *LL WHP*, 1:151–152; WHP to House, 20 December 1913, SI: SC, Box 86, EMHP. For Page's snubbing of Prince Louis, see Diary Entry, 19 June 1913, Series II: Diary (hereafter SII:D), Box 296, EMHP.

that this act violated the 1901 Anglo-American Hay-Pauncefote Treaty, which held that the canal would be open to ships of all nations on "terms of entire equality." Wilson was sympathetic to the British view, and Page's pleas in favor of non-discrimination helped convince the president to call for repeal of the law. The Senate and House of Representatives complied in early 1914. Page could look back on the opening act of his diplomatic service with satisfaction.[8]

The only matter that distressed Page prior to the outbreak of hostilities in Europe was financial. He discovered that he could not afford the expenses that the ambassadorship entailed: renting and furnishing a house; hosting receptions several times a week; paying the salaries of clerks, interpreters, messengers, and housekeepers. Congress, with its customary penuriousness, only provided an annual allowance of $17,500 – as compared to the $85,000 that the British ambassador to Washington received. Page spent over $30,000 of his personal savings in the first year. "Had I known that ... the obligatory cost was so great," he wrote Wilson, "I should not have dared to come. But nobody was frank with me about this aspect of the post." He regretfully informed the president that he would have to resign unless he received additional funds, and that he felt compelled to "tell the public the whole truth, that we can have only rich men for ambassadors." Wilson would not hear of Page stepping down. He and House worked out an arrangement whereby the millionaire Democratic Party stalwart Cleveland Dodge contributed $25,000 a year for the duration of Page's ambassadorship. Relieved of economic worries, Page could report home, "Everything is lovely and the goose hangs high. ... Lord! Lord! The fun I've had, the holy joy I am having!" He added, "Only, only, only – I do wish to do something constructive."[9]

His wish came true in the grisliest sense as July 1914 gave way to August and first one nation and then another plunged into the abyss

---

[8] Hay-Pauncefote Treaty cited in Hersch Lauterpacht, *International Law* (Cambridge: Cambridge University Press, 1975), 2:118. For Wilson's Mexican policy, see Peter V. N. Henderson, "Woodrow Wilson, Victoriano Huerta, and the Recognition Issue in Mexico," *Americas* 41 (October 1984): 151–176. For the canal issue, see William S. Coker, "The Panama Canal Tolls Controversy," *Journal of American History* 55 (December 1968): 555–564.

[9] WHP to Wilson, 5 June 1914, Correspondence between Walter Hines Page and Woodrow Wilson (hereafter CWHP-WW), Volume 1, WHPP; WHP to House, 28 July 1913, SI:SC, Box 86, EMHP; WHP to House, 23 November 1913, ibid. For Dodge as Page's benefactor, see Diary Entry, 5 September 1914, SII:D, Box 299, EMHP.

of war. Britain was the last major power to become involved, taking up arms on 5 August. Page suddenly found himself overwhelmed with work. Thousands of American tourists descended on the embassy and demanded transportation home. Inquiries as to the fate of loved ones stranded on the Continent poured in. The German and Austro-Hungarian governments asked Page, as representative of the leading neutral nation, to take over their London embassies. By all accounts, Page handled his new responsibilities well. He put in twenty-hour days for weeks on end, driving his small staff mercilessly, and while he did not manage to satisfy everyone, he earned the admiration of most who witnessed his labors. The *New York Times* lauded him for accomplishing a task that required "the wisdom of Solomon and the patience of Job." Possibly his greatest achievement was his selection of Herbert Hoover, an American engineer headquartered in London, to run the Committee for Relief in Belgium. Under Hoover's inspired leadership, the CRB saved millions of Belgians from starvation.[10]

Page initially endorsed without scruple Wilson's policy toward the conflict in Europe, even when the president took the extraordinary step of asking Americans to "be impartial in thought as well as in action." Like Wilson, Page was aghast at the horrors of modern war and grateful that the United States was able to stay out of it. "Again and again I thank heaven for the Atlantic Ocean," the ambassador wrote his boss. "Ours is the only great government in the world that is not in some way entangled. How wise our no-alliance policy is!"[11]

It did not take long, though, for Page to conclude that American neutrality was self-defeating – and, what was worse, immoral. Just weeks after the outbreak of hostilities, Page was advising the White House and State Department that an Allied victory was essential to America's survival as a democracy. "If German bureaucratic force would conquer Europe," he argued, "presently it would try to conquer the United States; and we should all go back to the era of war as man's chief industry and

---

[10] *New York Times* cited in Gregory, *Walter Hines Page,* 51. Page's letters to Wilson, House, and others give a detailed account of the embassy's ordeal. See for example WHP to Wilson, 9 August 1915, *LLWHP,* 1:303–305; WHP to Wilson, 23 August 1914, WHPP; WHP to House, 11 October 1914, SI:SC, Box 86, EMHP. For Page's role in getting Hoover to lead the CRB, see Cooper, *Walter Hines Page,* 282–283.

[11] Appeal by the President to the Citizens of the Republic, 19 August 1914, *FRUS,* 1914 (Washington, D.C.: U. S. Government Printing Office, 1928), Supplement, 552; WHP to Wilson, 29 July 1914, CWHP-WW, Volume 1, WHPP; WHP to Wilson, 2 August 1915, ibid.

back to the domination of kings by divine right." Besides, he said, American rectitude mandated a pro-Ally policy. The conduct of German troops in Belgium and other conquered territories put them beyond the pale. "[T]he Germans have perpetrated some of the most barbarous deeds in history," Page declared. "Those who have violated the Belgian treaty, ... those who have dropped bombs on Antwerp and Paris indiscriminately with the idea of killing whom they may strike, have taken to heart [German scholar Friedrich von] Bernhardi's doctrine that war is a glorious occupation. Can any one longer disbelieve the completely barbarous behavior of the Prussians?" All evidence indicates that the ambassador expected his friend Wilson, with whom he agreed about so many things, to share his sentiments and enlist America on the Allied side, if not to the extent of becoming a full-blown belligerent, at least in terms of waging pro-Ally neutrality.[12]

He was therefore disappointed by the president's lack of response. Wilson did not write to Page at all during the early stages of the war – the German drive on Paris, the retreat of the French government to Bordeaux, the arrival of the British Expeditionary Force, the first Battle of the Marne – and he continued to stress the importance of strict impartiality in his public statements. More worrisome to the ambassador was a brief, businesslike cable from Secretary of State Bryan instructing him to "inquire of the British government whether they are willing to agree that the laws of naval warfare laid down by the Declaration of London, 1909, shall be applicable to naval warfare during the present European conflict." Bryan noted that "acceptance of these laws by the belligerents would prevent grave misunderstandings which may arise."[13]

Thus began Page's first row with State. British policymakers refused to abide by the Declaration of London, and Page did not blame them. That declaration – an international code of maritime law in wartime that grew out of a 1909 conference between delegates from the leading European naval powers, the United States, and Japan – defined contraband and blockade in ways more favorable to neutrals than belligerents. It excluded from its definition of contraband food, clothing, and other such items of importance to a war, and it mandated that a blockade, to be legal, had to be made effective through the stationing of an adequate number of ships near the mouth of an enemy port. It also included a provision protecting

[12] WHP to House, 22 September 1914, SI:SC, Box 86, EMHP; WHP to Wilson, 11 September 1914, *LLWHP*, 1:325–326.
[13] Bryan to WHP, 6 August 1914, *FRUS*, 1914, Supplement, 216.

neutral-to-neutral commerce. None of the states represented at the conference had ratified the declaration by 1914, and the British Parliament had rejected it, fearful that Britain's belligerent status in a future war would be hindered by such liberal rules. Grey told Page that his government could not adopt the declaration without shackling its greatest military asset: the navy. The declaration's narrow definition of contraband allowed such articles as copper and rubber to get through to the enemy, which was unacceptable, and its requirement that a blockading power station ships just outside the three-mile limit of German-controlled ports was suicidal in a war that involved long-range guns and submarines. As for neutral-to-neutral trade, Grey insisted that Britain had a right to stop merchant ships sailing to neutral countries adjacent to Germany, like Holland, or near enough to Germany, like Sweden, to function as conduits to the Reich. Because of these considerations, Grey declared, London had to make approval of the declaration "subject to certain modifications and additions ... indispensable to efficient conduct of ... naval operations." Grey's explanation struck Page as sensible and he passed it along to State, assuming that the subject was closed.[14]

Foggy Bottom pushed back. Robert Lansing, counselor of the department and, in Bryan's absence, acting secretary, sent a long cable noting that the governments of Germany and Austria-Hungary had agreed to observe the Declaration of London if the Allies did, and that Britain's refusal to "accept the declaration as a whole" struck Washington as "a matter of grave concern" that, if publicized, would "arouse a spirit of resentment among the American people toward Great Britain." Lansing instructed Page to "impress upon Sir Edward Grey the president's conviction of the extreme gravity of the issue" and to urge British compliance with the declaration.[15]

Page thought he understood his government's viewpoint. America had traditionally been a champion of neutral rights. The war trade with Europe was profitable. Washington did not want British restrictions to hamper Americans' ability to make money. But, the ambassador asserted, Britain was fighting for its life against an adversary who was pure evil, and one could hardly blame London for placing national survival ahead of the interests of U.S. businessmen. Page observed that Germany and Austria-Hungary, being land powers, would sacrifice nothing by embracing the Declaration of London, but Britain would

---

[14] Grey cited in WHP to Bryan, 26 August 1914, *FRUS*, 1914, Supplement, 218–220.
[15] Lansing to WHP, 26 and 28 September 1914, *FRUS*, 1914, Supplement, 225–233.

cut its own throat. Furthermore, Page noted, the United States had abandoned its neutral-rights axioms during the Civil War, citing military necessity. It was hypocritical for Washington to expect London to respect those rules when the Kaiser's armies were thundering toward Paris. "The British purpose," Page cabled Lansing, "is to prevent the enemy from receiving food and materials for military use and nothing more." Surely, under the circumstances, Lansing could appreciate why Grey had to decline State's appeal.[16]

Lansing would not let the matter rest. When he saw a draft of a new British Order in Council enlarging the contraband list, he sent another protest to Embassy London. "This government would view with eminent satisfaction British acceptance of [the] declaration without change," he wrote. "It would also quiet public unrest, which is increasing, as to present British action." Page dutifully presented this message to Grey, who reiterated the British case: wartime needs dictated that His Majesty's government name as contraband the widest variety of items and exert control over cargoes bound for neutral ports. If Britain did as State suggested, it would lose the war. Britain might perhaps adopt the declaration in principle, but only with the understanding that "the present hostilities" had created unprecedented conditions that justified exceptional measures.[17]

Grey, fearful of alienating his nation's most powerful ally, was unfailingly polite. Page was less so. Convinced that State did not comprehend the life-and-death stakes of the situation, he went over Lansing's head with a cable marked "confidential for the president." Britain, he wrote Wilson, had "shown a sincere desire to meet all our wishes" except for permitting war material to reach Germany. "That it will not yield. We would not yield it if we were in their place. Neither would the Germans. The English will risk a serious quarrel or even war with us rather than yield. This you may regard as final." What Americans needed to grasp, Page contended, was that "[t]his is not a war in the sense we have hitherto used the word. It is a world-clash of systems of government, a struggle to the extermination of English civilization or of Prussian military autocracy. Precedents have gone into the scrap heap." In other words, it was not an occasion to quibble over "a few shippers' theoretical rights." Three times Page described the controversy as "academic," and he implored Wilson,

---

[16] WHP to Lansing, 29 September 1914, *FRUS*, 1914, Supplement, 233.
[17] Lansing to WHP, 4 October 1914, *FRUS*, 1914, Supplement, 243–244; Grey cited in WHP to Lansing, 9 October 1914, ibid., 244–246.

"Look a little further ahead. If Germany wins, it will make no matter what position Great Britain took on the Declaration of London. We shall see our Monroe Doctrine shot through." To forestall such a calamity, the least Washington could do was convey its "substantial acceptance" of British reinterpretation of maritime law. "I know that this is the correct, larger perspective," the ambassador said.[18]

He reinforced his cable with a handwritten letter sent to Wilson via steamship that made the same argument in stronger terms, asserting the need to "cut out Prussian war-culture as one would cut out a cancer." German victory would reduce the Monroe Doctrine to "less than a scrap of paper – the mere faded breath of a dead man," Page pronounced. Lansing's messages "read as if they came out of a sort of Hague-book in time of peace" while the British were "listening lest the very pillars of civilization give way and the last crash comes." Page assured Wilson that there would be time enough for State's hairsplitting "when this deadly business is ended – some years hence, I fear."[19]

"BE CAREFUL NOT TO EXPRESS ANY UN-NEUTRAL FEELING"

To Page's shock, the president's reply was a dressing-down. "Beg that you will not regard the position of this government as merely academic," Wilson cabled back. "Contact with opinion in this side of the water would materially alter your view." The same day, Page received a message from State containing bizarre instructions. Lansing had hit on a scheme he believed "would meet the wishes of this government and at the same time accomplish the ends which Great Britain seeks." The acting secretary proposed that the British publicly accept the declaration without amendments and then proclaim, on the basis of trumped-up evidence, that "a port or territory of a neutral country is being used as a base for the transit of supplies for an enemy government." This "excuse" would enable the British to maintain that the country in question was not covered by the declaration. Lansing told Page to broach this plan to Grey "in an entirely personal way, ... stating very explicitly that it is your personal suggestion and not one for which your government is responsible."[20]

[18] WHP to Wilson, 15 October 1914, *FRUS*, 1914, Supplement, 248–249.
[19] WHP to Wilson, 15 October 1914, Reel 63, WWP.
[20] Wilson to WHP, 16 October 1914, *FRUS*, 1914, Supplement, 252–253; Lansing to WHP, 16 October 1914, ibid., 249–250.

The double whammy of Wilson's reprimand and Lansing's order jolted Page. Clearly, the president was more committed to neutrality than Page had thought. That was bad enough. But for State to instruct the ambassador to present Lansing's stratagem as though it were his own was, Page felt, outrageous. House once remarked that Page's greatest weakness as a diplomat was "that he is so open, frank, and honest that he believes everybody is as much so as himself." Page had no intention of deceiving Grey, and he certainly would not lend his name to so shady a device. He delivered State's recommendation without saying whose idea it was.[21]

Grey issued the expected rebuff. Like Page, the foreign secretary was troubled by the dishonesty of the plan, and he also considered it politically unacceptable. Parliament, having vetoed the declaration in peacetime, would not countenance Whitehall's embracing it unaltered in the midst of the bloodiest combat in history. Page relayed this information to State with the comment, "This finally ends all hope of [Grey's] acceptance of the declaration entire. He is courteous, appreciative, and willing to go to any length he can to meet us, but he will not accept the declaration."[22]

The ambassador's letters and memoranda reveal the strain he was under. "If I were commanded to find the most unwelcome task that an English-speaking man may now have," he wrote, "I should say that this was it." Torn between loyalty to the land of his birth and that of his assignment, Page "turned the subject over in my mind, backward and forward, 100 times a day." Was he wrong to oppose Washington's policy? Instinct and observation told him that he was not. "A man has nothing but his own best judgment to guide him," he concluded. "If he follow that and fail – that's all he *can* do." His health suffered: "For the first time … my appetite disappeared and my digestion went bad." These symptoms would worsen in the coming months and lead to his death in 1918.[23]

Anxious and overwrought, Page wrote two messages that he felt might be among his final acts as ambassador. To Wilson he explained, "When I telegraphed you that the discussion is 'academic,' I did not mean that the subject itself is academic, but that our exceedingly argumentative treatment of it seemed academic to me – e.g. our continued insistence on the

[21] House to Wilson, 9 March 1915, Reel 69, WWP; WHP to Wilson, 21 October 1914, Reel 64, WWP.
[22] WHP to Lansing, 19 October 1914, *FRUS*, 1914, Supplement, 253.
[23] WHP to Wilson, 28 October 1914, Reel 64, WWP; Undated Memorandum, *LLWHP*, 1:387 (emphasis in the original).

Declaration of London after England's positive declination four times to accept it." He told the president that he could not obey Lansing's order. "It is one thing to present a question informally, which doesn't bind anybody," he wrote, "but it is a different thing to say that the idea is wholly my own and not my government's, when it isn't. .... My relations with Sir Edward have not been built up on this basis and could not survive this method of dealing long." Again Page begged Wilson to think of the big picture. "Wise diplomacy regards the next decade – the next 25 years," he declared. If Washington persisted in its foolish course, "the two governments that are the only hope of human freedom and human progress will be at ill will," and the consequences for humanity would be hideous.[24]

The ambassador then fired off a furious letter to House blasting State's "sheer idiocy" and threatening, "If Lansing again brings up the Declaration of London, after four flat and reasonable rejections, I shall resign. I will not be the instrument of a perfectly gratuitous and ineffective insult to this patient and fair and friendly government. ... It would be too asinine an act ever to merit forgiveness." Page could not understand State's failure to perceive basic facts. "The case is plain enough to me," he wrote. "England is going to keep war-materials out of Germany as far as she can. We'd do it in her place. Germany would do it. Any nation would do it." And yet Lansing kept insisting that London adopt a policy that would render the British fleet "useless" in the contest against the Central Powers. "If that isn't playing into the hands of the Germans, what would be?" Page demanded. "I pray you, good friend, get us out of these incompetent lawyer-hands." Aware that Wilson trusted House more than any other adviser, Page sought to use the colonel as a vehicle to get through to the president.[25]

How much Page's appeals influenced Wilson's decision to give up on the Declaration of London cannot be determined. We know that the ambassador's threat to resign made no difference, because Wilson directed State to drop its insistence that Britain observe the declaration two days before Page made that threat. Still, it is likely that Page played a role. Wilson respected him, even if he did not share his Manichean view of the war, and the sheer number and forcefulness of Page's messages could not have failed to engage the president's attention. Several historians have

---

[24] WHP to Wilson, 21 October 1914, Reel 64, WWP.

[25] WHP to House, 22 October 1914, *LLWHP*, 2:380–384. See also House to Wilson, 21 October 1914, *The Intimate Papers of Colonel House*, Charles Seymour, ed. (Boston: Houghton Mifflin, 1926) (hereafter *IPCH*), 1:305.

noted that Wilson was unusually unmindful of policymaking at this time, grief over his wife's recent death having incapacitated him. In the absence of strong presidential leadership, State had taken the reins of foreign policy, and it required a ferocious blast of dissent to make Wilson pay heed to how America dealt with the European conflict. Page supplied that thunderclap. In late October, Lansing informed the British ambassador to Washington, Cecil Spring-Rice, that the Wilson administration was withdrawing from the Declaration of London. He then cabled Page the news.[26]

Ecstatic, Page rushed to tell Grey. He had prevailed, but at a price. Relations between State and Embassy London, never warm, grew downright hostile. "I have an irresistible impulse to tell you that the State Department lacks guts," Page wrote House. Although he had not yet begun to question the president's motives, Page was convinced that Bryan and Lansing did not measure up to the challenge of the moment, and he was not reticent in expressing this view. In letters to friends and family members, he raged against Foggy Bottom's narrow focus on "the letter of international law" to the exclusion of "the larger *ethical* facts." Britain was fighting civilization's battle, the ambassador asserted, while State quibbled over definitions of contraband. Anglo-American friendship was "the only thing that now holds the world together. That's the big fact. A cargo of copper, I grant you, may be important, but it can't be as important as our friendship. It's the big and lasting things that count now." And it was those big and lasting things that State, with its forest-for-the-trees policy, repeatedly missed.[27]

The president, meanwhile, was losing patience with his defiant ambassador. "I am a little disturbed by the messages Walter Page is sending recently," Wilson wrote House. "We are very much helped by his advice, but ... it would be very unfortunate if he were to ... forget the temper of

[26] Lansing to Wilson, 20 October 1914, *FRUS, The Lansing Papers, 1914–1920* (Washington, D.C.: U.S. Government Printing Office, 1939) (hereafter *LP*), 1:255–256; Lansing to WHP, 22 October 1914, *FRUS, 1914*, Supplement, 257–258. For Wilson's inattentiveness during this period of mourning, see A. Scott Berg, *Wilson* (New York: G. P. Putnam's Sons, 2013), 333–340; John Milton Cooper, Jr., *Woodrow Wilson* (New York: Alfred A. Knopf, 2009), 258–264; Phyllis Lee Levin, *Edith and Woodrow: The Wilson White House* (New York: Charles Scribner's Sons, 2011), 46–51; Edwin A. Weinstein, *Woodrow Wilson: A Medical and Psychological Biography* (Princeton: Princeton University Press, 1981), 254–262.

[27] WHP to House, 25 October 1914, SI:SC, Box 86, EMHP; WHP to House, 20 July 1915, ibid.; WHP to House, 9 November 1914, ibid. (emphasis in the original). See also WHP to House, 10 September 1914, *LLWHP*, 1:410–411; WHP to Fuller, 29 December 1915, WHPP.

the folks at home." While Wilson's sentiments inclined toward the Allies, an attitude he knew most Americans shared, he was determined to keep the United States out of the war, and the surest means to that end, he believed, was a rigid neutrality. At the president's behest, House wrote Page instructing him to "be careful not to express any un-neutral feeling either by word of mouth or by letter, and not even to the State Department."[28]

Page made no attempt to obey Wilson's order. Indeed, his verbal and written attacks on Germany increased in truculence after American abandonment of the Declaration of London. Germany, he wrote the president, "has reduced this desperate struggle to the level of a ravaging cutthroat. All along the battle line, the Red Cross flag is a joke, the white flag is laughed at." If Americans could but understand "the character of the Germans," they would applaud Britain's taking liberties with traditional maritime rules. To House, Page argued that the war could only end when "this military war-party, which now *is* Germany ... quits dreaming of and planning for universal empire and quits maintaining a great war-machine which at some time for some reason must attack *somebody* to justify its existence."[29]

The ambassador also refused to moderate his attitude toward State. When Bryan, misinterpreting one of Page's messages, cabled Embassy London with an admonition not to assist the British in working out export arrangements with neutral nations, Page responded intemperately. "Now what damn fool in the State Department supposed that I was making agreements with any government?" he demanded. "I don't know, nor care to know. ... But – *but* you can't help doubting the *intelligence* of a man (whoever he is) that breaks loose with a sermon about my making 'agreements with other governments,' and you don't know how much dependence to put in the next telegram about something else that comes from the same source." Page did not identify Bryan or Lansing by name in this letter, a display of self-censorship he would rarely repeat, but it was obvious whom he was talking about.[30]

---

[28] WW to House, 23 October 1914, SI:SC, Box 86, EMHP; House to WHP, 4 December 1914, ibid. House noted in his diary that Wilson "asked me to caution Walter Page about being pro-British. Page is writing letters to the State Department which excite attention." Diary Entry, 3 December 1915, SII:D, Box 299, EMHP.

[29] WHP to Wilson, 19 March 1915, Reel 68, WWP; WHP to House, 12 December 1914, SI: SC, Box 86, EMHP (emphasis in the original).

[30] Bryan to WHP, 12 November 1914, *FRUS*, 1914, Supplement, 395; WHP to House, 12 December 1914, SI:SC, Box 86, EMHP (emphasis in the original).

Page's next quarrel with his superiors arose out of the announcement, in early February 1915, that Berlin intended to establish a war zone around the British Isles. All enemy ships in that area would be liable to destruction without warning. This measure was necessary, the German government asserted, because of British attempts to starve Germany into submission by an illegal blockade. Berlin's escalation of the war forced American policymakers to confront the problem of the submarine, a weapon the framers of international law had failed to anticipate. According to rules drawn up in the days of the sailing ship, no belligerent vessel could sink an enemy merchant ship without first stopping it, confirming its identity, and providing for the safety of passengers and crew. The submarine, however, relied on surprise for its effectiveness; it would surrender that advantage if it surfaced and gave the conventional warning. Submarines were moreover too small to take on hundreds of people from a ship about to be sunk. Finally, U-boats were so fragile that a single shot or a well-directed prow could send them to the bottom. With these considerations in mind, the German Admiralty proclaimed that "it may not always be possible to save crews and passengers." Berlin advised neutral merchant ships to stay out of the war zone to avoid cases of mistaken identity, a real possibility given British ships' practice of flying the American flag.[31]

Wilson's initial response to this proclamation was militant. He declared that he would not tolerate any abridgment, accidental or otherwise, of America's "acknowledged rights" at sea, and that if American vessels or lives were lost as a consequence of German actions, Berlin would be held to "strict accountability." Diplomatic language did not get much stronger, and Page was delighted by the president's hard line. Soon, however, the situation grew confused as the government of British Prime Minister Herbert Asquith made an unofficial proposal to Washington that Britain might "not put food on the absolute contraband list" if Germany promised to stop its submarine attacks on merchant ships. Almost simultaneously, Berlin intimated to State that British relaxation of the blockade could cause Germany to soften its U-boat policy. Seeing in these two overtures a chance to broker a compromise, Bryan, with Wilson's assent, suggested that Britain permit foodstuffs into Germany in exchange for a German pledge to give up unannounced submarine attacks. To sweeten the pill for the British, Bryan volunteered to set up an

[31] Gerard to Bryan, 4 February 1915, *FRUS*, 1915 (Washington, D.C.: U.S. Government Printing Office, 1928), Supplement, 94.

agency to ensure that food reached "solely the non-combatant population" of Germany.[32]

By the time Bryan's proposal arrived in London, Downing Street had thought better of its initial offer and decided to withdraw it, a move Page approved. He joined Grey in concluding that any arrangement that weakened the blockade would operate too heavily to the advantage of the Central Powers. Wilson, however, thought the Bryan formula had merit. To House, who was in London on an ill-conceived peace mission, Wilson urged vigorous advocacy of State's plan. "Please say to Page," the president cabled, "that he cannot emphasize too much in presenting the note to Grey the favorable opinion which would be created in this country if the British government could see its way clear to adopt the suggestions made there."[33]

Again, Page disobeyed orders. With House looking over his shoulder, the ambassador had to go through the motions of attempting to sell Grey on the compromise, but his lack of enthusiasm was obvious. "I ... tried to get him to make as strong a protest as our government desired him to make to the British government," House recorded in his diary, "but I could not get him to do so. He put it very mildly to the British government, although his instructions were to make it very strong." The colonel, alarmed at Page's performance, urged him to try again. He told the ambassador that Wilson wanted "the matter presented with all the emphasis in his power." Page agreed to meet with Grey a second time, but, House noted, "one could see he had no stomach for it." House ultimately gave up on Page and met one-on-one with Grey to pressure the foreign secretary into endorsing Bryan's modus vivendi. He enjoyed no greater success. The British would not ease their blockade, which they considered essential to victory. On 1 March 1915, London formally announced its intention to "prevent commodities of any kind from reaching or leaving Germany."[34]

Doubts as to the seriousness of Berlin's submarine policy were dispelled that spring, as German U-boats sank ninety ships in two months. The *Falaba*, a British passenger vessel, went to the bottom with the loss of one American life. Americans also perished on the U.S. oil tanker

---

[32] Bryan to Gerard, 10 February 1915, *FRUS*, 1915, Supplement, 99; WHP to Bryan, 17 February 1915, ibid., 111; Gerard to Bryan, 19 February 1915, ibid., 112–115; Bryan to WHP, 20 February 1915, ibid., 199–120.

[33] Wilson to House, 20 February 1915, SI:SC, Box 86, EMHP.

[34] Diary Entries, 20 and 22 February 1915, SII:D, Box 300, EMHP; Spring-Rice to Bryan, 1 March 1915, *FRUS*, 1915, Supplement, 128.

Gulflight, which the Germans torpedoed but did not sink. While these attacks galvanized anti-German sentiment in the United States, they were minor incidents compared to the sinking of the British liner *Lusitania* on 7 May, a tragedy in which almost 1,200 people died, including 128 Americans. For the first time, there seemed a real possibility that Washington might be drawn into the Great War. Page believed America had no choice. "[T]he United States must declare war or forfeit European respect," the ambassador cabled State. "So far as I know, this opinion is universal." He forecast grand things for his country in cobelligerency: "If the United States comes in, the moral and physical effect will be to bring peace quickly and give the United States a great influence in ending the war and in so reorganizing the world as to prevent its recurrence." Conversely, a timid response would result in Washington having "no voice or influence in settling the war nor in what follows for a long time to come."[35]

This was an appeal to Wilson's messianic progressivism, but it also reflected Page's true feelings. While he had been pro-British since the start of his ambassadorship, the *Lusitania* tragedy convinced him beyond question that Britain was on the side of the angels and that the United States needed to help the Allies purge Europe of German barbarism. "Ambassador violent for war," Page's daughter Katharine noted in her journal on the day the *Lusitania* went down. From that moment, Page dropped any pretense of neutrality or decorum. His cables and letters to the White House, State, and assorted relatives and friends were variations on a single theme. "We've got to get in," he wrote House in a typical dispatch. The Germans were "the damnedest pirates that ever blew up a ship. . . . By dallying with them we do not change the ultimate result, but we take away from ourselves the spunk and credit of getting in instead of being kicked and cursed in." Page's insistence that America join the Allies contributed to his estrangement, already well advanced, from Foggy Bottom and led to a falling-out with House and the president, but he kept up the epistolary barrage, generating in the process the fieriest diplomatic correspondence Washington had seen since Nicholas Trist laid down his pen.[36]

The ambassador's commentary on Wilson's handling of the *Lusitania* affair was a case in point. Three days after the liner was sunk, the

[35] WHP to Bryan, 8 May 1915, *FRUS,* 1915, Supplement, 385–386.
[36] Katharine Page cited in Cooper, *Walter Hines Page,* 307; WHP to House, 21 July 1915, *LLWHP,* 2:25–26.

president gave a speech in Philadelphia in which he proclaimed, "There is such a thing as a man being too proud to fight. There is such a thing as a nation being so right that it does not need to convince others by force that it is right." Page, appalled, cabled Wilson that such an apparent rationale for inactivity struck Britons as "moral failure on the part of the United States." At minimum, Page noted, His Majesty's Government expected a break in relations between America and Germany, and he concluded ominously that "failure to act ... will shut the United States out of British, and, I should guess, out of all European respect for a generation."[37]

To a degree, Wilson seemed to follow Page's advice. His first official note to Berlin on the *Lusitania* disaster affirmed that Americans had an "indisputable right" to travel on the high seas and demanded German disavowal of the submarine commander's "inhumane" conduct. Yet Page could not help noticing that this was not an ultimatum; it contained no indication that America might break relations. A second *Lusitania* note, issued after Berlin refused to admit wrongdoing, was sterner in tone but also bereft of any warning of a diplomatic rupture – and, like the first note, it elicited a defensive German response. There followed a third note, in which Wilson threatened that Washington would regard the sinking of another passenger ship as "deliberately unfriendly." By this point Page was near despair. Days had passed since the *Lusitania*'s torpedoing, and Wilson seemed content to fight back with words. "We're in danger of being feminized," Page wrote his son Arthur. "Petticoats where breeches ought to be and breeches where petticoats ought to be; white livers and soft heads and milk-and-water. ... As for being kicked by a sauerkraut caste – O Lord, give us backbone!" Page, a lifelong Democrat, was no admirer of Theodore Roosevelt, but he sounded like the ex-Rough Rider when he vented his spleen against Wilson's vacillating.[38]

There was, however, a silver lining for Page in the *Lusitania* affair: Bryan's resignation. The secretary felt that Wilson's protest notes to Berlin should be balanced by an equivalent warning to London about the blockade, and, when the president refused to heed his counsel, Bryan withdrew from the cabinet. Page had never cared for Bryan, considering him a pious buffoon and pro-German besides. Word of his departure

[37] Wilson cited in Tucker, *Woodrow Wilson and the Great War*, 111; WHP to Bryan, 11 May 1915, *FRUS*, 1915, Supplement, 391–392.
[38] Gerard to Bryan, 29 May 1915, *FRUS*, 1915, Supplement, 419–421; Lansing to Gerard, 9 June 1915, ibid., 436–438; Gerard to Lansing, 22 June 1915, ibid., 450; Lansing to Gerard, 21 July 1915, ibid., 480–482; WHP to Arthur Page, 6 June 1915, WHPP.

prompted a torrent of derision from Embassy London, as Page congratu-
lated Wilson for being a good "executioner" and pronounced, "There
always was a yellow streak in [Bryan], and now he shows a white liver. . . .
Conscience he has about little things – grape juice, cigarettes, etc. – but
about a big situation, such as embarrassing a president, he is fundamen-
tally immoral. Well, cranks always do you a bad turn, sooner or later.
Avoid 'em, son! Avoid 'em!" When House informed Page that Bryan was
planning to visit Europe to "try peace negotiations," the ambassador
jeered, "Send him over here if you want to get rid of him. He'll cut no
more figure than a tar-baby at a Negro camp meeting. If he had come
while he was secretary, I should have jumped off London Bridge and the
country would have had one ambassador less."[39]

Wilson apparently gave some thought to asking Page to succeed Bryan,
but decided against it. Lansing, who got the nod instead, recalled that the
crucial factor was Page's "lack ... of conformity with the president's
policy of preserving a neutral attitude toward all the belligerents." The
new secretary of state would soon infuriate Page more than Bryan had.[40]

"NOT A COURTEOUS WORD"

Shortly after Lansing took over the top job at State, and with passions still
aroused by the *Lusitania* catastrophe, a German submarine commander
torpedoed the *Arabic*, a British passenger vessel, killing two Americans.
Page was out of town when the attack occurred. Upon hearing the news,
he raced back to London, expecting to learn that the United States had
broken relations with Germany. Wilson, though, refused to be stampeded
into war, and he informed the press through intermediaries that he was
collecting facts and weighing his options. Page was beside himself. What
was there to weigh? "The facts about the *Arabic* seem so clear here as to
leave no doubt of her deliberate sinking by the German submarine without any provocation," he cabled State, warning that "delay in action"
would "deepen the impression throughout Europe that the United States

---

[39] WHP to Wilson, 12 June 1915, Reel 68, WWP; Diary Entry, 9 June 1915, Diary, WHPP;
House to WHP, 12 August 1915, *LLWHP*, 2:12; WHP to House, undated, ibid.,
2:13–17.

[40] Robert Lansing, *War Memoirs of Robert Lansing* (Indianapolis: Bobbs-Merrill, 1935),
15–16. See also House to WHP, 17 June 1915, SI:SC, Box 86, EMHP. Ironically, Lansing
got off to a genial start with Page, cabling the ambassador to congratulate him on "the
very remarkable record which you have made in London." Lansing to WHP, 22 December 1915, Volume 15, Robert Lansing Papers, Library of Congress.

is seeking to maintain peace at the price of humiliation." Page observed that British newspapers had adopted "a tone of open ridicule" toward Washington. As for the Germans, "they have a contempt for the United States as they had for England, and they hope to keep her writing letters at which they laugh." How much longer did the president intend to endure such treatment?[41]

Wilson scored an apparent triumph when the German ambassador to the United States expressed regret for the *Arabic*'s sinking and offered an indemnity. The so-called *Arabic* pledge followed, with Berlin assuring Washington that "orders issued by His Majesty the Emperor to the commanders of German submarines ... have been made so stringent that a recurrence of incidents similar to the *Arabic* case is considered out of the question." Although the chief justice of the U.S. Supreme Court acclaimed this as "the greatest victory for American diplomacy in a generation," it brought no joy to Embassy London. Page complained to Wilson that the *Arabic* pledge was insincere and that, moreover, it did not address the gorilla in the room. "We shall not get credit in English opinion for a decisive diplomatic victory over Germany," Page wrote, "until the *Lusitania* case is satisfactorily closed." Berlin had yet to apologize for that atrocity, and Washington's refusal to press the issue was destroying America's reputation in Britain. According to Page, "The British people ... and a considerable part of the government, don't care a fig what we say, do, or think, or whether we exist."[42]

America sank still lower in British eyes in succeeding weeks. Foggy Bottom had not abandoned its goal of getting London to alter its naval strategy. If Lansing no longer insisted on British adherence to the Declaration of London, he nonetheless still found Britain's blockade of northern Europe objectionable, and he sought to persuade policymakers in London to adopt a narrower definition of contraband. He also wanted the British to slacken their grip on U.S. commerce with neutral nations. When State informed Page that a new protest note to Whitehall was impending, the ambassador reacted with alarm. He told Lansing that the "government and public opinion here are in about the same mood that Northern opinion and Lincoln's administration were in the week after Bull Run."

---

[41] WHP to Lansing, 24 August 1915, *FRUS*, 1915, Supplement, 524–525.
[42] Bernstorff to Lansing, 1 September 1915, *FRUS*, 1915, Supplement, 530–531; Bernstorff to Lansing, 5 October 1915, ibid., 560; Lansing Memorandum, 5 October 1915, *FRUS, LP*, 1:486–488; justice cited in Kevin O'Keefe, *A Thousand Deadlines: The New York City Press and American Neutrality* (New York: Springer Science, 1972), 106; WHP to Wilson, 16 October 1915, CWHP-WW, Volume 3, WHPP.

Page thought it madness to expect men like Grey to attend to petty points of law when thousands of Britons were being slaughtered in the Gallipoli campaign and the Balkans were in turmoil. "[T]he note will receive no serious attention by the government until the present tension is relaxed," Page warned, "and its presentation at this moment is likely to result in a public reception that may tend to defeat its purpose."[43]

Lansing sent the note anyway. Fifty-five pages long, it exceeded Page's worst expectations. He called it "an uncourteous monster of 35 heads and 3 appendices." Most distressing was section thirteen, wherein Lansing observed that British trade had increased with the same neutral countries with which the United States was forbidden to deal. The secretary condemned this as "manifest injustice" and insisted that the United States would not "permit the rights of its citizens to be so seriously impaired." State had come as close to accusing the British of bad faith as one could without leveling the charge outright.[44]

Page was disgusted – as much, he said, by the "manner" of the note as by its "matter." "There is not a courteous word," he complained to House, "nor a friendly phrase, nor a kindly turn in it, not an allusion even to an old acquaintance, to say nothing of an old friendship. . . . There is nothing in its tone to show that it came from an American to an Englishman. It might have come from a Hottentot to a Fiji-Islander." Page protested that he had received no advance notice of State's "many-headed, much appendiced ton of stuff," and that if he had, "I should have suggested a courteous short note saying that we are obliged to set forth such and such views about marine law." That would have been a polite, constructive approach. Instead, thanks to Foggy Bottom's insensitive and bullying treatment, "English good-feeling toward us" was at a "low-water mark."[45]

Before showing the note to Grey, Page asked Lansing if he could delete section thirteen, with its "imputation of bad faith." Lansing irritably replied that the section should "stand as it is." The ambassador then delivered State's message to the foreign secretary, explaining that it was not as long as it seemed – the second half was appendices – and that much of it was intended for domestic consumption. Wilson, Page said, had to demonstrate to pro-German elements in the mid- and far West that he was not favoring

---

[43] WHP to Lansing, 15 October 1915, *FRUS, LP*, 1:303.
[44] WHP to House, 12 November 1915, WHPP; Lansing to WHP, 21 October 1915, *FRUS, 1915, Supplement*, 581–582.
[45] WHP to House, 12 November 1915, WHPP.

the British. Grey accepted Page's argument, and the Foreign Office responded to this protest note the way it had responded to the others: with delay – State did not receive an answer for over six months – and empty promises. "His Majesty's government desire to assure the United States government," the reply read, "that they will continue their efforts to make the exercise of what they conceive to be their belligerent rights as little burdensome to neutrals as possible." They would not, however, budge an inch on the blockade, contraband, or neutral-to-neutral trade.[46]

It was during this uncertain period, the winter of 1915–1916, that Page made one of the most notorious statements in the history of U.S. foreign relations. Grey recorded the event in his memoir:

Page came to see me at the Foreign Office one day and produced a long dispatch from Washington contesting our claim to act as we were doing in stopping contraband going to neutral ports. "I am instructed," he said, "to read this dispatch to you." He read and I listened. He then said, "I have now read the dispatch, but I do not agree with it; let us consider how it should be answered."

This anecdote provoked outrage when it became public in the mid-1920s. Even the *New York Times*, a pro-Ally paper, found it inexcusable, editorializing,

For a parallel to this action the records of diplomacy would probably be searched in vain. An ambassador is right in doing all he can to help maintain friendly relations between his own government and the one to which he is accredited. . . . But an ambassador's first duty is, after all, to the government which he represents. If he disagrees with its policy, he must keep still about it while in office abroad. Should his dissent be too strong for him to endure, he can always resign. But to act as Ambassador Page did was to follow a course for which it would be difficult to find a precedent and which could not be made common in diplomatic practice without demoralizing and disastrous consequences.

Wilson, of course, did not know of Page's remark to Grey. Had he been aware that the ambassador was presenting State Department messages in this fashion, he surely would have fired him. America's foreign service was more permissive than any other country's, but some actions were out of bounds. Fortunately for the cause of Anglo-American friendship, both Page and Wilson were dead when Grey published his account.[47]

---

[46] WHP to Lansing, 4 November 1915, *FRUS*, 1915, Supplement, 609; Lansing to WHP, 4 November 1915, ibid., 609–610; Spring-Rice to Lansing, 24 April 1916, *FRUS*, 1916 (Washington: U.S. Government Printing Office, 1929), Supplement, 380. For Page's meeting with Grey, see Gregory, *Walter Hines Page*, 134, 136–137.

[47] Edward Grey, *Twenty-five Years, 1892–1916* (New York: Frederick A. Stokes Co., 1925), 2:110–111; *Times* cited in Barnes, *Genesis of the World War*, 604–605.

"A COG THAT REFUSES TO WORK SMOOTHLY"

Page reached the height of impropriety during House's second peace mission to Europe in the early months of 1916. Convinced, like his hosts, that the war must continue until Germany surrendered unconditionally, Page objected to any attempt at mediation. He also resented Wilson's sending an emissary to assume duties properly belonging to the ambassador. Thus he was hardly in a mood to cooperate with House upon the latter's appearance in London on 5 January. Rather, Page used House as a verbal punching bag, venting over a year's frustration with American statecraft.[48]

House's diary, in which he kept a detailed record of these days, reads as black comedy. "The ambassador called at the Ritz Hotel a half hour after our arrival," House noted. "He was full of the growing unpopularity of the president and the United States in Great Britain. He questioned whether the president would ever take decisive action." At an embassy dinner, "my entire evening was spent listening to his denunciation of the president and Lansing, and of the administration in general." While Page pilloried Wilson – "everything the president was doing was wrong" – he saved his fiercest blows for State. "He thought the State Department should be 'cleaned out from top to bottom,'" House wrote of one afternoon's encounter. "He suggested that the Department should not remain in the same quarters, but should take a large tent and place it on the green near the Washington Monument in order to raze the present building to its foundations and start afresh." Sometimes the colonel let Page rant: "I sat still and quiet, looking into the fire, until he had relieved his mind. ... One might as well argue with a petulant woman." On other occasions, House leaped to the administration's defense: "I literally flayed him, and I was surprised that he took it so kindly." House and Page met often in January and February 1916, and in each exchange the ambassador "harp[ed] upon the same subject, that is, the density of the administration in dealing with the foreign situation." The colonel had to admit that "Page is a man of high character"; nonetheless, "It has become a

---

[48] "With House in mind," Page wrote the president, "a questioner asked Sir Edward Grey in the House of Commons yesterday whether the government meant to send a special diplomatic envoy to Washington. The answer was: 'No. His Majesty's government have complete confidence in its ambassador to the United States.'" Page wondered why his own government did not have similar confidence in him. WHP to Wilson, 1 June 1916, CWHP-WW, Volume 1, WHPP.

punishment for me to be with him, because he is so critical of the president, Lansing, and our people generally." Toward the close of his mission, House complained to a friend that "a large part of my time here was spent arguing with Page."[49]

They argued principally about two subjects. First, and most important, was a plan House and Wilson had contrived in late 1915 to lure the warring parties to a peace conference. House promised Grey that if Britain and France accepted Wilson's invitation to such a conference and Germany declined it, the United States would "probably" enter the war against the Central Powers; if the Germans accepted, and the conferees failed to secure peace, America would leave the conference a belligerent on the Allied side. This intrigue, known to history as the House-Grey Memorandum, received the British foreign secretary's tentative assent, but Page considered it a disgrace, even though it opened a possible path to U.S. belligerency. "Of course, the fatal moral weakness of the ... scheme is that we should plunge into the war, not on the merits of the cause, but by a carefully sprung trick!" the ambassador wrote in his diary. "Such a morally weak, indirect scheme is doomed to failure – is wrong in fact." Page told House to discard the plan, but the colonel, according to Page, said "that we must do it the president's own way." The ambassador refused. When House invited Page to participate in a meeting with British policymakers to discuss Wilson's proposal, Page told him no. "He was more depressing than ever," House recorded, "literally damning the president and Lansing for their lack of foresight." The meeting went forward without Page and resulted in the infamous memorandum, which House thought a great victory for the United States and for peace.[50]

The Allies soon shattered the American illusion. French politicians and military men still believed that they could force a German surrender. Intent on regaining the provinces they had lost in the 1870–1871 Franco-Prussian War, they had no interest in a negotiated settlement. As for the Asquith government, it twice declined to act upon the House-Grey Memorandum, reasoning that it could not take part in a peace conference at a time when Germany held the military advantage. (Of course, when

[49] Diary Entries, 9 February, 7 January, 10 February, 15 January, 14 February, 19 January 1916, SII:D, Box 296, EMHP.
[50] House-Grey Memorandum cited in Thomas H. Buckley and Edwin B. Strong, Jr., *American Foreign and National Security Policies, 1914–1945* (Knoxville: University of Tennessee Press, 1987), 38. See also Diary Entry, 9 February 1916, Diary, WHPP; Diary Entry, 11 February, SII:D, Box 296, EMHP.

the Allies were winning, they could not resist the temptation to press on to victory.) Page had gauged Allied sentiment better than had Wilson.[51]

House and Page also crossed swords over another scheme, this one of Lansing's device. The secretary had obtained Wilson's approval for a plan by which British merchantmen would remove their deck guns in exchange for a German pledge that U-boats would not attack non-combat vessels. This arrangement, Lansing argued, would relieve submarine commanders of the fear that a halted merchant ship might fire on them; they would therefore not object to following the traditional rules of visit and search, and a major source of tension between Washington and Berlin would disappear. Wilson thought the proposal "reasonable and thoroughly worth trying." Page disagreed. In concert with Grey, he told State that it was the most foolish American initiative "since our effort to have the Declaration of London adopted entire," that it was "wholly in favor of the Germans" and "wholly against the Allies," and that if Washington did not drop it, "the administration will forfeit the confidence [and] good will of England and France." What Lansing was in effect proposing, Page said, was American acceptance of the submarine as a legitimate means of waging war, which would constitute "a complete German victory over us in the U-boat controversy." House, by contrast, thought Lansing's idea had merit, but the negative reaction of the British government, to say nothing of Page's bellicose attitude, persuaded him that the time was not ripe for such a compromise. State ultimately withdrew its suggestion.[52]

Page was vexed by these unworkable plots, preferring a straightforward approach. "The only course to pursue is to cut off diplomatic relations with Germany at once," he wrote in a private memorandum. "We should declare an embargo against Germany and begin economic war. This would lead to actual war. We could use our navy and begin to prepare an army and – save our souls." Five days later, with House still in London, the ambassador sent one of his most strident cables to the

---

[51] For a keen analysis of the House-Grey Memorandum, see Charles E. Neu, *Colonel House: A Biography of Woodrow Wilson's Silent Partner* (New York: Oxford University Press, 2015), 213–218, 223–238.

[52] Lansing to Wilson, 7 January 1916, *FRUS, LP*, 1:334; Wilson to Lansing, ibid., 1:335; Lansing to Spring-Rice, 18 January 1916, *FRUS, 1916*, Supplement, 146–148; WHP to Lansing, 25 January 1916, ibid., 151–152; WHP to Lansing, 28 January 1916, ibid., 152–153; Lansing to House, 3 February, SI:SC, Box 69, EMHP. In an indication of Page's growing estrangement from State, Lansing conveyed his proposal through Cecil Spring-Rice, the British ambassador in Washington, rather than through Page, who did not learn of it until a week later.

president, imploring him to sever relations and take economic reprisals against the Central Powers. Page assured Wilson that if he followed this advice, "you will quickly end the war. ... The moral weight of the United States will be the deciding force in bringing an early peace for which you will receive immortal credit." Further hesitancy, on the other hand, "will bring us only a thankless, opulent, and dangerous isolation." Page acknowledged that such hard truths might be unwelcome in Washington, but insisted, "My loyalty to you ... would not be absolute if I shrank from respectfully sending my solemn conviction of our duty." When House read a draft of this cable, he told the ambassador not to send it. Page ignored him.[53]

The bloom was off Page's friendship with House by the time the colonel finished his mission. "Last night House left London for Falmouth to sail for N.Y. on Friday," Page wrote in his diary. "He cannot come again – or I go." Page felt that House had done "a lot of harm here that I must somehow turn to good." House, for his part, concluded from his European errand that Page was hopeless. The colonel informed Wilson after arriving in Washington, "We have in Page a cog that refuses to work smoothly in the machinery you have set in motion to bring about peace." He advised the president to bring Page home "for consultations." A few weeks stateside might acquaint the ambassador with popular opinion and make plain to him that the majority of his fellow Americans wanted nothing to do with the European bloodbath. Wilson refrained from taking that step, but he was clearly dissatisfied with his representative in London. He wrote of House's report on Page's behavior, "It lowers my opinion of the man immensely."[54]

By this point, Page's opinion of Wilson was no higher. "There is a real lack of leadership," he confided to his diary. "Every American would follow gladly if the president were to hold up his hand and say 'Come on!'" Yet Wilson clung to the belief that "the country desires peace first, last, and all the time." He had surrounded himself with "pusillanimous men" like Bryan and Lansing – "Chautauqua-millennium, halo-crowned, angel-winged idiots" – who reinforced his worst tendencies. "I want a real army to clean this crowd up," declared the ambassador. "I'd hang old

[53] Memo: "A Programme," 12 February 1916, WHPP; WHP to Wilson, 17 February 1916, *FRUS, LP,* 1:705–706; Diary Entry, 15 February 1916, Diary, WHPP.
[54] Diary Entries, 24 and 13 February 1916, Diary, WHPP; House to Wilson, 10 May 1916, Reel 72, WWP; House to Wilson, 18 May 1916, ibid.; Wilson to House, 17 May 1916, SI:SC, Box 69, EMHP.

William J. [Bryan] for treason and hang his followers to the nearest lampposts and put up big, electric signs at night: 'Now we propose to become men!'"[55]

Such pronouncements verged on Rooseveltian self-parody and did little credit to their author, but they indicate the stress that Page was under. The first half of 1916 was the most taxing period of his ambassadorship, as the fortunes of war went against the Allies and it became apparent that they could not win without American participation. January saw the end of the Gallipoli campaign, February the start of the Battle of Verdun. "It's a periodical slaughter-pen," Page wrote his friend and business partner Frank Doubleday. "I'd as lief live in the Chicago stockyards. There they kill beeves and pigs. Here they kill men and (incidentally) women and children." Page was determined "to be of what service I can to these heroic people," but he felt increasingly ineffectual as his government sat on its hands, issuing occasional protest notes and refusing to acknowledge the snarling German wolf at the door.[56]

Wilson lived down to Page's expectations when a U-boat torpedoed the French passenger steamer *Sussex* in the English Channel on 24 March. Eighty persons, among them Americans, were killed or injured. This seemed a clear violation of the *Arabic* pledge, and Page begged Wilson to break relations with Germany. Such an act, he said, "would quickly end the war" and "save perhaps a million lives." Wilson instead waited nearly a month before giving notice that the United States would "sever diplomatic relations with the German Empire altogether" unless Germany halted its submarine attacks on passenger and merchant ships. Here was the ultimatum that Page thought ought to have been issued after the *Lusitania*'s sinking. Berlin, however, defused it by promising that its submarines would not sink merchantmen or passenger liners without warning and without appropriate humanitarian precautions – but only on condition that Washington forced London to relax its blockade. If that relaxation did not occur, the German government declared, Berlin "would then be facing a new situation in which it must reserve [to] itself complete liberty of decision." The "*Sussex* pledge" was therefore meaningless because Berlin qualified it by insisting on a proviso that Washington could not fulfill; the British had already demonstrated that they had no intention of altering their blockade. Wilson accepted the pledge but not the proviso, further muddying the diplomatic waters. While he had

---

[55] Diary Entry, 8 May 1916, Diary, WHPP; WHP to Loring, 3 April 1916, ibid.
[56] WHP to Doubleday, 29 May 1916, *LL WHP*, 2:134, 139.

averted hostilities with Germany in the short term, Page observed, he had failed to resolve the problem of the submarine or bring the war any closer to an end.[57]

The president compounded his *Sussex* blunder, in Page's eyes, with a speech to the League to Enforce Peace on 27 May 1916. This address represented Wilson's first public announcement of his idea for what would come to be known as the League of Nations – he called it "a universal association of the nations ... to prevent any war" – and he struck a typically lofty tone, refusing to identify any of the belligerents by name and invoking instead "the great interests of civilization." Much of the speech was unobjectionable, but one passage stuck in the Allied craw. With the war's "causes and objects," Wilson proclaimed, "we are not concerned. The obscure fountains from which its stupendous flood has burst forth we are not interested to search for or explore." Statesmen in Britain and France interpreted this as a claim that both sides in the Great War were equally at fault – a supreme insult given the sacrifices made. "[A]nother too-proud-to-fight," was Page's disgusted reaction; he warned State that "peace-talk doesn't go down here now, and the less we indulge in it, the better."[58]

Page had by now fallen completely out of favor with the White House. "He is clean, able, and honest," House noted in his diary, "and he may be right in his views, but they are not the president's views – hence the trouble." Wilson began giving thought to replacing his wayward ambassador. He floated the notion of "kicking [Page] upstairs" by appointing him secretary of agriculture, but decided against it because he did not wish to offend the current head of the agriculture department, David Houston. House advised giving the London post to Cleveland Dodge, Wilson's old friend and a generous contributor to Democratic Party causes. Dodge, House told the president, "is loyal and has good sense, and that is all you want in an ambassador." The colonel also recommended the minister to Belgium, Brand Whitlock, as a possible successor

---

[57] WHP to Lansing, 26 March 1916, *FRUS, LP*, 1:706; Lansing to Gerard, 18 April 1916, *FRUS*, 1916, Supplement, 232–237; Gerard to Lansing, 4 May 1916, ibid., 257–260; WHP to Arthur Page, 8 May 1916, WHPP.

[58] Woodrow Wilson, Address Delivered at the First Annual Assemblage of the League to Enforce Peace: "American Principles," 27 May 1916, *The American Presidency Project*, www.presidency.uscb.edu/ws/?pid=65391; WHP to House, 30 May 1916, *IPCH*, 2:302. See also Notes of a Private and Informal Conversation with Sir Edward Grey, 27 July 1916, *LLWHP*, 2:160–163; Notes on a Conversation with Lord Bryce, 31 July 1916, ibid., 2:164–166.

to Page. Wilson received these suggestions noncommittally. We cannot know from the record how close he came to dismissing the ambassador, but his ultimate decision was to keep him on. Whether because of personal loyalty, lack of a suitable replacement, or reluctance to damage Anglo-American relations, Wilson allowed Page to remain as the nation's most important diplomatic representative, and Page continued to chart his own course.[59]

The U-boats were on their good behavior for nine months following the *Sussex* pledge, and, as had been the case earlier when German-American relations improved, popular and official opinion in the United States turned increasingly anti-British. Two events in particular incensed millions of Americans against their former mother country. First, London savagely suppressed an Irish revolt in the spring of 1916. Downing Street viewed the so-called Easter Rising as a stab in the back and its leaders as traitors, undeserving of mercy. Roger Casement, a former British colonial official who sought German military aid for the rebels, was quickly tried and hanged, despite a U.S. Senate resolution urging commutation of his death sentence. Page had no sympathy for Casement or his cohorts; he noted in his diary that "Irish martyrdom is perhaps the cheapest thing in the world to achieve." Nonetheless, he was aware that the rebellion had caused Britain's reputation to plunge in the United States, especially among Irish-Americans, at an inopportune time.[60]

More troubling than the Easter Rising was the British proclamation of a blacklist of more than eighty American companies suspected of trafficking with the Central Powers. British subjects were henceforward forbidden to trade with these firms. While London was within its rights in drawing up the blacklist, it sparked bellows of protest in the United States from business leaders who felt that it discriminated against them. Wilson thought it an insult. "I am, I must admit, about at the end of my patience with Great Britain and the Allies," he wrote House. "This blacklist business is the last straw. ... I am seriously considering asking Congress to authorize me to prohibit loans and restrict exportations to the Allies." The president did in fact persuade Congress to clothe him with power to close U.S. ports to Britons who boycotted blacklisted firms. Wilson never

---

[59] Diary Entry, 17 May 1916, SII:D, Box 296, EMHP; Wilson to House, 2 July 1916, SI:SC, Box 121, EMHP; House to Wilson, 18 May 1916, Reel 72, WWP; House to Wilson, 14 May 1916, SI:SC, Box 69, EMHP.

[60] Diary Entry, 3 August 1916, Diary, WHPP. For the impact of the Irish rebellion in the United States, see *Ireland's Allies: America and the 1916 Easter Rising*, ed. Miriam Nyhan Grey (Dublin: University College of Dublin Press, 2016).

used this authority, but Congress's willingness to grant it indicated the sorry state of Anglo-American relations as the war moved into its climactic stage. Page observed with dismay that Washington was now taking almost as stern a position with London as with Berlin.[61]

"THE GREATEST ISSUE IN THE WORLD"

Bowing to advice from House and members of State, Wilson called Page home in late July. "It is our hope," the president told the colonel, "that he may get back a little way at least to the American point of view about things." House wrote State Department counselor Frank Polk that Wilson wanted Page to "get a complete bath of American opinion." Page did not understand the summons this way; he thought he was returning stateside to meet with the president, and the prospect delighted him. "Such a visit will be of infinite help to me," he wrote Wilson shortly before his ship left Liverpool. "And it will be a great pleasure, as well as a great benefit, to see you, Mr. President." Time and again, Page felt, he had been thwarted in his attempts to make the administration see reason because of the meddling of interlopers like Lansing, men who knew nothing of political and military realities in Europe but who had the advantage of being able to strong-arm Wilson in person rather than via letter-writing or telegraphy. Page was certain he could convince the president to take up arms against the Central Powers if he could speak to him face-to-face.[62]

He had by this point been away from home for three and one-half years, two of which had been consumed by the war. A certain culture shock upon arriving in a nation at peace was to be expected. In Page's case, however, the jolt was especially severe. He was flabbergasted by the apparent indifference of the president and his chief advisers to the death struggle being waged across the Atlantic. The day after Page's arrival in Washington, he lunched with Wilson at the White House, and the discussion consisted entirely of idle chat. "Not a word about England," Page

---

[61] Wilson to House, 23 July 1916, SI:SC, Box 121, EMHP; WHP to Wilson, 21 July 1916, Reel 72, WWP. For the blacklist controversy, see Thomas A. Bailey, "The United States and the Blacklist during the Great War," *Journal of Modern History* 6 (March 1934): 14–35. Page thought the blacklist a "gross ... mistake" and so informed Grey's second-in-command, Sir Robert Cecil. WHP to Lansing, 22 July 1916, *FRUS*, 1916, Supplement, 412–413. See also Diary Entry, 15 December 1915, Diary, WHPP.

[62] Wilson to House, 23 July 1916, SI:SC, Box 121, EMHP; House to Polk, 25 July 1916, Box 11, Frank Polk Papers, Sterling Library, Yale University, New Haven, Connecticut; WHP to Wilson, 21 July 1916, WHPP.

noted in his diary. "Not a word about foreign policy or foreign relations."
When the ambassador tried to broach war-related subjects, Wilson told
him that an impending railroad strike was engaging his full attention.
Page offered to meet with the president at a time when his mind was free.
Wilson then gave Page a broad hint. Did not the ambassador want to "go
off for a rest and come back?" Page said no. "I preferred to do my errands
with the Department," he recorded, "but I should hold myself at his
convenience and his command."[63]

Page's errands with Foggy Bottom were even more frustrating. He had
not met Lansing before, but he had formed an unfavorable impression of
him based on State's notes to the British government. The secretary soon
confirmed that impression. In their initial encounter, Page noted, Lansing
"betrayed not the slightest curiosity about our relations with England.
The only remark he made was that I'd find a different atmosphere in
Washington from the atmosphere in London." Subsequent meetings
added to Page's discomfort. At a luncheon with Lansing and other
cabinet members, the ambassador recalled, the "talk was solely jocular,
about the food, about all sorts of silly commonplaces; not a word was
said to indicate that any man of thought sat at the table, barely a word
which showed that anybody there knew that a war was going on." Page
met, by his count, five times with Lansing during his leave, and each
conference deepened his conviction that the secretary was not "equal to
the task" history had assigned him. He was "a mere routine clerk, law-
book precedent man, no grasp, no imagination, no constructive ability –
measuring Armageddon, if he tries to measure it at all, with a six-inch
rule. . . . O God! What a crime and what a shame to have this manikin in
that place now!" With Lansing running State, Page concluded, it was
little wonder that U.S. policy toward Britain was so legalistic, pedantic,
and shortsighted.[64]

The ambassador got his chance to reverse that policy two weeks into
his visit, or so he thought. Wilson invited him to dine again at the White
House. Also in attendance were Ambassador to France William Sharp (on
leave, like Page), Mrs. Wilson, and three of the president's cousins. Page
showed up prepared to make the case for cobelligerency, but, to his
chagrin, the conversation was once more all small talk. "Not one word
about foreign affairs," Page noted. "The war wasn't mentioned. Sharp

---

[63] Memorandum: "About Washington," 30 August 1916, WHPP.
[64] Diary Entry, 19 August 1916, Diary, WHPP; Memorandum: "Leave, 1916 – Lansing,"
ibid.; Memorandum: "About Washington," 30 August 1916, ibid.

and I might have come from Bungtown and Jonesville and not from France and England." Afterwards the party drove to Capitol Hill, where Wilson addressed Congress on the strike. Page then rode back to the White House in a separate car than Wilson and found, when he arrived, that the president was already inside and at work. "Does he expect me to go in and say goodbye?" Page asked a doorman, who told him no. "Thus," Page noted in his diary the following day, Wilson "had no idea of talking to me now, or ever. Not at lunch or after did he suggest a conversation about American-English affairs or say anything about my seeing him again." The ambassador could not help but wonder why he had been summoned home in the first place.[65]

"I'm not going back to London," Page wrote his secretary, Irwin Laughlin, "till the president has said something to me or at least till I have said something to him. I am now going down to Garden City and New York till the president send [sic] for me; or if he do [sic] not send for me, I'm going to his house and sit on his front steps until he come [sic] out." True to his word, Page spent the next two weeks either visiting his son Arthur in Long Island or catching up on publishing work at the Doubleday-Page offices in Garden City. In his spare time, characteristic-ally, he wrote – pages and pages of frantic commentary on the war and Wilson's response to it. "The P[resident] suppressed free thought and free speech when he insisted on personal neutrality," Page scribbled on the stationery of a New York hotel. "The mass of the American people found themselves forbidden to think or talk, and this forbidding had a sufficient impact to make them take refuge in indifference. ... That wasn't leader-ship in a democracy." Elsewhere, Page lamented that Wilson "missed the cue when he elevated the negative quality of neutrality into a positive virtue when the greatest issue in the world, or that has ever arisen in the world, is thrust upon the attention and conscience of men." While Ameri-cans "fell back at their intellectual and moral ease," the ambassador proclaimed, "absolutism and autocracy have grown in power and in range and in territory."[66]

Page's principal effort during this tense period was a fourteen-page *cri de coeur* titled "Notes toward an Explanation of the British Feeling toward the United States" that he intended to submit to Wilson when the two men next met. In it, he begged the president not to permit "trivial

---

[65] Memorandum: "About Washington," 30 August 1916, WHPP.
[66] Page cited in *LLWHP*, 2:179; Memorandum: "About Washington," 30 August 1916, WHPP; "Notes," September 1916, ibid.

trade disputes" to "imperil the natural development of the human race."
American policy, he said, had "caused the British to think that we regard
a technicality as important as a principle," and this was tragic because
London was "fighting for the preservation of free government" against
"the strongest and most arrogant military absolutism that ever existed."
Page conceded that the exigencies of war had obliged Britain to take
measures of questionable legality, but he insisted that such considerations
were negligible when weighed against "the ultimate triumph of international good will." If Americans would only adopt "the proper perspective on this present upheaval of the world," they would recognize that the
United States, no less than Britain, benefited from "the sympathetic
understanding of the English-speaking nations" and that Washington
was wrong to make "no moral distinction" between democracy and
"predatory absolutism." With considerable exaggeration, Page claimed
that "the moral judgment of practically the whole civilized world, outside
of Germany" was on Britain's side, "except only the government of the
United States." He urged Wilson to embrace America's role as "leader of
the English-speaking world" and join the British in "their struggle against
a destructive military autocracy." It was the same argument Page had
been making for years, grown more desperate as he observed the
maddening apathy of his fellow Americans toward the Great War.[67]

The ambassador finally managed to secure a one-on-one meeting with
Wilson by writing him, "I have ... a most important and confidential
message for you from the British government which they prefer should be
orally delivered." That was untrue – Page had no such message – but his
bluff worked; the president invited him to spend a night at Shadow Lawn,
the New Jersey seaside estate that served as a summer White House.
A wreck on the line delayed Page's train, and he arrived close to midnight,
too late to speak to Wilson. The two men did not sit down for their long-
awaited conference until the following morning.[68]

Records of this exchange are spotty. Wilson sent Lansing a short note a
week later in which he claimed to have "covered the whole subject ... in a
way which I am sure left nothing to be desired in the way of explicitness
and firmness of tone." Page's account, scrawled in his address book on
the ride back to New York, only recorded what the president said, either
because Wilson did most of the talking or because Page had presented the

[67] "Notes toward an Explanation of the British Feeling toward the United States," 14 September 1916, WHPP.
[68] WHP to Wilson, 21 September 1916, *LLWHP*, 2:183.

case for Anglo-American partnership so many times that he felt no need
to write it out again. In any event, he captured Wilson's anger at Britain
and France. "The P[resident] said he started out as heartily in sympathy
w[ith the] Allies as any man could be," Page noted. "But Eng[land] had
gone on doing anything she wished, regardless of the rights of others, &
Amer[ican] pride (*his* pride) was hurt." To Page's distress, Wilson once
more appeared to put Britain and Germany on the same level: "He
described this war as a result of many causes, some of long origin. He
spoke of England's having the earth, of Germany's wanting it. Of course,
the German system is opposed to everything American. But this didn't
seem to him to carry any very great moral reprehensibility." Wilson also
complained about the "long English delay in answering our notes," a
practice that, he said, "showed contempt." When Page urged the president not to make any further attempts to secure an armistice, Wilson
bristled, insisting that he would be "glad" to participate in any "proposal
looking towards peace." Page also received a negative response to his
request that Wilson refrain from exercising the retaliatory powers Congress had conferred upon him. The most Wilson would promise was that
he would not invoke the legislation until after the election, "lest it might
seem playing politics." If he were reelected, however, and there were
"continued British provocations afterwards, ... then he would." Page
handed the president a German medal commemorating the sinking of
the *Lusitania*, but Wilson was unimpressed; he inspected the item briefly
and set it aside. By the time Wilson rose to signal that the meeting was
over, Page must have felt like a beaten man.[69]

He left Shadow Lawn shortly thereafter. Prior to departing, he gave
Wilson his fourteen-page plea for solidarity among the English-speaking
peoples, but he cannot have had much hope that it would sway the
president. His only other significant conference before returning to
London was a stormy encounter with House in which he condemned
Wilson, Lansing, and every other major policymaker in Washington. "He
is," House noted in his diary, "as pro-British as ever and cannot see the
American point of view. ... He declares none of us understand the
situation or the high purposes of the British in this war." House defended

[69] Wilson to Lansing, 29 September 1916, *FRUS, LP*, 1:319; Entry, Address Book, 1916,
WHPP (emphasis in the original). For Page's furnishing of the *Lusitania* medal, see
LLWHP, 2:185. The ambassador wrote about the encounter only once again, in a diary
entry composed on the eve of American belligerency. Wilson, he noted, "showed a great
deal of toleration for Germany and was, during the whole morning I talked with him,
complaining of England." Diary Entry, 1 April 1917, Diary, WHPP.

the administration, lashed the British for their "cant and hypocrisy," and otherwise made plain how utterly another of Page's friendships had foundered on the rocks of U.S. foreign policy. The ambassador's six-week journey home, begun in frustration, ended in despair.[70]

"*I* HAVE *ACCOMPLISHED SOMETHING*"

Wilson won reelection in November, largely on the strength of the unauthorized campaign slogan "He Kept Us out of War," and, as was customary for ambassadors at the close of a presidential term, Page submitted his resignation. It was, unsurprisingly, a long, passionate letter, a pull-out-all-the-stops effort that appealed to Wilson's morality, patriotism, and ego. Page volunteered to "lay down my work here" if the president so wished, but he felt bound to reiterate his point that "only some sort of active and open identification with the Allies can put us in effective protest against" the "German system" that sought to "reduce Europe to the vassalage of a military autocracy, which may then overrun the whole world or drench it in blood." This course, Page insisted, was the one "our fathers would surely have wished us to take – and would have expected us to take – and that our children will be proud of us for taking." He assured the president that if America intervened now on the Allied side, it "would probably not cost us a man in battle nor any considerable treasure." And the payoff would be magnificent: "The United States would stand, as no other nation has ever stood in the world – predominant and unselfish – on the highest ideals ever reached in human government. It is a vision as splendid as the Holy Grail [*sic*]." House, upon reading this message, remarked to Wilson that Page obviously hoped to have his resignation rejected.[71]

The president, however, seemed inclined to accept it. Apparently, the conference at Shadow Lawn had caused Wilson to question once more whether he wanted Page heading Embassy London. A week after the election, House met Wilson for an extended discussion about the ambassador in which, according to the colonel's journal, "we talked ... of the impossibility of using him to advantage." Both House and Wilson agreed

---

[70] Diary Entry, 25 September 1916, *IPCH*, 2:318–319. For an incisive treatment of Page's visit, see Ross Gregory, "The Superfluous Ambassador: Walter Hines Page's Return to Washington, 1916," *The Historian* 28 (May 1966): 389–404.

[71] WHP to Wilson, 24 November 1916, *LLWHP*, 2:190–195. For House's reaction, see Cooper, *Walter Hines Page*, 352.

that Page was "perfectly honest in his belief that the best thing that could happen to this country was an alliance between Britain and the United States," but they also thought that "he is so obsessed with this idea that it is practically impossible to make him view the situation from any other angle." Wilson spoke of "recalling Page," declaring that "no man must stand in the way" of peace. House, while not averse to this move, pointed out a potential problem: "practically every member of our London Embassy" shared Page's views. Getting rid of the ambassador would entail replacing the whole embassy staff. Wilson declined to take any action for the present, but he raised the issue again two weeks later when, as House recorded, "he expressed indifference to Page's attitude" and remarked that he "felt quite content to have him resign." Again, House urged caution. If Page resigned, "saying he did not approve the president's [peace] overtures," House noted, that would make the ambassador "popular in England" and Wilson "correspondingly unpopular." That objection found its mark, and Wilson stayed his hand.[72]

By mid-December, though, House was eager to see Page go. Hugh Wallace, a friend of both House and Page, showed the colonel a letter he had received from the ambassador, in which, House noted, "He [Page] strikes at the president covertly and cruelly. ... He thinks half or two thirds of the administration and those near the president, which I suppose includes me, should be discarded for better men." This was too much for House, who in his next meeting with Wilson recommended two candidates to replace Page: Wallace or Thomas Jones, a former Princeton classmate of the president. Both, the colonel observed, were staunch Democrats whose personal fortunes would enable them to meet the financial requirements of the London ambassadorship. Wilson demurred; he did not think Jones could be confirmed by the Senate, and Wallace, he said, was not "sufficiently serious minded." The president preferred Cleveland Dodge, the wealthy campaign contributor whom House had earlier suggested for Embassy London. At a mid-January 1917 meeting with House, Wilson identified Dodge as a likely candidate and spoke, House wrote, "of his determination to accept" Page's resignation. Wilson went so far as to offer Dodge the London post, but Dodge turned it down, citing ill health. In a remarkable diary entry composed a few weeks later, House recorded the president sighing that "we would be compelled to have a British-American representing the United States at the Court of

---

[72] Diary Entries, 14 and 26 November 1916, SII:D, Box 296, EMHP.

St. James." Among the reasons for keeping Page on, Wilson said, was the fact that he "could not find a suitable man to take his place."[73]

Page was unaware of how tenuous his position was, and it is unlikely that he would have behaved differently had he known. During the final months before U.S. entry into the war, he worked to undermine Wilson's last-ditch peacemaking efforts. In late December 1916, the president directed Lansing to send a proposal to the ambassadors of all the belligerent countries affirming that "the objects which the statesmen ... on both sides have in mind in this war are virtually the same." Wilson invited the Allied and Central Powers to state plainly "the precise objects which would, if attained, satisfy them and their people." He expressed confidence that "the terms which the belligerents on one side and on the other would deem it necessary to insist upon are not so irreconcilable as some have feared." Washington, he said, stood ready to facilitate peace. Lansing's covering telegram instructed Page to press the president's proposition "with the utmost earnestness."[74]

The ambassador could not obey that order. From his perspective, Wilson was making the same mistake he had made earlier by presuming equivalence between Britain and Germany. Page lost no time in relaying the British reaction to Washington. It was, he cabled, "a deep feeling of disappointment and in many quarters even of anger." He observed that the "British feel that that this is a holy and defensive war which must be fought to a decisive conclusion to save free government in the world from military tyranny." The president, by "placing the Allies and the Central Powers on the same moral level" had shown "a misunderstanding of the aims of the Allies" and caused "surprise and depression" throughout Britain. When Page was summoned to Whitehall by Undersecretary of State for Foreign Affairs Lord Robert Cecil to defend Wilson's message, he instead joined Cecil in denouncing it. According to Cecil's memorandum of the meeting, Page said that "though his countrymen were fully aware of the facts of the war, they did not seem to appreciate what the German really was, or that Prussian militarism was, as he put it, 'an organized crime.'" Cecil called American policy pro-German in effect if not intention, and Page did not disagree. He apologized for Wilson's

---

[73] Diary Entries, 17 and 14 December 1916, 12 January 1917, 28 March 1917, SII:D, Box 296, EMHP. For Wilson's offering of the ambassadorship to Dodge, see Cooper, *Walter Hines Page*, 355.

[74] Lansing to the Ambassadors and Ministers of Belligerent Countries, 18 December 1916, *FRUS*, 1916, Supplement, 97–99; covering telegram cited in Gregory, *Walter Hines Page*, 182.

proposal and vowed to make the British case even more zealously to his stateside supervisors. Only Wilson's unawareness of this conversation saved Page's job.[75]

Page similarly worked at cross-purposes to Wilson when the president delivered his famous "peace without victory" address. This oration grew out of the refusal of both sets of belligerents to accede to Wilson's request for war aims. Berlin thought it insulting; Ambassador Sharp, cabling from Paris, reported that the British and French could not agree to it until the war had been brought to a "victorious close." Undaunted, Wilson addressed Congress, and the world, on 22 January 1917 with a speech that Senator Ben Tillman of South Carolina deemed the "noblest utterance since the Declaration of Independence." The president called for freedom of the seas, national self-determination for countries large and small, disarmament, and a league of nations to ensure world accord. He insisted that only a "peace without victory" would be lasting. Page saw an advance copy of the speech, and the notorious phrase leaped out. Frantic, he cabled Wilson with a request to change it to "peace without conquest" or something of the sort. He predicted that, unaltered, the address would "provoke a storm of criticism that may greatly lessen your influence hereafter." Wilson refused to change a word.[76]

"Peace without victory" hit London like a torpedo. Apart from again appearing to put Britain and Germany on the same plane, the speech was spectacularly ill timed, as David Lloyd George, the new British prime minister, had just proclaimed that there could be no peace without victory. Page, in anguish, raged in private memoranda against Wilson. The president, he wrote, "does not at all understand ... that the [Allied] Powers ... cannot make 'peace without victory.' If they do, they will become vassals of Germany." Wilson's "distressing peace-move – utterly out of touch with the facts of the origin of the war or of its conduct or of the mood and necessities of Great Britain" was "a remote, academic deliverance, while Great Britain and France were fighting for their very lives." The ambassador was unable to justify or explain his government's policy to his hosts, and he made no effort to do so. He commiserated with

[75] WHP to Lansing, 22 December 1916, *FRUS,* 1916, Supplement, 108–109; Cecil cited in Gregory, *Walter Hines Page,* 184.

[76] Gerard to Lansing, 26 December 1916, *FRUS,* 1916, Supplement, 117–118; Sharp to Lansing, 10 January 1917, *FRUS,* 1917 (Washington, D.C.: U.S. Government Printing Office, 1931), Supplement, 1:8; Tillman cited in Bailey, *Diplomatic History of the American People,* 590; WHP to Lansing, 7 January 1917, *FRUS, LP,* 1:713–714. For Wilson's response, see Lansing, *War Memoirs,* 195.

Lloyd George and Arthur Balfour, Grey's successor as foreign secretary, and he hoped against hope that Berlin would take some action to force Wilson to face facts.[77]

Little did Page know that the German High Command had already initiated such a move. In early January 1917, Field Marshal Paul von Hindenburg, Quartermaster General Erich Ludendorff, and other leading military figures persuaded the Kaiser that an unrestricted submarine campaign would bring Britain to its knees before the Americans could mobilize and send troops across the Atlantic. Chancellor Theobald von Bethmann-Hollweg argued strenuously – and presciently – against this strategy, but the officers carried the day, and on 31 January the German ambassador to America informed Lansing that "all ships" found near British waters "will be sunk," without regard to their origin.[78]

Wilson had no choice. The *Sussex* pledge committed him to a diplomatic rupture, and, after several sleepless nights, he went before Congress to announce that the United States had broken relations with Germany. Page was, of course, overjoyed, but he tempered his enthusiasm, noting that Wilson had told legislators that this severance of diplomatic ties did not mean that the United States was at war. "I refuse to believe that it is the intention of the German authorities to do in fact what they have warned us they will feel at liberty to do," the president said. "Only actual overt acts on their part can make me believe it now." Page worried that Wilson might yet avoid hostilities by adopting a definition of "overt acts" that excluded everything short of a German attack on the U.S. mainland.[79]

The next two months were torture for Page, as Wilson refused to respond to increasingly flagrant provocations. U-boats sent one ship after another to the bottom, in some cases with Americans aboard. British intelligence intercepted and decoded a note from the German foreign minister, Arthur Zimmermann, to the German ambassador in Mexico City, proposing that Mexico become Berlin's ally against the United States; if the Central Powers were victorious, Zimmermann declared,

---

[77] Lloyd George cited in Gregory, *Walter Hines Page*, 186; Diary Entry, 16 January 1917, Diary, WHPP; WHP cited in *LLWHP*, 2:213–214.

[78] Bernstorff to Lansing, 31 January 1917, *FRUS*, 1917, Supplement, 1:97–102. For the Kaiser's fateful decision, which doomed his empire, see Dirk Steffen, "The Holtzendorff Memorandum of 22 December 1916 and Germany's Declaration of Unrestricted U-boat Warfare," *Journal of Military History* (January 2004): 215–224.

[79] Woodrow Wilson: Address to a Joint Session of Congress on the Severance of Diplomatic Relations with Germany, 3 February 1917. *The American Presidency Project*, www .presidency.ucsb.edu/ws/?pid=65397.

Mexico would recover Arizona, New Mexico, and Texas. Made public in early March, the Zimmermann telegram caused a wave of anti-German sentiment to sweep America. Still, Wilson hesitated. "I am now willing to record my conviction that we shall not get into war at all," Page confided to his journal. "The P[resident] is constitutionally unable to come to such a point of action."[80]

Yet matters had, in fact, become intolerable by early April. A Philadelphia newspaper aptly summarized the situation when it noted, "The only difference between war and what we have now is that now we aren't fighting back." Resistant to the last but finally resolved, Wilson called Congress into special session and asked its members to accept the status of belligerency that Germany had thrust upon the United States.[81]

Tellingly, the president's war message seemed cribbed from countless Page cables, letters, and notes. He called the German government a "natural foe to liberty" that waged "warfare against mankind," a "selfish and autocratic power" that "was not and could never be our friend," and a "little group of ambitious men" who had "thrown aside all considerations of humanity and of right." The United States must fight, he said, "to vindicate the principles of peace and justice in the world." At stake was nothing less than "civilization itself." Wilson at last acknowledged what Page had been insisting on for two years: "Neutrality is no longer feasible or desirable where the peace of the world is involved." The speech's most oft-cited phrases – "The right is more precious than peace"; "The world must be made safe for democracy" – echoed Page's thoughts, if not his exact words. Wilson could not have presented the Walter Hines Page case for belligerency more emphatically had he allowed the ambassador to write it himself.[82]

One can imagine Page's reaction to this message, and to the news that Congress had overwhelmingly approved the war resolution. It must have seemed the end to a long nightmare. His diary over the next few days was

[80] WHP to Lansing, 24 February 1917, *FRUS*, 1917, Supplement, 1:147–148; Diary Entries, 19 February 1917, 2 March, 1917, Diary, WHPP. For Zimmermann's message, probably the most famous piece of diplomatic correspondence in history, see Barbara W. Tuchman, *The Zimmermann Telegram*, Reprint Edition (New York: Random House, 1985).
[81] Newspaper cited in David Kennedy, Lizabeth Cohen, and Mel Piehl, *The Brief American Pageant: A History of the Republic*, Volume II, Ninth Edition (Boston: Cengage Learning, 2017), 503.
[82] Woodrow Wilson: Address to a Joint Session of Congress Requesting a Declaration of War against Germany, 2 April 1917. *The American Presidency Project*, www.presidency.ucsb.edu/ws/?pid=65366.

filled with accounts of British euphoria: Balfour warmly shaking his hand and declaring, "It's a great day for the world"; the king assuring him, "Ah – ah – we knew where you stood all the time." Page wrote his son, "I cannot conceal nor can I repress my gratification that we are in the war at last. ... I *have* accomplished something." He observed, "I have such a sense of relief that I almost feel my job is now done."[83]

That was a keener assessment than Page could have known. Ross Gregory, author of the most meticulous study of Page's ambassadorship, notes that "the ambassador was more a spectator than a participant" in the frenzied months after U.S. entry into the conflict. Affairs were in the hands of the military men, and "Page's war diplomacy virtually was over." It was just as well. The ambassador was a spent force, worn down by stress and overwork. He stayed in charge of Embassy London until the Central Powers capitulated, but his health was gone; he lost an alarming amount of weight and suffered acute respiratory problems. Gentle suggestions that he resign were turned aside. He was determined to stick it out to the end. While he had the satisfaction of seeing the Allies triumphant, his persistence in office ensured that he would be too far gone to recover after his return home, and he breathed his last on 21 December 1918.[84]

Eight years later, during the isolationist 1920s, Harry Elmer Barnes summed up the historiographical consensus on Page by writing that the ambassador bore "a greater degree of guilt and responsibility than any other single 'American' ... for the entry of the United States into the World War." Page would not have appreciated his nationality being put in quotation marks, but he would otherwise have worn Barnes's calumny as a badge of honor. Ironically, he himself was more modest in appraising his role. "I shall always wonder but never find out what influence I had in driving the president over," he noted in mid-1917. "All I know is that my letters and telegrams for nearly two years – especially for the last twelve months – have put before him every reason that anybody has expressed why we should come in – in season and out of season." And, Page might have added, he had waged his lonely battle in the teeth of opposition from officials who outranked him.[85]

[83] Diary Entries, 3 April 1917, 5 May 1917, Diary, WHPP; WHP to Arthur Page, 28 April 1917, ibid.
[84] Gregory, *Walter Hines Page*, 200.
[85] Barnes, *Genesis of the World War*, 587; WHP to Arthur Page, 28 April 1917, *LLWHP*, 2:238–239.

5

"No 'Rubber Stamp' Ambassador"

Kennedy Appeases the Dictators

At least one person in Joseph Patrick Kennedy's wide circle of friends, flacks, and sycophants attempted to rescue the multimillionaire would-be-diplomat from himself. Upon learning that President Franklin Delano Roosevelt had tapped Kennedy to be the next U.S. ambassador to the Court of St. James, conservative columnist Boake Carter wrote Kennedy a seven-page, single-spaced letter begging him to decline the appointment.

"I trespass upon our friendship," Carter noted, but "I'm trying to save you some heartaches." He reminded Kennedy that "there will never be sent to London a diplomate [*sic*] that is stronger than Roosevelt. ... No matter who is sent to London, he will remain there only so long as he does what he is told from Washington. The minute he shows independence, he's through." And Kennedy was nothing if not independent. "I know the spirit that runs through you," Carter wrote. "It is a spirit that likes to go out and do big things, fight big battles, win against huge odds – yet hates to get hurt, hates to be double-crossed, would hate to be bruised and battered by a set of forces not of your own creation." A man with such spirit had no business working for Foggy Bottom, especially in the Roosevelt administration: "The Boss is running the State Department today, more than ever before. If he thinks certain things should be done as far as Great Britain is concerned, which you may think are cockeyed, you'll either have to carry them out, à la order boy, or explode or resign." Neither option would advance Kennedy's reputation or ambition, said Carter, and "if you don't realize that soon enough, you're going to be hurt as you were never hurt in your life."[1]

Carter trespassed further upon his friendship with Kennedy by making the same argument in his nationally syndicated column. "To me, Joseph Patrick Kennedy of Boston has all to lose and nothing to gain in the course of his public career by going to London," Carter told readers. "Kennedy ... is not, nor will be, a 'yes man.' He does not pussyfoot. Neither does he work 'under orders' when he realizes some orders he may be called upon to execute are opposed to his own principles of what he believes to be the honest, sincere, and right thing to do." In other words, he was not ambassadorial material.[2]

Carter's wise words were drowned out in the chorus of media approval for Roosevelt's choice. Newspapers from coast to coast welcomed the prospect of Kennedy as U.S. envoy to Great Britain. "We are going to see Joe Kennedy big in the international picture in the next few years," noted columnist R. R. K. in the *Los Angeles Daily News*, predicting that members of the British government would soon "look up at Kennedy with awe." The *Portland* (Maine) *News* assured readers that "no one could better fill the role of ambassador to the Court of St. James than Joseph P. Kennedy." According to the *Atlanta Constitution*, Senate confirmation of Kennedy as ambassador "gives to this country a representative who, by every past record, will ably fill America's most important foreign diplomatic post." Press commentary elsewhere was similarly rhapsodic: "We miss our guess if Mr. Kennedy does not win laurels in the diplomatic service"; "He should be a great success at the Court of St. James"; "There need be no misgivings about his ability to discharge his duties with credit to himself and his country"; "He will make a worthy representative of the American nation in London"; "He will fill the post with dignity."[3]

---

[1] Carter to JPK, 28 December 1937, U.S. Maritime Commission: Correspondence, Box 90, JPKP.

[2] Carter, "But ...," *New York Daily Mirror*, 13 January 1938. For a stinging response to Carter, see James Morgan, "Why We Have No Foreign Policy," *Boston Morning Globe*, 16 January 1938.

[3] R. R. K., "Today and Tomorrow," *Los Angeles Daily News*, 18 February 1938; "A Valiant Ambassador," *Portland* (Maine) *News*, 25 February 1938; "A New Ambassador," *Atlanta Constitution*, 15 January 1938; "Our New Envoy to England," *Rock Island* (Illinois) *Argus*, 28 February 1938; "Two First-Rate Appointments," *Boston Transcript*, 13 January 1938; "Ambassador Kennedy," *Boston Herald*, 10 December 1937; "Joseph P. Kennedy," *National City* (California) *News*, 4 February 1938; "A Gain and a Loss," *Boston Post*, 10 December 1937.

The most effusive endorsement of Kennedy came from the *New York Times*. As a number of historians and biographers have established, Arthur Krock, chief of the *Times*'s Washington bureau, was a mouthpiece for Kennedy, virtually on his payroll. The two men met in 1932 on Roosevelt's campaign train, and Kennedy soon enlisted Krock as an unofficial publicist. Krock praised Kennedy in his columns, gave him political advice, wrote speeches for him, and ghosted his 1936 book *I'm for Roosevelt*, in which Kennedy made the case that the New Deal benefited American business. In exchange for these and other services, Kennedy lavished Krock with gifts, allowed him to vacation at the Kennedy Palm Beach estate, and pressured *Times* publisher Arthur Sulzberger to make Krock the newspaper's editor-in-chief. Predictably, the *Times* hailed Kennedy's new assignment as "a brilliant new step in a remarkable career" and asserted, "The acclaim which has followed publication of the news that the president intends to appoint Joseph P. Kennedy as our ambassador to the Court of St. James is a spontaneous testimonial to the respect and regard in which [he] . . . is held by his fellow-citizens, regardless of their politics." Soon after that puff-piece ran, Krock wrote Kennedy, "[Y]ou were born lucky, and . . . you were never more fortunate than when you were sent to Europe in such a time."[4]

Rarely has a forecast been wider of the mark. Kennedy himself gave a more accurate preview of his ambassadorship when he learned the Senate had confirmed him. "I don't know what kind of diplomat I shall be," he wrote Roosevelt. "Probably rotten." The line was tossed off in jest, but it proved prescient. Apart from his lack of foreign-policy experience – which, as we have seen, has not always been a disadvantage for American diplomats – Kennedy was intellectually and temperamentally unfitted for his new job. A brilliant businessman who managed to flourish during the depths of the Depression, he viewed the world, as one historian puts it, "through the bars of the dollar sign," convinced that every international

[4] "No Higher Post," *New York Times*, 13 December 1937; Krock to JPK, 17 March 1938, Ambassador: Correspondent File, Box 110, JPKP; Joseph P. Kennedy, *I'm for Roosevelt* (New York: Reynal & Hitchcock, 1936). For the Kennedy-Krock alliance, see Ronald Kessler, *Sins of the Father: Joseph P. Kennedy and the Dynasty He Founded* (New York: Warner Books, 1996), 117–118, 182; Koskoff, *Joseph P. Kennedy*, 37–38, 82, 140–141, 202–203, 234–235, 271; David Nasaw, *The Patriarch: The Remarkable Life and Turbulent Times of Joseph P. Kennedy* (New York: Penguin Books, 2012), 212, 229, 236–237, 247, 256, 316, 327–328, 395–396, 435–436; Richard J. Whalen, *The Founding Father: The Story of Joseph P. Kennedy* (London: Hutchinson, 1964), 145–147, 156–157, 181, 191, 284, 295–296, 328.

problem was, at its core, an economic problem. He never appreciated the ideological factors that drove Adolf Hitler's rampage through Europe from 1938 through 1940, and he was consequently incapable of formulating a realistic response to that onslaught. Furthermore, he suffered from mind-lock, a refusal to reconsider and revise assumptions no matter how much evidence accumulated indicating that those beliefs were incorrect. Shortsighted and bullheaded, he was miscast in a role calling for breadth and suppleness.[5]

Kennedy's ambassadorship played out as an Alice-in-Wonderland reenactment of Walter Hines Page's challenge to the White House and State Department, with the roles of interventionist and isolationist reversed. "Old Joe" was outspokenly pro-fascist, declaring on numerous occasions that he considered Hitler's territorial claims valid, that he saw no moral distinction between Britain and Germany, and that the British must not count on the United States to bail them out in the event of conflict. He was also flagrantly defeatist. Britain could not survive a German attack, he insisted. Hitler would need only a month to invade and conquer the country. Echoing the claims of his friend Charles Lindbergh, Kennedy declared that the Luftwaffe was more powerful than anything the British could deploy and that only a swift capitulation to Hitler would prevent Britain from being "finished off economically, financially, politically, and socially." Kennedy outdid even British Prime Minister Neville Chamberlain in his efforts to appease Germany, hewing to that course well after Whitehall and Downing Street abandoned it. The outbreak of hostilities in September 1939 drove Kennedy to despair. He sent long, Cassandra-like reports over the transatlantic line in which he forecast an imminent Nazi victory. When the Blitz began, he predicted, "Hitler will be in Buckingham Palace in two weeks."[6]

The ambassador would later claim that he had just executed policies drawn up in Washington only to have Roosevelt stab him in the back when prowar sentiment swept America. Evidence does not sustain that assertion. Indeed, as we shall see, Kennedy routinely disobeyed White House and State Department orders and misrepresented the Roosevelt

---

[5] JPK to Franklin Delano Roosevelt (hereafter FDR), 13 January 1938, President's Secretary's File (hereafter PSF), Box 37, Franklin Delano Roosevelt Library, Hyde Park, New York (hereafter FDRL); Jane Karoli Vieth, "Joseph P. Kennedy: Ambassador to the Court of St. James" (Ph.D. Dissertation: Ohio State University, 1975), 544.

[6] JPK to FDR, 3 November 1939 in *Hostage to Fortune: The Letters of Joseph P. Kennedy*, Amanda Smith, ed. (New York: Penguin Books, 2001) (hereafter *HTF*), 398; JPK cited in Nasaw, *Patriarch*, 474.

administration's position to his host government. He also boasted about his independence, telling colleagues that he had reached an "understanding" with Roosevelt that he was not to be "simply an errand boy in London." When, two weeks into Kennedy's tenure, Secretary of State Cordell Hull sharply edited a speech the ambassador planned to give on the grounds that it was too indulgent of Germany's annexation of Austria, Kennedy fought back by pressuring the secretary to cancel a foreign-policy address of his own. Thereafter he made public statements that contravened the administration's policy, eliciting progressively sterner rebukes from Hull and Roosevelt. Even when the president ordered Kennedy to say nothing without prior clearance, the ambassador could not control his trigger-happy tongue.[7]

Kennedy's appeasement extended to arranging unauthorized meetings with Nazi officials in which he issued some of the most shameful remarks ever uttered by an American diplomat, among them his claim to Ambassador Herbert von Dirksen that Hitler's critics in the Roosevelt administration were "afraid of the Jews" and did not "dare to say anything good about Germany." Kennedy repeatedly praised Hitler in his conversations with Dirksen and other Nazi diplomats in London and expressed an eagerness to sit down personally with the Führer "to create a better atmosphere in German-American relations." While he was never able to arrange such a conference, he did meet in mid-1938 with Helmuth Wohlthat, minister-director on Nazi Field Marshal Hermann Goering's staff, despite having been ordered not to by Hull and Roosevelt. These actions undermined the effectiveness of FDR's condemnations of German policy and lent considerable aid and comfort to the Reich.[8]

Ultimately, of course, Kennedy failed to deliver Europe into German hands, but it was not for lack of effort. By the time Roosevelt accepted Kennedy's resignation in late 1940, Britain stood virtually alone against fascist tyranny, and the Nazi-Soviet nonaggression pact seemed to

---

[7] JPK cited in Carter to JPK, 28 December 1937, U.S. Maritime Commission: Correspondence, Box 90, JPKP. The ambassador mounted a defense of his conduct in a memoir coauthored with aides James Fayne, James Landis, Paul Mallon, and Elizabeth Walsh. He chose not to publish the manuscript because he feared it would jeopardize the political careers of his sons. Various drafts of Kennedy's memoir, along with supplementary notes, can be found in Boxes 147–155, JPKP.

[8] JPK cited in Dirksen to Weizsacker, 13 June 1938, *Documents in German Foreign Policy, 1918–1945* (hereafter *DGFP*), From Neurath to Ribbentrop (Washington, D.C.: U.S. Government Printing Office, 1949), Series D, 1:714, 718.

guarantee Hitler free rein in the West. Few had done more to call forth this threat to human liberty than "Old Joe."

The literature on Kennedy's ambassadorship is vaster than on Page's, and it is remarkably consistent. With the exception of a spirited but unconvincing effort by Will Swift to rehabilitate the ambassador, two generations of historians have arrived at the same verdict. Conrad Black, speaking for the profession, judges Kennedy "one of the worst diplomatic appointments in the history of the United States." Biographer Ronald Kessler flays Kennedy for "well-documented anti-Semitism," "efforts to appease Adolf Hitler," "gullibility," "self-pity," and "monumental lack of faith in the American people and democracy." Kennedy "had neither the courage nor the will to fight," writes Kessler. "Like most bullies, he had little inner strength. When confronted with might, he caved." To these reproofs we might add that Kennedy, unlike other American rogue diplomats, did not advance his country's cause. On the contrary, his insubordination worked to the advantage of the Nazis. The pessimism and defeatism he repeatedly voiced stoked anti-American sentiment in Britain to the point where a public opinion poll conducted toward the close of his ambassadorship indicated that only 27 percent of Britons viewed the United States with favor. At a moment of supreme crisis, when the "special relationship" was more essential than ever to the survival of democracy, Kennedy all but scuttled it.[9]

---

[9] Conrad Black, *Franklin Delano Roosevelt: Champion of Freedom* (New York: Public Affairs, 2003), 439; Kessler, *Sins of the Father*, 2, 169, 174, 181, 184; poll cited in Mayers, *FDR's Ambassadors*, 186. In addition to Kessler's text, there are at least five biographies of Kennedy, all of which are critical of his service in London: William J. Duncliffe, *The Life and Times of Joseph P. Kennedy* (New York: McFadden, 1965); Koskoff, *Joseph P. Kennedy*; Nasaw, *Patriarch*; Ted Schwartz, *Joseph P. Kennedy: The Mogul, the Mob, the Statesman, and the Making of an American Myth* (Hoboken, NJ: Wiley, 2003); and Whalen, *Founding Father*. There are, moreover, two book-length accounts of Kennedy's ambassadorship that reach similar conclusions: Ralph F. de Bedts, *Ambassador Joseph Kennedy, 1938–1940: An Anatomy of Appeasement* (New York: Peter Lang, 1985); and Vieth, "Joseph P. Kennedy." See also Michael R. Beschloss, *Kennedy and Roosevelt: The Uneasy Alliance* (New York: Harper & Row, 1980), 158–233; William W. Kaufmann, "Two American Ambassadors: Bullitt and Kennedy" in *The Diplomats, 1919–1939, Volume II: The Thirties*, Gordon A. Craig and Felix Gilbert, eds. (New York: Atheneum, 1963), 649–681; Francis Russell, *The President Makers: From Mark Hanna to Joseph P. Kennedy* (Boston: Little, Brown, and Co., 1976), 325–392. Will Swift begins his revisionist account of Kennedy's diplomatic career by asking, "Was Kennedy really such a bad representative of his country?" Despite Swift's earnest attempts to argue the contrary, the reader puts his book down unpersuaded. Will Swift, *The Kennedys amidst the Gathering Storm: A Thousand Days in London* (New York: Smithsonian Books, 2008), xix. Indeed, Swift himself presents a condemnatory

"THE GREATEST JOKE IN THE WORLD"

To judge from his private papers and the testimony of friends and family, Kennedy wanted Embassy London because of the prestige it conferred, not because he had any interest in foreign affairs. He viewed the post as a springboard to the presidency, or at least the vice-presidency, and he was aware of the benefits his nine children would derive from having a father who had been U.S. ambassador to the Court of St. James. Equally important was his desire for payback. The grandson of an immigrant forced out of Ireland by the Great Famine, resentful of the slights he and his family had received at the hands of Boston Brahmins, Kennedy relished the prospect of being the first Irish-American and the first Catholic to represent the United States in London. That these motivations had nothing to do with the requirements for successful diplomacy was not lost on Roosevelt, who tried to get Kennedy to accept the secretaryship of commerce as a reward for past services, but Kennedy stood firm. He insisted that only Embassy London would square his accounts with the administration, and the president had little choice but to accede.[10]

FDR owed Kennedy a great deal. The bootstraps Irishman had donated substantial sums of money to the 1932 and 1936 presidential campaigns and had used his influence with Democratic Party luminaries to prevent a deadlocked convention in 1932 that would have denied Roosevelt the nomination. After FDR assumed office, Kennedy served him with distinction as chairman of two agencies, the newly created Securities and Exchange Commission and the Maritime Commission, and he tirelessly promoted the New Deal in right-wing circles, singing Roosevelt's praises to skeptics like isolationist publisher William Randolph Hearst and the borderline-fascist radio priest Charles Coughlin. The broad range of contacts Kennedy had built up in several careers – as banker, Great War shipyard manager, Hollywood studio boss, and Wall

picture of Kennedy in another publication, describing his ambassadorship as "disastrous." "Kennedy was unprepared for the job," Swift writes. "At that extraordinary moment in history, the role of ambassador required a talent for diplomatic nuance and a generous vision, qualities that were not in Kennedy's character." Will Swift, *The Roosevelts and the Royals: Franklin and Eleanor, the King and Queen of England, and the Friendship that Changed History* (Hoboken, NJ: Wiley, 2004), 166, 81.

[10] Of the Kennedy biographies, the most incisive in terms of dissecting the ethno-cultural determinants fueling his personal and familial ambition is Nasaw, *Patriarch*. For Kennedy's refusal of the secretaryship of commerce, see Arthur Krock, *Memoirs: Sixty Years on the Firing Line* (New York: Funk & Wagnalls, 1968), 333.

Street operator – made him an effective lobbyist. In addition, his religion and ethnicity gave him clout with one of the largest blocs of Democratic voters. He often boasted that he could draw 25 million Irish Catholics to the polls, an empty claim but one FDR apparently took seriously. By the time Robert Bingham, U.S. ambassador to Great Britain, returned home in late 1937 to begin treatment for the leukemia that would kill him, Roosevelt was deeply in debt to Kennedy and in no position to ignore his demand that he be named Bingham's successor.[11]

Still, the demand surprised FDR. While Kennedy had many gifts, he had never shown much flair for diplomacy. Quite the contrary: he had earned his reputation – and his fortune – by being, as Roosevelt put it, "a two-fisted, hard-hitting executive" who got things done but made enemies in the process. During his tenure at the SEC and the Maritime Commission, Kennedy had alienated such important New Dealers as Secretary of the Interior Harold Ickes, Secretary of Labor Frances Perkins, and Secretary of the Treasury Henry Morgenthau. He had a short fuse and a foul mouth. And, of course, he was an Irish Catholic new-money man applying for a post that had long been the preserve of Anglo-Scottish Protestant aristocrats. According to Roosevelt's son James, the president "laughed so hard he almost fell from his wheelchair" when Kennedy asked for Embassy London. FDR considered it "a great joke, the greatest joke in the world."[12]

When he stopped laughing, though, Roosevelt began to see an upside to the appointment. Kennedy would definitely work hard at representing his country. Say what you might about him, he was no slacker. He also met the financial requirement. In 1938, the annual salary for the U.S. ambassador to London was $17,500, with an additional expense allowance of $4,800. The opulent receptions the ambassador was expected to host burned up that much money every week. Every American who headed Embassy London had to be a millionaire prepared to spend six figures out of pocket every year. Bingham, a wealthy publisher, had been happy to lay out the money. Kennedy would be equally willing – and able.[13]

[11] For Kennedy's role in FDR's rise to the presidency, see Russell, *President Makers*, 346–354. For his subsequent pre-ambassadorial service to Roosevelt, see Beschloss, *Kennedy and Roosevelt*, 68–152.

[12] FDR cited in Nasaw, *Patriarch*, 279; James Roosevelt cited in Kessler, *Sins of the Father*, 147; FDR cited in Thomas Maier, *The Kennedys: America's Emerald Kings* (New York: Basic Books, 2003), 117.

[13] Kessler, *Sins of the Father*, 150.

The most significant factor influencing Roosevelt's decision was political. FDR considered Kennedy a rival, for good reason. Kennedy had
made no secret of his presidential ambitions, and his friends in the media,
notably Krock, were promoting him as Roosevelt's heir-apparent if, as
expected, the president chose not to run for an unprecedented third term
in 1940. Moreover, Kennedy, although unfailingly toadyish in Roosevelt's presence, had been issuing numerous anti-New Deal pronouncements to his Wall Street cronies and intimating that he, Kennedy, having
succeeded in every venture he undertook, would run a tighter and more
efficient ship of state than That Man in the White House. Roosevelt
wanted Kennedy's abrasive voice muffled by distance. Three thousand
miles of ocean would do the trick.[14]

FDR revealed the depths of his mistrust and resentment of Kennedy in
a remarkable conversation with Morgenthau shortly before the new
ambassador set sail. As Morgenthau noted in his diary, the president said
"that he considered Kennedy a very dangerous man and that he was going
to send him to Britain as ambassador with the distinct understanding that
the appointment was only good for six months." Roosevelt assured his
treasury secretary, "I have made arrangements to have Joe Kennedy
watched hourly, and the first time he opens his mouth and criticizes me,
I will fire him." According to Morgenthau, FDR declared several times
that "Kennedy is too dangerous to have around here." This did not bid
fair for smooth relations between the White House and Embassy London
at a harrowing moment in world history, but Kennedy, as usual, got what
he wanted.[15]

Ironically, in view of what came later, Londoners welcomed Kennedy
with open arms. Indeed, the British press was, if anything, more fulsome
than the American. "Mr Kennedy has tremendous energy" gushed the
Daily Mail the week the ambassador disembarked at Southampton. "He
is a man the English people will be apt to think typically American, so
forceful, so unconventional, so capable, so full of pep is he." Raved the
Observer, Kennedy "has already captured the imagination and friendship of the British people, who recognize in him a man of altogether
outstanding personality, able, vital, and attractive, certain to rank in
popularity with the most popular of his predecessors, and nothing
higher than that could be said." The *Daily Telegraph* described Kennedy

[14] Koskoff, *Joseph P. Kennedy*, 141.
[15] Diary Entry, 8 September 1937, Henry Morgenthau Diaries (hereafter MD), Volume
101, FDRL.

as "extraordinarily charming," and raised a point whose relevance would become apparent over future months: "Mr. Kennedy is ... certainly not the man to accept any job unless assured that he can run it with authority and without undue interference. . . . He will be no 'rubber stamp' ambassador."[16]

That was the impression Kennedy gave in his first press conference on British soil. In the sprawling head office of the American embassy at 1 Grosvenor Square, he popped a stick of gum into his mouth, leaned back in his reclining chair, put his feet up on his desk, and wisecracked, "You can't expect me to develop into a statesman overnight." A reporter asked about "the average American's interest in foreign affairs," and Kennedy's response was blunt: "Right now, he's more interested in how he's going to eat and whether his insurance is good. Some, maybe, are even more interested in how Casey Stengel's Boston Bees are going to do next season." With Japan having just launched an undeclared war against China, civil war raging in Spain, and Hitler poised to overrun Austria, this was not a message nervous Britons wanted to hear. Its stark isolationism seemed to contradict, or at least complicate, Roosevelt's recent Quarantine Speech, in which the president called on "peace-loving nations" to "quarantine" dictatorships spreading the "epidemic of world lawlessness." FDR had delivered that address because he was concerned that American inaction was encouraging the dictators in their bellicosity, but Kennedy seemed to suggest that the United States would continue to do nothing as aggressor nations bullied their neighbors.[17]

Kennedy's initial assessment of events on the Continent indicated how much he had to learn. He cabled Roosevelt shortly after Austrian Chancellor Kurt von Schuschnigg defied Hitler by announcing that he would hold a plebiscite on Austria's independence. "[N]othing is likely to happen except to have Schuschnigg eventually give in," the ambassador predicted, "unless there is some indication that France and England are prepared to back him up." Since neither of Europe's two leading democracies wanted to go to war to defend Austria, Kennedy believed the situation would be resolved peacefully. "My own impression," he wrote, "is that Hitler and [Italian leader Benito] Mussolini, having done so very

[16] "Mr. Kennedy Comes to Town," *Daily Mail*, 22 February 1938; "New American Ambassador," *Observer*, 6 May 1938; "Aims of New U.S. Ambassador in Britain," *Daily Telegraph*, 23 February 1938.

[17] JPK cited in "Ambassador Kennedy Visits Chamberlain," *New York Times*, 5 March 1938; FDR, Quarantine Speech, 5 October 1937, Miller Center, University of Virginia, millercenter.org/president/speeches/detail/3310.

well for themselves by bluffing, they [*sic*] are not going to stop bluffing until somebody very sharply calls their bluff."[18]

Hitler was not bluffing. Less than a day after Kennedy sent that cable, the Wehrmacht invaded Austria and annexed it to the Reich, sending shock waves through the world. Kennedy remained unperturbed. "The march of events in Austria made my first few days here more exciting than they might otherwise have been," he wrote Krock, "but I am still unable to see that the Central European developments affect our country or my job." In other words, while Hitler's Anschluss may have been a violation of the Versailles Treaty ending World War I, it was not, from Kennedy's perspective, an American problem.[19]

Kennedy did better at forging ties with the British government than at forecasting developments in Europe. He got along famously with Chamberlain, whom he described in his diary as "a strong, decisive man, evidently in full charge of the situation here." Like Kennedy, Chamberlain had been a businessman and, the ambassador noted, he could "see the advantages to business in fair and generous dealings." Kennedy also admired Foreign Secretary Edward Wood, Viscount Halifax, "a scholar, sportsman, and everything that an upper-class Englishman who gives his life to public service ought to be." Both Chamberlain and Halifax embraced the policy of appeasement, meaning accommodation, with Hitler and Mussolini, and Kennedy saw no reason to question their judgment. In his view, war had to be avoided at all costs. The economic consequences were too awful to contemplate. "I can talk Chamberlain's language and Halifax's language," Kennedy informed Secretary of State Cordell Hull in late March 1938. Unfortunately, Hitler's language, a toxic mix of grotesque racial theories and blood-and-soil nationalism that scorned financial matters as unworthy, proved beyond the ambassador's comprehension.[20]

To the surprise of observers on both sides of the Atlantic, Kennedy conquered British high society as effortlessly as he had the British cabinet. His rough-diamond reputation did not prevent him and his wife Rose from hobnobbing almost round-the-clock with what he called "topside people." Along with being weekend guests at Windsor Castle, the

---

[18] JPK to FDR, 11 March 1938, PSF, Box 37, FDRL.
[19] JPK to Krock, 21 March 1938, James Roosevelt Papers (hereafter JRP), Box 40, FDRL.
[20] Diary Entry, 4 March 1938, Diary, Box 100, JPKP; Diplomatic Memoir (hereafter DM), 10:5, Box 147, JPKL; JPK to Krock, 21 March 1938, JRP, Box 40, FDRL; JPK to Hull, 22 March 1938, Ambassador: Correspondent File, Box 109, JPKP.

Kennedys took in Ascot and the Derby, became members of the Royal Thames Yacht Club, attended extravagant house parties at grand country estates, and hosted bluebloods in the six-story, fifty-two-room mansion they rented just off Hyde Park. "Well, Rose, this is a helluva long way from East Boston," Kennedy remarked while dressing for dinner, a statement indicative of the social climbing that patrician New Dealers from the president on down found petty and ridiculous.[21]

Kennedy's drive to be accepted by topside people led to the first critical commentary he received in the American press. He became friends with Viscountess Astor (nee Nancy Langhorne of Danville, Virginia), one of the most prominent hostesses in Britain, and he was a frequent visitor at the Astors' estate at Cliveden. Lady Astor was notoriously anti-Semitic and pro-fascist, as was her husband, William Waldorf, Viscount Astor. Prior to Kennedy's appointment as ambassador, the term "Cliveden set" had entered the British and American lexicons to refer to the circle of appeasers allegedly presided over by the Astors, and Kennedy would have been well advised to steer clear of Cliveden, but he could not resist the glittering company and made no effort to stay away.[22]

Drew Pearson and Robert Allen, whose "Washington Merry-Go-Round" column commanded a broad readership, found Kennedy's closeness with the Astors disturbing. Although they had previously praised the ambassador, they reported in April that he was the "[l]atest American to be wooed by the Clivedon [*sic*] group," with its "Nazi-Fascist theories," and expressed hope that he would "snap out of it." Enraged, Kennedy fired off a telegram to Pearson denouncing the story as "complete bunk." A week later, his temper having cooled, he sent Lady Astor a clipping of the column and an attached note. "Well, you see what a terrible woman you are," he quipped, "and how a poor little fellow like me is being politically seduced. Oh weh ist mir!"[23]

---

[21] JPK cited in Garry Wills, *The Kennedy Imprisonment: A Meditation on Power* (New York: Mariner Books, 2002), 76.

[22] When Lady Astor asked Kennedy to address a gathering in Plymouth, his reply went beyond standard courtesy. "[I]f you asked me to go to Plymouth or anywhere else you were interested in," he declared, "I would get on a bicycle and go there." JPK to Lady Astor, 8 December 1938, Ambassador: Correspondent File, Box 101, JPKP. For Kennedy's defense of his membership in the Cliveden set, see DM, 5:4–6, Box 147, JPKP. The best biography of Lady Astor is Christopher Sykes, *Nancy* (Chicago: Academy Chicago Publishers, 1972).

[23] Drew Pearson and Robert Allen, "Washington Merry-Go-Round," 22 April 1938, www .aladin.wrlc.org/gsdl/collect/pearson/pearson.shtml; JPK to Pearson, 3 May 1938, *HTF*, 255; JPK to Lady Astor, 10 May 1938, ibid., 256.

That jaunty Yiddishism, written at a time when the plight of Europe's Jews could not have been direr, raises a delicate issue. Several historians and journalists have accused Kennedy of anti-Semitism, and when the Kennedy family allowed biographer David Nasaw unfettered access to Joseph P. Kennedy's papers, they did so in part out of the hope that Nasaw would establish that he was *not* biased against Jews. Sadly, while Nasaw does absolve Kennedy of some of the claims made against him over the years – that he was a bootlegger, that he traded stocks after entering government service, and other canards – he demonstrates beyond doubt that the ambassador shared in the anti-Semitism of his generation. Kennedy accepted many prevailing myths about Jews, especially that they exercised undue influence over the media, and his correspondence is littered with anti-Semitic remarks. He did have a number of Jewish friends, Krock among them, and he did make an effort, albeit not a very effective or consistent one, to find a haven for German and Austrian Jews in the British Empire, but overall the charge of bigotry sticks. Kennedy's tasteless sign-off to Lady Astor was not an aberration.[24]

---

[24] For a typical condemnation of Kennedy for anti-Semitism, see Schwartz, *Joseph P. Kennedy*, 239–241. For arrangements between Nasaw and the Kennedys, see Christopher Buckley, "Family Guy," *New York Times*, 15 November 2012. For Nasaw's debunking of longstanding Kennedy legends, see Nasaw, *Patriarch*, 71, 79–81, 437–438. A great deal has been written about the so-called "Kennedy Plan" for relocating Jews, and the subject attracted considerable press attention in America during Kennedy's ambassadorship, but Ralph de Bedts makes plain that it was much ado about nothing. Kennedy knew from the outset that Chamberlain was unwilling to open up any part of the Empire for resettlement, and his high-profile campaigning on behalf of the Jews was conducted with an eye on the U.S. media in anticipation of a 1940 presidential run rather than out of any sincere belief that he could alleviate persecution. De Bedts notes, "In the many works, scholarly and popular, written on the sad plight of the Jewish refugees from Adolf Hitler, the full variety of resettlement and escape plans and suggestions was recorded and explained. In none of these works was there any mention of a 'Kennedy Plan.'" De Bedts, *Ambassador Joseph Kennedy*, 119. For present purposes, the most important feature of the "Kennedy Plan" is that the ambassador did not coordinate his efforts with the White House or State and, in fact, left his superiors in the dark about what he was doing. In mid-November 1938, Undersecretary of State Sumner Welles was forced to admit to British Ambassador to Washington Ronald Lindsay that Kennedy had not informed State of his activities with respect to Jewish refugees. "I told the ambassador," Welles recorded, "that if Mr. Kennedy had any plan, he had not reported it to us. . . . [T]his government had not sent any instructions to Mr. Kennedy in the matter, nor had it instructed him to present any plan." The rogue diplomat was charting his own course, with no oversight from Washington. Memorandum of Conversation, 17 November 1938, *FRUS, 1938* (Washington, D.C.: U.S. Government Printing Office, 1955), General, 1:831.

It was Lady Astor who introduced the ambassador to one of his most important contacts – and a crucial instrument in his rogue diplomacy – at a lunch at Cliveden in early May. Colonel Charles Lindbergh, the famous aviator and leader of the America First movement to keep the United States out of war, was fresh from a credulous inspection tour of Germany's air forces in which he concluded, erroneously, that the Nazi Luftwaffe was more powerful than anything Britain or France could mobilize. He had been telling anyone who would listen that appeasement was the only sensible policy for the democracies to pursue, and, as this was an argument likely to fall on receptive ears at Cliveden, he had been a regular guest of the Astors. After meeting Kennedy, Lindbergh noted in his diary that the ambassador "interested me greatly. . . . His views on the European situation seem intelligent and interesting. I hope to see more of him." The two men did in fact meet often over the course of Kennedy's stint in the diplomatic corps, and Lindbergh markedly influenced the ambassador's view of how Washington ought to respond to fascist aggression.[25]

Kennedy got his first chance to promote that view in a speech to the Pilgrims Society, a group devoted to improvement of Anglo-American relations. It had become a tradition by 1938 for U.S. ambassadors to address the Pilgrims, and Kennedy knew about this event long before he arrived in London. Aware that the speech would receive close media scrutiny, he engaged Krock and other *New York Times* reporters to compile a draft, which he forwarded to State for approval. Hull delegated the task of vetting the text to J. Pierrepont Moffat, chief of the Western European division. Moffat was alarmed by the non-interventionist note Kennedy struck, which seemed inappropriate given the Anschluss and the Roosevelt administration's ongoing attempts to find some latitude in its interpretation of Congressional neutrality laws. After proposing what he described as "seven brief changes," Moffat passed the draft along to Hull, who found it more objectionable than Moffat did. As Moffat noted in his

---

[25] Diary Entry, 5 May 1938, *The Wartime Journals of Charles A. Lindbergh* (New York: Harcourt Brace Jovanovich, Inc., 1970), 26. The colonel's wife, Anne Morrow Lindbergh, recorded, "C[harles] has a good time talking to Kennedy – I cannot tear him away." Diary Entry, 5 May 1938, *The Flower and the Nettle: Diaries and Letters of Anne Morrow Lindbergh, 1936–1939* (New York: Harcourt Brace & Co., 1976), 262. For Charles Lindbergh's isolationism, see A. Scott Berg, *Lindbergh* (New York: Berkeley Books, 1998), 384–432; William L. O'Neill, *A Democracy at War: America's Fight at Home and Abroad in World War II* (Cambridge, MA: Harvard University Press, 1993), 33–50. For the Kennedy-Lindbergh partnership, see Wayne S. Cole, *Roosevelt and the Isolationists, 1932–1945* (Lincoln: University of Nebraska Press, 1983), 276–290.

diary, the secretary felt that Kennedy had "swung far too much toward the isolationist school" and that the speech needed deeper cuts.[26]

Hull had cause for distress. Kennedy's draft asserted, among other things, that Americans "do not see how we could usefully participate in the adjustments of international relations" and were "not now convinced that any common interest exists between them and any other country." The most troubling line read: "It must be realized, once and for all, that the great majority of Americans oppose any alliance, agreement, or understanding for joint action with any foreign country, even though the arrangement might be temporary and designed only for the prevention of war." Hull excised those passages, and, before sending the revised version to Kennedy, gave it to Roosevelt for a once-over. The secretary told the president that he thought the cuts "advisable in view of the present tense and critical situation." FDR concurred.[27]

It fell to Moffat to break the news to Kennedy that the speech was "no longer the rather virile document it once was." Moffat explained that the "German rape of Austria" had aroused American popular opinion against Hitler and that any public statement by a U.S. representative "will be read as having been written with the Austrian situation in view." Hull reinforced that message when he sent Kennedy the abridged address, remarking in his cover note, "We are inclined to think that the tone of the speech is a little more rigid, and hence subject to possible misinterpretation, than would appear advisable at this precise moment." The secretary also told Kennedy that he was planning to give a speech of his own, "with the president's approval," the day before the Pilgrims address, in which he would "set forth as our governmental policy our effort to avoid the extremes of isolationism and internationalism."[28]

A typical career diplomat would have accepted the department's judgment with grace. Kennedy, however, felt that Hull was making a mistake.

---

[26] DM, 3:7–8, Box 147, JPKP; Draft of Ambassador Kennedy's Speech for Pilgrims Dinner on 18 March, 10 March 1938, Speeches, Box 169, JPKP; Diary Entry, 11 March 1938, Diaries, Washington, 1938, Volume 1, J. Pierrepont Moffat Diplomatic Papers, Houghton Library, Harvard University, Cambridge, Massachusetts (hereafter JPMP); Diary Entry, 12 March 1938, ibid. For FDR's struggle with the neutrality acts of 1935, 1936, 1937, and 1939, see Dallek, *Franklin D. Roosevelt and American Foreign Policy*, 199–232.

[27] Color-coded version of JPK's speech to the Pilgrim's Club, 14 March 1938, President's Official File (hereafter POF), Box 1, FDRL; Hull to FDR, 14 March 1938, ibid.

[28] Diary Entry, 11 March 1938, Diaries, Washington, 1938, Volume 1, JPMP; Moffat to JPK, 14 May 1938, Correspondence: A-L, JPMP; Hull to JPK, 14 March 1938, POF, Box 1, FDRL.

Hours after he received the condensed version of his speech from State, he had a distressing encounter with Viscount Astor at the embassy in which, according to his diary, Astor "impressed me that some of the leading men here believe that immediate war is a greater danger than they like to let the public know." Astor warned Kennedy that the anti-appeasement bloc in Parliament was gaining in strength and that any indication from Washington that the Anschluss had nudged the United States closer to Europe's democracies would embolden those statesmen, Winston Churchill foremost among them, who wanted their government to stand up to Hitler. It was essential, Astor said, that the Roosevelt administration refrain from giving any encouragement to the Churchill group and allow Chamberlain to pursue his appeasement policy unimpeded.[29]

Kennedy phoned State imploring Hull to cancel or postpone his speech. As Moffat noted, the ambassador "said that England was in a serious situation, ... that within two or three days it would be necessary for the British government to make a decision one way or the other, and he feared that anything the secretary might say at present would be distorted by one faction or other in England to suit their partisan purposes." Hull listened civilly. After Kennedy rang off, the secretary called in the department's top officials, including Undersecretary of State Sumner Welles. All agreed that Hull should deliver his speech as scheduled. "A few of them," Moffat recorded, "were quite brutal in their comment that Kennedy wanted the secretary's speech canceled in order that his own, which was more isolationist in trend, would receive a better play." That was an accurate, if incomplete, reading of Kennedy's motivations. His principal objective was to prevent war, but he also did not like sharing the limelight, even with his boss.[30]

The ambassador's conduct in this affair was, to say the least, irregular. It amounted to an effort to promote his own beliefs as U.S. policy when he knew they differed from the line decided upon by the White House and State. Nothing in Kennedy's public or private papers indicates that he recognized how unusual this was. He simply assumed that, as ambassador, he would be a policy*maker* rather than an agent who implemented policies devised in Washington. This notion was, as we have seen, characteristic of several American diplomats who preceded Kennedy, but few were as brazen in asserting it or as impervious to efforts by their superiors to rein them in.

[29] Diary Entry, 15 March 1938, Diary, Box 100, JPKP.
[30] Diary Entry, 15 March 1938, Diaries, Washington, 1938, Volume 1, JPMP.

Kennedy's speech, delivered on 18 March to a white-tie audience of Pilgrims Society members at the resplendent Claridge's Hotel, packed a wallop even in its truncated form. "The present state of world affairs, it seems to me, calls for something more than the usual diplomatic niceties," Kennedy declared. He promised to be "frank and straightforward" about "certain factors in American life which have a greater influence than some of you may realize on the attitude of my countrymen toward the outside world." Britons, he said, "might just as well realize, at the outset, that the average American has little interest in the details of foreign affairs.... It must be realized that the great majority of Americans oppose any entangling alliances. ... We cannot see how armed conflict can be expected to settle any problem." He did not mean to imply that America "would not fight under any circumstances short of actual invasion." Nonetheless, he warned his listeners not to assume that "the United States could never remain neutral in the event a general war should unhappily break out." That, he insisted, was a "dangerous sort of misunderstanding."[31]

Later, Kennedy noted in his diary that "parts of" the address "fell flat. ... I had to tell my British hosts a few homely truths, and they could not be expected to cheer their heads off." The cheering would grow fainter over the coming months.[32]

"PREPARED TO SUPPORT GERMANY'S DEMANDS"

One of Kennedy's main responsibilities in London was communicating regularly with ambassadors of other nations, a duty that he feared would be "a terrible chore" but that turned out to be "quite enjoyable." Indeed, the only problem, he recalled, was that "the staff had not allowed me enough time to talk to these men as long as I should have liked to do." Especially compelling were his encounters with German ambassadors. Joachim von Ribbentrop did not serve long in that capacity after Kennedy arrived, being called home by Hitler to become foreign minister in early 1938. Still, Kennedy established a rapprochement with the prickly aristocrat, unlike almost any other American who encountered him. The two officials had what Ribbentrop described as a "lengthy conversation" in which Kennedy deplored anti-German statements in the American media and promised to "do everything in his power to stem this press agitation."

[31] JPK Speech, Pilgrims, 18 March 1938, Speeches, Box 155, JPKP.
[32] Diary Entry, 18 March 1938, Diary, Box 100, JPKP.

The impression the American ambassador left with his German counterpart was, as Ribbentrop reported, that "[h]is main objective was to keep America out of any conflict in Europe." That was, needless to say, a message calculated to go over well in Berlin.[33]

Kennedy formed closer ties with Ribbentrop's successor, Herbert von Dirksen, with whom he had several talks before the German was expelled from Britain on the eve of war. In their first, exploratory encounter, Kennedy, according to Dirksen's memorandum, said that "he would like to do his very best to improve German-United States relations" and that he intended to "approach President Roosevelt" during his next stopover in Washington with that "amelioration" in view. While Dirksen was unsure of "whether Kennedy possesses the influence which he ascribes to himself," he did note that the American ambassador was "a close friend of President Roosevelt." Consequently, Dirksen concluded that it would be "wrong to rebuff him."[34]

Kennedy's subsequent meetings with Dirksen constituted the vilest chapter in American diplomacy during World War II. Most of them were quite long, lasting over an hour, and in each of them Kennedy misrepresented his government's attitude toward Nazi behavior, made light of Hitler's anti-Semitic policies, praised the Führer's accomplishments, and asserted that the Reich should enjoy dominance in Eastern and Southeastern Europe. "Old Joe" moreover undercut London's negotiating position with Berlin by stating that Chamberlain was anxious for an Anglo-German settlement, an accurate claim but one that was improper for Kennedy to make. Finally, as if to complete the outrage, Kennedy reported just one of his visits with Dirksen to State, and even on that occasion he only revealed what the German had said, leaving out his own side of the conversation. It was, by any measure, a disgraceful performance.[35]

The conference of 13 June 1938 was representative. Kennedy began by inflating his role in policymaking circles, telling Dirksen that "neither Secretary of State Hull nor any of the other cabinet members" could give him orders and that the "only one whom he had to recognize as superior was President Roosevelt." FDR, Kennedy said, "was not anti-German"

[33] Diary Entry, 11 March 1938, Diary, Box 100, JPKP; Ribbentrop to Weizsacker, 10 June 1938, *DGFP*, From Neurath to Ribbentrop, Series D, 1:713.

[34] Dirksen to Weizsacker, 31 May 1938, *DGFP*, Germany and Czechoslovakia (Washington, D.C.: U.S. Government Printing Office, 1949), Series D, 2:368–369.

[35] I am obliged to David Koskoff for pointing out Kennedy's failure to inform State. Koskoff, *Joseph P. Kennedy*, 292, 521–522.

and "desired friendly relations with Germany." Unfortunately, "there was no one who had come from Europe who had spoken a friendly word to him regarding present-day Germany and her government. . . . Most of them were afraid of the Jews and did not dare to say anything good about Germany." Kennedy promised to correct these impressions on his next visit home. He would, he said, inform the president that "the present government had done great things for Germany and that the Germans were satisfied and enjoyed good living conditions."

According to the report submitted by Dirksen to German State Secretary Baron Ernst von Weizsacker, the discussion turned to "the Jewish question." Kennedy, Dirksen wrote, said that "it was not so much the fact that we wanted to get rid of the Jews that was so harmful to us, but rather the loud clamor with which we accompanied this purpose. He himself understood our Jewish policy completely. . . . In the United States . . . such pronounced attitudes were quite common, but people avoided making so much outward fuss about it." If Hitler just lowered the volume a bit, Kennedy was sure Berlin and Washington could finesse this issue.

Dirksen then complained about "the poisonous role of the American press in the relations between the two countries," and Kennedy nodded in sympathy, noting that "the press on the East Coast was unfortunately predominant in the formation of public opinion and that it was strongly influenced by Jews." Nonetheless, Kennedy declared, "public opinion in the United States was by no means so unfavorable toward Germany" as some Germans believed. "The average American . . . had no prejudice against Germany" and "did not have any particular liking for England," either. Kennedy assured Dirksen that "the overwhelming majority of the American people wanted peace and friendly relations with Germany." Germans ought not to be misled by "3½ million Jews" who did not speak for over 130,000,000 of their fellow citizens.

Kennedy concluded the exchange by asking "what the further aims of the Führer actually were," to which Dirksen replied that Hitler aimed "to put an end to the disenfranchisement of the Sudeten Germans" on the frontiers of Czechoslovakia. The American did not disapprove; indeed, Dirksen noted, Kennedy "repeatedly expressed his conviction" that "Germany had to have a free hand in the East as well as the Southeast." Unsurprisingly, Dirksen came away from the meeting with what he termed "a very good impression of Mr. Kennedy." In a later encounter with Dirksen, Kennedy volunteered to travel to Berlin to meet with Hitler and iron out German-American differences. Dirksen was receptive to the offer. "From his whole personality," the German ambassador wrote, "I believe that he would get on well with the Führer."[36]

Shortly after making Dirksen's acquaintance, Kennedy was back in the United States. He had asked for a home leave to attend his eldest son's graduation from Harvard and to confer with Roosevelt and Hull, and, although he had only been on the job for two months, his request was granted. This was the first of what would be many vacations. Indeed, of the thirty-three months Kennedy served as ambassador, ten, nearly a third of the time, were spent someplace other than London. No other U.S. ambassador of the era was absent from his post for so long, a fact that contributed to Kennedy's declining popularity in both Britain and America.[37]

Kennedy's homecoming was awkward. Roosevelt, displeased with the ambassador's insubordination, kept their meeting brief. Kennedy did not mention it in his diary, and in an unpublished memoir written a decade later he merely noted that FDR was "interested in my personal experiences with and reactions to the English scene." The president was tight-lipped with the press, stating that he had had an "informative talk with Ambassador Kennedy" in which everything he had heard "only confirmed the opinions" he had formed on "the European political situation." When Kennedy met with Hull, he lectured the secretary on defects in Embassy London's staff, who, he said, spent "far too much time ... attending teas, receptions, and other gala occasions" instead of gathering information from reputable sources. Hull heard him out respectfully. Still, Kennedy sensed a chill. Worried that he had fallen out of favor with the administration, he arranged another audience with FDR in which he declared that he did not want to return to Britain unless he had the president's full confidence. Roosevelt told him that he did. "In this way he assuaged my feelings," Kennedy recalled, "and I left again for London, but deep within me I knew that something had happened."[38]

The ambassador returned briefly to his job, arriving in early July and then joining his family for a vacation a month later on the French Riviera. While in London, he met with Chamberlain to discuss the Czech situation, and the prime minister seemed sanguine. As Kennedy reported to

[36] Dirksen to Weizsacker, 13 June 1938, *DGFP*, Series D, 1:713–718; Dirksen to Weizsacker, 13 October 1938, *DGFP*, The Aftermath of Munich (Washington, D.C.: U.S. Government Printing Office, 1951), Series D, 4:636.

[37] De Bedts, *Ambassador Joseph Kennedy*, 243.

[38] DM, 9:5,8,9, Box 147, JPKP; FDR cited in "Roosevelt Rushes His Work on Bills; Silent on Kennedy Talk," *New York Times*, 22 June 1938.

Hull, Chamberlain was "convinced that nothing is going to happen." Kennedy also had a conference with Dirksen in which he again misrepresented Washington's policy toward the Reich. "President Roosevelt," he declared, "would be prepared to support Germany's demands vis-à-vis England or to do anything that might lead to pacification." As Dirksen noted, Kennedy's "remarks showed very clearly that the present government of the United States supports the Chamberlain cabinet and assists it in overcoming all difficulties." Neither Roosevelt nor Hull had said or written anything to Kennedy to warrant such assertions. In fact, there was considerable coolness in Washington towards Chamberlain's appeasement, although the general trend was to back him. By portraying the administration's policy in this fashion, Kennedy made it more likely that Hitler would take an uncompromising stance with regard to the Sudetenland and other potential conquests.[39]

Kennedy soaked up the sun in Cap d'Antibes for three weeks before the worsening Czech crisis drew him back to London. Chamberlain's view had changed. "[H]e is very much disturbed," Kennedy cabled Hull. "All the information that he gets ... is that Hitler has made up his mind to take Czechoslovakia peacefully if possible but with arms if necessary." As alarming as the prime minister's outlook was his appearance. Kennedy thought him "a very sick looking individual," gaunt and shaky. Nonetheless, Kennedy still considered him "the best bet in Europe today against war."[40]

The ambassador did not include his own contribution to this exchange, which, as recorded by Halifax, who was present, was another misrepresentation of the administration's policy. Halifax noted that Kennedy said "that he was convinced that President Roosevelt had decided 'to go in with Chamberlain; whatever course Chamberlain desires to adopt he would think right.'" Again, no one in State or the White House had given Kennedy any reason to believe that this was the case. Roosevelt and Hull still hoped for a peaceful settlement in Europe, but they had begun to question whether further concessions to Hitler were the best means of achieving that end. The Anschluss and the increasing oppression of Jews in Germany led the president and his chief cabinet officer to conclude that perhaps Chamberlain ought to show some backbone, that German demands for the Sudetenland, to say nothing of all of Czechoslovakia,

---

[39] JPK to Hull, 6 July 1938, *FRUS*, 1938, General, 1:57; Dirksen to Weizsacker, 20 July 1938, *DGFP*, From Neurath to Ribbentrop, Series D, 1:721–723.

[40] JPK to Hull, 30 August 1938, PSF, Box 21, FDRL.

should be challenged rather than accommodated. Had Kennedy conveyed these views to Chamberlain, he might have induced him to take a harder line. Failing that, he would at least have put the prime minister on notice that he could not count on U.S. support no matter how cravenly he prostrated himself before the Führer. But Kennedy once more put forward his own ideas as though they were American policy, and Chamberlain, imperfectly informed, continued down the appeasement route, confident that he and Roosevelt were of one mind.[41]

Shortly after he assured Chamberlain of U.S. backing, Kennedy had a meeting with Halifax in which the foreign secretary was uncharacteristically brusque. "Public opinion here is definitely against going to war for Czechoslovakia," Halifax declared, adding, "The French do not want to fight either." As Kennedy reported to Hull, "Halifax asked me what would be the reaction in America if the Germans went into Czechoslovakia, with the Czechs fighting them, and England did not go along." This was an explosive question, requiring the utmost tact, but Kennedy did not even wait for a reply from Hull before informing newsmen of Halifax's inquiry. He also gave a telephone interview to the *Boston Evening American* that same day without obtaining permission from State. "I can promise you there is nothing this A.M. to lend further fears to the European situation," Kennedy declared. He told readers to "keep cool – things aren't as bad as they seem." Apart from the lack of discretion displayed by the ambassador in making these statements on his own authority, Kennedy's appraisal of conditions in Europe was so unrealistic as to be scandalous. The Continent was in fact closer to war than at any time since 1918, with Hitler's pressure on the Czechs increasing and the leaders of the democratic countries beginning to question whether German land hunger could ever be satiated.[42]

When Roosevelt learned of Kennedy's airing of Halifax's question, he was furious. He told Hull to inform Kennedy that he would not announce, in advance, how Washington might react to the theoretical scenario Halifax had described and to chew the ambassador out for granting interviews to newspapers. Hull was happy to oblige. "I feel," he cabled Embassy London, "that the recent public speeches and public

---

[41] Halifax cited in de Bedts, *Ambassador Joseph Kennedy*, 81. For the Roosevelt administration's evolving perspective on appeasement, see Cole, *Roosevelt and the Isolationists*, 284, 287–288, 342, 397–400.

[42] JPK to Hull, 31 August 1938, *FRUS*, 1938, General, 1:565; David Darrah, "British Criticize U.S. Envoy, Say He Talks Too Much," *Chicago Tribune*, 3 September 1938; JPK cited in DM, 13:15–16, Box 147, JPKP.

statements of the president and myself, which were prepared with great care, accurately reflect the attitude of this government toward the European and world situation, and that it would not be practicable to be more specific as to our reaction in hypothetical circumstances." With regard to the *Boston American* interview, Hull icily observed, "This will undoubtedly be regarded as unfair to other agencies and would, if the practice were pursued by our representatives abroad, result in great confusion." Kennedy responded petulantly. "It is my custom to answer any telephone call that comes from Boston, because that is where my family is," he wrote the secretary. "I'm sorry if everybody was disturbed." FDR himself finally intervened, sending Kennedy a cordial message that was nonetheless unmistakably a note of remonstrance. He repeated Hull's point about not going beyond previous administration statements with regard to policy and told the ambassador that he had been "greatly disturbed by the appearance of an 'exclusive' message of advice from you which was published as having been given to the *Boston American*." If every U.S. ambassador did as Kennedy did, the president observed, it would be almost impossible for State to coordinate policy. "I know you will understand," FDR wrote.[43]

Kennedy did not, but he was perceptive enough to recognize that he was losing ground with the administration and concerned lest he widen the gulf. He therefore dutifully sent State a draft of his next speech, scheduled to be delivered a week later at Aberdeen Cathedral in Scotland. Several passages were marked as possibly objectionable "on broad political grounds," chief among them the following paragraph:

I should like to ask you all if you know of any dispute or controversy existing in the world which is worth the life of your son, or of anyone else's son. Perhaps I am not well informed of the terrifically vital forces underlying all this unrest in the world, but for the life of me I cannot see anything involved which could be remotely considered worth shedding blood for.[44]

That was an apt summation of the ambassador's views, but it caused consternation at Foggy Bottom and the White House. Assistant Secretary of State for Latin American Affairs Adolf Berle thought that if Kennedy delivered those lines, he would "serve notice on Germany that, so far as the United States was concerned, Germany could go as far as she liked."

[43] FDR to Hull, 1 September 1938, POF, Box 1, FDRL; Hull to JPK, 1 September 1938, PSF, Box 37, FDRL; JPK to Hull, 3 September 1938, ibid.; FDR to JPK, 7 September 1938, ibid.

[44] JPK to Hull, 31 August 1938, PSF, Box 37, FDRL.

Moffat felt the paragraph "could only be interpreted as meaning that the
United States would never fight and practically advising the British not to
fight." Berle, Moffat, and Assistant Secretary of State George Messer-
smith met with Hull to review Kennedy's draft and they swiftly concluded, as Moffat noted in his diary, that Hull should receive
"presidential authority to reject the paragraph."[45]

FDR inspected the speech at a meeting attended by Morgenthau, whose
diary portrayed a president still fuming at Kennedy for having publicly
revealed Halifax's what-America-would-do-if-and-when question. Roosevelt, Morgenthau recorded, thought "that not only was Kennedy talking
to the press, but he was definitely trying to force the president's hand in
this manner in his process of playing the Chamberlain game." Morgenthau, who disliked Kennedy, stoked the president's fury by ridiculing
the Aberdeen address. What Kennedy was in effect saying, he declared,
was "'I can't for the life of me understand why anybody would want to go
to war to save the Czechs.'" Roosevelt snorted, "That young man needs
his wrists slapped rather hard." The offending passage was cut.[46]

"PEACE IN OUR TIME"

Had the president slapped Kennedy's wrists, really disciplined him beyond
editing his speech and sending mild reprimands, the ambassador might
have behaved differently in the fateful three weeks before the Munich
agreement. Alas, as Nasaw and other scholars have shown, Roosevelt
could not risk a full-blown comeuppance. He could not afford to have
the thin-skinned Kennedy resign and come home determined to sabotage
FDR's run for a third term. The Kennedy war chest could prove decisive
for another Democrat seeking the nomination, or a moderate Republican
acceptable to more conservative members of the New Deal bloc. Kennedy's connections in big business, show business, and the national press had
been invaluable assets in 1932 and 1936, and FDR had suffered some
setbacks since reelection, notably the failed court-packing scheme and the
so-called "Roosevelt recession" of 1937–1938. The president remained
popular, and he might be able to prevail in 1940 without Kennedy's

[45] Diary Entry, 1 September 1938, *Navigating the Rapids, 1918–1971: From the Papers of Adolf A. Berle*, Beatrice Bishop Berle and Travis Beal Jacobs, eds. (New York: Harcourt Brace Jovanovich, 1973), 183; Diary Entry, 31 August 1938, Diaries, Washington, 1938, Volume 2, JPMP.
[46] Diary Entry, 1 September 1938, MD, Volume 138, FDRL.

support, but the prospect of Kennedy as an enemy was daunting. So Roosevelt spared the rod, with calamitous results.[47]

On 12 September, Hitler delivered a speech demanding self-determination for the Sudeten Germans. His rhetoric was incendiary, but he did not declare war on Czechoslovakia, as many had feared. Kennedy thus saw reason to hope that peace might be preserved. "The speech contained highly offensive expressions," the ambassador admitted in a cable to Hull. "It does not seem, however, that Hitler has closed the door entirely nor yet put his hand to the trigger." When Kennedy canvassed the cabinet, he found them grasping at the same straw. Chamberlain, Halifax, and Chancellor of the Exchequer John Simon "felt there was more hope in the situation," Kennedy reported, although he had to add, "All this group in referring to Hitler always call him the mad man."[48]

This specious optimism collapsed when the Sudeten Germans began rioting. Czech president Edward Beneš declared martial law. Konrad Henlein, Czech Nazi Party chief, demanded that the government stop all police actions in the Sudetenland. Sir Nevile Henderson, British ambassador to Germany, reported home that the Germans stood ready to invade Czechoslovakia and would refrain from doing so only if Prague allowed the Sudetenland to become part of the Reich.[49]

Desperate to avert war, Chamberlain telegrammed Hitler for a one-on-one meeting. Hitler agreed, and Chamberlain flew to Munich, from whence he was conveyed to Berchtesgaden to confer with the Führer. Upon his return to London the next day, Chamberlain relayed Hitler's terms to Kennedy. They were not encouraging. Hitler insisted on "self-determination" for the Sudetenland, meaning its absorption by Germany. When Chamberlain asked if Hitler would take up arms to achieve this end, Hitler responded, "Absolutely, and I will chance a world war if necessary." Chamberlain then pathetically inquired what "assurances" Hitler could give that "the rest of Czechoslovakia would not sooner or later fall into his hands." The Führer declared that he "had no interest in

[47] See de Bedts, *Ambassador Joseph Kennedy*, 72–74; Nasaw, *Patriarch*, 332–333; Swift, *Kennedys amidst the Gathering Storm*, 4–6.

[48] JPK to Hull, 12 September 1938, *FRUS*, 1938, General, 1:591; JPK to Hull, 13 September 1938, ibid., 1:592.

[49] For the escalating Czech crisis in mid-September 1938, see Ian Kershaw, *Hitler: 1936–1945, Nemesis* (New York: Norton, 2000), 108–110; William L. Shirer, *The Rise and Fall of the Third Reich: A History of Nazi Germany* (New York: Simon & Schuster, 1960), 382–384; J. W. Wheeler-Bennett, *Munich: Prologue to Tragedy* (New York: Viking Press, 1963), 90–93.

the rest of Czechoslovakia," and that, in fact, he had "no further interest in the acquiring of any lands in Europe." Chamberlain felt the democracies had to trust Hitler, despite his record of broken promises, and Kennedy agreed. Both the ambassador and the prime minister decided to accept Hitler's demands, although they knew such acquiescence would be unpopular in many quarters.[50]

Kennedy enlisted Lindbergh in the campaign to appease Germany. According to the colonel's diary, Kennedy cabled him in Paris and asked him to "come to London as soon as possible." Lindbergh complied, and the two men met for lunch at Prince's Gate, where Kennedy revealed the details of Chamberlain's visit to Berchtesgaden. He told Lindbergh that Chamberlain might not be able to avoid hostilities because "English opinion" did not favor giving Hitler the Sudetenland. Lindbergh was horrified. "The English are in no shape for war," he observed. "They do not realize what they are confronted with. They have always before had a fleet between themselves and their enemy, and they can't realize the change aviation has made." Kennedy asked Lindbergh to compose a report detailing what would happen if Hitler unleashed the Luftwaffe against Britain. The colonel readily consented.[51]

As Kennedy foresaw, Lindbergh's report was a doomsday scenario. "Without doubt the German air fleet is now stronger than that of any country in the world," Lindbergh pronounced. "Germany now has the means of destroying London, Paris, and Prague if she wishes to do so. England and France together have not enough modern war planes for effective defense or counter-attack." The democracies, and that included the United States, needed to recognize that a new era had dawned: "For the first time in history, a nation has the power either to save or ruin the great cities of Europe. Germany has such a preponderance of war planes that she can bomb any city in Europe with comparatively little resistance." Kennedy circulated the report among British cabinet members and sent it to Hull with the suggestion that "it might be of interest not only to the State Department but also to the president and the War and Navy Departments." He did not inform the secretary that he had asked Lindbergh to write it.[52]

---

[50] Hitler and Chamberlain cited in JPK to Hull, 17 September 1938, *FRUS*, 1938, General, 1:607; JPK to Hull, 17 September 1938, ibid., 1:609–612.

[51] Diary Entries, 19–22 September 1938, *Wartime Journals*, 71–73. See also Diary Entries, 19–21 September 1938, *Flower and the Nettle*, 407–410.

[52] Lindbergh cited in DM, 15:3–5, Box 147, JPKP; Transcript of Transatlantic Telephone Conversation between Hull and JPK, 24 September 1938, Diary, Box 100, JPKP.

Lindbergh stayed on in London at the ambassador's invitation. "Kennedy wants me to talk to some of the British officials," the colonel noted in his diary. Over the next few days, Lindbergh met with the air secretary and other military figures, repeating his hair-raising prognosis. John Slessor, marshal of the Royal Air Force, prepared a memorandum of a conversation with Lindbergh that would have delighted Kennedy had he known of it. Slessor described Lindbergh as "a man of outstanding character" who was "entirely sympathetic with the British" but who believed that certain facts had to be faced. "His whole attitude," Slessor recorded, "was that Germany was immensely formidable in almost every way both in her spirit, her national organization, and particularly her air force, which, he says, is incomparably the strongest in the world. . . . He is convinced that our only sound policy is to avoid war now at almost any cost." The impact of such warnings, while impossible to determine, was doubtless significant.[53]

It seemed for a moment that the crisis had been defused when Beneš agreed to the cession of all Czech districts with populations more than 50 percent German in return for a multipower guarantee against further dismemberment. An international commission would oversee the complicated process of drawing new Czech borders. Chamberlain, elated, flew to Bad Godesberg in the Rhineland to finalize what he thought was an accomplished fact, and he was stunned when Hitler said the concessions were not enough. The Führer would not accept a gradual district-by-district transfer of territory, insisting that the entire Sudetenland be handed over by 1 October. Furthermore, he demanded that Czech military installations be left intact for incorporation into Germany's army, and he would not allow the dispossessed Czechs to take their livestock or household goods with them. If Prague did not comply by Hitler's deadline, meaning in less than two weeks, he would take the Sudetenland by force. Chamberlain tried to argue with Hitler, and then agreed to present those demands to Beneš. The following morning, he flew back to London, appalled and disheartened.[54]

Undersecretary Sir Alexander Cadogan briefed Kennedy on Hitler's new terms on 24 September. The ambassador was aghast. He now virtually gave up hope. "Hitler not only wants what everybody was

<hr/>

[53] Diary Entry, 22 September 1938, *Wartime Journals*, 73; Note on Conversation with Colonel Lindbergh, 22 September 1938, John Slessor, *The Central Blue* (New York: Praeger, 1957), 218–222.
[54] Kershaw, *Nemesis*, 112–115; Wheeler-Bennett, *Munich*, 128–139.

willing to give him but it looks as if he wants a great deal more," he cabled State. Chamberlain had concluded, Kennedy wrote, that "there is no sanity left in the man" and that "it is only a question now of hours" before hostilities erupted. Kennedy told Hull that Chamberlain still sought "peace at any price," but that some members of the cabinet, including Halifax, had begun to defect from this policy. There might soon be a rash of resignations that would paralyze the government.[55]

Britain began bracing for war. "All over London," Kennedy wrote years later, "people were being fitted for gas-masks. In the churches, in the theaters, at the sports matches, announcements were made of the depots to which they should go. ... All during the night of September 26–27, men were busily digging trenches in the parks under the glare of flashlights." Kennedy sent his children to Ireland to be out of harm's way.[56]

Roosevelt cabled a plea to all of the interested parties, but obviously pitched to Hitler. "The fabric of peace on the Continent of Europe, if not throughout the rest of the world, is in immediate danger," the president proclaimed. "For the sake of humanity everywhere, I most earnestly appeal to you not to break off negotiations." Chamberlain ordered Sir Horace Wilson, his most trusted adviser, to Berlin to implore Hitler for "negotiation as against violence." Hitler's response to both appeals was uncompromising. The day he received FDR's message, he delivered an address at a Nazi rally at Berlin's Sportspalast in which he declared that he would seize the Sudetenland by 1 October, the following Saturday. He also sent FDR a telegram proclaiming, "It does not rest with the German government, but with the Czechoslovakian government alone, to decide whether it wants peace or war." To Wilson, he was more direct. In the event Prague dragged its feet in complying with his terms, he said, "I will smash the Czechs."[57]

The day following Wilson's return to London, Chamberlain addressed the House of Commons in what everyone expected would be his last

---

[55] JPK to Hull, 24 September 1938, *FRUS*, 1938, General, 1:642–643; JPK to Hull, 25 September 1938, ibid., 1:652.

[56] DM, 15:11, 16:7, Box 147, JPKP.

[57] The President's Message to Czechoslovakia, Germany, Great Britain, and France Seeking a Peaceful Solution of the Threat of War, 26 September 1938, *Public Papers of the Presidents: Franklin Delano Roosevelt, 1938* (Washington, D.C.: U.S. Government Printing Office, 1939), 531–532; Chamberlain cited in Nasaw, *Patriarch*, 342; Hitler cited in Swift, *Kennedys amidst the Gathering Storm*, 94; Hitler to FDR, 26 September 1938, *FRUS*, 1938, General, 1:672; Hitler cited in H. W. Brands, *Traitor to His Class: The Privileged Life and Radical Presidency of Franklin Roosevelt* (New York: Anchor Books, 2008), 509; Kershaw, *Nemesis*, 118.

speech before war broke out. He spoke for almost an hour, laying out chronologically the negotiations with Hitler, and as he approached his climax, Cadogan burst into the chamber bearing a message from the Foreign Office. The peers passed the letter to Halifax, who interrupted the prime minister to hand it to him. Chamberlain read the contents over. His face brightening, he announced that Hitler had agreed to postpone mobilization for twenty-four hours and to meet him in conference with Mussolini and French President Edouard Daladier.[58]

Pandemonium ensued. The applause and cheers were deafening. Practically the entire House rose to give Chamberlain a standing ovation. Some MPs wept, while others climbed over each other to shake the prime minister's hand. No one cheered more lustily than Kennedy. "I was never so thrilled in all my life," he noted in his diary. "Tonight a feeling is spreading all over London that this means war will be averted." The ambassador issued a rhapsodic report to State, pronouncing, "The president can feel that God was on his side." Before heading to bed, Kennedy remarked jovially to the embassy staff, "Well, boys, the war is off."[59]

Chamberlain flew to Munich the next day, where he, Daladier, Mussolini, and Hitler agreed to the cession of the Sudetenland to Germany, evacuation to commence on 1 October and be completed by 10 October. Along with giving the Reich 2,800,000 Sudeten Germans and 800,000 Czechs, the conferees took away 86 percent of Czechoslovakia's chemicals; 80 percent of its cement, lignite, and textiles; 70 percent of its iron, steel, and electrical power; 76 percent of its railway car works and most of its railway system; 40 percent of its timber; and two-thirds of its coal. Czechoslovakia also lost its mountainous fortifications along the German border, the strongest defensive line in Europe. Chamberlain and Daladier signed a pact guaranteeing the integrity of what remained of Czechoslovakia, but this was, as Hitler later described it, "worthless." Equally valueless was a document Chamberlain got Hitler to initial pledging that Britain and Germany would never go to war again.[60]

The prime minister returned home to wild acclaim. Stepping off the plane at Heston aerodrome outside London, he pulled out the piece of

[58] Chamberlain cited in Keith Feiling, *The Life of Neville Chamberlain* (London: Macmillan, 1970), 374. See also Diary Entry, 28 September 1938, *The Diaries of Sir Alexander Cadogan, 1938–1945*, David Dilks, ed. (New York: G. P. Putnam's Sons, 1971), 109.

[59] Diary Entry, 28 September 1938, Diary, Box 100, JPKP; JPK to Hull, 28 September 1938, Ambassador: Dispatches, Box 170, JPKP; JPK cited in DM, 16:16, Box 147, JPKP.

[60] All figures from Shirer, *Rise and Fall of the Third Reich*, 421–422; Hitler cited in ibid., 437.

paper with the Führer's signature and told the gathered throng that it
signified "peace in our time." His listeners roared their approval. The
nine-mile drive from Heston to Whitehall lasted nearly two hours, so
dense were the crowds. Margot Asquith, widow of the prime minister
who oversaw Britain's entry into World War I, called Chamberlain the
greatest Englishman who ever lived. Kennedy might have agreed.[61]

Munich has deservedly become diplomatic shorthand for cowardice
and gullibility. The sellout of Czechoslovakia in late September 1938 was
a geopolitical disaster of the first magnitude. Had Britain and France
stood by their earlier pledges to the Czechs, Hitler would have had to
back down or absorb a battlefield defeat, either of which would have
weakened his hand and conceivably averted a general war in Europe.
Even fighting alone, Czechoslovakia might have been able to foil Hitler's
plans. As a number of Hitler's generals later confirmed, Germany was not
strong enough at the time of the Munich Conference to forcibly seize the
Sudetenland. Indeed, several army officers, among them Hitler's chief of
staff, were resolved to overthrow the Führer if he went to war with
Czechoslovakia. Their plot, aborted when Beneš gave up the Sudetenland
peacefully, represented the last organized opposition to Hitler for years.[62]

Not only did Hitler score a diplomatic victory at Munich; he vastly
improved Germany's military position. With the Czech frontier defenses
now part of the Reich, there was no possibility of Prague offering armed
resistance to a German invasion. Moreover, the massive Czech armaments industry, one of the mightiest in Europe, fell within the zone taken
over by Berlin. Without firing a shot, Hitler acquired enough weaponry to
equip eighty divisions. By caving in to the Führer at Munich, the democracies ensured that they would face a more formidable adversary when
they chose to draw the line against Nazi aggression.[63]

The American ambassador bore a share of responsibility for the
Munich debacle. Lindbergh exaggerated when he wrote in his diary,
"Kennedy has taken a large part in bringing about the conference between
Hitler, Chamberlain, Mussolini, and Daladier." That was untrue: the

[61] Chamberlain cited in Henry Kissinger, *Diplomacy* (New York: Simon & Schuster, 1994),
315; Asquith cited in David Dutton, *Neville Chamberlain* (New York: Oxford University
Press, 2001), 52.
[62] For the postwar testimony of German military leaders about the Reich's unpreparedness
for combat in September 1938, see Shirer, *Rise and Fall of the Third Reich*, 423–424. For
the conspiracy to topple Hitler, see ibid., 404–414.
[63] For the impact of Hitler's acquisition of Czech armaments, see Ian Kershaw, *Hitler:
A Biography* (New York: W. W. Norton, 1998), 474–475.

chief orchestrator of Munich was Chamberlain, and to him belonged most of the blame. Still, Kennedy contributed. His friendship with the prime minister gave him an uncommon degree of influence over British policy. Days after signing away the Sudetenland, Chamberlain told Kennedy that he had relied more on him "for judgment and support" during the Czech crisis than anyone else, including members of his cabinet. Kennedy's assurances that the White House embraced appeasement as enthusiastically as Downing Street did, a misrepresentation no competent diplomat would have made, enabled Chamberlain to proceed on the assumption that he enjoyed unconditional American backing, and this relieved him of the task of rethinking his strategy in the face of Hitler's increasingly irrational behavior. Despite indications that appeasement had fallen into disfavor among leading figures in the Roosevelt administration, including the president and the secretary of state, Kennedy gave Chamberlain no reason to suspect that the Anglo-American policy front was anything but united.[64]

Lindbergh's report on the military aviation situation in Europe, commissioned by Kennedy without the consent or knowledge of State, was also important. As noted above, its effect can only be guessed at, and such evidence as exists is anecdotal. Along with Slessor's memorandum, we have the 29 September diary entry of Tory MP Thomas Jones, who recorded, "Since my talk with Lindbergh on Monday, I've sided with those working for peace at any cost in humiliation, because of the picture of our relative unpreparedness in the air and on the ground which Lindbergh painted, and because of his belief that the democracies would be crushed absolutely and finally." American muralist Ione Robinson, working in London at the time, similarly noted in her diary that many British politicians, although "not admirers of Mr. Chamberlain" were "affected by the rumors circulated in England by Lindbergh." Not everyone accepted Lindbergh's assessment – conservative MP Hugh Dalton scoffed that the colonel was "no more an authority on air forces than Amy Johnson," a well-known aviatrix of the day – but the dire predictions of the world's most acclaimed flier did little to stiffen British morale at a time when Hitler was still eminently beatable.[65]

---

[64] Diary Entry, 29 September 1938, *Wartime Journals*, 79; Chamberlain cited in Entry, 6 November 1938, Diary, Box 100, JPKP. Czech President Beneš likewise blamed Kennedy to a considerable extent for Munich. See *Memoirs of Dr. Edward Beneš*, trans. G. Lias (Boston: Houghton Mifflin, 1954), 172.

[65] Diary Entry, 29 September 1938, Thomas Jones, *A Diary with Letters, 1931–1950* (New York: Oxford University Press, 1954), 411; Diary Entry, 10 September 1938, Ione

Kennedy never admitted that Munich had been a mistake. To the end of his days, he insisted that Chamberlain had had no choice but to sacrifice the Sudetenland because of Germany's greater armed might, especially in the air. Even after historians and Hitler's own military experts established that the Lindbergh report was inaccurate, that German airplane production was never close to the volume Lindbergh attributed to it, that Reich Commissioner of Aviation Hermann Goering persistently failed to correct the technical bugs that kept output low, Kennedy stuck to his guns. He also endorsed another post-facto argument put forth by many appeasers: that Munich bought Britain two years of time to rearm, so that it was better able to thwart Nazi assaults when Hitler launched Operation Sea Lion, the invasion of the United Kingdom. The purchased-time thesis, however, overlooked the fact that the two years' grace worked to Germany's advantage, not Britain's. Britain did build up its defenses, but not as rapidly as Hitler developed his Wehrmacht. As a totalitarian leader, Hitler did not have to govern through persuasion in an open society; he was therefore able to make better use of the time than Chamberlain. In addition, Czechoslovakia's fearsome Škoda armaments plant, surrendered to Hitler in the Munich agreement, generated more ordnance over the course of two years than all of Britain's munitions plants put together. Munich gained Britain nothing and benefited Hitler enormously. Yet Kennedy's don't-confuse-me-with-the-facts mindset allowed him to avoid recognizing the catastrophe he had helped bring about.[66]

"THERE CAN BE NO PEACE"

The ambassador again ran afoul of the White House and State when he addressed the annual Trafalgar Day dinner of the Navy League two weeks after Munich. For the most part, his speech was innocuous, but it took a disastrous turn when he advanced "a theory of mine that it is unproductive for both democratic and dictator countries to widen the divisions now existing between them by emphasizing their differences." Kennedy recommended that "instead of hammering away at what are regarded as irreconcilables," dictatorships and democracies ought to

---

Robinson, *A Wall to Paint On* (New York: E. F. Dutton, 1946), 315; Dalton cited in de Bedts, *Ambassador Joseph Kennedy*, 93.

[66] For a demolition of the bought-time argument, see Martin Gilbert and Richard Gott, *The Appeasers* (London: Weidenfeld & Nicolson, 1963), 11–13.

"bend their energies toward solving their common problems." While acknowledging that "democratic and dictator countries have important and fundamental divergencies of outlook," he contended, "There is simply no sense ... in letting those differences grow into unrelenting antagonisms. After all, we have to live together in the same world, whether we like it or not." The British press response to these remarks was muted, but American columnists erupted in outrage. Typical was a *New York Post* editorial that declared, "For Mr. Kennedy to suggest ... that the United States make a friend of the man who boasts that he is out to destroy democracy, religion, and all the other principles which free Americans hold dear, ... that passes understanding."[67]

Roosevelt and Hull were incensed by Kennedy's address, all the more so because the ambassador had submitted a draft for review and it had been approved. The passage of this speech through State Department bureaucracy had been a comedy of errors. Moffat noted in his diary that Kennedy expected a one-day turnaround after having spent ten days working on the speech, which Moffat considered unreasonable. Moffat had seen the explosive potential of the dictatorship-democracy paragraph, but noted, "being expressly advanced as the ambassador's personal views, there was nothing to do but pass it." Hull demanded to know why Welles had not recognized the speech's inappropriateness, and Welles protested that he had been focused on the ongoing oil expropriation crisis in Mexico and had "initialed blind," assuming that Hull had already approved the speech. Blame finally came to rest on Moffat, who noted in his diary, "[A] 'goat' is needed and I shall have to be the goat. In the long run, however, no one is going to be hurt unless it is Mr. Kennedy himself."[68]

That proved true. Along with the pummeling Kennedy took from influential columnists like Walter Lippmann, he had to absorb the closest thing to a dressing-down from FDR and Hull that he had received thus far in his ambassadorship. The morning after the Trafalgar Day address, Hull held a press conference to announce that Kennedy had been speaking for himself, not the administration. Roosevelt enlisted Berle and Moffat to, as Moffat recorded, "prepare a fifteen-minute speech" that would "undo the damage done by Kennedy's recent speech, [and] would make it clear that our foreign policy was unchanged." The two officials obliged, but their draft was too tepid for the president. Moffat noted in

[67] JPK Speech, Trafalgar Day, 19 October 1938, Speeches, Box 155, JPKP; *Post* cited in Koskoff, *Joseph P. Kennedy*, 159.
[68] Diary Entries, 18 and 21 October 1938, Diaries, Washington, 1938, Volume 2, JPMP.

his diary that FDR "dramatized" it to make clear that coexistence between democracies and dictatorships was impossible. In a scalding radio broadcast from the White House, the president proclaimed, "There can be no peace if the reign of law is to be replaced by a recurrent sanctification of sheer force. There can be no peace if national policy adopts as a deliberate instrument the threat of war." Roosevelt did not mention Kennedy by name, but his address was so clearly a repudiation of the ambassador that no one, least of all the hypersensitive Kennedy, could have missed its intent.[69]

As before, Kennedy could not understand why his behavior had occasioned such disapproval. He complained in a phone call with Moffat that "I have just received a week's batch of newspaper clippings and I should judge by them that I have never been right about anything since the war broke out in 1914." From Kennedy's perspective, what he had said in his Trafalgar Day speech was nothing more than common sense. The democracies faced two alternatives – war or appeasement – and since the dictatorships were so much stronger, Kennedy had indicated the only realistic course. As he wrote his friend Tom White, "I believe that unless England and France are prepared to fight and endanger civilization, ... then there is no point in staying on the sidelines and sticking your tongue out at somebody who is a good deal bigger than you are." He added, "75% of the attacks made on me ... were by Jews." That was bilge: the only Jewish columnist who criticized him was Lippmann, and his reproof was not as severe as that issued by Gentiles like Heywood Braun, Hugh Johnson, and Dorothy Thompson. Furthermore, Kennedy's staunchest defender in the American media, Krock, was Jewish.[70]

In mid-December, Kennedy returned to the United States for another vacation. He met briefly with Roosevelt, bringing with him a memorandum prepared by his staff detailing the ghastly consequences of war and

---

[69] Hull cited in "No Policy Changes in Kennedy Speech," *New York Times*, 21 October 1938; Diary Entry, 26 October 1938, Diaries, Washington, 1938, Volume 2, JPMP; FDR cited in "Text of Roosevelt's Talk to Forum," *New York Times*, 27 October 1938.

[70] JPK cited in Diary Entry, 4 November 1938, Diaries, Washington, 1938, Volume 2, JPMP; JPK to White, 12 November 1938, *HTF*, 299. Over a decade later, in his diplomatic memoir, Kennedy still expressed amazement at the "viciousness of the onslaught" he received from the media and blamed it on "Jewish publishers and writers." "The tactics of this group may someday be analyzed," he snarled. "Some of them in their zeal did not hesitate to resort to slander and falsehood to achieve their aims." DM, 18:4–5, Box 147, JPKP. I am obliged to David Nasaw for pointing out the gulf between Kennedy's claims and the actual number of Jewish commentators who found fault with his Trafalgar Day speech. Nasaw, *Patriarch*, 356–357.

recommending appeasement. America's goal, he insisted, should be "a world divided into totalitarian and democratic areas, together with a recognition that each within its sphere was its own master." He complained to FDR that the White House and State had disregarded his counsel and failed to stand up for him in the face of newspaper attacks. Renewing his offer of the previous June, he volunteered to "step out at any time" the president wanted him to. Roosevelt assured him that he was doing a good job and that no one sought his resignation or dismissal. Later that day, Kennedy dropped by Moffat's office at Foggy Bottom to vent. "He is bitter at the attitude of the press toward him," Moffat noted in his diary. "He attributes this to the Jews who dominate our press. If Europe goes to war, he thinks that the Jews will have a large share of blame." Kennedy then left for what was intended to be six weeks of R and R in Palm Beach.[71]

The holiday was shorter than planned, because Chamberlain, perhaps irritated by Kennedy's long absences from his post, as were many Britons (and Americans), had Cadogan cable State that it might be good "for Mr. Kennedy's own education to resume his contacts here." Hull called Kennedy in Florida and asked him to cut short his leave. Piqued, Kennedy obeyed, sailing for Britain on the *Queen Mary* on 11 February 1939.[72]

Upon his return, he conferred with Chamberlain, who was still optimistic about preserving European peace. As Kennedy reported to State, the prime minister felt that the "general outlook" was "much better" than in late 1938, that there was no possibility of a Nazi-Soviet pact – "they are both so distrustful of each other that it would never work out" – and that Munich had proven that the democracies could "do business with Hitler."[73]

Kennedy would have liked to believe that prognosis, but consultations with members of the Foreign Office revealed that most British policy-makers did not share Chamberlain's sentiments. They pointed out to Kennedy that Munich had not reduced tensions as dramatically as had been hoped. Less than two weeks after Chamberlain and Daladier gave Hitler the Sudetenland, the Nazi pogrom on Kristallnacht, in which more than 1,000 synagogues were burned, thousands of Jewish businesses and

---

[71] JPK to FDR, 16 December 1938, PSF, Box 37, FDRL; DM, 20:1, 21:1–3, Box 147, JPKP; Diary Entry, 16 December 1938, Diaries, Washington, 1938, Volume 2, JPMP.

[72] Cadogan cited in de Bedts, *Ambassador Joseph Kennedy*, 122; Diary Entry, 9 February 1939, Diary, Box 100, JPKP.

[73] JPK to Hull, 17 February 1939, *FRUS*, 1939 (Washington, D.C.: U.S. Government Printing Office, 1956), General, 1:14–17.

schools were vandalized, and 30,000 Jews were arrested and sent to concentration camps, had shocked the civilized world. The German press, government controlled, had become violently anti-British. Hungary was a virtual Nazi satellite. Hitler threatened to annex what remained of Czechoslovakia. Kennedy observed that the "long-term outlook for England . . . seems to me exceedingly dark."[74]

He sent FDR another alarmist memo, bleaker than the one he had brought with him to Washington. If America took up arms against the dictatorships, he warned, "the dislocation in the American economy and the necessary heavy armament expenses would so alter the balance of economic forces in the United States as to require a regimented industrial order under government control. Such centralization would tend to reproduce . . . the basic features of the fascist state: to fight totalitarianism, we would have to adopt totalitarian methods." The only way to avoid this fate, Kennedy insisted, was for America to stay out of any European conflict, even if the British were drawn in. Roosevelt did not reply.[75]

Kennedy was attending the papal coronation in Rome in mid-March when Nazi tanks crossed the Czech border. The Czechs, deprived of their best fortifications and munitions factories at Munich, could offer no opposition. Within a few hours, the Germans controlled Prague. Hitler entered the former Czech capital in a limousine and proclaimed, "Czecho-slovakia has ceased to exist." For the second time in a year, he had bloodlessly conquered a neighboring country. This was something new, though: by annexing a non-German population, the Führer went beyond his oft-proclaimed goal of returning Teutons to the Fatherland. William Bullitt, U.S. ambassador to Paris, remarked, "It is no longer possible to have confidence in any promises he may make."[76]

Chamberlain came to the same conclusion. He gave a cringing speech before the House of Commons in which he refused to honor Britain's guarantee to a state that no longer existed, but when public reaction in Britain was overwhelmingly negative, he reversed himself and delivered an address in Birmingham condemning Hitler's aggression. "No greater mistake could be made," he proclaimed, "than to suppose that, because it believes war to be a senseless and cruel thing, this nation has so lost its

[74] JPK to Hull, 23 February 1939, *FRUS*, 1939, General, 1:22. For an overview of this anxious period, see Donald Cameron Watt, *How War Came: The Immediate Origins of the Second World War, 1938–1939* (New York: Pantheon Books, 1989), 76–108.

[75] JPK to FDR, 3 March 1939, PSF, Box 37, FDRL.

[76] Hitler cited in Wheeler-Bennett, *Munich*, 346; Bullitt to Hull, 17 March 1939, *FRUS*, 1939, General, 1:48.

fiber that it will not take part to the utmost of its power in resisting such a challenge." Two weeks later, Chamberlain was even more emphatic. Since Poland was Hitler's presumed next target, Chamberlain told Commons that Britain would defend Poland against any attack. The French, he said, would do the same. That speech marked the end of Chamberlain's appeasement policy.[77]

It did not mark the end of Kennedy's. Despite the fact that Hitler had shown that he could not be trusted, that his aggression was motivated by something more than the drive to liberate Germans denationalized by the Versailles settlement, Kennedy continued to search for some way to placate him. The ambassador placed an urgent call to Hull and recommended that Roosevelt consider offering Hitler an arrangement whereby the United States would use its financial resources and know-how to help Germany transform its war machine into a prosperous, full-employment, free-trading society with no need for territorial aggrandizement. "What has to be done for [Hitler] is beyond anyone's conception yet," Kennedy declared. "He has no money, and he can't change all those people who are engaged in war-time activities into peace-time activities without having a terrific problem." A businessman to his marrow, Kennedy could not conceive of a political problem that did not have an economic solution. If Hitler could be assured that his country, which had suffered the ravages of depression, would enjoy a booming future, then, Kennedy believed, Germany would rejoin the ranks of peace-loving nations. The keys were such bread-and-butter matters as jobs, trade agreements, currency convertibility, and gold reserves. It was, in short, a pocketbook issue. Hull, as was his wont, listened and made no comments.[78]

Kennedy took his campaign for economic appeasement a step forward in early May 1939. James Mooney, president of General Motors Overseas, called on Kennedy at the embassy and informed him of discussions he had been having with Emil Puhl, director of the Reichsbank, and Helmuth Wohlthat, Goering's chief economic adviser. Both officials had told Mooney that Hitler would agree to peace terms and a general disarmament if Washington and London removed embargoes on German goods, restored colonies taken from Germany at the end of World War I, and gave the Reich a gold loan totaling between $500 million and $1 billion. Kennedy, sensing a once-in-a-lifetime opportunity to avert cataclysm, asked Mooney to return to Berlin to tell Puhl and Wohlthat that

[77] Chamberlain cited in Feiling, *Life of Neville Chamberlain*, 399–400.
[78] JPK cited in Nasaw, *Patriarch*, 382.

the American ambassador in London "might be able to go over to Paris,
ostensibly for a weekend visit" and meet with them "quietly and privately." Mooney hastened back to Germany to do Kennedy's bidding.[79]

Only after sending Mooney on his way did Kennedy cable a decep-
tively casual dispatch to Welles in which he noted that Mooney had
invited him to dine in Paris the coming Saturday. "Another party at the
dinner will be a personal friend of Hitler and high in influence in the
Reichsbank," Kennedy wrote. "This man is in the inner circle, from what
Mooney said. ... Do you perceive any objection to my going, and have
you any suggestions to make?"[80]

State reacted with horror. "The secretary and I have talked over your
message," Welles cabled back, "and it is our feeling, very strongly, that it
would at this time be almost impossible to prevent your trip to Paris and
the names of the persons you will see there from being given much
publicity. If the wrong impression were given here in the press to your
conference with the person in question from Germany, it would most
certainly create unfortunate comment." Therefore, Welles declared,
"I hope that you will not at this moment undertake this trip."[81]

Instructions could hardly be clearer, but Kennedy would not be
deterred. He went over Hull's head to Roosevelt, imploring the president
that he be allowed to meet Puhl and Wohlthat in Paris. Roosevelt refused
on the same grounds that Hull had. When Mooney returned to London
and learned of FDR's verdict, he complained to Kennedy that it would be
"unpardonable" to cancel the meeting he had arranged. Kennedy vowed
to try again. According to Mooney's unpublished memoir, when he called
on Kennedy the following morning, he "found a gloomy ambassador
awaiting me. He had been up half the night, he said, getting the telephone
call through to the White House, only to be refused permission for a
second time."[82]

Kennedy had been told unambiguously by the president and secretary
of state to have nothing to do with Puhl and Wohlthat. Still, he persisted.
After wrestling with the problem for a few days, he suggested to Mooney
that the two German officials come to London. Roosevelt and Hull had
vetoed a Paris meeting, he argued, but they had said nothing about an
interview in the British capital! While Mooney must have been startled by

[79] JPK cited in Kessler, *Sins of the Father*, 188.
[80] JPK to Welles, 4 May 1939, *HTF*, 331–332.
[81] Welles to JPK, 4 May 1939, Ambassador: Dispatches, Box 174, JPKP.
[82] Mooney cited in Seymour Hersh, *The Dark Side of Camelot* (Boston: Little, Brown), 68.

the audacity of this proposal, he passed it along. Wohlthat agreed to move the meeting. He arrived in London on 8 May and sat down with Kennedy the following morning at the Berkeley Hotel. "Each man made an excellent impression on the other," Mooney recalled. "It was heartening to . . . witness the exertion of real effort to reach something constructive."[83]

The encounter bore no fruit, however, and, as Hull and Welles had predicted, the British press got wind of Wohlthat's visit. "Goering's Mystery Man Is Here" blared the front-page headline of the *Daily Express* days after the Nazi banker conferred with Kennedy. Fortunately for the ambassador, he was not named in the article, but his stateside commanders had little difficulty reading the tealeaves. In the months following Kennedy's reckless meeting with Wohlthat, the White House and Foggy Bottom became progressively less discreet in criticizing him and bypassing the embassy in their dealings with the British government.[84]

"IT'S THE END OF THE WORLD"

Despite the volatility of the European scene, Kennedy went off for another vacation in late July. While he initially intended to return to America, he chose instead to give the South of France a second whirl, renting the grand chateau Domaine de Ranguin outside Cannes, leasing a yacht, and entertaining a parade of luminaries, among them the film star Marlene Dietrich. In a spare moment, he wrote Roosevelt to complain about how he had been treated. "I recognize that in this day and age an ambassador may be hardly more than a glorified errand boy," he declared, but that was not the assignment he thought he had taken on. "I have said repeatedly that in the two important positions I held in the United States, I never received one word of dictation or even suggestion as to the policy I should adopt, and that it is only working under such conditions that I could be at all happy." Yet his initiatives had been repeatedly countermanded by State and it seemed as though no one in the administration listened to his advice. This caused him to "wonder whether my experience and knowledge were not being completely wasted." He ended by pledging his "gratitude and loyalty" to the president, but the letter read as though dictated through clenched teeth.[85]

[83] Mooney cited in Swift, *Kennedys amidst the Gathering Storm*, 158.
[84] *Daily Express* cited in ibid., 158.
[85] JPK to FDR, 9 August 1939, PSF, Box 37, FDRL.

Announcement of the Nazi-Soviet nonaggression pact brought Kennedy's vacation to an end. This agreement, finalized between German Foreign Minister von Ribbentrop and his Soviet counterpart, Vyacheslav Molotov, gave the Nazis a green light in Eastern Europe. Kennedy flew back to London to find the government torn over its pledge to defend Poland. Chamberlain had bound Britain to come to that country's aid in the event of attack, but a glance at a map showed that logistics made such a venture fruitless. Halifax, Kennedy reported, said that "England will definitely go to war if Poland starts to fight." At the same time, the ambassador observed, "I have a distinct feeling that they do not want to be more Polish than the Poles and that they are praying that the Poles will find some way of adjusting their differences with the Germans."[86]

That was Chamberlain's view, one Kennedy shared. Kennedy's first meeting with the prime minister upon returning to London was alarming. "He looks very bad and is terribly depressed," Kennedy informed Hull. "He says the futility of it all is the thing that is frightful; after all, they cannot save the Poles; they can merely carry on a war of revenge that will mean the destruction of the whole of Europe." Kennedy advised State that "the only hope is for some action of the Poles in negotiating with the Germans which will make another delay possible." He recommended that Roosevelt personally "work on [Minister for Foreign Affairs Jozef] Beck in Poland. ... [T]o make this effective it must happen quickly."[87]

Kennedy was advising FDR to strong-arm the Poles into doing what the Czechs had done: surrender land in exchange for peace. Given how that policy had worked out for Prague, the ambassador must have been aware of the likely outcome on this go-round. Berle caught the cynicism in Kennedy's approach when he noted in his diary, "I am not quite clear how you would word a strong message to Poland. It would have to begin, 'In view of the fact that your suicide is required, kindly oblige by' etc."[88]

Chamberlain, a wreck of a man already feeling the effects of the cancer that would end his life the following year, seemed resigned to a fight he felt his country would lose, but Kennedy had not lost faith in appeasement. He stayed awake most of the night on 24 August trying to get a call

---

[86] JPK to Hull, 23 August 1939, *FRUS*, 1939, General, 1:341.

[87] JPK to Hull, 23 August 1939, *FRUS*, 1939, General, 1:355–356.

[88] Diary Entry, 24 August 1939, *Navigating the Rapids*, 243.

through to the White House, finally succeeding at midnight. Welles, who was in conference with the president, picked up the phone. Kennedy, according to his diary, asked Welles "if he understood the import of my request for the president to get in touch with Poland." The undersecretary replied that FDR understood, but that he could not pressure the Poles in the way Kennedy had suggested. "I don't care how it is done," the ambassador shouted, "as long as something is done and done quickly!" There was a pause, and then Kennedy heard Roosevelt's voice in the background. "All right," the president said. "Something will be done tonight." Kennedy went to bed assuming that FDR would put the squeeze on Warsaw to give Hitler what he wanted.[89]

He was mistaken. Hull tersely noted in his memoirs, "Neither the president nor I felt any disposition to bring any pressure to bear on Poland." When a punch-drunk Kennedy arrived at the embassy the following morning, he discovered that Roosevelt had merely asked Hitler and Polish President Ignacy Mościcki to continue negotiating in hope of achieving a peaceful settlement. FDR would not play the timid role demanded by his ambassador.[90]

That same day, Hitler made what he said was his final offer to British Ambassador Henderson. Two historic injustices rendered by the Treaty of Versailles – the demilitarized "free city" of Danzig on the Baltic and the Polish Corridor, the strip of land given to Poland to assure access to the sea – must be ceded to the Reich immediately or, Kennedy reported, "it was going to be a war worse than '14–18." The time for negotiations had seemingly passed.[91]

After Kennedy read this take-it-or-leave-it deal, he joined Chamberlain, Cadogan, and other officials in the cabinet room, where he again revealed how delusional he had become on the European situation. He suggested that, in exchange for "a reasonable Polish settlement," London "could get the U.S. and other countries to get together on an economic plan that would certainly be more important to Germany than what he [Hitler] could possibly get out of anything in Poland." As Kennedy put it, "You must pass the hat before the corpse gets cold." Chamberlain asked what Kennedy meant. Kennedy replied,

[89] Diary Entry, 24 August 1939, Diary, Box 100, JPKP; Welles and FDR cited in DM, 33:5, Box 148, JPKP. See also Diary Entry, 24 August 1939, Diaries, Washington, 1939, Volume 1, JPMP.
[90] Hull, *Memoirs*, 1:662; Diary Entry, 25 August 1939, Diary, Box 100, JPKP.
[91] JPK to Hull, 25 August 1939, *FRUS*, 1939, General, 1:369–370.

You have to make your solution more attractive to Germany than what she is trying to get out of Poland. Do it this way: Propose a general settlement that will bring Germany economic benefits more important than the territorial annexation of Danzig. Get the United States now to say what they would be willing to do in the cause of international peace and prosperity. After all, the United States will be the largest beneficiary of such a move. To put in a billion or two now will be worth it, for if it works we will get it back and more.

As Kennedy recorded in his diary, "When I left No. 10, I thought to myself, that incident has probably been the most important thing that has ever happened to me. Here was I, an American ambassador, called into discussion with the P[rime] M[inister] and foreign secretary over probably the most important event in the history of the British empire. I had been called in before the cabinet and had been trusted not only for my discretion but for my intelligence. It was a moving experience."[92]

It may have been moving, but it had no effect on British policy. Chamberlain and his cabinet rejected Kennedy's suggestions out of hand. The ambassador was proposing more appeasement, an approach Chamberlain had abandoned. No rational observer of Hitler's conduct over the preceding year could imagine that the Führer would be diverted from his course by financial inducements. No one attuned to the tides of British public opinion could believe that Chamberlain's government would survive a second attempt at appeasement. And, needless to say, Kennedy's recommendations did not reflect the views of the White House or State. He had not cleared them with his superiors. As had been the case since he arrived in London eighteen months earlier, he ran his own show.

Early in the morning on 1 September, Hitler brought the suspense to an end by sending fifty-seven divisions across the Polish border in the first exercise of what would come to be known as Blitzkrieg, or lightning war. Kennedy thought Britain would declare war at once, but Chamberlain waited two days before bowing to the inevitable. His official announcement was somber and dignified. "This is a sad day for all of us," he proclaimed, "and to none is it sadder than to me. ... I trust I may live to see the day when Hitlerism has been destroyed and a liberated Europe has been reestablished." Kennedy struck a different note. He telephoned Roosevelt at 3:00 a.m., Washington time, and repeated over and over, "It's the end of the world, the end of everything." The president, who disliked displays of emotion and needed a steady hand on the tiller in

---

[92] JPK and Chamberlain cited in Diary Entry, 25 August 1939, Diary, Box 100, JPKP; DM, 33:7–8, Box 148, JPKP.

London, would later mimic his ambassador's lament to deadly effect before colleagues and members of the press.[93]

From Kennedy's perspective, his chief task now was to keep his country out of the war, and the most effective way of doing that was by bringing it to an end as quickly as possible. Accordingly, just ten days after Hitler's invasion of Poland, Kennedy sent a "Triple Priority" telegram labeled "Strictly Confidential and Most Personal for the Secretary and the President." In it, he talked about meeting with the king, queen, and Home Secretary Sir Samuel Hoare, and the conclusions drawn from those talks: that Poland would soon be defeated, that Hitler would forward a proposal "to France and England to put a stop to this war," and that the Chamberlain government would then be in the impossible position of either accepting the offer and being voted out of office or rejecting it and condemning their country to an unwinnable conflict. Given those circumstances, Kennedy said, the only solution was for FDR to act where the British could not by working out an agreement with Hitler. "It appears to me," the ambassador wrote, "that this situation may resolve itself to a point where the president may play the role of savior of the world. As such, the English government definitely cannot accept any understanding with the present German chancellor, but there may be a situation when President Roosevelt himself may evolve world peace plans."[94]

Roosevelt and Hull were flabbergasted by the naiveté of Kennedy's proposition, which amounted to rewarding Hitler for his aggression at a time when even the staunchest believers in that policy had renounced it. Hull responded within two hours. "The people of the United States," he declared, "would not support any move for peace initiated by this government that would consolidate or make possible a survival of a regime of force." FDR told his postmaster general, James Farley, that Kennedy had sent "the silliest message to me I have ever received."[95]

By this point, Kennedy had lost all influence in the White House, a fact that gradually dawned on him and filled him with rage. Tellingly, the

[93] Chamberlain, 3 September 1939, avalon.law.yale.edu/wwii/gb2.asp; JPK cited in Joseph Alsop and Robert Kintner, *American White Paper: The Story of American Diplomacy and the Second World War* (New York: Simon & Schuster, 1940), 68; Swift, *Kennedys amidst the Gathering Storm*, 190.
[94] JPK to FDR and Hull, 11 September 1939, HTF, 376.
[95] Hull to JPK, 11 September 1939, FRUS, 1939, General, 1:424; FDR cited in James A. Farley, *Jim Farley's Story: The Roosevelt Years* (New York: McGraw-Hill, 1948), 198–199.

same day he received Kennedy's peace proposal, Roosevelt initiated a secret channel of communication with Churchill, bypassing the embassy. When Churchill, who had been brought into the wartime cabinet as first lord of the admiralty, told Kennedy about this private contact, the ambassador fumed in his diary, "Another instance of Roosevelt's conniving mind, which never indicates he knows how to handle any organization. It's a rotten way to treat his ambassador. . . . I am disgusted." The following day, Kennedy wrote, "Again I am amazed at Roosevelt's complete lack of understanding of organization. He calls Churchill up and never contacts me. A rotten way to win men's loyalty. . . . I'll have my say some day!"[96]

The fact that Churchill was expected to succeed Chamberlain as prime minister made FDR's surreptitious correspondence with him particularly troubling to Kennedy, who never liked the silver-tongued, hard-drinking aristocrat. "I can't help feeling he's not on the level," Kennedy noted in his diary. "He's just an actor and a politician. He always impressed me that he'd blow up the American Embassy and say it was the Germans if it would get the U.S. in. Maybe I do him an injustice, but I just don't trust him." And yet Roosevelt apparently trusted him more than his own ambassador![97]

Exacerbating the differences between Kennedy and Churchill was the latter's unflagging optimism. If Churchill sometimes doubted whether the British Army and Royal Air Force could conquer Germany outright, he was confident from the day war broke out that they could prevent Hitler from overrunning the British home islands. By contrast, Kennedy's reports to the White House and State were unrelievedly gloomy and defeatist. The British, he cabled FDR, were waging a "hopeless struggle" that "means the complete collapse of everything we hope and live for. . . . I have yet to talk to any military or naval expert . . . who thinks that, with the present and prospective set-up of England and France on one side and Germany and Russia and their potential allies on the other, England has a Chinaman's chance." In a follow-up cable sent the same evening, Kennedy despaired of the British government's "ever leading the people out of the valley of the shadow of death" and predicted the rise of fascism in Britain. "England passed her peak as a world power some years ago and

[96] Diary Entries, 5 and 6 October 1939, Diary, Box 100, JPKP. I am obliged to Nasaw for pointing out that FDR opened this channel after receipt of Kennedy's plan. Nasaw, *Patriarch*, 414.
[97] Diary Entry, 5 October 1939, Diary, Box 100, JPKP.

has been steadily on the decline. War ... will merely hasten the process. ... Nor do I think this war is a holy war, despite the fact that most of the people I see here sincerely believe that it is." To Missy LeHand, Roosevelt's private secretary (and mistress), Kennedy wrote, "Of course, I am not carried away by this war for idealism. I can't see any use in everybody in Europe going busted and having communism run riot. ... But, of course, one isn't supposed to say this out loud."[98]

No, one was not, especially if one was a diplomat. It would have been bad enough had Kennedy confined such sentiments to his private correspondence, but he aired them publicly. "To anyone who comes within hailing distance," Joe Alsop and Bob Kintner reported in their nationally syndicated column, "our ambassador to England freely predicts the collapse of capitalism, the destruction of democracy, and the onset of the dark ages. He says that only an early peace, at almost any price, can save the world." When Lippmann, perhaps the most influential columnist in America, visited Kennedy in London, the ambassador told him that Hitler had "every reason to go to war and is able to win. The British fleet is valueless. The German submarines can cut off shipping in the Atlantic. ... All Englishmen ... in their hearts *know* this to be true." Exercising more discretion than the ambassador, Lippmann did not include these comments in his column. Later, he described Kennedy as "more than an appeaser – he was actually pro-Nazi and strongly anti-Semitic."[99]

With the Germans and the Soviets dividing Poland and Hitler's armies poised to charge west, it seemed an odd time for Kennedy to take another vacation, but he asked for and received permission to come home. This furlough would last over three months and further strain relations both with the Roosevelt administration and the government in London. Kennedy covered himself by having his gastroenterologist write FDR that he needed the break because of his "chronic gastritis, which at the present time is in an acute phase." The president had little choice but to consent.[100]

Kennedy stopped over in Washington on his way to Florida and presented a funereal assessment of the situation. "Joe Kennedy was

[98] JPK to FDR [two cables], 30 September 1939, PSF, Box 37, FDRL; JPK to LeHand, 3 October 1939, Tully Archive, Box 10, FDRL.

[99] Alsop and Kintner cited in Alan Axelrod, *Lost Destiny: Joe Kennedy and the Doomed World War II Mission to Save London* (New York: St. Martin's Press, 2015), 23; JPK and Lippmann cited in Kessler, *Sins of the Father*, 190 (emphasis in the original); Ronald Steel, *Walter Lippmann and the American Century* (New York: Vintage, 1980), 376.

[100] Jordan to FDR, 13 December 1939, POF, Box 1, FDRL.

utterly pessimistic," FDR told Ickes. "He believes that Germany and Russia will win the war and that the end of the world is just down the road." Kennedy also dropped in on Moffat at State and indulged in some conspiracy-mongering, noting, "Churchill ... wants us in as soon as he can get us there. He is ruthless and scheming. He is also in touch with groups in America which have the same idea, notably certain strong Jewish leaders." In a hint that he had grown tired of his London assignment, Kennedy said that his "main work was now done." Moffat noted, "I gathered that he would prefer a key job here in Washington."[101]

The ambassador then left for Palm Beach, where, he recalled, "I could read detective stories and sleep and swim and sleep again."[102]

"NOTHING BUT SLAUGHTER AHEAD"

While Kennedy sunbathed and dozed, events in Europe rushed forward. Persecution of Jews intensified in the now-expanded Reich. The Soviets attacked and occupied Finland. Germany bombed the Scapa Flow naval base in Scotland. Rumors that Hitler was about to turn his Wehrmacht westward gained credence when a German military plane was shot down over Belgium. The Chamberlain government instituted rationing. American and British journalists came to call this period the Phony War, or Sitzkrieg, but it did not lack crises or drama.[103]

In late February 1940, Kennedy flew from Palm Beach to New York City, where he boarded the *Manhattan*, bound for Naples. This was a logical point of debarkation, since Italy, unlike Britain or France, was still neutral. Nonetheless, one might have expected Kennedy to race back to London to resume his duties after such a long absence. Instead, he lingered, striking up a dalliance with the playwright Clare Boothe Luce, visiting Pompeii, taking in the opera in Rome, visiting Milan for a private viewing of Leonardo da Vinci's *Last Supper*, and otherwise conducting himself like a tourist rather than an ambassador in wartime. He did not return to London until 9 March.[104]

Roosevelt, by this time disgusted with Kennedy, announced that he was sending Welles on a fact-finding mission to Europe to provide the

---

[101] Diary Entry, 10 December 1939, *The Secret Diary of Harold L. Ickes, Volume II: The Lowering Clouds, 1939–1941* (New York: Simon & Schuster, 1955), 85; Diary Entry, 8 December 1939, Diaries, Washington, 1939, Volume 2, JPMP. See also Diary Entry, 10 December 1939, Diary, Box 100, JPKP.
[102] DM, 37:22, Box 148, JPKP.   [103] Shirer, *Rise and Fall of the Third Reich*, 633–683.
[104] DM, 40:1–2, Box 148, JPKP; JPK to Rose Kennedy, 14 March 1940, HTF, 406–409.

administration with an eyewitness account of the Continent's conditions. This was a clear sign that the president did not trust his ambassadors, Kennedy in particular, to supply accurate information, and Kennedy's response was predictably irate. "It's just like Roosevelt," he snapped at U.S. Ambassador to the Vatican Myron Taylor. "He does these things." The Welles mission featured a galling moment when Kennedy was left off the invitation list for the undersecretary's visit to tea with the king and queen. Kennedy interpreted this as an indication of royal disfavor, which it probably was, and Welles's intervention to have the ambassador included did nothing to cool Kennedy's wrath. "Somebody is going to have to explain," he growled, "why I was left out intentionally."[105]

One of the purposes of Welles's European tour was to determine if there was any possibility of ending the war before it began again in earnest, and the undersecretary was forced to conclude, after visits to London, Berlin, Paris, and Rome, that the odds against an early peace were overwhelming. Hitler confirmed that verdict days after Welles sailed home by initiating conflict with Denmark and Norway. The Danes surrendered without a fight; the Norwegians chose to resist. A British intervention in Norway was turned back with such ease that Chamberlain's government barely survived a vote of censure in Parliament. Kennedy's fatalistic reports, however unwelcome in Washington and London, seemed to have been vindicated.[106]

On 10 May, the dam burst. Hitler unleashed an assault on the Netherlands and Belgium with 136 divisions and wave after wave of warplanes. The same day, he launched the Blitzkrieg against France, attacking through the Ardennes forest and outflanking the supposedly impregnable Maginot Line. Chamberlain, recognizing that his support had evaporated, resigned, and the king asked Churchill to form a government. Kennedy considered this change in leadership catastrophic. Following his first meeting with the new prime minister, Kennedy noted in his diary, "I couldn't help but think as I sat there talking to Churchill how ill-conditioned he looked and the fact that there was a tray with plenty of liquor on it alongside him and he was drinking a scotch highball, which I felt was indeed not the first one he had drunk that night." Although

---

[105] JPK cited in Vieth, "Joseph P. Kennedy," 361; Diary Entry, 11 March 1940, Diary, Box 100, JPKP; DM, 40:22, Box 148, JPKP.

[106] Laurence Thompson, *1940* (New York: William Morrow and Company, 1966), 49–87. For Welles's efforts, see "The Welles Mission in Europe, February–March 1940: Illusion or Realism?" *Journal of American History* 58 (June 1971): 93–120.

Churchill, who also assumed the post of defense minister, spoke in confident tones, the ambassador perceived "a very definite shadow of defeat hanging over" the cabinet.[107]

Hitler's juggernaut appeared unstoppable. Germany needed only four days to conquer the Netherlands. Less than 100 hours after the panzer tanks rolled into the Ardennes, Paul Reynaud, the French premier, telephoned Churchill to tell him that the road to Paris was open and that further resistance was futile. Churchill summoned Kennedy, who could not have been less encouraging. As Kennedy reported to Roosevelt and Hull, "I inquired what the United States could do to help that wouldn't leave us holding the bag for a war which the Allies expected to lose." Churchill replied that he intended to ask for American aircraft and "a loan of 30 or 40 ... old destroyers." Kennedy expressed doubt that this would make any difference. Churchill, wrought up, thundered that Britain would never surrender, even if the nation were burned to the ground. "The government will move," he said, "take the fleet with it to Canada, and fight on."[108]

This never-say-die tenacity, Churchill's most prominent trait and the key to his greatness, struck Kennedy as suicidal. Britain was obviously going to lose the war. The only questions were how badly it was going to lose and whether it would draw the United States in. From Kennedy's perspective, the sensible course was to cut a deal with Hitler that acknowledged his dominance of continental Europe, saved France from the shame of utter defeat, preserved as much of the British Empire as possible, and kept America at peace. Yet Churchill seemed hellbent on not only destroying Europe's remaining democracies but sacrificing Kennedy's homeland as well.[109]

Conditions in France grew bleaker by the hour, with Luftwaffe bombers and panzer divisions battering the French army and the British Expeditionary Force from the air and on the ground. Kennedy's correspondence, both private and official, was frantic. "I think the jig is up," he wrote his wife. "The situation is more than critical. It means a terrible finish for the Allies. ... What will happen is probably a dictated

---

[107] Diary Entry, 15 May 1940, Diary, Box 100, JPKP.

[108] JPK to FDR and Hull, 15 May 1940, PSF, Box 3, FDRL.

[109] "Churchill is a remarkable man," Kennedy said sarcastically to a friend as he waited for the Nazis to capture Paris, "or as remarkable as any man can be who's loaded with brandy by ten o'clock in the morning. And when he succeeds in bringing America into the war, he'll reach for that brandy glass, lift his hand on high, and say, 'I have discharged my duty.'" Cited in Vieth, "Joseph P. Kennedy," 405.

peace with Hitler probably getting the British Navy, and we will find ourselves in a terrible mess. My God, how right I've been in my predictions." To Hull, Kennedy cabled, "My impression of the situation here now is that it could not be worse. Only a miracle can save the British Expeditionary Force from being wiped out or ... surrender." The Allies, Kennedy declared, had no option but to raise the white flag: "I suspect that the Germans would be willing to make peace with both the French and the British now – of course on their own terms, but on terms that would be a good deal better than they would be if the war continues."[110]

Kennedy failed to take any relish in the miracle of Dunkirk, when an improvised flotilla of warships, tugs, and private boats managed to rescue some 338,000 troops from that port city town despite pounding by the Luftwaffe. Churchill's "We shall fight on the beaches" address to the House of Commons and the world on 4 June left the ambassador cold. He wrote his eldest son, "With the French out of the way and the Germans in control of all the ports, I can see nothing but slaughter ahead." On the day Reynaud resigned and turned over power to the octogenarian war hero Marshal Philippe Pétain, who was known to favor capitulation, Kennedy raged in his diary, "If Roosevelt had followed my advice, we'd have stopped the war." The insulting terms Hitler imposed – whereby Germany occupied northern France, the French army was reduced to 100,000 men, and France paid the Reich $120 million to cover the costs of occupation – seemed to Kennedy a preview of what the British could expect unless they abandoned Churchill's lunatic policy.[111]

Shortly after the fall of France and Mussolini's belated declaration of war against the democracies, Roosevelt sent another fact-finding mission to Britain. At the president's behest, Secretary of the Navy Frank Knox enlisted Medal-of-Honor winner Colonel "Wild Bill" Donovan, along with foreign correspondent Edgar Mowrer, to evaluate London's survivability. Kennedy found out about this secondhand, and he furiously cabled Hull that the U.S. embassy was more than capable of "getting all the information that can possibly be gathered." For the White House "to send a new man here, at this time," Kennedy sputtered, "with all due

[110] JPK to Rose Kennedy, 20 May 1940, *HTF*, 432–433; JPK to Hull, 27 May 1940, *FRUS*, 1940 (Washington, D.C.: U.S. Government Printing Office, 1957), General, 1:233.
[111] JPK to Joseph Kennedy, Jr., 6 June 1940, Family Correspondence, Box 2, JPKP; Diary Entry, 16 June 1940, Diary, Box 100, JPKP.

respect to Colonel Knox, is to me the height of nonsense and a definite blow to good organization."[112]

The Churchill government, seeing in Donovan a chance to counteract Kennedy's defeatism, gave the colonel unprecedented access to top-secret information. For two and a half weeks, Donovan and Mowrer met with lords of the admiralty, senior air commanders, and economists for briefings on Britain's ships, planes, industrial output, and food reserves. They also received reports from British intelligence, or MI6, and saw firsthand how the new British technological breakthrough, radar, worked. While Welles had at least been courteous and sought to include Kennedy in all the meetings he attended while in London, Donovan and Mowrer kept the ambassador at arm's length. They met with Kennedy's military attachés, but not with Kennedy himself. Upon their return to Washington, they gave Roosevelt a more encouraging assessment of the situation than the president had been receiving from Kennedy. Donovan said that Britain's army and navy were prepared to fight, and morale was superb. The dispersal of RAF bases and radar warning stations made a Luftwaffe triumph unlikely. Although Britain had been slow to gear up for war, aircraft and munitions production were now at an impressive level and were improving every day. In short, Britain could hold out, especially with American backing.[113]

Leaving nothing to chance, Roosevelt sent a third fact-finding mission to London, this one more narrowly focused. Whereas Donovan and Mowrer had had to assess a range of factors – military, industrial, political, and even psychological – the new delegation concentrated solely on Britain's military preparedness. FDR instructed General George Strong and Admiral Robert Ghormley to confer with British army, navy, and air officers and conduct a close inspection of military installations, arms and aircraft plants, and RAF command centers and airfields. Again, Kennedy was not informed of this mission in advance. When he found out, he exploded in a cable to Hull, "Now there is probably a good reason why it is necessary to go around the ambassador in London and take up the matter with the British before he knows about it. However, I do not like it and I either want to run this job or get out. . . . Not to tell me is very poor treatment of me." Hull deputized Welles to offer Kennedy the excuse that

[112] JPK to Hull, 12 July 1940, Ambassador: Dispatches, Box 176, JPKP.
[113] For the Donovan-Mowrer mission, see Anthony Cave Brown, *The Last Hero: Wild Bill Donovan* (New York: Vintage, 1984), 147–151; Joseph E. Persico, *Roosevelt's Secret War: FDR and World War II Espionage* (New York: Random House, 2001), 63–70; Douglas Waller, *Wild Bill Donovan: The Spymaster Who Created the OSS and Modern American Espionage* (New York: Free Press, 2011), 58–68.

State had not informed the embassy because the president wanted to "avoid publicity," an absurd claim given that the appearance in London of high-level U.S. military figures was sure to attract press attention.[114]

Kennedy graciously greeted Strong and Ghormley on their arrival, but he stewed at the humiliation of having his judgment questioned by the president. Even more offensive, from Kennedy's perspective, was the fact that, while the delegation was in London, negotiations were going on between the Roosevelt administration and the Churchill government over what was known as the destroyers-for-bases deal. This arrangement, proposed by Churchill, involved America giving Britain fifty destroyers of World War I vintage in exchange for ninety-nine-year leases on British naval and air bases in the Western Hemisphere. The rationale behind the swap was that it would furnish naval assets to Britain while enabling Roosevelt to sidestep isolationist opinion at home by claiming that he was strengthening American defense, not pushing the United States into the overseas conflict.[115]

This was the most important foreign-policy initiative of 1940, and Kennedy, not unreasonably, felt he should be part of it. He wanted to attach a strict condition: that Britain give the United States a guarantee that London would move the British fleet to Canada in the event the Nazis overran the United Kingdom. Churchill said he could not agree to that quid pro quo; the mere mention of such an arrangement, he argued, would weaken British morale. When Kennedy pressed his point, Churchill detoured the negotiations around the ambassador and dealt directly with Roosevelt and State through the British ambassador in Washington, Philip Kerr, Lord Lothian. Kennedy would have had no knowledge of these talks had Churchill not occasionally let slip a few details. Livid, Kennedy sent a cable to FDR. "I am sure you must be aware of the very embarrassing situation I feel myself in," he complained. "If I am not acquainted with facts of vital importance to both countries, I fail to see how I can function with any degree of efficiency. . . . Frankly and honestly, I do not enjoy being a dummy. I am very unhappy."[116]

---

[114] JPK to Hull, 7 August 1940, Ambassador: Dispatches, Box 176, JPKL; Welles cited in Nasaw, *Patriarch*, 465.

[115] The best treatment of the destroyers-for-bases deal is Robert Shogan, *Hard Bargain: How FDR Twisted Churchill's Arm, Evaded the Law, and Changed the Role of the American Presidency* (New York: Charles Scribner's Sons, 1995).

[116] JPK to FDR, 27 August 1940, HTF, 463. See also Memorandum for the President, 2 August 1940, *FRUS, 1940* (Washington, D.C.: U.S. Government Printing Office, 1958), The British Commonwealth, the Soviet Union, the Near East, and Africa, 3:58; Diary Entry, 14 August 1940, Diary, Box 100, JPKP.

FDR replied with a consoling message. "There is no thought of embarrassing you and only a practical necessity for personal conversations makes it easier to handle details here," the president wrote. "Don't forget that you are not only not a dummy but are essential to all of us." Kennedy was momentarily placated, but erupted in fury again when, a few days later, Ghormley informed him that the destroyers-for-bases arrangement was to be signed the following day. FDR and Hull had not seen fit to tell Kennedy when the deal was finalized. Conrad Black, Roosevelt's biographer, concludes that the president's treatment of his ambassador was "sadistic," and that judgment seems warranted.[117]

In a final slap at Kennedy, Ghormley and Strong, after returning to Washington, corroborated Donovan's report. The Luftwaffe could not defeat the RAF, they said, and therefore the Germans could not invade the island. Britain was unafraid, unified, primed for battle, and, of course, worth rescuing. In short, everything Kennedy had said for months was wrong.[118]

"DESERTING HIS POST"

On 7 September 1940, the London Blitz began. For fifty-six of the following fifty-seven days and nights, the Luftwaffe assaulted the British capital. Two hundred planes descended nightly, raining death on Londoners of every class, from the king and queen in Buckingham Palace to the East End slums, docks, and warehouses. Over 300,000 people lost their homes, and around 8,500 were killed. Never before had a city, in this case the world's largest, faced such a continuous aerial barrage.[119]

Morale would not crack. Indeed, many Londoners, as a sign of defiance, ignored their government's orders to evacuate. They remained in their homes, huddled in improvised shelters, or went underground into tube stations. As soon as the "all clear" sounded, they picked their way

---

[117] FDR to JPK, 28 August 1940, PSF, Box 37, FDRL; Diary Entry, 2 September 1940, Diary, Box 100, JPKP; Black cited in Swift, *Kennedys amidst the Gathering Storm*, 272.
[118] Ghormley and Strong cited in de Bedts, *Ambassador Joseph Kennedy*, 210.
[119] The Blitz has not lacked for scholarly attention. Studies include Amy Helen Bell, *London Was Ours: Diaries and Memories of the London Blitz* (New York: I. B. Tauris, 2011); Anthony J. Bird, *London's Burning* (New York: Endeavor Press, 2015); Constantine Fitzgibbon, *The Winter of the Bombs: The Story of the Blitz of London* (New York: Scholar's Choice, 2015); Gavin Mortimer, *The Blitz: An Illustrated History* (London: Osprey Publishing, 2010).

through the rubble and resumed daily routines as if nothing was amiss. Hundreds sat in deck chairs in the parks, reading newspapers. Movie theaters, restaurants, and pubs remained open, some filled to capacity. A few brave souls played golf, went horseback riding, or even held outdoor parties despite the roar of bombers overhead, the shriek of air-raid sirens, the rattle of anti-aircraft barrages, the explosions of shells. There were instances of panic, some looting, and even a few suicides, but overall it was the most legendary display of stiff-upper-lip in history. "They are a strange people," an uncomprehending Kennedy noted in his diary. "I can't make out whether they're stupid, courageous, or complacent."[120]

Whatever else they may have been, they were winning. The Germans could not establish supremacy in the air. Luftwaffe losses exceeded those of the RAF, often by a ratio as high as three to one. RAF bases were superbly dispersed and camouflaged, making them impossible to knock out, and radar ensured that they were rarely caught by surprise. Most important, German intelligence had underestimated the productive capacity of British aircraft factories, which turned out Hurricanes and Spitfires in greater numbers than Goering thought possible. Hitler inflicted terrific suffering on the British in the fall of 1940, but he never cleared the airspace over the English Channel. Consequently, he canceled his planned invasion of Britain and turned his attention east.[121]

No one in London knew of Hitler's decision, however, and the bombs kept falling. Churchill continued to urge his people to resist, they responded magnificently, and Kennedy, oblivious to the obvious, sang his signature dirge. "I cannot impress upon you strongly enough my complete lack of confidence in the entire conduct of this war," he cabled State, insisting that the British had nothing "to offer in the line of leadership or productive capacity in industry that could be of the slightest value to us." If America made the mistake of joining the war, he warned, "it will be the United States aided by a badly shot-to-pieces country which, in the last analysis, can give little if any assistance to the cause." He added, "It breaks my heart to draw these conclusions about a people that I sincerely hoped might be victorious," but facts were facts. Still convinced by Lindbergh's appraisal of the strength of the Luftwaffe, Kennedy told British correspondent George Bilainkin that the "Germans are not using [one] twentieth or thirtieth of their bomber strength against

---

[120] Diary Entry, 15 September 1940, Diary, Box 100, JPKP.
[121] Kershaw, *Nemesis*, 302–310.

Britain. [The a]ir war has not really begun." When the Führer really unloaded, he thought, London and every other major city in the Empire would be a moonscape. *Then* the White House and Foggy Bottom would appreciate what their much-maligned ambassador had been trying to save them from![122]

As biographer David Nasaw notes, Kennedy was now in the odd position of being angry with the RAF for winning the Battle of Britain. Kennedy saw this as prolonging Britain's inevitable defeat and making progressively likely American entry into the war. He would have been happier had the RAF failed quickly, forcing the government to sue for peace. Every day Britain held out gave hope to the interventionist faction in the United States, aggravated the damage done to already war-torn London, and, not incidentally, increased the physical danger to Kennedy himself. The ambassador had no desire to join the lists of the dead and wounded and had long since moved out of his official residence at 14 Prince's Gate in Grosvenor Square to spend his evenings and weekends at the sixty-room mansion of St. Leonard's, some twenty-five miles west of the capital. This earned him a great deal of invective from Londoners who thought he should share their plight. A common joke among the upper classes ran, "I thought my daffodils were yellow until I met Joe Kennedy."[123]

That was not entirely fair. Kennedy ran his share of risks – during one raid, the car carrying him was thrown onto the sidewalk by a bomb, although he escaped injury – and bombs destroyed several cottages near St. Leonard's. A German Messerschmitt 109, shot down in a dogfight, crash-landed so close to Kennedy's countryside estate that, according to the ambassador, he could "see the fuzz on [the pilot's] face and count the buttons on his uniform." Kennedy, although anxious to end his stint in Britain, was aware of the public-relations value of appearing fearless in the face of such an onslaught. His pitchman Krock published a piece in the *New York Times* calling Kennedy "Our Most Bombed Ambassador." Kennedy told Bilainkin, "I think I'll have my baptism of fire here, go through one good raid, before I quit and go back," a remark that suggested he was more interested in establishing his machismo than in

---

[122] JPK to Hull, 27 September 1940, *FRUS*, 1940, The British Commonwealth, the Soviet Union, the Near East, and Africa, 3:48–49; JPK cited in Diary Entry, 19 September 1940, George Bilainkin, *Diary of a Diplomatic Correspondent* (London: Allen & Unwin, 1942), 213.

[123] Nasaw, *Patriarch*, 477; joke cited in Thompson, 1940, 180.

fulfilling his duties – which, now that war had arrived, he considered more or less at an end.[124]

He knew, however, that Roosevelt wanted to keep him in London because of his possible impact on the 1940 election. "An emotional fellow, [Kennedy] has strong convictions and less than no remaining fondness for his chief," Alsop and Kintner noted in their column. "He will certainly express his opinions to every available American listener the instant he gets through the customs." A few addresses condemning FDR's foreign policy as likely to draw the United States into war might suffice to leverage the Republican candidate, Wendell Willkie, into the White House. "In short," Alsop and Kintner concluded, "the president has repeatedly urged Kennedy to remain in London in order to keep him quiet."[125]

Two days after that article ran, Kennedy spoke with Welles on the phone. According to his diary, he told the undersecretary that "I planned to leave here the week after next. If the Department wanted to call me home for consultation, well and good; if, however, they did not want to call me home, then I would extend my resignation, to take effect here and at once." Kennedy was not above threatening his bosses to secure his recall. Krock remembered Kennedy informing Welles that if he was not summoned home, he would return anyway and tell the American people that the destroyers-for-bases deal was "the worst ever."[126]

Roosevelt gave in. In his telegram calling Kennedy back to the United States, however, he warned the ambassador not to sound off to journalists. "The press will be very anxious to get some statements from you," the president wrote, "and no matter how proper and appropriate your statements might be, every effort will be made to misinterpret and to distort what you say. I am, consequently, asking you specifically not to make any statement to the press on your way over nor when you arrive in New York until you and I have had a chance to agree upon what should be said." At this juncture, Roosevelt was trying to avoid being painted as a warmonger by Willkie backers while at the same time pressing Congress to pass legislation amending U.S. neutrality laws. It was a political

[124] JPK cited in Robert Kennedy to JPK, undated, HTF, 474; Krock, "Our Most Bombed Ambassador," New York Times, 8 October 1940; JPK cited in Diary Entry, 28 June 1940, Bilainkin, Diary of a Diplomatic Correspondent, 135.

[125] Alsop and Kintner, "Advice Ignored, Kennedy Determined to Come Home Soon," Boston Globe, 7 October 1940.

[126] Diary Entry, 11 October 1940, Diary, Box 100, JPKP; Krock cited in Nasaw, Patriarch, 482.

challenge requiring tact and cunning, and FDR needed Kennedy to keep his mouth shut.[127]

Members of the Churchill government managed to restrain whatever sorrow they felt at Kennedy's departure. As the ambassador made the diplomatic rounds and bade his farewells to the cabinet, his military attaché, General Raymond Lee, noted, "From a soldier's point of view, he is deserting his post at a critical time." Kennedy had lunch with the king and queen at Buckingham Palace, returning later in the afternoon for tea with Princesses Elizabeth and Margaret, and he was photographed shaking hands with Churchill at 10 Downing Street. In all these formalities there was a frosty undercurrent that smiles and expressions of mutual esteem could not disguise.[128]

The one heartfelt encounter Kennedy had before taking his leave was with a terminally ill Chamberlain at the latter's country house. Chamberlain clasped Kennedy's hand and said, "This is goodbye. We will never see each other again." Moved, Kennedy sent the former prime minister a handwritten note the next day declaring, "Your conception of what the world must do in order to be a fit place to live in is the last sensible thing we shall see before the pall of anarchy falls on us all. . . . My job from now on is to tell the world of our hopes." And Kennedy would do that. For the rest of his life, he would defend Chamberlain's appeasement policy as the only sensible response to Hitler's aggression, insisting that Britain was able to stave off a Nazi invasion in 1940 because the Munich agreement purchased precious time to build up British defenses. That was a spurious argument, demolished by scholars in the years following World War II, but Kennedy gripped it with the rigor of death.[129]

Kennedy traveled to Lisbon, the only safe place from which to make a transatlantic flight, and when he arrived an embassy counselor handed him a note from Roosevelt instructing him come immediately to the White House upon his return to the United States. According to Kennedy's diary, the president told him to "make no statements to the newspapermen." FDR had already given Kennedy this order, and the fact that he felt

---

[127] FDR to JPK, 17 October 1940, *HTF*, 475.
[128] Diary Entry, 16 October 1940, *The London Observer: The Journal of General Raymond E. Lee, 1940–1941*, ed. James Leutze (London: Hutchinson, 1971), 95.
[129] Chamberlain cited in Diary Entry, 19 October 1940, Diary, Box 100, JPKP; JPK to Chamberlain, 22 October 1940, Ambassador: Correspondent File, Box 104, JPKP. See also DM, 50:11, Box 148, JPKP.

the need to repeat it irked the ambassador. "I was, of course, indignant," Kennedy recalled. But, for once, he did as he was told.[130]

The press was out in force to welcome Kennedy when his Pan Am clipper landed at LaGuardia Field in New York City. "Mr. Kennedy looked for all the world like a man bursting with things to say," observed the *New York Times*, "but in the interval between his arrival and his departure by plane for the capital, he limited himself to these words: 'I have nothing to say until I have seen the president.'" Kennedy did promise reporters that he would "talk a lot" after his conference with FDR. He also brandished a souvenir of the Blitz, an air-raid siren that he said would be used to call his children to meals at the Kennedy compound in Hyannis Port. Then, after a tearful reunion with his family in the terminal building, he was aloft again, flying with Rose to Washington.[131]

Roosevelt had arranged for South Carolina Senator James Byrnes and his wife to join the Kennedys at what he called a "little family dinner" at the White House. "When we were about half through the dinner," Kennedy recorded in his memoir, "Jim Byrnes, acting as though a wonderful idea had just struck him, said he thought it would be a great idea if I would go on the radio" and endorse Roosevelt for a third term. Kennedy, caught short, swiftly recognized that he could not refuse. However angry he might be with the president, FDR had honored him with Embassy London, and if Kennedy came out for Willkie he would look like an ingrate. In addition, he would damage his sons' political prospects. He therefore agreed, as he put it, to "make the God damned speech," but he insisted on writing it himself. "I don't want anyone else to do it for me," he snapped. "I am not going to show it to anyone. You will all trust me or you won't get it."

Kennedy then unloaded two and a half years of frustration on the bewildered Roosevelt, addressing him as though he were a Wall Street colleague rather than the president of the United States. "I am damn sore at the way I have been treated," Kennedy declared. "I feel that it is utterly unreasonable and I don't think I rated it." He listed his grievances: "First, because Donovan was sent to London without consulting me; secondly, your sending a general there and Britain's knowing about it before I did; thirdly, carrying on negotiations on destroyers and bases through [British

[130] Diary Entry, 22 October 1940, Diary, Box 100, JPKP; Hull to JPK, 25 October 1940, ibid.
[131] "Kennedy Sees Roosevelt at White House; Envoy Is Silent on Arrival from London," *New York Times*, 28 October 1940.

Ambassador Lord] Lothian and not through me; and fourthly, the State Department's never telling me about what was going on. All these things were conducive to harming my influence in England." Kennedy protested that he had always been loyal to FDR, supporting him even "when there was a great doubt amongst a great many people" about the president's policies. "[I]n spite of all that," the ambassador said, "you have given me a bad deal."

Roosevelt denied having undermined Kennedy's ambassadorship and blamed his problems on State, which, he said, was in the hands of "career men [who] always did things wrong." There would be a top-to-bottom housecleaning at Foggy Bottom after the election, he promised. Incompetents like Welles would be shown the door. FDR reaffirmed his friendship with Kennedy, praised his performance in London, and hinted that he would find him a prominent position in the administration after appointing another U.S. ambassador to Britain. Kennedy calmed down, but he knew better than to take Roosevelt at face value. "Somebody is lying very seriously," he wrote later, "and I suspect the president." Nonetheless, there would be no public break with FDR.[132]

Although the president invited the Kennedys to spend the night at the White House, they took a late night flight back to New York, where Joe secluded himself in a suite at the Waldorf Hotel to work on his speech. He issued a press release announcing that he would address the nation from CBS headquarters over 114 stations on Tuesday, 29 October. The sponsors, he said, would be his wife and the nine Kennedy children. He gave no indication of what he planned to say.[133]

The speech was a mix of pessimism and peevishness, hardly typical campaign oratory. Kennedy did endorse Roosevelt's bid for a third term, but he did so on the premise that FDR was likelier than Willkie to keep the United States at peace. "I am more convinced than ever that America should stay out of this war," Kennedy declared. "From the day I went to the Court of St. James until this minute I have never given to one single individual in the world any hope whatsoever that at any stage or under any conditions could the United States be drawn into the war." Apart from economic factors, Kennedy argued, the strategic challenges of

---

[132] FDR cited in Beschloss, *Kennedy and Roosevelt*, 215; DM, 51:6, Box 148, JPKP; Account of Ambassador's Trip to United States on Clipper, undated, Diary, Box 100, JPKP. See also James Byrnes, *All in One Lifetime* (New York: Harper & Brothers, 1958), 126–128; Krock, *Memoirs*, 335–336.

[133] "Kennedy to Speak on Radio Tonight," *New York Times*, 29 October 1940.

fighting Germany were insurmountable: "Where would an [American] army disembark, with Hitler holding nearly all the ports of continental Europe?" Kennedy defended his friend Chamberlain. "In the last year, I have read a lot of irresponsible writing, most of it of a critical nature, about the Munich pact," he said. "The criticism in my judgment is not justified. . . . Can anyone imagine what would have happened to England if the Blitzkrieg of the summer of 1940 had occurred in September of 1938?" He also defended himself: "[I]f, as some of my critics say, I am 'steeped in gloom,' let me ask you, what is there in the world picture that gives any excuse for gaiety? . . . Gloom, under such circumstances, is nothing more than 'facing the facts.'" He concluded on a personal note. "I have a great stake in this country," he stated. "My wife and I have given nine hostages to fortune. Our children and your children are more important than anything else in the world. . . . In the light of these considerations, I believe that Franklin D. Roosevelt should be reelected president of the United States."[134]

Press reaction to the speech was generally favorable, and Roosevelt was pleased with it, although it did not compare in tone to the enthusiastic addresses Kennedy had given in support of FDR in 1932 and 1936. In any event, a week later Roosevelt won reelection by taking thirty-eight states with 449 electoral votes. Several days after the votes were in, Kennedy stopped by the White House to congratulate the president and submit his letter of resignation. Roosevelt asked him to stay on until he had found a replacement. Kennedy replied, "That's OK, just so long as I'm out."[135]

"DEMOCRACY IS ALL DONE"

In Kennedy's defense, it should be noted that he was in an emotionally fragile state when he gave the interview that destroyed what remained of his reputation. On 9 November, he learned of Chamberlain's death, writing in his diary, "I had hard work to keep from crying because I was closer to Neville Chamberlain than I was to anyone in England. . . . He was noble. He was kind and fair and brave. The world and particularly England will miss his counsel." Given how hard the news hit, Kennedy would have been wise to cancel or postpone a meeting he

[134] JPK Speech, CBS Radio, 29 October 1940, Speeches, Box 157, JPKP.
[135] JPK cited in Diary Entry, 1 December 1940, Diary, Box 100, JPKP. For media response to Kennedy's address in America and Britain, see Vieth, "Joseph P. Kennedy," 509–510.

had agreed to two days earlier with reporters for the *Boston Globe*, but he pulled himself together and sat down with Louis Lyons, Charles Edmondson, and Ralph Coglan in a room at the Ritz-Carlton.[136]

"Joe Kennedy poured out his views about America and the war in a torrent that flowed like the free, full power and flood of the Mississippi River," Lyons told readers the following day. It was a vivid example of "the color and force and pungency that makes [*sic*] Joe Kennedy one of the leading figures on the world stage." The ambassador did not equivocate. "There's no sense in our getting in the war," he said. "We'd just be holding the bag." He reiterated a theme from his radio speech: "People call me a pessimist. I say, 'What is there to be gay about?' Democracy is all done." That statement stunned Lyons, who asked, "You mean in England or this country too?" Kennedy responded, "Well, I don't know. If we get into war, it will be in this country too. A bureaucracy would take over right off. Everything we hold dear would be gone."

Kennedy insisted that Britain was not "fighting for democracy. That's the bunk. She's fighting for self-preservation." Americans should not allow hands-across-the-sea sentiment to blind them to the facts of the situation, he declared. Instead, they should be "coldly realistic and for America all the time."

The ambassador assured his listeners, "I know more about Europe than anybody else in this country because I've been closer to it longer," and his experience, he said, led to one conclusion: "It would be senseless to go in. What would we be fighting for?" Again, he declared, "Democracy is finished in England. It may be here. Because it comes to a question of feeding people. It's all an economic question. I told the president in the White House last Sunday, 'Don't send me 50 admirals and generals. Send me a dozen real economists.'" Despite abundant evidence that the conflict roiling the Continent grew out of factors other than the purely economic, Kennedy continued to view events through the bars of the dollar sign. When Coglan noted popular fears that "we wouldn't trade with Europe . . . if Hitler wins the war," Kennedy scoffed, "That's nonsensical."

Kennedy dug himself into a deeper hole with ill-considered remarks about Queen Elizabeth and Eleanor Roosevelt. "Now, I tell you when this thing is finally settled," he said, "and it comes to a question of saving what's left for England, it will be the queen and not any of the politicians who will do it. She's got more brains than the cabinet." Kennedy had been

---

[136] Diary Entry, 9 November 1940, Diary, Box 100, JPKP.

in London for nearly three years, but that claim made it appear as though he did not grasp that it was the MPs, not the king and queen, who made political decisions. His assertion was moreover offensive to the Churchill government, whose members did not appreciate having their intelligence belittled by an ambassador accredited to their country. As for the first lady, Kennedy said that she was a lovely person but that "she bothered us more in our jobs in Washington to take care of the poor little nobodies who hadn't any influence than the rest of the people down there together. She's always sending me a note to have some little Susie Glotz to tea at the embassy." "Susie Glotz" was taken to be an anti-Semitic slur in many quarters, and for good reason.

"I'm willing to spend all I've got left to keep us out of the war," Kennedy said towards the close of the ninety-minute interview. "I say we aren't going in. Only over my dead body." Edmondson, an isolationist and admirer of Lindbergh, commented, "I'm happy to see that you aren't another Walter Hines Page," which was true, if not in the sense Edmondson intended.[137]

The story ran in the *Globe* and was picked up by other newspapers nationwide. Editorial comment was universally negative and often hostile. Even the *New York Times* condemned Kennedy as a "defeatist propagandist." Alsop and Kintner observed, "The history of American diplomacy is replete with fantastic incidents, but a good many State Department officials agree that the recent interview given by Joseph P. Kennedy . . . comes near to winning the prize." They claimed that Kennedy had been "frightened into something approaching a fit" and that he planned to "peddle appeasement all across the United States." Massachusetts Representative George Tinkham inserted a copy of the *Globe* article in the *Congressional Record*. An avalanche of letters and telegrams descended on the White House demanding that Roosevelt repudiate his ambassador.[138]

Kennedy tried damage control. He issued a formal statement asserting that he had told the reporters that "I should be very happy to give them

---

[137] Louis M. Lyons, "Kennedy Says Democracy All Done in Britain, Maybe Here," *Boston Globe*, 10 November 1940.

[138] "Kennedy Linked with Lindbergh," *New York Times*, 24 November 1940; Alsop and Kintner cited in Vieth, "Joseph P. Kennedy," 529–531; Nasaw, *Patriarch*, 500. For mail received by the White House concerning Kennedy's speech, see POF, Box 2, FDRL. Not surprisingly, the British press was even more damnatory. Typical was a piece in the *London Daily Mail* that directly addressed the ambassador: "Perhaps you were always a defeatist and never owned up to it in public. . . . We can forgive wrongheadedness, but not bad faith." Cited in Vieth, "Joseph P. Kennedy," 534.

my thoughts off the record, but I would make no statements that should be printed at this time. ... It was on this basis that our conversation proceeded." Many of the comments attributed to him, he said, were "inaccurate" and "create[d] a different impression entirely than I would want to set forth." He called the article "the first serious violation of the newspaper code on an off-the-record interview that I have ever experienced." In a subsequent press release, he proclaimed, "I have never made anti-British statements or said – on or off the record – that I do not expect Britain to win the war." That was, of course, a lie, and everyone in the White House, State, Downing Street, and Foreign Office knew it.[139]

The ambassador may have been chastened, but he committed another foot-in-mouth outrage a week after the *Globe* interview. He flew west to see his son Jack, who was taking classes at Stanford, and while there he accepted an invitation to speak at a luncheon at Warner Brothers studio. The speech was extemporaneous and lasted an astonishing three hours. Producer Douglas Fairbanks, Jr. wrote Roosevelt that Kennedy "suggested that the Lindbergh appeasement groups are not so far off the mark when they suggest that this country can reconcile itself to whomever wins the war and adjust our trade and lives accordingly." Kennedy, Fairbanks noted, "threw the fear of God into many of our producers and executives by telling them that the Jews were on the spot, that they should stop making anti-Nazi pictures or using the film medium to promote the cause of 'democracies' versus 'dictators.' He said that anti-Semitism was growing in Britain and that the Jews were being blamed for the war." While Fairbanks was certain that "there is not one half of one percent of truth in such a statement," he worried that Kennedy, still the U.S. ambassador to Britain, was "voicing administration thoughts." If that was not the case, Fairbanks said, then Roosevelt should "disown" Kennedy and "accept his resignation." After all, anyone who "believe[d] that a dictator's promise can be trusted" had no business representing America overseas.[140]

Kennedy had become an embarrassment, and although Roosevelt had yet to choose his successor, the president permitted him to release a

---

[139] JPK cited in "Kennedy Disavows Interview on War," *New York Times*, 12 November 1940; "Pessimism on Britain Is Denied by Kennedy," *New York Times*, 30 November 1940. FDR was unimpressed by Kennedy's pleadings. Ickes noted in his diary, "The president said that in his opinion the interview obtained with Kennedy in Boston a couple of weeks ago was authentic, despite its subsequent denial by Kennedy." Diary Entry, 1 December 1940, *Lowering Clouds*, 386.

[140] Fairbanks, Jr. to FDR, 19 November 1940, PSF, Box 37, FDRL.

statement to the press announcing, "I shall not return to London." Few Britons outside of the Cliveden set were sorry to hear the news.[141]

Shortly thereafter, there was an ugly encounter between Kennedy and Roosevelt at the president's Hyde Park estate, where the ex-ambassador went in early December to explain his *Globe* interview. Eleanor Roosevelt picked up Kennedy at the train station and brought him to see FDR at the main house. As she recalled twenty years later, the two men met behind closed doors for a few minutes before Roosevelt asked Kennedy to step out of his office and called the first lady in. "I never want to see that son of a bitch again as long as I live," FDR said, his face white with rage. "Take his resignation and get him out of here." Eleanor reminded her husband that the next train did not leave for four hours, to which he exploded, "Then you drive him around Hyde Park, give him a sandwich, and put him on that train!" Eleanor complied.[142]

Thus concluded Kennedy's years of public service. The man once touted as a good bet to become America's first Catholic president never held another government job.

*   *   *   *

Joseph P. Kennedy was nothing if not consistent. No U.S. diplomat, rogue or otherwise, clung more doggedly to a rooted notion regardless of facts and developments. Five months after the end of World War II, with Nazism overcome, millions liberated from concentration camps, and democracy restored in most of Western Europe, Kennedy met briefly with Churchill, who was touring the United States. It was an awkward faceoff, as both men knew they detested one another, but they managed to make small talk for a while before the former ambassador blurted out, "After all, what did we accomplish by this war?"

Churchill, for one of the few times in his life, was at a loss for words.[143]

[141] JPK Press Release, 1 December 1940, *HTF*, 497.
[142] Eleanor Roosevelt and FDR cited in Beschloss, *Kennedy and Roosevelt*, 229; Swift, *Kennedys amidst the Gathering Storm*, 294.
[143] JPK cited in Nasaw, *Patriarch*, 580.

6

"We Can't Fire Him"

Lodge Engineers a Coup

Despite patriotic myths to the contrary, the United States has always had an aristocracy, and in the early 1960s Henry Cabot Lodge II stood at its apex. American blood did not get bluer. The chiseled, lanky New Englander counted among his ancestors Frederick Frelinghuysen, a delegate to the Continental Congress; George Cabot, a founding member of the Federalist Party; John Davis, a representative, senator, and three-time governor of Massachusetts; and, of course, Henry Cabot Lodge I, one of the principal promoters of American empire at the turn of the century.[1]

Given that pedigree, it is unsurprising that Cabot Lodge II dedicated his life to public service. From boyhood, he had drilled into him the message that, as a member of America's ruling elite, he was expected to pursue a career in government, either elective or appointive. He made his debut in politics in 1932, winning a seat in the House of Representatives, and he was reelected in 1934. Two years later, he beat Democrat James Curley to become a senator. Reelected after U.S. entry into World War II, he resigned in 1944 to join the army, the first senator since the Civil War to give up his seat to fight for his nation. When he ran again for the Senate after returning home, he triumphed by an awesome

---

[1] For an informative if uncritical biography, see William Miller, *Henry Cabot Lodge* (New York: James H. Heineman, 1967). See also Alden Hatch, *The Lodges of Massachusetts: An Intimate Glimpse into the Lives and Careers of One of Our Country's Great Political Families* (New York: Hawthorn Books, 1973). Lodge's memoir is gossipy and anecdotal. See Henry Cabot Lodge, *The Storm Has Many Eyes: A Personal Narrative* (New York: W. W. Norton and Company, 1973).

plurality, but he was defeated in his campaign for a fourth term by John F. Kennedy.[2]

This turned out to be a blessing in disguise, as the just-inaugurated Dwight Eisenhower nominated Lodge to be U.S. ambassador to the United Nations. Swiftly confirmed, he occupied the post for almost eight years, earning a nationwide reputation. The new medium of television brought him into America's living rooms as the ruggedly handsome champion of democracy squaring off against communists, among them Andrei Vishinsky, the chief Russian delegate to the UN. Lodge and Vishinsky engaged in numerous verbal sparring sessions that drew a wide TV audience and made Lodge, by the end of the Eisenhower administration, one of the preeminent personalities in American life.[3]

At the UN, as during every stage of his public career, Lodge's conduct was grounded in an attitude of noblesse oblige that would have been familiar to patrician rogue diplomats like Robert Livingston. While willing to make any sacrifice for the good of his country, Lodge felt entitled by birth and breeding to follow his own judgment and have that judgment respected. Thus, when in 1953 a resolution was proposed in the UN on the Korean conflict, Lodge disregarded a State Department directive to vote yes. Upon reading in the newspapers that Lodge had voted no, Robert Murphy, assistant secretary of state for UN affairs, put through an urgent call to the ambassador in New York. "Apparently our instructions failed to reach you?" he asked. "Instructions?" Lodge repeated. "I am not bound by instructions from the State Department. I am a member of the president's cabinet and accept instructions only from him." Murphy protested, "But you also are head of an embassy, and our ambassadors accept instructions from the secretary of state." After a pause, Lodge said, "I take note of the department's opinions." Murphy, nonplused, declared, "This is a new situation to me, and I'll have to discuss it with the secretary." Lodge replied airily, "Yes, do that. He will set you straight."

[2] Lodge, *Storm Has Many Eyes*, 49–127; Miller, *Henry Cabot Lodge*, 104–255. For Lodge's loss to Kennedy, see Thomas J. Whalen, *Kennedy versus Lodge: The 1952 Massachusetts Senate Race* (Boston: Northeastern University Press, 2000). Lodge styled himself "Henry Cabot Lodge, Jr." while running for office, which was technically incorrect: the original Henry Cabot Lodge was his grandfather; his father was the author George Cabot Lodge. But "Henry Cabot Lodge II" sounded too snobbish for the campaign trail.
[3] Lodge, *Storm Has Many Eyes*, 127–155; Miller, *Henry Cabot Lodge*, 257–332.

As remarkable as that exchange was what happened afterwards. When Murphy told Secretary of State John Foster Dulles about Lodge's misdeed, Dulles thought about it for a moment and said, "This is one of those awkward situations which require special consideration. If it happens again, just tell me and I'll take care of it." State never issued another order to Lodge, who, Murphy recalls in his memoir, "interpreted his functions as much broader than those of an ordinary ambassador. He believed that his position in New York entitled him to help formulate policy as well as execute it."[4]

This was the man who Eisenhower's successor, John F. Kennedy, picked to head the U.S. Embassy in South Vietnam during the so-called Buddhist crisis of 1963. No one familiar with Lodge's record should have been shocked that he proved difficult to control while in Saigon. Indeed, as we shall see, he was the most obstreperous rogue diplomat sent abroad by the White House since President Kennedy's own father took up residence in London in the 1930s. In an irony so glaring that an author would be censured for inventing it, JFK found his Vietnam policy hijacked by an envoy from the same Boston Brahmin class against whom the Kelly-green Kennedys competed so often and so successfully.

The Buddhist crisis – and its culmination, the overthrow of South Vietnamese President Ngo Dinh Diem – has received considerable scholarly attention, more than most episodes in America's much-examined thirty-year engagement with Southeast Asia. Early journalistic treatments by John Mecklin, Robert Shaplen, and especially David Halberstam portray Lodge favorably, as a strong-willed individual who took charge of a challenging situation and helped get rid of a brutal and incompetent dictator. More recent works, drawing upon declassified government documents and other primary sources unavailable in the 1960s and 1970s, offer a more nuanced appraisal. Anne Blair, whose *Lodge in Vietnam* is probably the most thorough treatment of his ambassadorship, gives him high marks for "patriotism" and "character" but ultimately concludes that he "was out of his depth in Vietnam," confounded by an alien culture and prone to "dr[a]w speedy conclusions on the basis of preconceived notions." She also argues that he was "a poor choice as the official to coordinate the U.S.

---

[4] Murphy, Lodge (hereafter HCL), and Dulles cited in Robert Murphy, *A Diplomat among Warriors: The Unique World of a Foreign Service Expert* (Garden City, NY: Doubleday, 1964), 367–368. I am indebted to Anne Blair for drawing my attention to this vignette. Anne Blair, *Lodge in Vietnam: A Patriot Abroad* (New Haven: Yale University Press, 1995), 1.

mission" because he had "no experience as an administrator" and operated in "nineteenth-century diplomat-as-lone-wolf fashion."[5]

That point is a common theme in accounts of Lodge's stint in Saigon. Terrence Maitland and Stephen Weiss contend that he "ran the U.S. mission largely as a one-man operation, insulating himself from the general embassy staff." Geoffrey Stewart similarly faults him for "approach[ing] international relations in the tradition of a nineteenth-century diplomat who acted independently and kept his own counsel." According to David Kaiser, the ambassador "utterly lacked devotion to team play" and "insist[ed] upon defining and executing his own policy."[6]

Related to this lone-wolf charge is a conclusion drawn by virtually all studies: that Lodge, more than any other American, was responsible for the deposal and assassination of Diem and his brother, Ngo Dinh Nhu. Max Boot calls the ambassador "the architect of the coup." Robert Mann agrees: "Lodge was the primary American architect of Diem's downfall." Kaiser finds him "the most critical player in the drama," while George Herring, dean of American Vietnam War historians, concludes that he was "the primary architect." Such near-unanimity is rare in scholarship on this most controversial of wars, and attests to the voluminous paper trail Lodge generated as he wrenched control of Vietnam policy from the

[5] John Mecklin, *Mission in Torment: An Intimate Account of the U.S. Role in Vietnam* (Garden City, NY: Doubleday, 1965); Robert Shaplen, *The Lost Revolution: The Story of Twenty Years of Neglected Opportunities in Vietnam and of America's Failure to Foster Democracy There* (New York: Harper & Row, 1965); David Halberstam, *The Making of a Quagmire* (New York: Random House, 1965); Halberstam, *The Best and the Brightest* (New York: Random House, 1969); Blair, *Lodge in Vietnam*, 156–158, 35, 18, 38. For a rare critical contemporary assessment of Lodge, see Marguerite Higgins, *Our Vietnam Nightmare* (New York: Harper & Row, 1965). For other accounts of this fraught period, see Ellen J. Hammer, *A Death in November: America in Vietnam, 1963* (New York: Oxford University Press, 1987); Howard Jones, *Death of a Generation: How the Assassinations of Diem and JFK Prolonged the Vietnam War* (New York: Oxford University Press, 2003); John M. Newman, *JFK and Vietnam: Deception, Intrigue, and the Struggle for Power* (New York: Warner Books, 1992); Francis X. Winters, *The Year of the Hare: America in Vietnam, January 25, 1963–February 15, 1964* (Athens: University of Georgia Press, 1999).
[6] Terence Maitland and Stephen Weiss, *The Vietnam Experience: Raising the Stakes* (Boston: Boston Publishing Company, 1982), 85; Geoffrey C. Stewart, "Henry Cabot Lodge, Jr.: An American Proconsul in Diem's Vietnam" in *Diplomats at War: The American Experience*, eds. J. Simon Rofe and Andrew Stewart (St. Louis, MO: Republic of Letters Publishing, 2013), 232; David Kaiser, *American Tragedy: Kennedy, Johnson, and the Origins of the Vietnam War* (Cambridge, MA: Belknap Press of Harvard University Press, 2000), 233–234.

White House, State Department, Pentagon, and Central Intelligence Agency in the summer and fall of 1963.[7]

Writers who believe that Diem's elimination was a mistake, that the Vietnam War might have been won if Washington had stuck with him, have harsh words for Lodge. Phillip Jennings slams him as an "arrogant ambassador" who brought about "the biggest American foreign policy blunder of the twentieth century." Arthur Dommen considers Diem's overthrow "the greatest communist victory since Dien Bien Phu" and accuses Lodge of acting more dishonorably than the worst colonial administrator: "[N]o French high commissioner or governor general ever condemned an Indochinese head of state to death and presided over his murder." Mark Moyar is particularly vehement, calling the coup "by far the worst American mistake of the Vietnam War"; denouncing Lodge's "deviousness," "biased analysis," and "cultural ignorance"; and making a bold charge: "U.S. Ambassador to South Vietnam Henry Cabot Lodge ... instigated the coup without notifying Kennedy and in direct violation of presidential orders."[8]

That accusation, while not wholly incorrect, is overstated. Examination of the archival record reveals that Kennedy never flatly ruled either against or in favor of a coup and that the directives he sent, or allowed subordinates to send, to the embassy in Saigon were often vague, contradictory, or susceptible to different interpretations. It *is* true, however, that Lodge routinely disobeyed orders. He ignored no fewer than five commands by Secretary of State Dean Rusk to meet with Diem and instead pursued a policy of calculated standoffishness that he felt would be more effective. He also habitually withheld vital information from Washington and refused, despite orders, to collaborate with his military counterpart, General Paul Harkins, head of the Military Assistance Command Vietnam (MACV). Aware that Harkins disapproved of a coup, Lodge

---

[7] Max Boot, *The Road Not Taken: Edward Lansdale and the American Tragedy in Vietnam* (New York: Liveright Publishing Corporation, 2018), 426; Robert Mann, *A Grand Delusion: America's Descent into Vietnam* (New York: Basic Books, 2001), 457; Kaiser, *American Tragedy*, 233; George C. Herring, *America's Longest War: The United States and Vietnam, 1950–1975*, Fifth Edition (New York: McGraw-Hill, 2014), 130.

[8] Phillip Jennings, *The Politically Incorrect Guide to the Vietnam War* (Washington, D.C.: Regnery Publishing, 2010), 58; Arthur J. Dommen, *The Indochinese Experience of the French and the Americans: Nationalism and Communism in Cambodia, Laos, and Vietnam* (Bloomington: Indiana University Press, 2001), 563, 572; Mark Moyar, *Triumph Forsaken: The Vietnam War, 1954–1965* (Cambridge: Cambridge University Press, 2006), xvii, 245, 253, 273.

circumvented him time and again as he encouraged a cabal of South Vietnamese generals to rise up against their leader.

Like other rogue diplomats, Lodge forced through his policy against the wishes of higher-ranking stateside officials. While Kennedy, as noted, wavered back and forth with respect to a coup, his most trusted advisers staunchly opposed it: Secretary of Defense Robert McNamara, Chairman of the Joint Chiefs of Staff General Maxwell Taylor, CIA Director John McCone, Vice President Lyndon Johnson, and most importantly Attorney General Robert Kennedy all maintained that Diem, despite his faults, was preferable to any of his rivals and ought to be supported. In addition, the top three Americans in South Vietnam at the time of Lodge's appointment were pro-Diem: Harkins, Ambassador Frederick Nolting, and CIA station chief John Richardson. Lodge prevailed over them all.

The ambassador's disobedience was unprofessional and high-handed, but it benefited the United States. Those scholars who claim that the war was winnable under Diem are simply wrong. As a number of works have documented, Diem was losing ground to the communist Viet Cong (VC) toward the end of his regime. He and his representatives had been passing on misleading statistics to impress their American backers, but in fact the Army of the Republic of Vietnam (ARVN) was on the ropes in late 1963. Moreover, an abundance of evidence supports the conclusion that Diem was, if not insane, at least mentally imbalanced at the time of the Buddhist crisis; he was incapable of exercising responsible leadership and ought to have been removed from command. Nhu, his chief counselor, was even worse off psychologically, and his growing dependence on drugs made him a dangerous man to have in power. It was in the interest of South Vietnam and the United States that these two men step down, voluntarily or otherwise. Finally, the Diem regime's treatment of rebellious Buddhists, along with thousands of other South Vietnamese caught up in the crisis, was barbaric; for the Kennedy administration to have endorsed it would have cost America prestige, especially in the developing world, which Washington was attempting to woo. Lodge did the right thing, however unorthodox his methods, by bringing down the regime. He bought Washington time in Vietnam, and perhaps a second chance.[9]

[9] For the Diem government's flagging fortunes in the field, see Lawrence Freedman, *Kennedy's Wars: Berlin, Cuba, Laos, and Vietnam* (New York: Oxford University Press, 2000), 401; Kaiser, *American Tragedy*, 268; Fredrik Logevall, *Choosing War: The Lost Chance for Peace and the Escalation of War in Vietnam* (Berkeley: University of California Press, 1999), 438; Newman, *JFK and Vietnam*, 419–422; William Prochnau, *Once upon a Distant War: David Halberstam, Neil Sheehan, Peter Arnett – Young War*

From a twenty-first-century perspective, and in light of the consensus among most Vietnam War scholars that America's military effort would have come a cropper no matter who was in charge in Saigon, Lodge's ambassadorship does not seem as consequential as that of, say, Livingston. Viewed in the context of the time, however, it was a major watershed, and it constituted as brazen a demonstration of rogue diplomacy as one can find in the history of U.S. statecraft.

"MY POSITION WAS WHAT HIS FATHER'S HAD BEEN"

Vietnam was not high on John F. Kennedy's list of priorities when he assumed office in January 1961. The new president faced a daunting array of crises. Fidel Castro had established a potential communist beachhead ninety miles from Florida, rebels in the Dominican Republic seemed on the verge of turning their country into another Cuba, the Congo had lapsed into near-anarchy after the assassination of its leader, and Soviet premier Nikita Khrushchev was threatening to force the Americans out of West Berlin. Worst of all was the situation in Laos, where a three-sided civil war between the U.S.-backed Royal Lao Government, the communist Pathet Lao, and a neutralist front appeared about to conclude with the reds in charge. Vietnam, by contrast, barely registered as a concern. During the confused early weeks of the administration, when the journalist Stanley Karnow told Robert Kennedy that Vietnam might soon pose problems for America, RFK brushed off the suggestion by scoffing, "We have thirty Vietnams a day here."[10]

To be sure, conditions in South Vietnam were not ideal. That small country had led a precarious existence since its creation at the

Correspondents and Their Early Vietnam Battles (New York: Random House, 1995), 361; Neil Sheehan, *A Bright Shining Lie: John Paul Vann and America in Vietnam* (New York: Random House, 1988), 366. For a pugnacious but unpersuasive attempt to rebut this verdict, see Moyar, *Triumph Forsaken*, 247, 462.

[10] RFK cited in Halberstam, *Best and the Brightest*, 79. Laos topped the agenda when Eisenhower briefed Kennedy on the eve of the latter's inauguration. See Persons Memorandum for the Record, 19 January 1961, Eisenhower, Dwight D., Post-presidential Papers, 1961–1969, Augusta-Walter Reed Series, Box 2, Dwight D. Eisenhower Library, Abilene, Kansas; Clifford Memorandum on Conference, 24 January 1961, President's Office File (hereafter POF), Special Correspondence, Box 29a, JFKL; Herter Memorandum for the Record, 19 January 1961, Bureau of Far Eastern Affairs, Assistant Secretary for Far Eastern Affairs, Subject, Personal Name, and Country Files, 1960–1963, Box 5, Record Group 59, General Records of the Department of State, National Archives II, College Park, Maryland.

1954 Geneva Conference, which provisionally divided Vietnam at the
17th parallel. (The division became permanent when Diem refused to go
along with planned nationwide elections in 1956.) Diem had always
been a difficult ally: stubborn, unwilling to delegate authority, resistant
to American advice. A Catholic in a predominantly Buddhist country, he
was respected but not beloved by the South Vietnamese, and he had
survived a number of challenges to his rule: the 1955 "Battle for
Saigon," when he crushed South Vietnam's preeminent criminal organization; an assassination attempt two years later in which the gunman's
weapon jammed; and a nearly successful coup in 1960 that saw para-
troop battalions bombard the presidential palace for thirty-six hours
before loyal units from the countryside came to Diem's rescue. As years
passed, Diem had grown increasingly isolated and autocratic. He relied
more and more upon his brother, Nhu, a ruthless and mercurial man,
for advice, and upon Nhu's wife, the beautiful but poison-tongued
Madame Nhu. His regime had trouble suppressing the communist
insurgency sponsored by Ho Chi Minh's government in North Vietnam.
Still, compared to the civil war in Laos and other cold war flashpoints,
South Vietnam appeared stable.[11]

That changed on 7 May 1963, when Buddhists in the old imperial
capital of Hue joined in festivities commemorating the 2,527th birthday
of the Buddha. Many homes and pagodas were hung with Buddhist flags,
and the deputy province chief in charge of security, a Catholic major

[11] Scholarship on Washington's so-called "Diem experiment" is massive and contentious.
Probably the most authoritative study, drawing on both American and Vietnamese
records, is Edward Miller, *Misalliance: Ngo Dinh Diem, the United States, and the Fate
of South Vietnam* (Cambridge, MA: Harvard University Press, 2013). See also Philip
E. Catton, *Diem's Final Failure: Prelude to America's War in Vietnam* (Lawrence:
University Press of Kansas, 2002); Jessica M. Chapman, *Cauldron of Resistance: Ngo
Dinh Diem, the United States, and 1950s Southern Vietnam* (Ithaca: Cornell University
Press, 2013); Edward Miller, "Religious Revival and the Politics of Nation Building:
Reinterpreting the 1963 'Buddhist Crisis' in South Vietnam," *Modern Asian Studies* 49
(2015), 1903–1962; Miller, "Vision, Power, and Agency: The Ascent of Ngo Dinh Diem,
1945–1954," *Journal of Southeast Asian Studies* 35 (October 2004): 433–458; Geoffrey
C. Stewart, *Vietnam's Lost Revolution: Ngo Dinh Diem's Failure to Build an Independ-
ent Nation, 1955–1963* (Cambridge: Cambridge University Press, 2017). For accounts
focusing on the American side of this partnership, see Seth Jacobs, *America's Miracle
Man in Vietnam: Ngo Dinh Diem, Religion, Race, and U.S. Intervention in Southeast
Asia, 1950–1957* (Durham, NC: Duke University Press, 2004); Jacobs, *Cold War Man-
darin: Ngo Dinh Diem and the Origins of America's War in Vietnam, 1950–1963*
(Lanham, MD: Rowman & Littlefield, 2006); Jacobs, "'Our System Demands the
Supreme Being': The U.S. Religious Revival and the 'Diem Experiment,' 1954–1955,"
Diplomatic History 25 (December 2002): 589–624.

named Dang Xi, chose this inopportune moment to invoke a law banning the display of religious flags without government permission. At Xi's command, police pulled down the Buddhist banners. The following day, thousands of Buddhists gathered in front of Hue's radio station to protest the flag ban, and the chief bonze of central Vietnam, Thich Tri Quang, prepared to deliver an address over loudspeakers. Bonzes and Buddhist laymen in attendance called upon the station director to broadcast the speech, but he refused, instead phoning Xi, who arrived with a company and five armored cars. Xi ordered the protestors to disperse. When they did not comply, he told his troops to fire. The soldiers shot directly into the crowd, killing nine people and wounding fourteen.[12]

Diem dealt with this tragedy poorly. He blamed the affair on the VC, claiming that a communist agent had thrown a grenade, sparking a melee, and that the nine victims had been trampled to death as people fled the scene. Xi, an official statement announced, had done nothing wrong. This only stimulated further protests. In a demonstration in Hue on 10 May, Tri Quang proclaimed a "manifesto of the monks" that demanded freedom to fly the Buddhist flag, legal equality between Buddhists and Catholics, compensation for the families of the victims of the massacre, and punishment for the officials responsible. Diem at first refused to consider these demands, but as demonstrations spread throughout South Vietnam, he began to heed the advice of Ambassador Nolting, who told him that American press coverage of the crisis was making it difficult for Washington to continue its support of the Diem regime. At Nolting's urging, Diem met with a representative of the General Association of Buddhists in a conference at which the two sides agreed on truce terms. In return for a Buddhist pledge to "cease all demonstrations," Diem promised to permit religious flags to be flown on holidays and to guarantee freedom of religion throughout South Vietnam. The crisis appeared resolved.[13]

Discrimination and violence against Buddhists continued, however, and on 11 June an event occurred that all but doomed Diem's government. Thich Quang Duc, a seventy-three-year-old bonze, sat down in the middle of one of Saigon's major boulevards and performed his final act of devotion. After another bonze emptied a gasoline can over his head, Quang

---

[12] Helble to Rusk, 9 May 1963, *FRUS*, 1961–1963 (Washington, D.C.: U.S. Government Printing Office, 1991), Vietnam: January–August 1963, 3:277–278.

[13] "Manifesto of Vietnamese Buddhist Clergy and Faithful," 10 May 1963, *FRUS*, 1961–1963, Vietnam: January–August 1963, 3:287–288; agreement cited in Trueheart to Rusk, 5 June 1963, National Security File (hereafter NSF), Countries – Vietnam, Box 197A, JFKL.

Duc lit a match. His body burst into flames, and for ten minutes the inferno devoured him, while a young monk repeated over and over into a microphone, first in Vietnamese and then in English, "A Buddhist priest becomes a martyr." When a fire truck arrived, monks threw themselves in front of its wheels and prevented it from getting close enough to extinguish the blaze. Malcolm Browne, the Saigon bureau chief of the Associated Press, was among the spectators, and, despite being sickened by the odor of roasting flesh, he had the presence of mind to take photographs.[14]

The images captured by his camera leaped off the front page of newspapers everywhere the following day. John F. Kennedy saw a photo of Quang Duc's suicide by fire while talking to his brother Robert on the phone. The attorney general was giving his views on the civil-rights struggle unfolding in Alabama when suddenly JFK exclaimed, "Jesus Christ!" The president later remarked to a friend that "no news picture in history has generated so much emotion around the world as that one [has]."[15]

To meet the crisis, JFK decided to install a new U.S. ambassador in Saigon. Nolting was considered too pro-Diem and his relations with the American press corps were terrible. Young journalists like David Halberstam, Neil Sheehan, and Peter Arnett resented the ambassador's inaccessibility and found his reports of progress in the fight against the VC not only inaccurate but ludicrous. Nolting concedes in his memoir, "As ambassador I certainly was not successful with the press." He insists, however, that Halberstam and his colleagues were biased against the regime and seized on a few isolated events to manufacture a religious crisis almost entirely out of whole cloth. Whatever the merits of this claim – and a few historians take Nolting's side – JFK had lost faith in the Saigon embassy's capacity to manage affairs by mid-June.[16]

Kennedy initially intended to replace Nolting with Edmond Gullion, who had represented America in the Congo, but Rusk persuaded him to give Embassy Saigon to Lodge instead. Lodge was an appealing candidate

[14] Monk cited in Maitland and Weiss, *Raising the Stakes*, 75; Jacobs, *Cold War Mandarin*, 147–149.
[15] JFK cited in Richard Reeves, *President Kennedy: Profile of Power* (New York: Simon & Schuster, 1993), 517; Vietnam Memoir, Reel 26, Henry Cabot Lodge Papers, Massachusetts Historical Society, Boston, Massachusetts (hereafter HCLP).
[16] Frederick Nolting, *From Trust to Tragedy: The Political Memoirs of Frederick Nolting, Kennedy's Ambassador to Diem's Vietnam* (New York: Praeger, 1988), 92. See also Frederick Nolting, Oral History, 14 May 1966, JFKL. For two scholars who are especially spirited in their defense of Nolting and denunciation of the U.S. press, see Dommen, *Indochinese Experience*, and Moyar, *Triumph Forsaken*.

for several reasons. He spoke French, which would enable him to converse directly with Diem rather than through an interpreter. He had visited Vietnam on his honeymoon in the 1930s, so the country would not be completely unfamiliar to him. Most important, he was a Republican. Appointing him was a way for Kennedy to maintain bipartisan support for his Vietnam policy and ensure that, in the event of a VC triumph, there would be no GOP backlash.[17]

Lodge was not surprised when Kennedy offered him the assignment. He had been angling for an overseas post for some time, informing Rusk that he felt he had another "tour of public service" in his "system," and that he would be eager to go abroad for his country "even though there was a Democratic administration, provided the post was one of real interest." JFK summoned Lodge to the White House on 12 June, the day after Quang Duc's self-immolation, and told him that "the bad situation in Vietnam" endangered America's "position in all the surrounding countries." Would Lodge agree to head Embassy Saigon and clear things up? Lodge said he would need to consult with his wife before accepting, but both men knew that meant yes, and, as Lodge recalled, the president then observed that the Diem government was "entering a terminal phase." He also declared, "I suppose these are the worst press relations to be found in the world today, and I wish you, personally, would take charge of press relations." Lodge, who had enjoyed an excellent rapport with reporters and editors during his tenure at the UN, was confident he could repair the damage Nolting had caused. According to Lodge's journal, just before the meeting broke up, "I said that in general my position was what his father's had been," in that Joseph P. Kennedy had been a media darling when Franklin Roosevelt chose him to head Embassy London. JFK, Lodge recorded, "laughed at this."[18]

The Senate confirmed Lodge unanimously, and he began preparing for his new job: receiving briefings at State and the Pentagon, attending lectures

[17] For Rusk's recommendation of Lodge for the position, see Dean Rusk (as told to Richard Rusk), *As I Saw It* (New York: Penguin Books, 1990), 440; Dean Rusk Oral History Interview, 9 December 1969, JFKL. Former President Eisenhower told Lodge that while the Saigon appointment was a "nasty, mean job," it was Lodge's "Constitutional duty" to accept it – but, Ike insisted, "you must always make it clear that you are a Republican, and that you are doing this as a matter of bipartisan duty." Diary Entry, 18 June 1963, Reel 17, HCLP.

[18] HCL and JFK cited in Dean Rusk Oral History, 9 December 1969, JFKL; HCL Oral History, 4 August 1965, JFKL; Journal Entry, 12 June 1963, Reel 17, HCLP; Lodge, *Storm Has Many Eyes*, 205.

on counterinsurgency at the Foreign Service Institute in Virginia, and enduring a round of inoculations against yellow fever, polio, cholera, tetanus,
typhus, typhoid, and smallpox. Of all the conferences Lodge had during
these days, the one that made the profoundest impact on him was with
Madame Tran Van Chuong, South Vietnam's observer at the UN, wife of
South Vietnam's ambassador to America, and mother of the notorious
Madame Nhu. Over dinner, Madame Chuong told Lodge that the "oppressive acts of the [Diem] regime – the arbitrary arrests, imprisonments, and
executions, and the general reign of terror" would "make assassination
inevitable." Unless a new government was instituted in Saigon, she said,
there was "no power on earth that can prevent the assassination of Madame
Nhu, her husband Mr. Nhu, and his brother Mr. Diem."[19]

That Madame Chuong would say such things about her own family
deeply affected Lodge, as did Madame Nhu's infamous interview for CBS
television shortly thereafter in which she sneered, "What have these so-
called 'Buddhist leaders' done? ... All they have done is to barbeque a
bonze, and that not even with self-sufficient means, since they had to use
imported gasoline." These statements, in concert with JFK's claim that the
Diem government was entering a terminal phase, led Lodge to approach
his posting to Embassy Saigon with an anti-Diem cast of mind. He did not
go to South Vietnam, as CIA Director McCone later charged, with
presidential instructions to "bring about a change in the top leadership";
nonetheless, he was more inclined to countenance a coup – and even
assassination – than Nolting had been.[20]

"A PASSION PLAY OF REVENGE AND TERROR"

As Lodge got ready to take over Embassy Saigon, Nolting continued his
efforts to defuse the Buddhist crisis. It was a hopeless task, but the lame-
duck ambassador did his best. His last month in South Vietnam featured
near-constant meetings with Diem, who railed against the Buddhists, the
American press, and the VC in equal measure while Nolting tried to
explain that the White House could not appear to be a handmaiden to
dictatorship. Even if Diem had just cause for placing barbed wire around

---

[19] Madame Chuong cited in Vietnam Memoir, Reel 26, HCLP. For Lodge's preparation, see
Miller, *Henry Cabot Lodge*, 334–338.
[20] Madame Nhu cited in Higgins, *Our Vietnam Nightmare*, 59; McCone cited in George
Kahin, *Intervention: How America Became Involved in Vietnam* (New York: Anchor
Books, 1987), 151.

pagodas and having military police beat and arrest unarmed monks and nuns, these actions were destroying his image in the United States and generating pressure on JFK to dissociate his administration from the South Vietnamese government.[21]

Diem would not listen. He assumed an increasingly confrontational stance toward the Buddhists throughout the summer of 1963. In mid-July, he announced that an investigation into the Hue massacre had confirmed what he had been saying all along: the VC were responsible and the regime blameless. No one believed these claims, and they only spurred further Buddhist demonstrations in the streets and agitation in the pagodas. During a demonstration at Giac Minh Pagoda in Cholon, government police kicked, punched, and clubbed hundreds of bonzes and laypeople and carted them off to jail in American trucks decorated with the "clasped hands" symbol of U.S. aid. Nolting persuaded Diem to make an appeal for calm over nationwide radio, but if the ambassador nourished any hopes that this gesture would lead to a breakthrough in the crisis, they were dashed when he heard Diem's address, a lecture that lasted less than two minutes and announced the formation of a cosmetic commission to investigate Buddhist grievances.[22]

Apart from this speech, which probably created more unrest than it prevented, Nolting had little to show for his final days in Saigon. Three more Buddhists burned themselves to death in late July and early August. One eighteen-year-old chopped off her hand in an act of protest. Madame Nhu's public statements became more indefensible. She told a correspondent for *Life* magazine that the Buddhists were "crypto-communists" and promised, "Once this affair is finished, it will be finished for good. Buddhism will die in this country." The torch suicide of a Buddhist nun drew a shrug and a sneer: "[I]f they burn thirty women, we will go ahead and clap our hands." *Time* magazine published a cover story titled "The Queen Bee" that portrayed Madame Nhu as the real power in Saigon and noted that her only criticism of the government's anti-Buddhist policies was that they were too mild; if she had her way, South Vietnam's first lady boasted, she would punish the Buddhists ten times more severely than her brother-in-law.[23]

---

[21] Nolting, *From Trust to Tragedy*, 111–121.

[22] Memorandum of Conversation, 18 July 1963, NSF, Countries – Vietnam, Box 198, JFKL; Nolting to Rusk, 19 July 1963, ibid. See also Jones, *Death of a Generation*, 288–294.

[23] Madame Nhu cited in Clyde Edwin Petit, *The Experts* (Secaucus, NJ: Lyle Stuart, 1975), 141; Prochnau, *Once upon a Distant War*, 355; "South Viet-Nam: The Queen Bee," *Time* 86 (9 August 1963): 22.

Nolting left the country on 15 August, reputation in tatters, destined never again to work for the U.S. Foreign Service. His final meeting with Diem was, he reported, "a rather strenuous goodbye," although he did get the president to agree to issue another public statement calling for reconciliation. Its content and audience were left unspecified, however, and the two men said their adieus. Just before Nolting flew out of Tan Son Nhut Airport, Diem granted an interview to journalists in which he declared that compromise had been his policy all along; moreover, he said, this policy was "irreversible." The ambassador, ever prone to put the best face on matters, considered the announcement a sincere pledge by Diem that he would work to mollify the Buddhists and appease world opinion.[24]

How naïve this attitude was became clear less than a week later, when government forces armed with rifles, submachine guns, grenades, and tear-gas canisters launched a midnight raid on pagodas throughout South Vietnam. Halberstam called it "a horror spectacle, ... a passion play of revenge and terror." In Saigon, squads of soldiers smashed down Xa Loi Pagoda's iron-grilled gates and stormed through the temple, arresting hundreds of monks and nuns. Those who resisted were stomped with boot heels and battered with rifle butts and bayonets. The gong in the pagoda's tower clanged an alarm, but it was drowned out by the bursts of automatic-weapons fire, the crump of exploding grenades, and the crash of shattering glass. The violence in Hue was worse, as monks and nuns barricaded themselves inside Dieu De Pagoda and fought off troops and police for eight hours before the government brought in armored cars; by the time the pagoda was overrun, 200 people were wounded, and ten truckloads carted off to prison. Monks and nuns put up similar resistance at Hue's Tu Dam Pagoda, with similar consequences: many Buddhists were shot or clubbed, a statue of Buddha was toppled, and, for good measure, government forces set off an explosion that nearly leveled the building. In all, some 2,000 pagodas were raided and more than 1,400 monks, nuns, student activists, and ordinary citizens arrested. The number killed was never confirmed, but some sources placed it as high as several dozen. In a ghoulish move, soldiers ransacked the University of Hue and confiscated the charred heart of a monk who had burned himself to death.[25]

---

[24] Nolting to Rusk, 14 August 1963, NSF, Countries – Vietnam, Box 198, JFKL; Diem cited in Note 7, *FRUS*, 1961–1963, Vietnam: January–August 1963, 3:566.

[25] Halberstam, *Making of a Quagmire*, 231. For the pagoda raids, see Jones, *Death of a Generation*, 297–300; Stanley Karnow, *Vietnam: A History* (New York: Penguin Books, 1997), 301–302; Maitland and Weiss, *Raising the Stakes*, 80–81; Prochnau, *Once upon a Distant War*, 366–372; Sheehan, *Bright Shining Lie*, 354–358.

At daybreak, Diem spoke over Saigon Radio, declaring that negotiations had failed to achieve a settlement and that, for the good of the nation, he was placing South Vietnam under martial law. Until further notice, there would be a 9:00 p.m. to 5:00 a.m curfew – troops and police had orders to shoot anyone on the streets between those hours – and public gatherings were prohibited. The army had taken over civilian functions. Military censorship was in effect for outgoing press cables. The country was, in short, an armed camp. There seems little doubt that Diem deliberately took these measures at a time when the U.S. embassy was leaderless. He intended to present the incoming ambassador with a fait accompli, a crisis that had been resolved not through compromise but force.[26]

Lodge was in Tokyo en route to his post when news of the raids on the pagodas arrived. He had planned a leisurely trip, with time for recreation in Hong Kong – his assignment was not supposed to start until September – but Rusk called him in the middle of the night informing him of Diem's action and directing him to South Vietnam immediately. State sent a plane to pick up the ambassador on the morning of 22 August to fly him to Saigon.[27]

The media-savvy Lodge's arrival at Tan Son Nhut was effective diplomatic theater. His Lockheed Constellation touched down at 9:30 p.m, when the city was under curfew, and he and his wife stepped out into blast-furnace heat, drizzling rain, and the glare of TV floodlights. Shielding his eyes with a straw hat, he delivered a short speech he had prepared in Washington. "Many years have elapsed since we were here last," he said into a microphone. "Yet the memory of Saigon has remained vivid and we think we are lucky indeed to be here. ... I look forward to my accreditation to your chief of state and to living here among you all." Then he asked, "Where are the gentlemen of the press?" Directed to where Halberstam, Sheehan, Arnett, Browne, and about forty other journalists were assembled, Lodge brushed past Harkins and U.S. Embassy Chargé William Trueheart to introduce himself to the people who would be covering his ambassadorship. He addressed them respectfully, telling them they played an essential role in ensuring the survival of

[26] Trueheart to Rusk, 21 August 1963, *FRUS*, 1961–1963, Vietnam: January–August 1963, 3:595–597; Department of State Daily Staff Summary, 21 August 1963, ibid., 3:598–599; Carroll to McNamara, 21 August 1963, ibid., 3:600–601. See also Miller, *Misalliance*, 277–278.
[27] Blair, *Lodge in Vietnam*, 33–34.

democracy and promising to do whatever he could to help them fulfill that role. He pointed out that no fewer than four journalists had accompanied him on the flight from Tokyo, and that he had solicited their advice and shared information with them; he hoped, he said, to be able to establish a similar working relationship with the Saigon press corps. John Mecklin, head of the United States Information Service in Saigon, recalled, "the so-called press problems ended then and there."[28]

As Lodge and his wife rode from the airport with a police escort, he noted that the streets of the city were deserted except for soldiers posted at every intersection. All Saigonese who valued their lives were at home with doors locked and shades drawn. Lodge had the impression that he was entering a city in a state of siege. That South Vietnamese troops now occupied their own capital seemed proof that Diem had lost the support of his people. Any lingering hopes that the Diem government might be salvageable evaporated for Lodge when, after he arrived at the ambassador's residence, a staff member took him aside and warned him that Nhu was plotting to have him killed and blame the assassination on the VC.[29]

A cable awaited Lodge at the embassy requesting his assessment of the situation. State wanted to know "who is running the show" and the "relative power situation of specific groups and individuals, both military and civilian." After briefings by mission officials, Lodge informed his bosses that the "influence of the Nhus has not diminished." He also reported, "Should [the] regular army decide to take over in earnest, i.e. depose Diem, [the] possibility of serious fighting in Saigon would be considerable." For the present, Lodge recommended a wait-and-see approach.[30]

On his first full day in South Vietnam, the new ambassador took two swipes at Diem, whom he had yet to meet. First, he publicly sided with the Buddhists against the government. Two monks had taken shelter in the U.S. Operations Mission Building next door to the recently raided Xa Loi Pagoda, and the Saigon police chief was demanding that the Americans turn them over. Lodge decided he would not, on the grounds that their release would imply U.S. approval of Diem's crackdown on

[28] HCL cited in Rusk to Nolting, 23 July, NSF, Countries – Vietnam, Box 197A, JFKL; Mecklin, *Mission in Torment*, 190.
[29] HCL Oral History Interview, 4 August 1965, JFKL.
[30] Ball to HCL, 22 August 1963, *FRUS*, 1961–1963, Vietnam: January–August 1963, 3:604; HCL to Rusk, 23 August 1963, ibid., 3:605–606.

the pagodas. Instead, as his first official act, Lodge greeted the bonzes, inquired as to their health, and, upon learning that they were vegetarians, ordered a supply of fresh fruit and vegetables. He also posed for pictures with the bonzes. Many more Buddhists soon sought asylum in the USOM Building – and the American Embassy, which became known as "the Buddhist Hilton."[31]

In his second PR-driven broadside against the Diem regime, Lodge cemented his bond with the press corps by inviting several of its members to lunch in the drawing room of the embassy. Sheehan admits in his memoir to being flattered that this venerable, aristocratic figure, descended from some of America's most prominent families, treated him, a correspondent in his twenties, as an equal. When Lodge asked his guests for their assessment of conditions in South Vietnam, they spilled their guts. According to Sheehan, the young men told Lodge that Diem and Nhu were "so mad and hated that they were incapable of governing," that the "Viet Cong were gaining rapidly in the countryside," and that "if Diem and his family stayed in power the war was certain to be lost." Noting Lodge's impassive expression, Sheehan asked, "And what's your impression, Mr. Ambassador?" Lodge replied, "About the same as yours."[32]

More significant than his chumminess with the bonzes and correspondents was Lodge's receptivity to signals from Diem's enemies. Whereas Nolting refused even to discuss the possibility of a coup with dissident generals, Lodge pounced on every hint of rebelliousness in the ARVN and sought to exploit it. The ambassador determined from the start of his mission that the ARVN presented the only credible alternative to Diem; South Vietnam's civil bureaucracy, he felt, had been so purged of strong personalities that any non-military solution to the crisis was unrealistic. Therefore, Lodge told his subordinates – notably Lucien Conein, a CIA agent – to make contact with high-ranking South Vietnamese officers and let them know that the United States would not look unfavorably on a change in government. Lodge wanted to find out which ARVN generals seemed most capable of unseating Diem, how much support they would require, and how soon they would be prepared to move. Conein proved suited to the task of digging up this information because he was friendly

---

[31] Vietnam Memoir, HCLP, Reel 26; Blair, *Lodge in Vietnam*, 37. See also Rusk to HCL, 4 September 1963, NSF, Countries – Vietnam, Box 199, JFKL.

[32] Sheehan and HCL cited in Sheehan, *Bright Shining Lie*, 359–360. See also Moyar, *Triumph Forsaken*, 238–239.

with most of the generals, having fought alongside them against the Japanese in World War II.[33]

Less than twenty-four-hours after his arrival at Tan Son Nhut, Lodge received the first of several reports from Conein about prospective insurrectionists. Conein submitted a memorandum on 23 August detailing his conversation with General Tran Van Don, who Diem had just placed in charge of the ARVN. It was a bizarre account, filled with salacious details – among other things, Don informed Conein that Diem "has never had sexual relations" and "likes good looking men around him" – but its central point was that the much-despised Nhu had taken over the government. Nhu, Don declared, was Diem's "thinker," and "[a]s time went on, Diem has allowed Nhu to do most of the thinking." Don revealed that Nhu had been responsible for the recent pagoda raids, and that while many South Vietnamese still respected Diem, it was essential to get rid of Nhu to prevent a communist takeover of the country. Unfortunately, Don noted, separating Diem from Nhu would be "impossible"; Diem would not permit it. If the United States wanted to eliminate Nhu, it would have to eliminate Diem as well.[34]

That same day, a report landed on Lodge's desk from Rufus Phillips, the chief American adviser to the strategic hamlet program, Nhu's ill-conceived initiative to relocate peasants into secure villages and thereby deprive the VC of grassroots support. Phillips had just conferred with Brigadier General Le Van Kim, and their discussion mirrored that between Don and Conein. Kim expressed hatred for Nhu, who he claimed had turned the ARVN into his "puppet." The general confided that all of the "explosives and arms found in the pagodas" after the raids of 21 August, which Diem had used to justify martial law, had been "planted" by Nhu's secret police. The Buddhists posed no threat to the government; the real problem, Kim proclaimed, was Nhu, and if the United States supported action to remove Nhu from power, the ARVN "would be able to carry it out." All that was required was a signal from Washington. Nguyen Dinh Thuan, South Vietnam's secretary of state, likewise spoke to Phillips that day, arguing that the

---

[33] For Conein's role in the coup, I draw principally on his testimony before the U.S. Senate Select Committee to Study Governmental Operations with Respect to Intelligence Activities, 20 June 1975, Church Committee Records, Box 47, Record Group 46, National Archives II, College Park, Maryland (hereafter Conein Testimony, 20 June 1975, RG 46).

[34] CIA Agency Saigon to Agency, 24 August 1963, *FRUS, 1961–1963, Vietnam: January–August 1963,* 3:614–620. See also Tran Van Don, *Our Endless War: Inside Vietnam* (San Rafael, CA: Presidio Press, 1978), 90–91.

ARVN "would turn firmly against Nhu" if it could count on the Kennedy administration's support.[35]

Lodge passed these reports along to State, as well as other dispatches suggesting that Nhu was about to conclude a deal with Hanoi that would sell out South Vietnam's independence and force the Americans to withdraw. Taken together, these documents seemed to make a formidable case for a U.S.-supported coup, but Lodge stepped back from that precipice. "[The s]uggestion has been made that [the] U.S. has only to indicate to [the] 'generals' that it would be happy to see Diem and/or [the] Nhus go, and [the] deed would be done," the ambassador noted. "[The s]ituation is not so simple." No clear coup leader had emerged, and several military commanders were still presumed loyal to the regime. Lodge also did not have enough information to gauge the balance of power; Diem might still have an edge over his rivals. Therefore, Lodge concluded, "[a]ction on our part in these circumstances would be [a] shot in the dark." He recommended deferring any decision on a coup, while keeping the lines of communication to the generals open and "continuing to watch [the] situation closely."[36]

"NO RESPECTABLE TURNING BACK"

That disclaimer was not enough to counteract the tone of recent messages from Saigon, especially when those messages were augmented by sensationalist accounts of the Buddhist crisis in America's leading newspapers. Halberstam in particular seemed determined to use the pagoda raids as a means of promoting a coup against Diem. One day after Don and Kim opened up to sympathetic American listeners, Halberstam's front-page story in the *New York Times* proclaimed that Nhu had "effectively taken power" in South Vietnam and depicted Madame Nhu as "exuberant" over the pagoda raids. A front-page headline in the *Washington Post* read "POWER SHIFT TO NHU SEEN IN VIET-NAM"; Sheehan's accompanying article described Diem's brother as "the real ruler of the

---

[35] Kim cited in HCL to Rusk, 24 August 1963, *FRUS*, 1961–1963, Vietnam: January–August 1963, 3:613–614; Thuan cited in HCL to Rusk, 24 August 1963, ibid., 3:611–612. By far the best study of the strategic hamlet program is Stewart, *Vietnam's Lost Revolution*.

[36] HCL to Rusk, 24 August 1963, *FRUS*, 1961–1963, Vietnam: January–August 1963, 3:621. For Nhu's alleged flirtation with the North, a topic on which a great deal of ink has been spilt, see Mieczyslaw Maneli, *War of the Vanquished*, Maria de Gorgey, trans. (New York: Harper & Row, 1971), 125–152.

country." The *Times* and the *Post* ran these pieces on the same morning that cables summarizing Don's and Kim's anti-Nhu tirades arrived at State, accompanied by other telegrams setting forth the groundswell of military and civilian support for Nhu's expulsion. It was Saturday, 24 August, and most of the top officials in the Kennedy administration were out of town or otherwise indisposed.[37]

As fate would have it, the response Lodge received from Washington was drafted primarily by Roger Hilsman, assistant secretary of state for Far Eastern affairs, with the collaboration of roving Ambassador Averell Harriman and Michael Forrestal of the National Security Council. These were Diem's bitterest opponents in the administration, and they took advantage of their superiors' absence to compose what one historian calls the "most controversial cable of the Vietnam War," a wire that "mired Kennedy in a plot to overthrow Diem."[38]

Washington "cannot tolerate [a] situation in which power lies in Nhu's hands," the cable read. "Diem must be given [a] chance to rid himself of Nhu. . . . If, in spite of all your efforts, Diem remains obdurate and refuses, then we must face [the] possibility that Diem himself cannot be preserved." Lodge was instructed to tell "military leaders" that the "U.S. would find it impossible to continue to support [the] GVN [government of Vietnam]" unless Buddhist grievances were redressed and Nhu divested of power. The cable also ordered the ambassador to "examine all possible alternative leadership and make detailed plans as to how we might bring about Diem's replacement if this should become necessary."[39]

The words "coup" and "overthrow" never appeared in this directive, but it was equivalent to ordering Diem's ouster, as its drafters must have realized. Harriman, Hilsman, and Forrestal had issued a command to change South Vietnam's government at a time when the four most important members of the administration were out of the policymaking loop: President Kennedy was spending the weekend in Hyannis Port at his Cape Cod estate, Rusk was in New York attending a session of the UN, and McNamara and McCone were on vacation. Taylor later called the cable an "egregious end-run" by an anti-Diem faction in the government.[40]

[37] David Halberstam, "Anti-U.S. Feeling Rises in Vietnam as Unrest Grows," *New York Times*, 24 August 1963; Neil Sheehan, "Power Shift to Nhu Seen in Viet-Nam," *Washington Post*, 24 August 1963.

[38] Newman, *JFK and Vietnam*, 346.

[39] Ball to HCL, 24 August 1963, FRUS, 1961–1963, Vietnam: January–August 1963, 3:628–629.

[40] Maxwell Taylor, *Swords and Plowshares* (New York: W. W. Norton, 1972), 292.

Taylor exaggerated somewhat: both Kennedy and Rusk cleared the cable, although hastily and over the phone, and Undersecretary of State George Ball studied it carefully before giving his approval. While there is no question that this message ought to have been handled more conscientiously, the fact is that it was never rescinded. When Kennedy consulted his senior advisers on Monday, 26 August, in the first of many angry meetings touched off by the cable, he asked each man in turn if he stood by it or wanted it withdrawn. No one voted to back off, although McNamara, Taylor, McCone, and William Colby, chief of the CIA's Far Eastern division, denounced what Harriman, Hilsman, and Forrestal had done. Taylor later explained his vote to let their cable stand by arguing, "You can't change American policy in twenty-four hours and expect anyone ever to believe you again." Colby offered a different rationale: "It is difficult indeed to tell a president to his face that something he has approved is wrong and to do so without anything positive to offer in its place." Kennedy came to regret having authorized the 24 August missive. Weeks before his assassination, he made an audiotape in which he admitted, "[T]hat wire was badly drafted. It should never have been sent on a Saturday. I should not have given my consent to it without a roundtable conference. ... [T]hat wire encouraged Lodge along the course to which he was, in any case, inclined."[41]

Lodge would later claim that he had been "thunderstruck" by the 24 August cable and that he felt the administration was moving too fast. As he noted, "They were asking me to overthrow a government I hadn't

<hr>

[41] Taylor cited in Jones, *Death of a Generation*, 319; William Colby with James McCargar, *Lost Victory: A Firsthand Account of America's Sixteen-Year Involvement in Vietnam* (Chicago: Contemporary Books, 1989), 138; Dictated Memoir Entry, Dictation Belt 52.1, 4 November 1963, POF, Presidential Recordings, JFKL. This cable has been studied to death, and one wonders what new there is to say about it. The most even-handed treatment is probably Kaiser, *American Tragedy*, 229–238. See also Rudy Abramson, *Spanning the Century: The Life of W. Averell Harriman, 1891–1986* (New York: William Morrow and Company, 1992), 619–623; Freedman, *Kennedy's Wars*, 368–371; Jones, *Death of a Generation*, 314–321; Karnow, *Vietnam: A History*, 302–305; Moyar, *Triumph Forsaken*, 235–238, 243; Newman, *JFK and Vietnam*, 345–351; Reeves, *President Kennedy*, 560–568; William J. Rust, *Kennedy in Vietnam: American Vietnam Policy, 1960–1963* (New York: Charles Scribner's Sons, 1985),111–120. For accounts by participants, see George W. Ball, *The Past Has Another Pattern: Memoirs* (New York: W. W. Norton & Company, 1983), 371–373; Roger Hilsman, *To Move a Nation: The Politics of Foreign Policy in the Administration of John F. Kennedy* (Garden City, NY: Doubleday & Company, 1967), 483–494; Robert S. McNamara with Brian VanDeMark, *In Retrospect: The Tragedy and Lessons of Vietnam* (New York: Random House, 1995), 51–55; Rusk, *As I Saw It*, 437–438 – in addition to the Colby and Taylor memoirs cited above.

even presented my credentials to!" The directive did in fact run counter to Lodge's advice to adopt an approach of watchful waiting. Still, the ambassador not only endorsed the shift in policy; he encouraged Washington to go further. Since "the chances of Diem's meeting our demands are virtually nil," he observed, there was no point in presenting the South Vietnamese president with another ultimatum. That strategy had never worked – it only made Diem more stubborn – and it might "give Nhu [a] chance to forestall or block action by the military." Lodge therefore proposed that he say nothing to Diem about U.S. demands but go directly to the generals and tell them that "we [are] prepared [to] have Diem without [the] Nhus, but it is in effect up to them whether to keep him." In other words, if the generals decided that neither Diem nor Nhu could remain in power, Washington would support the removal of both men, and American aid would continue to flow to South Vietnam. Undersecretary Ball replied at once: "Agree to modification proposed."[42]

The following evening, four days after Lodge's touchdown at Tan Son Nhut, he finally met Diem. This lag time between arrival and introduction was strategic; the American wanted the Vietnamese to know that circumstances had changed, that he was not a stooge like Nolting, and that negotiations would henceforth be conducted at Washington's pace, not Saigon's. Towering a foot over Diem, and appearing even taller, the ambassador radiated confidence. He appeared to justify the taunts of bureaucrats in the U.S. Embassy to South Vietnamese officials: "Our old mandarin can whip your old mandarin."[43]

Despite his cable to State, Lodge could not resist laying down the law. When Diem welcomed him at Gia Long Palace, the ambassador did not give his host the opportunity to plunge into one of his legendary monologues. Instead, he delivered his own speech. "I want you to be successful. I want to be useful to you," Lodge declared. "I don't expect you to be a 'yes man.' I realize that you must never appear – let alone be – a puppet of the United States." Nonetheless, he insisted that Diem had to face the fact that American public opinion had turned against him. The United States, Lodge asserted, "favors religious toleration," and Diem's policies were "threatening American support of Viet-Nam." Diem had to get his house

[42] HCL cited in Michael Charlton and Anthony Moncrieff, *Many Reasons Why: The American Involvement in Vietnam* (New York: Penguin Books, 1979), 95; Newman, *JFK and Vietnam*, 350; Forrestal to JFK, 25 August 1963, *FRUS, 1961–1963*, Vietnam: January–August 1963, 3:634–635; Ball to HCL, 25 August 1963, ibid., 3:635.
[43] Embassy workers cited in Prochnau, *Once upon a Distant War*, 347.

in order, and that meant dismissing Nhu, silencing Madame Nhu, punishing the officials responsible for the 8 May massacre in Hue, and conciliating the Buddhists. Washington was no longer prepared to support the Diem regime unconditionally. It had to reform itself, or the $1.5 million in aid being spent in South Vietnam every day would be cut.

Lodge had spoken to the president with a brusqueness no other American had even attempted. Diem was not intimidated. He looked at this imperious Brahmin, lit the first of many cigarettes, and did something out of character: he made a joke. Madame Nhu was definitely a problem, he admitted, and said that more than once he had "threatened to take a wife" to make his sister-in-law "keep quiet." Then, switching gears, he went on the offensive, insisting that the Buddhists demonstrating against his regime represented only a "small percentage" of South Vietnam's population. Just because most South Vietnamese were Buddhists, Diem argued, Lodge ought not to assume that the VC-controlled agitators at Xa Loi Pagoda spoke for them all. Diem produced a booklet called "Buddhism in Viet-Nam" that, he claimed, made clear that less than 1 million Buddhists supported the anti-regime movement, or around 15 percent of the Buddhists in the country. Lodge, who was not inclined to put much faith in Diem's figures, tried to steer the conversation back to the issue of American public opinion, but Diem gave his guest no opportunity to speak. As Lodge reported wrathfully to State, "The next two hours were spent by him in a remarkable discourse about his own family and [the] extent to which Viet-Nam was an underdeveloped country." Diem justified his centralization of power as necessary in view of South Vietnam's "lack of educated people" and proclaimed that he had received information from reliable sources about "a well organized plan to create unrest around the country" by using pagodas as control points for subversion and espionage. This was why he had decreed martial law, he said, and "under these circumstances" he could not say for certain "how long martial law would continue." Diem closed with a threat of his own, expressing hope that there would be "discipline, particularly as regards the United States's activities in Saigon." He did not want to hear any more "reports of diverse activities interfering in Vietnamese affairs by various United States agencies," by which Lodge assumed he meant the CIA.[44]

---

[44] Diem and HCL cited in HCL to Rusk, 26 August 1963, *FRUS*, 1961–1963, Vietnam: January–August 1963, 3:644–645; Blair, *Lodge in Vietnam*, 21; Winters, *Year of the Hare*, 61–63.

The ambassador left the meeting in a rage, resolved to avoid further contact. For weeks, he did not speak to Diem or any member of his government. When a reporter asked Lodge why he had not visited the palace, he responded, "They have not done anything I asked. They know what I want. Why should I keep asking? Let them come to me." Lodge could be just as stubborn as Diem, and he had the might of the world's greatest economic and military superpower backing him up. Moreover, as a prestigious public servant from the opposition party who had accepted Embassy Saigon as a favor to Kennedy, Lodge retained the option of resigning his post. Should he exercise that option and dump Vietnam into the Democrats' laps, it would hardly hurt his standing among Republicans. On the other hand, as Diem surely recognized, the Saigon government was so unpopular in the United States that if it were overthrown, the coup would redound to Lodge's political benefit. Lodge, in other words, held all the advantages in this game of chicken, and he knew it.[45]

Lodge's approach, whatever its merits, did not align with the wishes of the secretary of state. Rusk, who had sat silently through most of the high-volume conferences following the dispatch of the 24 August cable, still felt that Diem was reachable through persuasion. Three times in late August, and twice in early September, he instructed Lodge to meet with the South Vietnamese president. "You should initiate [a] dialogue with Diem soon," Rusk declared, and "make him understand that . . . we have a common problem to work out to permit us to proceed together towards our joint objective of winning the war against the Viet Cong." If Lodge confronted Diem "man-to-man" in "candid and critical talks," Rusk believed that the Saigon regime had enough time to "take actions to restore its image."[46]

The ambassador ignored each command. He was confident that his strategy of what one historian calls "proconsular aloofness" was correct, and, as during his years at the UN under Eisenhower, he did not consider himself subject to State's direction. Days passed in stalemate, with Diem and Lodge waiting for the other to make the first move. "[T]he United States," Lodge cabled Hilsman, "must maintain its posture of silent

[45] HCL cited in Maitland and Weiss, *Raising the Stakes*, 82. See also Roger Hilsman Oral History Interview, 14 August 1970, JFKL.

[46] Rusk to HCL, 28 August 1963, *FRUS, 1961–1963, Vietnam: August–December 1963* (Washington, D.C.: U.S. Government Printing Office, 1991), 4:15–16; Rusk to HCL, 29 August 1963, ibid., 4:33–34; Rusk to HCL, 3 September 1963, ibid., 4:104–106; Rusk to HCL, 6 September 1963, ibid., 4:128–129. See also Ball to HCL, 24 August 1963, ibid., 3:628–629.

disapproval. In fact, I have never realized before in my life how much attention silence could attract. As you know, Madame Nhu is attacking me for being so silent!" To Rusk's pleas that he "have frequent conversations with Diem," Lodge responded with the same silence, and he never received a rebuke, much less a dressing down.[47]

Lodge knew Rusk well enough to recognize that he ran no great risk by disobeying him. As the secretary's own colleagues have admitted, he was a diffident administrator who more or less surrendered Vietnam policy-making to anti-Diem subordinates like Harriman and Hilsman. State, Lodge was certain, would not interfere with his activities in Saigon.[48]

The Pentagon, and especially the MACV, posed more of a problem. Harkins contended that there was no guarantee that a new government would do better than Diem had done and that, moreover, the coup plotters might not have a sufficient military advantage to force Diem from office. The general also believed it was possible to get rid of Nhu without overthrowing Diem. At least, Harkins argued, Washington should "give Diem a chance" to remove his brother before the United States started down a road that could lead to catastrophe. "In my opinion," he cabled the White House, "as things stand now, I don't believe there is sufficient reason for a crash approval [of a coup] on our part."[49]

Lodge disagreed, insisting in one of the strongest dispatches of his mission,

We are launched on a course from which there is no respectable turning back: the overthrow of the Diem government. There is no turning back in part because U.S. prestige is already publicly committed to this end in large measure and will become more so as facts leak out. In a more fundamental sense, there is no turning back because there is no possibility, in my view, that the war can be won under a Diem administration.

---

[47] Winters, *Year of the Hare*, 170; HCL to Hilsman, 4 September 1963, Roger Hilsman Papers (hereafter RHP), Countries, Box 4, JFKL; Rusk to HCL, 12 September 1963, *FRUS*, 1961–1963, Vietnam: August–December 1963, 4:195. McCone complained about Lodge in late September, "We have been issuing instructions for three weeks for him to see that fellow, and he just won't see him." Memo of Phone Conversation between Hilsman and McCone, 23 September 1963, RHP, Countries, Box 4, JFKL.

[48] Though it pains him, McNamara concedes this point in his memoir: "Dean – one of the most selfless, dedicated individuals ever to serve the United States – failed utterly to manage the State Department and supervise Lodge." McNamara, *In Retrospect*, 70. See also, *Robert Kennedy in His Own Words*, Edwin O. Guthman and Jeffrey Shulman, eds. (New York: Bantam Books, 1989), 403.

[49] Harkins to Taylor, 29 August 1963, *FRUS*, 1961–1963, Vietnam: August–December 1963, 4:10–11.

The ambassador rejected Harkins's advice about asking Diem yet again to dismiss Nhu. "I believe that such a step has no chance of getting the desired result," he declared, "and would have the very serious effect of being regarded by the generals as a sign of American indecision." Such signs needed to be avoided, because the generals were already unsure about U.S. intentions and might get cold feet if they sensed that Washington was thinking about pulling back its go-ahead.[50]

Kennedy, upon receipt of Lodge's cable, issued the first of a series of ambivalent directives that the ambassador twisted into an anti-Diem mandate. "We will do all that we can to help you conclude this operation successfully," the president told Lodge. But Kennedy had reservations and insisted on his "right to change course and reverse previous instructions" if necessary. With the fiasco at Cuba's Bay of Pigs fresh in his memory, JFK observed, "I know from experience that failure is more destructive than an appearance of indecision. . . . [I]t will be better to change our minds than fail." He therefore ordered Lodge to furnish him with "a continuing assessment of the prospects for success" and requested "your candid warning if [the] current course begins to go sour."[51]

Lodge's response, a deft parry, split the difference between reassurance and rebuttal. He acknowledged Kennedy's presidential prerogative while at the same time discounting its feasibility. "I fully understand that you have the right and responsibility to change course at any time," he declared. "Of course, I will always respect that right." On the other hand, he noted, "[t]o be successful, this operation must be an essentially Vietnamese affair with a momentum of its own. Should this happen, you may not be able to control it, i.e., the 'go signal' may be given by the generals."[52]

The generals, however, were reluctant to give that go signal, and Lodge soon realized that his primary task would be to light a fire under the anti-Diem forces rather than rein them in. As August gave way to September, none of the generals had taken charge of the coup planning process and none seemed eager to lead an ARVN revolt. "The days come and go and nothing happens," Lodge complained to Rusk. "I am sure that the best

[50] HCL to Rusk, 29 August 1963, *FRUS*, 1961–1963, Vietnam: August–December 1963, 4:21–22.
[51] JFK to HCL, 29 August 1963, *FRUS*, 1961–1963, Vietnam: August–December 1963, 4:35.
[52] HCL cited in Footnote 2, *FRUS*, 1961–1963, Vietnam: August–December 1963, 4:36.

way to handle this matter is by a truly Vietnamese movement, even if it puts me rather in the position of pushing a piece of spaghetti."[53]

All the participants in this still inchoate conspiracy had a number of reasons to resist the ambassador's pushing. First, they had yet to receive the kind of cue from Washington that would convince them that the Americans were behind a coup. Lodge had suggested to Kennedy that a cutoff in aid to the Diem regime would constitute such a high sign, but JFK had thus far demurred. Also, the dissident generals were anxious about John Richardson, the CIA station chief in South Vietnam, who had worked with Nhu in developing the regime's intelligence capacity and who was rumored to be on intimate terms with the Ngo family. What if Richardson tipped off Nhu about an impending coup? Finally, there was the lack of cohesion in the generals' own ranks. No one trusted any of the others not to divulge their plans to the government, and all knew the consequences of such a betrayal. When an aide asked Lodge why the generals were slow to take action, he replied, "Perhaps they're afraid to die, like everyone else."[54]

Of the crew of ARVN commanders, the figure who appeared most capable of rallying the rest was General Duong Van Minh, known as "Big" Minh because he stood six feet tall – rare for a Vietnamese – and weighed over 200 pounds. While hardly a deep thinker, Minh was well liked by the troops and had a reputation as a man of action. His upper front teeth had been snapped off at the roots by Japanese interrogators during World War II, and he refused to have the teeth replaced; the gap in his smile was, for him, a testament to his toughness. He had proven himself in combat on numerous occasions, notably in the 1955 Battle for Saigon, when he helped Diem crush South Vietnam's crime lords. According to one U.S. correspondent, Minh was "possibly the most popular man in the country." More important, for Lodge's purposes, was the fact that the burly general bore a grudge against Diem, who had relieved him of much of his authority and "promoted" him to a meaningless post as military adviser to the president. Minh suspected, with justification, that Diem considered him a rival and sought to sidetrack his career. The general required little prodding from Conein to reveal his interest in a coup.[55]

---

[53] HCL to Rusk, 30 August 1963, *The Pentagon Papers: The Defense Department History of United States Decisionmaking on Vietnam*, Senator Mike Gravel Edition (Boston: Beacon Press, 1975) (hereafter *PP*), 2:739–740.

[54] HCL cited in Hilsman, *To Move a Nation*, 493.

[55] Correspondent cited in Prochnau, *Once upon a Distant War*, 439; Conein Testimony, 20 June 1975, RG 46.

Yet Minh was no more inclined than the other generals to become a martyr, and he informed Lodge on 31 August – through Harkins, significantly – that he had "called off the planning." The generals, he said, "were not ready, as they did not have enough forces under their control compared to those under the president." Neither he nor his co-conspirators wanted "to start anything they could not successfully finish." Lodge, disgusted, complained to Rusk that "there is neither the will nor the organization among the generals to accomplish anything." Washington had no choice, the ambassador said, but to stick with Diem a bit longer while attempting to reactivate the coup planners. CIA Station Chief Richardson, who was delighted with the turn events had taken, cabled his stateside superiors, "This particular coup is finished."[56]

"CHANGES ... WITH PERSONNEL"

Kennedy's top advisers shared Richardson's sentiments. During the daily meetings at the White House that took place throughout the initial phase of Lodge's ambassadorship, it became evident that the highest ranking officials were pro-Diem – or at least anti-coup. The conferences were often heated, and Diem's detractors, in particular Harriman and Hilsman, made their case for throwing out the president with great force, but they failed to convince the big guns. McNamara maintained that there was "no valid alternative to the Diem regime." McCone expressed "doubt that alternative leadership exists in Vietnam." Vice President Johnson likewise saw "no alternative" to Diem and declared that he had "never been sympathetic with our proposal to produce a change of government in Vietnam by plotting with Vietnamese generals." Taylor was especially outspoken. "Diem is not ideal," he admitted. "He is a terrible pain in the neck in many ways. But he is an honest man; he is devoted to his country, and we are for him until we can find someone better." As Rusk understates in his memoir, "Clearly, Henry Cabot Lodge was more supportive of a coup than we were in Washington."[57]

[56] Minh cited in Harkins to Taylor, 31 August 1963, *FRUS, 1961–1963, Vietnam: August–December 1963*, 4:64–65; HCL to Rusk, 31 August 1963, ibid., 4:66; Richardson to McCone, 31 August 1963, ibid., 4:64.

[57] Memorandum of Conference, 29 August 1963, *FRUS, 1961–1963, Vietnam: August–December 1963*, 4:27; Memorandum of Conversation, 10 September 1963, ibid., 4:170; Memorandum of Conversation, 31 August 1963, ibid., 4:74; Taylor cited in Rust, *Kennedy in Vietnam*, 114; Rusk, *As I Saw It*, 440. In an indication of his uneasiness

One reason for Lodge's eagerness to eject Diem was the president's ongoing brutality in suppressing demonstrations against his regime. Many urban, young South Vietnamese, previously apolitical, were radicalized by Diem's crackdown on the Buddhists and defied the government's ban on public gatherings by holding anti-Diem rallies. Students at Saigon University boycotted classes and rioted in protest against Diem and Nhu. Diem had the students arrested, the ringleaders beaten, and the university shut down. He also closed South Vietnam's other university at Hue. Then the high school students demonstrated, and Diem was compelled to arrest them; one morning, army trucks hauled more than 1,000 students from the nation's finest high school to indoctrination centers. Eventually, Diem closed the high schools, too. Nhu's secret police rounded up hundreds of dissidents, some of them children caught scribbling antigovernment graffiti on walls. The South Vietnamese foreign minister, Vu Van Mau, resigned his post, shaved his head like a Buddhist monk, and asked Diem for permission to leave the country on a religious pilgrimage. Diem threw him in jail. South Vietnam's ambassador to the United States, Tran Van Chuong, also resigned in protest, telling American reporters that Diem had "cop[ied] the tactics of totalitarian regimes." Chuong, reporters could not help but note, was Madame Nhu's father.[58]

Matters were spinning out of control. Xa Loi, the premier pagoda in Saigon, became a center of dissident activity, where laymen and bonzes held press conferences denouncing Diem, mimeographed thousands of antigovernment pamphlets, and organized mass meetings. They proved skillful at using American correspondents to publicize their cause. From the beginning, they printed their protest signs and press releases in English as well as Vietnamese, and they selected one of the few English-speaking bonzes in Vietnam to be their spokesman. Diem, furious that the American press would dignify these people with a hearing, proclaimed repeatedly that there was no religious persecution in his country, that South

---

about a coup, JFK invited Nolting to join these conferences, and the former ambassador did not mince words. "Only Diem can hold this fragmented country together," he insisted. "Supporting a coup is bad in principle and sets a bad precedent." This was too much for Harriman, who barked at Nolting, "You've been wrong from the beginning. No one cares what you think!" – to which the president replied that he liked Nolting and wanted to hear his views. Memorandum of Conference, 28 August 1963, *FRUS, 1961–1963*, Vietnam: August–December 1963, 4:3, 6; Harriman cited in Reeves, *President Kennedy*, 570; JFK cited in Jones, *Death of a Generation*, 332.

[58] Chuong cited in Maitland and Weiss, *Raising the Stakes*, 81. For Diem's campaign of repression, see Karnow, *Vietnam: A History*, 300–302; Mecklin, *Mission in Torment*, 196–200.

Vietnam's Buddhists supported the government, and that the bonzes stirring up all of this trouble were VC agents. Madame Nhu went further. American journalists in Saigon, she told an interviewer, were either "communists" themselves or "as bad as the communists," while the Buddhists –"senseless people, eternal slaves" – "will be the pariahs of our new society forged in the heroic resistance struggle."[59]

Worse than Madame Nhu's comments were the interviews her husband gave to the media despite American admonitions to stay quiet. Stanley Karnow of Time-Life remembers that he "saw Nhu periodically in those days, and he appeared to me to be approaching madness." While Karnow could not substantiate charges that the president's brother was smoking opium – and even supplementing it with heroin – he noted that "he often ranted and raved like a drug addict." Nhu charged American officials with "destroying the psychology of our country" and "initiating a process of disintegration." He called Lodge "a man of no morality." To Joseph Alsop, one of the few American reporters sympathetic to the Diem regime, Nhu boasted that he was the "unique spine" of the anti-communist struggle in Vietnam and the "only serious modern theorist of guerrilla war." Bounding to his feet, he declared, "Even if you Americans pull out, I will still win the war here at the head of the great guerrilla movement which I have prepared." In another interview, Nhu again had trouble staying in his seat. Strutting back and forth, gesticulating wildly, he denounced his father-in-law, former Ambassador Chuong. "If he comes to Saigon, I will have his head cut off," Nhu proclaimed. "I will hang him in the center of a square and let him dangle there. My wife will make the knot on the rope because she is proud of being a Vietnamese and she is a good patriot." These displays lent urgency to Lodge's campaign to spark a coup.[60]

---

[59] Madame Nhu cited in Robert J. Manning, Report on the Saigon Press Situation, undated, NSF, Countries – Vietnam, Box 198, JFKL. See also Hammer, *Death in November*, 134–142.

[60] Karnow, *Vietnam: A History*, 281, 311; Nhu cited in HCL to Rusk, 17 October 1963, NSF, Countries – Vietnam, Box 198, JFKL; Joseph Alsop, "In the Gia Long Palace," reprinted in *Reporting Vietnam, Part One: American Journalism, 1959–1969* (New York: Library of America, 1998), 91; HCL to Rusk, 7 October 1963, *FRUS, 1961–1963*, Vietnam: August–December 1963, 4:386. Dang Duc Khoi, a recently ousted government official, told officials at the U.S. Embassy that Nhu was a "fanatic," a "philosopher gone crazy," a "nut," and a "crackpot." Khoi cited in Memo of Conversation, 18 September 1963, Box 519, W. Averell Harriman Papers, Library of Congress, Washington, D.C. (hereafter WAHP).

That Diem was aware of American involvement in the brewing conspiracy against him became obvious when Paul Kattenburg, chairman of Kennedy's Interdepartmental Working Group on Vietnam, traveled to Saigon in late August and interviewed the beleaguered South Vietnamese leader. Kattenburg, who had previously worked for the U.S. Foreign Service in Southeast Asia, considered Diem a friend and admired his courage, but he was shocked by the president's behavior during their three-hour conversation. "More than on earlier occasions," Kattenburg reported to State, Diem "talked largely to himself. . . . [The] impression of growing neurosis cannot be escaped." Kattenburg was "unable to break in more than once or twice," as the torrent of words poured out, angry, defensive, self-pitying, supplicatory, always returning to the same theme: that American policymakers and journalists were encouraging Buddhist "agitators" as they "played on [the] traditional primitive proclivities" of the Vietnamese. Did Washington want the communists to triumph in Vietnam? If not, then the "'technical cadres' among [the] American services" who were "organizing [the] U.S. press corps against him" had to "stop their insane activities." Toward the end of the discussion, Diem declared, "I'm ready to die, at once, if [the] sweat and blood of [the] last nine years [is] now to be sacrificed to [a] small group of agitators in Buddhist disguise." Kattenburg, rattled, told Diem "frankly, as [a] friend" that "his image abroad" had "deteriorated." Perhaps it would be wise for him to appear before the National Assembly and explain the government's actions, at least insofar as they related to the pagoda raids of 21 August and ideally with regard to the 8 May massacre in Hue as well. Diem might even announce that he was holding elections. This would persuade people in the United States that he was breathing some democratic life into what had become known as "Diem-ocracy." Diem, Kattenburg recorded, said "he was studying [the] possibility [of] meeting [the] Assembly [and] failed to respond to [the] question on elections." As Kattenburg rose to take his leave, Diem begged him "with great sincerity" to "try [to] help us." Kattenburg could only reply: "[P]lease try to do [the] same for us."[61]

Four days after Kattenburg's encounter with Diem, President Kennedy gave the dissident ARVN generals the signal they required when he sat for an interview with Walter Cronkite, news anchor for CBS, at the Kennedy estate in Hyannis Port. The president's appearance was the highlight of

---

[61] Diem and Kattenburg cited in HCL to Rusk, 29 August 1963, *FRUS*, 1961–1963, Vietnam: August–December 1963, 4:18–20.

CBS's first half-hour evening news program – the network had for years been cramming world events into a fifteen-minute broadcast – and JFK knew the interview would attract a large audience. He chose his words with care. When Cronkite asked him about the progress of the war in Vietnam, he responded, "I don't think that unless a greater effort is made by the government to win popular support that the war can be won." Cronkite asked, "Do you think this government has time to regain the support of the people?" Kennedy's reply must have drawn howls of outrage from Gia Long. "I do," he said. "With changes in policy and perhaps with personnel, I think it can win. If it doesn't make those changes, I would think that the chances of winning would not be very good."[62]

Those three words – "changes ... with personnel" – constituted, one historian notes, "the public equivalent of the August 24 telegram." Tran Van Don, asked years later how he interpreted the American president's statement, replied that it seemed as though Kennedy "would support any change, any change." At least the Cronkite interview let Diem know that Washington would tolerate no more procrastination on the question of his younger brother and political counselor. Either Diem must rid himself of Nhu, or the Americans would rid themselves of Diem.[63]

The president underscored the seriousness of this warning in late September when he sent McNamara and Taylor on a ten-day fact-finding mission to South Vietnam. Lodge was not pleased to learn of their visit. "It is inconceivable to me that questions asked on a whirlwind tour of the countryside can elicit any new and deep insights into the situation," the ambassador cabled State. He was aware that the two men opposed a coup, and he worried that their trip would oblige him to make contact with Diem, whom he had been avoiding since their first encounter. If he escorted the defense secretary and the JCS chairman to the palace, Lodge complained, "[t]his will be taken as a sign that we have decided to forgive and forget and will be regarded as marking the end of

[62] JFK concluded the interview with kind words for Lodge, who Cronkite called "a political enemy of yours over the years." The ambassador, JFK said, should be commended for rising above partisanship and agreeing to serve in a Democratic administration: "[H]e has strong feelings about the United States, and, surprisingly as it seems, he put this ahead of his political career. Sometimes politicians do those things, Walter. ... And we are fortunate to have him." Interview for CBS News, 2 September 1963, *Public Papers of the President: John F. Kennedy, 1963* (Washington, D.C.: U.S. Government Printing Office, 1964), 650–653.
[63] Reeves, *President Kennedy*, 587; Don cited in Charlton and Moncrieff, *Many Reasons Why*, 99.

our period of disapproval of the oppressive measures which have been taken." In other words, it would negate the work Lodge had done over the previous month.[64]

Told by Rusk that the mission could not be called off, Lodge determined to control it. He arranged for McNamara to be his houseguest, and went so far as to have two staff members block Harkins when McNamara and Taylor descended from their plane at Tan Son Nhut. While the ambassador greeted the two emissaries, Harkins was stranded behind a human barrier, protesting, "Please, gentlemen, please let me through."[65]

McNamara and Taylor maintained a punishing schedule, working from six in the morning until eleven at night, and although the military controlled the itinerary, Lodge usually managed to get in the last word. On the second day of the mission, Harkins and the MACV staff presented a favorable picture of the war, stressing the robustness of the strategic hamlet program and the improved ARVN position. The VC, they claimed, were on the run. Lodge let his colleagues finish, then contradicted everything they had said. "The current government is probably beginning its terminal phase," he said, echoing what Kennedy had told him in Washington. "We must get ready for some really tough weather because it is at least theoretically possible that this thing will disintegrate to a point where the Vietnamese army cannot cope with it." Lodge insisted that Washington had to sacrifice Diem to save South Vietnam: "Our interest in the people is such that it transcends the question of who happens to be in control of the government."[66]

The ambassador orchestrated a meeting between the two envoys and South Vietnamese Vice President Nguyen Ngoc Tho five days later that drove his point home. Lodge had met Tho shortly after his arrival in Saigon, and while he considered the vice president too meek to succeed Diem, he felt he was a competent bureaucrat who could lend a civilian gloss to whatever military regime took charge after a coup. Tho gave the visiting Americans a different appraisal of the strategic hamlet program than that offered by the MACV. He said that the peasants dragooned into the hamlets resented being forced off ancestral lands and disliked having to pay taxes both to the government and the VC. Taylor protested that in a "properly defended hamlet" the VC ought not to be able to collect

[64] HCL cited in Blair, *Lodge in Vietnam*, 60; HCL to Rusk, 18 September 1963, *FRUS, 1961–1963, Vietnam: August–December 1963*, 4:255.

[65] Harkins cited in Halberstam, *Best and the Brightest*, 283.

[66] For the MACV report, see *PP*, 2:248; HCL cited in Vietnam Memoir, Reel 26, HCLP.

taxes, to which Tho responded, "Why, General Taylor, there are not more than 20 or 30 properly defended hamlets in the whole country."[67]

More compelling than Tho's testimony was the impression McNamara and Taylor received of Diem during a meeting prior to their return to Washington. As in his encounter with Kattenburg, Diem talked nonstop, giving his guests no opportunity to speak for two hours. Chain-smoking and referring to maps and charts, the president described progress in the strategic hamlet program, the war against the VC, and other initiatives undertaken by his government, forecasting that "in two or three more years, Viet-Nam will be a model democracy." McNamara waited until "a suitable pause occurred in the monologue," and then expressed concern about South Vietnamese political unrest. The "recent wave of repressions," McNamara contended, had "alarmed public opinion" and caused people in the Kennedy administration and Congress to worry that "the war effort would be damaged." Diem dismissed such concerns as the byproduct of "attacks of the American press on his government"; there was no repression in South Vietnam, and his regime enjoyed broad support. According to the minutes of the meeting, Diem "said nothing to indicate that he accepted the thesis that there was a real problem ... [and] displayed no interest in seeking solutions or mending his ways."

McNamara would not be diverted, however, and explained that while he was "willing to acknowledge that some press accounts may have been in error," this did not alter the fact that many Americans had lost faith in the Diem regime and were questioning the "necessity of the United States government's aiding a government that was so unpopular." The secretary also raised the touchy subject of Madame Nhu, producing from his pocket a number of newspaper clippings containing her "unfortunate declarations." Madame Nhu's outbursts, McNamara insisted, were "offensive to American public opinion" and "the American people would flatly refuse to send out the best of their young officers to face mortal perils to support an effort that had such irresponsible spokesmen." Diem, never one to brook criticism of his family, fired back that "one cannot deny a lady the right to defend herself when she has been unjustly attacked." His sister-in-law, he claimed, had been under a "scurrilous press attack" for a long time, and if she became "exasperated," this ought to be forgiven.

---

[67] Taylor and Tho cited in HCL to Rusk, 30 September 1963, *FRUS*, 1961–1963, Vietnam: August–December 1963, 4:321–323.

Then came the most bizarre stage of the conversation, as Diem turned to his difficulties with South Vietnam's Buddhist majority. He bore a "certain responsibility" for the crisis, he admitted, because he had been "too kind to the Buddhists," extending "so much assistance that the number of Buddhist temples in the country had doubled" in the past nine years. This had given the Buddhists a sense of entitlement and led them to demand special treatment from the government. Now they were holding "orgies in pagodas" and engaging in other depraved activities. He would have to be stricter with them in the future. Apart from that, the minutes noted, "Diem offered absolutely no assurances that he would take any steps in response to the representations made to him by his American visitors."[68]

Lodge, keeping his own counsel, must have relished every minute. South Vietnam's president seemed lost in a dreamworld. McNamara and Taylor left Gia Long shaken, and Lodge had every reason to suppose that they would return to Washington avid for a coup.

He was accordingly disappointed in their report, an awkward attempt to harmonize the irreconcilable views they had heard. They praised the accomplishments of ARVN and MACV, even to the point of speculating that one thousand U.S. advisers could be withdrawn from Vietnam by the end of the year. On the other hand, they had doubts about Diem. "There are serious political tensions in Saigon," McNamara and Taylor observed. They deplored Diem's handling of the Buddhist crisis and acknowledged that "[f]urther repressive actions by Diem and Nhu could change the present favorable military trends." Consequently, they advised taking sanctions "to impress upon Diem our disapproval." They wanted to suspend funding for the Commodity Import Program (CIP), an economic aid project that provided South Vietnam with many of its commercial imports and most of the revenue for its army, and they proposed an elimination of financial support to Diem's Special Forces, six battalions of soldiers who now operated more as the president's "praetorian guard" than counterinsurgency troops. As for a coup, Taylor and McNamara shared Kennedy's conviction that failure would be worse than indecisiveness. They were not so much opposed to helping the generals overthrow Diem as worried that they might not prevail. From what Taylor and McNamara had been able to observe, the generals' chances did not look good; ARVN's top officers

---

[68] Memorandum of Conversation, 29 September 1963, *FRUS*, 1961–1963, Vietnam: August–December 1963, 4:310–321.

had been "neutralized by a combination of their own inability and the regime's effective countermeasures." The Taylor-McNamara report thus concluded: "There is no solid evidence of the possibility of a successful coup." Given the odds, Washington should not "encourage actively a change in government," but Taylor and McNamara did urge the embassy in Saigon to "identify and build contacts with alternative leadership if and when it appears."[69]

"NO WAY TO RUN ANYTHING"

JFK adopted McNamara's and Taylor's advice, suspending shipments of tobacco, rice, and milk under the CIP and cutting funding for the Special Forces. He also sent Lodge another diffident cable that must have made the ambassador's gorge rise. "[N]o initiative should now be taken to give any active covert encouragement to a coup," the president said. "There should, however, be [an] urgent covert effort with closest security under [the] broad guidance of [the] ambassador to identify and build contacts with possible alternative leadership." Aware by now that Lodge was trying to wrestle American policy off the cautious path favored by State, Defense, and the CIA, Kennedy emphasized, "We repeat that this effort is not to be aimed at active promotion of a coup but only at surveillance and readiness." So Lodge, who had already tried to set a coup in motion and who was known throughout Saigon's top political and military echelons as an opponent of the regime, had somehow to "identify and build contacts with possible alternative leadership" without conveying the message that Washington welcomed a change in command. It was an impossible directive.[70]

Lodge could at least take solace in the fact that the aid cuts did not have the desired effect. Rather than making Diem more compliant, they reinforced his stubbornness. He and Nhu refused to institute any of the reforms the White House demanded. The government-controlled *Times of Vietnam* became more outspoken against Kennedy. Diem also pushed through austerity measures to help South Vietnam get along with less U.S. assistance. Combined with the cuts in aid, these measures caused economic stress and turned more people against the Diem regime. Most

---

[69] Memorandum for the President, 2 October 1963, NSF, Meetings and Memoranda, Box 314, JFKL.

[70] Rusk to HCL, 5 October 1963, *FRUS, 1961–1963, Vietnam: August–December 1963,* 4:371–379; Bundy to HCL, 5 October 1963, ibid., 4:379.

important, Washington's financial pressure convinced the military leadership in Saigon more forcibly than JFK's 2 September interview that the Americans wanted Diem gone. As Minh told a journalist shortly thereafter, "The aid cuts erased all our doubts."[71]

Galvanized by Washington's tightening the screws on Diem, Minh met Conein and informed him that a coup was in the offing. In fact, it was going to occur "within the very near future." Minh told the American that Diem needed to be deposed because "the situation is deteriorating rapidly and ... action to change the government must be taken or the war will be lost to the Viet Cong." He insisted that he did not expect "any specific American support"; all he wanted was "American assurances" that Washington would "not attempt to thwart this plan" and that there would be "a continuation of American military and economic aid" after Diem was overthrown.[72]

The instant Conein related this conversation to Lodge, the ambassador decided to give the generals the assurances they needed, and his resolve deepened when, later that day, a bonze burned himself to death in Saigon's central marketplace. It was the first self-immolation since the pagoda raids a month earlier, and it gave the lie to Diem's assertions that the Buddhist crisis was under control. This torch suicide, the eighth overall, was especially distressing for the Kennedy administration because it was the first such spectacle to be photographed and filmed in color, which made viewing it on American television screens or in the pages of American magazines even more horrific. Also, secret police in the marketplace made no attempt to beat out the flames; instead, they attacked American newsmen, particularly those with cameras. Grant Wolfkill of NBC had his 16-millimiter Bolex ripped from his hands before a rifle butt struck him in the face and knocked him to the pavement. John Sharkey, an NBC stringer-correspondent, and the ubiquitous Halberstam joined in the melee, kicking and punching, briefly recovering the camera, and making a vain attempt to reach the Caravelle Hotel, five blocks away, before the police caught up with them and battered them unconscious. One policeman pounded on the fallen Sharkey's head with a sidewalk-café bar stool. The next morning, the *Times of Vietnam* reported that not

[71] Minh cited in Higgins, *Our Vietnam Nightmare*, 208. See also HCL to Rusk, 7 October 1963, *FRUS*, 1961–1963, Vietnam: August–December 1963, 4:385–386; CIA Report: "Events and Developments in South Vietnam, 5–18 October," 19 October 1963, NSF, Countries – Vietnam, Box 201, JFKL.

[72] Minh cited in HCL to Rusk, 5 October 1963, NSF, Countries – Vietnam, Box 204, JFKL. See also Conein Testimony, 20 June 1975, RG 46.

only were the correspondents responsible for the market battle; they had staged the suicide as well.[73]

This was madness, Lodge cabled Washington, and could not be allowed to continue. He recommended that Minh be told that "the U.S. will not attempt to thwart his plans." Furthermore, Conein should "[a]ssure Minh that U.S. aid will be continued to Vietnam" after Diem was unseated.[74]

Kennedy took four days to reply, an eternity in the age of cable. He told Lodge to obey the earlier directive to avoid giving "active covert encouragement to a coup" while "indentify[ing] and build[ing] contacts with possible alternative leadership." He also declared, "While we do not wish to stimulate [a] coup, we also do not wish to leave [the] impression that [the] U.S. would thwart a change of government or deny economic and military assistance to a new regime if it appeared capable of increasing [the] effectiveness of [the] military effort." Then came the crucial passage:

With reference to [the] specific problem of General Minh, you should seriously consider having [your] contact [i.e. Conein] take [the] position that in [the] present state [of] his knowledge he is unable [to] present Minh's case to responsible policy officials with any degree of seriousness. In order to get responsible officials even to consider Minh's problem, [your] contact would have to have detailed information clearly indicating that Minh's plans offer a high prospect of success. At present, [your] contact sees no such prospect in the information so far provided.[75]

Lodge's response to this directive was revealing. He did not disobey it in its entirety. On 10 October he ordered Conein to inform Minh, as per Kennedy's instructions, that the White House "would not stand in the way of a coup if it took place, and ... if it was successful and a new regime could improve military morale, ... it would receive aid." But Lodge did *not* tell Conein to communicate the administration's misgivings about Minh's prospects, and the generals consequently never learned this vital information. Conein thus left the impression that Washington was as gung-ho for a coup as the rebels were, which was hardly the message Kennedy wanted to send. By failing to transmit the president's doubts,

---

[73] Prochnau, *Once upon a Distant War*, 444–446.
[74] HCL to Rusk, 5 October 1963, *FRUS, 1961–1963*, Vietnam: August–December 1963, 4:367.
[75] JFK to HCL, 9 October 1963, *FRUS, 1961–1963*, Vietnam: August–December 1963, 4:393.

Lodge steered American policy in a direction his superiors had not approved.[76]

As Arthur Schlesinger, Jr., JFK's friend and court historian, wrote years later, "Lodge was a strong man with the bit between his teeth," and he seemed to have overborne the will of the Kennedy administration by late October 1963. Just as the coup Lodge had lobbied to bring about was on the verge of erupting, however, Harkins threatened to foul up the ambassador's plans. Harkins encountered Don at a party at the British Embassy and remarked that it would be unwise to launch a coup because the war was going well. Don pretended to know nothing of any anti-government plotting, but he rushed away from the gathering and sent a desperate message to Conein requesting that the two men meet the following day. When they met at a Saigon dentist's office, Don demanded to know what Washington's policy was. Did the White House intend to stand by Diem, and were Don, Minh, and their cohorts facing execution? Conein assured Don that Harkins's remarks had been "inadvertent" and were "contrary to presidential guidance." The Kennedy administration, he said, would not obstruct a coup and would continue aid at the present level to a new regime. Mollified, Don went to strategize with the other rebel generals and met Conein again the next morning to deliver bracing news: the coup would take place on 2 November or earlier.[77]

That information delighted Lodge, but he had a problem. Harkins's comment to Don, and his apparent awareness that a coup was afoot, forced the ambassador to divulge more to the Oval Office than he wanted to. Lodge was certain that Harkins would mention his meeting with the South Vietnamese general to Taylor, McNamara, or even Kennedy, and he resolved to steal a march on his military counterpart. He therefore sent

[76] HCL cited in Shaplen, *Lost Revolution*, 203–204. See also Don, *Our Endless War*, 97; *PP*, 2:257–258; Conein Testimony, 20 June 1975, RG 46; Lucien Conein and John Richardson, "History of the Vietnamese Generals' Coup," U.S. Senate Select Committee to Study Governmental Operations with Respect to Intelligence Activities, Church Committee Records, Box 47, Record Group 46, National Archives II, College Park, Maryland (hereafter Coup History, RG 46). I am indebted to Moyar for drawing my attention to Lodge's deviousness on this occasion. Moyar, *Triumph Forsaken*, 255–256.

[77] Arthur M. Schlesinger, Jr., *Robert Kennedy and His Times* (New York: Ballantine Books, 1978), 771; Don, *Our Endless War*, 98; Anne L. Hollick, *U.S. Involvement in the Overthrow of Diem, 1963*, U.S. Congress, Senate, Committee on Foreign Relations, Staff Study No. 3, 92nd Cong., 2nd sess. (Washington, D.C.: U.S. Government Printing Office, 1972), 14; Conein Testimony, 20 June 1975, RG 46; Editorial Note, *FRUS*, 1961–1963, Vietnam: August–December 1963, 4:427; Footnote 5, ibid., 423–424; HCL to Rusk, 23 October 1963, NSF, Countries – Vietnam, Box 204, JFKL.

the president a cable in which he asserted, "Circumstances compel me to say that, in the contest with the Viet Cong, we at present are not doing much more than holding our own." Over 24,000 VC had been killed since JFK's inauguration, he noted, and yet VC troop strength was "reckoned at a higher figure than it was two years ago." Why? Because "hatred of the government continues to be an incentive for young men to join the Viet Cong." Diem was so unpopular that the communists had little difficulty replacing and augmenting their forces. "All this could be quickly changed," Lodge declared, by "a change in government," but if Diem remained in control, "the hatred is bound to grow." This was why the U.S. mission in Saigon, under Lodge's direction, had "creat[ed] favorable conditions for a coup," and the ambassador was pleased to report that "our actions" would soon enable America "to discharge its moral responsibility for the behavior of this government, which surely would not stay in office without us."[78]

Lodge's cable landed like a grenade in the White House. He had all but admitted disobeying Kennedy's orders, and seemed to be suggesting that rebellion was imminent. In a meeting of high-level advisers summoned to discuss Lodge's actions, McNamara denounced the ambassador and his go-between. "We ought to take our association with [the coup] out of the very amateurish hands that have been controlling it," the defense secretary declared. "Those hands are, particularly, Lodge and Conein." From McNamara's perspective, the embassy was intriguing with rebel generals behind Washington's back, and "that's no way to run anything. ... It's the damnedest arrangement I've ever seen." McNamara wanted Lodge and Conein replaced by "experienced men of sound judgment." Kennedy agreed that they might have to remove Conein, and perhaps other anti-Diem figures in the mission, but he drew the line at recalling Lodge. He knew the ambassador could exploit his dismissal for political advantage, and the 1964 presidential election was only a year away. JFK wanted to run against a beatable Republican like Barry Goldwater. Lodge, with his imposing résumé, famous name, and deep pockets, would be a more daunting opponent, especially if he could woo voters with the message that he had stood up for American values in Vietnam while the incumbent administration coddled a mad tyrant. "Everybody on this issue has more or less the same reservations about Lodge's conduct," the president stated. "But he's there, and because he's there we can't fire him. So we're

[78] HCL to JFK, 23 October 1963, *FRUS, 1961–1963*, Vietnam: August–December 1963, 4:421–424.

going to have to give him direction. ... We've got to end up where we want him to go, not end up where he wants us to go."[79]

Unable to dismiss Lodge but troubled by his behavior, JFK had National Security Adviser McGeorge Bundy send the ambassador a cable informing him that "[c]ertain aspects of the Don-Conein contacts give us considerable concern." Washington needed more "information regarding Don's real backing" and some evidence that "real capabilities for action have been developed." Repeating the objection raised in Kennedy's earlier message, Bundy wanted to know what proof the administration had that the Don-Minh group could succeed in unseating Diem. Lodge did not address this point in his response, but he assured the White House that if the coup misfired, "I believe that our involvement to date through Conein is still within the realm of plausible denial." He also insisted that Washington must not stand in the way of the rebel generals because "it is at least an even bet that the next government would not bungle and stumble as much as the present one has."[80]

With Lodge hellbent on deposing him, Diem made a rare conciliatory gesture. He invited the ambassador and his wife to accompany him to Dalat to attend the inauguration of an atomic energy center. Diem wanted the Lodges to stay with him at one of his villas in the mountain resort. Lodge, surprised, accepted the invitation, even though he expected the generals to rise up against Diem at any moment. Some in State thought Diem's olive twig might indicate that he was "moving in [the] direction we desire," which would obviate the need for a coup, but Lodge had long since decided that South Vietnam could not survive under Diem. He never considered reversing course.[81]

Indeed, the morning he flew out of Saigon on Diem's personal plane, Lodge met with Don to discuss the coup. Lodge had never previously spoken face-to-face to Don – the general had preferred to use Conein as an intermediary – but Don had been alarmed by another encounter with Harkins at which the MACV commander said that Washington would not condone Diem's removal. Panicking, awash in sweat, Don showed up at Tan Son Nhut at 7:00 a.m. on 27 October, fifteen minutes before Diem arrived, to confront Lodge. The general demanded to know whether Harkins or Conein spoke for the Kennedy administration.

---

[79] Meeting, Tape 117/A53, 25 October 1963, POF, Presidential Recordings, JFKL.
[80] Bundy to HCL, 24 October 1963, *FRUS, 1961–1963*, Vietnam: August–December 1963, 4:429; HCL to Bundy, 25 October 1963, ibid., 4:434–435.
[81] Rusk to HCL, 28 October 1963, NSF, Countries – Vietnam, Box 204, JFKL.

Lodge assured Don that Harkins was wrong, that Conein in encouraging a coup did represent the White House's views, and that Washington would neither impede the generals in their attempt to topple Diem nor reduce aid in the aftermath of a successful rebellion. Now Don had the word of the U.S. ambassador. He left Tan Son Nhut with doubts dispelled.[82]

The Lodges spent the next two days being entertained by Diem. First came an inspection tour of a strategic hamlet near Dalat, interrupted by a seven-course meal served on antique settings from Gia Long. When the party arrived at Diem's villa, they enjoyed another extravagant meal that lasted until 1:30 in the morning. Diem then showed the Lodges to his guest house, where they spent the night on beds covered with silk quilts. The following day was the inauguration ceremony for the atomic energy laboratory, preceded by a sumptuous luncheon. Lodge had to admit in his account of the visit that "Diem was at his best. ... He is very likable."

All tender feelings vanished, however, when the discussion turned to those issues plaguing U.S.-South Vietnamese relations. On this score, as always, Lodge found Diem "simply unbelievably stubborn." The president would not change his position on any matter of substance. When Lodge asked if Diem intended to "liberate those Buddhists and others who were in prison," Diem replied that every inmate who deserved to be released had already been set free. To Lodge's protests about "newspapermen being beaten up," Diem responded that "newspapermen shouldn't go into the center of a riot [or] they could expect to be beaten." When Lodge pointed out that "you don't get anywhere in the U.S. by beating up newspapermen," Diem shot back, "I will not give in." He went on to declare that "the U.S. press is full of lies, a concert of lies ... orchestrated by the State Department" and that Madame Chuong acted "like a prostitute." She even "jumped on priests," he insisted. He offered alibis, rationalizations, and complaints, but not one meaningful concession. "When it was evident the conversation was practically over," a frustrated Lodge reported, "I said: 'Mr. President, every single specific suggestion I have made you have rejected. Isn't there some one thing you may think of that is within your capabilities to do and that may favorably impress U.S. opinion?' As on other previous occasions when I asked him similar questions, he gave me a blank look and changed the subject." Lodge

---

[82] Vietnam Memoir, Reel 26, HCLP.

returned to the U.S. Embassy in Saigon more certain than ever that Diem had to go.[83]

"WE THINK IT WOULD BE DISASTROUS TO PROCEED"

As before, the White House was on a different page. When Kennedy brought together his senior advisers on 29 October, he heard some persuasive anti-coup counsel, especially from his brother, whom he trusted more than anyone. "I don't see that this makes any sense," Robert Kennedy declared. "We're putting the whole future of the country – and, really, Southeast Asia – in the hands of somebody that we don't know." RFK pointed out that "Diem is a fighter. ... He's a determined figure who's going to stick around, and, I should think, go down fighting. And he'll have some troops there that will fight for him too. If it's a failure, we risk just a heck of a lot." As far as the younger Kennedy was concerned, "we're just going down the road to disaster." Taylor agreed, and went, in his words, a "step further" by asserting that "even a successful coup, I would think, would be an immediate setback to the cause of this war" because "we'll have a completely inexperienced government." McCone felt the same way: "Even a successful coup ... would create a period of political confusion that would seriously affect the war for a period of time ... and might be disastrous." Only Harriman was pro-coup, and he was the lowest-ranking official in the room. His immediate superior, Rusk, was undecided. In all, JFK's chief consultants opposed overthrowing Diem. Before the meeting broke up, the president stated that, given what he understood of conditions in Saigon, "it wouldn't make any sense to have a coup. ... It seems to me that [Lodge] should discourage it at this time."[84]

---

[83] HCL to Rusk, 29 October 1963, NSF, Countries – Vietnam, Box 204, JFKL. Lodge's wife Emily, who may or may not have been present at this conversation, wrote to a friend that Diem "was charming, a brave little man, but how his mind appears closed." Emily Lodge to "Nancy," 30 October 1963, Reel 25, Emily Sears Lodge Papers, Massachusetts Historical Society, Boston, Massachusetts. See also NSF, Countries – Vietnam: CIA Memorandum, "The Current Situation in South Vietnam," 30 October 1963, Box 201, JFKL. An indication of Diem's retreat from reality was his conclusion that the encounter had been a success. "At last," he noted afterwards, "Mr. Lodge understands what I am trying to do!" Diem cited in Catton, *Diem's Final Failure*, 1.

[84] Meeting, Tape 118/A54, 29 October 1963, POF, Presidential Recordings, JFKL. McCone recalled advising JFK, "Mr. President, if I was manager of a baseball team [and] I had only one pitcher, I'd keep him in the box whether he was a good pitcher or not." McCone Testimony, 6 June 1975, U.S. Senate Select Committee to Study Governmental Operations with Respect to Intelligence Activities, Church Committee, Box 47, Record Group 46, National Archives II, College Park, Maryland.

At JFK's behest, Bundy cabled Lodge with instructions to tell the generals that Washington did not believe there was a "substantial possibility of quick success" for a coup and that since "prolonged fighting or even defeat" could "result in jeopardizing [the] U.S. position in Southeast Asia," all operations were to be held in abeyance pending a thorough review by the embassy, MACV, and CIA. Bundy also instructed Lodge that "there be [the] fullest consultation [with] Harkins." Lodge's repeated evasion of the MACV commander had not escaped the White House's attention.[85]

Again, Lodge disobeyed orders. He never instructed Conein to convey the message to the generals that the White House told him to transmit. And, believing the momentum of events to be running against Diem, he took his time replying. Although he received Bundy's cable on the morning of 30 October, he did not send a response until that evening. It was a melodramatic wire that included the declaration: "My general view is that the U.S. is trying to bring this medieval country into the 20th century and that we have made considerable progress in military and economic ways but to gain victory we must bring them into the 20th century politically." He could not cancel the coup, he said, except by betraying the plotters to Diem, and that would "make traitors of us"; no South Vietnamese – no *Asian* – would trust America's word again. With regard to the administration's doubts about a coup's prospects, Lodge argued, "I do not know what more proof can be offered than the fact that these men are obviously prepared to risk their lives." The ambassador agreed that "a miscalculation could jeopardize [our] position in Southeast Asia," but noted, "We also run tremendous risks by doing nothing." In a concluding sentence that pushed the boundaries of the term *understatement* to the rupturing point, Lodge observed, "Gen. Harkins has read this and does not concur."[86]

Harkins was, in fact, furious with Lodge and sent no fewer than three messages to Kennedy that same day complaining that "the ambassador is forwarding military reports and evaluations without consulting me" and that "Ambassador Lodge did not see fit to utilize my suggestions to any

---

[85] Bundy to HCL, 29 October 1963, *FRUS, 1961–1963, Vietnam: August–December 1963,* 4:473–475. Harriman wrote to Bundy after Diem's overthrow detailing a conversation with Lodge in which the ambassador declared, "Paul Harkins just wasn't bright." HCL cited in Harriman to Bundy, 30 November 1963, Box 484, WAHP.

[86] HCL to Rusk, 30 October 1963, *FRUS, 1961–1963, Vietnam: August–December 1963,* 4:484–488. I am indebted to Karnow for drawing my attention to Lodge's flouting of Kennedy's order. Karnow, *Vietnam: A History,* 316.

significant degree." Rising to rhetorical heights as least as lofty as that of his civilian counterpart, Harkins thundered, "In my contacts here I have seen no one with the strength of character of Diem, at least in fighting communists. Certainly, there are no generals qualified to take over. ... [R]ightly or wrongly, we have backed Diem for eight long, hard years. To me, it seems incongruous now to get him down, kick him around, and get rid of him."[87]

These messages, along with the other advice he was receiving, shook JFK. At an 11:00 a.m. meeting on 30 October, he noted that Lodge was "much stronger for [a coup] than we are here." Since no one knew the "correlation of forces in Saigon" between rebels and loyalists, the president said, "There is a substantial possibility of a prolonged fight." Bundy added, "Or even defeat." JFK repeated, "Or even defeat. This being true, we think it would be disastrous to proceed." A failure "could in one blow defeat our whole effort in South Vietnam." Exasperated, the president said, "This is Lodge's fault, because he hasn't brought Harkins in," to which McNamara declared, "There has been a failure of communication on many subjects. ... Lodge obviously fears that Harkins might put a coup down." Kennedy instructed Bundy to send another cable to the ambassador ordering him to tell the generals not to initiate any operation that did not have a strong chance of triumphing.[88]

Bundy complied. His message was almost hostile in tone. "We do not accept as a basis for U.S. policy that we have no power to delay or discourage a coup," he said. The administration had "never considered any betrayal of [the] generals to Diem"; in fact, it had "explicitly rejected that course." All it sought was some assurance that a policy shift that risked so much in the way of U.S. prestige be more than a roll of the dice. "Once a coup under responsible leadership has begun," Bundy wrote, "it is in the interest of the U.S. government that it should succeed." Again, Bundy ordered Lodge to keep "Harkins fully informed at all stages" of the enterprise. Lodge, who was unlikely to depart from his lone-wolf course now, tersely replied, "Thanks [for] your sagacious instruction. Will carry [it] out to the best of my ability."[89]

---

[87] Harkins to Taylor, 30 October 1963, *FRUS, 1961–1963*, Vietnam: August–December 1963, 4:479–482; Harkins to Taylor, 30 October 1963, ibid., 4:496–498; Harkins to Taylor, 30 October 1963, ibid., 499.

[88] Meeting, Tape 118/A54, 30 October 1963, POF, Presidential Recordings, JFKL.

[89] Bundy to HCL, 30 October 1963, *FRUS, 1961–1963*, Vietnam: August–December 1963, 4:500–502; HCL cited in Footnote 5, ibid., 502.

"U.S. POLICY HAS BEEN VINDICATED"

Diem and Lodge met for the last time on the morning of 1 November. The ambassador and Admiral Harry Felt, commander in chief of U.S. Pacific forces, paid a courtesy call on Diem at 10:00 a.m. at Gia Long and were treated to a typical two-hour monologue. The Americans sat uncomfortably in brocade armchairs while Diem held forth, his ashtray filling with cigarette butts. As the visit drew to a close, however, Diem surprised his guests by noting that there were rumors of a coup. The Americans should not be alarmed, he said; he had everything under control. Referring to the fact that Lodge would soon be returning to Washington to brief Kennedy on the progress of the war, Diem joked, "There's an old saying here that every time the American ambassador leaves, there is a coup against the government." Lodge laughed nervously. Then Diem became serious; just as the ambassador rose to depart, Diem took him aside and said, "Please tell President Kennedy that I am a good and frank ally. ... I take his suggestions very seriously and wish to carry them out." Lodge interpreted this as "a reference to a possible coup" and reported, "In effect, [Diem] said: tell us what you want and we'll do it."[90]

A different ambassador might have seized on this as cause to give Diem a reprieve, but Lodge was months past that point. While he did forward a summary of the meeting to Washington, he sent it as a cable of the lowest priority, and it did not arrive at State until hours after the White House began receiving reports of a coup. He also did not lead off with Diem's plea for reconciliation, which would seem to have been appropriate, but buried that information at the end of his wire. With rebel troops already beginning to deploy around Saigon, he was not interested in postponing the fall of the House of Ngo.[91]

The coup began at 1:45 in the afternoon. It was over in less than a day, to the relief of JFK and others who worried that the rebel generals would only be able to manage a stalemate against forces loyal to Diem, thereby plunging South Vietnam into civil war. Such fears proved unfounded. There was no nationwide conflagration, the fighting did not spread

---

[90] Diem cited in A. J. Langguth, *Our Vietnam: The War, 1954–1975* (Simon & Schuster, 2002), 251; HCL to Rusk, 1 November 1963, *FRUS, 1961–1963*, Vietnam: August–December 1963, 4:516–517.

[91] I am indebted to Blair for pointing out Lodge's designation of the cable as "priority" rather than "critical flash" and his choice to smother its key point. Blair, *Lodge in Vietnam*, 68.

beyond Saigon, and despite concern about the generals' professionalism, rebel troop movements were carried out with precision. Moreover, the balance of forces turned out to be overwhelmingly in favor of the insurgents: rebels outnumbered loyalists from the start, and defections to the rebel side swelled their ranks as the coup played itself out. The rapidity of the government's collapse testified to Diem's unpopularity and to the eagerness of millions of South Vietnamese to be rid of him.[92]

Yet it was not immediately apparent that the rebels would win. Diem's Special Forces mounted a spirited defense of Gia Long, manning machine guns and fighting with grenades and rifles from behind barricades, and the president defied increasingly strident demands by Minh and Don to surrender. He and Nhu also attempted to summon friendly units from the provinces. A few division commanders remained loyal; if they could get their troops to the capital in time, Diem might hang on to power. Thus, when Diem contacted Lodge by phone at the embassy, the success of the coup was not assured. The transcript of their exchange, as published by the *New York Times*, is painful to read:

DIEM: Some units have made a rebellion, and I want to know what is the attitude of the U.S.

LODGE: I do not feel well enough informed to be able to tell you. I have heard the shooting, but I am not acquainted with all the facts. Also, it is four-thirty A.M. in Washington and the U.S. government cannot possibly have a view.

DIEM: But you must have some general ideas. After all, I am a chief of state. I have tried to do my duty. I want to do now what duty and good sense require. I believe in duty above all.

LODGE: You have certainly done your duty. As I told you only this morning, I admire your courage and your great contribution to your country. No one can take away from you the credit of all you have done. Now I am worried about your personal safety. I have a report that those in charge of the current activity offer you and your brother safe conduct out of the country if you resign. Had you heard this?

DIEM: No. [Pause.] You have my telephone number.

LODGE: Yes. If I can do anything for your physical safety, please contact me.

DIEM: I am trying to reestablish order.

Diem's bodyguard recalls a more heated conversation that concluded with Diem shouting, "Mr. Ambassador, do you realize who you are

---

[92] There are a number of excellent accounts of the coup. The best include Hammer, *Death in November*, 280–311; Jones, *Death of a Generation*, 407–422; Karnow, *Vietnam: A History*, 317–327; Langguth, *Our Vietnam*, 251–260. See also Conein Testimony, 20 June 1975, RG 46; Coup History, RG 46.

talking to? I would like you to know that you are talking to the president of an independent and sovereign nation. I will only leave this country if it is the wish of my people. I will never leave according to the request of a group of rebellious generals or of an American ambassador." Diem then slammed down the receiver.[93]

Another witness to this exchange, embassy official Frederick Flott, remembers Lodge flattering Diem and making promises that exceeded his authority. According to Flott, Lodge said, "You're a great man. You've done great things for your country. I think the prudent thing for you to do would be to get out of here and not fight it further," whereupon he offered to fly Diem to the Philippines aboard a U.S. plane that was standing by at Tan Son Nhut to take the ambassador to Washington. "I would be prepared to send my car and one of my officers whom you know to meet you," Lodge said. "And we can get you on my jet aircraft, and I'm sure I can deliver on that." Diem turned Lodge down. "No, no, you're panicking," he said. "I cannot agree to fleeing, because this is all just a tempest in a teapot; it's a couple of hothead generals who don't speak for the army, and I know that the real troops are loyal to me." Flott recalled that Diem "didn't even thank Lodge graciously for the offer."[94]

The ambassador's official record of his activities, reproduced in the *Pentagon Papers*, contends that this conversation, whichever version of it one accepts, "was the last that any American had with Diem." Most chroniclers of the coup take Lodge at his word, but the journalist Zalin Grant raises the provocative question of why, if Lodge had expressed such concern for Diem's safety, the South Vietnamese president did not get in touch with him when the rebels overran the palace. Diem and Nhu had escaped via a tunnel and were hiding out in the house of an associate in Cholon, Saigon's Chinese district. They knew that Minh, Don, and the rest of the victorious junta might order their assassination. Why did they not reach out to Lodge? John Michael Dunn, Lodge's senior aide in 1963, told Grant almost thirty years later that the brothers did in fact telephone the embassy early in the morning of 2 October. Lodge, roused from sleep, got on the line and, as Dunn recalled, "told Diem he would offer them

---

[93] Diem and HCL cited in "Lodge's Last Talk with Diem," *The Pentagon Papers: New York Times Version* (New York: Quadrangle Books, 1971), 238; Jacobs, *Cold War Mandarin*, 2.

[94] Diem, HCL, and Flott cited in Jones, *Death of a Generation*, 413; Moyar, *Triumph Forsaken*, 269.

asylum" – but did not renew his offers of plane transportation or a special escort. Indeed, when Dunn volunteered to pick up the Ngo brothers, Lodge forbade it. "We can't," he said. "We just can't get that involved." Dunn remembered protesting, "They are going to kill them," but the ambassador was immovable. Having closed off Diem's last avenue of escape, he returned to bed.[95]

While Dunn's story is amazing, there are reasons to believe it. First, Dunn had no motive to slander the ambassador; indeed, he confessed to Grant, "I loved Lodge. I make no bones about it. I don't think there was ever anybody I liked as much." Lodge saved Dunn from a court-martial in 1964, and Dunn remained grateful for the rest of his life. Why would he invent a story that cast Lodge in a bad light? Second, Dunn's recollection is consistent with Lodge's entire ambassadorship. If the 2 October conversation did take place, and Lodge never reported it to State – well, he had done a lot of things since coming to South Vietnam that he had not told his superiors about. Also, the ruthlessness Dunn remembered rings true. Lodge had repeatedly taken whatever measures he felt were necessary to achieve his objectives, so his alleged about-face – offering the jet and his car when the outcome of the coup was in doubt, withdrawing the offer when the rebels had clearly triumphed – would not have been out of character. Nor would it have been likely to trouble his sleep.[96]

Spurned by the ambassador, Diem and Nhu left the Cholon safe house and took refuge in a Catholic Church, from which Diem contacted the generals and offered to surrender. An armored car arrived to pick up the brothers. During the trip to army headquarters, they were sprayed with bullets and stabbed with knives and bayonets. Their bodies were buried in a prison cemetery.[97]

As news of the assassinations went out over the radio, Saigon exploded in rejoicing. Spontaneous celebrations broke out all over the city, as crowds tore up Diem's portrait wherever it was displayed, offered food and liquor to the coup troops, and hailed every American they saw. The Saigonese, at least, had no illusions about U.S. complicity

---

[95] *PP*, 2:269; Dunn and HCL cited in Zalin Grant, *Facing the Phoenix: The CIA and the Political Defeat of the United States in Vietnam* (New York: W. W. Norton and Company, 1991), 210–211. For monographs that accept Lodge's chronology, see for example Karnow, *Vietnam: A History*, 322–323; Langguth, *Our Vietnam*, 254; Maitland and Weiss, *Raising the Stakes*, 87; Mann, *Grand Delusion*, 297; Sheehan, *Bright Shining Lie*, 370.

[96] Dunn cited in Grant, *Facing the Phoenix*, 197, 213.

[97] Karnow, *Vietnam: A History*, 325–326.

in the coup. More than one reveler told U.S. journalists that if Lodge ran for president of South Vietnam, he would win in a landslide. "Every Vietnamese has a grin on his face today," a gleeful Lodge cabled Washington. In some instances, demonstrations in support of the coup threatened to develop into riots. The homes of Diem's ministers, deputies, and other officials were sacked and set ablaze, as were the offices of the *Times of Vietnam* and the headquarters of Madame Nhu's Women's Solidarity Movement. From Hue, the American consul reported "considerable jubilation. . . . Americans here [are] greeted with [a] smile and [the] feeling is frequently expressed that U.S. policy has been vindicated." Lodge certainly felt that way, and insofar as it was really *his* policy rather than the White House's, he must have considered this the crowning accomplishment of his public career.[98]

JFK, however, was appalled. He heard the news that Diem was dead during a meeting with advisers on 2 November. Forrestal presented the president with a cable from Saigon that claimed Diem and Nhu had committed suicide, an assertion that Kennedy, a practicing Catholic like the Ngo brothers, recognized as false. Taylor recalled that "Kennedy leapt to his feet and rushed from the room with a look of shock and dismay on his face." Kennedy's revulsion was exacerbated when he learned two days later that an "unimpeachable source" who had examined Diem's and Nhu's bodies found that both men had had been shot and stabbed many times. JFK considered this a shabby conclusion to nine years of U.S.-South Vietnamese cooperation and a blot on his administration. Whatever South Vietnam's first president might have become toward the end of his life, Kennedy declared to one of his advisers, "Diem had fought for his country . . . and it should not have ended like this."[99]

Now that the deed was done, though, the president could not repudiate his ambassador. How would it look if he publicly admitted that he had lost control of U.S. foreign policy? After waiting a few days, he cabled Embassy Saigon: "Your leadership in pulling together and directing the whole American operation in South Vietnam has been of the greatest importance, and you should know that this achievement is recognized here. . . . [O]ur actions made it clear that we wanted improvements, and when those were not forthcoming from the Diem government, we

[98] HCL to Rusk, 2 November 1963, NSF, Countries – Vietnam, Box 201, JFKL; Helble to Rusk, 2 November 1963, ibid.

[99] Taylor, *Swords and Plowshares*, 301; HCL to Rusk, 4 November 1963, NSF, Countries – Vietnam, Box 201, JFKL; JFK cited in Newman, *JFK and Vietnam*, 415.

necessarily faced and accepted the possibility that our position might encourage a change of government." In fact, the president had never faced and accepted that possibility, while Lodge had done so almost from the moment he arrived in Saigon, but Lodge had the discretion not to challenge Kennedy's version of recent history.[100]

The White House's primary objective at this ticklish stage was to avoid any appearance of American collusion. Officials told newsmen – falsely – that the plot had been organized and executed by the Vietnamese and that it had taken Washington by surprise. Rusk cabled Lodge that State wanted to underscore that "this was not so much a coup as an expression of national will." Therefore, Lodge was instructed to discourage rebel generals from visiting the U.S. Embassy as though they were "reporting in." Lodge, of course, disobeyed that order.[101]

---

[100] JFK to HCL, 6 November 1963, *FRUS, 1961–1963*, Vietnam: August–December 1963, 4:580.

[101] Rusk cited in *PP*, 2:270; Karnow, *Vietnam: A History*, 327. Jim Rosenthal, the duty officer at the embassy in the days following the coup, told journalist Tim Weiner that Minh, Don, and other insurgent generals called on the ambassador, "and Lodge greeted them. ... Here were the guys who had just carried out a coup, killed the chief of state, and then they walk up to the embassy, as if to say, 'Hey, boss, we did a good job, didn't we?'" Rosenthal cited in Tim Weiner, *Legacy of Ashes: The History of the CIA* (New York: Doubleday, 2007), 221.

Conclusion

The wildest revelation in Bob Woodward's 2018 bestseller *Fear: Trump in the White House* involved American foreign policy. According to Woodward, United States President Donald Trump was at one point on the verge of signing and sending a letter to South Korean President Moon Jae-in that would have aborted the U.S.-South Korean Free Trade Agreement, known as KORUS. Trump was angry that America had an $18 billion annual trade deficit with South Korea and spent $3.5 billion a year to keep 28,500 U.S. troops in that country. He felt that Seoul was "ripping us off."[1]

Trump's advisers, in particular Secretary of Defense James Mattis, had repeatedly told the president that KORUS could not be viewed in isolation, that it was part of the overall relationship between America and South Korea, and that the national-security benefits of that relationship outweighed the financial costs. Among other things, Seoul permitted Washington to conduct Special Access Program (SAP) intelligence operations south of the 38th parallel that could detect an ICBM launch from North Korea within seven seconds. (America's SAP mission in Alaska took fifteen minutes to perform the same task.) Mattis and others begged Trump not to jeopardize this asset by scuttling KORUS, which the South Koreans considered essential to their economy. Trump let the issue lie for a while, but by early September 2017 he had had enough. Bypassing Staff Secretary Rob Porter, he had a low-ranking White House aide draft a

---

[1] Trump cited in Bob Woodward, *Fear: Trump in the White House* (New York: Simon & Schuster, 2018), 304.

note to President Moon that announced Washington's withdrawal from the trade agreement.

Fortunately, Woodward reported, at the eleventh hour a savior appeared: Gary Cohn, former president of Goldman Sachs and Trump's principal economic counselor, who dropped by the Oval Office on an unrelated matter and saw the letter on the president's desk. Aghast, Cohn pocketed it, later remarking to a friend, "He's never going to see that. . . . Got to protect the country." Thereafter Cohn worked with Porter to ensure that every time a document terminating KORUS made its way to Trump, it disappeared before the president could sign it. Cohn also thwarted Trump's attempts to pull out of the deal by raising numerous objections, largely procedural: that a decree of this nature had to go through the proper vetting channels, that it required legal clearance, and so on. The president, Cohn knew, had a fitful attention span, and he counted on Trump to become distracted, forget about the subject, and move on to something else. This strategy of delay and obstruction paid off, or at least it had by the time *Fear* hit the bookstores; the U.S.-South Korean alliance, while frayed, remained intact, and senior Trump White House functionaries could congratulate themselves, in Mattis's words, for having "prevent[ed] World War III."[2]

Woodward recognized the dramatic effectiveness of the filching-papers-off-the-president's-desk anecdote, and he opened *Fear* with it, even though that required him to circle back in time seven years to Trump's fateful first meeting with Steve Bannon, the man who would ultimately manage the billionaire reality star's successful presidential campaign. Nearly all reviews in the mainstream press mentioned Cohn's mutinous deed, most casting it in a favorable light. George Packer of the *New Yorker* called it "an act of patriotism," while the *Washington Post*'s Jill Abramson noted that "Cohn comes as close as anyone in the book to being a principled character." The *New York Times* spoke for much of the fourth estate when it told its audience, "Cohn is in some ways this

---

[2] Cohn cited in ibid., xix; Mattis cited in ibid., 305. See also ibid., xvii–xxiii, 105–107, 224–225, 232–233, 263–265, 303–308. Woodward was "scooped" to a degree by a *New York Times* op-ed that appeared shortly before *Fear*'s publication. The *Times* described the unidentified author as "a senior official in the Trump administration," and he or she announced that there were "unsung heroes" in the West Wing who were "working diligently . . . to frustrate parts of [Trump's] agenda and his worst inclinations." "[W]e believe our first duty is to this country," the editorial read, "and the president continues to act in a manner that is detrimental to the health of our republic." Anonymous, "The Quiet Resistance inside the Trump Administration," *New York Times*, 6 September 2018.

book's moral center." If *Fear* were a first-person novel, critic Dwight Garner mused, Cohn "would be its narrator."[3]

What Woodward and his reviewers missed was how singularly *American* Cohn's behavior was. Such intrigue was inconceivable in the administrations of British Prime Minister Theresa May, French President Emmanuel Macron, German Chancellor Angela Merkel, or any other first-world leader. It would never have occurred to a non-American government official to purloin papers from the boss's desk because of disagreements over policy. British, French, and German political advisers might challenge a given course of action – and resign if unable to make their views prevail – but to steal an executive order would have been out of the question, treasonous. Only in the United States, with its proud tradition of diplomatic indiscipline, could Cohn have acted as he did.

Readers familiar with the history of American rogue statecraft will detect familiar features in Cohn's pre-Trumpworld résumé. A multimillionaire many times over, Cohn earned $22 million annually as Goldman Sachs CEO and accepted a severance package of $285 million when he joined his friend Donald's administration. Upon assuming control of the National Economic Council, he informed journalists that his salary would be just $30,000 a year, much less than other top White House officials. His foray into public service, in other words, was not financially motivated. Nor was it prompted by party loyalty: Cohn was a registered Democrat and had donated extensively to Democratic politicians. Like Henry Cabot Lodge II, who served a president from the opposition party out of a sense of noblesse oblige, Cohn felt at liberty to take whatever measures he felt would "protect the country," even if that meant pre-empting presidential prerogatives. Hence his subterfuge with the KORUS letter, which Woodward dramatically – and accurately – described as "no less than an administrative coup d'état, an undermining of the will of the president of the United States."[4]

Some may object that Cohn was not a true rogue diplomat in that he was serving stateside rather than at an overseas post. For his

---

[3] George Packer, "Scary Stuff," *New Yorker* 95 (24 September 2018): 66; Jill Abramson, "Bob Woodward's Meticulous, Frightening Look inside the Trump White House," *Washington Post*, 6 September 2018; Dwight Garner, "In 'Fear,' Bob Woodward Pulls Back the Curtain on President Trump's 'Crazytown,'" *New York Times*, 5 September 2018.

[4] Larry Buchanan, Andrew W. Lehren, Jugal K. Patel, and Adam Pearce, "How Much People in the Trump Administration Are Worth," *New York Times*, 3 April 2017; Lorraine Woellert, "Cohn Says He's Still a Democrat," *Politico*, 2 November 2017; Woodward, *Fear*, xix.

rebelliousness to fit the pattern of the preceding chapters, he would have to have been the U.S. ambassador to South Korea or a special envoy sent there by Trump to iron out a problem. This would be true had typical conditions obtained in late 2017, but at that stage there *was* no American ambassador or official of comparable rank in Seoul. Trump famously declared after his inauguration that most positions at the State Department were "unnecessary" and that "I'm the only one that matters," an attitude translated into policy by his secretary of state, Rex Tillerson, who slashed State's budget by over one-third and gutted the senior ranks of the diplomatic corps. Meanwhile, Trump declined to nominate candidates for open positions at embassies worldwide, among them the embassy in South Korea, despite his repeated claims that Pyongyang posed the most immediate threat to U.S. national security. (Key ambassadorships in countries like Saudi Arabia, Jordan, and Cuba also remained empty.) In the absence of a diplomatic first line of defense at the 38th parallel, Cohn stepped into the breach and kept a vindictive, mercurial president from taking the nation down a path whose consequences were too ghastly to contemplate – just as Nicholas Trist had done 160 years earlier.[5]

If Cohn's sedition had ample antecedents in the history of U.S. foreign relations, so too did Trump's contempt for diplomacy. As I note in the introduction, U.S. politicians and pundits have traditionally derided diplomats as perfidious and superfluous, despite the fact that many of America's greatest foreign-policy triumphs were achieved not on the battlefield but at the negotiating table. Americans feel differently about the military – they are willing to tolerate gargantuan expenditures to field the largest, best-equipped armed forces on earth, and they would have risen up in protest had Trump attempted to hollow out the Pentagon instead of State – but they generally have no quarrel with keeping the United States's diplomatic establishment on a starvation diet. There have, to be sure, been some reforms in the machinery of American statecraft since Benjamin Franklin, John Adams, and John Jay journeyed to Paris in the 1780s. Slow-dawning awareness that diplomacy requires training led to the creation of a U.S. Foreign Service – over a century after America's military developed a professional structure at West Point – and Congress has taken steps to increase diplomats' salaries and provide job security. Still,

---

[5] Trump cited in Heather Digby Parton, "'I'm the Only One That Matters': Trump's Chilling Imperial Power Grab," *Salon*, 6 February 2017. For Tillerson's evisceration of State, see Ronan Farrow, *War on Peace: The End of Diplomacy and the Decline of American Influence* (New York: W. W. Norton and Co., 2018).

compared to other countries, the United States spends a paltry percentage of its Gross National Product on diplomacy and reserves a huge share of its ambassadorial appointments for amateurs.

Trump did not invent this system, but his administration exacerbated it. Along with downsizing State, firing dozens of career men and women serving abroad, and leaving the top position at many embassies vacant, the president showed an alarming – and very American – preference for campaign donors and friends when he *did* nominate ambassadors. A case in point was David Friedman, Trump's emissary to Israel. Friedman, a lawyer, had known the president since the early 1990s, when he represented the Trump Organization in bankruptcies involving Trump's Atlantic City casinos. During the 2016 campaign, Friedman advised Trump on Jewish issues and contributed lavishly to the Republican National Committee. He had no diplomatic experience, but Trump did not see this as a problem. After the votes were in and Democratic candidate Hillary Clinton conceded defeat, Trump announced that Friedman was his choice for Embassy Tel Aviv, probably the most sensitive post in the world.[6]

Friedman's nomination met spirited opposition from liberal activist groups who deplored his many public statements denouncing a two-state solution and supporting Israel's settlement policies. Among the nominee's most inflammatory assertions was the claim that members of J Street, a left-wing Jewish advocacy organization, were "far worse than kapos – Jews who turned in their fellow Jews in the Nazi Death Camps." Five former U.S. ambassadors to Israel signed a letter to Trump declaring Friedman "unqualified." The Tel Aviv job required knowledge, tact, and skill, they said; it was absurd to install a dilettantish blowhard bereft of "the balance and the temperament to represent the United States." Trump stood by his man and Friedman was ultimately confirmed by the Senate.[7]

No other great power would have given Friedman this assignment. His lack of foreign-policy training alone would have disqualified him, to say nothing of his controversial views. Trump appeared to be courting disaster. But, as this study has demonstrated, America's tradition of sending nonprofessionals to do the nation's overseas business has often worked

---

[6] See David A. Graham, "Trump's Pick for Israel Ambassador Is No Diplomat," *Atlantic* 318 (16 December 2016): 19.

[7] Friedman cited in the Editorial Board, "A Dangerous Choice for Ambassador to Israel," *New York Times*, 16 December 2016; ambassadors cited in Anne Gearan and Karoun Demirjian, "Trump Pick for Ambassador to Israel Has Contentious Senate Audition," *Washington Post*, 16 February 2017.

out better than anticipated. Talent has proven to be at least somewhat fungible. Many of the people named ambassador, having earned distinction in another field, have been able to adapt to their new tasks surprisingly well. Some of them, although by no means all, have also effectively drawn upon the expertise of a permanent staff of secretaries and counselors at the embassy.

Most important, as short-term appointees, with no thought of making diplomacy a life's work, they have felt sufficiently liberated from executive control to either challenge or disobey orders they deemed counterproductive. In this regard, Friedman had some advantages over a career diplomat. Unlike the latter, who might think it wisest, for the sake of his or her position, not to present facts the boss finds painful to accept, Friedman could afford to be brutally honest. He could also draw upon over two decades of friendship with Trump to ensure that his advice received a respectful hearing in the White House. And if Trump, regardless of Friedman's counsel, persisted in a policy the ambassador thought contrary to American interests, Friedman might, à la Walter Hines Page, undermine that policy by obfuscation, misrepresentation, and foot-dragging. Or – the nuclear option – he could resign, an act that would damage his reputation in some quarters but enhance it in others and would carry no financial penalty. Whatever course he chose, he would not, if history is any indication, be content to serve as a passive conduit and would feel much freer than diplomats from other countries to articulate, in his own fashion, the sentiment so pungently expressed by William Watts in 1970. Watts, an aide to National Security Adviser Henry Kissinger, was appalled when he learned of President Richard Nixon's plans to use American ground forces in an invasion of Cambodia, and announced his intention to resign from the National Security Council in protest. Alexander Haig, Kissinger's deputy, admonished Watts that he could not disobey "an order from your commander in chief."

To which the rogue diplomat responded, "Fuck you, Al. I just did."[8]

---

[8] Haig and Watts cited in Loren Baritz, *Backfire: A History of How American Culture Led Us into Vietnam and Made Us Fight the Way We Did* (Baltimore: Johns Hopkins University Press, 1985), 208.

Bibliography

ARCHIVAL COLLECTIONS

Bureau of Far Eastern Affairs, Assistant Secretary for Far Eastern Affairs, Subject, Personal Name, and Country Files, 1960–1963, Record Group 59, General Records of the Department of State, National Archives II, College Park, Maryland

Dwight D. Eisenhower Library, Abilene, Kansas
    Post-presidential Papers, Augusta-Walter Reed Series

Diplomatic Instructions of the Department of State, 1801–1906, Mexico, Record Group 59, National Archives II, College Park, Maryland

Dispatches from U.S. Consuls in Havana, 1783–1906, Record Group 59, National Archives II, College Park, Maryland

W. Averell Harriman Papers, Library of Congress, Washington, D.C.

Edward M. House Papers, Sterling Library, Yale University, New Haven, Connecticut
    Series I: Select Correspondence
    Series II: Diary

John F. Kennedy Library, Boston, Massachusetts
    Roger Hilsman Papers
        Countries
    Joseph Patrick Kennedy Papers
        Ambassador: Correspondent File
        Ambassador: Dispatches
        Diary
        Diplomatic Memoir
        Family Correspondence
        Speeches
        U.S. Maritime Commission: Correspondence
    National Security File
        Countries – Vietnam
        Meetings and Memoranda

Oral History
   Roger Hilsman
   Henry Cabot Lodge II
   Frederick E. Nolting
   Dean Rusk
President's Office File
   Presidential Recordings
      Meetings
      Dictation
   Special Correspondence
Robert Lansing Papers, Library of Congress, Washington, D.C.
Robert Livingston Papers, New York Historical Society, New York City, New York
Emily Sears Lodge Papers, Massachusetts Historical Society, Boston, Massachusetts
Henry Cabot Lodge II Papers, Massachusetts Historical Society, Boston, Massachusetts
   Vietnam Memoir
   Journal
William L. Marcy Papers, Library of Congress, Washington, D.C.
   Outgoing Correspondence, Vols. 13, 14
J. Pierrepont Moffat Diplomatic Papers, Houghton Library, Harvard University, Cambridge, Massachusetts
   Correspondence: A–L
   Diaries, Vols. 1, 2
Walter Hines Page Papers, Houghton Library, Harvard University, Cambridge, Massachusetts
   Diary
   Correspondence between Walter Hines Page and Woodrow Wilson, Vols. 1, 3
   Unprocessed Correspondence and Memoranda
Frank Polk Papers, Sterling Library, Yale University, New Haven, Connecticut
James Knox Polk Papers, Library of Congress, Washington, D.C.
Franklin Delano Roosevelt Presidential Library, Hyde Park, New York
   Henry Morgenthau Diaries
   President's Official File
   President's Secretary's File
   James Roosevelt's Papers
   Tully Archive
Nicholas Philip Trist Memorial to Congress, 7 August 1848, Record Group 58, National Archives, Washington, D.C.
Nicholas Philip Trist Papers, Library of Congress, Washington, D.C.
Nicholas Philip Trist Papers, Southern Historical Collection, Louis Round Wilson Special Collections Library, University of North Carolina, Chapel Hill, North Carolina
U.S. Senate Select Committee to Study Governmental Operations with Respect to Intelligence Activities, Church Committee, Record Group 46, National Archives II, College Park, Maryland
Woodrow Wilson Papers, Library of Congress, Washington, D.C.

GOVERNMENT PUBLICATIONS

American State Papers: Foreign Relations. Washington, D.C.: Gales and Seaton, 1832. Vol. 2.

Barnes, William and John Heath Morgan. *The Foreign Service of the United States: Origins, Development, and Functions.* Washington, D.C.: Department of State, Historical Office, Bureau of Public Affairs, 1961.

Compilation of Reports of Committee on Foreign Relations, United States Senate. Washington: U.S. Government Printing Office, 1901. Vol. 3.

Congressional Globe. Washington, D.C.: Blair & Rives, 1848. Vol. 19.

Congressional Globe. Washington, D.C.: John C. Rives, 1860. Vol. 35.

Congressional Record. Washington, D.C.: U.S. Government Printing Office, 1885. Vol. 16.

Congressional Record. Washington, D.C.: U.S. Government Printing Office, 1908. Vol. 42.

The Debates and Proceedings of the Congress of the United States. Washington, D.C.: Gales and Seaton, 1851. Vol. 12.

Documents in German Foreign Policy, 1918–1945: From Neurath to Ribbentrop. Washington, D.C.: U.S. Government Printing Office, 1949. Series D, Vol. 1.

Documents in German Foreign Policy, 1918–1945: Germany and Czechoslovakia. Washington, D.C.: U.S. Government Printing Office, 1949. Series D, Vol. 2.

Documents in German Foreign Policy, 1918–1945: The Aftermath of Munich. Washington, D.C.: U.S. Government Printing Office, 1951. Series D, Vol. 4.

Foreign Relations of the United States, The Lansing Papers, 1914–1920. Washington, D.C.: U.S. Government Printing Office, 1939.

Foreign Relations of the United States, Supplement, 1914. Washington, D.C.: U.S. Government Printing Office, 1928.

Foreign Relations of the United States, Supplement, 1915. Washington, D.C.: U.S. Government Printing Office, 1928.

Foreign Relations of the United States, Supplement, 1916. Washington, D.C.: U.S. Government Printing Office, 1929.

Foreign Relations of the United States, Supplement, 1917. Washington, D.C.: U.S. Government Printing Office, 1931.

Foreign Relations of the United States, Supplement, 1918. Washington, D.C.: U.S. Government Printing Office, 1933.

Foreign Relations of the United States, 1938, General. Washington, D.C.: U.S. Government Printing Office, 1955. Vol. 1.

Foreign Relations of the United States, 1938, The American Republics. Washington, D.C.: U.S. Government Printing Office, 1956. Vol. 5.

Foreign Relations of the United States, 1939, General. Washington, D.C.: U.S. Government Printing Office, 1956. Vol. 1.

Foreign Relations of the United States, 1940, General. Washington, D.C.: U.S. Government Printing Office, 1957. Vol. 1.

Foreign Relations of the United States, 1940, The British Commonwealth, the Soviet Union, the Near East, and Africa. Washington, D.C.: U.S. Government Printing Office, 1958. Vol. 3.

Foreign Relations of the United States, 1961–1963, Vietnam: January–August 1963. Washington, D.C.: U.S. Government Printing Office, 1991. Vol. 3.

Foreign Relations of the United States, 1961–1963, Vietnam: August–December 1963. Washington, D.C.: U.S. Government Printing Office, 1991. Vol. 4.

Gravel, Mike, ed. *The Pentagon Papers: The Defense Department History of United States Decisionmaking on Vietnam*. Boston: Beacon Press, 1975. Vol. 2.

Hollick, Anne L. *U.S. Involvement in the Overthrow of Diem, 1963*, U.S. Congress, Senate, Committee on Foreign Relations, Staff Study No. 3, 92nd Cong., 2nd sess. Washington, D.C.: U.S. Government Printing Office, 1972.

Hunt, Galliard, ed. *Journals of the Continental Congress, 1774–1789*. Washington, D.C.: U.S. Government Printing Office, 1912. Vol. 5.

Madden, R. R. *A Letter to W. E. Channing, D. D., on the Subject of the Abuse of the United States in the Island of Cuba*. Boston: William D. Ticknor, 1839.

Manning, William R., ed. *Diplomatic Correspondence of the United States: Inter-American Affairs, 1831–1860*. Washington, D.C.: Carnegie Endowment for International Peace, 1937. Vol. 8.

Miller, Hunter, ed. *Treaties and Other International Acts of the United States of America*. Washington, D.C.: U.S. Government Printing Office, 1931. Vol. 2.

Public Papers of the President: Franklin Delano Roosevelt, 1938. Washington, D.C.: U.S. Government Printing Office, 1939.

Public Papers of the President: John F. Kennedy, 1963. Washington, D.C.: U.S. Government Printing Office, 1964.

Public Documents Printed by Order of the Senate of the United States. Washington, D.C.: Gales and Seaton, 1845. Vol. 3.

Public Documents Printed by Order of the Senate of the United States during the Second Session of the Twenty-Sixth Congress. Washington, D.C.: Blair & Rives, 1841. Vol. 3.

Register of Debates in Congress. Washington, D.C.: Gales and Seaton, 1835. Vol. 10.

Report from the Committee on Commerce, to Whom Was Referred the Petition of Certain Shipmasters, Shipowners, and Other Citizens, in Relation to the Conduct of N. P. Trist, Consul of the United States in Havana. Washington, D.C.: U.S. Government Printing Office, 1840.

Reporting Vietnam, Part One: American Journalism, 1959–1969. New York: Library of America, 1998.

Richardson, James D., ed. *A Compilation of the Messages and Papers of the Presidents, 1789–1897*. Washington, D.C.: U.S. Government Printing Office, 1898. Vol. 5.

State Papers and Correspondence Bearing upon the Purchase of the Territory of Louisiana. Washington, D.C.: U.S. Government Printing Office, 1903.

Treaties and Conventions Concluded between the United States of America and other Powers since July 4, 1776. Washington, D.C.: U.S. Government Printing Office, 1889.

The Treaty between the United States and Mexico: Proceedings of the Senate Thereon. Washington, D.C.: U.S. Government Printing Office, 1848.

Wharton, Francis, ed. *The Revolutionary Diplomatic Correspondence of the United States.* Washington, D.C.: U.S. Government Printing Office, 1889. Vols. 4, 5, 6.

NEWSPAPERS AND MAGAZINES

Atlanta Constitution
Atlantic
American Heritage
Boston Globe
Boston Herald
Boston Post
Boston Transcript
Chicago Tribune
Harvard Crimson
Huffington Post
Guardian
Harper's
Daily Mail
Daily Telegraph
Observer
Los Angeles Daily News
Los Angeles Times
National City [California] News
New York Daily Mirror
New York Post
New York Times
New York Tribune
New Yorker
Pittsburgh Daily Dispatch
Politico
Portland [Maine] *News*
Rock Island [Illinois] *Argus*
Salon
Time
Washington Daily Union
Washington National Intelligencer
Washington Post

AUTOBIOGRAPHIES, DIARIES, EDITED COLLECTIONS, LETTERS, MEMOIRS, SPEECHES

Adams, Charles Francis, ed. *The Works of John Adams.* Boston: Little, Brown, and Company, 1851. Vol. 3.

Ball, George W. *The Past Has Another Pattern: Memoirs*. New York: W. W. Norton & Company, 1983.

Barbé-Marbois, François. *The History of Louisiana, Particularly of the Cession of that Colony to the United States*, trans. William Beach Lawrence. New York: Carey and Lea, 1830.

Bell, Amy Helen. *London Was Ours: Diaries and Memories of the London Blitz*. New York: I. B. Tauris, 2011.

Beneš, Edward. *Memoirs of Dr. Edward Beneš*, trans. G. Lias. Boston: Houghton Mifflin, 1954.

Berle, Beatrice Bishop and Travis Beale Jacobs, eds. *Navigating the Rapids, 1918–1971: From the Papers of Adolf A. Berle*. New York: Harcourt Brace Jovanovich, 1973.

Bilainkin, George. *Diary of a Diplomatic Correspondent*. London: Allen & Unwin, 1942.

Byrnes, James. *All in One Lifetime*. New York: Harper & Brothers, 1958.

Chamberlain, Neville. Declaration of War against Hitler's Germany, 3 September 1939, avalon.law.yale.edu/wwii/gb2.asp

Clark, Ferdinand. *The American Captives in Havana, Being Ferdinand Clark's Reply to Nicholas P. Trist, Consul at That Place*. Boston: Jonathan Howe, 1841.

Colby, William with James McCargar. *Lost Victory: A Firsthand Account of America's Sixteen-Year Involvement in Vietnam*. Chicago: Contemporary Books, 1989.

Daniels, Josephus. *Shirt-Sleeve Diplomat*. Chapel Hill: University of North Carolina Press, 1947.

Dean, William, ed. *Life and Writings of Benjamin Franklin*. New York: Derby and Jackson, 1859. Vol. 1.

Dilks, David, ed. *The Diaries of Sir Alexander Cadogan, 1938–1945*. New York: G. P. Putnam's Sons, 1971.

Don, Tran Van. *Our Endless War: Inside Vietnam*. San Rafael, CA: Presidio Press, 1978.

Farley, James A. *Jim Farley's Story: The Roosevelt Years*. New York: McGraw-Hill, 1948.

Ford, Paul Leicester, ed. *Works of Thomas Jefferson*. New York: G. P. Putnam's Sons, 1899. Vol. 10.

Ford, Worthington Chauncey, ed. *Writings of John Quincy Adams*. New York: Macmillan, 1916. Vol. 6.

Franklin, William Temple, ed. *The Private Correspondence of Benjamin Franklin*. London: Henry Colburn, 1817.

Freeman, Landa M., Louise V. North, and Janet M. Wedge, eds. *Selected Letters of John Jay and Sarah Livingston Jay*. Jefferson, NC: McFarland & Co., 2005.

Gibbs, George, ed. *Memoirs of the Administrations of Washington and Adams Collected from the Papers of Oliver Wolcott*. New York: Printed for Subscribers, 1846.

Giunta, Mary, ed. *Documents of the Emerging Nation: U.S. Foreign Relations, 1775–1779*. Wilmington, DE: Scholarly Resources, 1998.

Grey, Edward. *Twenty-five Years, 1892–1916*. New York: Frederick A. Stokes and Co., 1925. Vol. 2.

Guthman, Edwin O. and Jeffrey Shulman, eds. *Robert Kennedy in His Own Words*. New York: Bantam Books, 1989.

Hackett, Mary A., J. C. A. Stagg, Jeanne Kerr Cross, Susan Holbrook Perdue, and Ellen J. Barber, eds. *The Papers of James Madison: Secretary of State Series*. Charlottesville: University Press of Virginia, 1998. Vol. 4.

Hamilton, Stanislaus Murray, ed. *The Writings of James Monroe*. New York: G. P. Putnam's Sons, 1900. Vol. 4.

Hendrick, Burton J., ed. *The Life and Letters of Walter H. Page*. Garden City, NY: Doubleday & Company, 1922. Vol. 2.

Hilsman, Roger. *To Move a Nation: The Politics of Foreign Policy in the Administration of John F. Kennedy*. Garden City, NY: Doubleday & Company, 1967.

Hunt, Galliard, ed. *Papers of James Madison*. New York: J. & H. G. Langley, 1841. Vol. 1.

Ickes, Harold L. *The Secret Diary of Harold L. Ickes, Volume II: The Lowering Clouds, 1939–1941*. New York: Simon & Schuster, 1955.

Jay, William, ed. *The Life of John Jay: With Selections from His Correspondence and Miscellaneous Papers*. New York: J. & J. Harper, 1833. Vol. 1.

Johnston, Henry P., ed. *The Correspondence and Public Papers of John Jay*. New York: G. P. Putnam's Sons, 1890. Vol. 2.

Jones, Thomas. *A Diary with Letters, 1931–1950*. New York: Oxford University Press, 1954.

Kennedy, Joseph P. *I'm for Roosevelt*. New York: Reynal & Hitchcock, 1936.

Klingelhofer, Herbert E. "Matthew Ridley's Diary during the Peace Negotiations of 1782." *William and Mary Quarterly* 20 (January 1963): 95–133,

Krock, Arthur. *Memoirs: Sixty Years on the Firing Line*. New York: Funk & Wagnalls, 1968.

Lansing, Robert. *War Memoirs of Robert Lansing*. Indianapolis: Bobbs-Merrill, 1935.

Leutze, James, ed. *The London Observer: The Journal of General Raymond E. Lee, 1940–1941*. London: Hutchinson, 1971.

Lindbergh, Anne Morrow. *The Flower and the Nettle: Diaries and Letters of Anne Morrow Lindbergh, 1936–1939*. New York: Harcourt Brace & Co., 1978.

Lindbergh, Charles A. *The Wartime Journals of Charles A. Lindbergh*. New York: Harcourt Brace Jovanovich, 1970.

Lodge, Henry Cabot. *The Storm Has Many Eyes: A Personal Narrative*. New York: W. W. Norton and Company, 1973.

Malone, Dumas, ed. *Correspondence between Thomas Jefferson and Pierre Samuel du Pont de Nemours, 1798–1817*. Boston: Houghton Mifflin Company, 1930.

Maneli, Mieczyslaw. *War of the Vanquished*, Maria de Gorgey, trans. New York: Harper & Row, 1971.

McNamara, Robert S. with Brian VanDeMark. *In Retrospect: The Tragedy and Lessons of Vietnam*. New York: Random House, 1995.

Mecklin, John. *Mission in Torment: An Intimate Account of the U.S. Role in Vietnam*. Garden City, NY: Doubleday & Company, 1965.

Monaghan, Frank, ed. *The Diary of John Jay during the Peace Negotiations of 1782, Being a Complete and Faithful Rendering of the Original Manuscript, Now Published for the First Time*. New Haven: Bibliographical Press, Yale University, 1934.

Monroe, James. *The Autobiography of James Monroe*, Stuart Gerry Brown, ed. Syracuse, NY: Syracuse University Press, 2017.

Murphy, Robert. *A Diplomat among Warriors: The Unique World of a Foreign Service Expert*. Garden City, NY: Doubleday & Company, 1964.

Nolting, Frederick. *From Trust to Tragedy: The Political Memoirs of Frederick Nolting, Kennedy's Ambassador to Diem's Vietnam*. New York: Praeger, 1988.

Oberg, Barbara B., ed. *Papers of Thomas Jefferson*. Princeton: Princeton University Press, 2014. Vol. 40.

O'Keefe, Kevin. *A Thousand Deadlines: The New York City Press and American Neutrality*. New York: Springer Science, 1972.

Parsons, Edward Alexander, ed. *The Original Letters of Robert R. Livingston, 1801–1803*. New Orleans: Louisiana Historical Society, 1953.

The Pentagon Papers: New York Times Version. New York: Quadrangle Books, 1971.

Quaife, Milo Milton, ed. *The Diary of James K. Polk*. Chicago: A. C. McClurg & Co., 1910. Vols. 2, 3.

Robinson, Ione. *A Wall to Paint on*. New York: E. F. Dutton, 1946.

Roosevelt, Franklin Delano. Quarantine Speech, 5 October 1937, Miller Center, University of Virginia, millercenter.org/president/speeches/detail/3310

Rusk, Dean as told to Richard Rusk. *As I Saw It*. New York: Penguin, 1990.

Ryerson, Richard Alan, Joanna M. Revelas, Celeste Walker, Gregg G. Lint, and Humphrey G. Costello, eds. *The Adams Papers: Adams Family Correspondence*. Boston: Massachusetts Historical Society, 1993. Vol. 5.

Schultz, George P. *Turmoil and Triumph: Diplomacy, Power, and the Victory of the American Ideal*. New York: Charles Scribner's Sons, 1993.

Sparks, Jared, ed. *The Works of Benjamin Franklin*. Philadelphia: Childs and Peterson, 1840. Vol. 9.

Seymour, Charles, ed. *The Intimate Papers of Colonel House*. Boston: Houghton Mifflin Company, 1926.

Slessor, John. *The Central Blue*. New York: Praeger, 1957.

Smith, Amanda, ed. *Hostage to Fortune: The Letters of Joseph P. Kennedy*. New York: Penguin, 2001.

Syrett, Harold C., ed. *The Papers of Alexander Hamilton*. New York: Columbia University Press, 1962. Vol. 3.

Taylor, Maxwell. *Swords and Plowshares*. New York: W. W. Norton, 1972.

Wilson, Woodrow. Address Delivered at the First Annual Assemblage of he League to Enforce Peace: "American Principles," 27 May 1916, *The American Presidency Project*, www.presidency.uscb.edu/ws/?pid=65391

    Address to a Joint Session of Congress on the Severance of Diplomatic Relations with Germany, 3 February 1917, *The American Presidency Project*, www.presidency.ucsb.edu/ws/?pid=65397

Address to a Joint Session of Congress Requesting a Declaration of War against Germany, 2 April 1917, *The American Presidency Project*, www.presidency.uscb.edu/ws/?pid=65366

BOOKS AND ARTICLES

Abramson, Rudy. *Spanning the Century: The Life of W. Averell Harriman, 1891–1986*. New York: William Morrow and Company, 1992.

Adair, Douglass. "Hamilton on the Louisiana Purchase: A Newly Identified Editorial from the New York Evening Post." *William and Mary Quarterly* 12 (April 1955): 268–281.

Adams, Henry. *History of the United States of America during the First Administration of Thomas Jefferson*. New York: Charles Scribner's Sons, 1909.

Adams, Mary P. "Jefferson's Reaction to the Treaty of San Ildefonso." *Journal of Southern History* 21 (May 1955): 173–188.

Alexander, R. S. *Napoleon*. New York: Oxford University Press, 2001.

Alsop, Joseph and Robert Kintner. *American White Paper: The Story of American Diplomacy and the Second World War*. New York: Simon & Schuster, 1940.

Ambrose, Stephen E. and Douglas G. Brinkley. *The Mississippi and the Making of a Nation: From the Louisiana Purchase to Today*. Washington: National Geographic, 2003.

Ambrose, Stephen E. *Rise to Globalism: American Foreign Policy since 1938*, Seventh Edition. New York: Penguin, 1993.

Ammon, Harry. *James Monroe: The Quest for National Identity*. Charlottesville: University Press of Virginia, 1990.

Asprey, Robert B. *The Rise of Napoleon Bonaparte*. New York: Basic Books, 2000.

Augur, Helen. *The Secret War of Independence*. New York: Greenwood Press, 1955.

Axelrod, Alan. *Lost Destiny: Joe Kennedy and the Doomed World War II Mission to Save London*. New York: St. Martin's Press, 2015.

Bailey, Thomas A. *A Diplomatic History of the American People*, Seventh Edition. New York: Appleton-Century-Crofts, 1964.

"The United States and the Blacklist during the Great War." *Journal of Modern History* 6 (March 1934): 14–35.

Baritz, Loren. *Backfire: A History of How American Culture Led Us into Vietnam and Made Us Fight the Way We Did*. New York: Ballantine Books, 1986.

Barnes, Harry Elmer. *The Genesis of the World War*. New York: Alfred A. Knopf, 1929.

Bauer, K. Jack. *The Mexican War, 1846–1848*. New York: Macmillan, 1974.

Bemis, Samuel Flagg. *The Diplomacy of the American Revolution*, Second Edition. Bloomington: Indiana University Press, 1965.

A Diplomatic History of the United States. New York: Henry Holt, 1946.

Bendiner, Elmer. *The Virgin Diplomats*. New York: Alfred A. Knopf, 1976.

Berg, A. Scott. *Lindbergh*. New York: Berkeley Books, 1998.

Wilson. New York: G. P. Putnam's Sons, 2013.

Beschloss, Michael R. *Kennedy and Roosevelt: The Uneasy Alliance*. New York: Harper & Row, 1980.

Bill, Alfred H. *Rehearsal for Conflict: The War with Mexico, 1846–1848*. New York: Alfred A. Knopf, 1947.

Billington, Ray A. *Westward Expansion*. Albuquerque: University of New Mexico Press, 2001.

Bird, Anthony J. *London's Burning*. New York: Endeavor Press, 2015.

Black, Conrad. *Franklin Delano Roosevelt: Champion of Freedom*. New York: Public Affairs, 2003.

Blair, Anne. *Lodge in Vietnam: A Patriot Abroad*. New Haven: Yale University Press, 1995.

Boot, Max. *The Road Not Taken: Edward Lansdale and the American Tragedy in Vietnam*. New York: Liveright Publishing Corporation, 2018.

Bourne, Edward Gaylord. "A Trained Civil Service." *North American Review* 169 (October 1899): 528–535.

———. "The United States and Mexico, 1847–1848." *American Historical Review* 5 (April 1900): 491–502.

Brands, H. W. *Traitor to His Class: The Privileged Life and Radical Presidency of Franklin Roosevelt*. New York: Anchor Books, 2008.

Brecher, Frank W. *Securing American Independence: John Jay and the French Alliance*. Westport, CT: Praeger, 2003.

Brent, Robert A. "Reaction in the United States to Nicholas Trist's Mission to Mexico, 1847–1848." *Revista de Historia de América* 35 (January–December 1953): 105–118.

Brinton, Crane. *The Lives of Talleyrand*. New York: W. W. Norton and Company, 1963.

Broers, Michael. *Europe under Napoleon, 1799–1815*. London: Arnold, 1996.

Brown, Anthony Cave. *The Last Hero: Wild Bill Donovan*. New York: Vintage, 1984.

Bruno, James. *The Foreign Circus: Why Foreign Policy Should Not Be Left in the Hands of Diplomats, Spies, and Political Hacks*. Canastota, NY: Bittersweet House Press, 2014.

Buckley, Thomas H. and Edwin V. Strong, Jr. *American Foreign and National Security Policies, 1914–1945*. Knoxville: University of Tennessee Press, 1987.

Bush, Robert B. *The Louisiana Purchase: A Global Context*. New York: Routledge, 2014.

Byrnes, Mark E. *James K. Polk: A Biographical Companion*. Santa Barbara: ABC-CLIO, 2001.

Cannon, Lou, and Carl M. Cannon. *Reagan's Disciple: George W. Bush's Troubled Quest for a Presidential Legacy*. New York: Public Affairs, 2007.

Catton, Philip E. *Diem's Final Failure: Prelude to America's War in Vietnam*. Lawrence: University Press of Kansas, 2002.

Cerami, Charles A. *Jefferson's Great Gamble*. Naperville, IL: Sourcebooks Incorporated, 2003.

Chamberlain, Eugene Keith. "Nicholas Trist and Baja California." *Pacific Historical Review* 32 (February 1963): 49–63.

Channing, Edward. *History of the United States.* New York: Macmillan, 1926. Vol. 4.

Chapman, Jessica M. *Cauldron of Resistance: Ngo Dinh Diem, the United States, and 1950s South Vietnam.* Ithaca: Cornell University Press, 2013.

Charlton, Michael and Anthony Moncrieff. *Many Reasons Why: The American Involvement in Vietnam.* New York: Penguin, 1979.

Chavez, Thomas E. *Spain and the Independence of the United States: An Intrinsic Gift.* Albuquerque: University of New Mexico Press, 2002.

Christensen, Carol and Thomas Christensen. *The U.S.–Mexican War.* San Francisco: Bay Books, 1998.

Cogliano, Francis D. *Emperor of Liberty: Thomas Jefferson's Foreign Policy.* New Haven: Yale University Press, 2014.

  Thomas Jefferson: Reputation and Legacy. Charlottesville: University of Virginia Press, 2006.

Coker, William S. "The Panama Canal Tolls Controversy." *Journal of American History* 55 (December 1968): 555–564.

Cole, Wayne S. *Roosevelt and the Isolationists, 1932–1945.* Lincoln: University of Nebraska Press, 1983.

Combs, Jerald A. and Arthur G. Combs. *The History of American Foreign Policy,* Second Edition. New York: McGraw-Hill, 1997.

Cooper, Jr., John Milton. *Walter Hines Page: The Southerner as American, 1855–1918.* Chapel Hill: University of North Carolina Press, 1977.

Cooper, *Woodrow Wilson.* New York: Alfred A. Knopf, 2009.

Corwin, Edward S. *French Policy and the American Alliance.* Princeton: Princeton University Press, 1916.

Costigliola, Frank and Michael J. Hogan, eds. *America in the World: The Historiography of American Foreign Relations since 1941,* First Edition. Cambridge: Cambridge University Press, 1995.

  eds. *America in the World: The Historiography of American Foreign Relations since 1941,* Second Edition. Cambridge: Cambridge University Press, 2013.

  eds. *Explaining the History of American Foreign Relations,* Third Edition. Cambridge: Cambridge University Press, 2016.

Craig, Gordon A. and Felix Gilbert, eds. *The Diplomats, 1919–1939, Volume II: The Thirties.* New York: Atheneum, 1963.

Cronin, Vincent. *Napoleon Bonaparte: An Intimate Biography.* New York: William Morrow and Company, 1972.

Cronon, E. David. *Josephus Daniels in Mexico.* Madison: University of Wisconsin Press, 1960.

Cunningham, Jr., Noble E. *Jefferson and Monroe: Constant Friendship and Respect.* Chapel Hill: University of North Carolina Press, 2003.

Dallek, Robert. *Franklin D. Roosevelt and American Foreign Policy, 1932–1945.* New York: Oxford University Press, 1995.

Dangerfield, George. *Chancellor Robert Livingston of New York, 1746–1814.* New York: Harcourt, Brace, and Company, 1960.

De Bedts, Ralph F. *Ambassador Joseph Kennedy, 1938–1940: An Anatomy of Appeasement.* New York: Peter Lang, 1985.

DeConde, Alexander. *A History of American Foreign Policy*, Second Edition. New York: Charles Scribner's Sons, 1971.

    The Quasi-War: The Politics and Diplomacy of the Undeclared War with France, 1797–1801. New York: Charles Scribner's Sons, 1966.

    This Affair of Louisiana. Baton Rouge: Louisiana State University Press, 1976.

DeRoach, Andrew. *Andrew Young: Civil Rights Ambassador*. Wilmington, DE: Scholarly Resources, 2003.

Divine, Robert A. *Perpetual War for Perpetual Peace*. College Station: Texas A & M University Press, 2000.

Dommen, Arthur J. *The Indochinese Experience of the French and the Americans: Nationalism and Communism in Cambodia, Laos, and Vietnam*. Bloomington: Indiana University Press, 2001.

Drexler, Robert W. *Guilty of Making Peace: A Biography of Nicholas P. Trist*. Lanham, MD: University Press of America, 1991.

Dull, Jonathan R. *A Diplomatic History of the American Revolution*. New Haven: Yale University Press, 1985.

    The French Navy and American Independence: A Study of Arms and Diplomacy, 1774–1787. Princeton: Princeton University Press, 1975.

Duncliffe, William J. *The Life and Times of Joseph P. Kennedy*. New York: McFadden, 1965.

Dumbrell, John. *A Special Relationship: Anglo-American Relations from the Cold War to Iraq*, Second Edition. London: Palgrave, 2006.

Dutton, David. *Neville Chamberlain*. New York: Oxford University Press, 2001.

Eisenhower, John S. D. *So Far from God: The U.S. War with Mexico, 1846–1848*. Norman: University of Oklahoma Press, 1989.

Elliott, Charles W. *Winfield Scott: The Soldier and the Man*. New York: Macmillan, 1937.

Ellis, Joseph J. *American Sphinx: The Character of Thomas Jefferson*. New York: Vintage Books, 1998.

Ellis, L. Nathan. *A Short History of American Diplomacy*. New York: Harper & Brothers, 1951.

Englund, Steven. *Napoleon: A Political Life*. New York: Charles Scribner's Sons, 2004.

Esposito, David M. *The Legacy of Woodrow Wilson: American War Aims in World War I*. Westport, CT: Praeger, 1996.

Farnham, Thomas J. "Nicholas Trist and James Freaner and the Mission to Mexico." *Journal of the Southwest* 11 (Autumn 1969): 247–260.

Farrow, Ronan. *War on Peace: The End of Diplomacy and the Decline of American Influence*. New York: W. W. Norton and Company, 2018.

Feiling, Keith. *The Life of Neville Chamberlain*. London: Macmillan, 1970.

Ferrell, Robert. *American Diplomacy: A History*. New York: W. W. Norton and Company, 1959.

Fitzgibbon, Constantine. *The Winter of the Bombs: The Story of the Blitz of London*. New York: Scholar's Choice, 2015.

Fleming, D. F. *The Cold War and Its Origins, 1917–1960*. Garden City, NY: Doubleday & Company, 1961.

Fleming, Thomas. *The Louisiana Purchase*. New York: Wiley, 2003.

The Perils of Peace: America's Struggle for Survival after Yorktown. New York: Smithsonian Books, 2007.

Flood, Ryan M. *Abandoning American Neutrality: Woodrow Wilson and the Beginning of the Great War, August 1914–December 1915*. London: Palgrave-Macmillan, 2013.

Foley, William E. *The Genesis of Missouri: From Wilderness Outpost to Statehood*. Columbia: University of Missouri Press, 1989.

Fowler, William M. *American Crisis: George Washington and the Dangerous Two Years after Yorktown, 1781–1783*. New York: Walker & Company, 2011.

Santa Anna of Mexico. Lincoln: University of Nebraska Press, 2007.

Freedman, Lawrence. *Kennedy's Wars: Berlin, Cuba, Laos, and Vietnam*. New York: Oxford University Press, 2000.

Fuller, John D. P. *The Movement for the Acquisition of All Mexico, 1846–1848*. Baltimore: Johns Hopkins University Press, 1936.

Gelfand, Lawrence E. "Towards a Merit System for the American Diplomatic Service, 1900–1930." *Irish Studies in International Affairs* 2 (1988): 49–63.

Gilbert, Felix. *The Beginnings of American Foreign Policy: To the Farewell Address*. Princeton: Princeton University Press, 1961.

Gilbert, Martin and Richard Gott. *The Appeasers*. London: Weidenfeld & Nicolson, 1963.

Gilje, Paul A. *Free Trade and Sailors' Rights in the War of 1912*. Cambridge: Cambridge University Press, 2013.

Gordon, Meryl. *Mrs. Astor Regrets: The Hidden Betrayals of a Family beyond Reproach*. Boston: Houghton Mifflin, 2008.

Graebner, Norman A. *Empire on the Pacific: A Study in American Continental Expansion*. New York: Ronald Press Company, 1955.

"Party Politics and the Trist Mission." *Journal of Southern History* 19 (May 1953): 137–156.

Graebner, Norman A., Richard Dean Burns, and Joseph M. Siracusa. *Foreign Affairs and the Founding Fathers: From Confederation to Constitution, 1776–1789*. Santa Barbara: ABC-CLIO, 2011.

Grant, Zalin. *Facing the Phoenix: The CIA and the Political Defeat of the United States in Vietnam*. New York: W. W. Norton and Company, 1991.

Grattan, C. Harley. "The Walter Hines Page Legend." *American Mercury* 6 (September 1925): 39–51.

Gregory, Ross. "The Superfluous Ambassador: Walter Hines Page's Return to Washington, 1916." *The Historian* 28 (May 1966): 389–404.

Walter Hines Page: Ambassador to the Court of St. James. Lexington: University of Kentucky Press, 1970.

Grey, Miriam Nyhan, ed. *Ireland's Allies: America and the 1916 Easter Rising*. Dublin: University of Dublin Press, 2016.

Halberstam, David. *The Best and the Brightest*. New York: Random House, 1969.

The Making of a Quagmire. New York: Random House, 1965.

Hammer, Ellen J. *A Death in November: America in Vietnam, 1963*. New York: Oxford University Press, 1987.

Harris, Robin. *Talleyrand: Betrayer and Savior of France*. London: John Murray, 2007.

Harvey, Robert. *The War of Wars: The Great European Conflict, 1793–1815*. New York: Carroll and Graf, 2006.

Hatch, Alden. *The Lodges of Massachusetts: An Intimate Glimpse into the Lives and Careers of One of Our Country's Great Political Families*. New York: Hawthorne Books, 1973.

Haynes, Sam W. *James K. Polk and the Expansionist Impulse*. New York: Longman, 1997.

Heidler, David and Jeanne Heidler. *The Mexican War*. Westport, CT: Greenwood Press, 2006.

Henderson, Peter V. N., "Woodrow Wilson, Victoriano Huerta, and the Recognition Issue in Mexico." *Americas* 41 (October 1984): 151–176.

Henderson, Timothy J. *A Glorious Defeat: Mexico and Its War with the United States*. New York: Hill and Wang, 2007.

Henry, Robert Selph. *The Story of the Mexican War*. New York: Da Capo Press, 1950.

Herring, George C. *America's Longest War: The United States and Vietnam, 1950–1975*, Fifth Edition. New York: McGraw-Hill, 2014.

    From Colony to Superpower: U.S. Foreign Relations since 1776. New York: Oxford University Press, 2008.

Hersh, Seymour. *The Dark Side of Camelot*. Boston: Little, Brown, and Company, 1998.

Higgins, Marguerite. *Our Vietnam Nightmare*. New York: Harper & Row, 1965.

Hilton, Stanley E. "The Welles Mission to Europe, February–March 1940: Illusion or Realism?" *Journal of American History* 58 (June 1971): 93–120.

Hoffman, Ronald and Peter J. Albert, eds. *Diplomacy and Revolution: The Franco-American Alliance of 1778*. Charlottesville: University Press of Virginia, 1981.

    eds. *Peace and the Peacemakers: The Treaty of 1783*. Charlottesville: University of Virginia Press, 1986.

Hogan, Michael J. and Thomas Paterson, eds. *Explaining the History of American Foreign Relations*, First Edition. Cambridge: Cambridge University Press, 1991.

Horsman, Reginald. *The Diplomacy of the New Republic, 1776–1815*. Chicago: Harlan Davidson, 1985.

Hosmer, James K. *History of the Louisiana Purchase*. New York: D. Appleton and Company, 1902.

Hughes, Nathaniel Cheairs and Roy P. Stonesifer, Jr. *The Life and Wars of Gideon Pillow*. Chapel Hill: University of North Carolina Press, 1993.

Humphrey, Carol Sue. *The Press of the Young Republic, 1783–1833*. Westport, CT: Greenwood Press, 1996.

Hutson, James H. *John Adams and the Diplomacy of the American Revolution*. Lexington: University Press of Kentucky, 1980.

Ilchman, Frederick Warren. *Professional Diplomacy in the United States*. Chicago: University of Chicago Press, 1961.

Jacobs, Seth. *America's Miracle Man in Vietnam: Ngo Dinh Diem, Religion, Race, and U.S. Intervention in Southeast Asia, 1950–1957*. Durham, NC: Duke University Press, 2004.

Cold War Mandarin: Ngo Dinh Diem and the Origins of America's War in Vietnam, 1950–1963. Lanham, MD: Rowman & Littlefield, 2006.

"'Our System Demands the Supreme Being': The U.S. Religious Revival and the 'Diem Experiment, 1954–1955.'" *Diplomatic History* 25 (December 2002): 589–624.

James, C. L. R. *Toussaint L'Ouverture: The Story of the Only Successful Slave Revolt in History*. Durham, NC: Duke University Press, 2013.

Jennings, Phillip. *The Politically Incorrect Guide to the Vietnam War*. Washington, D.C.: Regnery Publishing, 2010.

Jett, Dennis C. *American Ambassadors: The Past, Present, and Future of America's Diplomats*. New York: Palgrave, 2014.

Johnson, Dennis W. *The Laws That Shaped America: Fifteen Acts of Congress and Their Lasting Impact*. New York: Routledge, 2009.

Johnson, Ronald Angelo. *Diplomacy in Black and White: John Adams, Toussaint L'Ouverture, and Their Atlantic World Alliance*. Athens, GA: University of Georgia Press, 2013.

Johnston, Willis Fletcher. *America's Foreign Relations*. New York: Appleton-Century-Crofts, 1916.

Jones, Howard. *Crucible of Power: A History of American Foreign Relations to 1913*, Second Edition. Lanham, MD: Rowman & Littlefield, 2009.

Death of a Generation: How the Assassinations of Diem and JFK Prolonged the Vietnam War. New York: Oxford University Press, 2003.

Kahin, George. *Intervention: How America Became Involved in Vietnam*. New York: Anchor Books, 1987.

Kaiser, David. *American Tragedy: Kennedy, Johnson, and the Origins of the Vietnam War*. Cambridge, MA: Belknap Press of Harvard University Press, 2000.

Kammen, Michael, ed. *The Past Before Us: Contemporary Historical Writing in the United States*. Ithaca: Cornell University Press, 1980.

Kaplan, Lawrence F. *Colonies into Nation: American Diplomacy, 1763–1801*. New York: Macmillan, 1972.

Entangling Alliances with None: American Foreign Policy in the Age of Jefferson. Kent, OH: Kent State University Press, 1987.

Karnow, Stanley. *Vietnam: A History*. New York: Penguin, 1997.

Kennedy, David, Lizabeth Cohen, and Mel Piehl. *The Brief American Pageant: A History of the Republic*, Ninth Edition. Boston: Cengage Learning, 2017. Vol. 2.

Kershaw, Ian. *Hitler: 1936–1945, Nemesis*. New York: Norton, 2000.

Hitler: A Biography. New York: W. W. Norton, 1998.

Kessler, Ronald. *Sins of the Father: Joseph P. Kennedy and the Dynasty He Founded*. New York: Warner Books, 1996.

Kilpatrick, Carroll. *Roosevelt and Daniels: A Friendship in Politics*. Chapel Hill: University of North Carolina Press, 1952.

Bibliography

King, Victor T., ed. *Explorers of Southeast Asia: Six Lives*. New York: Oxford University Press, 1995.

Kissinger, Henry. *Diplomacy*. New York: Simon & Schuster, 1994.

Kluger, Richard. *Seizing Destiny: The Relentless Expansion of American Territory*. New York: Alfred A. Knopf, 2005.

Knight, Roger. *Britain against Napoleon: The Organization of Victory, 1793–1815*. New York: Penguin, 2013.

Knott, Sarah. *Sensibility and the American Revolution*. Chapel Hill: University of North Carolina Press, 2008.

Koskoff, David E. *Joseph P. Kennedy: A Life and Times*. Englewood Cliffs, NJ: Prentice Hall, 1974.

Kukla, John. *A Wilderness So Immense: The Louisiana Purchase and the Destiny of America*. New York: Alfred A. Knopf, 2003.

Lawday, David. *Napoleon's Master: A Life of Prince Talleyrand*. New York: Thomas Dunn, 2007.

LaFeber, Walter. *The American Age: U.S. Foreign Policy at Home and Abroad, 1750 to the Present*, Second Edition. New York: W. W. Norton and Company, 1994.

Lamar, Quentin Curtis. "A Diplomatic Disaster: The Mexican Mission of Anthony Butler, 1829–1834." *The Americas* 45 (July 1988): 1–17.

Langguth, A. J. *Our Vietnam: The War, 1954–1975*. New York: Simon & Schuster, 2002.

Lauterpacht, Hersch. *International Law*. Cambridge: Cambridge University Press, 1975. Vol. 2.

Learned, Henry Barrett. "Cabinet Meetings under President Polk." *Annual Report of the American Historical* Association: Washington, D.C., 1916: 229–242.

Leonard, Thomas M. *James K. Polk: A Clear and Unquestionable Destiny*. Lanham, MD: Scholarly Resources, 2001.

Lever, Maurice. *Beaumarchais*, trans. Susan Emanuel. New York: Farrar, Straus, and Giroux, 2009.

Levin, Phyllis Lee. *Edith and Woodrow: The Wilson White House*. New York: Charles Scribner's Sons, 2011.

Logevall, Fredrik. *Choosing War: The Lost Chance for Peace and the Escalation of the War in Vietnam*. Berkeley: University of California Press, 1999.

Lopez, Claude-Anne. *Mon Cher Papa: Franklin and the Ladies of Paris*. New Haven: Yale University Press, 1966.

Lyon, E. Wilson. *The Man Who Sold Louisiana*. Norman: University of Oklahoma Press, 1974.

Mackesy, Piers. *The War for America, 1775–1783*. Cambridge, MA: Harvard University Press, 1964.

Madelin, Lewis. *Talleyrand: A Vivid Biography of the Amoral, Unscrupulous, and Fascinating French Statesman*. New York: J. Rolls Book Company, 1948.

Mahin, Dean B. *Olive Branch and Sword: The United States and Mexico, 1845–1848*. Jefferson, NC: McFarland & Co., 1997.

Maier, Thomas. *The Kennedys: America's Emerald Kings.* New York: Basic Books, 2003.

Maitland, Terence and Stephen Weiss. *The Vietnam Experience: Raising the Stakes.* Boston: Boston Publishing Company, 1982.

Mann, Robert. *A Grand Delusion: America's Descent into Vietnam.* New York: Basic Books, 2001.

May, Ernest R. *The World War and American Isolation, 1914–1917.* Cambridge, MA: Harvard University Press, 1959.

Mayers, David. *FDR's Ambassadors and the Diplomacy of Crisis.* Cambridge: Cambridge University Press, 2013.

McCormac, Eugene Irving. *James K. Polk: A Political Biography.* New York: Russell & Russell, 1922.

McCoy, Donald R. *Calvin Coolidge: The Quiet President.* Lawrence: University Press of Kansas, 1988.

McCullough, David. *John Adams.* New York: Simon & Schuster, 2001.

McElroy, Robert. *The Winning of the Far West.* New York: Carpenter Press, 1914.

McKercher, B. J. C. *Britain, America, and the Special Relationship since 1941.* London: Routledge, 2016.

Melton, Jr., Buckner F. *Aaron Burr: Conspiracy to Treason.* New York: Wiley 2002.

Merry, Robert W. *A Country of Vast Designs: James K. Polk, the Mexican War, and the Conquest of the American Continent.* New York: Simon & Schuster, 2009.

Middlekauff, Robert. *The Glorious Cause: The American Revolution, 1763–1789,* Second Edition. New York: Oxford University Press, 2005.

Miller, Edward. *Misalliance: Ngo Dinh Diem, the United States, and the Fate of South Vietnam.* Cambridge, MA: Harvard University Press, 2013.

——— "Religious Revival and the Politics of Nation Building: Reinterpreting the 1963 'Buddhist Crisis' in South Vietnam." *Modern Asian Studies* 49 (2015): 1903–1962.

——— "Vision, Power, and Agency: The Ascent of Ngo Dinh Diem, 1945–1954." *Journal of Southeast Asian Studies* 35 (October 2004): 433–458.

Miller, William. *Henry Cabot Lodge.* New York: James H. Heineman, 1967.

Millis, Walter. *Road to War: America, 1914–1917.* Boston: Houghton Mifflin Company, 1935.

Monaghan, Frank. *John Jay.* New York: Bobbs-Merrill, 1935.

Morgan, Edmund S. *The Birth of the Republic, 1763–1789,* Second Edition. Chicago: University of Chicago Press, 1977.

Morgan, Robert. *Lions of the West: Heroes and Villains of the Western Expansion.* Chapel Hill: Algonquin Books, 2011.

Morris, Richard B. *The Peacemakers: The Great Powers and American Independence.* New York: Harper & Row, 1965.

Morton, Brian N. and Donald C. Spinelli. *Beaumarchais and the American Revolution.* Lanham, MD: Lexington Books, 2003.

Mortimer, Gavin. *The Blitz: An Illustrated History.* London: Osprey Publishing, 2010.

Moskin, J. Robert. *American Statecraft: The Story of the U.S. Foreign Service.* New York: St. Martin's Press, 2013.

Mowat, R. B. *The Diplomacy of Napoleon.* New York: Russell and Russell, 1971.

Moyar, Mark. *Triumph Forsaken: The Vietnam War, 1954–1965.* Cambridge: Cambridge University Press, 2006.

Murat, Ines. *Napoleon and the American Dream,* trans. Frances Frenaye. Baton Rouge: Louisiana State University Press, 1976.

Murphy, Orville T. *Charles Gravier, Comte de Vergennes: French Diplomacy in the Age of Revolution.* Albany: State University of New York Press, 1982.

Nasaw, David. *The Patriarch: The Remarkable Life and Turbulent Times of Joseph P. Kennedy.* New York: Penguin, 2012.

Newman, John M. *JFK and Vietnam: Deception, Intrigue, and the Struggle for Power.* New York: Warner Books, 1992.

Newman, Simon P., ed. *Europe's American Revolution.* New York: Palgrave, 2006.

Neu, Charles E. *Colonel House: A Biography of Woodrow Wilson's Silent Partner.* New York: Oxford University Press, 2015.

Ogg, Frederick Austin. *The Opening of the Mississippi: A Struggle for Supremacy in the American Interior.* London: Greenwood Press, 1904.

Ohrt, Wallace. *Defiant Peacemaker: Nicholas Trist and the Mexican War.* College Station: Texas A & M University Press, 1997.

O'Neill, William L. *A Democracy at War: America's Fight at Home and Abroad in World War II.* Cambridge, MA: Harvard University Press, 1993.

Onuf, Peter S., ed. *Jeffersonian Legacies.* Charlottesville: University Press of Virginia, 1993.

Parton, James. *The Presidency of Andrew Jackson.* New York: Mason Brothers, 1861. Vol. 3.

Paterson, Thomas G., J. Gary Clifford, Shane J. Maddock, Deborah Kisatsky, and Kenneth J. Hagan. *American Foreign Relations: A History,* Seventh Edition. Boston: Wadsworth, 2010.

Paul, Joel Richard. *Unlikely Allies: How a Merchant, a Playwright, and a Spy Saved the American Revolution.* New York: Riverhead Books, 2009.

Pellew, George. *John Jay.* Boston: Houghton Mifflin Company, 1890.

Perkins, Bradford. *Castlereagh and Adams: England and the United States, 1812–1823.* Berkeley: University of California Press, 1964.

The Creation of an American Empire, 1775–1865. Cambridge: Cambridge University Press, 1993.

Persico, Joseph E. *Roosevelt's Secret War: FDR and World War II Espionage.* New York: Random House, 2001.

Peterson, Merrill D. *Thomas Jefferson and the New Nation: A Biography.* New York: Oxford University Press, 1970.

Petit, Clyde Edward. *The Experts.* Secaucus, NJ: Lyle Stuart, 1975.

Pletcher, David M. *The Diplomacy of Annexation: Texas, Oregon, and the Mexican War.* Columbia: University of Missouri Press, 1973.

Pratt, Julius W. *A History of United States Foreign Policy.* Englewood Cliffs, NJ: Prentice Hall, 1955.

Prochnau, William. *Once upon a Distant War: David Halberstam, Neil Sheehan, Peter Arnett – Young War Correspondents and Their Early Vietnam Battles.* New York: Random House, 1995.

Rafferty, Matthew. "Our (Unhappy) Man in Havana: Nicholas Trist, American Networks of Capital, and U.S. Consular Authority in Cuba, 1833–1845." *Society for Historians of American Foreign Relations 2015 Annual Meeting.* Washington, D.C.: June 2015.

Reeves, Jesse S. *American Diplomacy under Tyler and Polk.* Baltimore: Johns Hopkins University Press, 1906.

Reeves, Richard. *President Kennedy: Profile of Power.* New York: Simon & Schuster, 1993.

Ritcheson, C. R. "The Earl of Shelburne and Peace with America, 1782–1783: Vision and Reality." *International History Review* 5 (August 1983): 322–345.

Rives, G. L. *The United States and Mexico.* New York: Charles Scribner's Sons, 1914. Vol. 2.

Roberts, Geoffrey. *Molotov: Stalin's Cold Warrior.* Washington, D.C.: Potomac Books, 2012.

Rofe, J. Simon and Andrew Stewart, eds. *Diplomats at War: The American Experience.* St. Louis, MO: Republic of Letters Publishing, 2013.

Ronning, C. Neale and Albert P. Vannucci. *Ambassadors in Foreign Policy: The Influence of Individuals on U.S.-Latin American Policy.* New York: Praeger, 1987.

Rossbach, Niklas. *Heath, Nixon, and the Rebirth of the Special Relationship: Britain, the U.S., and the EC.* London: Palgrave, 2009.

Rotter, Andrew J. "Christians, Muslims, and Hindus: Religion and U.S.-South Asian Relations, 1947–1954." *Diplomatic History* 24 (Fall 2000): 593–619.

Russell, Francis. *The President Makers: From Mark Hanna to Joseph P. Kennedy.* Boston: Little, Brown, and Company, 1976.

Rust, William J. *Kennedy in Vietnam: American Vietnam Policy, 1960–1963.* New York: Charles Scribner's Sons, 1985.

Santoni, Pedro. *Mexicans at Arms: Puro Federalists and the Politics of War, 1845–1848.* Fort Worth: Texas Christian University Press, 1996.

Schiff, Stacy. *A Great Improvisation: Franklin, France, and the Birth of America.* New York: Henry Holt and Company, 2005.

Schlesinger, Arthur M. *Robert Kennedy and His Times.* New York: Ballantine Books, 1978.

Schoenbrun, David. *Triumph in Paris: The Exploits of Benjamin Franklin.* New York: Harper & Row, 1976.

Schom, Alan. *Napoleon Bonaparte.* New York: Harper-Collins, 1997.

Schulzinger, Robert D. *The Making of the Diplomatic Mind: The Training, Outlook, and Style of United States Foreign Service Officers, 1908–1931.* Middletown, CT: Wesleyan University Press, 1975.

Schwartz, Ted. *Joseph P. Kennedy: The Mogul, the Mob, the Statesman, and the Making of an American Myth.* Hoboken, NJ: Wiley, 2003.

Scott, James Brown. *The United States and France: Some Opinions on International Gratitude.* New York: Oxford University Press, 1926.

Sears, Louis Martin. "Nicholas P. Trist: A Diplomat with Ideals." *Mississippi Valley Historical Review* 11 (June 1924): 85–96.

Semmel, Bernard. *The Rise of Free-Trade Imperialism: Classical Political Economy, the Empire of Free Trade, and Imperialism, 1750–1850.* Cambridge: Cambridge University Press, 1970.

Shaplen, Robert. *The Lost Revolution: The Story of Twenty Years of Neglected Opportunities in Vietnam and of America's Failure to Foster Democracy There.* New York: Harper & Row, 1965.

Shavit, David. *The United States in Latin America: A Historical Dictionary.* New York: Greenwood Press, 1992.

Sheehan, Neil. *A Bright Shining Lie: John Paul Vann and America in Vietnam.* New York: Random House, 1988.

Shirer, William L. *The Rise and Fall of the Third Reich: A History of Nazi Germany.* New York: Simon & Schuster, 1960.

Shogan, Robert. *Hard Bargain: How FDR Twisted Churchill's Arm, Evaded the Law, and Changed the Role of the American Presidency.* New York: Charles Scribner's Sons, 1995.

Shurbutt, T. Ray. *United States-Latin American Relations, 1800–1850: The Formative Generations.* Tuscaloosa: University of Alabama Press, 1991.

Singletary, Otis A. *The Mexican War.* Chicago: University of Chicago Press, 1960.

Smith, Arthur D. Howden. *Old Fuss and Feathers: The Life and Exploits of Lt.-General Winfield Scott.* New York: Greystone Press, 1937.

Sprague, Marshall. *So Vast, So Beautiful a Land: Louisiana and the Purchase.* Boston: Little, Brown, and Company, 1974.

Stahr, Walter. *John Jay: Founding Father.* New York: Bloomsbury Academic, 2005.

Steel, Ronald. *Walter Lippmann and the American Century.* New York: Vintage, 1980.

Steffen, Dirk. "The Holtzendorff Memorandum of 22 December 1916 and Germany's Declaration of Unrestricted U-Boat Warfare." *Journal of Military History* (January 2004): 215–224.

Stephenson, Nathaniel W. *Texas and the Mexican War.* New Haven: Yale University Press, 1971.

Stewart, Geoffrey C. *Vietnam's Lost Revolution: Ngo Dinh Diem's Failure to Build an Independent Nation, 1955–1963.* Cambridge: Cambridge University Press, 2017.

Stinchcombe, William C. *The American Revolution and the French Alliance.* Syracuse, NY: Syracuse University Press, 1969.

Stuart, Graham H. *American Diplomatic and Consular Practice.* New York: Appleton-Century-Crofts, 1952.

    The Department of State: A History of Its Organization, Procedure, and Personnel. New York: Macmillan, 1949.

Swift, Will. *The Kennedys amidst the Gathering Storm: A Thousand Days in London.* New York: Smithsonian Books, 2008.

    The Roosevelts and the Royals: Franklin and Eleanor, the King and Queen of England, and the Friendship that Changed History. Hoboken, NJ: Wiley, 2004.

Sykes, Christopher. *Nancy.* Chicago: Academy Chicago Publishers, 1972.

Tansill, Charles Callen. *America Goes to War*. Boston: Little, Brown, and Company, 1938.

Thompson, Buchanan Parker. *Spain: Forgotten Ally of the American Revolution*. North Quincy, MA: Christopher Publishing House, 1976.

Thompson, Laurence. *1940*. New York: William Morrow and Company, 1966.

Tuchman, Barbara W. *The Zimmermann Telegram*, Reprint Edition. New York: Random House, 1985.

Tucker, Robert W. and David C. Hendrickson. *Empire of Liberty: The Statecraft of Thomas Jefferson*. New York: Oxford University Press, 1999.

Tucker, Robert W. *Woodrow Wilson and the Great War: Reconsidering America's Neutrality, 1914–1917*. Charlottesville: University of Virginia Press, 2007.

Van Alstyne, R. W. *Empire and Independence: An International History of the American Revolution*. Hoboken, NJ: Wiley, 1965.

Van Deusen, Glyndon. *The Jacksonian Era*. New York: Harper & Brothers, 1959.

Van Doren, Carl. *Benjamin Franklin*. New York: Viking Press, 1939.

Van Tyne, C. H. "French Aid before the Alliance of 1778." *American Historical Review* 31 (October 1925): 21–31.

"Influences Which Determined the French Government to Make the Treaty with America, 1778." *American Historical Review* 21 (April 1916): 528–541.

Waller, Douglas. *Wild Bill Donovan: The Spymaster Who Created the OSS and Modern American Espionage*. New York: Free Press, 2011.

Watt, David Cameron Watt. *How War Came: The Immediate Origins of the Second World War*. New York: Pantheon Books, 1989.

Weiner, Tim. *Legacy of Ashes: The History of the CIA*. New York: Doubleday, 2007.

Weinstein, Edwin A. *Woodrow Wilson: A Medical and Psychological Biography*. Princeton: Princeton University Press, 1981.

Whalen, Thomas J. *Kennedy versus Lodge: The 1952 Massachusetts Senate Race*. Boston: Northeastern University Press, 2000.

Wiltse, Charles M. *John C. Calhoun: Nationalist, 1782–1828*. Indianapolis: Bobbs-Merrill, 1944.

Whalen, Richard J. *The Founding Father: The Story of Joseph P. Kennedy*. London: Hutchinson, 1964.

Wheeler-Bennett, J. W. *Munich: Prologue to Tragedy*. New York: Viking Press, 1963.

Wills, Garry. *The Kennedy Imprisonment: A Meditation on Power*. New York: Mariner Books, 2002.

Winsor, Justin, ed. *Narrative and Critical History of America*. Boston: Houghton Mifflin Company, 1888. Vol. 7.

Winters, Francis X. *The Year of the Hare: America in Vietnam, January 25, 1963– February 15, 1963*. Athens: University of Georgia Press, 1999.

Wood, Gordon. *The Americanization of Benjamin Franklin*. New York: Penguin, 2004.

Woodward, Bob. *Fear: Trump in the White House.* New York: Simon & Schuster, 2018.
Young, G. M. *Portrait of an Age: Victorian England.* New York: Oxford University Press, 1936.

THESES AND DISSERTATIONS

Buttram, Timothy Evans. "'Swallowing Mexico without Any Grease': The Absence of Controversy over the Feasibility of Annexing All Mexico." Ph.D. Dissertation: University of New Hampshire, 2008.
Brent, Robert A. "Nicholas P. Trist: Biography of a Disobedient Diplomat." Ph.D. Dissertation: University of Virginia, 1950.
  "Nicholas Philip Trist's Search for a Career." M.A. Thesis: University of Virginia, 1946.
Schuster, Alice Katherine. "Nicholas Philip Trist: Peace Mission to Mexico." Ph.D. Dissertation: University of Pittsburgh, 1947.
Vieth, Jane Karoli. "Joseph P. Kennedy: Ambassador to the Court of St. James." Ph.D. Dissertation: Ohio State University, 1975.

Index

Abramson, Jill, 354
Adams, Henry, 79
Adams, John:
  Andrew Young compared with, 16
  and the Convention of 1800, 6
  Plan of 1776 drafted by, 36
  and Vergennes instructions, 46, 70–71
  – and the Anglo-American treaty (1783):
    and American fisheries, 27–28, 71
    consequences of his diplomatic
      disobedience, 25–29
    coordination with Jay, 67, 70–71
    on the "glory" of having broken the
      Continental Congress' directives, 14,
      67
    and the precedent set by his, Franklin's,
      and Jay's insubordination, 23, 29–31
Adams, John Quincy:
  reservations about diplomacy expressed
    by, 3
  secretary of state. See Clay, Henry
  stroke on the House floor, 187
  and the Treaty of Ghent, 6
Allen, Robert, 250
Alliance of 1778:
  and American dependence on France,
    39–40
  Article 2 stipulation of prior consent, 25,
    37
  signing of, 35–36
  and territory acquired as a result of the
    war, 40

and the treaty of amity and commerce, 36
– and Vergennes's instructions
  acceptance by Congress, 42, 58–59
  and American claim to fisheries off the
    Grand Banks, 60
  criticism of, 42
  Franklin's circumvention of, 46–51
  issuing of (1779), 40–41
  Jay, Adams, and Franklin's differing
    reactions to, 45–51
  reactions expressed to Livingston,
    44–46
Alsop, Joseph, 331
Alsop, Joseph and Robert Kintner, 283,
  293, 299
American diplomatic service:
  exam system, 7–10
  and the Rogers Act (1924), 8–9
  and the Stone-Flood Act (1915), 8
  suspicion and distaste for professional
    diplomacy, 2–4, 7–8, 356–357
  and the twenty-first century, 23
American diplomatic service –
    ambassadorial appointments:
  amateurism of, 5, 9, 11, 19–22,
    200–201
  and the Moses-Linthicum Act (1931),
    10–11
  pay-to-play arrangements, 9, 19
  and personal relationships with the
    president, 10, 20–21
  and political appointees, 21

American diplomatic service –
ambassadorial appointments: (cont.)
  underfunding of, 5–6, 9, 245–246,
    355–357
  See also Adams, John; Cohn, Gary;
    Daniels, Josephus; Kennedy,
    Joseph P.; Page, Walter Hines;
    Trist, Nicholas Philip; Wilson,
    William
  – and disobedience:
  and American pre-Civil War ministers,
    15
  non-American diplomatic history
    compared with, 1–2, 14–15, 22, 44,
    355
  and the precedent set by the Anglo-
    American treaty (1783), 29–31
  and the profit America gained from
    insubordination, 1, 13–14, 79–81,
    121, 125, 187, 198–199, 307–308,
    354–356
American isolationism:
  and challenges faced by Franklin, Deane,
    and Lee in forging the Franco-
    American alliance, 35, 37–38, 72
  and Livingston and Monroe's defense for
    departing from their instructions,
    113
  as a theme in U.S. history, 37
  See also Page, Walter Hines – and
    American isolationism
Amiens. *See* Treaty of Amiens
Anaya, Pedro:
  negotiations with Trist in Hidalgo,
    174–175
  official statement praising Trist for his
    negotiations, 190–191
  as president *ad interim* of Mexico, 158,
    175
  and Trist's recall to Washington,
    159–162
Anglo-American treaty (1783):
  criticism of, 25–29
  and freedom of navigation and commerce
    on the Mississippi River, 24, 64–67,
    71
  management of it criticized. *See*
    Livingston, Robert – as secretary of
    foreign affairs
  as a precedent for America's foreign
    policy, 29–31

and restitution of property and estates,
    66, 72
signing of, 24–25, 30, 72–73, 76
Vergennes misled by Adams, Franklin,
    and Jay during the final stage of
    negotiations, 71
See also Franklin, Benjamin – and the
    Anglo-American settlement (1783);
    Jay, John – and the Anglo-American
    treaty; Oswald, Richard – and the
    Anglo-American treaty
Anglo-Spanish treaty outlawing the slave
    trade, and Trist's views on slavery,
    135–139
Arabic sinking and the *Arabic* pledge,
    216–217, 224
Aranda, Pedro Pablo Abarca de Bolea,
    Conde de, 53–55, 61
Arnett, Peter, 311, 316
Asquith, Herbert, 212, 221
Asquith, Margot, 268
Astor, Nancy, Viscountess Astor, 250, 252
Astor, Viscount, 253–254

Bailey, Thomas A., 116, 168
Baldwin, Robert, 189
Balfour, Arthur, 198, 238
Ball, George W., 322–323
Bankhead, Charles, 146–147
Bannon, Steve, 354
Barbé-Marbois, François de:
  and American claim to fisheries off the
    Grand Banks, 60
  and the Anglo-American treaty, 27
  and Livingston's memorandum,
    93–94
  meetings with Napoleon, 103–104
  terms for purchasing Louisiana offered to
    Livingston in a midnight meeting,
    107–109, 121
Barnes, Harry Elmer, 198–199, 238
Battle of Buena Vista, 126, 169
Battle of Churubusco, 150
Battle of Monterey, 126, 169
Beck, Jozef, 278
Bemis, Samuel Flagg, 24, 30, 36, 42
Beneš, Edward, 263, 265, 269
Berle, Adolf, 261–262, 278
Bilainkin, George, 291
Bingham, Robert, 245–246
Black, Conrad, 244, 290